# Organizational Behavior

## Concepts and Applications

Third Edition

Jerry L. Gray
Frederick A. Starke

Faculty of Administrative Studies
The University of Manitoba

Charles E. Merrill Publishing Company
A Bell & Howell Company
Columbus    Toronto    London    Sydney

Published by Charles E. Merrill Publishing Co.
A Bell & Howell Company
Columbus, Ohio 43216

This book was set in Optima.
Copyeditor: Eloise Thompson
Cover Design Coordination: Tony Faiola
Text Designer: Michael J. Benoit
Cover painting by Marko Spalatin
Production Coordination: Jeffrey Putnam

Library of Congress Catalog Card Number: 83-43158
International Standard Book Number: 0-675-20098-9
Printed in the United States of America

2 3 4 5 6 7 8 9 10   88 87 86 85 84

Our basic objective in this Third Edition is the same as that in the first two editions: *to teach students and managers to think analytically about human behavior in organizations.* In order to apply organizational behavior theories effectively, managers must be able to think in analytical terms about the various theories. Analytical thinking requires an open mind about issues and a willingness to look at research evidence that has been developed on these issues. Much of the first chapter orients the reader to think in analytical terms, a prerequisite, we think, to acquiring the necessary skills for effective use of organizational behavior theory. If nothing else, we hope this book encourages students and managers to be more critical thinkers.

The text is designed to stand on its own as a classroom text for a one-semester or one-quarter undergraduate organizational behavior course or for graduate students who have no behavioral science background. We have left considerable scope for instructors to move about within the areas covered and to supplement our materials with their own. The text assumes no prior knowledge of organizational behavior, although, like any book in the field, students with organizational experience may find it easier to relate to some of the applications and examples. An *Instructor's Manual* is available for those who wish to use our experiences with the material.

## ☐ Changes in the Third Edition

There are several changes in the third edition. *First,* the material in all chapters of the second edition has been updated. Since the study of organizational behavior is developing rapidly, it is necessary to include the latest theoretical and empirical work in the field. By doing this, students will be able to see more clearly how knowledge about human behavior in organizations is developing.

*Second,* four new chapters have been added:
*Issues and Research Methods in Organizational Behavior*—This chapter presents an introductory treatment of some basic issues in organizational behavior and a description of several research methods used to gather data about people in organizations.

# Preface

*Behavioral Aspects of Decision Making*—A description of the important process of decision making in organizations is presented. The way in which human idiosyncracies complicate this process is stressed.

*Organizational Politics*—Human behavior in organizations is not always rational or directed toward achieving organizational goals. This new chapter analyzes both why people pursue their own goals at the expense of the organization and the overall effect of political behavior on individuals and the organization.

*Managing Change*—One of the most important and critical activities of management is implementing change. The reasons why people resist change and ways of dealing with this resistance are the focus of this chapter.

*Third,* the chapters have been organized into four basic sections. Section I, *Foundations of Organizational Behavior,* contains a chapter which introduces the subject of organizational behavior and a chapter on basic research methods in organizational behavior. Section II, *Behavioral Processes in Organizations,* deals with several important processes that occur in organizations, including motivation, organizational behavior modification, structure and behavior, leadership, communication, and decision making. Section III, *Behavioral Consequences in Organizations,* stresses the outcomes of people's behavior, and includes chapters on the informal organization, small group behavior, conflict, and politics. Section IV, *Adapting Organizations to Changing Conditions,* focuses on ways to promote organizational adaptation, and includes chapters on managing change, organizational development, and the future of organizational behavior.

Finally, summaries indicating how actual companies manage people have been added to each chapter; the summaries tell how various theories are applied and how well they are working.

## ☐ Chapter Features

Each chapter contains a variety of features designed to stimulate student interest and understanding of the field of organizational behavior:

**Chapter Objectives**   Each chapter begins with a set of action objectives, which help students anticipate the important points that will be made in the chapter. Once students have finished reading a chapter, they can return to the objectives to determine how well they have mastered the material.

**Key Terms**   The key terms are listed at the start of each chapter. When these terms are encountered in the chapter, they will be recognized as particularly important.

**Chapter Outline**   The order of topics is indicated at the beginning of each chapter. This gives the student an overview of a particular topic (e.g., leadership) and its components.

**Opening Incident**   Each chapter begins with a realistic incident that deals with a specific problem commonly found in organizations. The problem in the opening incident relates directly to the material presented in the chapter.

**Boxes**   Several controversial, humorous, or interesting issues are raised in boxed inserts. These increase student interest in the field of organizational behavior and further motivate them to think analytically about the management of people.

**Organizational Reality**   Since actually dealing with people is an important part of organizational behavior, each chapter contains several "organizational realities." These are reports of how real companies deal with employees. These realities are ruled inserts which are placed close to the appropriate theoretical material in the chapter.

**Applications**   Most chapters contain an applications section which indicates how the theories discussed in the chapter can be applied to problems commonly found in organizations. In several chapters, there is no separate applications section because the applications are an integral part of the material discussed in the chapter.

**Opening Incident Revisited**   The opening incident is analyzed using the material presented in the chapter. This is yet another vehicle for helping students apply the material they have studied.

**Summary**   The material presented in the chapter is briefly summarized. The summary is not a substitute for reading the chapter, but it does help students recall its main points.

**Review Questions**   These questions are designed to test the students' ability to recall specific facts, as well as their ability to think analytically about the topics presented in the chapter.

**Exercises**   Two or three exercises are presented at the end of each chapter. These are generally incidents which focus on issues discussed in the chapter. Questions at the end of each incident guide students in their analysis. Comprehensive cases are contained at the back of the book.

## ☐   Acknowledgements

Several individuals and groups have made important contributions to the third edition. Our students have been very helpful. It is always with mixed emotions that we require our students to buy our own book, but they have given us many ideas on how to improve the book. Their feedback has always been frank, open and supportive. We must also recognize the supportive role that our former dean, Dr. John Mundie, and our present dean, Dr. Roland Grandpré, have played from the very start.

Academically speaking, we have received much help from our colleagues, friends, adopters, and reviewers. The feedback from all of them has been invaluable. But despite their assistance, any errors remain our responsibility.

We are grateful to our reviewers, whose comments helped us communicate more effectively: Tom Bateman of Texas A&M University; Mark Hammer of Washington State University; Rick Rogers of Bentley College; Jean McGuire of the University of Massachusetts-Amherst; and Thomas Ingram of the State University of New York-Oswego.

Thanks must also go to our secretarial and word processing staff who helped in this revision: Diana Sokolowski and Sue Harder. Without their help, the revision would not have been completed on schedule.

The alphabetical listing of the authors' names reflects the equal contribution of each.

Jerry L. Gray
Frederick A. Starke

# Contents

*To Lynda and Derek*
*Aurelia, Eric, and Grant*

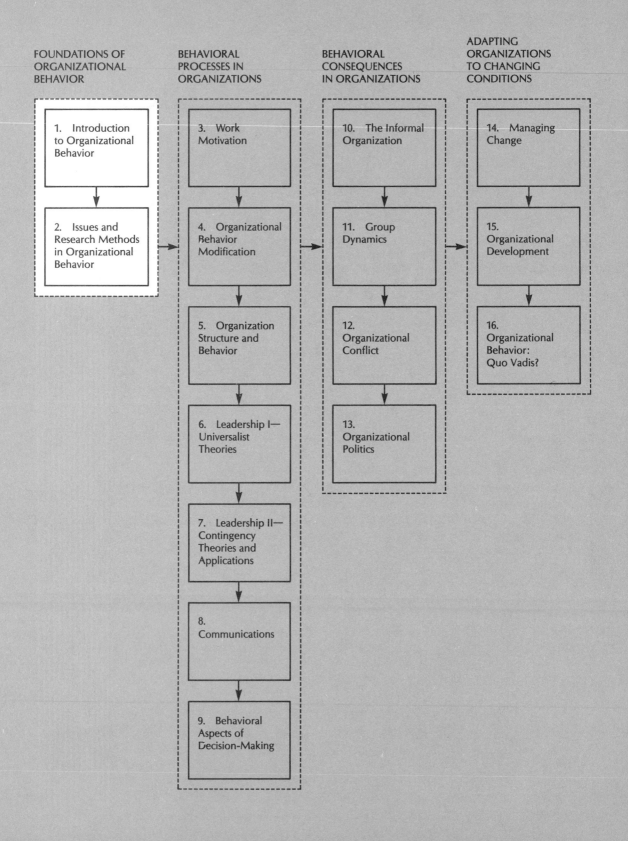

FOUNDATIONS OF
ORGANIZATIONAL
BEHAVIOR

1. Introduction to Organizational Behavior

2. Issues and Research Methods in Organizational Behavior

BEHAVIORAL
PROCESSES IN
ORGANIZATIONS

3. Work Motivation

4. Organizational Behavior Modification

5. Organization Structure and Behavior

6. Leadership I— Universalist Theories

7. Leadership II— Contingency Theories and Applications

8. Communications

9. Behavioral Aspects of Decision-Making

BEHAVIORAL
CONSEQUENCES
IN ORGANIZATIONS

10. The Informal Organization

11. Group Dynamics

12. Organizational Conflict

13. Organizational Politics

ADAPTING
ORGANIZATIONS
TO CHANGING
CONDITIONS

14. Managing Change

15. Organizational Development

16. Organizational Behavior: Quo Vadis?

# Foundations of
# Organizational Behavior

# SECTION I

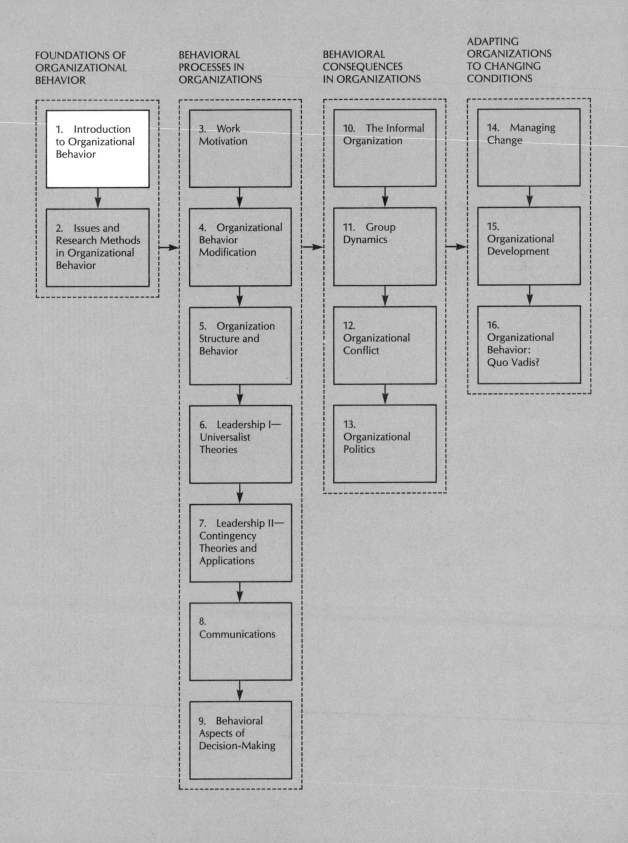

FOUNDATIONS OF
ORGANIZATIONAL
BEHAVIOR

BEHAVIORAL
PROCESSES IN
ORGANIZATIONS

BEHAVIORAL
CONSEQUENCES
IN ORGANIZATIONS

ADAPTING
ORGANIZATIONS
TO CHANGING
CONDITIONS

1. Introduction
to Organizational
Behavior

2. Issues and
Research Methods
in Organizational
Behavior

3. Work
Motivation

4. Organizational
Behavior
Modification

5. Organization
Structure and
Behavior

6. Leadership I—
Universalist
Theories

7. Leadership II—
Contingency
Theories and
Applications

8. Communications

9. Behavioral
Aspects of
Decision-Making

10. The Informal
Organization

11. Group
Dynamics

12. Organizational
Conflict

13. Organizational
Politics

14. Managing
Change

15. Organizational
Development

16. Organizational
Behavior:
Quo Vadis?

# Introduction to Organizational Behavior

## ■ Learning Objectives

After studying this chapter, you should be able to:

☐ Understand the origins of the study of organizational behavior and how it developed to its current state.

☐ Understand what organizational behavior attempts to do for the manager.

☐ Understand why the management of people is not an exact science.

☐ Understand how organizational behavior can affect your managerial career.

# Chapter 1

# ■ KEY TERMS

**Analytical thinking**
**Scientific management**
**Human Relations movement**
**Hawthorne experiments**
**Technical career**
**Managerial career**

# ■ CHAPTER OUTLINE

I. Organizational Behavior: The Subject
   A. The Manager As an Analyst
II. The History, Nature, and Scope of Organizational Behavior
   A. Early History and Background
   B. The Nature of Organizational Behavior
   C. The Scope of Organizational Behavior
III. A Model of Organizational Behavior
   A. Foundations of Organizational Behavior
   B. Behavioral Processes in Organizations
   C. Behavioral Consequences in Organizations
   D. Adapting Organizations to Changing Conditions
IV. Summary

## *Opening Incident—George Skelton*

George Skelton, regional sales manager for the Power Manufacturing Company and manager of twenty-five salespeople scattered throughout the state, was seated in his office contemplating several pressing problems when he heard a knock at the door. Martha Clark, the company controller, entered his office and asked to speak with him for a few minutes.

"I've got something here that you're not going to like," she said.
"What's that?" said Skelton.
"I've had my suspicions now for several months, but it's only recently that the evidence is fairly clear. Several of the people in our office thought that some of

the expenses turned in by your staff looked kind of fishy. So we've done some checking and sure enough, some of the expenses have been faked," said Clark.

"You mean some of the salespeople are padding their expense accounts?" asked Skelton.

"Yes. At least the information we have suggests that."

"What are you going to do about it?" Skelton asked.

"I'm not going to do anything," replied Clark, "except to tell the president that I've told you. As far as I'm concerned, it's your responsibility after that." With that, she got up and walked out of Skelton's office.

Skelton was in somewhat of a state of shock for a few minutes. After all, he had hired and trained practically all of the sales staff himself. While some were better at sales than others, he considered all of them to be basically good people. He certainly had never had any problems of this sort with them before. It was then that Skelton realized that he had not even asked Clark which salespeople were padding their accounts.

"Was I afraid to ask for fear of what I might find out?" he thought to himself.

At any rate, Clark was already gone and he would have to find out later. For the time being, he settled back in his chair and contemplated the problem from a general perspective. After giving considerable thought to possible solutions, he came up with the following list:

1. Dismiss the offenders and hope that the example would cause others not to fake expenses in the future;
2. Institute tighter controls over expense accounts for all sales personnel;
3. Ignore the problem for the time being on the grounds that only a few were doing it and it was possibly not an ongoing problem;
4. Eliminate all expense account controls and instruct the sales staff to spend "whatever amount necessary to generate maximum sales";
5. Let the salespeople padding their accounts know they were caught and let them off with a severe warning.

Though all the solutions appeared to have possibilities, after considerable thought, Skelton was at a loss to decide which alternative to choose.

# ■ ORGANIZATIONAL BEHAVIOR: THE SUBJECT

Why do people behave the way they do? What causes different people to react differently to the same situation? Why are some organizations more successful than others, even though they appear to be managed in the same manner? And why do managers spend so much of their time trying to "figure out what makes people tick"? All of these questions—and more—are the substance of what organizational behavior is all about. An understanding of the behavior of people in organizations has become increasingly important as more and more of us find ourselves involved with organizations and the management of people, not only at work, but in all facets of our lives.

Even though one might not be a manager, it is still important to understand as much as possible about how people behave at work if we want to make our organizational lives more pleasant and productive. Consider the following situations as a few examples that illustrate common patterns of behavior in organizations:

1. The manager of an accounting department finds that the accounting clerks are beginning to make errors in calculations that were seldom made before.
2. A police chief notices an improvement in job attitudes of patrolmen after their supervisor retired and was replaced.
3. The foreman in a production department is faced with consistently high absenteeism on Mondays and Fridays.
4. The director of nursing in a small rural hospital discovers that the surgical nurses resent being transferred temporarily to the hospital information desk during slack periods in the surgical ward.
5. The president of an organization realizes that the vice-presidents seem reluctant to offer new ideas on how the company should be managed.
6. A new employee in the typing pool notices that none of the other typists are acting very friendly.
7. A college dean notices improved communication and greater faculty commitment after a reorganization of the academic unit.
8. The committee chairman of a local volunteer fund-raising drive is informed that most of the volunteers have requested to be dropped from the committee after the current drive is over, even though more funds have been raised than ever before.
9. The personnel manager of a manufacturing organization notices that the company is having increased difficulty recruiting new production workers, even though its wage rate is the highest in the local area.

These examples illustrate the need for understanding behavior at all levels of management and in all types of organizations: manufacturing firms, government agencies, volunteer organizations, the military, churches, service organizations, etc. In virtually all cases, it is desirable, if not imperative, to have the ability both to solve problems and to prevent them from occurring. *To have this ability we must have an understanding of why people behave as they do.*

An examination of the case studies at the end of this book will illustrate the value of preventing problems from occurring rather than attempting to resolve a situation after a sequence of events has already happened. If one has the ability and knowledge to understand *why* people behave the way they do, then foresight, anticipation, and prevention of problems become more probable.

## ☐ The Manager As an Analyst

Learning about organizational behavior is more than simply storing up facts about people. It requires studying organizational relationships, patterns of behavior, and theories about organizational behavior. The ultimate goal is an increased understanding of cause-and-effect relationships, i.e., the "whys" of behavior in organizations. We emphasized in the preface that one of our objectives in writing this book is to increase the reader's ability to think analytically about organizational behavior. As we hope to demonstrate, analytical thinking results from a clear understanding of the (1) content of various theories and (2) manner in which they can be applied. To get from (1) to (2) requires an awareness of the research available for a given theory. In other words, we must learn *how* the theory works, *when* it works, and most importantly, *why* it works.

To emphasize the analytical approach to studying organizational behavior, and to increase the reader's ability to think in analytical terms, most chapters in this book have sections entitled "empirical evidence." These sections present at least the basics of the research available on the topic and provide some interpretation and application of the findings. *It is our firm belief that we can increase the analytical skills of readers through this method and thereby increase their effectiveness as managers.* Or, looked at another way, if managers can increase their understanding of cause-and-effect relationships in organizations, they will be able to make more effective decisions. One should always remember that managers are paid mostly for their ability to diagnose situations and develop decisions which will increase the organization's effectiveness; often, the "mechanical" implementation of the decision is passed on to lower levels.

In our case, we are interested in developing the reader's analytical skills regarding "people" problems. This may or may not mean that the manager has the *ability* to *apply* solutions effectively. Therefore, sound analytical thinking developed through the study of organizational behavior is a necessary—but not sufficient—condition to increase one's managerial effectiveness.

This introductory chapter provides some groundwork the reader can use in understanding and evaluating the material in the remaining chapters. In Chapter 2, *Issues and Research Methods in Organizational Behavior,* you will be given additional information that will assist in developing your analytical skills in organizational behavior. We now begin your exposure to the field of organizational behavior by exploring its historical origins and how it got to where it is today.

# ■ THE HISTORY, NATURE, AND SCOPE OF ORGANIZATIONAL BEHAVIOR

## ☐ Early History and Background

Using our definition of the study of organizational behavior as *the study of why people behave the way they do in organizations,* it is safe to say that the field has existed for many thousands of years. People have always attempted to understand and predict how other people will behave in work situations of all types, but the magnitude of this need is largely determined by the sizes and types of organizations in existence. By size we mean the number of individuals working together toward a specific set of goals; by type we mean whether membership in the organization is voluntary or involuntary.

It has only been since the Industrial Revolution of the nineteenth century that relatively large numbers of individuals have been required to work together in manager-subordinate relationships.[1] Prior to this, most organizations were of the "mom and pop" type in which few formal organizational relationships were required. In addition to the size differences among organizations, there are also differences in the influence systems that can be used to affect behavior. Many of the large organizations that did exist before the Industrial Revolution were military ones in which the authority of the leader was supreme and practically unquestioned, since membership was not voluntary. Behavioral problems, assuming they exist, are relatively easy to deal with under these conditions. It is certainly no accident that much of our current knowledge about human behavior has been derived from organizations in which influencing behavior consists of more than just giving orders.

If we add the term "scientific" to the definition suggested above, the study of organizational behavior then becomes *the scientific study of why people behave the way they do in organizations.* Although it is not possible here to discuss all the implications of scientific versus nonscientific investigations, suffice it to say that it takes us out of the realm of "seat-of-the-pants" reasoning into something of a more systematic (and therefore more useful) nature. We discuss the importance of this in more detail in Chapter 2. For the moment, we will examine two of the earliest scientific approaches to the study of management—Scientific Management and the Human Relations movement—since it was in them that modern organizational behavior theory had its beginnings.

**Scientific Management**  Most textbooks agree that the Scientific Management movement was epitomized by the work of Frederick W. Taylor in his time-and-motion studies at the Midvale Steel Company in the early 1900s. Today we would call Taylor an efficiency expert. As an industrial engineer, he was concerned with inefficiencies in manual labor jobs and believed that by scientifically studying the specific motions that made up the total job, a more rational, objective, and effective method of performing the job could be determined. In his early years as a

# Box 1-1: Is Taylorism Really Dead?

Fred Taylor took a lot of flack during his heyday. Unions were suspicious of him, employers were skeptical of his claims, and the government thought he needed to be investigated. Taylor's philosophy permeated his whole life. Sudhin Kakar, in his study, *Frederick Taylor: A Study in Personality and Innovation* (Cambridge: MIT Press, 1970), notes that he did such strange things as experiment with his legs on cross-country walks to discover the step that would cover the greatest distance with the least expenditure of energy; as a young man, before going to a dance, he would conscientiously and systematically list the attractive and unattractive girls with the object of dividing his time equally between them; and he often incurred the wrath of his playmates when he was more concerned that the playing field for sports be scientifically measured than he was with actually playing the game.

Taylor's "one best way" philosophy has often been misunderstood; though he believed that in terms of physical motions there should be "one best way," he also recognized that the equipment needed to perform the "one best way" would vary from person to person. His famous example of equipping a large man and a small man with shovels of different sizes to match their respective strengths proved how important it was to match the equipment with the person.

While it is fashionable today to blast Taylor as being insensitive to human needs and treating people like machines, it is painfully obvious that his influence is probably as great now as it ever was. Though Taylor is criticized for treating people only as economic beings, surveys show that dollar motivation is still strong, particularly in manufacturing organizations. If one includes managerial personnel who are on some type of bonus or profit-sharing scheme, then we probably have more people today on economic incentive systems than ever before.

foreman in the steel industry, he saw different workers doing the same job in different ways. It was his opinion that each man could not be doing his job in the optimal way, and he set out to find the "one best way" to perform the job efficiently. His argument proved to be correct and in some instances "Taylorism" resulted in productivity increases of 400 percent! In almost all cases, his methods improved productivity over existing levels.

Coupled with Taylor's logical, rational, engineering-like approach to management was a simple theory of human behavior: people are primarily motivated by economic rewards and will take direction if offered the opportunity to better their economic positions. Put simply, Taylor's theory stated that:

1. Physical work could be scientifically studied to determine the optimal method of performing a job.

2. Workers could thereafter be made more efficient by being given prescriptions for how they were to do their jobs.
3. Workers would be willing to adhere to these prescriptions if paid on a "differential piecework" basis.[2]

Many have criticized Taylor's work for dehumanizing the work place and treating workers like machines, but his overall contribution to management was significant. Although others were studying similar methods at the same general time, Taylor was one of the first to take the theory and practice of management out of the realm of intuitive judgment and into the realm of scientific inquiry and reasoning. Prior to this, management was largely a "seat-of-the-pants" type of activity with few generalizable principles. While his work had some serious implications for managers and workers alike, and was therefore quite controversial, Taylor nevertheless made major advances in the field by showing that management could be studied and developed scientifically.

As one would expect in a situation involving "greatness," Taylor's ideas have been evaluated many times since his death. More recently his efforts have received more favorable evaluations than they did years ago. For example, Peter Drucker believes that Taylor's work has had the same degree of impact upon the world as the work of Karl Marx or Sigmund Freud.[3] On the other hand, Taylor has been accused not only of lying about some of his experiments, but also of stealing his ideas from others researching industrial management at the same time.[4] On balance, however, the evaluations of Taylor's work are positive. In a review of Taylor's ideology and relevance to today's managerial practices, Locke maintains that Taylor's ideas on time study, standardization of work practices, goal setting, money as a motivator, scientific selection of workers, and rest pauses have all proved to be successful techniques of management today.[5]

**The Human Relations Movement**    The second major step on the way to current organizational behavior theory was the Human Relations movement that began in the 1930s and continued in various forms until the 1950s. Popularized by Elton Mayo and his famous Hawthorne studies conducted at the Hawthorne Plant of the Western Electric Company, in many ways it remains the foundation of much of our management thinking today.[6] The initial experiments reflected strongly the physical orientation of Scientific Management, since they were designed to explore the relationship between lighting and productivity. The rational approach of Scientific Management predicted a positive relationship; i.e., as lighting increased, productivity would increase—up to a point, of course. Logically, at some (high) level of illumination, productivity should begin to decline, so the original experiment was designed to determine the optimal level of illumination. However, the researchers found no predictable relationship between lighting and output and, because the research results could not be explained by existing knowledge, the researchers were forced to find new explanations. Further research indicated that the lack of a predictable relationship between lighting and output was related to the *mental and emotional* side of organizations rather than the physical, mechanistic side recognized by Scientific Management. Additional studies showed that economic factors, such as incentive systems, were equally poor in predicting behavior.

A summary of the purposes of the Hawthorne experiments, the types of variables that were studied, and the conclusions drawn is contained in Table 1-1. It should be noted that the physical variables studied included such things as illumination, rest periods, length of work periods, and length of work week—all in an attempt to find the optimal level of each. But as the experiments continued, nonphysical variables were also studied, such as improved human relations, supervisory methods, social interactions, incentive systems, and worker autonomy. In general, the researchers concluded that *social* factors were more important determinants of employee behavior and productivity than were physical and economic factors. Something called "morale" was suggested as being related to productivity and morale was found to be related to factors such as style of supervision, personal relationships on the job, freedom to choose work methods, and a concept called "group norms." The recognition of the importance of these factors opened up much opportunity for advances in the theory and practice of management.

The Human Relations movement, like Scientific Management, is not without its shortcomings. Because of the nature of its findings and the resulting lessons for managers, it has been criticized as "cow sociology" (so-called because happy cows presumably give more milk). This simplistic view of the relationship between morale and productivity is something that existing research has not been able to verify.[7] The view has also caused misconceptions about what "correct" management methods are. A common interpretation of the Human Relations movement is that managers need only treat their employees well to generate maximum productivity. This conclusion is unfortunate for two reasons. First, as the material in subsequent chapters will show, it is oversimplified and therefore often inaccurate. Second, those who do not agree with this conclusion might be labeled advocates of poor treatment of employees—which, of course, is also false. Quite possibly, the positive but simplistic philosophy of human relations has actually hindered needed research into organizational behavior.

In recent years attempts have been made to reexamine the Hawthorne experiments in light of new research regarding the relationship between morale and productivity. In a classic review of Mayo's major work, *Management and the Worker,* Landsberger states:

> Far outweighing its limitations is the positive effect which *Management and the Worker* had (1) in showing that empirical research within industry and organizations in general was at all possible; (2) in broadening and profoundly changing one well-established subdiscipline, that of industrial psychology; and (3) in touching upon most of the problem areas into which the field of human relations in industry is now breaking up. This breakup was delayed for some ten years by a misreading of the lessons of the book not only by its critics, but also by its friends.[8]

**TABLE 1-1.  The Flow, Content, and Conclusions of the Hawthorne Studies**

| Flowchart | Experimental Variables Manipulated or Observed | | | | Description and Conclusion |
|---|---|---|---|---|---|
| | Physical work environment | Physical work requirements | Management and supervision | Social relations of workers | |
| (1) ILLU—MINATION | X | | | | Three exploratory studies that suggested human factors, rather than physical working conditions, determined worker satisfaction and performance. |
| (2) FIRST RELAY | X | X | X | X | The major Hawthorne experiment, testing effects on performance of rest pauses, shorter work periods, increased worker autonomy, and small-group incentive pay. This study concluded that benefits to worker performance resulted from improved human relations, and to a lesser extent from rest pauses. |
| (3) SECOND RELAY | | | X | | Derivative experiment suggesting only moderate effects of small-group incentive pay upon worker performance. |
| (4) MICA SPLITTING | | X | | | Derivative experiment suggesting only moderate effects of rest and shorter work periods upon worker performance. |
| (5) INTER-VIEWING | | | X | X | Derivative survey reinforcing prior conclusions regarding importance of social interactions (worker-worker and worker-supervisor) in the satisfaction of workers. First indications, during intensive interviews early in 1931, of problems resulting from employee inter-relations, especially in restriction of output. |

**TABLE 1-1 (continued).**

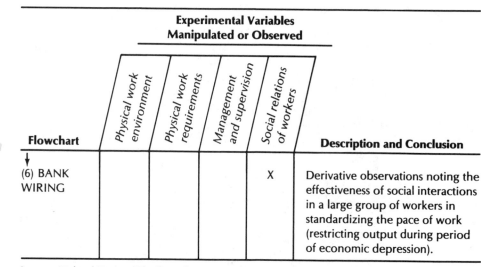

| Flowchart | Physical work environment | Physical work requirements | Management and supervision | Social relations of workers | Description and Conclusion |
|---|---|---|---|---|---|
| ↓<br>(6) BANK WIRING | | | | X | Derivative observations noting the effectiveness of social interactions in a large group of workers in standardizing the pace of work (restricting output during period of economic depression). |

Source: Richard Herbert Franke and James D. Kaul, "The Hawthorne Experiments: First Statistical Interpretation," *American Sociological Review* (October, 1978): 626. Used with permission.

In contrast, a more recent study reexamined all of the original Hawthorne research data, using more sophisticated research techniques. The study concluded that:

> The first statistical interpretation of the major Hawthorne experiment leads to conclusions different from those heretofore drawn. Most of the variance in production rates during the first relay experiment could be explained by measured variables. To assume that output changes resulted from unmeasured changes in the human relations of workers therefore seems injudicious, even though it was the assumption of the Hawthorne researchers and has been accepted and built upon by many social scientists over the past several decades. . . . Quantitative analyses of the data from Hawthorne, as well as empirical studies of work groups in the decades subsequent, . . . unfortunately do not support a contention that improvements in human relations lead to improved economic performance.[9]

This does not necessarily mean that an understanding of human relations is not useful; it may have a payoff in areas other than performance, such as absenteeism, turnover, etc. This possibility is explored in greater detail in Chapter 3, Work Motivation.

The Human Relations movement is sometimes referred to as a backlash to the economic and rational approach of the Scientific Management movement, but this point of view tends to cast Scientific Management in an unfair light. Because of his shop-floor experience, Taylor realized before Mayo and his colleages did that there were "goldbrickers," that group norms might restrict output, and that workers generally preferred their own ways of doing things. Perhaps the major shortcoming of Taylor's philosophy was his underestimation of the magnitude of

## Box 1-2: Do Happy Cows Give More Milk?

The Human Relations school of thought has been accused of advocating "cow sociology" as a method of managing people, i.e., since happy cows can give more milk, it follows that happy people will produce more. But *do* happy cows give more milk? Or, perhaps more importantly, how can you tell if cows are happy? In our quest for an answer to these important questions we asked farmers, dairies, and professors of agriculture; we read journals *(Journal of Dairy Science)*, textbooks on dairy management, and popular farm publications. We even assigned a graduate student to research the question. But alas, we could not uncover any *scientific* evidence proving it to be true (although everyone we spoke to believed it to be true). In one study we found, an author noted the importance of "psychological and stress" factors which affect milk production, but declined to study them because "they were too difficult to measure." So at least for the present, we must scientifically conclude that the question is yet unanswered. Nevertheless, we were impressed by one textbook in dairy science in which the author prescribes several techniques to maximize milk production:

1. Cows become accustomed to a regular routine; disturbing this routine disturbs them and causes a decrease in milk production.
2. Attendants should come into close contact with the cows, and it is important that the best of relations exist between the cows and keepers.
3. The cows should not be afraid of the attendants.
4. Cows should never be hurried.
5. Chasing cows with dogs or driving them on the run should never be allowed.
6. In the barn, attendants must work quietly; loud shouting or quick movements upset cows and cause them to restrict production.

Now the question is, can these principles be applied to people?

Source: Clarence H. Eckles, *Dairy Cattle and Milk Production* (New York: Macmillan, 1956), pp. 332–33.

these feelings in relation to his economic man concept. Taylor believed that in the final analysis, workers are rational, logical people who would change their behavior in the interest of their economic well-being. Mayo, on the other hand, attempted to show that man is also an emotional, nonlogical being who often reacts unpredictably to the work environment.[10]

The influence of the human relations philosophy can be seen in many management training programs today. Topics such as communications, counseling, understanding people, and leadership are common ingredients in many training programs and reflect the findings of the original Hawthorne studies. Often, participants are taught that improved communications, etc., will increase morale.

Unfortunately, these topics can erroneously be seen as the totality of the manager's job, thereby increasing the probability that employee morale may increase and productivity may decrease.[11]

**Conclusions**   Today it is common to picture modern management theory as a blend of the extremes of the principles contained in Scientific Management and Human Relations, with each contributing valuable insights for managing organizations. We now recognize that the study of human behavior in organizations is a multifaceted subject involving combinations of the rational and the emotional, the physical and the mental, and the logical and nonlogical.

Regardless of one's interpretation of the Hawthorne experiments, or perceptions of their social significance, that series of investigations stands as a monumental research study in the field of management and organizational behavior. Mayo continued in the tradition of Scientific Management by showing other ways that the process of management could be studied scientifically and how these studies could lead to other fruitful areas of inquiry. The fact that hindsight and sophisticated mathematical techniques have questioned the true meaning of the Hawthorne experiments should not deter us from crediting Elton Mayo and his associates with being the founding fathers of modern organizational behavior concepts.

## ☐  The Nature of Organizational Behavior

Organizational behavior is not a discipline in the usual sense of the term, but rather an eclectic field of study that integrates the behavioral sciences (psychology, sociology, anthropology, etc.) into the study of human behavior within organizations. Although those who research organizational behavior often come from business schools, they may have their roots in diverse areas such as political science, cultural anthropology, or social psychology.

Although organizational behavior uses the relatively exact tools of mathematics and statistics in its research methods, it is far from an exact science itself. Because it is such a young field of inquiry, at least in terms of the use of scientific techniques, comparatively little progress has been made in providing specific answers to specific organizational problems. This can be quite frustrating for the teacher as well as the student of organizational behavior. Managers feel a need for precise answers as they face important day-to-day problems; teachers, on the other hand, knowing that organizational behavior is a "soft" area, are reluctant (or should be) to be too precise in teaching "how-to-do-it" methods. The net result is a feeling of irritation by the student ("why study something that won't give me an exact answer?") and a feeling of inadequacy by the teacher ("I wish I had something more concrete to give them"). But to learn that human behavior in organizations is not an exact science is, in itself, a significant realization. One of the failings of the Scientific Management movement was its belief that human behavior was easily predicted. So while the field of organizational behavior may be inexact, it is realistic.

**Organizational Behavior: an Art or a Science?**   Whether or not organizational behavior (or management, for that matter) is an art or a science is an age-old question with a relatively obvious answer: it is both. The knowledge *about* human behavior in organizations lies toward the science end of the continuum; the skill in *applying* that knowledge clearly leans toward the art end, recognizing that individual differences in managerial style can vary considerably. In some circumstances this question would be of little importance, but since we are attempting to emphasize both the theory and application of organizational behavior in this book, we must at least recognize the significance of the differences between the science and the art. These differences will become more important later in Chapter Two when we discuss the differences and similarities between theory and practice.

**Is Organizational Behavior Common Sense?**   Part of the problem in answering this question is agreeing upon a definition of "common sense." There are certainly some things that cannot be learned from a book, but this does not mean they have not been learned from other sources. Does this make them common sense? And if organizational behavior is common sense, then it should easily be taught to others (or learned by others very quickly), and the application of this common sense should show positive results right away.

We cannot deny that some people have wisdom and unusual insight into behavioral problems, but we cannot explain why such people have these skills. They, of course, call it "common sense," but recognize the frustration of attempting to teach someone else the sense of wisdom or of insight. Even in colleges and universities, it is generally understood that we cannot teach students to use better judgment, but only to use the ideas, concepts, theories, and knowledge available to analyze the bases for judgment.

What the field of organizational behavior attempts to do is add a degree of scientific thinking to what might already exist as common sense. In some cases, the scientific approach may only confirm what common sense believed all along, and this is useful since science can be taught, common sense cannot. It is also probable, however, that science will counter what was previously thought to be common sense, or will add a dimension of precision to it. In such cases—becoming more predominant as people become more complex—common sense becomes a weak foundation for analyzing and solving complex managerial problems.

The primary difference between sound organizational behavior and common-sense is in the precision of knowledge. Most commonsense statements are so broad that they offer little guidance in specific instances. It is difficult to disagree with them since they are so general. For example, the commonsense statement "money is important to people" generates more questions than it answers: how important is it? under what conditions? how should money be used? is a salary system more effective than a bonus system? and so forth. These critical and precise questions constitute the essence of organizational behavior.

## ☐ The Scope of Organizational Behavior

Since we earlier defined organizational behavior very broadly as "the scientific study of why people behave the way they do in organizations," it follows that its scope is quite wide—wide enough, in fact, that it is necessary for us to set some limits on the subject area so that our discussion can be reasonably contained.

In many situations it may be permissible to use the terms **organizational behavior** and **management** interchangeably. A good case can be made for doing so since both involve the study of organizations. But since we have excluded many management topics from this book, it is important that we distinguish between the two, lest the reader get a one-sided view of the manager's job. It is sometimes convenient to divide the term *management* into two areas: the behavioral side and the managerial process side. As we have mentioned, the behavioral side concerns why people behave the way they do in organizations; the process side, which has its origins in the classical "principles of management," concerns the managerial processes of planning, organizing, controlling, etc., as well as the management science (quantitative) aspects of management. While it is convenient to make this arbitrary division, it must be understood that organizational behavior is affected by management processes. By excluding this interaction through the omission of certain topics, we possibly run the risk of oversimplification. Yet, in an attempt to make some sense out of the wealth of literature regarding the behavioral side, we find it necessary to oversimplify to some extent. In Chapter 5 we have included one of the major process variables—organization structure—in our discussion because of its profound impact upon behavior.

Generally speaking, organizational behavior is relevant for all types of organizations, although much of the research in the area has been conducted in business and government organizations. In an introductory text, usually it is not necessary to explore the finer points of difference in comparative organizational behavior, though such differences do exist. For example, the leadership style appropriate to lead a group of Red Cross volunteers may be different from that required of a drill sergeant with a new group of recruits. However, we do hope to provide the reader with sufficient data so that detection of differences will be possible through analytical thinking. For example, rather than to state that different styles of leadership may be required in different organizations, we prefer to describe the conditions in which various types of leaders have been effective, leaving it to readers to analyze their own situations according to the criteria stated.

**Organizational Behavior and Your Career**　It was mentioned earlier that organizational behavior is not a discipline in itself. Similarly, organizational behavior is not a functional area within organizations (i.e., one does not find a vice-president of organizational behavior in companies).[12] It is a tool area that can be applied across functional lines and should be useful to anyone who interacts in a work setting with other people (which includes just about everyone).

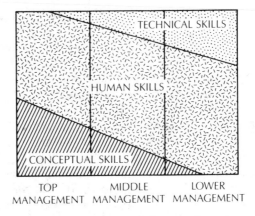

**FIGURE 1-1.   Importance of Different Skills at Various Organizational Levels**

The role of organizational behavior in your own career development can best be understood by examining the differences between technical education and managerial education. Most readers of this text will be preparing themselves for a technical career, i.e., engineer, accountant, home economist, pharmacist, or some other specialty. Your first job will be that of a technical specialist, i.e., actually doing a specific set of tasks for which you were trained. However, at some point in your career, you will likely become a manager or supervisor. As Figure 1-1 suggests, the technical skills you have studied and mastered will become secondary to human relations skills when you begin managing people. As you acquire more and more managerial responsibilities, your technical skills become less and less important, and give way to human relations skills and conceptual (decision-making) skills.

All this suggests that most of us spend most of our formal education studying something that will become less and less important to us as we progress through our managerial careers. So, although it is not possible to become "vice-president of organizational behavior," the concepts covered in this book will be relevant throughout your managerial career.

## ■ A MODEL OF ORGANIZATIONAL BEHAVIOR

Our purpose in this text is to present the most important topics that are needed for an introduction to organizational behavior. Rather than view all these topics as separate, we prefer that you see them as a logical progression of concepts that are interrelated. This does not mean that the concepts occur in sequence, but rather that we think it is possible to gain a better understanding of cause and effect if the topics are presented in some coherent fashion. Our model of organizational behavior describes the relationships that exist between the topics covered in this book, and is illustrated in Figure 1-2.

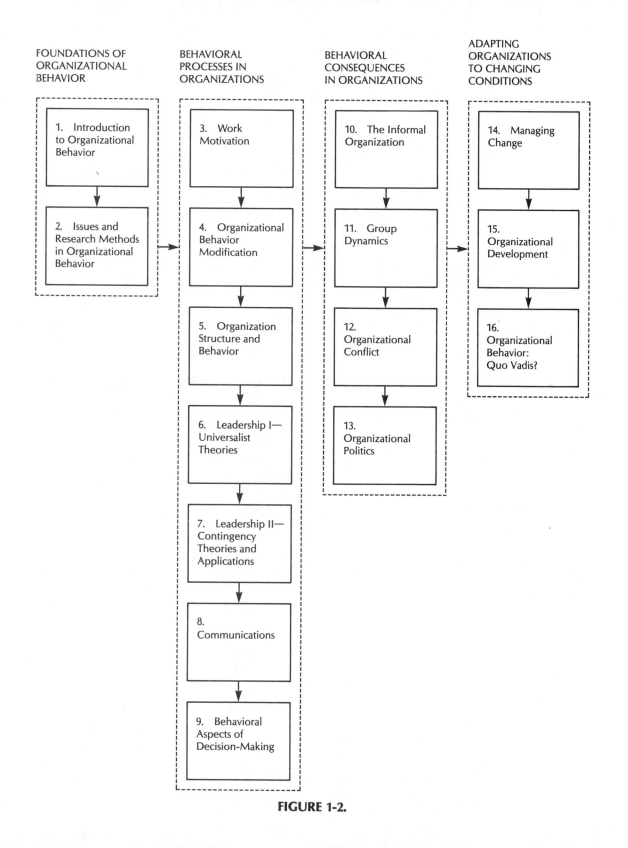

**FOUNDATIONS OF ORGANIZATIONAL BEHAVIOR**

1. Introduction to Organizational Behavior

2. Issues and Research Methods in Organizational Behavior

**BEHAVIORAL PROCESSES IN ORGANIZATIONS**

3. Work Motivation

4. Organizational Behavior Modification

5. Organization Structure and Behavior

6. Leadership I—Universalist Theories

7. Leadership II—Contingency Theories and Applications

8. Communications

9. Behavioral Aspects of Decision-Making

**BEHAVIORAL CONSEQUENCES IN ORGANIZATIONS**

10. The Informal Organization

11. Group Dynamics

12. Organizational Conflict

13. Organizational Politics

**ADAPTING ORGANIZATIONS TO CHANGING CONDITIONS**

14. Managing Change

15. Organizational Development

16. Organizational Behavior: Quo Vadis?

**FIGURE 1-2.**

## ☐ Foundations of Organizational Behavior

Because organizational behavior is not an exact science, it is important to understand where it comes from, how knowledge in the field is generated, and what can be done with that knowledge. This chapter has briefly discussed the historical origins of the field and presented some initial thoughts on the purpose, breadth, and depth of organizational behavior. In the next chapter, *Issues and Research Methods in Organizational Behavior,* we discuss the fundamentals of organizational behavior research and the issues that must be considered in applying the findings of that research.

The foundations of organizational behavior serve a secondary purpose—to give you a greater appreciation for the value of science, scientific thinking, and analytical methods. As managers you will eventually be in the position of having to sort out cause and effect, not only in what you do but in what you read as well. A basic knowledge of research methods and the differences between theory and practice will be a useful tool for your future.

## ☐ Behavioral Processes in Organizations

As shown in Figure 1-2, we begin the study of organizational behavior itself in Chapter 3 by examining the basic processes that occur in any organization. These are the events and behaviors that set the stage for organizational effectiveness. They determine the success or failure of the people side of organizations. Chapter 3, *Work Motivation,* reviews the current theories of motivation and integrates them into a motivational framework for managers. The research evidence for each of the theories is reviewed and examples of the applications of motivation theory are presented. Chapter 4, *Organizational Behavior Modification,* is a more specific study of motivation. This chapter reviews how reward systems affect performance on the job, and shows how managers can design more effective reward systems to improve performance.

All organizational behavior occurs within a formal system of roles, role relationships, job descriptions, policies, procedures, and rules. Put together, these describe the organizational structure of an organization. Chapter 5, *Organization Structure and Behavior,* describes the alternative structures available, and how these structures affect behavior.

The research on leadership has developed two approaches: the universalist approach and the contingency approach. Chapter 6 reviews the "one best way" approaches (universalist), and Chapter 7 presents the contingency viewpoint. These two chapters are important for managers, since they describe what leadership styles are available and the situations in which various styles have proved to be effective.

It is often said that communications are the lifeblood of any organization. Chapter 8 examines the communications process from both a theoretical and practical perspective. The theoretical portion describes the basic communications models and gives examples of their effect in organizations. The practical side of this topic shows specific-skill applications of communications.

Chapter 9, *Behavioral Aspects of Decision Making,* describes how managers make decisions. Rather than concentrating on decision-making techniques, the focus of this chapter is on examining the forces that influence the process itself. Understanding these behavioral processes is necessary for making effective decisions.

## ☐ Behavioral Consequences in Organizations

The behavioral processes just presented lead to a number of outcomes or consequences in organizations. They are neither good nor bad, but simply natural outcomes of the basic processes.

Although behavior exists within a formal structure, informal structures result from the interaction of people at work. These structures can be as important as, or, in some circumstances more important, than the formal ones. Chapter 10, *Informal Organization,* and Chapter 11, *Group Dynamics,* describe the informal relationships that inevitably occur, and how these social systems can affect performance.

An inevitable result of behavior in the organization is conflict. Because individuals and groups have different personal and organizational objectives, conflict results. Conflict can be either positive or negative, depending upon how it is managed. Chapter 12 analyzes the sources of conflict and how the energy inherent in conflict can be channeled toward more productive results.

Although we often do not like to admit it, political behavior is a normal outcome of people at work. This is the "it's not what you know but who you know that counts" syndrome. Chapter 13 examines political behavior from a scientific perspective and shows how politics can affect everything from decisions to careers. While we do not necessarily recommend political behavior, we do believe that a proper understanding of it will improve one's life at work.

## ☐ Adapting Organizations to Changing Conditions

If anything is certain about the future, it is the fact of change. Because people, technologies, and environments are constantly changing, organizations must change as well. This section examines both the micro aspects of change (i.e., implementing change within a small group or organization), as well as the macro aspects (i.e., adapting a total organization to the environment). Chapter 14, *Managing Change,* examines why people resist change and how change can be implemented by the manager. Chapter 15, *Organizational Development,* discusses how major system-wide changes can be implemented and why they are necessary. The final chapter, *Organizational Behavior: Quo Vadis?* looks at the future and analyzes how organizational behavior can be used as a tool for predicting the nature of our organizations in the years to come.

## *Opening Incident Revisited—George Skelton*

When we left George Skelton at the start of this chapter, he was trying to decide which of his five solutions was the right one. One reason he was having difficulty deciding was that he did not know *why* the salespeople were padding their expense accounts. The correct solution to this problem will depend upon two things: (1) what George Skelton's objectives are and (2) why each of the salespeople is behaving the way he is.

Going to (1) first, if Skelton's objectives are to stop the padding (and only that), then he probably should try solutions (1), (2), or (5). However, if his objectives are somewhat broader than that, then solutions (3) and (4) are more likely possibilities. But in all cases, *he will be unable to apply the correct solution until he knows why the salespeople are doing it.* While it may seem unlikely at first glance, Skelton must realize the possibility that each salesperson may be doing it for different reasons, i.e., their motivations may be different. For example, one salesperson may be padding because she is basically a dishonest person. In such a case, dismissal may be in order. However, another may be padding because he feels his commission schedule is unfair and this is his way of making the situation more equitable. If this is true, then a raise in pay may be in order! If George Skelton is like most of us, he will assume a single motivation for all of them and apply the same solution to all. And if he does, he will likely cause additional—and possibly more severe—problems in the future.

## ■ SUMMARY

In this introductory chapter we have attempted to provide the reader with a broad conceptual and historical base from which the subjects to be encountered in later chapters can be viewed. We have described how the study of organizational behavior grew out of two major movements in organizations: the Scientific Management ideology of Frederick W. Taylor, and the Human Relations movement of Elton Mayo.

We have indicated the importance of viewing organizational behavior as more than just a commonsense approach to managing people. A good comprehension of the field can add significantly to your success as a manager. Organizational behavior is primarily related to the "people" side of organizations, the other being the technical and management-process side.

This chapter also presented a model of organizational behavior which constitutes the plan of this book. Basic understanding of the field is achieved through the *Foundations of Organizational Behavior* section; the fundamental concepts are contained in the *Behavioral Processes in Organizations* section, which result in the *Behavioral Consequences* section. The processes and consequences are then used to discuss change in the section, *Adapting Organizations to Changing Conditions.*

# ■ REVIEW QUESTIONS

1. Why is it important to understand why people behave the way they do in organizations?

2. Why are "scientific" investigations in organizational behavior important for the manager?

3. How did Scientific Management contribute to the development of organizational behavior theory?

4. How did the Human Relations movement contribute to the development of organizational behavior theory?

5. Is organizational behavior an art or a science? Why?

6. What are the limitations of the "commonsense" approach to organizational behavior?

7. How is organizational behavior related to the study and practice of management?

# ■ EXERCISE 1-1: MODERN QUALIFICATIONS FOR SUPERVISORY POSITIONS

The following ad appeared in the *Chicago Tribune* a few years ago. Perhaps you would like to try the little test that the advertiser suggests for a foreman. Could you qualify?

### HELP WANTED

"Our firm is one of the Midwest's largest galvanizers. We are looking for someone with at least five years of first-line supervisory experience. He/she will join us as Special Assistant to the Plant Manager during the period of indoctrination, and as quickly as his/her abilities, aptitudes, and familiarity with the business permit, will take over as General Foreman, and thereafter as Division Superintendent. The person will replace a man whose shoes are going to be hard to fill, but the constant growth of this company requires promotion of the Division Superintendent as soon as he can be relieved by this competent successor. Knowledge of our industry is helpful, but not essential."

Test Your Ability as a Manager:

Indicate whether you think the following statements are true or false based on your experience with people:

|  |  | T | F |
|---|---|---|---|
| 1. | It is good policy for a supervisor or manager to assume that a group will accept him/her as their natural leader. | ( ) | ( ) |
| 2. | People always appreciate improvement in working conditions. | ( ) | ( ) |
| 3. | The best way to change a deep-seated, fixed, emotional attitude toward anything is to provide all the facts on the issue. | ( ) | ( ) |
| 4. | Where people are happy, satisfied, and content, their productivity will be high. | ( ) | ( ) |
| 5. | Communications should be primarily and heavily concerned with transmitting objective data, facts, theories, figures, statistics, ideas, knowledge and information—up, down, and horizontally in the organization. | ( ) | ( ) |

## ■ EXERCISE 1-2: COMMON SENSE IN ORGANIZATIONAL BEHAVIOR

This exercise contains 20 pairs of statements about organizational behavior. For each pair, circle the letter preceding the statement which you think is most accurate. Circle only *one* letter in each pair.

After you have circled the letter, indicate how certain you are of your choice by writing 1, 2, 3, or 4 on the line following each item according to the following procedure.

Place a "1" if you are *very uncertain* that your choice is correct.

Place a "2" if you are *somewhat uncertain* that your choice is correct.

Place a "3" if you are *somewhat certain* that your choice is correct.

Place a "4" if you are *very certain* that your choice is correct.

Do not skip any pairs.

1. a) A supervisor is well advised to treat, as much as possible, all members of his/her group exactly the same way.

   b) A supervisor is well advised to adjust his/her behavior according to the unique characteristics of the members of his/her group.    _____

2. a) Generally speaking, individual motivation is greatest if the person has set goals for himself/herself which are *difficult* to achieve.

   b) Generally speaking, individual motivation is greatest if the person has set goals for himself/herself which are *easy* to achieve.    _____

3. a) A major reason why organizations are not so productive as they could be these days is that managers are too concerned with managing the work group rather than the individual.

b) A major reason why organizations are not so productive as they could be these days is that managers are too concerned with managing the individual rather than the work group. _____

4. a) Supervisors who, sometime prior to becoming a supervisor, have performed the job of the people they are currently supervising are apt to be *more* effective supervisors than those who have never performed that particular job.

   b) Supervisors who, sometime prior to becoming a supervisor, have performed the job of the people they are currently supervising are apt to be *less* effective supervisors than those who have never performed that particular job. _____

5. a) On almost every matter relevant to the work, managers are well advised to be completely honest and open with their subordinates.

   b) There are very few matters in the work place where managers are well advised to be completely honest and open with their subordinates. _____

6. a) One's *need for power* is a better predictor of managerial advancement than one's *motivation to do the work well.*

   b) One's *motivation to do the work well* is a better predictor of managerial advancement than one's *need for power.* _____

7. a) When people fail at something, they try harder the next time.

   b) When people fail at something, they quit trying. _____

8. a) Performing well as a manager depends most on how much *education* you have.

   b) Performing well as a manager depends most on how much *experience* you have. _____

9. a) The most effective leaders are those who give more emphasis to *getting the work done* than they do to *relating to people.*

   b) The effective leaders are those who give more emphasis to *relating to people* than they do to *getting the work done.* _____

10. a) It is very important for a leader to "stick to his/her guns."

    b) It is *not* very important for a leader to "stick to his/her guns." _____

11. a) *Pay* is the most important factor in determining how hard people work.

    b) The *nature of the task people are doing* is the most important factor in determining how hard people work. _____

12. a) *Pay* is the most important factor in determining how satisfied people are at work.

    b) The *nature of the task people are doing* is the most important factor in determining how satisfied people are at work.   _____

13. a) Generally speaking, it is correct to say that a person's *attitudes cause his/her behavior.*

    b) Generally speaking, it is correct to say that a person's *attitudes are primarily rationalizations for his/her behavior.*   _____

14. a) Satisfied workers produce *more* than workers who are not satisfied.

    b) Satisfied workers produce *no more* than workers who are not satisfied.   _____

15. a) The notion that most semiskilled workers desire work that is interesting and meaningful is most likely *incorrect.*

    b) The notion that most semiskilled workers desire work that is interesting and meaningful is most likely *correct.*   _____

16. a) People welcome change for the better.

    b) Even if change is for the better, people will resist it.   _____

17. a) Leaders are born, not made.

    b) Leaders are made, not born.   _____

18. a) Groups make better decisions than individuals.

    b) Individuals make better decisions than groups.   _____

19. a) The statement, "A manager's authority needs to be commensurate with his/her responsibility" is, practically speaking, a *very meaningful statement.*

    b) The statement, "A manager's authority needs to be commensurate with his/her responsibility" is, practically speaking, a *basically meaningless statement.*   _____

20. a) A major reason for the relative decline in North American productivity is that the division of labor and job specialization *have gone too far.*

    b) A major reason for the relative decline in North American productivity is that the division of labor and job specialization *have not been carried far enough.*   _____

Source: Adapted from Robert Weinberg and Walter Nord, "Coping with 'It's All Common Sense,'" *Exchange: The Organizational Behavior Teaching Journal* 7 no. 2 (1982): 29–32. Used with permission.

# ■ ENDNOTES

1. In our relatively egalitarian society, we have recently found that some people are turned off by the term "manager-subordinate" or, worse yet, "superior-subordinate" relationships. We must point out that these terms refer to roles, not people. Organizationally speaking, those reporting to a manager are in a subordinate role, which makes their manager's role a superior one. This does not mean that one individual is inferior to another.

2. It is not our intent to suggest that this is the totality of Scientific Management or that Taylor was the only person who scientifically studied the field. The movement encompassed many areas of organizational analysis, including organizational design and selection and testing, to name but a few. But since much of the theory was based on the physical aspects of work and a set of rigid assumptions about human behavior, we use only this portion, which relates to the development of organizational behavior. For a more detailed discussion of Scientific Management, see James G. March and Herbert A. Simon, *Organizations* (New York: John Wiley & Sons, 1958).

3. P. F. Drucker, "The Coming Rediscovery of Scientific Management," *The Conference Board Record* 13, no. 6 (1976): 23–27.

4. C. D. Wrege and A. G. Perroni, "Taylor's Pig-Tale: A Historical Analysis of Frederick Taylor's Pig-Iron Experiments," *Academy of Management Journal* 17 (1974): 6–27.; and C. D. Wrege and A. M. Stotka, "Cooke Creates a Classic: The Story Behind F. W. Taylor's Principles of Scientific Management," *Academy of Management Review* 3 (1978): 736–749.

5. Edwin A. Locke, "The Ideas of Frederick W. Taylor: An Evaluation," *Academy of Management Review* 7, no. 1 (1982): 14–24.

6. For a detailed discussion, see F. Roethlisberger and W. J. Dickson, *Management and the Worker* (Cambridge: Harvard University Press, 1935).

7. See Chapter 3 on Motivation for a more detailed discussion of this relationship. An interesting criticism has come from the engineering ranks as well; they maintain that the Hawthorne studies set experiments on lighting back fifty years.

8. Henry A. Landsberger, *Hawthorne Revisited* (Ithaca, N.Y.: Cornell University, New York State School of Industrial and Labor Relations, 1958): p. 115.

9. Richard Herbert Franke and James D. Kaul, "The Hawthorne Experiments: First Statistical Interpretation," *American Sociological Review* 43 (October 1978): 638.

10. It is important to note the differences between "nonlogical" and "illogical." The former suggests that the person is responding to a set of values or criteria that are relatively unknown to us and their responses are different from what we would expect (according to our value system). An illogical response is one that is inappropriate to mutually agreed-upon values and can therefore be called a mistake in judgment. Mayo, recognizing that worker responses were not consistent with existent research findings, preferred to stick with the much broader definition of rationality and called their responses "nonlogical." Today, we would call them "complex."

11. Such results have been shown in studies evaluating the effects of management training programs. For an excellent summary of this research, see J. Campbell et al., *Managerial Behavior, Performance, and Effectiveness* (New York: McGraw-Hill, 1970), Chapter 10.

12. This situation can create problems for university graduates. If students concentrate their studies in organizational behavior, they run the risk that prospective employers will not know what they are trained to do; recruiters may be accustomed to hiring majors in production, marketing, personnel, etc. The personnel area is probably the most common field associated with organizational behavior.

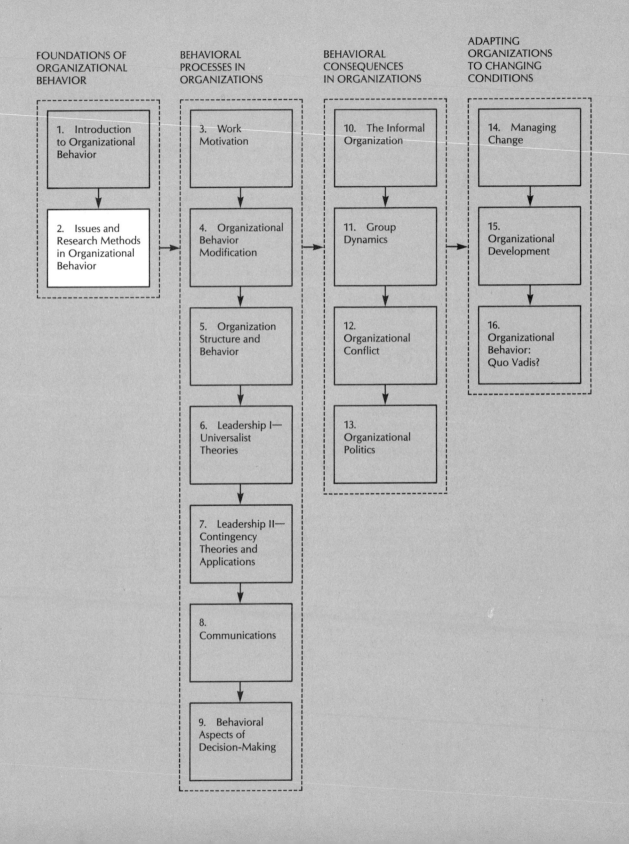

FOUNDATIONS OF
ORGANIZATIONAL
BEHAVIOR

1. Introduction to Organizational Behavior

2. Issues and Research Methods in Organizational Behavior

BEHAVIORAL
PROCESSES IN
ORGANIZATIONS

3. Work Motivation

4. Organizational Behavior Modification

5. Organization Structure and Behavior

6. Leadership I— Universalist Theories

7. Leadership II— Contingency Theories and Applications

8. Communications

9. Behavioral Aspects of Decision-Making

BEHAVIORAL
CONSEQUENCES
IN ORGANIZATIONS

10. The Informal Organization

11. Group Dynamics

12. Organizational Conflict

13. Organizational Politics

ADAPTING
ORGANIZATIONS
TO CHANGING
CONDITIONS

14. Managing Change

15. Organizational Development

16. Organizational Behavior: Quo Vadis?

# Issues and Research Methods in Organizational Behavior

## ■ Learning Objectives

After a thorough reading of this chapter you should be able to:

☐ Identify the major issues of controversy surrounding the application of organizational behavior principles.

☐ Understand why research into organizational behavior is important for the manager.

☐ Understand the basic research methods used and their advantages and disadvantages.

☐ Identify the major theories of organizational behavior and relate them to the various research methods.

☐ Understand the basic differences between theory and practice in organizational behavior.

# Chapter 2

# ■ KEY TERMS

**Dependent variables**
**Correlation analysis**
**Case studies**
**Field experiments**
**Simulations**
**Internal validity**
**Predictive theories**
**Universalist theories**
**Systems theories**
**Independent variables**
**Cause and effect**
**Laboratory experiments**
**Survey research**
**External validity**
**Descriptive theories**
**Prescriptive theories**
**Contingency theories**
**Experiential learning**

# ■ CHAPTER OUTLINE

I. Concepts in Organizational Behavior Research
   A. Dependent and Independent Variables
   B. Correlation Analysis
II. Basic Research Methods
   A. Case Studies
   B. Laboratory Experiments
   C. Field Experiments
   D. Survey Research
   E. Simulations
   F. Dilemmas in Research
   G. Conclusions: Basic Research Methods
III. Theories of Organizational Behavior
   A. Descriptive, Predictive, and Prescriptive Theories
   B. Universalist and Contingency Theories
   C. Systems Theories

# *Opening Incident*

Ted Loewen, vice-president for human resources at Inter-System Manufacturing Company stared in amazement at the three students in his office.

"You think I should what?" he asked again.

"Our survey shows that you have some serious morale problems here at your plant, and we think there are some obvious steps you should take to improve the situation. All of our recommendations are covered in the summary, but it looks as though your operation could use some T-group training, improved communications, and vastly improved salary structure. Also, all of your managers could use training in participative management methods and how to implement job enrichment. The survey is very clear on that," replied one of the students.

Loewen paused for a moment to rethink how he got into this situation. Oh yes, he thought, it all started when he met Professor Grastark at a luncheon one day and Grastark asked him if he would be willing to let a team of organizational behavior students undertake a research study at Inter-System. Since the professor stated that the data would be confidential and the study wouldn't take much of the employees' time, he had agreed. After all, maybe they might find out something worthwhile. And now this! At least now the memo he received from the union president made sense. Yesterday he had received a note to the effect that the union did not appreciate outsiders hired by management poking into the personal affairs of union members, and that no matter what they found out, the union would not let the information influence the bargaining which was scheduled to begin in two weeks. Loewen quickly made an excuse about being late for a meeting, and ushered the students out of his office. He then reached for the phone to call Professor Grastark.

Organizational behavior study is part of the social sciences. As such, there are some philosophical, ethical, and research issues that, while somewhat abstract, nevertheless have important implications for applying organizational behavior theory. Though the same issues are characteristic of the physical sciences, they tend to assume a more important role in an area such as organizational behavior, which contains knowledge used (or misused) by so many people in their everyday lives. In astronomy, for example, there are questions of a philosophical nature that must be addressed, but they are of little consequence to the average person, since they do not affect daily life.

All of us, however, are in constant interaction with other people at home, work, and in leisure activities. This makes a discussion of some of the major issues in organization behavior imperative, both for the theoretician and the practicing manager. In fact, in many ways practitioners are theoreticians because all managers make decisions based upon some "theory" about how their environment operates. This chapter will show how research methods are used to design and evaluate theories, the problems likely to be encountered in that process, and the impact of personal values in the application of theories. Once these kinds of things are known, students and managers can be better judges of good and bad theories.

We are undecided whether to put the discussion of issues and research methods in the opening section of the book or at the close, since some of the issues may make more sense after the reader has been exposed to the content of organizational behavior. We have chosen to present them here so that the reader can be on guard for them as they crop up throughout the rest of the book, especially in sections where we review research findings and suggest applications. However, we also think you would find it useful to review this section after the book has been completed.

# ◼ CONCEPTS IN ORGANIZATIONAL BEHAVIOR RESEARCH

In order to study human behavior in organizations effectively, researchers have developed certain procedures (methodologies) that can be used to gather information. This information, referred to in this book as "empirical evidence" is then used to refine theories of human behavior. Empirical evidence differs from other types of information in that it is generated from scientific procedures rather than seat-of-the-pants types of efforts. The object of research into organizational behavior is to gather as much empirical evidence as possible, weigh the evidence against scientific criteria, and then formulate (or revise) theories about human behavior in organizations.

Before we examine the various research methods used to generate empirical evidence, we must clarify two methodological concepts that often cause confusion. These are the concepts of (1) dependent and independent variables, and (2) correlation analysis.

## ☐ Dependent and Independent Variables

When organizational researchers study human behavior in organizations, they usually try to draw conclusions about what causes what. For example, does high job satisfaction cause employees to work harder? Does an enriched job increase an employee's sense of competence? Does democratic leadership cause employees to have higher morale? In order to answer these and many other questions, we need to think carefully about the relationships between these variables. When doing this, researchers usually think in terms of independent and dependent variables.

An independent variable is one that is believed to be a cause of something, while a dependent variable is that which is being caused. For example, in a thunderstorm, lightning (the independent variable) causes thunder (the dependent variable). We would therefore hypothesize (as amateur weather forecasters) that as the amount of lightning increases, so will the amount of thunder. This, then, identifies the relationship between the dependent and independent variables.

In the natural sciences it is easy to find clear-cut examples of independent and dependent variables, such as the thunder-lightning relationship. However, when we are dealing with people in organizations, the situation is more complex. The difficulty is twofold: first, it is sometimes hard to tell which is the independent and which is the dependent variable, and second, it is even more difficult to determine what the relationship between them is.

As an example, suppose we want to examine the relationship between satisfaction and performance and our case study is a student who has just received an "A" on an exam. The student will probably feel very satisfied about this. Now, what is the independent variable here? If we say "satisfaction" we would be arguing that satisfied students study hard for exams, hence *satisfaction causes performance*. This sounds very reasonable on the surface. However, the argument that performance is the independent variable also has merit, i.e., the student (for whatever reason) scored well on the exam and that caused the student to feel satisfied. Thus, *performance caused satisfaction*. This example demonstrates the difficulties encountered in defining dependent and independent variables in the social sciences.

## ☐ Correlation Analysis

Perhaps the most commonly used statistical technique in the social sciences is correlation analysis. For this reason we will describe it briefly here. Correlation analysis can be used with any of the basic research methods discussed below.

Simple correlation analysis is used to determine what kind of relationship (if any) exists between two or more variables. In order to use correlation analysis, the variables under study must be measured (i.e., quantified). This means that in order to correlate variables like satisfaction, morale, and motivation, some sort of numerical scale must be developed for each of these variables. Correlation coefficients (or measures of relationships) range from −1.0 (a perfectly inverse relationship between two variables) to +1.0 (a perfectly direct relationship between two variables). Thus, a .97 correlation between, say, the number of students in a course and the number of textbooks sold would indicate that as the number of students in the course increases, the number of textbooks sold increases as well. We would be able to predict almost perfectly how many textbooks would be sold. Similarly, if the correlation was −.97 we could still predict accurately, except that now as the number of students increases the number of books sold decreases.

In more general terms, a positive correlation means that two variables move in the same direction, i.e., as variable *A* increases (or decreases), variable *B* moves in the same direction. A negative correlation means that they move in opposite directions, i.e., if variable *A* increases, variable *B* decreases. The strength of the relationship, regardless of the direction, is specified by the *coefficient of correlation*. For example, we might observe a relationship of −.10 between two variables. The −.10 indicates the relationship is a negative one, but not very large.

One caution about correlation analysis: a positive or negative correlation between two variables does not necessarily mean there is a cause-and-effect relationship present. In our earlier example of the lightning and thunder, we might observe that the occurrence of lightning and thunder are closely related, but we would need additional information before we could conclude that lightning causes thunder (or that thunder causes lightning, for that matter). In some situations the nature of the causal relationship is intuitively obvious. We know, for example, that students buy textbooks so we can be reasonably confident that increases in the number of students will cause an increase in the number of textbooks bought, but often situations are not this simple.

## Box 2-1: The Case of the Alcoholic Teachers

Several years ago a study was done that showed a positive correlation between the number of elementary school teachers and the total amount of alcohol consumed. Does this mean that teachers are big drinkers? Perhaps, but correlation analysis cannot be used to prove the point. A more likely explanation is that as the population grows, more teachers are needed and more alcohol is also consumed. The two variables of interest are therefore not *causally* related, they simply have a *correlational* relationship. Such relationships are also called *spurious correlations*.

Since many organizational behavior studies use correlation analysis, we must be careful when drawing conclusions about what is reported in them. Unfortunately, most organizational behavior studies aren't as obvious in their relationships as thunder and lightning, or textbooks sold and numbers of students. First, correlations in the range of plus or minus .90 are rare, and second, intuitive causal judgments about two variables are extremely hazardous. Strong relationships are more frequent and meaningful when measurement of the variables is precise. Measures of items such as job satisfaction, morale, and feelings of competence are not hard and fast measures. Even if they could be measured successfully, it would be difficult to exclude from the study other variables that could influence correlation. The net effect is that we must be quite cautious in judging the findings of correlational studies.

# ■ BASIC RESEARCH METHODS

Throughout this book we will make reference to studies investigating human behavior in organizations. In order for the reader to be able to make an informed judgment regarding the conclusions drawn from the studies cited, it is important that we briefly describe the research methods most commonly used in organizational behavior and note the strengths and weaknesses of each method. The five most common research methods are (1) case studies, (2) laboratory experiments, (3) field experiments, (4) survey research, and (5) simulations.

## □ Case Studies

The principal method of research in organizational behavior is the case study. In the case-study method, the researcher observes what happens in an organization and reports the observations. The method is best known for its use in anthropological studies in which the anthropologist visits communities, tribes, or other groups and observes the cultural, economic, social, and family affairs of the group. Because anthropologists have been doing case studies for many years at many different locations, much data has accumulated regarding the behavior patterns of different cultures. These data are then used to compare various cultures and to observe differences and similarities.

The case study is one of the earliest methods used in organizational behavior research, and is an excellent method for gathering information about an organization, a society, or any definable problem, if very little is known about it. Because of its observational nature, it is well suited to initial investigations. However, there are difficulties with case studies, the major one being that there is no control over the variables in which the researcher is interested. For example, if a case writer observes low morale in an organization, it is difficult to attribute the low morale to a definable set of causes, since the case study is limited to *description* of sets of variables. This description is useful for additional analysis, but cause-and-effect findings are not possible. Since causal analysis is important in organizational behavior research, the case study method then has a major shortcoming insofar as increasing our knowledge of human behavior in organizations is concerned.

Another problem is the potential bias of the case writer. When a person enters an organization or society as an observer and then attempts to draw some conclusions, it is always possible that the researcher will impose his or her own values, opinions, attitudes, or beliefs on the event witnessed. It is sometimes said that case studies reveal more about the case writer than they do about the organization studied. As an example, several years ago the newspapers reported about an anthropologist from the United States who married a New Guinea tribal chief. We could speculate that this researcher would have difficulty making unbiased observations about the tribe in view of her relationship to the chief executive of the tribe.

In spite of the shortcomings noted above, case studies are a useful tool for gathering initial information about social systems in organizations. Case studies tend to generate a wealth of data about a social system, which is a useful first step towards increased understanding of the system. Cases also contribute to a better understanding of the interaction of the variables, since the data are seen as a part of the total picture. And finally, case research assists in the teaching of social systems concepts, since the data are the result of real-life experiences. Organizational behavior researchers must be careful to keep in mind the two shortcomings noted above and to use more powerful (and unbiased) research methods like those discussed below, once some understanding of the situation is achieved. Case study research can be enhanced if more rigorous research methods are employed in the study itself.[1] Whatever their research limitations might be, however, case studies have proved to be excellent vehicles for teaching about organizational behavior and for understanding applications of the theory.[2]

## ☐ Laboratory Experiments

The goal of laboratory experiments is to measure the impact of independent variables on the dependent variable by isolating and controlling the important variables in an artificial environment designed by the experimenters.[3] By comparing the behaviors of two groups, a *control group* and an *experimental group*, any differences can usually be attributed to the experimental design. In the experimental group the independent variable is manipulated, and the results are compared to the control group, in which the independent variable is held constant. If the control of the independent variable is successful, then any differences in the behavior of the dependent variable between the two groups can be attributed to the change in the independent variable.

As an example, we might design a laboratory experiment in which labor and management representatives bargain with each other on the understanding that if they do not reach agreement at the end of a specified time, they will be forced to submit their final position to an arbitrator. Half of the participants (the control group) might be told that the arbitrator will use a certain method to reach a decision, while the other half (the experimental group) might be told a different method will be used. We could then observe how this anticipation of arbitrator decision methods (the independent variable) influences the negotiating behavior of the participants (the dependent variable). With this experimental design, we could draw some specific conclusions about the relationship between the two variables.

Within the history of social science research, literally thousands of laboratory experiments have been conducted on a wide variety of topics. In spite of this diversity of activity, all laboratory experiments have two properties in common:

tight control of the independent variables, and a close examination of how changes in the independent variables are related to changes in the dependent variable. This control allows stronger conclusions about cause-and-effect relationships. In the bargaining experiment referred to above, we might find that bargainer expectations about arbitrator decisions did indeed influence negotiating behavior in measurable ways. In a laboratory experiment we can draw conclusions about the impact of arbitrator decisions on negotiator behavior with much more confidence than we could if we had done a case study and simply observed people bargaining with each other.

## Box 2-2: Ethics in Laboratory Research

As laboratory research has become more widely used in organizational behavior, the problem of ethics in laboratory research has also become important. Only a minority of the population has expressed concern over how animals are treated in laboratory research, but the advent of research in the social sciences, particularly as applied to organizations, has surfaced concerns about human subjects. The ethical problem is basically this: in order to probe the inner feelings and motivations of people, potential biases must be removed through deception so that the responses, either verbal, written, or behavioral, will be "uncontaminated."

One of the most common biases that can creep into a laboratory study is the participants' knowledge of its purpose, i.e., what the study is attempting to show. To overcome this problem, researchers must engage in "deception" (a much nicer word than lying) which has been accepted as a necessary research strategy for the advancement of knowledge. The problem is to determine how much deception is too much. When does the researcher overstep reasonable bounds and take a questionable moral posture, even though the deception is in the interests of science? As an example, it is interesting to note that one area in which we have relatively little knowledge about human behavior is in the area of death and dying, and the little knowledge we have is from case study research. The major reason for this is, so far at least, researchers have not been willing to deceive people for experimental purposes into believing they are dying. Imagine the fate of the researcher who, after gathering the completed questionnaires on "Attitudes Toward Dying," tells the experimental group, "O.K., people. We were just kidding. You aren't really dying after all. Thanks for your help!"

In spite of the gains achieved by controlling independent variables, laboratory experiments are not without difficulties. The problem raised by most critics is that the artificiality or contrived nature of the experiment is unrealistic, since these same conditions do not exist in the real world. If, for example, we are conducting a laboratory experiment to assess the effects of certain leadership behaviors on employee morale and productivity, some critics might argue that the artificial environment created is nothing like the real situation that would exist in an actual employment situation. Accordingly, they would argue that laboratory experiments are not very worthwhile because of this major limitation.

While it is certainly true that laboratory experiments do involve artificial environments, we must be careful to keep in mind the goal of laboratory experiments: controlling independent variables in order to draw cause-and-effect conclusions in specific circumstances. If this goal is kept in mind, then the conclusions drawn in many laboratory experiments can be useful. It is important to examine the relationship between independent and dependent variables in a simplified environment to gain understanding of how they interact. Once this causal understanding is gained, additional research can study the same variables in a more complex environment, more closely approximating real-world conditions.

## ☐   Field Experiments

Since what is true in the laboratory environment may be true only to a slight degree in the "real world," field experiments are useful to further refine our understanding of certain issues or problems. Field experiments are essentially laboratory experiments conducted in actual organizations. Once some laboratory research has been done on the relationship between specific variables, researchers can then analyze the same phenomenon in an actual organization.

Field experiments are a powerful research method because the manipulation of independent variables takes place in the environment in which they naturally occur. However, like all research methods, field experiments do have limitations. The major limitation is the practicality of conducting an experiment in an organization. For example, consider a researcher wanting to examine the effects of advertising on sales volume. The researcher might like to have the company advertise heavily in one market and very little in another so that the sales volume from the two levels of advertising could be compared. Imagine, however, the reaction from the sales manager to such a proposal: "You can't really expect us to cut advertising in one region—our competitors will kill us!" The sales manager's concern is a very real one for which there is no easy solution.

Another problem is the difficulty in assigning individuals to the various experimental conditions in the field experiment. To minimize the possibility of bias in the participants, ideally they should be divided randomly into the experimental groups. In organizations, however, this may be impossible, since people cannot be moved around at the experimenter's will or treated unequally. Imagine the effects of a field experiment, designed to study the effect of pay upon motivation, in which half the employees have their pay reduced by 2 percent!

The net result of these two problems is that the typical field experiment may not be a true experiment, but a "quasi-experiment" where only some of the rules for scientific experimentation are satisfied.[4] Nevertheless, even with these limitations, the control over the independent variables possible in field experiments allows the researcher to make some reasonably strong cause-and-effect conclusions.

## □ Survey Research

Perhaps the most popular of all basic research methods in organizational behavior is survey research. It involves developing a series of questions on the subject to be researched. A relevant sample of individuals is chosen, they complete the questionnaire, and their responses are analyzed. Obviously, this kind of approach can be used in a variety of situations that involve people and organizations. For example, we could ask people to comment on how they feel about their jobs, how satisfied they are with their pay, the quality of their working life, and a host of other items. Survey research is relatively inexpensive and it allows the researcher to sample a large number of opinions regarding the topic.

The common problem with survey research is that the answers given may or may not be indicative of respondents' true feelings. In many studies a problem called "social desirability bias" has been noted.[5] This refers to the tendency of respondents to reply in a manner they believe the researcher (and others) will find acceptable. For example, if a person responds to the question, "What do you like most about your job?" by saying, "I like the responsibility and the challenge," this *might* be an example of social desirability bias, since this answer is often considered more acceptable than to say, "I like the money." Social desirability bias (or any distortion of true feelings) can be a major problem not only because it gives a false measure of how a person feels, but also because the researcher has no way of knowing that the bias exists. Some attempts have been made to identify individuals who are especially prone to giving socially biased responses, but it is still a problem for survey research.[6]

Another problem is that the questions may not be clear to respondents. Two people may interpret the same question differently, hence their responses will not be comparable. Again, the researcher has no way of knowing for sure how questions were interpreted. Overall, since survey research usually uses large samples, there is some insurance against misinterpretation of the results. Even if a few people misinterpret questions, the vast majority will likely interpret them properly and give an honest answer. The larger the sample, the greater the chances that most answers will be adequate reflections of peoples' feelings. Misinterpretations of questions can also be minimized by pretesting question-naires before the actual research study.

## □ Simulations

When people decide to do something they have never done before, most try to find out a little about the situation, to increase the chances they will succeed. At some point, however, they actually have to get involved in the new activity. If things don't work out to their satisfaction, then it's "back to the drawing boards." The same is often true for an organization that decides to innovate in some aspect of its management; it could be a new compensation program, building a new plant, or introducing a change in work methods. In any case, there are often unexpected human and technical complications that can arise. Avoidance or minimization of these complications can be achieved through simulation.

Simulation is the approximating of a real-life situation by developing a model composed of the important variables in the situation. This involves obtaining an understanding of how the relevant real-world system operates and then developing a model, often physical or mathematical, which captures the dynamics of the actual situation.

## Box 2-3: Using Simulation Methods

Simulation is a common technique for approximating the real-world environment. Here are a few examples:

Economists have developed a model of the U.S. economy that contains scores of variables (e.g., the prime rate, unemployment rate, government expenditures, etc.). This model can be used to answer questions like "What will happen to unemployment if the prime interest rate increases by two percentage points?" Other variables can be changed and the results simulated until a satisfactory result is obtained relative to the economic goals set.

Many business schools use simulation games as a teaching device. Students run their own companies, usually simulated by a computer. They make decisions on price, advertising budgets, quality control, etc. The computer takes all decisions together and simulates what would happen in a real industry. The results can be used as feedback to students to make additional decisions, while learning how the industry operates.

As another example, the Air Force has developed sophisticated devices that simulate a plane in flight. Pilots in training spend many hours on these simulators, partly because they are cheaper than tying up a regular aircraft, but also because many more events can be simulated on the simulator than can be experienced in real life. Pilots report that the simulators are incredibly realistic, even to the point of causing air sickness!

The examples in Box 2-3 indicate the major advantage of simulations: researchers can try out solutions without actually having to spend the time and money normally required, not to mention running the risks normally involved. If the idea doesn't work in the simulation, it likely won't be tried in the real world.

Simulations in organizational behavior generally are of two types: those that set up a general structure for people to act in roles, and those that attempt to quantify behavioral areas into computerized models. In the first instance, the simulations are designed to give participants a chance to practice behavioral skills without the risk associated with real-life problems. To simulate the effect of one-way communications, for example, an instructor might ask one member of the class to communicate a message to the class using one-way techniques with no feedback.[7] More recent research has attempted to quantify certain variables in organizational behavior so that behavioral processes can be simulated on the computer.[8]

It should be understood that the advantages of simulation accrue only if the simulation model is accurate. If the model developed behaves like its real-world counterpart, obviously it will be very valuable; if not, at best it may be an interesting exercise and, at worst, may be misleading in what it teaches those who experience it. At present, the simulation technique is the least frequently used of the research methods in organizational behavior, partly because human behavior does not lend itself to precise model building. However, as our understanding of computerized model building increases, simulation techniques will no doubt become more valuable as research techniques.

## ☐ Dilemmas in Research

One of the major issues in research methodology concerns the degree of rigor used in formulating the theory and collecting data to test it. As you read the research findings discussed in this book, it will become obvious that the theories incurring the most criticism are those of which the initial findings could not be replicated. One of the strongest influences affecting scientific findings is the personality (or social skills) of the researchers. In interviewing, for example, the personal style of the interviewer can affect the quality and type of information gathered.

When we move from qualitative to quantitative approaches to research, the potential impact of the researcher is reduced. Not surprisingly, research findings that have resulted from qualitative approaches are very slow to be accepted.[9] In the ideal situation, the perfect research study in organizational behavior would be one in which, regardless of the research method used, similar results would be obtained if the same research question were examined many times. Practically speaking, this is not possible in organizational behavior, since it is impossible to identify and control all the variables affecting a research study. Consequently, researchers must settle for less consistent results while still attempting to be as rigorous as possible in their research methods.

Another dilemma lies in the area of internal and external validity of research studies. *Internally valid* means that a study is internally consistent with regard to the experimental variables in question, and therefore the conclusions derived from the study are valid insofar as the experiment is concerned. However, since experiments are artificial and contrived examples of the real world, the findings may have little *external validity*, i.e., relevance to similar situations external to the laboratory. Similarly, a field experiment may have high external validity in that the situation researched is a valid example of how the real world operates; however, due to the large number of uncontrolled variables in the study, its findings may be suspect. For example, case study research generally has high external validity but low internal validity. Laboratory experiments, on the other hand, tend to have high internal validity but low external validity.

Another dilemma pertains to the practical value of research findings. Much organizational behavior research is oriented toward finding predictable relationships between variables, and yet the research is not designed to give specific answers to specific problems. The dilemma here is this: if a theory is too general, then it is relatively useless in practice, since it provides too few guidelines; but if it is too specific, then it is too narrow to be of use to anyone but a select few. Research on specific problems is inefficient research since, by definition, it has limited application.[10] So, assuming one could find a "correct" theory, it would probably be applicable only to a specific organization, or possibly even to one individual. Researchers must, therefore, walk the fine line between the two extremes and engage in research that is not so general as to be useless, yet not so specific as to be generally irrelevant.

## ☐ Conclusions: Basic Research Methods

Two observations are in order as we conclude this brief overview of research methods. First, there is no such thing as *the* definitive research study, and there is no single research method that is better than all the rest. Rather, the most powerful findings concerning human behavior in organizations are those based upon many different studies, using a variety of research methods. If many different studies using different research methods arrive at the same conclusion about the relationship between a set of variables, then we can have considerable confidence in the results.

Second, although the research methods described have been discussed individually, they can be used in combination with each other. For example, in the typical laboratory experiment, survey research is also used to get subject opinions and reactions to issues central to the experiment. In major research projects, several of the research methods may be used as the findings from earlier parts of the research suggest new lines of inquiry and new methods for pursuing these lines of inquiry. Overall, researchers are limited only by their ingenuity in combining the methods of examining human behavior in organizations.

# ■ THEORIES OF ORGANIZATIONAL BEHAVIOR

The fundamental purpose of research in organizational behavior is to test ideas about the relationship between certain variables. From this research new ideas or theories are constructed and refined through further research. However, new ideas about how to manage more effectively come from a variety of sources: management books, personal experiences, conversations with other managers, and management training programs, among others.

Regardless of the source of data, it is important for students of organizational behavior to have a system for evaluating each new theory encountered. This is especially important in this book, since we are emphasizing the applications of the theories. In this section we will describe several classifications of organizational behavior theories and illustrate how they are related to research methods.

## ☐ Descriptive, Predictive, and Prescriptive Theories

Three models classify the purpose of a theory and usually represent its state of development.[11] *Descriptive* theories of organizational behavior simply describe a series of events, relationships, or variables. The observer or researcher does not interject any judgments about whether or not what has happened is right or wrong, or what is causing what to happen.[12] This is a fairly "clean" type of research in the sense that it is not value-laden or full of platitudes regarding what managers should or should not do. Moreover, descriptive theories do not claim to specify that one type of behavior causes another to happen. The case study method mentioned earlier is an example of the descriptive model, since the cases only describe a set of circumstances.

*Predictive* theories of organizational behavior are those that attempt to specify cause-and-effect relationships in organizations. As noted earlier, they are typically designed using sophisticated quantitative research tools that allow the researcher to be reasonably confident that cause and effect has been demonstrated. Generally, predictive theories follow descriptive ones, since it is necessary to have an accurate picture of *what* is going on before we can specify *why*. Accurate predictive models are scarce in organizational behavior for all the reasons noted earlier in discussing cause-and-effect relationships. Predictive theories come about only through exhaustive and repetitive observations, and even then they are often questioned by other researchers using different research tools. One of the most important examples of a rejected predictive model is the one noted in Chapter 1, from the Hawthorne studies. These studies suggested a causal relationship between morale and productivity, but current research does not always verify this predicted relationship. For reasons to be discussed later, predictive models in organizational behavior, once they are constructed, have a way of becoming obsolete.

Another problem with predictive models is that they are often seen as unrealistic. This is largely because most predictive theories receive their strongest support from laboratory studies, which have already been described as artificial and contrived. Let us assume, for example, that we wish to create a model showing the effect of pay upon motivation. If we study normal people in their everyday situations, it is unlikely that we will discover any consistent relationship between pay and motivation because of the other uncontrollable factors—organizational and personal—affecting the relationship. In addition, to create such a model requires us to observe the effects of changes, something difficult to do since changes in pay are usually relatively small.

To overcome some of the problems of predictive models, extreme situations may be created in the laboratory that exaggerate the relationship between the independent and dependent variables. Other variables are controlled (or at least accounted for). Thus, we might observe a change in behavior when pay is either doubled or eliminated completely. And while we realize that in real life people's pay is unlikely to be doubled in a short period of time, this hypothetical situation will allow us to create a tentative predictive model regarding pay and motivation. The reason we choose to point out this characteristic of predictive models is that extreme examples are frequently used in this book. We give these examples, not to show what is typical, but to illustrate cause and effect.

The *prescriptive* or *normative* model prescribes a particular situation as "right" or a particular course of action as the best thing to do. In other words, given a problem, a prescriptive model will tell a manager what course of action to take. Much of the original human relations theory about how people should be treated falls into this category. It should be obvious from our previous discussion that the chances of generating reasonably useful prescriptive models is increased by first developing the descriptive and predictive sequences.

---

### Box 2-4: *Predicting and Prescribing Pay Levels*

Professor Elliott Jaques of Brunel University in England has spent many years examining the relationships among pay, levels of responsibility, and age. Scientifically speaking, his findings are reasonably sound. Given knowledge about your earnings history and your age, Jaques can *predict* reasonably accurately what your earnings will be during the rest of your working life. Also, based on additional research into equitable pay levels, he can *prescribe* the level of pay that norms of society have stated as fair for given levels of responsibility. Reactions to this model are interesting. When informed of the availability of such a predictive model, individuals are dying to know what this "crystal ball" says about their future earnings; when they find out, they spend a considerable amount of time arguing about why it is not true. And despite the predictive validity of the equity model, there is not a single organization in the world that uses the model as its major determinant of salary structures, and only a handful of companies that use the model as a secondary compensation tool. Assuming for the moment that the model is valid, why would this be so?

---

Prescriptive statements, by definition, presume an accurate knowledge of both the situation (description) and the cause-and-effect relationships with the system (predictive). For example, to correctly prescribe that "A manager should adopt a democratic style of leadership" is based upon the assumptions that (1) we *know* what democratic leadership is and how it relates to the specific situation in question, and (2) we *know* the effect democratic leadership will have upon the other important variables (such as productivity). Any time a manager faces a choice of solutions to a problem, the situation must first be clarified, followed by an accurate analysis of why the problem has developed. Then, and only then, can an effective solution be determined.

It should be no surprise that the bulk of organizational behavior theories are descriptive in nature. Since organizational behavior is not an exact science, very little can be prescribed (except in the most general sense) and it is likewise difficult to consistently predict the behavior of people in organizations. Prediction on a large scale is often possible, but individual factors frequently cloud theories that have been based upon data gathered from large groups. For example, we can predict with reasonable accuracy what proportion of employees will be absent on a given day, but not precisely who the employees will be.

This is not to say that organizational behavior theories are of no value. Far from it. As will be seen in the later chapters, the repeated observation and description of an event or series of events allows one to make some cautious but useful generalizations about relationships, and then to make some reasonable prescriptive statements for managers. In essence, this is what we have done in the "applications" sections of each chapter.

A more detailed discussion of the relationship between theory and practice is contained in the final section of this chapter.

## ☐ Universalist and Contingency Theories

Another system for categorizing organizational behavior theories is the universalist/contingency framework. Universalist theories are those proposing a "one best way" for resolving organizational behavior problems. They ignore individual differences and the environment in which behavior occurs. Contingency theories start from the assumption that different situations (and individuals) require different treatment. Rather than a focus upon "one best way," the philosophical cornerstone of contingency theories is "it all depends." Because they consider individual differences and situational determinants, contingency theories tend to be more complex than the universalist theories.[13]

Examples of the *universalist* approach are the beliefs that (1) democratic leadership is always superior to autocratic leadership, (2) everyone desires more challenge and responsibility on the job, (3) everyone is motivated by money, or (4) low morale leads to lower productivity. In general, any theory or model which proposes (either explicitly or implicitly) that all people react the same way to the same stimulus is a universalist theory.

Examples of *contingency* approaches are (1) designing organizations around individual capabilities, (2) using different leadership styles to be effective in a variety of situations, or (3) tailoring job incentives to individual needs. As might be expected, contingency organizational behavior requires greater analysis than the simplistic approach of the universalist theories. The more recent research on contingency theory suggests that organizational behavior relationships are even more complex than previously proposed.[14] More will be said about these two approaches later in this book.

## ☐ Systems Theories

Systems theories are logical extensions of the contingency approach. The systems approach means that all the variables in a system are viewed as both consequences and determinants of each other. In other words, all parts of the system are interrelated. Therefore, changing one factor in the system has an effect, albeit quite small in some cases, on every other variable. Systems are composed of mutually interdependent entities involving a variety of controllable and uncontrollable variables.

## Box 2-5: The Shower Problem: A Contingency Analysis

To demonstrate the contingency versus universalist approach in real life, consider the following example. Imagine yourself in the shower at home; you adjust the water temperature to your desired level and you proceed to shower. Suddenly, the water pressure drops noticeably. Moments later, the water temperature also drops. You leap out of the way of the now-cold water and flatten yourself against the wall of the shower, wondering what in the world has happened. Moments later, both the water pressure and temperature return to normal.

At this point you may be tempted to develop a universalist theory of showers, i.e., you say to yourself, "Whenever the pressure drops, I will leap out of the way to avoid the cold water that is sure to come."

You continue to shower warily, and sure enough, several minutes later the pressure drops again. Having learned your universalist lesson, however, you flatten yourself against the shower wall in anticipation of the cold burst to come. However, this time, as you gingerly reach your hand out under the spray, you notice that the water temperature has not changed. Your universalist theory failing, you must now think in contingency terms if you intend to solve this annoying problem.

The key question is this: Under what circumstances does a drop in water pressure also lead to a drop in water temperature? The answer becomes clear when you recall that when two taps in a home are turned on you will not get as much pressure out of either tap as you would if only one were on. Most people also know that if one tap is running a mixture of hot and cold and another hot water tap is turned on, the temperature of the first tap will be affected. This information can be used to construct our contingency theory of the shower problem. In the first instance (where the drop in water pressure also resulted in a drop in water temperature) we can hypothesize that one of the other hot water taps in the house was turned on. This extra usage of hot water diverted some hot water from your shower and hence the temperature dropped along with the pressure. In the second instance (when the temperature did not drop with the pressure), we can hypothesize that someone else turned on both the hot and cold water at the same time, thus causing a drop in pressure but not in temperature.

Armed with this contingency perspective, you can not only take showers in peace, but also manage people more effectively.

Systems theory is heavily dependent upon description and prediction. In fact, the simulation method discussed previously is frequently a major tool in understanding how variables in the system interact. A simulation model allows the researcher to change one variable in the system and observe how it affects other variables.

Systems analysis is not so much a theory of organizational behavior as it is a way of looking at behavior in organizations. Awareness of the systems perspective forces researchers to go beyond the obvious and examine the rest of the system for cause-and-effect relationships. For example, today it is recognized that while leadership and motivation are "separate" topics, they are intricately related. Similarly, job design is not independent of leadership style, nor is communication distinct from motivation.

The major disadvantage of the systems perspective is complexity. Social systems are extremely dynamic and complex entities which often defy description and analysis. One can easily get lost attempting to sort out all the cause-and-effect relationships. In this book we attempt to point out systems ramifications of certain theories when appropriate and when research justifies it. In real life, managers must likewise view their decisions from a systems viewpoint to ascertain the effects throughout the organization.

# ■ PHILOSOPHICAL AND ETHICAL ISSUES

## □ How Much Behavior Change?

Probably the most important philosophical and ethical issue in organizational behavior concerns the question of how much behavior we want to be able to predict. Since we have hinted that one of the ultimate objectives of organizational behavior is to increase the predictability of human behavior in organizations, we must then face up to the question of how much? In other words, there are many potential problems associated with being able to predict what people will do in a given situation. As an example, consider the stock market. A considerable amount of research effort is directed at developing a model that will accurately predict the behavior of stock prices. Yet, it is equally well-known that should researchers ever succeed, it would mean the end of the stock market as we now know it; the value of the stock market as a means of equity funding is at least partially dependent upon its *unpredictability*, i.e., the risk associated with the uncertainty of stock prices.

A similar problem exists in organizational behavior. We want to predict human behavior, yet we realize that should we ever achieve that goal, managers' jobs would change substantially. This is because the responsibility of the manager is to analyze a situation, make a judgment (decision) based upon knowledge and interpretation of the relevant facts, and then implement the decision. Should human behavior become completely predictable, the need for judgment would be removed and decision making would be more computational than judgmental. As is noted in Chapter 9, *Behavioral Aspects of Decision Making,* computational decisions require technicians, not managers.

The dilemma of organizational behavior, then, is to attempt to increase the predictability of human behavior (probably the main reason why you are reading this book!), yet at the same time to be cognizant of the difficulties that may arise if we succeed. Fortunately (or unfortunately, depending upon your point of view) in much of the organizational behavior theory available, we have few worries in this area. However, there are some areas of research in which this is a nagging question, e.g., the research and practice of reinforcement theory as applied to organizational behavior.[15] It should be noted also that the dilemma is not peculiar to organizational behavior but is characteristic of all the social sciences. For example, if social workers do their jobs well we will have no need for social workers; if ministers are truly effective, they will no longer have a mission, and so forth.[16]

## ☐  The Use of Knowledge

A second problem related to the above concerns not the amount of knowledge that we possess, but what we do with whatever knowledge is available. This is an important issue in organizational behavior, since the fundamental design of organizations places individuals in superior/subordinate relationships, allowing superiors to attempt to control subordinates' behavior.

Since managers are in a position to influence behavior, the degree of influence will depend at least partially on the manager's knowledge of human behavior. Knowledge can be misused and it is not difficult to find instances in which knowledge about human behavior has been used to manipulate people. But this raises the question, "What is manipulation?" If a manager used a monetary incentive to motivate an employee, isn't this a "manipulation" of the employee? Or, if a manager solicits ideas from employees to increase their commitment to the work unit, isn't this manipulating them? As these examples indicate, there is a very fine line between manipulation and "sound organizational behavior practices." It is our belief that manipulation occurs when one person gets what he or she wants at someone else's expense (which usually involves deceiving the other person). But in the above examples, if the manager is getting what he or she wants and the employee is simultaneously reaching personal objectives, then manipulation—in the negative sense—does not occur, in our judgment.

In the final analysis, the distinction between good human relations and manipulation is a value judgment—a judgment that must be exercised by each individual from his or her own frame of reference. This is not to say that the perceptions of others are not important (in fact, the individual may value other peoples' opinions highly and use them as the major criterion). We mean to emphasize that, barring the extremes, we cannot dictate to others what is good and bad managerial behavior.[17] If individuals differ over what constitutes good and bad practice, it is likely that they are reacting to different value systems. The importance of personal value systems in understanding and using organizational behavior theory is very great, indeed.[18]

## ☐  Understanding vs. Changing Behavior

A critical issue in the study of organizational behavior relates to understanding behavior versus changing it. The reason that this is critical is because understanding is a scientific concept which is neutral in its approach, whereas changing behavior involves a value judgment on the part of the one doing the changing, in our case a manager. To understand this issue, it will help to recall our earlier analysis of descriptive, predictive, and prescriptive models in organizational behavior. The *understanding* of human behavior comes about through scientific observation, using both descriptive and predictive types of research designs. The prescriptive model, on the other hand, contains value judgments about a correct decision or course of action. If you believe a particular course of action is the "correct" one, your decision is influenced by your personal values. Because value systems vary considerably among individuals and groups, the relative scarcity of accepted prescriptive models is understandable. Therefore, because of the ethical and moral implications of prescribing behavior for others, much of the theory in organizational behavior—and this book—takes the more neutral position of attempting to *understand* behavior, not necessarily to change it.

## Box 2-6: *The Problems with Changing Behavior*

As only one example of how managers can face ethical and moral dilemmas in changing employees' behavior, consider the following hypothetical (but realistic) example. Assume that an employee is a relatively shy, reserved person who is noted for being unaggressive in dealing with others. The employee's manager believes that promotion will not be possible until the employee becomes more aggressive and assertive with others. The employee is therefore sent to a training program (with his consent) to train him to become more assertive. Because the program is a good one, the training "takes," the new behaviors are reinforced back on the job, and the employee becomes more assertive.

Unfortunately, these new behaviors antagonize the employee's wife considerably. She is not used to this "new" person and finds life quite unsatisfactory. The situation worsens (partly, no doubt, due to the fact that the new assertiveness has also changed the employee's methods of dealing with conflict) so the wife leaves and takes the kids. Now feeling distraught over his broken marriage, the employee blames the company for the unhappy state of his personal life. Was the company wrong in changing this employee's behavior?

There are some important exceptions to the neutral position of organizational behavior. For example, there is a body of literature relating to organizational development and change (i.e., the planned change of behavior in organizations). However, we will see that these changes are only prescribed for situations in which (1) sufficient evidence is available to make prescriptive statements, and (2) the values affected are held by sufficiently large numbers of individuals. You will find examples of these in the "applications" sections of subsequent chapters, as well as in Chapter 14, *Managing Change*, and Chapter 15, *Organization Development*.

The practical implications of the value of understanding rather than trying to change behavior are often underestimated. Managers often fail to realize that making significant changes in behavior in the short run is difficult, and in many cases impossible. Behavior patterns are a function of many things, all of which have occurred over long periods of time for individuals. Similarly, large changes in behavior normally occur over extended periods (notwithstanding the apparent exception noted in Box 2-6), and it is for this reason that people tend to resist attempts to change their behavior quickly. To attempt to make a significant change in a person's behavior in the short run is analogous to pressing on the accelerator and brake of your car simultaneously. The net result is two opposing forces acting at the same time, with much wasted energy and little, if any, change in direction.

A good example of this understanding vs. changing phenomenon occurred in the Canadian north when contractors hired Indian workers for construction crews to erect power transmission lines. One day none of the crew showed up for work, and investigations showed that all had gone to work their trap lines, something they had been taught to do for generations. The mere fact that they had accepted employment by another organization did not affect their cultural heritage. Rather than dismiss the workers or attempt to change their behavior, the company instituted policies which allowed the Indians to maintain their previous behaviors, and found productivity to be satisfactory.

Consistent with the descriptive and predictive approaches in organizational behavior, our philosophy is that understanding the behavior of others leads to *coping* in the short run (as shown by the example above) rather than changing. If managers are aware of *why* something is happening, then they are in a better position to cope with it over the short run (maybe even use it), and then make a judgment about the long-run possibilities for change.

To use a case from the physical sciences to emphasize our point, airplane pilots realize it is useless to try to change existing wind directions and foolish to ignore them. But by *understanding* their nature, i.e., their direction and magnitude, they are still able to reach their objective, sometimes even using the winds to assist them. So by studying the *description* of existing weather conditions, pilots are better able to *predict* the behavior of their flight and allow for the various forces that may be affecting the attainment of their objective. As we mentioned earlier, although prediction in the social sciences cannot yet approximate that which is possible in the physical sciences, the basic principles still hold.

# ■ APPLYING BEHAVIORAL THEORIES TO ORGANIZATIONS

One of the objectives of this book is to relate theory and practice in organizational behavior. A common statement made by managers is, "That's fine in theory, but in practice it doesn't work!" Moreover, the managers are probably correct, i.e., in their experience the theories they have tried have not worked. This state of affairs is unfortunate, since the real world is the ultimate laboratory for the social scientist; if theories are created that do not work, then the gap between theoretician and practitioner is widened. It therefore seems important to discuss some common reasons why theories may not work in practice.

## ☐ Why Do Theories Fail?

It would be foolish to deny that theories occasionally fail to work. In the real world it is not difficult to find examples of theories that have failed to produce expected results and have consequently cost organizations considerable sums of money. But the reasons for each failure are perhaps more important than the failure itself. If these reasons are understood, managers can improve their skills in choosing and implementing theories. Some of the most common reasons why theories fail are discussed below.

**The Theory Is Not Properly Understood.**   In many cases, the individual applying the theory does not fully understand it. Lack of complete understanding can cause a manager to apply something other than the theory in question, or to apply the theory to an inappropriate situation (i.e., use the correct solution for the wrong problem). This might occur, for example, in using job enrichment.[19] A manager who does not fully understand what job enrichment is might overload (instead of enrich) a worker's job, or he might enrich a job that is grossly underpaid in relation to market conditions.

**The Theory Is Designed for General, Not Specific, Cases.**   As mentioned earlier, sound theories are developed using scientific methods on relatively large numbers of observations, repeated many times. Consequently, theories developed tend to apply to individuals collectively, but not to any one specific person. A manager may attempt to apply a prescriptive statement from a general theory to a specific situation that does not fit the general requirements of the theory. For example, it is common to encounter theories that state "generally speaking, money is not a motivator." A manager may mistakenly apply this theory to one individual who, because of his particular background, status factors, experience, etc., is actually highly motivated by money.

**All Relevant Variables Are Not Identified.**   One of the major problems in designing a theoretical model is identifying the number and magnitude of the relevant variables. Since theories are designed for the general case, such models will specify the most important variables that are predicted to affect a situation. This still leaves the possibility, though, that other variables may enter into the problem, thus rendering the original model unworkable. As an example, one of the authors discussed the application of several behavioral science theories with a manager who was attempting to solve a problem of consistent tardiness on the part of one of his women employees. After exhausting all the obvious possibilities of trying to explain the motivations behind her behavior, the manager was asked if there was any other information that might bear upon the problem. He replied that the subordinate was also the wife of his boss, who himself was constantly late to work! General theories cannot possibly account for circumstances like this.

**No Consideration Is Given to Systems Effects.**    One of the most common experiences of managers who try new theories is that, while they may solve their original problem, occasionally new problems are created as a result of their action, and the managers end up thinking they were better off before applying the theory. By remembering that all behavioral systems are interdependent, managers can be on the lookout for potential implications resulting from their decisions. Theoretical models, because they must be limited to a relatively small number of variables, tend to neglect the "systems effect" of introducing change into a social system. For example, a manager who after reading about how increased status for a work group may motivate that group to higher productivity, may overlook the fact that increasing the status of one group may mean lowering the status of another.

**The Ability to Apply the Theory Is Assumed.**    We mentioned earlier the differences between the art and science of organizational behavior and described science as knowledge *about* organizational behavior and art as the *application* of that knowledge. By definition, theoretical models cannot include the art of application. They are designed from a conceptual point of view rather than from a skills perspective, and therefore tend to assume the factor of personal styles and ability to apply a theory properly. We must always recognize that sound theory can be improperly applied by an unskilled practitioner.

**The Theory Is Wrong.**    We must also recognize that "incorrect" theories are created. They may be incorrect for a variety of reasons: (1) the environmental conditions under which the theory was created have changed,[20] (2) incorrect conclusions were drawn from good data, (3) correct conclusions were drawn from poor data, and (4) experimenters overlooked other significant influences that affected their results. Probably the best example of a theory that is now considered to be "wrong" (at least our perceptions of it have been modified) is the theory that money is a motivator of behavior. This theory had been prominent for many years and was one of the cornerstones of scientific management and other theories of employee motivation. However, because additional research has not yet verified a consistent relationship between pay and productivity, the importance of pay is now suspect. The common explanation for the difference in findings is the environmental one, i.e., the conditions under which the original conclusions were drawn no longer exist.

**Cultural Problems Affect Application.**    Finally, there is also reason to believe that differences between cultures can affect the application of theory. A theory based upon data from one culture may be totally inappropriate for other cultures that have significantly different norms and values.[21] A recent example of this potential problem is the publicity given to the Japanese style of management;[22] the success of this style is readily apparent but it is not yet clear whether the system can be used effectively in other cultures. Although one recent study proposed that the Japanese method is not based upon any unique cultural attributes, there have not been enough actual applications of the total system to draw firm conclusions.[23] In any case, most of the research on this problem to date has been concerned with the transferability of North American management methods to other cultures and these have confirmed the transferability problem.

---

## Box 2-7: The Test of a Good Theory

What is a good theory? How would you know one if you found it? These are the questions addressed by two organizational behavior theorists in an attempt to point the directions for future research. They first note that any theory must be of practical relevance for managers. That is, it must be useful. To be useful, the researchers suggest five conditions that must be met:

1. DESCRIPTIVE RELEVANCE—the theory must accurately describe the phenomena actually encountered by the manager;
2. GOAL RELEVANCE—the theory must relate to something that the manager wishes to influence;
3. OPERATIONAL VALIDITY—the theory must relate to variables that the manager can control;
4. NONOBVIOUSNESS—the theory must add something beyond the "commonsense" level of knowledge;
5. TIMELINESS—the theory must be available at the time when managers need it.

Source: Kenneth W. Thomas and Walter G. Tymon, Jr., "Necessary Properties of Relevant Research: Lessons from Recent Criticisms of the Organizational Sciences," *Academy of Management Review 7*, no. 3, (1982): 345–352.

---

## ☐ The Value of Theory

Despite problems that may be encountered in using organizational behavior theories, the theories do have considerable value. Because this is a book that uses a theoretical base to present some practical considerations, it is important to understand the value of theory in everyday life. A good understanding of what theory is and what it can do will assist managers in analyzing problem areas as well as in preventing problems from developing.

Theory is the main vehicle by which an accepted body of knowledge is communicated. Without theoretical concepts, managers would be left with only their personal experiences. Without a systematic method by which the experiences can be related, the value of the experiences is decreased considerably. By combining a series of experiences into a general statement about human behavior, theories are created. Granted, there are better and worse methods of combining experiences, but all theories result from this same general process.

Another way of putting it is to say that managers *will* have theories about organizational behavior; the major question is, how valid will they be? A random combination of experiences is a disjointed and limited framework from which one can learn about human behavior. A systematic, scientific study of experiences, on the other hand, can yield some valuable principles that will help managers perform their jobs more effectively.

Theory also minimizes personal influences, or at least attempts to account for them. If managers attempt to learn only by experience, they are faced with the problem of attempting to sort out what effect they personally had on outcomes. A common example is one manager communicating to another about a successful experience he or she has had. The listener (or learner) has the problem of trying to decide if this person has discovered a new theory or if his or her success is due to personal factors that are not obvious. Thus, what textbook theory loses in its specific applicability, it gains in its generalizability.

One of the major advantages of studying and practicing theory is that it trains the mind to think in an abstract and analytical fashion. For this reason alone, it would be helpful if every manager were partly a theoretician. To put it another way, probably one difference between successful and unsuccessful managers is that successful managers are able to *learn* and *abstract* from their previous experiences; they are able to formulate a principle that can be applied to the general case, thus providing themselves with a new tool with which to work.[24]

In sum, studying theories of organizational behavior can make managers more effective. Although any specific theory may not be able to provide immediate solutions to a problem, the analytical process that must occur is useful, since it teaches the manager to think in scientific terms. A manager who can abstract, learn, and reason has a significant advantage over one who must inefficiently experience every principle of organizational behavior before it is learned.

## ☐ The Value of Experience

Some readers will no doubt think we have been unduly harsh on the practitioner in our discussion of theory versus practice. So far we have not credited experience with being very useful. Such is not our intent. Just as all experience with no theoretical background is undesirable, the "egghead" approach to organizational behavior (i.e., all theory, no practical experience) is equally inappropriate.

Experience is the final test of theory and without it we would be in poor shape, indeed. It is only because experience is sometimes so unscientific that we

> ## Box 2-8: If Professors Are So Smart, Why Aren't They Rich?
>
> Well, first of all, some of them *are*. But not many. Why not? It would seem logical that if someone has all the "answers," then he or she should put this knowledge to good use and make a fortune. But let's look at it from the opposite point of view. If rich people are so smart, why aren't they teaching? In other words, if a rich person really had all the answers, then these answers could be sold for a fortune. But they aren't. Why not? If you can answer this question, then you will have the answer to the first one; if you get that one, then you have a good grasp of what this section is all about. Advance to "GO" and collect your $200.

must be cautious of its meaning and value. Managers who use their experiences as a learning device, have had some valuable experiences that will doubtless make them more effective managers. Experienced managers are certainly more adept in the application of knowledge than the inexperienced academic, but the magnitude of their adeptness will depend on their ability to learn from their experiences. It is an old saying in the personnel field that ten years' experience may only be one year's experience ten times!

## ☐ Experiential Learning

Practicing managers can take pride in the fact that the academic world recognizes the value of using personal experiences in teaching. One method of teaching organizational behavior and management is the use of experiential exercises, which provide students with actual experiences from which they can learn. The experiences are contrived and controlled to illustrate general phenomena about a topic such as leadership, motivation, communications, etc.

The traditional method of teaching leadership, for example, is to lecture *about* leadership concepts. This is typically done by reviewing the theories themselves, examining the research evidence on the theories, and then coming to a general conclusion regarding their relative validity and applicability. Experiential learning, on the other hand, presents the student with a minimum of descriptive theory about leadership and then creates a situation in which the student must either be a leader in a group or a member of a group engaged in completing a task. In either case, the student *experiences*—and therefore feels—something about leadership in addition to simply studying it.

Predictably, experiential learning in the classroom tends to be highly effective (i.e., what is learned becomes internalized) but also highly inefficient in that comparatively fewer concepts are learned. Whereas a good lecturer could explain a large part of leadership theory in perhaps an hour or two, it may require an experiential exercise of four or five hours (including analysis) to experience the difference between autocratic and democratic leadership styles.

One reason why teaching techniques have begun to stress experience is because learning is a personal phenomenon. We spoke earlier of the importance of value judgments in organizational behavior theory, and the concept is equally important here. Experiential learning allows students to integrate the theoretical concepts into their own value systems. It recognizes that behavior is appropriate or inappropriate only in relation to personal goals and values. Experience allows the comprehension of the theoretical concepts in a particular exercise and also permits students to make their own decisions about the appropriateness of behaviors studied and experienced.

# *Opening Incident Revisited—Ted Loewen*

Ted Loewen is obviously upset with Professor Grastark, and justifiably so. What started as an innocent student research project has now ballooned into a major problem for Loewen and an embarrassing situation for Professor Grastark. The project conducted by the students was a combination field study and survey research design. You have now learned that intervening in a social system, no matter how small the intervention, will have effects throughout the system. Professor Grastark was off base in not communicating those risks to Loewen.

The students have learned a valuable lesson about research: field experiments and/or survey research is often fraught with contaminating elements beyond the researcher's control. The fact that union negotiations were about to begin has possibly influenced the responses of participants. Complicating the situation is that most people apparently were naive regarding the purpose of the study, a phenomenon that can strongly influence participants in a field study (recall that this was considered an asset in laboratory studies). The students, obviously not well taught by Professor Grastark, have jumped into a series of prescriptive statements based upon suspicious empirical evidence. Not only have they not considered the systems effects of their recommendations, but they have placed far too much weight on the validity of their findings. Loewen could encounter great trouble if he attempted to implement their recommendations based upon this single research study.

All need not be lost, however. The study could serve as the basis for discussions concerning future changes. Additional evidence, both quantitative and qualitative, could be collected and serve as a more solid foundation for change strategies. For example, the students' findings regarding a poor salary structure could be examined in relation to other data such as turnover, comparable salary structures in the area and industry, and attitudes of employees. What all have realized from this experience is that research is a necessary component in understanding organizational behavior, but inadequate understanding of the role of research can create serious problems.

# ■ SUMMARY

Our primary purpose in this chapter has been to show that understanding the basic research methods and issues in organizational behavior is of importance to management. Although managers are not in the business of creating new theories of organizational behavior, they should always be testing their experiences against their own personal theories of how people behave in organizations. New "bandwagon" concepts are constantly paraded before managers in the popular journals, and managers need a scientific perspective from which the concepts can be evaluated. New knowledge, while often created in formal research studies, is always put to its final test in the field; this could be a field experiment, or a manager applying the concepts to his or her place of work. In either situation, the application of the theory will result in additional data being generated, which can then be used to refine the theory further.

Human behavior being as complex as it is, it is extremely unlikely that a single research study will come up with "the answer." Even if this were to happen, because people and conditions change over time, the conclusions of the study would probably be outdated very soon. So managers and students of organizational behavior must always be searching for new ideas, concepts, and theories, knowing full well that when they find something that works, it will probably soon become obsolete.

# ■ REVIEW QUESTIONS

1. What is the difference between dependent and independent variables?

2. What is the difference between positive and negative correlation?

3. Why does a high correlation not necessarily mean causation?

4. What are the advantages and disadvantages of case study research?

5. What are the advantages and disadvantages of laboratory research?

6. What are the advantages and disadvantages of field experiments?

7. What are the advantages and disadvantages of survey research?

8. What are the advantages and disadvantages of simulation research?

9. What is the difference between external and internal validity in research studies?

10. What are the differences between descriptive, predictive, and prescriptive models of organizational behavior?

11. What is the major difference between universalist and contingency theories of organizational behavior?

12. What is the "systems approach" to organizational behavior?

13. What are the major philosophical and ethical issues in organizational behavior?

14. What are the reasons why theories fail?

15. Of what value is theory to the practicing manager?

16. Of what value is experience to the practicing manager?

17. What are the advantages and disadvantages of experiential learning?

# ■ EXERCISE 2-1: THE BARREL OF LUG NUTS

Joe Milano worked on the assembly line in one of the major automobile manufacturing plants. He had been with the company for about three years. Joe's job was placing the wheels on the cars as they came down the assembly line. The wheels, previously programmed as far as size and styles were concerned, were already mounted on color-keyed rims. Joe worked with an electrically operated torque wrench that automatically tightened the lug nuts to a predetermined torque. At his work station, Joe had a waist-high barrel containing the lug nuts used to attach the wheels to the cars. Every morning when he arrived at work he found that his barrel had been filled during the night, giving him a fresh supply for the day's production.

Jim Miller, an experienced worker, was Joe's foreman. During the past year or so, he noticed that Joe's attitude toward his job seemed to be deteriorating. He didn't seem to care much about his job, his absenteeism had been steadily increasing, and Miller noticed an occasional car missing a lug nut or two. In speaking to Joe about this, he got the distinct impression that Joe really didn't care about his job or the company.

Since the company had a staff of highly educated industrial psychologists readily available, Miller decided one day to ask for a psychologist's help in improving Joe's attitude toward his job and, hopefully, his productivity. The psychologist agreed to help and went about gathering data to bear upon the problem. He interviewed Joe, Miller, and other employees. He watched Joe work for a while and examined many documents pertaining to Joe's work. After gathering a lot of data and retiring to his office, the psychologist returned in about a week to Miller with the following analysis:

"Joe, I believe, is performing poorly and exhibiting poor job attitudes because he does not feel important in his job. He is merely putting wheels on cars. Therefore, the solution to the problem is for you to make him feel more important."

After considering the psychologist's advice, the next day Miller decided to embark upon a concentrated campaign to make Joe feel more important. During the first coffee break of the day, he found Joe in a corner and said to him, "Joe, have I ever told you how important you are around here? Why, just think, if you weren't on the job, every car coming off this assembly line wouldn't have any wheels on it!"

Joe, of course, did think about it and it didn't take him too long to remember that last week he'd taken off one day to go deer hunting and when he came back, he didn't see any cars in the storage lot without wheels on them. The more he thought about it, the more angry he became until late in the afternoon he found himself purposely leaving off a lug nut here and there, under the pretense that the line was moving too fast to get them all on. Almost unconsciously, the next day he arrived at work fifteen minutes late and got a brief feeling of satisfaction as he watched Miller putting wheels on the cars while frantically looking for a "floater" to take over.

Miller, being a man of wide experience, realized that Joe's attitude had not improved and, if anything, had gotten worse. During the day, he also noticed the increased number of wheels with lug nuts missing and became even more concerned—enough so that he called the psychologist again to ask for help. The psychologist returned, listened to Miller's story, and asked for more time to gather more data and study the situation some more.

After more data-gathering and rethinking the problem, the psychologist returned to the foreman with the following analysis:

"The first time I was right, but I wasn't precise enough. Joe's real problem is that he doesn't feel as though he is accomplishing anything. All he does is put on lug nut after lug nut and he never sees that he is making any progress or getting anywhere. He needs some kind of challenge in his daily work life. Note, for example, that each day he comes to work facing a barrel of lug nuts that he cannot possibly finish off. By the end of a hard-working day, he has got the barrel down only halfway; the next day it is filled up again. The poor guy never gets any sense of accomplishment! I think a solution might be to get him a smaller barrel—about half the size he has now—so that by the end of the day he will see the bottom of the barrel and feel as though he has accomplished something."

The analysis made sense to Miller so the next day he ordered a smaller barrel, about half the size of the previous one, filled it with lug nuts and placed it at Joe's regular work station. When Joe arrived at work, he immediately noticed the smaller barrel, but before he could question the foreman about it, the line started and he had to jump right into his job. Nothing unusual happened during the day up until the afternoon break. During the break, Joe felt a little "different" but couldn't seem to analyze why he had the feeling. Before he knew it, the break was over and he was back putting wheels on the cars. Along about four o'clock—about a half hour before quitting time—something remarkable happened. While almost unconsciously probing the barrel for another handful of lug nuts, Joe saw the bottom of the barrel, and for the first time in his automotive career (as the psychologist had predicted), Joe's interest and motivation to produce increased sharply.

What do you think of the psychologist's solution? Why?

# ■ EXERCISE 2-2: DR. CLARK'S PROBLEM

Dr. Joseph Clark was in his first year of teaching and already was faced with a serious problem. He had just left his Dean's office and had one day to give the Dean an answer to the telephone call the Dean had just received.

Dr. Clark's problem was with one of his students in his evening class in organizational behavior. The class was composed largely of adults, many of whom held managerial jobs in the community. The previous week, Dr. Clark had graded the final examinations from the class and had recently forwarded the grades to the students. One student, Mr. Charles Wilson, had failed the course. Dr. Clark read his examination several times, but it was obvious that Wilson did not know the material. Clearly, a grade of "F" was deserved.

The telephone call the Dean received that morning was from Wilson. Wilson had just received his grade from Clark's class and was very upset. It turned out that he owned a local construction company which was quite successful. He told the Dean that he had built the company up from nothing, that the company's growth rate was over 20 percent per year, that he had never experienced any "people problems" as manager, and that he was known throughout the community as a good manager. How then, he demanded to know, could he fail an introductory course in organizational behavior?

As Dr. Clark, what would you tell the Dean?

# ■ ENDNOTES

1. Robert K. Yin, "The Case Study Crisis: Some Answers," *Administrative Science Quarterly* 26 (March 1981): 58–65.
2. For an example of how the case study method is used in teaching, see William E. Zierden, "Some Thoughts on the Case Method," *Exchange: The Organizational Behavior Teaching Journal* 6, no. 4, (1981): 19–22.
3. For a summary of the artificiality issue, see K. Weick, "Laboratory Experimentation with Organizations," in J. March, ed., *Handbook of Organizations* (Chicago: Rand-McNally, 1965), p. 194.
4. D. T. Campbell and J. C. Stanley, *Experimental and Quasi-experimental Designs for Research* (Chicago: Rand-McNally, 1963).
5. See, for example, D. Marlow and D. P. Crowne, "Social Desirability and Response to Perceived Situational Demands," *Journal of Consulting Psychology* 25 (1964): 109–115; and R. T. Golembeweski and R. Munzenrider, "Social Desirability As an Intervening Variable in Interpreting Organizational Development Effects," *Journal of Applied Behavioral Science* 11 (1975): 317–332.
6. H. Arnold and D. C. Feldman, "Social Desirability Response Bias in Self-Report Choice Situations," *Academy of Management Journal* 24 (1981): 377–385.
7. There are many exercises available to demonstrate practically every facet of organizational behavior. For example, see Kolb, Rubin, and McIntyre, *Organizational Psychology: An Experiential Approach*, 3rd ed. (Englewood Cliffs, N.J.: Prentice-Hall, 1980).
8. See, for example, R. I. Hall, "Managing a Magazine Publishing Company," University of Manitoba, 1974. This simulation is based upon research reported in R. I. Hall, "A System Pathology of an Organization: The Rise and Fall of the Old Saturday Evening Post," *Administrative Science Quarterly* 21 no. 2 (June 1976): 185–221.
9. Perhaps the best example of this phenomenon is in the area of salesmanship, an area noted (either rightly or wrongly) for emphasizing the importance of personality ("Good salesmen are born and not made"). Today it is unusual to find courses in salesmanship in university curricula, partly because its research base is suspect. As the research base of other areas increases, those areas replace salesmanship, which has yet to leave the personal-skill base.
10. In recent years the gap between problem-oriented research and pure research has narrowed. "Action research" is now an accepted form of research, provided that scientific principles are still used in gathering and interpreting data (see Chapter 15 for a discussion of action research). See also Virginia R. Boehm, "Research in the 'Real World': A Conceptual Model," *Personnel Psychology* 33 (1980): 495.
11. The discussion here draws heavily upon Fremont A. Shull, Jr., "The Nature and Contribution of Administrative Models in Organizational Research," *Academy of Management Journal* 5 (August 1962): 124–38.
12. Description can be in either qualitative form (e.g., case studies) or quantitative form (e.g., statistical analysis).
13. See for example, Jay W. Lorsch, "Making Behavioral Science More Useful," *Harvard Business Review* March–April (1979): 171–180.
14. Claudia B. Schoonhoven, "Problems with Contingency Theory: Testing Assumptions Hidden within the Language of Contingency 'Theory,'" *Administrative Science Quarterly* 26 (1981): 349–377.
15. See the discussion on operant conditioning in Chapter 4, as well as Chapter 16, where we address this issue.

16. All of these extreme examples assume, of course, that the individual or group has full control over all of the variables in question. This is highly unlikely.

17. For example, if an organization were to make a practice of shooting employees who are absent from work, we would call this a "bad" practice because of the widely held value of the importance of human life.

18. One of the authors once had this point driven home quite well while teaching a course in principles of management. During one of the early lectures, one of the students commented that the entire body of knowledge about management is based on the premise that higher profits are a desirable objective, and that if this premise were discarded, an entirely different set of principles of management could be designed. The student was rightfully concerned, since he thought he would have considerable difficulty getting a good grade in a course that was based upon a value system completely contrary to his.

19. Job enrichment theory proposes that giving individuals more responsibility in their job increases their motivation. We discuss this in more detail in Chapters 3 and 15.

20. This factor is elaborated upon in detail in James A. Lee, "Behavioral Theory vs. Reality," *Harvard Business Review* (March–April 1971).

21. John W. Hunt, "Applying American Behavioral Science: Some Crosscultural Problems," *Organizational Dynamics* (Summer 1981): 55–62.

22. See, for example, Richard Pascale and Anthony Athos, *The Art of Japanese Management* (New York: Simon & Schuster, 1981), and W. G. Ouchi and A. M. Jaeger, "Type Z Organization: Stability in the Midst of Mobility," *Academy of Management Review* 2 (1978): 305–314.

23. Nina Hatvany and Vladimir Pucik, "An Integrated Management System: Lessons from the Japanese Experience," *Academy of Management Review* 6, no. 3 (1981): 469–480.

24. At this point it seems appropriate to note another reason why there are so few prescriptive models in organizational behavior. Prescriptive statements allow for a minimum of learning on the part of the learner. This is because being provided answers to problems is probably one of the worst ways of learning. Teachers learned long ago that students who must work through problems themselves tend to learn more than those who are given the answer.

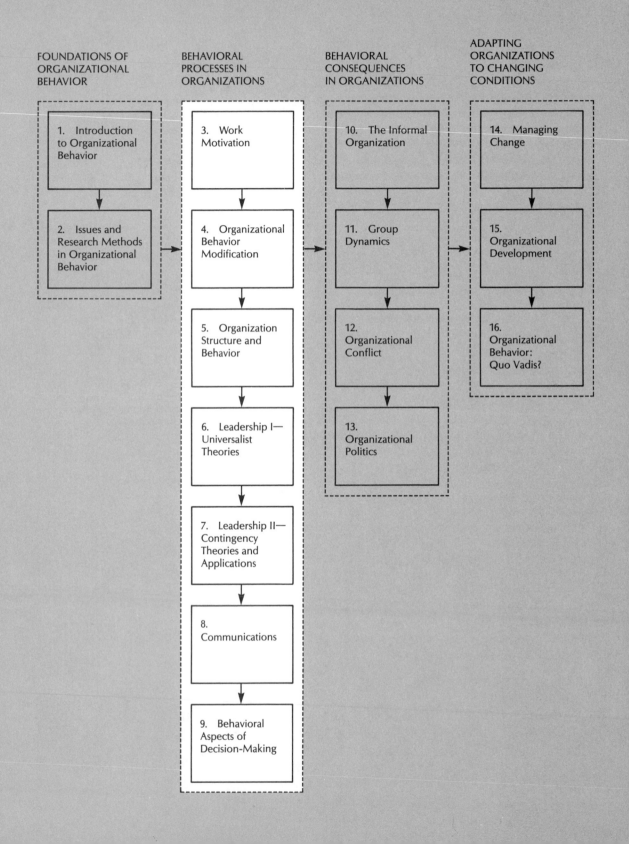

FOUNDATIONS OF
ORGANIZATIONAL
BEHAVIOR

1. Introduction to Organizational Behavior

2. Issues and Research Methods in Organizational Behavior

BEHAVIORAL
PROCESSES IN
ORGANIZATIONS

3. Work Motivation

4. Organizational Behavior Modification

5. Organization Structure and Behavior

6. Leadership I— Universalist Theories

7. Leadership II— Contingency Theories and Applications

8. Communications

9. Behavioral Aspects of Decision-Making

BEHAVIORAL
CONSEQUENCES
IN ORGANIZATIONS

10. The Informal Organization

11. Group Dynamics

12. Organizational Conflict

13. Organizational Politics

ADAPTING
ORGANIZATIONS
TO CHANGING
CONDITIONS

14. Managing Change

15. Organizational Development

16. Organizational Behavior: Quo Vadis?

# Behavioral Processes
# in Organizations

# SECTION II

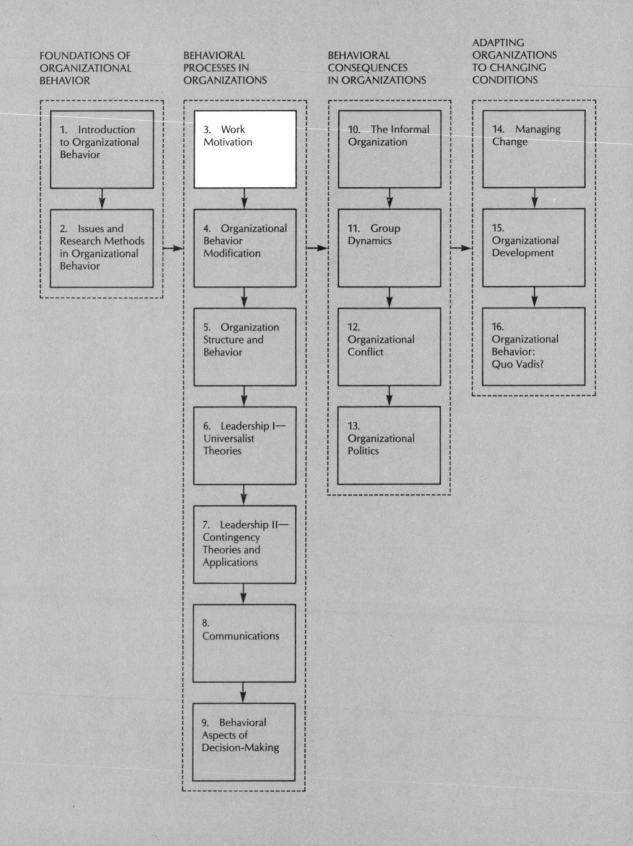

FOUNDATIONS OF
ORGANIZATIONAL
BEHAVIOR

1. Introduction to Organizational Behavior

2. Issues and Research Methods in Organizational Behavior

BEHAVIORAL
PROCESSES IN
ORGANIZATIONS

3. Work Motivation

4. Organizational Behavior Modification

5. Organization Structure and Behavior

6. Leadership I—Universalist Theories

7. Leadership II—Contingency Theories and Applications

8. Communications

9. Behavioral Aspects of Decision-Making

BEHAVIORAL
CONSEQUENCES
IN ORGANIZATIONS

10. The Informal Organization

11. Group Dynamics

12. Organizational Conflict

13. Organizational Politics

ADAPTING
ORGANIZATIONS
TO CHANGING
CONDITIONS

14. Managing Change

15. Organizational Development

16. Organizational Behavior: Quo Vadis?

# Work Motivation

## ■ Learning Objectives

After you have read and studied the material in this chapter you should be able to:

☐ Explain why an understanding of motivation is important for managers in all types of organizations;

☐ Describe the important variables that influence employee performance;

☐ Explain the difference between intrinsic and extrinsic motivation;

☐ Describe several well-known motivation theories and understand their basic assumptions and conclusions;

☐ Explain the relationship between job satisfaction and job performance;

☐ Use the motivation theories presented in this chapter to predict behavior in various situations.

# Chapter 3

# ■ KEY TERMS

**Motivation**
**Intrinsic motivation**
**Extrinsic motivation**
**Ability**
**Performance**
**Goal setting**
**Physiological needs**
**Safety needs**
**Social needs**
**Esteem needs**
**Self-actualization**
**Motivators**
**Hygienes**
**Need for achievement**
**Need for affiliation**
**Need for power**
**Equity theory**
**Expectancy theory**
**Valence**
**Instrumentality**

# ■ CHAPTER OUTLINE

I. Motivation: Some Introductory Observations
   A. What Is Motivation?
   B. The Importance of Motivation
   C. Intrinsic and Extrinsic Motivation
   D. Motivation, Ability, and Performance
   E. Goal Setting and Performance
II. Theories of Work Motivation
   A. Maslow's Hierarchy of Needs
   B. Herzberg's Two-Factor Theory
   C. Maslow and Herzberg Compared
   D. McClelland's Achievement Motivation Theory
   E. Equity Theory

## *Opening Incident—Neilsons*

Jack Daniels was the vice-president of operations for Neilsons, the oldest and largest department store in a major southern city. For the past twenty years the store had surveyed its customers annually about their feelings toward the store. The last three surveys had shown a disturbing trend—customers felt that the salesclerks in the store were unfriendly and not very helpful. These feelings had been reflected in sales; the data Daniels had before him revealed that both absolute sales volume and profit margins had declined for the last three years.

Daniels felt the problem was very serious, so he called a meeting of the executive committee to deal with it. In attendance were the vice-presidents of marketing, finance, personnel, and merchandising. After a lengthy meeting with considerable input from the personnel vice-president, it was decided that the real problem was low motivation levels on the part of the salesclerks. These low motivation levels apparently had resulted in indifferent attitudes towards customers. Several executives at the meeting commented that rumors had filtered up to them that clerks on the floor were not happy because they felt that they were being ignored by management.

The vice-president of personnel pointed out that Neilsons conducted attitude surveys of employees from time to time, and these revealed that (1) salesclerks did not find their jobs very interesting; (2) they received little feedback on how well they were doing; and (3) they felt that there were inequities across departments in terms of workload. A discussion then ensued about how these problems could be resolved. The vice-president of personnel pointed out that since the salesclerks were on straight salary, they were all paid the same amount of money regardless of their sales. She suggested that the clerks be put on commission; if this were done, she argued, salesclerks would show much more interest in customers and therefore would sell more. She cited evidence from a number of organizations showing that the introduction of an incentive system had resulted in increased output by employees and increased profit for the organization.

Some of the members of the executive committee thought that this was a rather drastic step to take and that employee turnover would surely increase if the system were implemented. They cited evidence from other companies where this had happened. Others felt that an incentive scheme really wouldn't solve the problem of poorly motivated employees because money wasn't a good motivator of people. In view of these disagreements, Daniels scheduled a second executive committee meeting for one week later, to allow the members time to mull over the problem and to come up with a workable solution.

Throughout human history, managers in all kinds of organizations have made assumptions about what motivates workers. In organizations that used slave labor, threats and abuse were common ways of motivating workers; paternalistic, conde-scending attitudes were also common. In organizations using paid labor, managers typically assumed that employees worked out of necessity, not out of a love for work. This assumption naturally led to the conclusion that money was an impor-tant motivator of work effort.

The view that money is a motivator was given support by Frederick Taylor in the context of the Scientific Managment movement. As we saw in Chapter 1, Taylor's concern for productivity led him to introduce payment schemes clearly based on the idea that money is a powerful motivator of behavior. Although this view is now recognized as an oversimplification, money *is* important to people, and many managers still use money to motivate workers.

By the 1930s, a major new idea about motivation emerged. The Hawthorne studies had shown that noneconomic factors (e.g., group norms and management concern for employees) could have a major impact on employee motivation and productivity. Many managers eagerly accepted these findings because they felt that if they could substitute "being nice" to employees for paying them a lot of money, the organization would benefit. In retrospect, this view is also an over-simplification of reality.

By the 1970s, managers were frequently encountering a "new breed" of worker who appeared to be suspicious of management, unimpressed by money, unconcerned about productivity, and very hedonistic and self-centered. Moti-vating workers with these views is a major challenge to management because a simple solution to the problem does not exist.

Until recently, concern for motivation centered on blue-collar workers, but there is increasing evidence that white-collar workers are also becoming more difficult to motivate. Executives, for example, are refusing transfers and promotions in the interest of pursuing leisure-time or family-oriented activities. Absenteeism is also common, and a general apathy seems to pervade the white collar ranks in some organizations. These and other conditions suggest that, if organizations are going to be effective, managers are going to need a much more sophisticated understanding of what motivates *all* organizational participants.

In order to deal with the complex subject of work motivation, in this chapter we will:

1. make some introductory observations about motivation, including defining the term, discussing its importance to organizations, distinguishing extrinsic and intrinsic motivation, and examining how motivation interacts with other variables to determine employee performance;
2. discuss the most widely known motivation theories and review the support for them;
3. analyze the relationship between job satisfaction and job performance;
4. discuss some common motivation problems and indicate how the various motivation theories discussed in this chapter can be useful in solving these problems.

# ■ MOTIVATION: SOME INTRODUCTORY OBSERVATIONS

## □ What Is Motivation?

During the last fifty years many individuals have developed definitions of motivation. In the nontechnical sense, the definitions have focused on how hard an individual works at trying to do a task. More technical definitions suggest that some unobservable psychological processes prompt behavior in the first place; these processes then direct the behavior to certain areas and determine how much persistence an individual will have in doing a task. Other definitions stress the importance of conscious goal setting in motivation.

All of the definitions have some merit. However, for purposes of simplicity, we propose the following:

> Motivation is the result of processes, internal or external to the individual, that arouse enthusiasm and persistence to pursue a certain course of action.

This definition recognizes the current debate in motivational research about *why* a person might be enthusiastic and persistent about a certain task. One view is that unobservable (internal) needs motivate behavior. This is a plausible argument, and we will look at several need-based motivation theories. However, as we shall see, these theories have to some extent fallen out of favor with motivational researchers and have been replaced with other types of theories. The most dramatic example of this latter trend is something called *behavior modification* (see Chapter 4), a theory that completely ignores needs as motivators of behavior and concentrates on environmental (external) factors.

Perhaps more important than the choice of a particular definition of motivation is the recognition that motivation has certain underlying properties:

*It is an individual phenomenon*—Each individual is unique, and this fact must be recognized in motivation research.

*Motivation is intentional*—When an employee does something it is because he or she has chosen to do it.

*Motivation has many facets*—Researchers have analyzed various aspects of motivation, including how it is aroused, how it is directed, what influences its persistence, and how it is stopped.

*The purpose of motivation theories is to predict behavior*—The distinction must be made between motivation, behavior, and performance. Motivation is what causes behavior; if the behavior is effective, high performance will result.[1]

## ☐ The Importance of Motivation

Most managers intuitively believe that if workers are enthusiastic and persistent about task accomplishment, the organization will benefit. On balance, this intuitive belief is correct (see Box 3-1 for some exceptions). Why do motivated employees make an organization more effective? First, motivated employees are always looking for better ways to do a job. This statement can apply to top managers who are looking for new corporate strategies, and to production

### Box 3-1: Is It Important to Have Motivated Workers?

A lot of time and money has been spent researching the topic of motivation. This expenditure is defended on the grounds that motivation is important. But important for what? For performance? A worker could be highly motivated and still be a poor performer if the worker did not possess skills or training relevant to the job.

In addition to this problem is the one created by industrial engineers who have been very successful in designing jobs that require very little motivation from employees. All that is required on many production-line jobs, for example, is worker presence at the machine and some slight willingness to do the simplified tasks. This phenomenon is best known in the automobile industry, where worker motivation is typically reported as very low, yet productivity is high.

On the other hand, there are many jobs where motivation *is* important for performance. Generally speaking, in any job where employee enthusiasm and innovative thinking are important, high levels of employee motivation will enhance productivity.

The important thing to remember is that high motivation levels may not always be necessary for employees to be productive.

workers who are looking for ways to do a specific job better. When people actively seek new ways of doing things they usually find them.

Second, a motivated employee generally is more quality-oriented. This is true whether we are talking about a top manager spending extra time on data gathering and analysis for a report, or a clerk taking extra care when filing important documents. In either case the organization benefits, because individuals inside and outside the organization see the organization as quality conscious.

Third, highly motivated workers are more productive than apathetic workers. Much has been written recently about the high productivity of Japanese workers and the fact that fewer workers are needed to produce an automobile in Japan than in the United States. The high productivity of Japanese workers is attributable to a variety of things, but motivation levels are prominently mentioned in many studies. Since increased productivity is a major concern of U.S. firms, and since motivation is an important element in productivity, managers are understandably concerned about employee motivation levels.

---

### Organizational Reality  3-1
### Stock Options and Motivation

Stock options are a good incentive in good times, but they can lose their luster when a recession shrinks share value. To get around this problem, Toronto-based Vickers and Benson, Ltd., one of Canada's largest ad agencies, has devised a unique incentive scheme.

Vickers and Benson divided itself into six autonomous subsidiaries, each with about $40 million in billings. Each company has its own account staff and creative staff, and each buys central services, such as accounting, from the holding-company parent, which controls all the companies. Up to 49 percent of each subsidiary can be purchased by its managers, who decide on the number of shareholders the subsidiary will have. The managers participate in dividends and stock appreciation, and there is a mechanism for selling back the shares as the managers approach retirement.

Burr Bremmer, Terry O'Malley, and Michael Koskie own 80 percent of the parent firm, but this will likely be reduced to 60 percent. "I've had people tell me Terry and I are crazy to give up our own equity," says Bremmer, "but five or ten years down the road I'll feel better having a lot of bright young people running a stronger company."

As shareholders of voting stock, the subsidiary managers are more intent on finding solutions that advance the firm. The parent executives note a new concern with delinquent accounts, a businesslike objectivity in decision making, and greatly increased motivation.

---

Source: "No More Fat Cats: How Vickers and Benson Makes Managers Lean—and Rich," *Canadian Business* (September 1982): 18.

---

### Organizational Reality   3-2
### *Improving Productivity at American Can Company*

The full-time job of about 100 employees of the American Can Company concerns productivity. The productivity groups work with plant managers, advising them and helping them carry out productivity improvements. Most of the improvements are pilot studies that are later adopted in other areas. The group also persuades managers to do more maintenance planning and control. To support the managers, American Can set up a Productivity Information Center at its headquarters. The center indexes magazine articles, books, and journals dealing with productivity and refers them to the appropriate managers. It also publishes a monthly bulletin listing articles concerned with productivity.

When the program began eight years ago it was confined mainly to plant operations that used traditional study techniques. The staff gathered all available information on productivity, and studied methods being used in plants within the corporation and in other firms with high productivity. With its Japanese licensee, the company's human resources staff studied the behavioral sciences and employee motivation programs.

Productivity is stressed in management training, so that managers understand the concept beyond the traditional idea of input/output. The company gives supervisors more management training and managerial tasks. It also encourages business-school graduates to go into production management. By giving them the experience of the shop floor the company hopes to make its managers more aware of the changing needs of the work force.

---

Source: *AMA International Forum* (March 1981): 31–32.

### ☐   Intrinsic and Extrinsic Motivation

There are many reasons why people work. If we accept the notion that people work for broadly defined "rewards" we can break these rewards down into two very general classes. *Extrinsic rewards* (e.g., pay, promotions, compliments, etc.) are independent of the task performed and are controlled by other people. *Intrinsic rewards* (e.g., a feeling of accomplishment of a task that was interesting and challenging) are an integral part of the task and are administered by the individual doing the task. Extrinsic motivation therefore results from anticipation of extrinsic rewards, and intrinsic motivation results from potential intrinsic rewards.

Consider two examples. Suppose you have difficulty in quantitative methods courses but resolve to do well on the next exam. If you study very conscientiously and receive a "B" on an exam, you will probably be elated, even though the instructor may give you no words of encouragement. In this case you were intrinsically motivated because you have rewarded yourself simply by doing well. As another example, if you successfully completed a complicated sale because it meant a bonus, you were extrinsically motivated because you anticipated a reward by someone else (you may also have been intrinsically motivated if you just wanted to do a good job).

If we accept the idea that intrinsic motivation is very powerful, ideally, a manager would determine the specific need structures of all employees and then allow them to work in such a way that intrinsic motivation would be maximized. For a variety of reasons this is usually not possible, so managers generally rely on extrinsic motivators.

Both intrinsic and extrinsic motivators are evident at the work place. Although that may seem appealing (two types of motivation are better than one), there may be significant problems that arise. One researcher argues that extrinsic rewards can actually reduce intrinsic motivation. In a laboratory experiment, students worked on several interesting puzzles. One half of the subjects were paid to work on the puzzles and the other half were not. Subjects were also given free time during the experiment when they could do whatever they wished. The activity they engaged in during their free time was used as an indicator of their intrinsic motivation. Students who were not paid spent significantly more free time working on the puzzles than did subjects who were paid.[2]

The notion that intrinsic motivation can be reduced when extrinsic rewards are given has potentially large practical implications. A person who is intrinsically motivated to do volunteer work may find, for example, that being paid for it reduces his or her intrinsic motivation. In the extreme, this suggests that the pay of workers should not be tied to performance. However, this conclusion contradicts a large body of research that says rewards should be contingent on performance. Which view is correct? The tentative contingency conclusion is that the type of task being performed influences the motivation. Where the reward is an integral part of the task (e.g., commission sales jobs), extrinsic rewards do not reduce intrinsic motivation. However, when the reward is not seen as an integral part of the task, extrinsic rewards may reduce intrinsic motivation.

## ☐ Motivation, Ability, and Performance

Researchers and practicing managers generally accept the idea that employee performance is the result of many factors, some of which are not known to the manager, and some of which may not even be consciously understood by the worker. There is also agreement that the two most important variables in explaining employee performance are (1) employee motivation, and (2) employee ability. These variables appear to be related as follows:

$$\text{Performance} = \text{motivation} \times \text{ability}$$

As we have already seen, motivation is the *enthusiasm* and *persistence* with which a person does a task. Ability, on the other hand, refers to a person's *task competence*. The distinction between ability and motivation is relevant for many situations. For example, if two offensive linesmen are vying for a starting position, they may do so with equal enthusiasm. However, if one of them weighs 175 pounds and the other weighs 250 pounds, the coach will likely pick the heavier player. In a business situation, two salespeople may pursue customers with equal vigor, but if one sells much more than the other, we would have to conclude that one has more ability at sales.

---

### *Organizational Reality   3-3*
### *Productivity Management at Ex-Cell-O*

Updating plant and equipment is a traditional way to increase productivity, but new programs dealing with the total needs of the employees can also be an effective method. Ex-Cell-O Corporation, a manufacturer of packaging and industrial machinery, credits its successful productivity effort to management's keen interest in employees' personal achievements. Robert Harris, manager of profit improvement at Ex-Cell-O, designed a unique three-phase program in which employees take part in their own development as well as that of the company.

In the "motivation" phase of Ex-Cell-O's program, employees complete written exercises that record their views of their jobs, interests, attitudes, and ambitions. On the basis of these answers, the employees and their supervisors arrive at a mutually agreed-upon job description designed for the individual's interests and abilities.

The "education" phase identifies projects for performance achievement. Before or immediately after becoming a member of a project team, an employee takes courses on creative thinking, problem solving, and how to sell ideas and recommendations. For the most part, emphasis is placed on writing reports and verbal presentations.

In the "innovation" phase, project teams analyze a particular work situation, provide solutions, and make formal recommendations to management. Management uses the recommendations to decide on the implementation of ideas, setting up plans, budgets, and timetables.

Plant managers reward volunteers. Recognition may take the form of letters of commendation through theatre tickets and publicity in plant or local newspapers.

---

Source: "Management in Practice," *Management Review* (February 1982): 43–44.

To be realistic, we must accept the fact that these two examples are somewhat extreme. Most managers face situations where (1) the difference between ability and motivation is not quite so clear, and (2) performance may not be clearly defined. Nevertheless, an understanding of the simple formula noted above gives considerable insight into an important part of a manager's job: getting employees to perform at a satisfactory level. The formula allows the manager to assess various situations much more effectively because emphasis can be placed on the variable which seems to be causing the lack of performance. In some situations employee motivation levels are the problem, but in others ability is the issue. The solutions to the problems of lack of ability and lack of motivation are quite different, and a manager will obviously be more effective if the correct problem is defined.

In the formula noted above, a very low score on either motivation or ability will result in low performance overall. For example, people who are extremely nervous about speaking in front of a large audience (low ability) will not perform well, no matter how motivated they are. The formula also implies that a high score on one variable can overcome a moderate score on the other variable. Thus, a person with relatively low ability (but high motivation) might outperform another person with high ability but low motivation. This situation occurs frequently in professional sports when a supposedly superior team (i.e., one with players with more ability) gets beaten by a team with less talented players.

## ☐ Goal Setting and Performance

Motivation and ability are not the only variables that influence employee performance. Various research studies have demonstrated that the setting of goals increases the likelihood of good performance.[3] Some studies also indicate that several characteristics must be evident if goal setting is to lead to improved performance:

First, goals should be *specific*. If the circumstances allow it, goals should be quantified. So, rather than simply exhorting production workers or salespeople to do their best, managers should set specific goals that employees can work toward.[4]

Second, employee performance will be higher if the goals which are set are *accepted* by those who must achieve them. One obvious way of increasing employee acceptance is for the employee to participate in the development of goals.[5]

Third, goals should be difficult enough that workers will have to *work hard* to achieve them, but not so difficult that the workers will give up. If goals are too easy to achieve, apathy and a lack of enthusiasm will be evident; if goals are too difficult, employees will perceive that the system is unfair and motivation will decline. Thus, goals in the middle range of difficulty are most effective at encouraging employees to perform well.

Finally, workers should get explicit *feedback* on their performance.[6] In order to give this feedback, managers must have previously set specific goals or they will be unable to comment on performance. When feedback on performance is combined with specific, reasonable, and accepted goals, the stage is set for improved performance in subsequent time periods.

Several interesting laboratory and field studies have been conducted that examined the effect of goal setting on performance.[7] Two field studies in the lumber business are typical of the results found in goal-setting research. In the first study, the productivity of 292 independent pulpwood producers was analyzed.[8] The highest productivity was found in logging crews where the supervisor (1) set specific production goals for the workers, and (2) stayed with them in the field when they worked. Productivity was high even in groups that did not have much mechanized equipment to aid in their work.

The organization that sponsored the study had emphasized increased mechanization as a way to improve productivity, so the findings were greeted with some skepticism. A second study was therefore conducted to determine if the first findings were normal findings.[9] In the second study, the behavior of 892 logging supervisors was analyzed. Once again, productivity was highest when supervisors stayed on the job with their workers and set specific production targets for them. Several other field studies were also conducted; these yielded consistent results favoring goal setting as a way to improve productivity.[10]

# ■ THEORIES OF WORK MOTIVATION

The motivation research that has been conducted during the last forty years has resulted in some important insights into what motivates people, but it has also resulted in a very large number of motivation theories vying for attention as the best explanation of human behavior. Unfortunately, it is not always clear under what conditions the various motivation theories predict individual effort. While it is quite likely that all motivation theories taken together predict most human behavior, it is often difficult to specify the exact situation in which a particular motivation theory will predict individual work motivation. In this section we will discuss only those motivation theories that have gained widespread acceptance. They are as follows:

1. Maslow's Hierarchy of Needs
2. Herzberg's Two-Factor Theory
3. McClelland's Need-for-Achievement Theory
4. Equity Theory
5. Expectancy Theory

## ☐ Maslow's Hierarchy of Needs

One of the most widely known motivation theories is the need hierarchy proposed by Abraham Maslow.[11] This theory argues for a "here-and-now" motivational state of individuals, and assumes that human behavior is affected when people try to satisfy their unsatisfied needs. The theory assumes that human needs are arranged hierarchically and that needs low in the hierarchy must be largely satisfied before needs further up the hierarchy will motivate behavior.[12] The specific needs and their arrangement are diagrammed in Figure 3-1 and are defined as follows:

1. *Physiological needs*—those needs concerned with the basic biological functions of the human body, such as eating and sleeping;
2. *Safety needs*—those needs concerned with protecting the person from physical and psychological harm.
3. *Belonging needs*—the need to associate with one's own kind; social interaction, love, acceptance, group membership.
4. *Esteem (status) needs*—the need to feel important, or to differentiate one's status from other comparable individuals' feelings of self-worth and self-importance.
5. *Self-actualization needs*—the need to reach one's ultimate goals in life; the need to fulfill one's own destiny.

The need hierarchy rests on two fundamental propositions (1) that unsatisfied needs motivate behavior, and (2) as a particular need becomes largely satisfied it becomes less of a motivator of behavior, while the next level of need becomes a greater motivator of behavior. For most people, higher-order needs will be less satisfied than lower-order ones. Differences in satisfaction levels are likely to

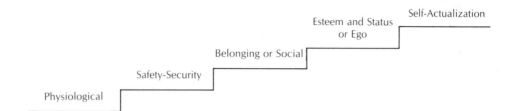

**FIGURE 3-1.    The Need Hierarchy of A. Maslow**

appear across cultures and individuals. In underdeveloped countries, for example, lower-order needs are often poorly satisfied, while in North America they are generally satisfied for most of the population.

Maslow is not the only theorist to suggest a hierarchy of needs; other researchers have also suggested that human needs are hierarchically arranged, but their proposals assume different numbers of levels they believe exist. For example, Alderfer has proposed the ERG theory, which says that there are just three basic needs: *E*xistence (e.g., good pay, job security, fringe benefits); *R*elatedness (e.g., friendship, acceptance by others); and *G*rowth (e.g., development of new skills, self-esteem).[13]

**Empirical Evidence and Comments**    Although widely accepted as an explanation of human behavior, Maslow's theory has not been supported by data gathered in organizations. A study of managers at A. T. & T. over a five-year period tested the extent to which need changes correlated with need strengths in accordance with the predictions of Maslow's theory; little support was evident for the need hierarchy.[14] Another study tested the prediction that changes in the satisfaction of needs in one category correlate negatively with changes in the importance of needs in the same category, and positively with changes in the importance of needs in the next higher category. Again, very little support was found for a hierarchical arrangement of needs.[15] In a third study, the enduring need strength of 547 recent high school graduates was measured three times over a two-year period.[16] Because Maslow's theory says that at a particular time one need is dominant, there should be a negative relationship between the importance of any two needs in the hierarchy. In this study, however the average correlation between needs was positive. Once again, Maslow's hierarchy was not supported. These studies obviously cast doubt on the descriptive accuracy of Maslow's hierarchy.

It is important to point out that Maslow himself cautioned against using the hierarchy to formulate theories of work motivation (such as the Theory X–Theory Y proposal of Douglas McGregor that is discussed in Chapter 6):

> After all, if we take the whole thing from McGregor's point of view of a contrast between a Theory X view of human nature, a good deal of the evidence upon which he bases his conclusions comes from my researches and my papers on motivation, self-actualization, etc. But I of all people should know just how shaky this foundation

is as a final foundation. My work on motivations came from the clinic, from a study of neurotic people. The carry-over of this theory to the industrial situation has some support from industrial studies, but certainly I would like to see a lot more studies of this kind before feeling finally convinced that this carry-over from the study of neurosis to the study of labor in factories is legitimate.[17]

Maslow's need hierarchy may have some validity if we view human behavior on a society-wide rather than an individual level. For example, during the last seventy-five years, employees as a whole seem to have become increasingly concerned with satisfying higher-order needs on the job. This is not to say that wages (which facilitate satisfaction of lower-order needs) are not important; rather, many employees wish to satisfy both lower- and higher-order needs. (For an analysis of the effects of money on worker motivation, see the "Compensation" section in this chapter.)

On an individual level, however, the hierarchy lacks the ability to predict behavior. One reason for this is that the hierarchy is a simplified model of human needs, and in order to be useful it must be used in a very rigid form. Research shows people to be quite complex, and thus it is very difficult to relate a particular behavior to a single need at a given time. This may be why the hierarchy has failed to confirm its existence through research. The hierarchy does serve, however, to give us a general perspective on motivation if used as an abstraction of individual behavior.

## ☐ Herzberg's Two-Factor Theory

A major departure from much of the thinking about work motivation was the "two-factor" theory proposed by Frederick Herzberg and his colleagues in 1959.[18] Prior to that time it was common for those researching work motivation to view the concept of job satisfaction as unidimensional, i.e., job satisfaction and job dissatisfaction were viewed as opposite ends of the same continuum. This meant that something that caused job satisfaction would cause job dissatisfaction if it were removed; similarly, something that caused job dissatisfaction, if removed, would result in job satisfaction. Based upon unstructured interviews with 200 engineers and accountants, Herzberg concluded that this view of job satisfaction was incorrect, and that satisfaction and dissatisfaction were actually conceptually different factors caused by different phenomena in the work environment. These two views of job satisfaction are shown in Figure 3-2.

In the research, the engineers and accountants were asked to think of a time when they felt especially good or bad about their jobs and to detail the circumstances leading to those feelings. After analyzing their responses, Herzberg concluded that one group of factors was causing job satisfaction and another group of factors was causing job dissatisfaction. He labeled the former "motivators" (which, when present, cause satisfaction) and the latter "hygienes" (which, when not present, cause dissatisfaction). The two groups of factors are indicated in Table 3-1. An analysis of the factors in Table 3-1 indicates that motivators are generally related to job *content* (the nature of the work itself), whereas hygienes are generally related to job *context* (the environment in which the job is per-

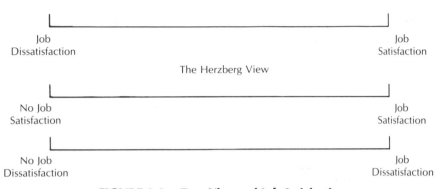

**FIGURE 3-2. Two Views of Job Satisfaction**

formed). Thus, Herzberg believes that job satisfaction and job dissatisfaction are different because *the sources of each are different.*

In Herzberg's view, it is possible to increase job satisfaction without reducing job dissatisfaction and vice versa. Moreover, because the sources of job satisfaction (the motivators) and dissatisfaction (the hygienes) are known, it is easier to predict the effect of a change in, say, working conditions versus a change in job content. To further clarify the Herzberg model, Figure 3-3 shows the theoretical relationship between motivators and hygienes in the work environment.

**Empirical Evidence and Comments** The Herzberg proposal has generated more controversy than any other motivation theory. Unlike the situation for Maslow's hierarchy, empirical evidence on the two-factor theory is abundant. While both supporting and nonsupporting data are available, generally the evidence suggests that Herzberg's proposal is an oversimplification of reality.[19] There are four important criticisms of Herzberg's proposal:

1. *The methodology causes the results.* Many researchers have found that unless Herzberg's methodology is used, it is very difficult to support his theory.

**TABLE 3-1. Motivators and Hygienes in Herzberg's Two-Factor Theory**

| Motivators | Hygienes |
| --- | --- |
| Achievement | Company policy, administration |
| Recognition | Technical supervision |
| Advancement | Interpersonal relations |
| Work itself | Salary |
| Possibility of growth | Job security |
| Responsibility | Personal life |
| | Working conditions |
| | Fringe benefits |
| | Status |

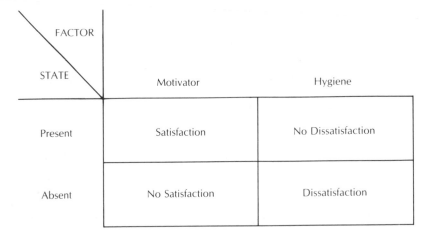

**FIGURE 3-3.   A Contingency Table of the Herzberg Model**

The research supporting this argument makes the validity of the two-factor theory particularly suspect, since conclusions based on what is essentially an artifact of the methodology are unlikely to give insights into human behavior in actual work situations.

2. *The two factors are not actually distinct.* While Herzberg argues for the existence of two distinct factors affecting motivation (motivators and hygienes), empirical studies indicate that specific *job content* factors are sometimes listed by individuals as hygienes, while *job context* factors (particularly pay) are sometimes listed as motivators.[20] This is most likely to be the case if two distinctly different groups are studied. For example, blue-collar workers may perceive pay as a motivator, whereas professional workers may not. Sex differences have also been found; female workers often list interpersonal relations as motivators, but male workers generally do not. Thus, the distinction between motivators and hygienes is often not so clear as Herzberg contends.

3. *Human nature explains Herzberg's findings.* Some researchers have suggested that human beings have a tendency to take credit for their achievements and to blame others, or the company, for their failures.[21] If this is so, it would account for the separate lists of hygienes and motivators that Herzberg "discovered." His proposal then becomes simply an after-the-fact clarification of human nature instead of a breakthrough in the field of motivation.

4. *Herzberg's influence has caused hygienes to be ignored.* Critics argue that the wide acceptance of Herzberg's theory has led to a tremendous emphasis on motivators, and that the importance of hygienes has been ignored. While Herzberg's findings may apply to professional workers, studies of blue-collar workers reveal a continuing concern about hygienes. In one such study, personal interviews with production workers revealed that they were less satisfied with the hygienes in their job than they were with the motivators.[22] This finding suggests that hygienes also play an important role. Thus, Herzberg's ideas may have led to

an overemphasis on high-level needs at the expense of basic needs that employees are concerned with.

Taken in its entirety, the empirical evidence (other than that supplied by Herzberg) does not strongly support the two-factor theory. It does not, however, clearly refute it. Perhaps the most important conclusion to be reached is that the dual continua of job satisfaction and job dissatisfaction have not been empirically demonstrated as *the* descriptive model of individual motivation. Yet, the recognition that such a possibility exists has certainly contributed to the clarification of the relationship between employee morale and productivity, an issue that is treated later in this chapter.

## ☐ Maslow and Herzberg Compared

The motivational proposals of Herzberg and Maslow have become very popular and have been widely accepted by both academics and managers. Does this mean that the theories have much in common and are complementary? Although there are some similarities in the two theories, many differences exist. Perhaps the most basic similarity is that they both assume that specific needs energize behavior. Furthermore, there appears to be a great deal of agreement as to the totality of human needs. Figure 3-4 shows how the needs in the two proposals might be related. It seems reasonable to argue that Herzberg's motivators satisfy Maslow's higher order needs, i.e., ego and self-fulfillment, while the hygiene factors are the equivalent of the physiological, safety, and social needs of the need hierarchy. If the assumption is made that, at least in North America, most people's lower-order needs have been relatively satisfied, then there is some logic in arguing that hygiene factors will not motivate them (a satisfied need is not a motivator of behavior, according to Maslow). In other words, the reason Herzberg's motivators motivate is because they appeal to the generally unsatisfied higher order needs of

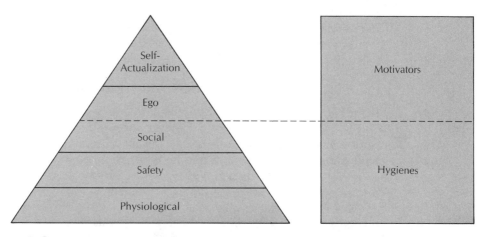

**FIGURE 3-4. A Comparison of Maslow's Need Hierarchy and Herzberg's Two-Factor Theory**

**TABLE 3-2.   Differences in Maslow's and Herzberg's Motivation Theories**

| Issue | Maslow | Herzberg |
|---|---|---|
| 1. Type of theory | Descriptive | Prescriptive |
| 2. The satisfaction–performance relationship | Unsatisfied needs energize behavior; this behavior causes performance | Needs cause performance |
| 3. Effect of need satisfaction | A satisfied need is not a motivator (except self-actualization) | A satisfied (hygiene) need is not a motivator; other satisfied needs are motivators |
| 4. Need order | Hierarchy of needs | No hierarchy |
| 5. Effect of pay | Pay is a motivator if it satisfies needs | Pay is not a motivator |
| 6. Effect of needs | All needs are motivators at various times | Only some needs are motivators |
| 7. View of motivation | Macro view—deals with all aspects of existence | Micro view—deals primarily with work-related motivation |
| 8. Worker level | Relevant for all workers | Probably more relevant for white collar and professional workers |

man. But again, caution must be used with these two models on an individual basis, since there are many exceptions to them. On a general level, however, the juxtaposition of the two models makes logical sense.

The differences in the two theories are presented in detail in Table 3-2. An analysis of this table reveals obvious differences in important underlying assumptions, yet many managers and academics seem to accept *both* theories. While this may not be quite so illogical as it appears at first glance, the fact remains that many individuals apparently have not clarified their own assumptions about work motivation prior to assessing the theories. Thus, the popular acceptance of these motivation theories may be based more on ease of understanding than on clear thinking.

## ☐ McClelland's Achievement Motivation Theory

In the late 1930s the Thematic Apperception Test (TAT) was developed by Murray.[23] Twenty pictures were shown to subjects who were asked to make up a dramatic story about each one. Based on the results, Murray argued that about twenty basic human needs that motivated behavior could be identified. Beginning in the early 1950s, McClelland and his associates began to research three of these needs extensively—power, affiliation, and achievement.[24]

McClelland believes that each person possesses all three needs (as well as others), but that people differ in the degree to which the various motives dominate their behavior. The motives are described as:

1. *Need for power (nPow)*—The individual exhibiting this need as the dominant one derives satisfaction from his or her ability to *control* others. Actual achieve-

> ## Box 3-2: How Can This Be?
>
> The motivation theories of Maslow and Herzberg are currently very popular and are widely accepted by students and practicing managers as being descriptive of employee motivation.
>
> Interestingly, Maslow and Herzberg make dramatically different assumptions about employees. Maslow argues that a satisfied need is not a motivator, whereas Herzberg believes that the reverse is true (for motivators). How can people accept both theories when these fundamental differences exist in the theories?

ment of desired goals is of secondary importance to the high nPow individual; instead the means by which goals are achieved (the exercise of power) are of primary importance. Individuals with a high nPow derive satisfaction from being in positions of influence and control. Organizations that foster the power motive tend to attract individuals with a high need for power (for example, military and political organizations).

2. *Need for affiliation (nAff)*—Individuals exhibiting this need as a dominant motive derive satisfaction from *social and interpersonal activities.* There is a need to form strong interpersonal ties and to "get close" to people psychologically. If asked to choose between working at a task with those who are technically competent and those who are their friends, high nAff individuals will choose their friends.

3. *Need for achievement (nAch)*—Individuals high in nAch derive satisfaction from *reaching goals.* The feeling of successful task accomplishment is important to the high achiever. Although individuals high in nAch are often wealthy, they are so largely because they are able to achieve goals, and in most societies this is rewarded financially. High achievers are not motivated by money per se, but instead use money as a method of "keeping score" of their achievements. High achievers prefer immediate feedback on their performance and they generally undertake tasks of moderate difficulty rather than those that are either very easy or very difficult. They also prefer to work independently so that successful task performance (or failure) can be related to their own efforts rather than the efforts of someone else. High achievers avoid gambling situations since they do not have control over the outcome.

Like Murray, McClelland uses the TAT to determine individual need dominance. Subjects are presented with a series of simple pictures and asked to write a short story of "what is going on" in the picture. "What is going on" is, of course, determined by the subjects' own perceptions. The comments made by individuals taking the test are converted to an objective measure of the strength of each of the three needs, using a scoring technique developed by McClelland.

Perhaps the most distinctive element of the achievement motivation theory is the claim by McClelland that the need can be learned (or unlearned). McClelland has reported numerous instances in which individuals with a low initial need to achieve were subjected to a series of classroom experiences that resulted in an increased need to achieve. He believes that cultures that are economically backward can be changed by inducing and stimulating the need to achieve; if McClelland is right, this gives the achievement motivation theory a distinct advantage over many other motivation theories, inasmuch as it can be taught to an individual or group.

Although much of the writing and research published has been concerned with the need to achieve, McClelland's work on motivation extends to the needs of power and affiliation as well. McClelland is most concerned with matching an individual's motivation patterns with the needs of the organization. In using the TAT test to determine people's motivation patterns, it may be discovered that an individual whose dominant motive is affiliation is working in an organization that rewards power-oriented behavior. The individual can then be placed in a program to enhance his or her own power motivation to more closely match that rewarded by the organization. Another example, more specific in nature, is the possibility that a social worker may find his or her dominant need to be achievement, a motive that research has shown to be inappropriate for this type of work.[25] Again, a development program may be undertaken to reduce the need to achieve, to

## Box 3-3: Why Are Certain Motivation Theories Popular?

Why is it that certain motivation theories catch the attention of academics and managers, while others languish in obscurity? The answer should be that the "right" theories become popular and the "wrong" ones don't. In the long run, this argument may be correct. (For example, in the three-thousand-year history of astronomy we have become increasingly knowledgeable through "right" theories about the universe.) In the short run, however, this argument doesn't explain things very well. Something else explains popularity. Let's try to discover what that "something else" is.

We can consider the five motivation theories presented in this chapter. Whereas the theories are very diverse in their approach to motivation, they all have a "high" view of human beings. They assume that we are thinking creatures with goals, feelings, and a capacity to learn. All of this is very flattering if you're a human being, much more flattering than a motivation theory that assumes that you are a more or less mindless organism going through life responding to stimuli from your environment. There is a motivation theory that makes precisely these assumptions (it is discussed in the next chapter) and it has been vigorously opposed by many researchers even though it predicts human behavior in many situations. So popularity may depend less on what is correct than on what is palatable for the population at a particular time (remember the earth-is-the-center-of-the-solar-system belief of the 1300s?).

bring it more in line with the other two needs. So, while the need to achieve has received the greatest publicity, McClelland's theory is actually concerned with matching individuals' motivation patterns to the organizations in which they are working.

**Empirical Evidence and Comments**   The bulk of the evidence cited as support for the relevance of nAch has been conducted by McClelland and his associates. In an analysis of grade-school readers, for example, it was found that over a twenty-five-year period, in some countries the readers increased their emphasis on the need to achieve (as measured by McClelland's scoring technique) while in others, Great Britain for example, the emphasis decreased drastically.[26] McClelland argues that it is important for those in positions of authority to seriously consider ways to continue an upward trend or reverse a downward one for the sake of the economic development of the country. It is his belief that the educational system reflects the presence or absence of the need to achieve and conditions the citizenry to behave in a certain fashion. Following are three major criticisms of McClelland's work.

First, the use of a projective technique such as the TAT to determine basic needs has been questioned. While projective techniques have many advantages over structured questionnaires, the interpretation of subjective comments is at best an art, and at worst an exercise indicating the bias of the researcher, not the subject. Because of this criticism, it is useful to use different techniques to measure McClelland's three needs. One promising approach is to look at the actual decision-making behavior of people and then deduce what needs are motivating the decisions. In one study designed to test this idea, respondents were asked to make job-choice decisions between jobs that were high in nPow, nAch, or nAff.[27] Three groups (scientists and engineers, graduate students, and executives) were used in the study. For both graduate students and scientists/engineers, nAch scores were higher than nPow and nAff scores. For executives, however, nPow scores were higher than nAff or nAch. (This latter finding is important, as we shall see later in Chapter 6.) These findings are exploratory in nature, but they do indicate that there are multiple ways to test a theory. If the various tests of the theory all yield consistent answers, then we can have increased confidence in what the theory says.

Second, the argument that the need for achievement can be taught to adults conflicts with the large body of psychological literature that argues that the acquisition of motives normally occurs in childhood and is very difficult to change, once it has been established. McClelland himself recognizes this problem, but argues that there is strong evidence from various fields (e.g., politics and religion) to indicate that adult behavior can be drastically altered in a relatively short period of time.

Third, McClelland's proposal has been questioned on grounds of permanence. While the need to achieve may be feasible to teach under carefully controlled conditions, it may be only a temporarily induced feeling rather than a permanent change in behavior. Critics compare McClelland's results with those one sometimes sees in emotionally charged groups such as evangelistic meetings or political rallies; through the atmosphere and emotion generated within these groups, people can exhibit changes in behavior within that environment, but once they return to their "normal" environment, the behavior is extinguished if not properly supported. McClelland himself has noted this problem when attempting to induce and maintain the need to achieve in members of minority groups. He has found that while nAch can be taught to a group of, say, disadvantaged minority members, once they return to the ghetto the need can be lost because of the nonsupportive environment.[28]

On balance, McClelland's work seems to have numerous practical applications, at least in the economic realm. It would appear that the current problem is to concentrate on the development of an environment that will support the desired need, be it affiliation, power, or achievement, or to change the need to fit the environment. In many respects, McClelland's work holds promise for work motivation.

## □ Equity Theory

As the name implies, this motivation theory is based on the assumption that individuals are motivated by their desire to be equitably treated in their work relationships. When employees work for an organization, they basically exchange their services for pay and other benefits. Equity theory proposes that individuals attempt to reduce any inequity they may feel as a result of this exchange relationship. For example, if employees feel either overpaid or underpaid, equity theory predicts they will be motivated to resolve the inequity.

The original statement of equity theory is generally credited to Adams, but other researchers have also contributed to its development.[29] Four important terms are defined by Adams:

1. Person—the individual for whom equity or inequity exists;
2. Comparison Other—any group or individual used by Person as a referent regarding inputs and outcomes;
3. Inputs—characteristics individuals bring with them to the job; these may be ascribed (e.g., race, sex, age, etc.) or achieved (e.g., education, experience, etc.). They are subjectively perceived by Person.
4. Outcomes—those things the individual receives from the job (e.g., pay, promotions, fringe benefits, etc.); these are also subjectively perceived by Person.[30]

The theory proposes that the motivation to act develops after the Person compares Inputs/Outcomes with the identical ratio of the Comparison Other. This process is shown in Figure 3-5. Inequity is defined as the perception that Person's job Inputs/Outcomes ratio is not equal to the Inputs/Outcomes ratio of the Comparison Other. Table 3-3 indicates how the magnitude of inequity is perceived by the Person; the level of felt inequity is scaled from 0 to 2, with 0, 1, and 2 indicating no, moderate, and great inequity, respectively.

The basic equity proposal assumes that, upon feeling inequity, the Person is motivated to reduce it. Further, the greater the felt inequity, the greater the

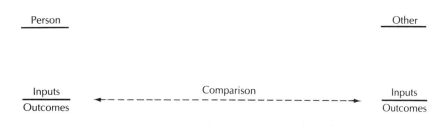

**FIGURE 3-5.  The Basic Equity Model**

motivation to reduce it. When attempting to reduce felt inequity, the Person may try a number of alternatives, some of which are:

1. The Person may increase or decrease Inputs or Outcomes relative to those of the Other;
2. The Person may subjectively distort perceptions of Person's own or the Other's Inputs or Outcomes;
3. The Person may change to a different Comparison Other;
4. The Person may leave the situation.

**Empirical Evidence and Comments**   A large number of empirical studies have tested equity theory under one of four conditions. These four conditions are two-way comparisons of the two control variables: method of payment (hourly or piece-rate) and magnitude of payment (overpayment or underpayment). The predictions for each situation and the empirical support for each are indicated in Figure 3-6. Overall, the support for equity theory is mixed, with the strongest support evident for predictions made when the Person is paid on a piece-rate basis. Support for predictions made when the Person is paid on an hourly basis is less consistent.[31]

   One field experiment tested the accuracy of equity theory in predicting the behavior of free-agent major-league baseball players.[32] The researchers predicted

**TABLE 3-3.  Amount of Inequity for Person as a Result of Different Inputs and Outcomes for Person and Other**

| Person | Inputs-Outcomes Other | | | |
| | Low-High | High-Low | Low-Low | High-High |
|---|---|---|---|---|
| Low-High | 0 | 2 | 1 | 1 |
| High-Low | 2 | 0 | 1 | 1 |
| Low-Low | 1 | 1 | 0 | 0 |
| High-High | 1 | 1 | 0 | 0 |

**Note:**   The first member of the pair indicates inputs and the second member Outcomes.

Source: J. S. Adams, "Toward an Understanding of Inequity," *Journal of Abnormal and Social Psychology* 67 (1963): 425. Reprinted by permission.

|  | Underpayment | Overpayment |
|---|---|---|
| **Piece Rate** | Predictions: Quantity will increase and quality will decrease as the individual attempts to resolve his underpayment situation.<br><br>Empirical Evidence: Support for the hypothesis. | Predictions: Quantity will decrease and quality will increase as the individual reduces output to avoid further inequity because of overpayment.<br><br>Empirical Evidence: Consistent support for the hypothesis. |
| **Hourly** | Predictions: Quality and quantity will decline as the individual reduces inputs in an attempt to achieve equity.<br><br>Empirical Evidence: Very few studies done; some preliminary support for the hypothesis. | Predictions: Quality and quantity will increase as the individual increases inputs in an attempt to achieve equity.<br><br>Empirical Evidence: Generally supports the hypothesis; however, the studies may have had methodological problems. |

**FIGURE 3-6. Equity Predictions and the Empirical Support for Them**

that since players playing out their options perceived themselves as underpaid, their performance in their option year should decline. An analysis of twenty-three individuals who were playing out their options in 1976 revealed that their performances (as measured by batting average, home runs, and runs batted in) dropped during their option year as compared to an average of their three previous years' performances. When the players joined their new teams in 1977 (at their new salaries), their performances returned to normal.

A second study, which analyzed the performance of free agents over a three-year period, found that there were no declines in performance for individuals in their option year.[33] The researchers attributed this finding to the fact that free agency was brand new in 1976 and had an unusual effect on players. Once it had become commonplace (and three years of data were available), the effects diminished markedly.

Equity theory is a promising motivation theory for predicting activities of employees; however, there are some areas of the theory that need clarification:

1. Is a given factor always an Input or an Outcome? For example, "responsibility" is viewed by some people as an Input and by others as an Outcome.
2. How does Person choose (or change) the Comparison Other? The process by which individuals decide with whom to compare themselves is not clearly understood at present.
3. Under what circumstances will each method of inequity resolution be used? The inequity level that induces one employee to quit his job may cause another

to simply change his Comparison Other. Individual differences obviously influence this activity.

4. What is the relationship between Inputs and Outcomes? If (as seems likely) they are perceived by employees to be interrelated (e.g., more outcomes cannot be attained without additional inputs), the prediction of employee behavior is more difficult.

5. Will the findings generated in laboratory experiments hold in actual organizations? One analysis of equity theory noted that most studies supporting it have been laboratory experiments with student subjects.[34] In these situations, the comparison person is usually specified and the over- or underpayment is obvious. In actual organizations these things are not nearly so clear.

Since equity theory was proposed only recently, it is not surprising that answers to these questions are not clear-cut. Further research will give us greater insights into the usefulness of equity theory for predicting employee behavior and motivational levels.

## ☐ Expectancy Theory

One of the basic assumptions made in expectancy theory is that people think quite a bit about doing things before they actually do them. In its simplest form, expectancy theory says that a person's motivation to behave in a certain way is determined by (1) outcomes the person sees as desirable and (2) the person's belief that these desired outcomes can be attained. Expectancy theory was first proposed by Vroom,[35] and has been elaborated and refined by other researchers.[36]

To understand expectancy theory, it is necessary to define the important terms in the theory and indicate how they interact to cause employee motivation. The terms and their interactions are as follows:

1. *Instrumentality*—This is the belief by an individual that certain work outcomes will lead to certain other desired outcomes. For example, successful completion of an important project may mean that an individual will get a promotion. One outcome (project completion) leads to another outcome (promotion). Instrumentality ranges from $-1$ (belief that one desired outcome is attainable only without the other) through 0 (belief that there is no relationship between the two outcomes) to $+1$ (belief that the first outcome is necessary and sufficient for the second outcome to occur).

2. *Valence*—This term refers to the degree of desirability of outcomes as seen by the individual. The valence of an outcome is positive when the individual desires it and negative when he or she wishes to avoid it; valences are therefore scaled over a wide range of positive and negative values. Expectancy theory emphasizes the idea that objective valences are unimportant; rather, the individual's perceptions are determinants of behavior. Two types of valence exist in expectancy theory. The valence of second-level outcomes ($V_k$) measures outcomes employees feel are desirable or undesirable. These include things like pay, job status, promotions, getting fired, etc.

Another kind of valence is the valence of job performance ($V_j$). This measures how desirable or undesirable employees see actual performance on the job. Instrumentality and the two kinds of valence are related as indicated in the formula below:

$$V_j = \sum_{k=1}^{n} (I_{jk} V_k)$$

where  $V_j$ = the valence of job performance level $j$
  $I_{jk}$ = the belief that outcome $j$ will lead to the desired second-level outcome $k$
  $V_k$ = the valence of second-level outcome $k$

What this formula is really saying is that employees will value actual job performance if the relationship between second-level outcomes ($V_k$'s) and instrumentality ($I_{jk}$) is "right" and will not value job performance if the relationship is "wrong." For example, if an employee viewed a bonus as having positive valence and the boss said, "If you get this project completed on time, there will be a big bonus in it for you," the valence of job performance would be positive and the employee would likely work very hard to finish the project. On the other hand, if a student didn't care about grades and the professor said, "If you don't turn in the assignment, you are going to flunk the course," the student might very well not turn in the assignment. In this case the valence of job performance (i.e., performing in the course) would probably be very low so the student would not be motivated to turn in the assignment.

To this point we have shown only how employees decide whether or not job performance ($V_j$) is desirable. Before employees actually demonstrate job behavior, expectancy theory says they also consider how likely it is that they will successfully complete tasks they attempt. Thus, in expectancy theory employee preferences for certain courses of action are affected not only by the desirability of the outcomes associated with them (valence) but also by the degree to which the outcomes are perceived as following from the act. Expectancy ($E_{ij}$) is the belief of an individual that an act on his or her part will actually result in a given outcome. The value of expectancy ranges from 0 (no relationship perceived) to +1 (complete certainty that the performance of the act will result in the outcome). Expectancy interacts with the valence of job performance ($V_j$) to cause employee motivation as follows:

$$F_i = \sum_{j=1}^{n} (E_{ij} V_j)$$

where  $F_i$ = the force (motivation) to perform act $i$
  $E_{ij}$ = the expectancy that outcome $j$ will follow from act $i$
  $V_j$ = the valence of outcome $j$ (the valence of job performance)

This is the key formula in expectancy theory and it simply says that if the relationship between $E_{ij}$ and $V_j$ is "right," motivation will be high and if it is "wrong," motivation will be low. For example, if a person feels it would be very desirable to be a physicist ($V_j$ is positive) and the person is a mathematical genius, the expectancy is positive and it is likely that the person will be motivated to do what is necessary to become a physicist. On the other hand, if an employee in a family-owned business feels it would be very desirable to be the company president ($V_j$ is positive) but knows that only family members can become president, expectancy ($E_{ij}$) = 0 and motivation = 0.

As the preceding paragraphs suggest, expectancy theory is a very complex motivation theory from the point of view of (1) assumptions made about employee decision processes and (2) the difficulty managers may have in understanding it. Figure 3-7 further clarifies the variables in the theory and the way in which they interact by showing the equivalent of what is algebraically represented in the two formulae above.

**Empirical Evidence and Comments**   A great deal of research has been conducted testing expectancy theory, most of it using survey research techniques, and as subjects, either students or managers in actual organizations.[37] The typical study involves gathering data from managers on valence, instrumentality, and expectancy. Effort is usually rated by the respondents and their superiors on the job (self-rated and superior-rated effort, respectively). To determine how well expectancy theory predicts behavior, correlation analysis is used; changes in the independent variables (valence, expectancy, and instrumentality) are correlated with changes in the dependent variable (effort). Generally, the correlations in these studies do not exceed 0.50, meaning that, at most, expectancy theory accounts for one-quarter (0.50 squared) of the variance in behavior. While these results are no worse than those for some other motivation theories, these relatively low correlations have led a number of researchers to propose refinements and alterations in the basic model so that it will more accurately account for human behavior. As it stands presently, expectancy theory exhibits a number of difficulties that need to be resolved.

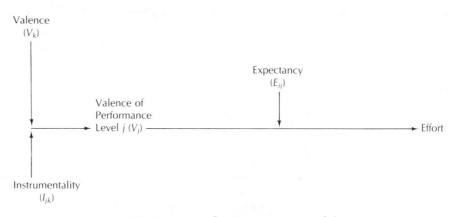

**FIGURE 3-7.   The Expectancy Model**

Source: Adapted from Herbert Heneman and Donald Schwab, "Evaluation of Research on Expectancy Theory Predictions of Employee Performance," *Psychological Bulletin* 78: 1-9.

First, the assumed connections among the variables may not be representative of reality. For example, the relationship between effort and performance may be much more complex than assumed in expectancy theory. As it stands, expectancy theory assumes that effort causes performance. In some situations, however, performance may cause effort. A student who scores well on an examination may suddenly find that he or she has become much more interested in the course. Here, performance (a good exam score) has caused effort (increased studying). To be realistic, however, we must admit that some effort must originally have gone into studying or a good exam score would not have occurred in the first place. The point is that the causal connections are not so simple as one might think.

Second, there are probably numerous instances where employees make work effort "decisions" with no conscious thought. This is particularly true for routine jobs. A related issue is whether employees are willing to engage, or are capable of engaging in the decision processes assumed by expectancy theory. Research indicates that people often make decisions and later try to rationalize them, rather than use the process indicated in expectancy theory to make the decision in the first place. (This question of how much thought employees give to actions before taking them is dealt with in some detail in the next chapter.)

Third, the predictive accuracy of the theory leaves much to be desired. Correlations of the magnitude mentioned above indicate that many factors besides those mentioned influence the amount of effort individuals are willing to put into the job.

## Box 3-4: *Thinking and Motivation*

There is much controversy at present about the importance of mental processes in employee motivation. At one extreme, some researchers argue that very little conscious thinking is done before people behave. These proponents can point to evidence that seems to support their argument. At the other extreme, the so-called "cognitive" researchers argue (again with supporting evidence) that human beings do a lot of thinking before they do things. Which of these views is the more reasonable? Or are they both right?

## ☐ Summary

In this section we have described several motivation theories. One obvious conclusion that can be made about these theories is that each appears plausible. However, when we begin examining the studies testing these theories, we find that often they are not supported very strongly. Although the studies testing the theories may have some methodological shortcomings, the fact remains that none of the motivation theories we have examined is a powerful predictor of individual behavior. The reason for this is that we simply have not yet developed an understanding of the human being sophisticated enough to predict individual behavior with accuracy. As additional research is conducted, a better understanding of people will probably emerge and better theories can be constructed.

The second observation is that, over time, motivation theories have become more complex. Equity and expectancy theory (developed in the 1960s) view the human being in a more complex light than Maslow's hierarchy of needs (developed in the 1940s). If this trend continues, extremely complex proposals will become the rule rather than the exception. However, these will probably be necessary to explain something as complex as human behavior.

---

### *Box 3-5: How Do You Tell What "Turns People On?"*

One of the things motivation theories clearly tell managers is that before they can really motivate their workers, they must have a good understanding of each worker's goals, likes, dislikes, and needs. How is the manager to get this understanding?

The obvious thing for the manager to do is to consult with each worker individually. If the relationship between the boss and the workers is good, this will probably work out very well. However, if the relationship is bad, this approach probably will accomplish little. The worker will probably be very defensive during the conference and will refuse to open up about what he or she really feels. Another approach is therefore necessary.

The manager can also ask people who are close friends of the person the manager wishes to know more about. This is a higher-risk strategy, however, since peers may not be willing to help the manager, or the person in question may get wind of what is going on and feel threatened by the activity.

A final alternative is for the manager to decide what the worker wishes. Managers typically have some knowledge about employees' interests both on and off the job and this can be pieced together over a period of time to get a pretty good idea of what will motivate a given employee.

Regardless of the method used, it is obvious that this activity is going to require a substantial amount of the manager's time. This time may simply not be available and the insights that might have been gained may never be perceived. So, while it is certainly logical to say that employees' needs must be understood before their energies can be fully mobilized, it may be difficult to get the information.

---

## ■ JOB SATISFACTION AND JOB PERFORMANCE

Now that we have reviewed a number of motivation theories and examined the research evidence for each, we are able to discuss motivation from a broader perspective, i.e., the relationship between job satisfaction and job performance.

Writers in this area are extremely cautious about assuming causal connections between these two variables, since there has been an abundance of evidence for a quarter of a century that there is no simple relationship. The discussion below traces the development of research in this important area and includes a suggested model of the relationship between job satisfaction and job performance.

## ☐ Assumptions About the Satisfaction–Performance Relationship

As might be expected, the intuitive argument that a satisfied worker is a productive worker was the first one to be made, largely as a result of the Human Relations movement in the early 1930s. From conclusions drawn during the Hawthorne experiments, for a number of years it was accepted that if management provided a positive work environment for employees, they would show their gratitude by producing more. Recently, Herzberg's work suggests that the addition of motivators (as opposed to hygienes) will lead to greater employee job satisfaction.

By the mid-1950s enough research evidence had accumulated to indicate that there was, at best, a tenuous relationship between workers' job satisfaction levels and their performance. In part as a result of a summary of research by Brayfield and Crockett in 1955,[38] investigators in the field began to question their assumptions about both the strength and direction of causation between the two variables. It was not until very recently, however, that researchers began seriously to consider the possibility that performance causes job satisfaction. Although this causal connection at first glance might seem illogical, a more thorough analysis reveals that the relationship may, in fact, be quite reasonable. The logic of this argument is demonstrated in the next few pages.

## ☐ Satisfaction and Motivation

Almost invariably, the question posed by academics and practitioners is formulated as follows: "Is a satisfied worker a productive worker?" A simple answer to this question has not been possible; some studies show a positive relationship between employee satisfaction and performance, some show a negative relationship, and others indicate no relationship at all. The failure to discover a consistent relationship may be due to oversimplifying the problem and asking the wrong question. Instead of asking, "Is a satisfied worker a *productive* worker?" we should first ask, "Is a satisfied worker a *motivated* worker?" This question should come first because motivation to perform is normally a prerequisite for performance on a job. Upon examination, this seemingly simple question becomes quite complex. An analysis of the assumptions underlying two of the most widely known motivation proposals reveals considerable difference.

Maslow argues that lower-level needs are prepotent, with higher-level needs emerging and influencing behavior only after lower-level needs are largely satisfied. The salient point about Maslow's need hierarchy is his assumption that a satisfied need is not a motivator. If his assumption is correct, satisfied employees are not motivated to expend further energy on tasks that give rewards for needs they have already satisfied.

Herzberg, on the other hand, argues that only the presence of motivators will lead to employee satisfaction and motivation. The salient point about Herzberg's proposal is his assumption that (for motivators) a satisfied employee is a motivated one. The proposals by Maslow and Herzberg thus seem to conflict at the very fundamental level of assumption making.

Job motivation is the enthusiasm and persistence exhibited by employees in the work situation as they attempt to satisfy their unsatisfied needs in their particular need structure. Job motivation is determined by three factors: the employee's need structure, the perceived opportunity to satisfy needs in the work situation, and the perceived opportunity to satisfy these needs outside the work situation. These determinants suggest that the manager should be aware not only of the needs that are most pressing for employees, but also of whether employees can satisfy those needs on or off the job.

The employee's job motivation is an indirect result of the rewards and need satisfaction supplied in the work place. Other factors, such as the organization's pay policies, the performance appraisal system, and benefits resulting from employment regardless of job motivation, also affect the rewards and need satisfaction supplied in the work situation. In some organizations, job behaviors have a more direct relationship to rewards and need satisfaction than in others. The manager's knowledge of how direct or indirect the relationship is for the particular organization will be useful for analyzing, understanding, and influencing individual behavior. Individuals will revise or reinforce their perceptions of the opportunity for satisfying needs in the work situation based on their experiences. Part of each person's need structure is satisfied through off-the-job behaviors. The combination of need satisfaction on the job and off the job defines how well the individual's total need structure is satisfied.

If the satisfaction of a particular need leads to the emergence of another, more potent one, the individual's need structure is modified. In this case Maslow's assumption holds; that is, a satisfied need is not a motivator. Likewise, if a need that was previously satisfied is no longer satisfied, it will reemerge. Once again, an unsatisfied need is a motivator. Another possibility involves continued potency for a particular need. For example, although an employee may have desired a promotion and obtained one, the employee may desire a further one. In this example, the employee's ego or self-actualization needs have reemerged and continuously motivate the individual. This analysis suggests that satisfaction does not lead to motivation; instead the reemergence of needs leads to motivation.

The individual with a high level of overall job satisfaction is more likely to continue employment. Through continued employment and the exhibition of job behaviors, this individual will obtain job rewards and some level of need satisfaction in the work place. The level of need satisfaction in the work place and the equity of these rewards leads to a general attitude toward the job. This attitude defines the overall job satisfaction of the individual.

Notice that, generally, satisfying an individual does not lead to job motivation; however, the individual with overall job satisfaction is more likely to remain with the organization (all other things being equal) and is therefore able to exhibit job behaviors that are indicative of job motivation. Herzberg's assumption that a satisfied individual is a motivated one may be interpreted in this context. The relationship between overall job satisfaction and motivation is, however, quite indirect and tenuous.

## ☐ Motivation and Performance

Once the relationship between need satisfaction and motivation has been determined, the relationship between employee motivation and performance can be analyzed.

The simplest model of motivation assumes that there is a direct positive relationship between motivation and productivity, i.e., high motivation causes high productivity. If managers use this model to guide them, emphasis will be placed on techniques that increase employee motivation. In this model the manager need not be concerned directly with productivity, since achieving a desirable level of motivation automatically achieves the desired level of productivity. Unfortunately, this approach is unrealistic. The relationship between motivation and productivity is not this simple; many factors other than employee motivational levels influence employee productivity.

What are these other factors and how important are they? There are at least five factors that are important: (1) task and technology, (2) individual, (3) group, (4) organizational, and (5) environmental factors.

1. *Task and technology factors*    If tasks to be performed by employees are poorly designed, productivity will be low regardless of individual motivational levels. A well-designed task system, on the other hand, can enhance productivity even if management is faced with low employee motivation. The technology used to perform the task affects the M-P link in two ways. First, it sets upper and lower limits on productivity regardless of effort other than that which is minimally acceptable for continued employment. Second, it may completely prevent productivity if it becomes inoperable, as when a machine breakdown occurs.

2. *Individual factors*    Many individual factors modify the M-P relationship. For example, if an individual's abilities with respect to the task are low, high motivation cannot lead to high productivity; in fact, low abilities in general will make the individual's motivational state irrelevant in predicting productivity. Or, if the individual's role perception (his or her view of what is "proper" job behavior) is inaccurate, the M-P relationship will be unclear to management.

Organizations have attempted to cope with individual factors by explicitly dealing with traits (hiring only those individuals who score well on personality tests), abilities (involving employees in training programs), and role perceptions (conducting orientation sessions for new employees).

3. *Group factors*    There are two fundamental elements of working in groups that directly affect the M-P relationship. First, the well-documented existence of group norms must be dealt with in any discussion of productivity. Taylor's observations on "soldiering," the Hawthorne findings on punishment (both physical and psychological) meted out to "rate busters," and other research studies have found persistent evidence that the work group is a powerful influence on indi-

vidual productivity. In any particular situation the group norms may function either to facilitate or to restrict individual productivity. Management must determine the type and magnitude of group norms operating in order to have a complete understanding of the M-P relationship.

Second, the amount of *within-group* coordination needed for high output affects individual productivity. For example, the coordination necessary for members of a basketball team to demonstrate high productivity (individual points scored, rebounds, and steals) is considerably higher than that necessary for members of a cross-country track team, where individual productivity is total minutes or minutes per mile.

4. *Organizational factors*   The individual employee performs within a specific group, which in turn functions as part of the total organizational environment. The degree of *between-group* coordination that exists will affect the productivity of individuals comprising each group. For example, a great deal of effort expended by one group may result in very little productivity (as measured by the total organization) if coordination with other groups is so poor that the total project is not completed.

5. *Environmental factors*   In addition to operating within groups in a single organization, individuals having direct contact with clients or customers and those above middle management operate in an environment composed of interacting social entities. These entities include other individuals, groups, or organizations external to their organization. The ease with which inputs are obtained from these other social entities aids or hinders individual productivity, irrespective of motivational levels. For example, the ability of the personnel department to obtain managerial talent is the measure of the "productivity" of the personnel function. If the firm has an excellent reputation, that productivity is achieved much more easily than if the firm has a poor reputation, regardless of the motivational levels of those in personnel.

## ☐  Integration of Important Variables

The above discussion suggests that the conflicting findings that have been generated over the years on the satisfaction–performance relationship are not surprising. An accurate understanding of the relationship will occur only if the variables affecting it are conceptualized very carefully before empirical evidence is gathered. Figure 3-8 incorporates the comments made to this point into a model linking the important variables.[39] This model can be used to guide managers in their attempts to improve employee productivity.

As indicated in Figure 3-8, the manager must first determine the interrelationship of need satisfaction, need structure, and job motivation for employees. If the manager is unable to influence motivation, directing managerial efforts toward other work-related areas (for example, improvements in job design) would be appropriate.

Once the satisfaction–motivation link has been clarified by the manager in a particular situation, the motivation–productivity link must be assessed. As indicated above, numerous factors moderate the motivation-productivity relationship,

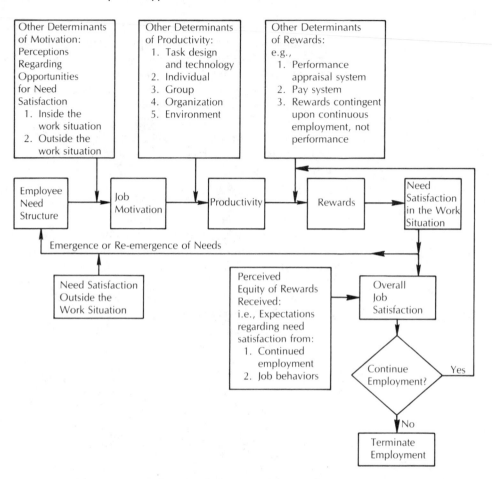

**FIGURE 3-8.    The Satisfaction-Motivation-Productivity Model**

Source: Thomas W. Ferratt and Frederick A. Starke, "Satisfaction, Motivation, and Productivity: The Complex Connection," in J. Gray and F. Starke, eds., *Readings in Organizational Behavior* (Columbus, Ohio: Charles E. Merrill, 1977), pp. 74–86. Used with permission.

and these must be taken into consideration when attempts are made to predict productivity from a knowledge of individual motivational states. The model indicates where these factors are important in the motivation–productivity link; however, the model does not give automatic answers to the manager. This relationship must be thought through by each manager, and the relevant factors in the situation must be noted. For example, for production-line workers in a mass-production type organization, task and technology factors are important moderators of the motivation–productivity relationship; in a service organization, however, environmental considerations might be dominant. Whatever the job in question, it is important that each situation be analyzed to determine which of the "other factors" significantly moderates the motivation–productivity relationship.

The level of productivity is one determinant of individual rewards and, thus, need satisfaction in the work situation. In most organizations there is some connection between productivity (performance) and rewards (pay increases, promotions, recognition, etc.). In some cases (e.g., commission selling) the connection is very direct whereas in others (e.g., upper-level managerial positions) the relationship is somewhat tenuous. The imperfect connection between productivity and rewards exists because some rewards result simply from holding the job. In any case, rewards and need satisfactions generally follow productivity and do not precede it; however, the continuous circle of need structure, motivation, productivity, and need satisfaction indicates that prior levels of need satisfaction affect later levels of productivity. Notice that need satisfactions are distinct from overall job satisfaction; the former refers to the level of need fulfillment whereas the latter is an attitude.

When employees receive rewards, they generally make comparisons to determine whether the rewards are equitable. The greater the agreement (as subjectively perceived by the employee) between the expectations of rewards and the rewards actually received, the greater the probability that overall job satisfaction will result.[40] Thus, need satisfaction and perceived equity of rewards cause overall job satisfaction with pay, supervision, co-workers, and so on. Research indicates that there are two distinct aspects of job satisfaction: facet satisfaction (i.e., satisfaction with specific facets of the job, of which pay is one) and overall job satisfaction (a composite of the individual facets). Despite satisfaction with some facets of the job, an employee may be dissatisfied with the overall job and vice versa.

In the model, overall job satisfaction determines whether employment is terminated or continued. This relationship is consistent with research showing that overall satisfaction is related to turnover. If employment is continued, rewards that are associated with continued employment also continue. *Overall job satisfaction is not in the causal chain for productivity, but need satisfaction is.* This distinction between need satisfaction and overall job satisfaction should help explain some of the inconsistent findings regarding satisfaction and productivity.

The connections between the variables of satisfaction, motivation, and productivity, as shown in Figure 3-8, indicate the complex relationship between employee satisfaction and performance and the need to avoid making simplistic assumptions about it.

The model in Figure 3-8 indicates only some of the reasons for the weak relationship between satisfaction and performance. Fisher has suggested additional reasons.[41] First, it may be difficult to find a relationship between an attitude (satisfaction) and a behavior (performance). In a given situation, people simply may not behave in a way that is consistent with the attitudes they say they have. Their general behavior pattern may be consistent with their attitudes, but most studies have focused on performance at only one point in time, not on general performance patterns over a period of time.

Second, if a person has a favorable attitude toward the job, this does not automatically mean that high performance will result, even if we assume that the person is good at the job. This is because performing well is only one of many responses a satisfied person could make to a job. If performance were more broadly defined to include other responses like absenteeism, horseplay, tardiness, goldbricking, etc. it would be more strongly related to job satisfaction.

Third, attitude measures are usually too general to predict performance. Various studies have shown that the more specific the attitude questions are, the higher the correlation between the attitude and the actual behavior of interest. For example, one study analyzed the attitude-behavior relationship in the purchase of lead-free gasoline.[42] Four levels of attitude questions were used, ranging from general questions about the environment to specific questions about buying lead-free gasoline. The more specific the questions were, the higher the correlation between respondent attitudes and behavior (actually buying lead-free gas). The logical extension of these findings into the job satisfaction–job performance area means that overall measures of job satisfaction will not predict job performance as well as specific measures. Thus, measuring an employee's attitudes toward a specific aspect of performing on the job will yield stronger relationships than simply measuring the employee's attitudes toward some vague notion of performance.

# ■ APPLICATION OF MOTIVATION THEORIES

A number of the motivation theories we have discussed in this chapter have been criticized for being "too theoretical," implying that while they may be interesting, they afford the practicing manager very little in the way of day-to-day suggestions for motivating employees. Though this complaint may be warranted for some of the proposals, most of the theories have some practical implications for everyday work situations. Rather than pointing out the implications of each theory individually, we discuss some general organizational problems and indicate how a particular theory may explain or predict behavior in that situation. Since it is difficult to be exhaustive in the problem areas, the reader should use the examples below as a springboard for analysis of other problems which are often encountered in organizations. An understanding of the theories and how they might be applied should develop the reader's skill to think analytically about other behavioral problems such as leadership, communication, work groups, etc.

The discussion of applications of motivation theories concentrates on the following organizational problems:

1. Job design and content
2. Employee compensation
3. Organizational climate

## □ Job Design and Content

One of the most frequently mentioned ways of motivating employees is through job enrichment, i.e., changing the content of the job to make fuller use of employee abilities. Job enrichment is an obvious practical application of the theoretical work of Herzberg and other need theorists who argue that individuals have higher-order needs that must be satisfied. The suggested method of harnessing potential motivation power for the organization is to design jobs that allow workers to satisfy these needs. Consequently, a new "science" has developed, using job enrichment as its conceptual base. (A detailed analysis of what job enrichment involves is presented in a later chapter.) There are numerous examples of the success of job enrichment programs.[43] Large companies such as A. T. & T., Texas Instruments, and the Bell System have reported major increases in productivity after the redesign of jobs.

The practical application of the job enrichment theories, while potentially beneficial, is not a cure-all for organizational ills. Even to the extent that job enrichment may provide a means of motivating some workers, it is not a universal tool that can be applied indiscriminately to any "unmotivated" employee. The success of job enrichment is probably dependent upon the following prerequisites:

1. The employee wants more responsibility. Clearly, attempting to give more responsibility to an employee who does not want it could lead to more serious problems.[44]
2. The remainder of the organizational environment is conducive to motivation. For example, job enrichment will have limited, if any, success if poor supervisory practices are evident.
3. The lower-order needs (hygiene factors) are relatively satisfied. Particularly in underdeveloped economies, in which lower-order needs are not relatively satisfied, higher-order needs (more responsibility) are probably meaningless.
4. The job can be redesigned. Some jobs, particularly those that are machine-paced, may be difficult to enrich.
5. The employee has positive experiences with job enrichment. If employees make mistakes in their new, redesigned jobs and are severely criticized instead of supported, they will quickly learn to avoid more responsibility.

As a summary statement regarding motivation through job content, the practicing manager should be aware of the limitations of the method, as well as its potential benefits. Before embarking on the job enrichment program, a thorough diagnosis of the internal organizational environment is advisable; otherwise, it is possible that the cure may be worse than the disease. On an individual level, however, managers are in a much better position to work out problems of job content and design since they may be personally aware of the needs of individuals in their work group. When job enrichment programs fail, they tend to do so because their application does not take individual differences into account. Individual managers can overcome this problem by becoming more skilled at recognizing individual differences.

---

### Organizational Reality   3-4
### The Three-Day Work Week As a Motivational Tool

The four-day weekend is a reality at the Meredith Corporation, where the printing plant employees and twenty computer operators each work three twelve-hour days for a thirty-six hour week. The shift system known as "3/36" began at Meredith's Des Moines, Iowa, printing plant under a collective agreement. Many factors prompted the introduction of the system. One was the need to keep the presses operating as continuously as possible. Also, the high capital expenditures required by high-speed presses meant that work weeks of only five days could not be justified.

The solution was to assign a fourth crew where there were previously three. The company also created two twelve-hour shifts to allow continuous operation of the two presses six days a week. The shifts are from 7:15 A.M. to 7:15 P.M. and from 7:15 P.M. to 7:15 A.M. One crew works each shift Monday through Wednesday, and the other two crews work Thursday through Saturday. When necessary, Sunday work is divided between the two shifts. Sunday work is paid at double time. Policies regarding holiday pay, vacation time and funeral leaves have been adjusted so that weekly earnings and benefits are not affected by the shorter work week.

The three-day work week attracts many employees to the press room. However, seniority determines who will remain there. The company plans to extend the 3/36 system to other capital-intensive operations where there is sufficient volume to support it. The new shift system has eliminated excessive overtime demands and also has resulted in a small increase in productivity.

---

Source: *Management Review* (January 1981): 31.

## ☐  Compensation

The extent to which pay motivates employees has been debated for many years.[45] Its early importance in management theory can be seen in the Scientific Management movement, which held the *economic man* assumption (man is motivated by money) to be its essential theory of motivation. Taylor predicated his philosophy of "the one best way" to do a job on the assumption that workers would change their ways of performing jobs if they were given the monetary incentive to do so. The economic man assumption was questioned in Taylor's time, and it appears even more suspect today. This relatively simple view of the nature of man is relevant only to a simple kind of worker. To state that man is so simple that his motivation can be attributed to a single phenomenon is a gross over-simplification of human motivation.

The function of pay in our society is quite complex and any simple statement regarding its importance in the work situation is inappropriate. For this reason, it is important to recognize the importance and relevance of each of the motivation theories in terms of compensation. The discussion below attempts to point out the major considerations in applying compensation systems to work organizations, recognizing that no single theory is able to explain all behavior.

One of the difficult aspects of compensation is that financial rewards have multiple meanings. In addition to being the obvious means by which workers can satisfy basic needs, pay is also an indication of social status, social value, and competence. Therefore, workers can also satisfy higher-order needs with their paychecks. To complicate the situation even more, their perceptions of the degree to which their lower-order needs are satisfied may change as their income rises, so that while workers may have their basic needs relatively satisfied, a pay increase may serve only to increase their level of expectations regarding the lower-order needs. For example, if eating hamburgers four times a week satisfies people's need for food, increasing their wages may simply cause them to change their eating habits from hamburger to steak; this would be a result of higher expectations of satisfaction. There is also the possibility that eating steak may satisfy other needs (e.g., status).

Perceptions of need satisfaction are determined by expectations, which are in turn determined by comparisons with what other individuals are receiving relative to the responsibility of their jobs. Individuals generally feel an inequity if comparisons show that they are receiving less than others with similar inputs. Equity theory is very useful here, since it tells us that the *relative levels of perceived pay* are as important as *absolute levels of actual pay*.

It is useful to explore the concept of piece-rate or commission payment (incentive) systems to determine their potential impact upon motivation. Perhaps the best way of doing this is to examine the assumptions that underlie the incentive system concept. These are as follows:

1. Employees desire to make more money and will change their behavior to meet this objective (economic man assumption).
2. Employees can see a relation between their efforts and the rewards they receive (expectancy theory).
3. Employees attach a net positive valence to increasing their efforts to produce more (expectancy theory).
4. Earning extra money will allow employees to either increase their perception of needs satisfaction or to satisfy needs not currently satisfied (Maslow).
5. Employees have the ability to increase output (physiological assumption).
6. Other conditions in the work environment do not override the desire to increase output for financial rewards (Herzberg, expectancy theory).
7. The worker perceives that other individuals in his or her comparison group receive similar rewards for similar efforts (equity theory).

It is not surprising that many piece-rate and commission payment systems are less than successful in view of all the criteria that should be met.

Gellerman has noted that in order for money to motivate, pay increases must be extremely large to create the feeling of "wealth."[46] If a worker sees that increased effort will lead to a significant change in his or her standard of living, then pay can be considered a motivator. It is for this reason that incentive systems at higher echelons of organizations tend to meet with more success than do those on production-line systems. If top executives improve their performance, they stand to gain considerably from their efforts since some company bonus systems increase executive pay by as much as 50 percent. Production workers, on the other hand, are limited to much smaller absolute increases.

Herzberg maintains that pay is not a motivator but a hygiene, i.e., if it is satisfactory, workers will not be dissatisfied. If pay meets their expectations, they will do nothing differently because of it. It is only when pay does not meet expectations that employees change their behavior. Consistent with both equity theory and Gellerman's position, payment above expectations will probably change behavior as the individual attempts to reduce the dissonance associated with the increased pay. Payment below expectations causes dissatisfaction and prevents a positive work environment from being established. The key point in this philosophy is that providing workers with what they expect will have no

---

### *Organizational Reality*   3-5
### *Pay and Performance*

If organizations were perfectly rational, the pay of top excutives would be tied to the company's performance on indicators such as average return on stockholders equity and the price of the firm's common stock. But there are numerous examples of top executives who are paid well in spite of poor performance by the company they head. For example, Rand Araskog (ITT) was paid $1,150,000 in 1981 while Tom Phillips (Raytheon) received $635,000. This was in spite of the fact that Raytheon substantially outperformed ITT on important performance indicators. As another example, in the pharmaceutical industry the top men at Smith Kline and French and Warner–Lambert received about the same money, even though Smith Kline and French's return on stockholders' equity far exceeded Warner–Lambert's.

If company performance doesn't determine pay, what does? One important variable is company size. A relatively high positive correlation exists between company size and executive compensation, but the correlation between pay and performance is relatively weak. The effect of size is particularly strong when two companies merge. When Dart industries merged with Kraft, the salary of the man who became president of the merged company went from $460,000 to $700,000. The usual argument for pay hikes like this is that the president of a larger firm is dealing with increased complexity and should therefore be paid more.

One obvious way to relate pay more closely to performance is to institute a rigorous bonus system for top managers. At H. J. Heinz, for example, no bonus is given for annual earnings per share growth of less than 7 percent, but if the company achieves 18 percent growth, the president will take home a healthy bonus. Presumably, the shareholders should be in favor of this kind of arrangement.

---

Source: Carol J. Loomis, "The Madness of Executive Compensation," *Fortune* (22 July 1982): 42–52.

appreciable effect on their behavior; it is only when expectations are not met that behavior is changed.

The varied role that pay can assume is further demonstrated when we consider McClelland's nAch theory. In the most literal sense, the high achiever is not motivated by pay. However, in actual on-the-job situations, it is easy to see how a supervisor can misinterpret the individual's motives and assume that the need for money—instead of the need for achievement—is operating.

## ☐ Organizational Climate

Renato Tagiuri has defined organizational climate as ". . . a relatively enduring quality of the internal environment of an organization that (1) is experienced by its members, (2) influences their behavior, and (3) can be described in terms of the values of a particular set of characteristics (or attributes) of the organization."[47] The climate within an organization is both a consequence and a determinant of motivation. Based on the research done on the effects of climate on motivation, it is perhaps best to view climate as something that can either facilitate or inhibit what is inherent in the individual.[48]

Organizations that are power-oriented (such as the military) tend to attract and support individuals with the need for power; similar observations can be made for the needs of achievement and affiliation. A manager who desires to develop and stimulate the need for achievement will want to design an internal organization environment that will both attract and maintain high achievers. Based upon McClelland's research and the description of achievers, this climate might have the following characteristics:

1. A reward system (e.g., pay) that is based upon achieved objectives;
2. A system of goal-setting that allows each worker to set his or her own goals in accordance with the organization's objectives;
3. Emphasis upon individual effort and accomplishment rather than group efforts;
4. A feedback system that supplies information on task performance as quickly as possible and provides immediate rewards for successful task performance;
5. A system that minimizes the degree of dependence each worker has upon other segments of the organization.

It should not be surprising to the reader that these characteristics are descriptive of most sales-oriented organizations. As an extreme example, note how insurance companies utilize this system to stimulate the achievement motive in their sales personnel.

Also of importance to the practicing manager is the view that climate is a predisposition to motivation, i.e., before motivation can occur, the organizational climate should be "positive." The Herzberg-Maslow theories are examples of this philosophy. Herzberg would maintain, for example, that if the hygiene factors were extremely poor, attempting to motivate through the "motivators" would be useless. McGregor maintains that the Theory Y manager motivates employees by providing the climate in which the motivation can occur through the inherent abilities of man. In other words, there are no "good" and "bad" people, only good and bad environments. (It should be noted that this is consistent with operant conditioning theory, which says that environmental characteristics shape what people are.)

---

### Organizational Reality   3-6
### Organizational Climate at Pepsi and J. C. Penney

The culture of a corporation, much like that of a country, plays a significant role in its actions, opinions, and policies. Such patterns instilled by founders are passed down the line from executives to middle managers to assembly-line employees.

A corporation's culture can be its major strength when it is consistent with its strategies. For example, at IBM, marketing drives an unparalleled service philosophy. The company maintains a twenty-four-hour, seven-days-a-week hotline to service IBM products. At Delta Airlines, Inc., commitment to customer service causes a high degree of teamwork. Employees will substitute in other jobs to keep planes flying and luggage moving.

However, culture has its negative side when it prevents a company from meeting competitive threats or from adapting to social or economic change. This type of culture can lead to company stagnation and demise unless a conscious effort is made to change. One company that successfully changed its culture from passivity to aggressiveness is Pepsico Inc.

Twenty years ago Pepsi was content to be number two, offering its product as a cheaper alternative to Coca Cola. Today a Pepsi employee quickly learns that beating the competition both inside and outside the company is the clearest road to success. Pepsi marketers now take on Coke directly in taste-test comparisons. That same confrontation occurs within the company where managers are pitted against one another to work harder and reap higher profits. Since winning is the highest priority, losing carries a heavy price; consistent runners-up find their jobs gone.

In contrast, at J. C. Penney Co., building long-term customer loyalty far outweighs a quick victory in the marketplace. The business style set by the company's founders still holds today. Customers know merchandise can be returned with no questions asked and suppliers know that Penney will not haggle over terms.

Employees at both Pepsi and J. C. Penney know the values that are used to measure individual performance. Not unlike tribal customs and taboos, corporate culture influences employees' actions toward customers, suppliers, and each other. Most often such rules are not neatly written down; instead they are laid down by a strong founder and hardened by success into action.

Because a company's culture is so encompassing, changing it is one of the most difficult tasks a chief executive can tackle. Corporations faced with changing economic, social, and political environments must drastically change their methods. Blocking the road to changes is not only the subtlety of culture, but also the fact that few executives recognize their company's culture and how it pervades all operations.

---

Source: "Corporate Culture," *Business Week* (27 October 1980): 148–160.

The concept of organizational climate is valuable in applying motivation theory, since it indicates that theories cannot be implemented without regard to other environmental considerations. One of the most important and difficult problems facing managers is how to intervene successfully in a social system. A clear understanding of the organizational climate and its determinants assists in these situations.

## □ Conclusions

The discussion of applications suggests that the ease of application of the various motivation theories varies widely. We might assume that ease of application (or the degree of relevance to the real world) is a function of the theoretical soundness of the model, and there are several explanations as to why some applications are more difficult than others.

Certain theories (e.g., Maslow's and Herzberg's) assume that basic needs exist almost universally across employees; these needs imply that certain motivational approaches are inherently superior to others. However, our ability to measure these needs accurately is, at present, questionable. Moreover, it is not known whether, in a given individual, these needs are innate or learned or whether they exist at all. Consequently, it is often difficult to apply these motivation theories with confidence, since any individual can be an exception to the general case.

Other motivation theories (e.g., equity and expectancy theory) do not assume universal needs but rather that each individual is different and that a person engages in relatively complex decision processes prior to expending effort on the job. Whether or not these theories are descriptively accurate remains open to debate.

One theory, McClelland's nAch (need for achievement) model, is quite specific and deals with the development of nAch in various populations. The extension of these findings to complex organizations is certainly possible, but considerable work must be done in developing the need to achieve. Whether or not individual managers are capable of stimulating this need is a subjective judgment at this point. It is possible, as mentioned in the discussion of organizational climate, for a manager to develop a system that encourages an achievement need already present, thus creating a climate that will support high achievers. This does not, however, answer the question of whether the need to achieve is a desirable characteristic in every occupation.

If managers have some understanding of the behavior of their subordinates, then there is a wealth of assistance available in the form of motivation theories that will provide the tools with which motivation can be achieved. One of the keys to successful human resource management is to know what tool to apply in what situation. If nothing else, we have learned in the course of motivation research that every individual is different and "universal" theories of motivation often fail because they ignore this fundamental fact.

As a final point, it is important to note that on certain occasions, the insights gained by managers as a result of studying motivation theories cannot be implemented because of inadequate authority. Knowing what to do and being unable to do it normally leads to increased frustration levels, which may have adverse effects on subordinates. Or, as has been said by many managers, "This is all fine and good, but when will *my* boss hear about it?"

## *Opening Incident Revisited—Neilsons*

If you were a member of the executive committee and attended the second meeting called by the president, what useful comments could you make about the role of money in motivation after reading this chapter? If we accept Herzberg's view of motivation, we would probably disagree with the vice-president of personnel's incentive scheme as a solution to the motivation problem. This is because Herzberg does not see money as a motivator. We would instead propose a restructuring of the job so that it would be psychically rewarding to employees and would motivate them to sell enthusiastically.

If we accept Maslow's arguments, the role of money as a motivator is less clear. Money could be a motivator for any need, but this would be particularly likely for physiological and safety needs. For some needs, however, money is only one of the ways to achieve satisfaction. The need for status, for example, may be satisfied by having a certain job title even though the job does not pay very well. Thus, the role of money in motivation in Maslow's theory is very dependent on the level of the hierarchy at which the individual finds himself as well as the general view of money the person has.

Equity theory says that money may be a motivator if the person is under- or overpaid. If the person perceives an inequity in the area of pay, he or she will be motivated to resolve it. This motivation may, of course, be positive or negative (the person may produce more *or* less). The company in this case would have to determine if salary schedules for sales clerks are perceived to be equitable before implementing the incentive scheme.

Expectancy theory argues that money is a motivator if it is positively valent and there are no organizational factors inhibiting task performance. In the case of Neilsons, management would have to insure that these two criteria are satisfied before an incentive scheme could be successfully implemented.

## ■ SUMMARY

In this chapter we have discussed the most popular motivation theories that have been developed during the last forty years. The theories of Maslow and McGregor assume that all human beings have a need to grow psychologically both on and off the job. Therefore the organizational application of these theories requires the design of jobs to fulfill these universal human needs. McClelland's nAch theory assumes that people can be taught the need to achieve, but for it to persist the organization must provide a proper climate. Equity and expectancy theory assume that each individual will respond to organizational conditions in a slightly different way. Hence, predicting human behavior is difficult, and more complex theories are necessary.

The relationship between job satisfaction and job performance is discussed in the context of work motivation. Reviews of research done in organizations suggest that there is no direct relationship between the two variables and the assumption that a satisfied worker is a productive worker is not reasonable.

# ■ REVIEW QUESTIONS

1. Describe the difference between "motivators" and "hygienes" in Herzberg's two-factor theory.

2. Compare the motivation theories of Herzberg and Maslow. How are they similar? How do they differ?

3. Discuss the need hierarchy of Maslow. What assumptions does Maslow make about motivation? To what extent have these assumptions been verified by research?

4. Describe the "traditional" view of job satisfaction and contrast it with Herzberg's view. Which is more reasonable?

5. Briefly describe the three needs that McClelland has studied. What are his conclusions about nAch? What are the implications of his findings for organizations?

6. Discuss some organizational problems that might be resolved using the motivation theories discussed in this chapter. What are the potential problems in using the theories?

7. Discuss the difficulties that are encountered when managers use motivation theories (e.g., equity and expectancy) that rely on subjective employee responses.

8. What is the relationship between job satisfaction and job performance?

9. Discuss how the motivation theories presented in this chapter can be useful in job design.

10. What is the role of money in motivation?

# ■ EXERCISE 3-1: THE CAVALIER EMPLOYEE

Donald Taylor was the office manager for Baker Trucking. As such, he supervised an office staff of seven. Taylor's boss, James Baker, the vice-president of operations, was becoming increasingly concerned about Taylor's midday absences from the office. Baker knew that Taylor was heavily involved in volunteer civic affairs and did not oppose this so long as these activities did not interfere with Taylor's performance. As of late, however, Baker was getting the feeling that the office staff needed more supervision and guidance in their daily work.

Baker decided one afternoon to call Taylor in and express his concerns. The following conversation took place:

BAKER:   Don, I'm going to get right to the point. I think you're spending too much time away from the office during the day. I think you're needed here to give direction to the office staff.

TAYLOR:   Are the staff complaining?

BAKER:   No, but I feel things would go more smoothly if you were here.

TAYLOR:   Is office staff performance below standard?

BAKER:   No, but I think their performance would be even better if you were here throughout the day.

TAYLOR:   I don't understand that argument. The office staff are very experienced. They certainly wouldn't appreciate my looking over their shoulder all day.

BAKER:   I'm not suggesting that you do that. What I am suggesting is that your enthusiasm for the job seems to have declined lately. I'd like to see you as interested in your job here as you seem to be in community affairs. If you were, perhaps you would come up with ideas that would improve the performance of the office staff.

TAYLOR:   I don't think that my community activities are relevant to this discussion. If my performance and that of my subordinates is satisfactory, that should be all you're concerned with.

The meeting ended shortly after this. As he reflected on the discussion, Baker wondered why Taylor was so willing to put in so much time and effort in unpaid community activities but was so nonchalant about his paid work activity.

1.   What factors should Baker take into consideration as he analyzes this problem?

2.   Why does Taylor put so much effort into unpaid community activities?

3.   What would you do to increase Taylor's on-the-job motivation?

## ■ EXERCISE 3-2: THE PROBLEM CHEMIST

Martin Stahl was the head of the research and development lab of Beltronics, Inc., a large manufacturing firm involved in the manufacture of plastic products for both consumer and industrial markets. In his role as head of R & D, Stahl supervised eleven chemists, all of whom had Ph.D.s in chemistry. The R & D laboratory had a dual responsibility: (1) to do "pure" research on various chemical compounds and how they behaved, and (2) to take any promising results from the pure research output and see how they could be applied in the manufacture of plastic products.

The R & D lab had an excellent reputation inside and outside the company. A steady stream of new ideas and compounds had emerged from the lab over the last ten years, and several important patents had been obtained during that period. Most of the members of Stahl's department had also published articles about their work in chemical trade journals. Stahl encouraged this because it gave the company a good reputation and it provided feedback and status to the chemists.

Stahl was on excellent terms with all but one of the staff chemists. Gary Blaski had been hired seven years ago to give some additional expertise in the pure research area. Blaski had gone to school with one of Stahl's group and on that person's recommendation, Stahl had hired Blaski. However, within about one year of Blaski's hiring, Stahl began to have major problems with him. In Stahl's view, Blaski didn't seem to be very motivated to do the kind of work the R & D lab was doing. Blaski showed little enthusiasm for the job, was often absent, and had very low productivity (as measured by new patents granted, trade journal publications, and research projects completed.)

Stahl had several discussions with Blaski about his performance, but Blaski rejected Stahl's position and argued that "You can't rush research." These discussions were often frustrating for Stahl, but he had gradually learned some things about Blaski. For example, he discovered that Blaski craved recognition of any sort, no matter how insignificant. Stahl had attempted to use this knowledge to motivate Blaski by suggesting that Blaski get some of his work patented; this would mean considerable recognition. Blaski seemed very interested in the idea, but somehow nothing ever came of it.

As time went on, Stahl became more and more unhappy with Blaski's nonchalant attitude and his subpar performance. He began putting increasing pressure on Blaski to improve his performance, but this simply worsened the interpersonal relations between the two. Stahl noticed that Blaski seemed to be more and more unhappy, and on one occasion Blaski offered the opinion that the other chemists didn't seem to like him very much. He even commented that his old school buddy seemed to be avoiding him. When asked why, Blaski said he didn't know, but that it was unfair that his peers didn't recognize his abilities.

One afternoon Blaski came to Stahl's office and requested permission to take time off from work (with pay) to attend a meeting of industrial chemists that was being held in another city. The following conversation took place:

BLASKI:   I'd like to go to the Industrial Chemists Association meetings. I think it's appropriate that the company pay for my travel and accommodations since I will be improving my work-related expertise by attending this meeting. I know you have re-imbursed other people in the lab, and I think I should be treated the same way.

STAHL:   I'm sorry, but I can't grant the request. Before laying out money for things like this, I need to see a considerable improvement in your work here.

BLASKI:   What do you mean?

STAHL:   You know exactly what I mean. Your nonchalant attitude has got to change and your productivity must improve.

BLASKI:   I've told you this before, but you just don't listen. You can't rush research.

STAHL:   The other chemists don't seem to be having any trouble meeting my productivity standards. I must not be "rushing" them. Why are you the only person who can't seem to do the job?

BLASKI:   You just don't realize that each person is unique. You're trying to make me fit into a certain mold and that's been weighing on my mind and reducing my productivity. If I were given more freedom to do my own thing, I would be more productive.

STAHL:   When you demonstrate some productivity you'll get some freedom!

After Blaski left, Stahl wondered if he had been too harsh with him. However, he was at the end of his rope and had exhausted all the avenues he knew of to motivate Blaski.

1.   Use each of the motivation theories in this chapter to analyze this problem. What solutions would each theory suggest?

2. Comment on Blaski's performance problems using the formula: performance = ability $\times$ motivation.

3. What should Stahl do to motivate Blaski?

# ■ EXERCISE 3-3: THE FILING SECTION

Dorothy Akers was the manager of the filing section of General Insurance, Inc. The section employed seven clerks whose major function was to file all active policies for ready reference by agents if inquiries arose. The section also informed the agent thirty days in advance of each policy's expiration date so that the agent could take the appropriate action.

Recently, Akers had become aware of two productivity problems—filing backlogs and errors in communicating policy expiration dates. Complaints were increasing from the agents and Akers decided some action must be taken. Accordingly, she called a meeting to allow the employees to indicate any problems they were having. Surprisingly, at the meeting, the employees said that they were very satisfied with their jobs and could offer no suggestions for improvement. Akers had a good working relationship with the employees and was confident that they weren't holding anything back. Akers thus found herself in the position of having satisfied employees with productivity problems and she wondered what to do next.

Use the model in Figure 3-8 to analyze this problem and to make suggestions to Akers about what she should do.

# ■ ENDNOTES

1. T. R. Mitchell, "Motivation: New Directions for Theory, Research, and Practice," *Academy of Management Review 7* (1982): 80–88.
2. E. L. Deci, "The Effects of Externally Mediated Rewards on Intrinsic Motivation," *Journal of Personality and Social Psychology* 22 (1972): 113–120.
3. For a review of this literature, see G. P. Latham and G. A. Yukl, "A Review of Research on the Application of Goal Setting in Organizations," *Academy of Management Journal* (1975): 824–845; see also J. B. Miner, *Theories of Organizational Behavior* (Hinsdale, Ill.: Dryden Press, 1980): pp. 168–200.
4. S. E. White, T. R. Mitchell, and C. H. Bull, "Goal Setting, Evaluation Apprehension, and Social Cues As Determinants of Job Performance and Job Satisfaction in a Simulated Organization," *Journal of Applied Psychology* 62 (1977): 665–673; see also R. M. Steers and L. W. Porter, "The Role of Task–Goal Attributes in Employee Performance," *Psychological Bulletin* 81 (1974): 434–452.
5. J. M. Ivancevich, "Effects of Goal Setting on Performance and Job Satisfaction," *Journal of Applied Psychology* 61 (1976): 605–612.
6. J. S. Kim and W. C. Hammer, "Effect of Performance Feedback and Goal Setting in Productivity and Satisfaction in an Organizational Setting," *Journal of Applied Psychology* 61 (1976): 45–57.
7. For an analysis of the laboratory evidence, see E. A. Locke, "Toward a Theory of Task Motivation and Incentives," *Organizational Behavior and Human Performance* (1968): 157–189.
8. W. W. Ronan, G. P. Latham, and S. B. Kinne, "Effects of Goal Setting and Supervision on Worker Behavior in an Industrial Setting," *Journal of Applied Psychology* 58 (1973): 302–307.
9. Ibid.
10. G. P. Latham and E. A. Locke, "Goal Setting—Motivational Technique That Works," *Organizational Dynamics* 8 (1979): 68–80.

11.  A. Maslow, "A Theory of Human Motivation," *Psychological Review* 50 (1943): 370–396.

12.  The term *largely* is extremely important in understanding the need hierarchy. It recognizes that individual differences may determine the level of satisfaction that is required before moving on to the next-order needs.

13.  C. P. Alderfer, *Existence, Relatedness, and Growth* (New York: Free Press, 1972).

14.  D. T. Hall and K. E. Nougaim, "An Examination of Maslow's Need Hierarchy in an Organization Setting," *Organizational Behavior and Human Performance* 3 (1968): 12–35.

15.  E. E. Lawler and J. L. Suttle, "A Causal Correlational Test of the Need Hierarchy Concept," *Organizational Behavior and Human Performance* 7 (1972): 265–287.

16.  J. Rauschenberger, N. Schmitt, and J. E. Hunter, "A Test of the Need Hierarchy Concept by a Markov Model of Change in Need Strength," *Administrative Science Quarterly* (1980): 654–670.

17.  A. Maslow, *Eupsychian Management* (Homewood, Ill.: Richard D. Irwin, 1965), pp. 55–56.

18.  F. Herzberg, B. Mausner, and B. Synderman, *The Motivation to Work* (New York: Wiley, 1959).

19.  R. House and L. Wigdor, "Herzberg's Dual-Factor Theory of Job Satisfaction and Motivation," *Personnel Psychology* 20 (Winter 1967): 369–389.

20.  Ibid.

21.  V. Vroom, *Work and Motivation* (New York: Wiley, 1964), p. 129; see also R. Bobbitt and O. Behling, "Defense Mechanisms As an Alternate Explanation of Herzberg's Motivator–Hygiene Results," *Journal of Applied Psychology* 56 (1972): 24–27.

22.  A. M. Whitehill, "Maintenance Factors: The Neglected Side of Worker Motivation," *Personnel Journal* (1975): 516–520.

23.  R. Murray, *Thematic Apperception Test Pictures and Manual* (Cambridge, Mass.: Harvard University Press, 1943).

24.  D. C. McClelland et al., *The Achievement Motive* (New York: Appleton-Century-Crofts, 1953).

25.  D. Kolb and R. Boyatzis, "On the Dynamics of the Helping Relationship," in *Organizational Psychology*, ed. D. Kolb, I. Rubin, and J. McIntyre (Englewood Cliffs, N. J.: Prentice-Hall, 1971).

26.  D. C. McClelland, "That Urge to Achieve," *Think* (published by IBM, 1966).

27.  A. M. Harrell and M. J. Stahl, "A Behavioral Decision Theory Approach for Measuring McClelland's Trichotomy of Needs," *Journal of Applied Psychology* 66 (1981): 242–247.

28.  McClelland, "That Urge to Achieve."

29.  L. Festinger, *A Theory of Cognitive Dissonance* (Evanston, Ill.: Row, Peterson, 1957).

30.  J. S. Adams, "Toward an Understanding of Inequity," *Journal of Abnormal and Social Psychology* 67 (1963): 425. Copyright (1963) by the American Psychological Association. Reprinted by permission.

31.  For a review of much of this research evidence, see Paul S. Goodman and Abraham Friedman, "An Examination of Adams' Theory of Inequity," *Administrative Science Quarterly* 16 (1971): 271–286.

32.  R. G. Lord and J. A. Hohenfeld, "Longitudinal Field Assessment of Equity Effects on the Performance of Major League Baseball Players," *Journal of Applied Psychology* 64 (1979): 19–26.

33.  D. Duchon and A. G. Jago, "Equity and the Performance of Major League Baseball Players: An Extension of Lord and Hohenfeld," *Journal of Applied Psychology* 66 (1981): 728–732.

34.  M. Carrell and J. Ditrich, "Equity Theory: The Recent Literature, Methodological Considerations, and New Directions," *Academy of Management Review* 3 (1978): 202–210.

35.  V. Vroom, *Work and Motivation* (New York: Wiley, 1964).

36.  See, for example, R. House, "A Path-Goal Theory of Leader Effectiveness," *Administrative Science Quarterly* 16 (September 1971): 321–338; also J. Campbell, et al., *Managerial Behavior, Performance, and Effectiveness* (New York: McGraw-Hill, 1970).

37.  See, for example, H. J. Arnold, "A Test of the Multiplicative Hypothesis of Expectancy–Valence Theories of Work Motivation," *Academy of Management Journal* 24 (1981): 128–141.

38.  A. H. Brayfield and W. H. Crockett, "Employee Attitude and Performance," *Psychological Bulletin* 52 (1955): 396–428.

39.  The basic relationships in the model were first proposed in L. W. Porter and E. E. Lawler III, *Managerial Attitudes and Performance* (Homewood, Ill.: Richard D. Irwin, 1968).

40. It is probably unreasonable to assume that the more rewards an employee receives, the more satisfied he or she will be. Individuals who receive considerably more rewards (e.g., pay) than they feel are reasonable will typically feel some anxiety and guilt and are therefore less satisfied.

41. C. D. Fisher, "On the Dubious Wisdom of Expecting Job Satisfaction to Correlate with Job Performance," *Academy of Management Review* 5 (1980): 607–612.

42. T. A. Heberlein and J. S. Black, "Attitudinal Specificity and the Prediction of Behavior in a Field Setting," *Journal of Personality and Social Psychology* 33 (1976): 474–479.

43. M. S. Myers, "Who Are Your Motivated Workers?" *Harvard Business Review* 34 (January–February 1964): 73–88; see also R. N. Ford, *Motivation Through the Work Itself* (New York: American Management Association, 1969).

44. This statement ignores a trend in much of the organizational development literature regarding changing behavior. It has been the common practice to attempt to change attitudes first, then hope for the behavioral change to follow. Trying to convince employees who do not want more responsibility that they should have more, would probably be a futile exercise. It is now being suggested that behavior should change first, followed by the change in attitude (e.g., "forcing" employees to accept more responsibility on the assumption that they will be reinforced by positive experiences). This strategy is discussed in more detail in Chapter 4.

45. For an in-depth review of much of this literature, see E. E. Lawler, *Pay and Organizational Effectiveness* (New York: McGraw-Hill, 1971).

46. S. W. Gellerman, *Management by Motivation* (New York: American Management Association, 1968).

47. R. Tagiuri and G. H. Litwin, *Organizational Climate* (Boston: Division of Research, Harvard Business School, 1967), p. 27.

48. G. H. Litwin and R. A. Stringer, *Motivation and Organizational Climate* (Boston: Division of Research, Harvard Business School, 1968).

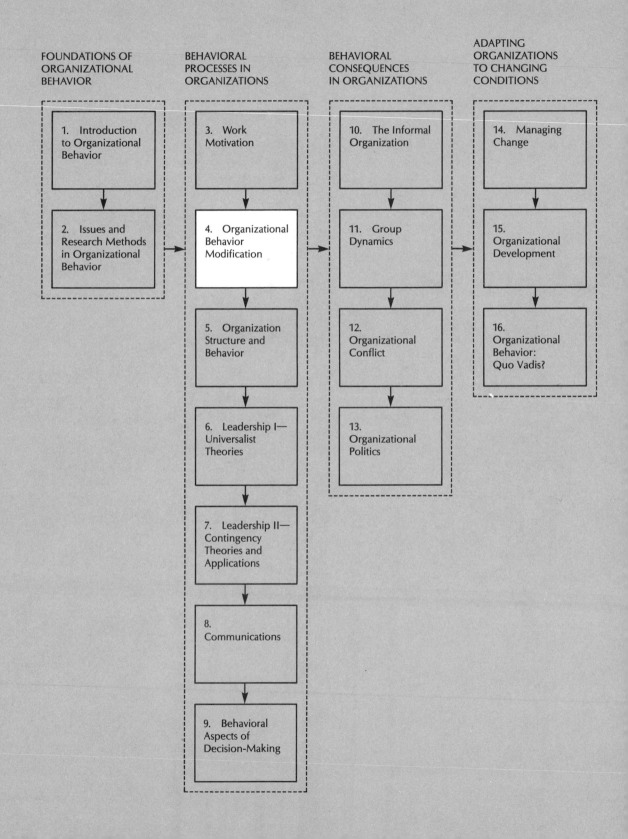

FOUNDATIONS OF
ORGANIZATIONAL
BEHAVIOR

BEHAVIORAL
PROCESSES IN
ORGANIZATIONS

BEHAVIORAL
CONSEQUENCES
IN ORGANIZATIONS

ADAPTING
ORGANIZATIONS
TO CHANGING
CONDITIONS

1. Introduction to Organizational Behavior

2. Issues and Research Methods in Organizational Behavior

3. Work Motivation

4. Organizational Behavior Modification

5. Organization Structure and Behavior

6. Leadership I—Universalist Theories

7. Leadership II—Contingency Theories and Applications

8. Communications

9. Behavioral Aspects of Decision-Making

10. The Informal Organization

11. Group Dynamics

12. Organizational Conflict

13. Organizational Politics

14. Managing Change

15. Organizational Development

16. Organizational Behavior: Quo Vadis?

# Organizational Behavior Modification

## ■ Learning Objectives

After thoroughly reading and studying this chapter you should be able to:

☐ Describe the differences between attitude and behavior;

☐ Define the major concepts in organizational behavior modification: conditioning, contingencies, positive reinforcement, negative reinforcement, and punishment;

☐ List the advantages and disadvantages of using positive reinforcement to shape behavior;

☐ List the advantages and disadvantages of using punishment to shape behavior;

☐ List the major limitations to using behavior modification principles in organizations;

☐ List the steps in designing an organizational behavior modification system;

☐ Design an organizational behavior modification system to improve performance on the job;

☐ Describe how different reinforcement schedules affect performance.

# Chapter 4

■ **KEY TERMS**

| | |
|---|---|
| **Attitudes** | **Avoidance learning** |
| **Behaviorists** | **Omission** |
| **Cognitive theories** | **Extinction** |
| **Mutual causality** | **Punishment** |
| **Learning theory** | **Reinforcement schedules** |
| **Classical conditioning** | **Continuous reinforcement** |
| **Involuntary response** | **Partial reinforcement** |
| **Stimulus** | **Intermittent reinforcement** |
| **Operant conditioning** | **Fixed-interval reinforcement** |
| **Instrumental conditioning** | **Variable-interval reinforcement** |
| **Consequences** | **Fixed-ratio reinforcement** |
| **Contingencies** | **Variable-ratio reinforcement** |
| **Reinforcement** | **Intrinsic rewards** |
| **Positive reinforcement** | **Extrinsic rewards** |
| **Negative reinforcement** | **Performance Management** |

■ **CHAPTER OUTLINE**

I. Historical Origins and Terminology

II. Understanding Behavior
   A. Determinants of Behavior
   B. Attitudes and Behavior
   C. The Importance of "Why"
   D. Mutual Causality
   E. So What Causes "B"?
   F. Conclusions

III. Central Concepts in Organizational Behavior Modification
   A. Learning
   B. Conditioning
   C. Contingencies
   D. Reinforcement
   E. Schedules of Reinforcement

IV. Using Punishment in Organizational Behavior Modification
   A. Criticisms of Punishment

# *Opening Incident—Pickerel Manufacturing Company*

The Pickerel Manufacturing Company was facing a serious problem. While absenteeism was usually slightly higher than was desired, on Mondays and Fridays it was particularly bad. On these days, about 15 to 20 percent of the work force was usually absent. Several years ago the company instituted a policy that required a doctor's certificate for each absence. Without the certificate, a worker was not paid for the days missed. When the policy was first instituted, absenteeism was reduced slightly, but was now worse than it had ever been.

Company officials were well aware of the basic causes of the absenteeism but felt powerless to do anything about it. It was clear that many of the workers preferred a day off now and then, regardless of the loss in pay, especially when they could choose which day it was. A three-day weekend had more appeal now than ever before, especially during the summer months. Most of the jobs in the factory were quite routine and job satisfaction was generally low, although working conditions were comparable to similar plants in the area.

One day the personnel manager had an idea based on a seminar in behavior modification he had recently attended. The idea seemed pretty far-fetched to others, but things were so bad that the company was willing to try almost anything. The personnel manager talked with the company accountant and they concluded that absenteeism was costing the company about $2,000 per week in net profits. The personnel manager persuaded the president to agree to spend one third—or $666 per week—on a system designed to reduce absenteeism.

The personnel manager's idea was to run a lottery with participation based on attendance. The plan went like this: there was to be a weekly lottery held every Friday afternoon just before quitting time. The time cards of workers who had been at work every day that week were placed in a basket and one was drawn out at random. The winner received a portable black-and-white television set. On the following Monday the lottery began again, and this was repeated each and every week. There was also a two-week lottery. The same rules applied, except this time workers had to have two weeks of perfect attendance to be eligible for the draw. The prize for the two-week lottery was a small color television set. There was also a four-week lottery (console color television set), a seven-week lottery (living room furniture set), and twelve-week lottery (bedroom set), a twenty-week lottery (week's vacation at a famous resort), and the grand prize, a yearly lottery in which the winner received a two-week vacation to Hawaii with salary and all expenses paid by the company.

As soon as the program was implemented, absenteeism dropped dramatically. Whereas previously the company experienced absenteeism of 15 to 20 percent on Mondays and Fridays, now absenteeism seldom went above 5 percent. The other days of the week averaged 3 to 4 percent.

After about a month the company had to make a change in the rules. It was discovered that people who were ill and should be staying at home were coming to work, thus presenting a health hazard to the rest of the work force. The rule change allowed for people with doctor's certificates to remain in the lottery provided their total absences did not exceed 10 percent of the eligible working days.

Probably no subject has generated so much controversy in the organizational behavior field as the topic of behavior modification. To some it smacks of manipulation, coercive control, and other Orwellian methods. To others it is a series of techniques that may be useful for getting dogs to salivate, pigeons to play ping-pong, and chickens to ring bells, but beyond this has no real relevance to management. Even within the scientific community there is disagreement about the theory, practice, and application of behavior modification. On the one hand, there are those who disagree with the basic concept because behaviorists (those who believe in behavior modification) "do not give people credit for thinking." On the other side of these debates are the behaviorists who believe that all behavior is learned through a process of experiencing rewards and punishments, and that all behavior can be accounted for by analyzing these experiences. We will explore the details of these positions later in this chapter.

Regardless of the pros and cons, it is a fact that behavior modification applied to organizations is receiving increased attention in both the scientific and practitioner communities. In some cases we are finding new applications for the uses of behavior modification in organizations and in others we are simply using behavior modification concepts to explain what and why certain events have occurred in the past. Since our major focus in this book is the application of theory, we will tend to minimize the semantic and theoretical arguments that excite academics and spend most of our time describing organizational behavior modification and showing how it can be applied to specific problem areas of management. The application of behavior modification to organizations has created a new field of study called *performance management,* and that is the final section of this chapter.

# ◼ HISTORICAL ORIGINS AND TERMINOLOGY

The concepts of organizational behavior modification are actually specific applications of the more general science of behavior modification. The origins of behavior modification are somewhat obscured by time as well as the vast numbers of individuals who have made significant contributions to the field. It is generally agreed that our current formulation of behavior modification began with "Watsonian behaviorism," the stimulus–response approach to behavior espoused in 1913 by psychologist John B. Watson.[1] Watson believed that behavior was a learned phenomenon and could be predicted by studying the organism's environment. Another influential psychologist was Edward L. Thorndike, who is best known for his formulation of the "law of effect."[2] Thorndike took Watson's basic premise of environmental influence but changed the emphasis from events *prior* to behavior to studying the effects of events *subsequent* to behavior. His basic formulation of the "law of effect" was as follows:

> When a modifiable connection between a situation and a response is made and is accomplished or followed by a satisfying state of affairs, that connection's strength is increased; when made or accompanied or followed by an annoying state of affairs, its strength is decreased.[3]

This statement of cause and effect in human behavior is the foundation for much of our current knowledge about behavior modification theory.

The most influential person in the field has been psychologist B.F. Skinner, of Harvard University, who is well known for his books and articles on the subject.[4] Skinner was the first to make the distinction between *operant* and *respondent* behavior, a topic covered in more detail later in this chapter. Without this distinction, behavior modification would not have the wide applicability that it does today.

In the pages that follow we develop the fundamentals of behavior modification theory. We use the term *behavior modification* in reference to the general concepts; *organizational behavior modification* is used to denote the specific applicability of the concepts to organizational behavior. We have not referenced the definitions of the concepts inasmuch as they are widely accepted. However, readers wishing to explore the concepts in greater depth are urged to examine the endnote references for other sources.

# ■ UNDERSTANDING BEHAVIOR

In Chapter 1 it was pointed out that managers could be more effective if they understood *why* people behave the way they do. In other words, if the underlying *causes* of behavior could be discovered, then the manager would be in a much better position of control. Up to this point, we have dealt with the causes of behavior in an intangible way (i.e., we have attributed causation of behavior to such things as needs, attitudes, beliefs, values, and so forth). For example, we have said that people *need* security (Maslow), or that they have a *need* for achievement (McClelland), or that responsibility will increase *satisfaction* (Herzberg). The one thing that most of these theories have in common is that they attribute motivation to states of mind whether they be attitudes, needs, drives, wants, etc. The assumption in these theories, therefore, is that if we improve the individual's state of mind, this will improve his or her motivation and, it is hoped, performance. Unfortunately, as pointed out in Chapter 3, we have not been extremely successful using these approaches. At best, we can say that the approaches work some of the time but it is difficult to specify exactly when and under what conditions.

The one exception to this causal model is the one developed in Chapter 3 which stated that an individual's attitude (i.e., satisfaction) is the *result* of some type of behavior, not the cause of it. However, we are still presented with some difficulty here if we try to sort out why each individual receives satisfaction from a particular type of behavior. It was also noted in Chapter 3 that some theories propose that individuals go through complex thought processes in an attempt to maximize their outcomes; unfortunately, we do not know much about these thought processes or how they cause behavior.

One of the contributions of the behaviorist approach pertains to the causes of behavior. As noted above, we are not able to peek inside employees' heads to see what goes through their minds. Many a manager has learned the hard way that what employees *say* their feelings are and what the people actually *do* are often quite different.[5] It is useful, therefore, to examine the determinants of behavior from a behaviorist's perspective.

## ☐ Determinants of Behavior

The strict behaviorist approach recognizes five phenomena that determine human behavior: hereditary factors, organizational or social roles, reward systems, experiences, and random behavior. Although there is some overlap between the categories, we will treat them as separate for the time being.

**Hereditary Factors** The importance of hereditary factors in our behavior has been the subject of controversy for years. It is an accepted fact that our biological development is a determinant of some behavior, although there tends to be less agreement regarding exactly how this development operates on behavior. We know that certain physical characteristics can be biologically determined (such as physical size or color of hair), and that some physical characteristics tend to have behavioral traits associated with them. For example, there are the stereotypes that short people are insecure, or that physically strong people are very confident. But we also know that not all short people are insecure, and not all strong people are confident. So as a predictor of behavior, the hereditary approach leaves much to be desired.

The hereditary approach also has limits in organizational behavior. Although it is agreed that hereditary factors influence behavior, it would appear to be in only a small part. Not only is it a small part, but we do not know *which* part falls into the hereditary category. And finally, even if we could solve these problems, hereditary behavior cannot be changed by managers anyway. The only potential value of the hereditary approach is in selection of employees, but our knowledge about the hereditary influences upon our behavior is not sufficient for this to be a useful managerial tool at this time.

**Social Roles** In the Shakespearean view, we are all actors on a stage. We occupy roles in our life and these roles have a significant impact upon how we behave. Just as an actor changes his behavior when playing a role in a stage play or movie, we also change our behavior as we move from role to role. Most people occupy several roles simultaneously, e.g., employee, mother, community worker, church member, etc., and we can observe changes in behavior as the roles change.

Social roles are defined by *expectations* by others. The people who interact with a role have certain behavioral expectations of the role and their behavior will be such that positive role behaviors are encouraged and negative role behaviors discouraged. For example, most people have a common expectation of how a church minister should behave (although even this differs between denominations). If a minister engages in behavior that is inconsistent with the role expectations, then pressure—either formal or informal—will be brought to bear to change his or her behavior.

The same is true for the organizational role. All members of the organization are faced with a series of expectations associated with their roles. These expectations come from various sources: supervisors, colleagues, subordinates, and to a lesser extent, others in the organization. Unless the persons occupying the roles wish to incur the wrath of others, they will engage in the behaviors expected of that role. This does not mean that individuals cannot interject something of themselves into their roles, but the primary role behaviors will be consistent with the expectations.

## Box 4-1: Using Role Theory to Modify Behavior

Understanding how roles affect our behavior leads to some useful techniques for modifying behavior. For example, one company (which, for reasons that will become obvious in a moment will remain anonymous), uses role theory to cure performance problems. On regular occasions, the department managers of this company meet to discuss the possibilities of trading their "worst" subordinates. This is done on the premise that poor performance is often a function of the role the person is occupying, i.e., that there are expectations that the person cannot meet. The company's philosophy is that there are no "bad" people in organizations, only people who are in roles that are unsuitable for them. The trading is done as a means of finding another role that is more suitable.

A major theoretical cornerstone to the program is the recognition that expectations can affect behavior, both positively and negatively. It is believed that part of the ongoing performance problem is the expectation of the manager and other co-workers; because they expect the person to perform poorly, the poor performance continues. When the person is transferred out of that environment into a new one, new expectations are able to influence behavior and the person is better able to shake the stigma of the previous role.

**Reward Systems**   Reward systems are the programs, policies, and behaviors of others that either reward or punish our behavior. They can be formal systems such as an incentive bonus program, or informal systems such as the interpersonal rewards and punishments that occur between individuals.

In the broadest sense, the reward system tells people what is acceptable and unacceptable behavior, i.e., the "rules of the game." For example, if a company wants its salespeople to sell more of a certain product, it might increase the commission rate on that product. This increase is the reward system that communicates to the salespeople the kind of behavior the organization wants. Examples of other reward systems are performance appraisal schemes, wage and salary policies, promotion policies, and disciplinary clauses of union contracts. Each of these specifies a certain set of behaviors as being desirable or undesirable, and then sets out a reward or punishment system designed to determine that behavior.

Every social system has a reward system of some type. It might be explicitly defined, as in the case of the commission program, or may be an unwritten practice, as would be the case with managers subconsciously rewarding certain kinds of behaviors of their subordinates. In all cases it is important to understand how reward systems affect behavior so they can be more scientifically designed. Otherwise, organizations may communicate unintentional signals to employees regarding the appropriate behaviors to be rewarded.

## *Box 4-2: You Get What You Reward*

An article by Steven Kerr titled, "On the folly of Rewarding A, While Hoping for B" points out many instances in which our reward systems in society and in organizations are counterproductive. Kerr suggests that many organizations reward one type of behavior but hope that a different type occurs. Several examples are:

1. Universities hope for good teaching, but reward good research and publishing activities.
2. Many budgeting processes in organizations hope managers will save money and not spend their entire budget, but the reward system rewards those who overspend. (Ask yourself, what is the reward for not spending your annual budget?)
3. Many companies have a sick-leave policy that rewards sick people and penalizes healthy ones who come to work.
4. Many companies speak of the importance of teamwork on the job, but the reward systems are usually individually based.

Given these examples, it is not surprising that many university students must take classes from someone who can't teach, that no money is ever saved by people spending less than their budget, that many people take the maximum number of paid sick days allowed each year, and that competition between individuals in organizations is more prevalent than cooperation.

Source: *Academy of Management Journal* 18, no. 4 (1975): 769–783.

**Experience**    The most general category recognized by behaviorists is that of experience. In fact, behaviorism views people as products of their experience in that they tend to repeat experiences that were rewarding and avoid experiences that were not rewarding or were unpleasant. The phrase "learning from experience" acquires a specific and significant meaning when one is studying organizational behavior modification. Therefore, present behavior is the result of past behavior and the environment's reaction to it.

The relationship between roles, reward systems, and experiences should be evident. Social roles and specific reward systems are simply experiences that we have. When occupying a new role, for example, our experiences with others will teach us whether we are exhibiting the proper behaviors. Similarly, the reward systems under which we operate will determine whether we have good or bad experiences. If a person reached a sales target last year and received a large bonus, then he or she is likely to attempt to reach that target this year, to repeat the experience. The primary value of studying roles and reward systems is that they provide us with possible strategies for changing behavior through changing experiences.

**Random Behavior**    Finally, we must recognize that some behavior occurs by chance, meaning that it cannot be explained by role theory, reward systems, or any previous experiences. The behavior may be purposeful (i.e., goal-oriented) but is not determined by previous learning. One example would be a new employee in a job who is given little direction or information about the system.

---

### Box 4-3: The "One-Minute Manager"

Professor Ken Blanchard (whose Situational Leadership theory is discussed in Chapter 7) has coauthored a book with Spencer Johnson, M.D. that utilizes the principle of random behavior and the importance of the consequences that follow the behavior. The book is titled *The One-Minute Manager* and is based on three specific managerial actions that can be used to motivate behavior: one-minute goal setting, one-minute praising, and one-minute reprimands.

Blanchard and Johnson maintain that the style of many managers is to "catch people doing things wrong" and then punish them for their errors. Most good performance, they maintain, is ignored, and this philosophy of management breeds poor motivation and deadwood in organizations.

The "one-minute praising" involves a reversal of this philosophy. The authors propose that better motivation will occur if managers spend their time "catching people doing things right." In other words, a manager should observe performance, and when the employee does something right, he or she should receive the one-minute praising. By practicing this philosophy, the good behaviors that originally occur through random (yet purposeful) methods will eventually become more frequent and determine performance. The "one-minute goal setting," of course, provides the objective for the employee to aim for, and also serves to give the behavior a purpose. The "one-minute reprimand" is used to provide a negative experience for employees who have the skill to perform but have an attitude problem.

Source: Kenneth Blanchard and Spencer Johnson, *The One-Minute Manager* (New York: William Morrow and Co., 1982).

That person may try several behavior patterns to see what is rewarded and what isn't. Therefore, while the behavior is goal-oriented (to have a rewarding experience), the person will behave in a random fashion attempting to figure out what works.[6]

With random behavior it is important whether the behavior is rewarded or punished. If it is punished (and the person associates the punishment with the behavior), then it is less likely the behavior will occur again. The opposite will be the case if the random behavior was rewarded. In either case, once the person has had an experience with the behavior, that behavior leaves the random category and becomes part of the individual's repertoire.

The important thing to remember about determinants of behavior in the behaviorist approach is that causation is attributed to some type of experience in the organism's past. Behaviorists are not comfortable with terms such as attitudes, feelings, values, beliefs, or other such states of mind. However, it is recognized that attitudes do exist so it is important to sort out the apparent difference between the behaviorists on the one hand, and the cognitive (e.g., thinking) approach on the other. This is the purpose of the following section.

## ☐  Attitudes and Behavior

As the opening section of this chapter noted, much of our current view regarding causes of behavior proposes that behaviors result from certain attitudes. This causal model can be represented as follows:

$$A \longrightarrow B$$

where *A* is attitude and *B* is behavior. Taking this literally, it means that if you want to change *B* (behavior), you must change *A* (attitude) first. Or, to put it in the context of many motivation theories, if you can improve an employee's attitudes, then this will generate a change in behavior. From a managerial perspective, then, this raises the question—how do you change someone's attitudes?

To answer this we have to go back to the causes of attitudes. What causes people to feel the way they do about certain things? Why do some people like their jobs and others don't? Why do some people have positive attitudes toward something and others negative ones? Why do some people like such-and-such and others don't? The common answer to all of these questions, according to the philosophy of behavior modification, is that *differences in attitudes are caused by differences in experiences.* If one person likes his or her job and another doesn't, it is because each has had different experiences on the jobs. If one person likes milk (i.e., has a positive attitude toward it) and another person doesn't (i.e., has a negative attitude toward it), it's because each has had different experiences with milk. And so it goes with any attitude toward anything.

To emphasize the importance of this position even more, consider the following example. Suppose you are a manager and one of your subordinates has a "bad attitude." You do not like this so you decide to talk with the employee, inform him of your concern, and make a request for a change. After doing this, the employee calmly replies, "O.K., boss, I've changed my attitude." Is this reasonable? Of course not, for you know that attitudes do not change that easily.

We can conclude, then, that attitudes are formed out of experiences and that the more experiences we have (providing they are reasonably consistent with one another), the stronger and deeper the attitudes we will develop. Similarly, a person who is "open-minded" is one who either has not had enough experiences with something to form an attitude, or has had a series of different experiences which have not formed a consistent pattern.

To put our model into the behaviorist philosophy, we need only substitute the word *behavior* for *experience*. This can be done by recognizing that an experi-

---

### Box 4-4: Want to Have a Free Car for the Weekend?

Anyone who has the task of changing someone else's attitude (or behavior) must know something about behavior modification in order to be successful. It is therefore no accident that salespeople tend to have a pretty good grasp of the fundamentals of behavior modification, even though they may not have had formal training in the subject or know the terminology. As customers, we can use their knowledge of human behavior to our own advantage once in a while.

Pick out any automobile dealership in your city, say a Ford dealer. Walk in the showroom late on a Friday afternoon, find a salesperson, and relate the following tale:

> I'm here shopping for a car. But before we get into this, I must tell you that my grandfather owned nothing but Chevrolets, my father owned nothing but Chevrolets, and I've had Chevrolets all my life. I happen to think that Chevrolets are the best car money can buy. Now, try and sell me a Ford.

If you've picked a successful, experienced salesperson, he or she will know that there is only one way to overcome your obviously strong attitudes about Chevrolets, and that is to give you such a positive experience with a Ford that it will change your attitude toward Chevrolets. The only way of providing this positive experience is to let you drive a Ford. But the salesperson also knows that there are many years of experiences to be undone. The necessary change is not likely to happen in a fifteen-minute drive around town. Therefore, the smart salesperson will hand you the keys to a new Ford for the whole weekend in the hope that this experience will change your attitude.

Keep in mind, however, that this method works only once with each dealership. But who knows? Maybe the experience will change your mind about Fords!

ence is really some type of behavior; for example, an experience with milk consists of drinking the milk (behavior). This changes our causal model to appear as follows:

$$B \longrightarrow A$$

Now the conclusion is that *if you want to change someone's attitude toward something, you must first change his or her behavior.* Referring to our previous example of the employee with the bad attitude, to change that attitude we must give the person a set of different experiences (behaviors) which will then affect that person's attitudes.

## ☐ The Importance of "Why"

One of the contrasts between the behaviorists and the nonbehaviorists is the question of why something happens. As we will see throughout this chapter, the pure behaviorist is unconcerned with why something affects a person in a given way—only that it does. In the statement regarding the milk, the behaviorist is not concerned with *why* someone has had a bad experience with milk, only that it was bad. The cognitive theorists, on the other hand, would be concerned with why on the grounds that a better understanding of that could lead to change if the reasons could be controlled.

To put this in an organizational context, assume that a supervisor reprimands a subordinate and we know that the employee doesn't like the reprimand. The cognitive approach would be concerned—at least partially—with why the employee did not like the reprimand, i.e., how will it affect his or her attitude? The behaviorist, on the other hand, will only be concerned with how this experience will affect the future *behavior* of the employee. Thus, the cognitive approach is concerned with how the employee *feels* about the reprimand, whereas behaviorists are concerned with what he or she will *do* about the reprimand.

This analysis is somewhat oversimplified since it implies that the cognitive approach is not concerned with how people behave, only how they feel. This is not true, since all motivation theories attempt to predict behavior. The difference between the two approaches lies mainly in the use of attitudes and their causal effect; the cognitive theorists use attitudes as an intervening variable in the causation of behavior and the behaviorists prefer to deal only with behavior itself.

## ☐ Mutual Causality

As usual, the most realistic position is a compromise between the two extremes. We have to acknowledge that attitudes are generated out of experiences, but also that attitudes, once formed, are determinants of behavior. Our model, therefore, can best be represented as follows:

$$B \longleftrightarrow A$$

The reader should note that this configuration reflects the thrust of the research evidence discussed in Chapter 3 on motivation. If we denote "attitude" as being synonymous with "job satisfaction," and "behavior" as synonymous with "productivity," we have the same conclusion as that reached in Chapter 3 (i.e., productivity and job satisfaction operate in a circular relationship, with productivity affecting satisfaction more than satisfaction affects productivity). Similarly, we can conclude that there is a circular relationship between behavior and attitudes, with behavior affecting attitudes more than attitudes affect behavior.

## □  So What Causes "B"?

Behaviorists see attitudes as resulting from behavior (although technically speaking, behaviorists would not even consider attitudes as important to an understanding of human behavior). We are therefore left with our original question of what causes B (behavior) to occur? Discounting for the time being the function of genes and other hereditary phenomena, behavior *first* occurs either on a random basis or as an imitation of others' behavior. In either case, behavior modification proposes that the probability of a behavior occurring in the future will be a function of the consequences attached to that behavior. The behaviorist philosophy is that all behavior is environmentally determined, i.e., depending upon the reaction of the environment to that behavior its frequency will either increase, decrease, or remain the same. If a person exhibits a specific behavior and has a

---

### *Organizational Reality   4-1*
### *Turning an Error Into a Positive Experience*

Heinz's highly successful frozen foods subsidiary Ore-Ida is using the basic principles of behavior modification to maintain a reasonable level of risk taking in the company. Recognizing that risk taking will result in frequent mistakes or dead ends, the company has instituted a program to turn mistakes into positive experiences.

Ore-Ida has carefully defined what it calls the "perfect failure," and has arranged for a cannon to shoot off every time one occurs. The cannon symbolizes that a mistake has been admitted and is to be recognized and then forgotten. Because failures are openly discussed, the behavior the company wants (i.e., continued risk taking) is not jeopardized as is often the case when failures are ridiculed and/or punished.

As a positive by-product of the program, the cannon has also legitimized mistakes and created positive feelings toward calling a quick halt to an obviously failing project. In contrast, in other organizations there is often pressure to have the project drag on and squander more funds in the hope that the failure will turn into a success.

---

Source: Thomas J. Peters and Robert H. Waterman, "How the Best-Run Companies Turn So-So Performers Into Winners," *Management Review* (November–December 1982): 8–16.

positive experience with it, then the probability of that behavior occurring again in the future increases; similarly, if the person has a negative experience, then the probability is decreased. Therefore, from the behaviorist point of view, what causes behavior to occur is the environment's reaction to that behavior. Our current behaviors have therefore been determined, both positively and negatively, by society's reactions to them.

## □ Conclusions

The behaviorist point of view has one significant advantage over the cognitive perspective. Behavior itself is directly observable, whereas attitudes, values, beliefs, etc., are not. If we observe an individual emitting a behavior in a certain set of circumstances, this is a measurable event that can be studied scientifically. However, attributing behavior to attitudes and states of mind presents severe measurement problems, since we are attempting to study something which, if it exists at all, cannot be measured accurately and reliably.

# ■ CENTRAL CONCEPTS IN ORGANIZATIONAL BEHAVIOR MODIFICATION

Most theories of human behavior have some jargon attached to them and organizational behavior modification is no different in this respect. However, unlike some other theories, the concepts and terminology of organizational behavior modification take on added importance since each concept has a specific meaning which must be understood before effective application is possible. In this section we present the central concepts necessary for a working knowledge of organizational behavior modification.

## □ Learning

The concept of learning is so common in our everyday lives that most people take it for granted and do not stop to think about what learning actually is. It is particularly important for organizational behavior modification since, for all practical purposes, the terms are snyonymous. If someone has learned something, then his behavior has been modified. Definitions of learning are widespread, but most behavioral scientists agree that *learning is a relatively permanent change in behavior that results from reinforced practice or experience.* Organizationally speaking, we are interested in learning, since this is the process by which employees acquire behavior patterns, both desirable and undesirable. It is implied that if we can control the reinforcements, then we can control learning.

## □ Conditioning

The concept of conditioning is in some ways similar to learning. Conditioning is the *process* by which learning occurs, and learning is the result of conditioning.

Conditioning describes how the environment reacts to behavior and the effect that it has upon behavior. If a person learns—through the environment—to exhibit a certain behavior, then we can say that person has been *conditioned,* or taught that behavior. There are two basic types of conditioning processes and they differ significantly in their relevance for management.

**Classical Conditioning**    Classical conditioning (also known as respondent conditioning and Pavlovian conditioning) places primary emphasis upon the relationship between the stimulus (cue) of the behavior and the response. The best-known examples of this are the experiments conducted by the psychologist Pavlov in which dogs were conditioned to salivate at the ringing of a bell because the bell had previously been associated with food (which also caused the dogs to salivate). The emphasis here was upon the stimulus (the food) which caused an *involuntary response* by the dog (salivation); when the food was subsequently paired with the ringing of a bell, the dog learned to associate the bell with the food and thus salivated at the sound of the bell. Classical conditioning therefore scientifically studied the relationship between the stimulus and the response and showed that responses could be controlled *involuntarily* by controlling the pre-conditioned stimulus.

Classical conditioning is generally not used in organizations for several reasons. First, to use it properly, managers would require laboratory-like conditions in order to control the conditioning process. This is because the pairing of the conditioned stimulus with the unconditioned one must be done carefully. Second, in order to control behavior, the manager would have to have control over the *stimulus,* not the response. This would be impossible in an organization because of the number of uncontrolled stimuli around. Third, it is generally agreed that this type of conditioning only accounts for a small part of learning—reflexive behavior—and therefore is limited in its applicability.

As an additional thought, it should be noted that much of the controversy surrounding behavior modification stems from the methods of classical conditioning. Since under classical conditioning the response is reflexive and therefore not under the control of the respondent, it is often thought that this gives the person doing the conditioning too much control over the organism. In the same sense that Pavlov's dog had no control over its salivation, it is thought that managers using the classical conditioning process would generate subordinates who had no control over their own behavior. Fortunately for managers, there is another method of conditioning that offers greater possibilities for organizational behavior modification.

**Operant Conditioning**    Whereas under the classical or respondent conditioning models the organism responded involuntarily, the operant model allows the person to *operate* on the environment to obtain the desired rewards (or avoid undesired punishments). In the operant model, the emphasis is upon the *consequences* of behavior, i.e., the outcomes in the environment that result from the behavior itself. In the classical model, behavior is controlled by controlling the stimulus; once the conditioning process has occurred, the same stimulus will generate the same behavior. In the operant model, a given stimulus can evoke a variety of responses, but these responses can be controlled by controlling the environmental events which follow the response.

For a manager, then, this allows many more possibilities for controlling the behavior of employees. Over time, employees can learn what behaviors result in what types of outcomes—both positive and negative. Once the consequences have been learned, employees can then "operate" on the environment to maximize their positive experiences and minimize their negative ones. This process is also called *instrumental conditioning* because the organism (employee) is instrumental in obtaining rewards and avoiding punishments. In other words, their behavior is not reflexive and involuntary but rather purposeful and voluntary.

As only one example of how operant conditioning influences behavior, let us assume that a given employee develops a habit of arriving late to work each morning. Let us further assume that the manager does not like this and therefore begins to reprimand the employee every time he is late for work. The employee does not like to be reprimanded and therefore begins coming to work on time every day. In our technical jargon, the example would read like this: an unconditioned response (coming to work late) has developed in the organism; the

---

### Organizational Reality   4-2
### Crown Zellerbach Lets Workers
### Operate on Their Environment

William Cresson, president of Crown Zellerbach, is getting cooperation from the International Woodworkers of America to cut logging costs and also halt the loss of hourly jobs. Under the experimental plan, the incentive to be more productive is that pay, excluding pension and health insurance benefits, will depend entirely on how much wood the crews produce each day. All workers in a crew will earn the same pay, which will be determined by the whole crew's performance.

In addition, the union has agreed to do away with up to twenty-five job classifications that pigeonholed workers into specific tasks. Both sides predict that eliminating these classifications will make the crews more productive.

The company would not have been able to make these changes, however, had it not also agreed to give union members much greater input into the design of their jobs and agreed to cease contracting out for cutting. The new wage structure will be developed by six joint union–management committees, corresponding to IWA locals, in the experiment. These committees will decide how many crews to form and which job functions will be included in each crew. The company will decide where to log, but the committees will decide how to organize the work. Since the workers will be paid by the amount they produce, they will also be motivated to suggest the most efficient plan possible.

---

Source: *Business Week* (29 November 1982): 35

manager specifies the consequences of the response (reprimand), which results in a bad experience for the organism; the organism operates on the environment (ceases to arrive late) to avoid the consequences (reprimand of the manager).

We noted in our discussion of classical conditioning that control of behavior rested with the person controlling the stimulus. In the operant model, control is still present but the control is over the *consequences,* not the *behavior.* In other words, the employee's choice is whether or not to come late to work but *not* whether to get the reprimand if he arrives late to work.

As another example, with our speed laws we are told what the desirable speed is and what the consequences are likely to be if we exceed those limits. As automobile drivers, our choice is whether or not we wish to adhere to those laws. But once we break the law, the consequences (i.e., speeding tickets) are beyond our control. In organizational behavior modification, the application of the operant model tells us that consequences should be clearly stated so that employees can be instrumental in obtaining their desired outcomes. We will discuss this concept more fully later in this chapter.

## ☐ Contingencies

The term *contingencies* is used to express the relationships of the stimulus, response, and consequence. It is generally used in the normative or prescriptive sense in that the relationships of the stimulus, response, and consequence should be in a *contingent* framework such that consequences are seen by the organism as being directly related to behavior. Recently, as organizational behavior modification has become popular, a new term, *contingency management,* has been created to describe how managers should specify the relationships of stimuli, behaviors, and outcomes to manage their employees more effectively.

## ☐ Reinforcement

It hasn't been easy, but so far we've tried to avoid using the term *reinforcement.* While it is likely the best-known term in behavior modification theory, it is often misunderstood. As will be seen shortly, organizational behavior modification goes far beyond the simple application of reinforcements, and a clear understanding of operant conditioning and other principles is necessary before discussing reinforcement.

Sometimes we take the terms *reinforcement* and *motivation* to be synonymous but this is not really the case. Motivation refers (usually) to the complex psychological processes that occur in the causation of behavior.[7] Recall that behaviorism does not really recognize these abstract concepts but rather attributes behavior to environmental events. To many behavior modification theorists, motivation is a nonsense term that defies definition, meaning, and measurement.

Reinforcement also differs from motivation in that reinforcement is an *event* that follows a behavior and is perceived as being contingent upon the behavior. This second condition is necessary since many events follow a behavior but relatively few are seen as being outcomes. For example, a salesperson may make a sale to a customer and this is followed by a complaint from another customer. The two events are sequential but there is no contingent relationship. In the theory of behavior modification, reinforcement is defined in terms of events. We can say that *reinforcement is any event that affects a response*. So if a student studies hard for an exam (response) and then receives a high grade (reinforcement), the chances that the student will study hard for the next exam are greater (i.e., the response is strengthened, all things being equal). Although there are minor differences, we can usually use *reinforcement* and *consequence* to mean the same thing.

Technically speaking, reinforcement is a neutral term, i.e., it only specifies that an event is contingent upon a response. In reality, there are several types of reinforcements and each has a different effect upon behavior. It is extremely important that managers understand the nature of the various reinforcements and their likely effects.

**Positive Reinforcement**  Positive reinforcement strengthens a response when presented contingent upon the response. As the name implies, the reinforcement event (consequence) consists of a positive experience for the individual. In more general terms, we often say that positive reinforcement consists of a reward for the individual and, when presented contingent upon behavior, tends to increase the probability that the behavior will occur again. For example, if an employee does something well and is complimented for it by the boss, this increases the probability that the employee will repeat the behavior.

While the concept of positive reinforcement has been scientifically verified in terms of its effect upon behavior, in managerial situations the principle is complicated by individual differences. While there are some things that practically all people find rewarding, there are also a lot of differences. For example, receiving a compliment from the boss would be a positive experience for most people but there are some for whom it would not. Similarly, giving employees more responsibility because they have performed well in the past could be rewarding for some, but for others the additional responsibility may be seen as only more headaches and hassles. It is extremely important that positive reinforcement always be given an individual interpretation. Also, if the reinforcement is not presented contingent upon the desired behavior, then the effect will not be the same. Managers who reward employees—but do not specify what the rewards are for —are not using their influence effectively.

**Negative Reinforcement**  At first glance it might appear that negative reinforcement is synonymous with punishment. The two appear to be so similar that they are assumed to have the same effects upon behavior, although this is not the case. Negative, like positive, reinforcement, *strengthens* behavior when it is contingent upon a response. The difference is that with negative reinforcement, the individual exhibits the desired behavior to *avoid* something unpleasant. Thus, the effect of negative reinforcement is often called *avoidance learning*. An example might be an employee who does something to avoid incurring a reprimand from

## Box 4-5: Using the Tools of Control on the Controller

The following story is passed around in practically every psychology department of every university, supposedly as a true story from that university. We suspect that it never really happened, but it still makes for an interesting possibility.

The story goes that a professor was teaching a class in behavior modification. Since the basics of behavior modification can be learned very quickly, after about two weeks into the term the students had a pretty good grasp of the fundamentals. In an informal bull session one day in the student lounge, the class decided to apply some behavior modification techniques to the professor during class. They decided that each time the professor wrote on the left side of the blackboard, everyone would take notes vigorously; when the professor wrote on the right-hand side of the blackboard, they would put their pencils down and just stare. Over the period of the semester, they gradually changed their reinforcement strategy until, at the end of the term, they had the professor writing in a space about 12 inches square!

(In case you weren't aware, most professors find it reinforcing to have students take notes.)

the supervisor. If an employee had developed a behavior pattern of arriving late to work, he or she may learn that this increases the probability of a reprimand; assuming this is an unpleasant experience, the employee may begin arriving on time to avoid the criticism.

Interestingly, we often think of pay as a positive reinforcer since employees engage in a behavior (come to work) and then receive a reward (pay). If pay is contingent upon performance (such as straight commission sales), then pay is being used as a positive reinforcer. However, if pay is not contingent upon performance, then a person may put forth only enough effort to *avoid* losing the pay (i.e., getting fired). In this latter case, pay is affecting the desired behavior but not in the same manner or to the same degree as the positive method.

**Omission**   Also referred to as "extinction," omission actually refers to the lack of a reinforcement—either positive or negative. It means that a given behavior is neither rewarded nor punished—simply ignored. While it may seem strange to classify this as a method of behavior modification since it really involves doing nothing, *it must be understood that omission does have an effect on behavior.* Since we know that reinforced behavior has a greater chance of occurring again, it follows that not reinforcing behavior (either positively or negatively) will reduce the chances of its recurring.

This principle has important implications for managers since it is common to think that if things are going well, people should just be let alone. This is often

## *Box 4-6: The Las Vegas Behavioral Scientists*

Knowledge about schedules of reinforcement can be of use to most anyone. However, one group whose very existence depends upon it is the gambling casino owners in Las Vegas. Their profits are assured by an astute knowledge of how people react to various reinforcement schedules.

Probably the best example is the slot machine. As far as the player is concerned, a slot machine pays off according to a random reinforcement schedule. If it were a fixed-ratio schedule, then one need only count the number of pulls on the handle between payoffs. Not only would this not be very profitable for the casino, it wouldn't be much fun to play. If the machine were on a fixed-interval schedule, then one would need only to watch the clock and count how many times per hour the machine paid off. Again, not much fun or profit. We know already that learning is more permanent when we reward desirable behavior only part of the time, hence the random reinforcement schedule. Individuals playing the slot machine have really no idea when the machine will pay off, but they do know that they will never win if they stop putting money into the machine.

Casino owners are very much aware of the danger of players (particularly inexperienced ones) not being reinforced quickly enough. They know that continuous reinforcement is the quickest method of establishing desirable behavior (in this case, putting money into the machine). However, to institute a continuous method at the outset would require either that the machine be rigged (which is against the law) or that they lose money (probably worse than breaking the law). So to approximate as closely as possible the continuous reinforcement schedule, the owners employ a concept known as "vicarious reinforcement," or reinforcement through another person's experiences. Each machine is wired into a central control, so that, when any machine hits the jackpot, sirens wail, lights flash, and bells ring. This lets everyone else in the casino know that reinforcement is possible—for those who continue to insert money!

referred to as the "don't rock the boat" strategy. Yet, our current knowledge about behavior modification principles tells us that if the desirable behavior is not reinforced, we are increasing the probability that it will become extinct. The reason this happens, of course, is because people will tend to seek out positive experiences and avoid negative ones. Since a positive experience is more rewarding than a neutral one, unrewarded behaviors have a greater chance of being dropped as the person experiments with other behaviors in an attempt to receive more rewards.

Another application of the omission principle pertains to undesirable behavior. If an employee is exhibiting an undesirable behavior, it follows that we can increase the chances that it will become extinct simply by ignoring it. But, in fact, a common strategy is to criticize the employee or apply some other type of negative reinforcement and in some cases to punish the employee. Each of these strategies can have undesirable effects not found in the extinction method. Suppose, for example, that employees find the manager's attention to be rewarding and that the only way to get the supervisor's attention is to do something wrong. In applying negative reinforcement or punishment to the undesirable behavior, the supervisor may actually be strengthening it!

Of course, there are times when extinction is not possible. A supervisor may face a problem in which one employee is arriving late to work—an undesirable behavior. It may well be that if the behavior is ignored, other employees may begin to do the same thing. In these cases more direct methods are necessary. This brings us to punishment.

**Punishment**    Punishment involves the presentation of an aversive or negative consequence contingent upon a response or removing a pleasant consequence contingent upon a response. In the first instance, when an undesirable response is emitted, it is contingently followed by a negative outcome. Since negative outcomes tend to be avoided, this decreases the chances the behavior will recur. In the second instance, a previously contingent reward is withheld because of the undesirable behavior. Since the individual wants the reward, the withholding of it is a punishment and has the effect of decreasing the chances the behavior will occur again. Because punishment is so often used by managers as a method of shaping behavior, we devote an entire section to it later in this chapter.

Positive reinforcement, negative reinforcement, omission, and punishment constitute the major strategies of influencing behavior in organizations. In one sense, their application is simple, since we know quite well the effect each has upon behavior. However, since they can be used in any combination, actual application becomes somewhat more complex. Examples of these applications are discussed later in this chapter.

## ☐  Schedules of Reinforcement

There are essentially two factors that influence behavior in organizations: the nature of the outcomes (rewards or punishments) and the manner in which they are applied. The nature of the outcomes was discussed in the previous section; in this section we present some thoughts on the *timing* of these outcomes which, in the language of organizational behavior modification, is referred to as the *schedule of reinforcement*.

Theoretically there are an infinite number of schedules, since rewards and punishments can be applied after each emitted behavior, every second one, every fourteenth one, and so on. But from years of research on the effects of various schedules in laboratory situations, two basic types have been recognized: *continuous* and *partial* reinforcement schedules.

**Continuous Schedules**    On a continuous reinforcement schedule, a reinforcement follows each time the desired behavior is emitted. A proud parent praising an infant son or daughter each time a puzzle is done correctly is an example of continuous reinforcement. This has the effect of increasing the desired response rapidly since the organism quickly learns that a reinforcement is forthcoming after (and only after) the desired response is emitted. Its disadvantage, however, is that if the continuous schedule is not maintained, the desired response decreases rapidly as well. It should be obvious that this is generally not recommended as a long-term managerial reinforcement strategy. It can require the constant presence of the manager to make sure the desired behavior is rewarded every time, thus making the manager very inefficient, since he or she has other things to do besides continually rewarding employees. However, it might be useful over short periods of time (particularly for new employees who are just learning their jobs) until other methods and types of reinforcements can be applied.

**Partial Schedules**    Partial reinforcement schedules are different from continuous ones in that correct behavior is rewarded only part of the time. Again, there are many possible schedules under this arrangement but the general principle is that *learning is more permanent when we reward behavior only part of the time.* At first glance, this appears to be a direct contradiction of what we have learned so far. It would initially appear that continuous reinforcement is the most effective in the ideal case even though it does have significant disadvantages (e.g., the time requirement for the manager). However, the difference lies in the *speed* of learning (i.e., how quickly one goes from a neutral state to one of emitting the desired behavior) and the *permanency* of learning (i.e., how long one keeps emitting the desired response once it is established). Continuous reinforcement starts up the desired response over a very short period of time. However, as we noted earlier, unless the continuous reinforcement is maintained, the desired response rate is likely to decrease.

Partial schedules of reinforcement have the disadvantage of being relatively slow in stimulating the desired behavior, but once established they are the most effective at maintaining the behavior and are therefore most often recommended for managerial application. Partial reinforcement schedules are also referred to as *intermittent* schedules, reflecting the fact that reinforcements are applied at various time intervals or response rates.

**Examples of Schedules**    Since there are a wide variety of partial schedules available, it is useful to classify them into two types: interval schedules and ratio schedules. *Interval schedules* are based on time, i. e., reinforcements are applied over a variety of time intervals; *ratio schedules* are based on the number of responses (i.e., reinforcements are applied following a number of behavioral responses). Each of these is explained below.

*Fixed interval*—In this type of schedule a reinforcement is applied regardless of the number of responses after a *known* time period. Notice the importance of the qualifier "known." If the manager were applying a fixed interval method but the subordinate did not know the schedule, then it would have the same effect as a ratio schedule.[8]

## Box 4-7: But Can These Results Be Generalized to People . . . ?

As has been pointed out earlier in this chapter, much of what we know about operant conditioning techniques has come out of laboratory experiments on various types of animals, very often rats and mice. Although some believe that these results cannot be extrapolated to managing people, there is increasing evidence that the results can be useful. Consider the following example.

In the 1950s two professors at Indiana University studied the differences between the relative strengths of continuous versus intermittent (partial) reinforcement schedules. The experimenters taught two groups of rats to press a lever to get a drink of water. Once this behavior was learned, the rats were separated into two groups. In group I, the rats were placed in a lever-equipped box for 180 minutes (in half-hour sessions) and were permitted to press the lever as often as they wished, but they were rewarded with water on the average of only once every two minutes, for a total of ninety rewards. Group II rats had the same time conditions but were rewarded *every time* they pressed the lever. They accumulated 2,400 reinforcements in their 180 minutes. Immediately following these experiences, extinction methods were instituted; all the rats were allowed to press the lever but no reward was given. They were tested this way daily for three one-hour periods.

Group I rats, given 90 *intermittent* rewards, pressed the lever 129 times during the extinction period, or over 140 percent of the number of previous reinforcements. The group II rats, given 2,400 *continuous* reinforcements in the original learning, yielded only 100 responses during the extinction period, or just slightly over 4 percent.

The lesson here: *the less consistently you reward, the stronger the learning.*

Source: W. O. Jenkins and M. K. Rigby, "Partial (Periodic) Versus Continuous Reinforcement in Resistance to Extinction," *Journal of Comparative and Physiological Psychology* 43 (1950): 30–40.

To show the relationship between the various schedules and their relative effectiveness, we will use a common example for all the schedules. Under the fixed interval method, our example would be that, as subordinates, we know that our manager visits our department once every fifth day. It follows that this method of reinforcement will have the strongest effect on our behavior on the fifth day, but very little on the other days, since we know that the reinforcement will not occur until the fifth day. While this type of schedule does have an effect upon behavior, it is limited compared to the other types of schedules.

*Variable interval*—Again, the schedule refers to the passage of time but the time period is *unknown* to the respondent. Note that if the interval were both variable and known, it would actually be a fixed-interval schedule, since the respondent would know the time at which the reinforcement would occur. In essence, the variable-interval schedule appears to be a random one for the respondent, since the intervals between reinforcements cannot be predicted in advance.[9]

Using our example above, variable-interval reinforcement would be a situation in which we know the manager visits our department once a week but we don't know when. The effects of this type of schedule are interesting. On Monday, our behavior is influenced somewhat as we estimate the probability of the manager's showing up. If the manager doesn't come on Monday, then the effect of the system on our behavior on Tuesday is greater and so on until the manager actually comes through the department. But once the manager has visited, regardless of the day, the effect of the system on our behavior decreases dramatically. The astute reader will note that this is actually not a "pure" random reinforcement method since we know that there are at least weekly visits. In this respect we do know something about the interval which makes it a little like a fixed-interval schedule. Technically speaking, the above example is a variable interval within a fixed-interval reinforcement schedule.

*Fixed ratio*—The ratio schedules pertain to reinforcement/response patterns rather than the passage of time. A reinforcement is applied after a fixed number of measurable behavioral responses. A continuous reinforcement schedule described earlier is a specific example of a fixed-ratio scale because the ratio is 1:1. The term is usually applied to other ratios, however, such as 1:10, 1:50, and so forth.

Our example of the manager's visiting the department now changes from a schedule based upon time to one based upon frequency of behaviors. Let us say that every fourth time our department meets its production quota, the manager comes to the department and congratulates us. This could be once a week, four times a week, etc., depending upon how often we meet our quota. Another example would be where workers are paid on a piece-rate basis and after a fixed number of pieces produced, they are given a bonus. This system tends to be more effective in determining behavior because the reinforcements are oriented to the frequency of desired behaviors and employees can influence the outcomes significantly by "playing the system" according to their objectives. It also has the advantage of communicating more effectively to employees the types of behavior that are desirable.

*Variable ratio*—The variable ratio schedule means that specific behaviors are reinforced at different response rates. Sometimes a reinforcement will occur after three behavioral responses, sometimes after ten, sometimes after fifty, and so forth. To the individual, of course, the reinforcement schedule will appear to be random as was the case with the variable-interval schedule. Research indicates that this method is the slowest to start up a desired behavior, but once established it is the most resistant to extinction methods (see Box 4-7). This happens because the person learns over time not to expect reinforcement at any predictable time but that reinforcement will be forthcoming eventually if the correct responses are continually emitted. It is this significant principle which, to a large degree, accounts for the success of gambling activities (see Box 4-6).

Taking this schedule literally and applying it to our earlier example, as subordinates we know that the manager comes through the department but we don't know when or specifically why. All that we do know is that at random times the manager visits us and reinforces—either positively or negatively—our previous behavior. This would have a significant effect on our behavior as we try to maximize our rewards and minimize our costs over time.

It may appear that the random method of applying reinforcements is more effective than other methods and this is true in most cases, providing certain conditions are met. But it should be understood that this does not apply to punishment, since it is designed to *extinguish* a specific behavior, not strengthen it, as reinforcement does. A manager who applies punishment on a random basis would surely generate a palace revolt in a short period of time. This is because we have learned through our previous experiences that punishment is only applied for specific, observable causes. However, there is an element of randomness present when punishment is related to events but the timing of the application of the punishment varies. For example, the police force relies heavily on the fact that most people will stay within the speed limits for fear of being punished if they are caught. In this way a relatively small number of police can control the speeding behavior of thousands of people. So there is a significant difference between applying punishment indiscriminately for unknown causes and punishing undesirable behavior on a (perceived) random basis. All of this, of course, reinforces the need for managers to understand clearly how the systematic application of rewards and punishments affects the behavior of employees. A summary of the various schedules and their effects is presented in Table 4-1.

**Research Evidence on OBM Schedules**     The theory behind reinforcement schedules is relatively straightforward, but as would be expected, when the schedules are applied in work organizations the effects are not nearly as neat and concise. For example, one of the major variables not specified in the theory of reinforcement schedules is the ability of the employee. As noted in Chapter 3, performance is a function of two major variables: ability and motivation. Regardless of the schedule used, if the employee's ability is limited, then different schedules of reinforcement will not change performance.[10]

A complicating factor in the research on reinforcement schedules is the infinite combination of schedules that can be used. For example, a variable-ratio schedule can be used anywhere from an average of two responses per reinforcement up to an extremely large number of responses. In addition, the period of time over which these responses occur can also influence the effectiveness of the schedule.[11]

Another variable that can alter the effects of a schedule is the size of the reinforcement. In fact, one of the underlying assumptions of behavior modification theory is that "more is better," thus emphasizing that the larger the reward, the

**TABLE 4-1.   Schedules of Reinforcement and Their Effects**

| Schedule | Description | Effects on Responding |
|---|---|---|
| Continuous (CRF) | Reinforcer follows every response. | (1) Steady high rate of performance as long as reinforcement continues to follow every response. (2) High frequency of reinforcement may lead to early satiation. (3) Behavior weakens rapidly (undergoes extinction) when reinforcers are withheld. (4) Appropriate for newly emitted, unstable, or low-frequency responses. |
| Intermittent | Reinforcer does not follow every response. | (1) Capable of producing high frequencies of responding. (2) Low frequency of reinforcement precludes early satiation. (3) Appropriate for stable or high-frequency responses. |
| Fixed ratio (FR) | A fixed number of responses must be emitted before reinforcement occurs. | (1) A fixed ratio of 1:1 (reinforcement occurs after every response) is the same as a continuous schedule. (2) Tends to produce a high rate of response which is vigorous and steady. |
| Variable ratio (VR) | A varying or random number of responses must be emitted before reinforcement occurs. | (1) Capable of producing a high rate of response which is vigorous, steady, and resistant to extinction. |
| Fixed interval (FI) | The first response after a specific period of time has elapsed is reinforced. | (1) Produces an uneven response pattern varying from a very slow, unenergetic response immediately following reinforcement to a very fast, vigorous response immediately preceding reinforcement. |
| Variable interval (VI) | The first response after varying or random periods of time have elapsed is reinforced. | (1) Tends to produce a high rate of response which is vigorous, steady, and resistant to extinction. |

Source: Fred Luthans and Robert Kreitner, *Organizational Behavior Modification* (Glenview, Ill.: Scott, Foresman, 1975), p. 51. Reprinted by permission.

less important the schedule. One study showed that this is not necessarily true and that offering too large an incentive can have negative repercussions. The researchers offered equity theory as one explanation for their findings, i.e., the size of the incentive was perceived as being so large that it was inequitable.[12] So with the confounding effects of size, length of reinforcement period, ability, and other factors, it is not surprising that the research evidence on schedules of reinforcement is mixed.

## Box 4-8: When Is a Fixed Schedule Not a Fixed Schedule?

In several places in this chapter we have referred to the importance of the *perception* of the organism in responding to a particular reinforcement schedule. It was noted, for example, that if a variable-interval schedule were *known* by the organism, then it would be perceived as a fixed *schedule* and the effect upon behavior would be the same as a fixed schedule. Similarly, if a variable-ratio schedule were *known*, we proposed that it would have the same effect as a fixed-ratio schedule. Our conclusion is based upon our belief that people can "think" about the differences between fixed and variables and this process can result in different responses.

Whether we are right or wrong, we must point out that the *reasons* for our conclusions are totally at odds with the view of the behaviorists, although all of us would agree with effects that both fixed and partial schedules have upon organisms. The behaviorists would say, for example, that rats and mice cannot deduce the nature of a reinforcement schedule; they merely respond in a predictable manner to how the reinforcements are applied. We have proposed, however, that people are capable of figuring out reinforcement schedules and their conclusions about what the schedules are will affect their behavior.

If you find these positions difficult to reconcile, then you have the essence of one of the key disagreements between behaviorists and the cognitive theorists.

There is some evidence to suggest that variable-ratio reinforcement schedules are superior to continuous schedules. However, the conclusions are situational. Latham and Dossett[13] were able to increase the productivity of beaver trappers in the northwest by 41 percent, compared to a 20 percent increase by those on a continuous reinforcement schedule The study also shows that continuous schedules were more effective for inexperienced trappers and the variable-ratio schedule was more effective for experienced ones. The same researchers conducted a follow-up study two years later and found the program still effective and the same differences between continuous and variable-ratio schedules. Their research in this phase explored the reasons why the variable-ratio schedule was superior and found that the employees perceived several job-enrichment factors such as recognition, task variety, task accomplishment, and feedback, to be operating in the variable-ratio schedule.[14] Several other studies have showed similar findings.[15]

Other studies, however, indicate that continuous-reinforcement schedules are at least equal to and sometimes superior to variable-ratio schedules. In an experiment with workers planting trees, one study found that the continuous schedule was superior to the variable-ratio schedule. In fact, under one variable-ratio schedule, performance actually decreased.[16] In another study designed to increase bus ridership, both incentive schedules increased ridership and there was no difference in the effectiveness of the two schedules.[17] Another study showed that incentive schedules were superior to hourly schedules, but there was no difference between the various incentive schedules.[18]

---

### Box 4-9: Mistakes in Rewarding Major-League Baseball Pitchers

All sports figures draw a lot of public attention, sometimes good and sometimes bad. The bad is often represented by the irate fans who are upset by a star who is paid several hundred thousand dollars per year but doesn't perform. All of us can think of a sports figure at some time who didn't seem to earn his or her enormous salary. Only one case comes to mind in which a player actually refunded part of his pay because he wasn't playing well. Is it true that many highly paid baseball stars do not earn their salaries, or is it just a figment of our imagination?

While most of us are content to argue these issues simplistically, three researchers decided to find out if it is really true that highly paid baseball stars don't earn their salaries. They examined the performance of major-league baseball pitchers who were on long-term guaranteed contracts with high rates of pay. Historically, players negotiated each yearly contract after the season and new contracts tended to reflect the previous season's performance. In 1977, multiyear guaranteed contracts were introduced, changing the system from a contingent one to a noncontingent reward system.

After studying the performance of seventy-six pitchers making a minimum of $100,000 per year for a minimum of three years, and comparing their performances with two control groups on annual contracts, the researchers concluded that the high-pay, long-term contracts coincided with significant deterioration in the pitchers' performances. The research team also noted that this evidence is contrary to equity theory, which would predict that a highly-paid poor performer would attempt in some way to reduce the inequity.

Source: Steven R. Howard, Robert W. Figlerski, and Richard M. O'Brien, "The Performance of Major-League Baseball Pitchers on Long-Term Contracts," in Richard M. O'Brien, Alyce M. Dickson, and Michael P. Rosow, eds., *Industrial Behavior Modification* (New York: Pergamon Press, 1982), pp. 91–114.

So where does this leave the manager who is trying to decide which type of incentive condition to implement? First, the evidence supports the fact that contingent reward systems generally are superior to fixed-interval (hourly) reward systems. Therefore, it would appear prudent for organizations to examine various incentive programs as alternatives to fixed-wage plans.

Second, the evidence is also relatively conclusive that continuous-reinforcement schedules are more appropriate for individuals who are learning their jobs, as opposed to more experienced employees. Third, the continuous schedule would have the greatest *practical* value to an organization because of the difficulty in administering a variable-ratio schedule. Not many employees, for example, would want to work for an organization in which they were paid on an intermittent basis. However, creative experimentation by organizations could conceivably overcome this difficulty.

Fourth, practicality juxtaposed with research evidence suggests that any variable-ratio reinforcement schedule should be *in addition* to a fixed base or interval reward. This serves to reduce the anxiety associated with the pure intermittent schedule, yet, providing the reinforcer is large enough, can improve performance beyond what the normal fixed-interval schedule usually generates.[19] Fifth and finally, the difficulties associated with the complexities of designing the "perfect" organizational behavior modification system might be reduced by involving the employees in the design of the plan itself. All of the studies noted have the common element that the reinforcement schedule studied was designed by someone other than the subjects. In the one case in which the subjects had an input into the system, not only did performance improve over the baseline level, but the variable-ratio schedule proved to be superior to the continuous schedule. This is significant for managers because variable-ratio schedules should be less expensive to operate than continuous schedules.[20]

# ■ USING PUNISHMENT IN ORGANIZATIONAL BEHAVIOR MODIFICATION

Punishment is a very complex behavior modification strategy that is often misunderstood. Because of its importance we devote a section specifically to the topic so that managers will be in a better position to decide when and if to use punishment. Most of the complexity associated with punishment is caused by the fact that a reasonable case can be made both for and against using punishment. In this section we present the essence of each of the positions and conclude with some general rules regarding the use of punishment in organizations.

## □ Criticisms of Punishment

In presenting the case against punishment we try to stick with the scientific approach rather than the emotional one. The use of punishment tends to bring out many emotional reactions in people, most dealing with personal philosophies of control. While that is an important issue with punishment, we can do nothing in this regard for the reader except reiterate the obvious positions. Instead, we will focus on what is known about the negative effects of punishment in the scientific sense.

1. *Punishment does not strengthen the desired response.* We must remember that the effect of punishment is to extinguish a response (presumably an undesirable one) and this it tends to do fairly effectively, all things being equal. However, it is not always true that a desirable response is the opposite of the undesirable one. Therefore, punishment is limited in that it may get rid of the undesirable behavior but does not necessarily stimulate the desirable one. For example, a sales manager may "chew out" a salesman who has lost an important sale because he used an inappropriate sales technique. The salesman will learn not to use that technique again (which in itself may be wrong since the technique may be appropriate for other customers) but the punishment does not teach him the proper technique to use.

2. *Surveillance by the manager is necessary.*[21] Punishment tends to be an inefficient form of control because the physical presence of the manager is usually required. Since by definition no one likes punishment, it is unlikely a person would make a self-report that would result in punishment.[22] Managers whose dominant control method is punishment-oriented will probably find that when they are away from the workers, their influence will be restricted to whatever evidence can be produced regarding the worker's behavior in their absence (e.g., spies). Even in the presence of the manager, the suppression of the undesirable behavior is only temporary.

3. *Punishment tends to lead to more punishment.*[23] Since punishment can result in only temporary improvement, the manager may become increasingly frustrated at the lack of permanent behavior change. Often this frustration manifests itself in the form of even more punishment, i.e., punishment directed at not respecting punishment.

4. *Punishment has emotional consequences.*[24] People who feel unjustly punished may take out their feelings in other nonproductive ways, in some extreme cases even in direct sabotage. More important, punishment tends to cause dislike of the punishing agent (the manager) and this can have repercussions for future relations.

5. *Punishment can cause behavior inflexibility.*[25] Punishment tends to be something that is administered for a particular behavior at a particular time. In the sense that it can extinguish that behavior quickly, this has to be seen as an advantage. However, people may generalize the punishment to the same behavior in other situations and refuse to emit the behavior, based on their previous experiences. The learning can be too permanent. For example, a new employee may try some innovative ideas on the job only to be criticized (punished) by the manager. Although the criticism may have been justified in this instance, the manager may wonder several years later why the employee refuses to innovate on the job.

6. *Punishment may have reinforcing consequences.* Finally, we must recognize that some people find punishment itself to be reinforcing. (Technically speaking, if one finds something rewarding, then it is not really a punishment; but in this instance we are referring to the perceptions of the manager). The manager may think he or she is punishing but in fact is applying a type of reinforcement. It is often pointed out that children, when feeling the neglect of their parents, will engage in behaviors they know will bring punishment (such as running wildly through the house) because they know this will get their parents' attention. Similarly, an employee may "create" a problem, knowing full well that this will result in more attention from the manager. The punishing behavior of the manager can actually generate more problems.

Before going into the positive side of punishment, we should examine the question, "If punishment is so undesirable, then why do so many managers (and parents) rely so heavily on it?" Luthans and Kreitner maintain that punishment is used often *because the act of punishing is reinforcing to the person applying the punishment.*[26] It may be that we apply punishment more for our own purposes (e.g. releasing emotional tension) than for the purpose of extinguishing the undesirable behavior. It is not likely, however, in such an emotional situation that a manager would stop to ponder the negative outcomes of the punishment process.

## ☐ Advantages of Punishment

All of the above would suggest that punishment should not be used as a method of controlling behavior. While this is true in the ideal sense, there are some important qualifiers. First, whether punishment is useful depends upon the manager's objectives. If the goal of a manager is to get rid of an employee and he or she does not have the authority to fire, applying punishment increases the likelihood that the employee will leave. Managers can actually take advantage of all the criticisms mentioned above to rid themselves of a problem employee. In most cases, however, we assume that the manager wants to influence an employee's behavior positively, and this places punishment in an unfavorable light.

Second, whether punishment is useful depends upon the situation. Generally speaking, if the costs of not punishing outweigh the advantages, then punishment is clearly an appropriate strategy. For example, to ignore your child when he or she is writing on your newly papered wall is a pretty expensive way of shaping behavior, since the extinction process would take quite some time. However, even here there might be ways of dealing with the problem other than punishment, such as providing the child with a writing pad. In either case, one has to keep in mind the child's motivation for emitting the behavior; if it is to get the parents' attention, then the writing pad will actually increase the problem. So within these broad qualifications, here are the generally accepted reasons for using punishment.

1. *Punishment is the fastest method of extinguishing undesirable behavior.* If speed is of the utmost importance, then punishment is a viable strategy. In most of these cases, other considerations are of lesser importance (e.g., those mentioned above as criticisms). If your child is running out into a dangerous street, the price of this behavior is so high that it outweighs any other consideration. You don't particularly care at this point whether your spanking will cause the child to have a long-term fear of automobiles.

2. *Punishment is a natural part of our physical and psychological growth.* Bandura suggests that much of our learning is through punishment from the environment (as opposed to managers, parents, etc.).[27] For example, we learn not to touch a hot stove by being punished (i.e., burned) when we do. Psychologically speaking, we learn to be shy by experiencing embarrassment when ridiculed by others, and so forth. Although some of this learning may be negative reinforcement instead of punishment, the fact remains that punishment is common in our experiences.

3. *Intrinsically rewarding behavior is difficult to extinguish through means other than punishment.* We first have to accept that intrinsic rewards (i.e., those given by persons to themselves) tend to have a stronger effect on behavior than extrinsic rewards (i.e., rewards conferred by others).[28] Given this, it follows that only the most powerful strategy (punishment) is likely to have any effect on the intrinsically rewarding behavior. If a worker gets extreme intrinsic satisfaction out of being the group leader in horseplay activities, omission (i.e., ignoring it) will probably not have any effect. Punishment would have the greatest chance of extinguishing the behavior, but even here, if the intrinsic rewards are strong enough, punishment may have only the effect of driving the behavior underground.

## ☐ Using Punishment Effectively

In a review of the literature regarding punishment, Arvey and Ivancevich point out that the topic of punishment has received little attention in organizational research. In examining what research there is, they note the following variables appear to influence the effectiveness of punishment in organizations: (1) the timing of the punishment; (2) its intensity; (3) the relationship with the punishing agent; (4) the schedule of punishment; (5) whether or not the rationale for punishment is clear; and (6) whether or not alternative responses are available to the person being punished.[29] The translation of these variables into prescriptive statements yields some suggestions as to how the positive aspects of punishment can be used by managers and the negative effects minimized. One such prescriptive list is provided by Hamner and Organ.

1. Punishment is more effective if it is applied before an undesired response has been allowed to gain strength.
2. Other things being equal, punishment is generally more effective when it is relatively intense and quick (i.e., administered as soon after the response as possible).

3. Punishment should focus on a specific act, not on the person or on his/her general patterns of behavior.
4. Punishment should be consistent across persons and across time.
5. Punishment should have informational value (i.e., it should be accompanied by an explanation of why the behavior is undesirable).
6. Punishment is most effective when it occurs in the context of a warm or nurtured relationship.
7. Punishment should *not* be followed by *noncontingent rewards* (often done as a means of relieving the guilt feelings of the person doing the punishing).[30]

If all of these factors are kept in mind when applying punishment in those situations in which it is deemed necessary, then there is less chance of negative side effects. It is interesting to note, however, that the essence of the above list is to make punishment less aversive—meaning less of a punishment. So we arrive at the seemingly paradoxical conclusion that punishment can be more effective if it is made less of a punishment!

---

## *Organizational Reality*   4-3
## *Sheraton's Superstars*

When the Sheraton Corporation purchased what is now the Sheraton Center in New York, it wanted to improve its employees' behavior toward its customers. Jean-Robert H. Cauvin, executive assistant to the vice-president, commented, "In the service industry, employees do not perform when morale is low. If employees do not perform, then guests don't receive services." Cauvin then started the "Superstar" program to improve and maintain the quality of services provided by the hotel's staff.

The program involves monthly Superstars, Super-superstars, and a Superstar contest. Hotel guests are given a "starcard" upon check-in and are encouraged to vote for their Superstar. The votes are tabulated and twenty Superstars are chosen based on the balloting, a review by the division supervisor, and past employment records. The Superstars and their achievements are then announced at a monthly meeting and winners are given a certificate and a check for $100. A Super-superstar is chosen from the twenty finalists and is given another $100 and a trophy. There is also a Super-superstar of the year who receives a trophy and a $1,000 check.

The contest consists of multiple-choice questions on hotel procedures and a bonus question asking the employee for a definition of quality of performance as it relates to his or her job. These questions require the employee to think about what good performance looks like. The first-place winner of the contest receives an all-expense-paid trip to Hawaii.

---

Source: *Personnel Journal* (February 1981).

# ■ CONCERNS AND LIMITATIONS OF ORGANIZATIONAL BEHAVIOR MODIFICATION

The controversy surrounding organizational behavior modification has become intense in recent years. Reactions tend to be at two extremes: those who are turned on by it and those who are not. As noted above, there are cognitive theorists, who propose that individuals engage in complex thought processes before emitting behavior, and behaviorists, who believe that people react primarily to their environmental history. The cognitive theorists are critical of behavior modification principles because they believe the principles ignore man's capability to consider rationally various alternative courses of action and innovative behaviors. Behaviorists, on the other hand, tend to exclude "thinking" from the behavioristic model and account for all behavior using operant concepts.

The fact that behavior modification principles can account for *any* behavior is both a strength and a weakness. We have already noted that rewards and punishments are defined in terms of their consequences, i.e., if a consequence strengthens a response, it is called a reward, and if it weakens a response, it is called a punishment. Scientifically speaking, this raises serious questions. Also, since we would like to *predict* behavior rather than simply account for it, behavior modification leaves something to be desired. It is, however, important to observe what individuals have responded to in the past because that can give us important clues to how they will respond in the future.

Much of the controversy surrounding behavior modification is highly technical and theoretical in nature. Since this book is primarily applications-oriented rather than research-oriented, we choose to mention only concerns and limitations that are of primary interest to the practicing manager.[31] Here we will be general in our remarks, saving the specific problems for the applications section of this chapter.

## ☐ "Too Much" Control?

Assuming for the moment that the concepts and principles proposed by organizational behavior modification are correct (i.e., that they work), then the ability to control subordinates is placed directly in the hands of the manager. Or, to put the matter another way, if the manager has control over the things that subordinates find reinforcing, then the potential control over the subordinates is increased. There is often a negative reaction by managers to this phenomenon, as though having control over someone else's behavior is wrong. It is almost as if managers expect subordinates to do the things the organization wants them to do for no reason at all or that subordinates should behave properly because they want to, not because of some external reward or punishment. We must recognize, of course, that any type of control can be misused, but this does not negate the need for control. We can imagine a manager using his or her influence to get an employee to break the law and everyone would agree that this is wrong. However, we must also remember that the major responsibility of a manager is to control the behavior of subordinates and anyone who believes that control is bad would make a poor manager, indeed. Bandura, in his classic book on organizational behavior modification, has noted this fact as follows:

> . . . all behavior is inevitably controlled and the operation of psychological laws cannot be suspended by romantic conceptions of human behavior, any more than indignant rejection of the law of gravity as antihumanistic can stop people from falling.[32]

## ☐ No Control Over Reinforcements

The successful application of organization behavior modification principles is limited by the extent that the manager can control reinforcements. Clearly, if a manager does not have control over the things an employee finds to be rewarding, then that manager will not have much influence over the employee. Take the case of a manager who has a subordinate who is a local sports hero—say an amateur bowler well known in the community for his or her bowling prowess. Assuming that the individual's major source of satisfaction (i.e., reinforcement) comes from bowling, it is unlikely that the manager will have much control over the subordinate's behavior unless job behavior can somehow be related to the bowling activity. This is not to say that the manager will have *no* control over the subordinate, only that this influence will be less than it would be if the person received his or her major rewards at work. As another example, many managers complain that union contracts prohibit them from doing certain things that would motivate workers. From a behavior modification perspective, this simply means that the manager has less influence (control) over the unionized workers than might otherwise be the case.

It should be noted that this limitation does not apply only to organizational behavior modification: *any theory of motivation is limited to the extent that the manager is able to control the variables in question.* To propose a facetious (but illustrative) example, if it were found that employees were motivated by the degree of sunlight in their work area, the manager's ability to influence their behavior would clearly be determined by his/her ability to control the amount of sunlight! The reader need only apply this reasoning to the various theories of motivation presented in Chapter 3 to see how important control is to the practicing manager.

## ☐ Behavior Modification and Group Theory

Whyte notes that there can be conflict between individual and group applications of organizational behavior modification.[33] He notes that managers may attempt to apply reinforcements on an individual level without realizing that reinforcements for groups may be different.[34] For example, job enrichment may be used as a method of motivating a given individual on the basis that the person will find the increased responsibility reinforcing. However, if the group norm restricts productivity, this may counteract the positive force of the enriched job. From the worker's point of view, a decision is made regarding the relative importance of the two reinforcements—job satisfaction versus group acceptance. If it is decided that group acceptance is worth more, then the enriched job would not be likely to produce any change in productivity.

We can broaden this concern and point out that often managers may find that reinforcements are in conflict, and the group versus individual phenomenon is only a specific case. For example, an employee may find a conflict between attempting to maximize earnings on a piece-rate system and the fear that the rate for the job will be lowered if too much is earned.

## ☐ Inability to Identify Proper Reinforcements

Many times managers are unable to identify what employees find reinforcing. While there are many things that most people find rewarding (e.g., pay, recognition, interesting job, etc.), it is not uncommon to find situations in which nothing appears to reinforce a particular worker. To solve this problem, we must first start with the premise that *everyone is motivated, everyone finds something to be reinforcing;* the key, of course, is to discover what it might be.

There is no fixed way of finding out what is reinforcing to a person. One can always ask but there is no guarantee that the answer will be totally honest and complete. Some may feel it is childish to admit to the things they want; others may be suspicious of a manager who is so direct. In the final analysis, observation is perhaps the best method of determining reinforcements. Through observation, the manager attempts to deduce what an individual has responded to in the past. This requires sensitivity on the part of the manager, particularly in the area of cause and effect. If no reasonable pattern emerges even after many attempts to figure out what a person finds rewarding, it may be best to look for rewards outside of the workplace as a possible answer.

---

### Box 4-10: Who Is Reinforcing Whom?

The point has been made that in the ideal state, reinforcement systems are mutual, i.e., each party to the interaction receives reinforcement from the other's behavior. One of the common jokes heard around behavioral science laboratories concerns this very thing. The story is told that two rats in the psychology laboratory are talking one day and one rat says to the other one, "Boy, have I got that lab technician conditioned. Every time I pull this lever, he gives me something to drink!"

---

## ■ APPLICATIONS AND PERFORMANCE MANAGEMENT

The study of applications of organizational behavior modification is by necessity somewhat different from that found in other chapters. Because behavior modification is basically a technology rather than an abstract theory, the applications of the concepts are revealed when learning about them. The entire chapter, therefore, is about the applications of organizational behavior modification principles.

The examination of how the principles operate in practice allows us to interject a new term—performance management. Since the practice of organizational behavior modification principles has received increased attention, the field has adopted the term "performance management" to emphasize that management's attention should be focused on performance, not attitudes, morale, or other intangible terms. The term also reflects the specific focus of behavior modification, i.e., the influencing of behavior toward the organizational goal of performance.

We will begin our study by examining in detail the two major components of performance management: goal-setting and feedback on performance. Using these as our foundation, we will then present some general principles of application, outline the steps for implementing an organizational behavior modification system, and then conclude with a review of how performance management has been applied in organizations.

## ☐ Goal Setting and Feedback

As we noted in Chapter 3, goal setting and feedback on progress toward goals are important ingredients in the determinants of motivation. It was pointed out that goals should be *specific, accepted, challenging,* and have *feedback.* It is no accident that these same characteristics are important in the application of performance management.

Assume, for example, that a manager wishes to improve the performance of an employee. The formula above suggests that:

1. The manager should set specific targets for behavior change. If the performance problem is poor quality of work, then the manager must specify exactly what good performance looks like. This then becomes the target.
2. Goals are meaningless if the employee is not committed to them. Employee participation in the goal-setting process is one way of overcoming this problem, but, according to research is not always necessary.[35] The more the manager and subordinate communicate about the performance problem and what good performance looks like, the more it is likely that the employee will work toward improvement.
3. The goal must be within the abilities of the employee. If the goal is unrealistic in expectation, the employee will not see it as being attainable, and may view the manager as setting him up for failure.
4. The feedback becomes important since it tells the employee how well he or she is progressing toward the goal. Working without feedback is like hitting a golfball in the dark. Your shot may feel good, but you don't really know how close you came to your target.

An additional point about goal setting is the number of goals that should be set. Generally speaking, the number of goals should be kept small. If there are too many goals, then the employee has a more difficult time sorting out priorities, and his or her energy must be divided between too many activities. Too many goals also complicates the feedback process since multiple feedback sources may get confused and not give a clear picture of progress toward the individual goals.[36]

**Propositions for Goal Setting and Feedback**   Because performance management is still a relatively new area of research in organizational behavior, there is a lot yet to examine about the effects of goal setting and feedback. However, various studies and reviews of the literature produce the following generalizations that would be of use to managers:

1. Feedback by itself is not sufficient to produce motivation.[37] For example, feedback on a goal not accepted by the employee would not improve performance.
2. Feedback and goal setting used in conjunction with each other are superior to goal setting alone.[38]
3. Harder goals are more motivating than easy goals only if the expected outcomes for the difficult goals exceed the expected outcomes from the easier goals.[39]
4. Inexperienced employees' goal setting and performance can be influenced by the goal setting and performance of high performers.[40] This has important implications for how organizations should train new employees.

---

### *Organizational Reality   4-4*
### *Using Feedback to Improve Productivity*

Mr. Peter Kirby, vice-president of human resources for Li'l General Food Stores reports on a case study in a manufacturing organization in which feedback was used to improve productivity. This particular company was having difficulty in the marketplace in keeping its products competitive. It was decided that the best way to keep the product line competitive was to reduce the labor costs associated with production.

Management established a production quota for each unit with no participation from the union. The goals, however, were widely circulated and all employees were kept informed.

Management then established feedback systems to keep employees informed as to how they were progressing toward their goal. Kirby emphasizes that the feedback systems need not be sophisticated, and that in most companies the information exists already. For example, in one department production was kept on a chalkboard and updated at the end of each shift.

The results of this program were positive. Productivity increases in each department were large and maintained over long periods of time. One department that had a history of labor problems began breaking previous production records when feedback was given regularly.

---

Source: Peter G. Kirby, "Productivity Increases Through Feedback Systems," *Personnel Journal* (October 1977): 512–515.

5. When the task itself provides feedback and knowledge, feedback from an external source may be unnecessary.[41]
6. Goal setting clarifies role expectations and reduces stress associated with role ambiguity.[42]
7. If a task or goal is accepted, performance on the task is higher when the goal is difficult than when it is easy.[43]
8. Both assigned and participative goals produce higher performance than the "do your best" instruction.[44]

Each of these conclusions should be viewed as tentative. There is research evidence to support them, but there may be contingent factors operating that might invalidate (or at least limit) the specific conclusions. Additional research that will no doubt be forthcoming will shed more light on these and other important issues. Meanwhile, we will use this evidence, as well as other research on organizational behavior modification, to discuss some general applications of performance management.

## □ General Concepts for Applications

All the concepts to this point provide a framework from which a set of useful principles can be designed. Effective application of organizational behavior modification begins with the following fundamental principles.

1. *Every manager already uses behavior modification.* One point that is often difficult to get across to many managers is that they are already using behavior modification principles in their jobs, usually without realizing it. In other words, any manager who exerts influence over subordinates(which is just about every manager) is already using rewards and punishments. It is hoped that by studying the principles of organizational behavior modification, managers can gain a better understanding of how their behavior (in the form of applying rewards and punishments) is affecting the behavior of employees. It is not a question of whether or not to use the concepts but rather how to use them effectively to attain desired objectives.

2. *Actions speak louder than words.* This is an old adage which has an important meaning in organizational behavior modification. People respond to the events that actually affect them, not to what they are told. A manager who tells employees one thing but whose behavior reflects something different will find that employees react to the behavior and not the words. For example, if a manager tells employees that *quality* of work is what is important but then rewards *quantity* of work produced, employees will soon respond to the quantity dimension, often at the expense of quality. Just as a small child learns that a parent gets upset when bothered while reading the evening paper despite a professed intention to play with the child, employees can read the *behavior* of their manager to learn his/her likes and dislikes.

3. *Doing nothing has reinforcing consequences.* Unfortunately, the strategy of "don't rock the boat" has an undeserved reputation for being an effective

management style. Our earlier discussion of the omission technique indicated that behavior that is ignored is less likely to occur again. This means that employees who are behaving properly may cease to exhibit desirable behaviors in order to get their manager's attention. Managers must constantly keep in mind that desirable behavior must be positively reinforced to maximize the chances that it will be continually exhibited.

4. *Reinforcers are individual in nature.* There can be important individual differences in reinforcements, although some reinforcers (such as pay) may be common to most people. We must also discriminate between the *type* of reinforcer used and its *importance* to a particular individual. Though two people may both find pay to be a positive reinforcement, it may be a much stronger reinforcer for one than the other.

5. *Reinforcers must be oriented toward specific behaviors.* It would be inappropriate to use reinforcement theory in an attempt to make someone "a better employee." Organizational behavior modification techniques can only be effective if applied to a specific, observable act of behavior. From the employee's point of view, he/she cannot really know what the manager feels "a better employee" is. Does the manager want a higher quantity of production? More quality? Better appearance? Or what? There are obviously a number of behaviors that constitute a person's total performance. To use behavior modification effectively, the employee must know specifically which behaviors the manager finds desirable and which are undesirable. Not knowing would only result in a very frustrated employee and a disappointed manager.

6. *Reinforcements must be "real."* This is another way of saying that the application of positive reinforcements cannot be treated as a gimmick to get employees to do things they would not normally do. The situation in which this is most likely to arise is the use of compliments by the manager to an employee. If the method of positive recognition is used in a situation in which the manager does not sincerely believe that the performance warrants the compliment, then the act is likely to be seen as insincere and will probably do more harm than good. Similarly if a manager overdoes the compliment routine, employees are likely to see the act as a gimmick and will respond in a negative manner.

7. *Reinforcements must be fair.* We learned in Chapter 3 the importance of the equity principle in determining individual motivation. This principle also has important implications for the use of organizational behavior modification techniques. It says that if people do not see the rewards as being commensurate with the required behaviors, then the reinforcement system will be ineffective. A manager can have a complete system designed using feedback, contingency frameworks, and identification of the correct reinforcements, but if the people in the system do not consider the rewards fair, then the system will not influence their behavior (except possibly in the negative sense that they feel cheated). For example, an incentive system that requires workers to expend 50 percent more effort for the opportunity to gain 10 percent more reward would probably be ineffective. This is a common problem with many formalized company suggestion systems: employees suggest methods that can save the company thousands of dollars only to receive a reward of $100.

8. *Reinforcements must be relatively quick.* Although the specific timing of the reward will vary with the situation, the general rule is that contingency arrangements should have as short a time horizon as possible. The reason that retirement plans are ineffective motivators, for example, is that employees must wait so long to receive the benefits. Similarly, many automobile insurance companies attempt to modify driving behaviors by offering reductions in insurance premiums if a person is accident-free for a certain period (usually one year). Unfortunately, few people will make a dramatic change in their behavior today for a small reward one year from now. The principles operate the same way within organizations. A common example is with employee incentive plans that attempt to relate productivity to financial rewards. To be successful, such plans must provide relatively quick rewards to the employee that can be specifically identified with productive behaviors. For example, all things being equal, a bonus system that rewards employees weekly is superior to one that pays off once every six months.

9. *Employees must be given feedback on their performance.* It is difficult for employees to change their behavior if they do not know what they are doing wrong. Feedback on performance is a necessary ingredient of any organizational behavior modification program. While the act of negative feedback may in itself not be rewarding, it is a necessary prerequisite for behavior change. Many managers find the feedback process to be an uncomfortable one and therefore avoid it as often as possible. Unfortunately, this can cause additional problems as the manager becomes increasingly frustrated with the lack of performance and the employees become frustrated trying to figure out what it is the manager wants.

## ☐ Steps in Designing an Organizational Behavior Modification Program

If the above concepts are kept in mind as a general framework, then it is possible, by going through a series of steps, to design a reinforcement system to modify a particular aspect of organizational behavior. Sequentially, the steps would be as follows:

1. *Identify the specific problem to be solved.* The manager must decide what specific behavior is to be eliminated or stimulated.

2. *Specify the behavior in observable, measurable terms.* The manager must then define what is to be changed and how it is to be measured. This will prevent the common problem of attempting to change employees' attitudes or to "make them better employees." If, for example, the problem to be solved is tardiness, the manager should define the desired behavior in terms of which employee should be at work by what time.

3. *Identify the reinforcements.* The manager must examine those reinforcers that appear to be common to most people, as well as the individual reinforcers. All things being equal, the individual ones are likely to be the more powerful reinforcers.

4. *Design the contingencies.* The manager designs a system which allows the desired reinforcements to be made contingent upon the desired behavior being emitted. If the manager can neither identify the reinforcements nor make them contingent upon the behavior, then behavior will not change.

5. *Insure that there is a method for applying the contingency relationship.* If the manager has specified a contingency relationship between behavior and rewards, then there must be some means of making sure that when the desired behavior is emitted, the reward will follow. In some cases this may only mean that the manager must learn about behavior through the normal feedback communication channels. But in other cases, such as when an employee is learning a new behavior, more immediate feedback may be in order. This may require the physical presence of the supervisor for a short period until the behavior is learned. In other cases, the method may be more mechanical in nature. For example, if a college professor wishes to reward students specifically for coming to class, then there must be a system by which attendance can be monitored.[45]

6. *Feedback to the employee how the system operates and what it takes to "win."* Before anyone can play the game successfully, they must know what the rules are and what behaviors are needed to get reinforced. In this step the manager must outline specifically what the employee is doing right and wrong, what the rewards are and how they will be applied, and the nature of the contingency relationship.

7. *Apply the system fairly and consistently.* Once the system is established, it should be maintained in a consistent manner. Nothing is more frustrating to employees than to have the rules changed on them midway through the system. And nothing will kill an effective behavior modification system more quickly than to change the contingencies unfairly. A good example of this is rate-cutting in piecework systems; employees are told they will be paid a given rate for production and then subsequently the rate is lowered, meaning that the employees have to work harder now for the same reward. It is for this very reason that many piecework incentive systems are ineffective.

If these guidelines seem very mechanical and impersonal, it is because our discussion has necessarily been brief. In actual practice, there should be considerable communication between managers and employees in designing a behavior modification system, a process which in itself can be reinforcing. In any case, if one examines a situation in which a manager has little control over subordinates, it will probably be found that one or more of these seven steps has been either ignored completely or at least not given the attention that it should have. Nevertheless, we must always keep in mind that a manager may not have control over the reinforcements necessary to change and/or control behavior, in which case the manager will have less influence over subordinates than would be desired.

## ☐ Research on Application of Performance Management

While many of the studies of performance management have been concerned with the refinement of organizational behavior modification theory (e.g., which schedules are most effective, etc.), considerable research has also been conducted into actual performance management programs. In these studies, the organization has identified a particular performance area that needs improvement; a behavior modification system is implemented, and the results are measured. Although the research methods vary considerably in these studies, they nevertheless give a good indication of the potential for performance management programs, as well as the areas in which they are likely to be effective.

Perhaps the granddaddy of all performance management studies is the Emery Air Freight case.[46] It is credited with being the case that has since promoted the interest in performance management concepts. Emery trained all supervisors and managers in positive reinforcement techniques. Then key performance areas were identified and positive reinforcement was applied to areas where a performance deficiency existed. In one area, the shipping department, performance rose from 45 percent of standard to 95 percent. Emery reported similar results in other areas of company operations.

Michigan Bell Telephone Company was another early example of performance management.[47] Their problem was high absenteeism among the telephone operators, which historically had averaged about 11 percent. Attendance records were kept for one group and posted on a weekly basis, and supervisors were encouraged to make positive comments about improved attendance. Within six weeks absenteeism dropped to 6.5 percent. When the rest of the company's Detroit operators went on the system, absenteeism dropped from 7.5 percent to 4.5 percent.

In another study involving a city transit company, behavior modification methods were applied to the safety record of the bus drivers.[48] Several experimental manipulations were conducted, but overall the system reduced accident rates by 24.9 percent. This program differed from the previous two not only in that feedback was provided on a daily basis, but "teams" were put in competition with each other, with the winning team receiving a choice of rewards ($5 worth of gas, free bus rides, etc.). The researchers concluded that the program resulted in a benefit/cost ratio to the company of over 3:1.

Another study reported on a hardware company that employed a variable ratio reinforcement schedule to reduce absenteeism and tardiness.[49] Employees who came to work on time each day for a month were eligible for a drawing at the end of the month, and employees who had perfect attendance for six months were placed in a lottery for a television set. The study reported that sick leave costs were reduced by 62 percent with this system. A similar study reported on an attempt to improve the attendance of school teachers (not students!).[50] Teachers who had a perfect attendance record for a semester were reinforced with $50. Over the five-year life of the program, perfect attendance averaged 50 percent, resulting in a significant savings in the cost of substitute teachers.

Performance management techniques are particularly relevant to sales positions, largely because performance in sales lends itself to specific goal setting and performance measurement. In SAS airlines, agents were trained in specific sales techniques, the key one being the "offer." An offer was the attempt by the agent to sell a specific seat to a customer who had called in for information. Sales supervisors were also trained in specific positive reinforcement techniques designed to improve the skills of the agents. By the end of the program, 84 percent of the potential-offer opportunities had offers being made, as compared to 34 percent at the beginning of the program. Since offers tend to result in bookings, the airline attributes its increased bookings during this period to the program.[51]

Behavior modification has also been used for sales training. In contrast to many sales training approaches that attempt to increase the motivation of sales people (e.g., by increasing enthusiasm), the performance management approach concentrates on the specific behaviors that have been empirically verified as improving the probabilities of the sale. For example, obtaining and using the customer's name has proven to lead to more sales, so this becomes an integral part of the training program. After the training program, follow-up results showed that obtaining and using the customer's name increased from a baseline of 18 percent to 79 percent. Similar results were reported for other behaviors as well.[52]

Although the evidence is clear that behavior modification principles offer considerable promise for organizational behavior, much research needs to be done, especially in the area of evaluation research. We need better experimental designs in field studies, and many more situations involving the application of performance management programs in which proper controls can be used to measure objectively the changes in behavior. Laboratory studies have been extremely useful in sorting out some of the technical aspects of behavior modification, but these principles need much more rigorous testing in the field. Unfortunately, many field studies still conclude with, ". . . the results were positive and performance improved," with little or no supporting evidence to substantiate the claim. As the interest in performance management increases in the coming years, additional research will no doubt be one positive result.

## ☐ Performance Management and Monetary Rewards

Knowledge of behavior modification and the effective use of rewards and punishments usually opens peoples' eyes to the fact that most organizations do not use their limited rewards in a very effective manner. In times when available rewards are being diminished, it becomes even more important to recognize how rewards affect behavior and how managers can more effectively utilize those rewards that are available. Since money is a common reinforcer and is available in various amounts in all organizations, it seems imperative that we spend some time discussing how money should be used to maximize its impact upon behavior.

*The most common reason that money is not used effectively is because it is often not awarded contingent upon desired behavior.* In many cases, employees receive their paychecks regardless of how they have performed over the relevant period. In most cases, the behavior of the employee only becomes important in the extreme, i.e., someone who is extremely bad is fired and someone who is extremely good is sometimes given a raise and/or promotion. But for the majority of employees who are somewhere in between these extremes, pay is often not related to on-the-job behavior.

There are some notable exceptions to the above. Commission sales, for example, is a good example of a contingency arrangement: no sale, no money.

# Box 4-11: Is Behavior Modification Really Different from Other Theories?

In any discussion of the various approaches to understanding motivation theories, the theories of Maslow, Herzberg, McClelland, and expectancy theory usually are in the forefront. Most people tend to think of behavior modification as a "different" approach. Yet, on closer examination, behavior modification is not really inconsistent with any of the other approaches.

Take Maslow for example. In his hierarchy of needs it is proposed that people gradually progress to higher and higher levels of need satisfaction and it is unsatisfied needs that motivate people. In behavior modification terminology, we need only say that the satisfactions are reinforcers: thus, if people are "motivated" by ego needs, we can also say that they will find events which increase their ego satisfaction to be reinforcing. Or, alternatively, if one wants to reinforce someone, one need only discover what level of need satisfaction is salient and apply the proper reinforcement.

Herzberg maintains that there is a difference between hygienes and motivators. Motivators, in Herzberg's terms, are really nothing more than specific reinforcers. Hygienes are reinforcers that have been saturated. The reader should recall that one of the shortcomings of Herzberg's theory is that hygienes and motivators have not been found to be consistent with all people; this can be explained by behavior modification, since we know that people find different things to be reinforcing. To say that a hygiene factor can also be a motivator recognizes that some people find hygiene items to be reinforcing. Why? Because their experiences have conditioned them to respond to hygienes.

A similar analysis can be applied to McClelland. McClelland notes that the needs of achievement, power, and affiliation determine our behavior. High achievers are people who have been conditioned to respond to achieving situations; people who have a strong need for power are those who have been conditioned to respond to influence, and so on. It is no accident that McClelland's method of inducing the need to achieve is through behavior modification techniques. Subjects are shown how high achievers behave and are then conditioned to imitate that behavior.

Expectancy theory refers to "outcomes," which is simply another term for reinforcement. Expectancy theory tells us that in order to motivate an employee, we have to match the employee's outcomes (reinforcements) with those of the organization, so that the parties are in a mutually reinforcing situation.

In sum, behavior modification can explain why other approaches to motivation work and also account for why they don't work.

Piece-rate systems (of which commission sales is only one example) are also behaviorally anchored in that rewards are based upon the number of pieces produced. This is not to say that all piece-rate systems are well-managed, but at least they satisfy the basic conditions for effective behavior modification.

Since there are many types of reward systems in organizations, it is interesting to look at the more common ones and use the principles of behavior modification to analyze their potential effects on behavior.

1. *Wages and salaries.* Usually ineffective since they are often related to time, not performance; they can be partially reinforcing, however, depending upon how they are administered. If the level of pay is determined by seniority, then pay reinforces longevity, but rarely productivity, in the work force.

2. *Commission schemes.* Usually highly effective, provided that (1) the employee has a reasonable chance of accomplishing what is necessary and (2) the amount of commission is sufficiently large to be reinforcing.

3. *Salary plus bonus systems.* Can be reasonably effective since the salary reinforces the workers' need for a predictable standard of living and the bonus—if contingent upon behavior—provides the opportunity to increase reinforcements. It is only effective, however, if the employee perceives that the bonus is contingent upon *personal* effort rather than something that is beyond his/her control. As an example, many company bonus systems are ineffective since the size of the bonus depends upon the total company operations (not the individual effort) and the time period is often too long between the behavior and the reward.

4. *Profit-sharing systems.* Usually ineffective in determining behavior, since too many variables affect profits. They can be useful for smaller companies where a more direct relationship between individual performance and reward exists.

5. *Retirement plans.* Usually ineffective for two reasons: first, it is impossible to see a relationship between individual effort and the rewards (the amount of money available for retirement); second, the time period for receiving the reward is far too long to have an appreciable effect upon behavior. As one grows closer to retirement, however, the effect of the system can increase, subject, of course, to the first qualification.

The above examples lead us to a series of conclusions regarding the effectiveness of pay. To put these principles into a prescriptive model, we propose the following list of principles that must be followed if monetary rewards are to be used effectively:

1. Pay must be reinforcing to the employee.
2. Pay must be made contingent upon previously agreed-upon behaviors.
3. The interval between behavior and receipt of pay must be as short as is administratively practicable.
4. The level of the pay (or size of the potential pay level) must be sufficiently large to overcome the effect of competing reinforcements.

# Opening Incident Revisited—
# The Pickerel Manufacturing Company

Having now read the chapter on behavior modification, the reader should not be surprised that the absenteeism lottery system was effective. Most of the principles of organizational behavior modification are embodied in the system, as compared to previous approaches which did not consider the principles of reinforcement. To use this example as a learning experience, let us now go through the program in a piecemeal fashion to analyze what the company did and why it worked.

First, we start with the simple fact that workers were not coming to work all the time before the program because they had no reason to. In other words, on several days during the week, the reasons for not coming to work outweighed (i.e., were more reinforcing than) the reasons for coming. Thus, what the company did was give them a reason to come to work every day. All an organizational behavior modification system does is give people a reason for doing what the organization wants them to do. Or, to put the matter another way, organizational behavior modification (practiced correctly) lets the employees satisfy their individual goals (i.e., get reinforced) while simultaneously allowing the company to satisfy its goals.

In this situation what the company wanted was more people at work more often. There was a contingent relationship present before the lottery system (i.e., nonmedical absences were docked a day's pay). However, since it did not have the desired effect upon behavior then, it evidently was not reinforcing enough to the workers. The company's problem, then, was to maintain the contingent relationship but increase the strength of the reinforcers. Here is where the lottery and prizes come in. In order to get one's name in the lottery, one had to have perfect attendance for the week, and in order to win one of the prizes, one had to be in the lottery. So these two items served as reinforcers in addition to the pay the worker avoided losing by coming to work.

The company also adequately considered the timing aspect. They realized that if there was only an annual lottery, those people who missed a day early in the year would have no incentive to better their attendance, since they were already eliminated from the lottery. On the other hand, if there were only weekly lotteries, both saturation and frustration could result. Saturation would be possible in the sense that not all workers necessarily needed a new television set, and frustration could result from the people who never won anything. The spacing of the different lotteries, then, was an attempt to overcome both of these problems. Even people who never won the weekly lottery were still in the running for the larger lotteries, and the chance of winning one of these was greater because of the lower number of people eligible. One can imagine the pressure on the workers to come to work toward the end of the year when comparatively few were eligible for the very large prizes! The workers who were absent for non-medical reasons were immediately placed back into the lotteries, so that the system had an immediate effect on their behavior even though they had been eliminated from the larger prizes.

A word of caution is in order, however. It was pointed out in this chapter that to apply behavior modification correctly, it must be addressed to a specific problem. The company did this in designing an organizational behavior modification system to increase attendance. But this says nothing about what the workers will do once they arrive at work. For example, it would be erroneous to conclude that this system makes the employees more productive or motivated; all it can do is condition them to come to work when they might otherwise stay at home. If the company wants to increase the productivity of workers once they are at work, it is likely that a different system is needed. Or, as someone once said in a skeptical vein, "With this system you will likely have about 50 to 75 people at work who would just as soon not be there. I wouldn't give you a dime for their productivity."

## ■ SUMMARY

In this chapter we have described how the concepts of behavior modification might be applied to organizational behavior. We began with a discussion of the determinants of behavior and pointed out the contrast between the cognitive theorists and the behaviorists. Behaviorists do not concern themselves with internal states of mind, particularly as causes of behavior. The cognitive theorists, on the other hand, believe that individuals engage in complex thought processes before deciding on a course of action. It was also noted that the behaviorists believe that all behavior is determined by environmental reactions, both positive and negative, to our behavior. The application of positive and negative reinforcements is the essence of behavior modification.

Discussion then turned to the central concepts in behavior modification: conditioning, contingencies, reinforcement, and learning theory. Each of these concepts is important to the successful application of behavior modification principles. Schedules of reinforcement pertain to the timing of rewards and punishments. Each schedule has a different effect upon people, and the manager should know how the timing of rewards can influence behavior.

One of the most common methods of shaping behavior in organizations is punishment. Punishment can be quite effective at reducing undesirable behavior, but it can also have some negative side effects. A proper understanding of how punishment operates and the effects it is likely to have is necessary for any manager.

Behavior modification is not without its limitations and criticisms. Some people are concerned that managers may have too much control over employees and that people are thereby deprived of their freedom and dignity. Behavior modification is limited in that if a manager does not have control over the reinforcements, then it will not be possible to exert any influence over employees. Since one of a manager's major responsibilities is to control the behavior of subordinates, it is imperative to have knowledge about how control can be used effectively.

The application of organizational behavior modification principles is called performance management. Performance management involves examining specific areas of performance that need changing, and designing a contingency system to modify that behavior. This chapter reviewed several studies conducted in organizations that illustrated how performance can be changed using this method.

Behavior modification applied to organizations is not just a trick or gimmick to get more out of people. Reinforcement must be a mutual process (i.e., one in which the employee and employer are mutually reinforced in the work situation). Since all managers already use behavior modification (in the sense that they apply rewards and punishments), then it is imperative that each manager be aware of the effect that his/her behavior can have on subordinates.

# ■ EXERCISE 4-1: ANALYZING YOUR CLASS

It has been established in the chapter that behavior modification is a technique used by everyone; most people just don't realize they are using it. But once a situation is analyzed according to behavior modification techniques, it is often apparent that rewards and punishments are not administered as effectively as they might be.

To gain experience in applying behavior modification concepts, this exercise requires you to analyze the class you are in now (or any other class for that matter) to see how behavior modification techniques are being utilized. To assist you in this task, below are some questions to stimulate your thinking.

1.  What rewards and punishments are evident in this class? (Examine the subtle ones as well as the obvious ones.)

2.  In your "reading" of the use of rewards and punishments, what behaviors does your instructor see as desirable and undesirable?

3.  Are there any examples of undesirable behavior that the instructor may be unconsciously conditioning?

4.  What major principles of behavior modification is the instructor violating?

5.  What types of reinforcers do the students give back to the instructor?

# ■ EXERCISE 4-2: THE OTHER SIDE OF THE COIN

Organizational behavior modification has generated considerable controversy in recent years. The grounds for the controversy have been many and varied, but one of the more common criticisms concerns the extrapolation of research findings from laboratory mice to human beings. The following quotation is representative of the criticism.

In the introductory sentences of this paper, I pointed out that operant conditioning has worked well with animals, mental patients, autistic children, and others. Here, I have said that the approach insults the intelligence of the average worker. The human subjects with whom it has worked well have had in common some impairment in their ability to fully utilize their intelligence. Even the literature dealing with the hard-core unemployables suggests that, because of environmental, cultural, or educational deficiencies, they cannot function properly. From these experiences, I infer that operant conditioning may be a very valuable aid in working with those who either have a low intelligence or cannot properly use their intelligence. It is a logical extension of this observation to conclude that operant conditioning works best for those whose level of functional intelligence allows them to see only very short-run, lowest-order needs, as described by Maslow. These individuals may have the capability of perceiving only the close relationship between an act and an immediate reward. The general run of workers, we hope, are beyond that stage, and, if so, O.B. Mod. cannot be expected to have the pervasive results claimed for it.[53]

Do you agree or disagree with the author? Why?

# ■ ENDNOTES

1. See John B. Watson, "Psychology As the Behaviorist Views It," *Psychological Review* 20 (1913): 158–77.

2. E. L. Thorndike, *Educational Psychology: The Psychology of Learning,* vol. 2 (New York: Columbia University Teachers College, 1913).

3. Ibid, p. 4.

4. See, for example, B. F. Skinner, *Science and Human Behavior* (Glencoe, Ill.: Free Press, 1953); *The Behavior of Organisms* (New York: Appleton-Century-Crofts, 1938); *Contingencies of Reinforcement* (New York: Appleton-Century-Crofts, 1969); and *Beyond Freedom and Dignity* (New York: Bantam Books, 1971).

5. In addition to the anecdotal evidence that could be offered for this statement, there is scientific evidence as well. As only one example, see James A. Breaugh, "Predicting Absenteeism from Prior Absenteeism and Work Attitudes," *Journal of Applied Psychology* 66, no. 5 (1981): 555–560. This study showed that previous behavior (absenteeism) was a better predictor of absenteeism than attitudes toward work.

6. Strictly speaking, of course, even this behavior would not be totally random, since the new employee has to have some type of previous organizational or social experience from which to learn something about acceptable and unacceptable behaviors. It might be more correct to state that the employee will exhibit a "wide range" of behaviors rather than just a random set.

7. Fred Luthans, *Organizational Behavior* (New York: McGraw-Hill, 1973), p. 374.

8. It should be noted that this statement is inconsistent with the "pure" theory of behavior modification. The statement implies that the organism plays an active role (i.e., thinking) in determining what the reinforcement schedule is. Because of our position on this, we would not be invited to the annual Behaviorists Picnic. See Box 4-8 for the reason for our position.

9. See Box 4-7.

10. Robert D. Pritchard, John Hollenback, and Philip J. Deleo, "The Effects of Continuous and Partial Schedules of Reinforcement on Effort, Performance, and Satisfaction," *Organizational Behavior and Human Performance* 25 (1980): 336–353.

11. Gary P. Latham and Dennis L. Dossett, "Designing Incentive Plans for Unionized Employees: A Comparison of Continuous and Variable Ratio Reinforcement Schedules," *Personnel Psychology* 31 (1978): 47–61.

12.  Abraham K. Korman, Albert S. Glickman, and Robert L. Frey, Jr., "More Is Not Better: Two Failures of Incentive Theory," *Journal of Applied Psychology* 66, no. 2 (1981): 255–259.

13.  Latham and Dossett, "Designing Incentive Plans."

14.  Lise M. Saari and Gary P. Latham, "Employee Reactions to Continuous and Variable Ratio Reinforcement Schedules Involving a Monetary Incentive," *Journal of Applied Psychology* 67, no. 4 (1982): 506–508.

15.  See, for example, G. A. Yukl, K. N. Wexley, and J. D. Seymour, "Effectiveness of Pay Incentives Under Variable Ratio and Continuous Reinforcement Schedules," *Journal of Applied Psychology* 56 (1972): 19–23; and Latham and Dossett, "Designing Incentive Plans."

16.  G. A. Yukl and G. P. Latham, "Consequences of Reinforcement Schedules and Incentive Magnitudes for Employee Performance: Problems Encountered in an Industrial Setting," *Journal of Applied Psychology* 60 (1975): 294–298.

17.  B. C. Deslauries and P. E. Everett, "Effects of Intermittent and Continuous Token Reinforcement on Bus Ridership," *Journal of Applied Psychology* 62 (1977): 369–75.

18.  Pritchard, Hollenback, and DeLeo, "Effects of Continuous and Partial Schedules."

19.  Interestingly, some studies have showed that changing from a piece-rate system to a weekly wage resulted in a drop in performance. See E. Jacques, A. Rice, and J. Hill, "The Social and Psychological Impact of a Change in Method of Wage Payment," *Human Relations* 4 (1951): 315–340; and H. Rothe, "Output Rates Among Welders," *Journal of Applied Psychology* 54 (1970): 549–551.

20.  For a more in-depth discussion of reinforcement schedules applied to industrial settings, see Teodoro Ayllon and David J. Kolko, "Productivity and Schedules of Reinforcement in Business and Industry," in Richard M. O'Brien, Alyce M. Dickinson, and Michael P. Rosow, eds., *Industrial Behavior Modification* (New York: Pergamon Press, 1982), pp. 35–50.

21.  W. Clay Hamner and Dennis W. Organ, *Organizational Behavior: An Applied Psychological Approach* (Dallas: Business Publications, 1978), p. 75.

22.  This is because the definition of punishing is "aversive." An event that one person finds pleasurable may be aversive to another, but each will find *something* to be aversive. Even a masochist (one who derives pleasure from pain) will find something to be aversive, most likely pleasure!

23.  Fred Luthans and Robert Kreitner, *Organizational Behavior Modification* (Glenview, Illinois: Scott Foresman, 1975), p. 119.

24.  Ibid., p. 120.

25.  Ibid., p. 121.

26.  Ibid., p. 116.

27.  A. Bandura, *Principles of Behavior Modification* (New York: Holt, Rinehart and Winston, 1969).

28.  William W. Notz., "Work Motivation and the Negative Effects of Extrinsic Rewards," *American Psychologist* (September 1975): 884–91.

29.  Richard D. Arvey and John M. Ivancevich, "Punishment in Organizations: A Review, Propositions, and Research Suggestions," *Academy of Management Review* 5, no. 1 (1980): 123–132.

30.  Hamner and Organ, *Organizational Behavior*, pp. 77–80.

31.  For a more detailed discussion of the controversy, see Edwin A. Locke, "The Myths of Behavior Mod in Organizations," *Academy of Management Review* 2, no. 4 (October 1977): 543–53; and Jerry L. Gray, "The Myths of the Myths About Behavior Mod in Organizations: A Reply to Locke's Criticisms of Behavior Modification," *Academy of Management Review* 4, no. 1 (1979): 121–29; and Edwin A. Locke, "Myths in the Myths of the Myths About Behavior Modification in Organizations," *Academy of Management Review* 4, no. 1 (1979): 131–36; Marcia Parmerlee and Charles Schwenk, "Radical Behaviorism: Misconceptions in the Locke-Gray Debate," *Academy of Management Review* 4, no. 4 (1979): 601–07; and Donald B. Fedor and Gerald R. Ferris, "Integrating OB Mod with Cognitive Approaches to Motivation," *Academy of Management Review* 6, no. 1 (1981): 115–25.

32.  Bandura, *Principles of Behavior Modification*, p. 85.

33.  William H. Whyte, "Pigeons, Persons, and Piece Rates," *Psychology Today* (April 1972): 67–68, 96, 98, 100.

34. The differences between individual and group theory are discussed in greater detail in Chapters 10 and 11.
35. See, for example, Paul D. Tolchinsky and Donald C. King, "Do Goals Mediate the Effects of Incentives on Performance," *Academy of Management Review* 5, no. 3 (1980): 455–467.
36. Kenneth Blanchard and Spencer Johnson, *The One-Minute Manager* (New York: William Morrow and Co., 1982). Blanchard and Johnson suggest that each employee should have no more than five to seven major goals. It is their contention that Pareto's Law is relevant to goal-setting, meaning that 20 percent of an employee's goals will account for 80 percent of his results. It is for this reason, they maintain, that managers can set goals in one minute. They also contend that the failure of many management-by-objectives programs (MBO) are due to too many goals being set.
37. Tolchinsky and King, "Do Goals Mediate Effects," 3:456.
38. Ibid., 3:457.
39. Tamao Matsui, Akinori Okada, and Reijii Mizuguchi, "Expectancy Theory Prediction of the Goal Theory Postulate, 'The Harder the Goals, the Higher the Performance,'" *Journal of Applied Psychology* 66, no. 1 (1981): 54–58.
40. Thomas L. Rakestraw, Jr. and Howard M. Weiss, "The Interaction of Social Influences and Task Experience on Goals, Performance, and Performance Satisfaction," *Organizational Behavior and Human Performance* 27 (1981): 326–344.
41. J. S. Kim and R. S. Schuler, "The Nature of the Task As a Moderator of the Relationship Between Extrinsic Feedback and Employee Responses," *Academy of Management Journal* 22 (1979): 157–62.
42. J. C. Quick, "Dyadic Goal Setting and Role Stress: A Field Study," *Academy of Management Journal* 22 (1979): 241–52.
43. As one example, see R. M. Steers and L. W. Porter, "The Role of Task–Goal Attributes in Employee Performance," *Psychological Bulletin* 81 (1974): 434–52.
44. Tolchinsky and King, "Do Goals Mediate Effects," 3:459.
45. Note that there may be other ways of conditioning students to come to class without the necessity for checking on their attendance. If students find the classes to be rewarding in themselves, this would increase the probability that more students would attend. The system mentioned in this example is only relevant for rewarding class attendance per se.
46. "At Emery Air Freight: Positive Reinforcement Boosts Performance," *Organizational Dynamics* (Winter 1973): 41–50.
47. "Where Skinner's Theories Work," *Business Week* (December 1972): 66.
48. Robert S. Haynes, Randall C. Pine, and H. Gordon Fitch, "Reducing Accident Rates with Organizational Behavior Modification," *Academy of Management Journal* 25, no. 2 (1982): 407–416.
49. Walter Nord, "Beyond the Teaching Machine: The Neglected Area of Operant Conditioning in the Theory and Practice of Management," *Organizational Behavior and Human Performance* 4 (1969): 375–401.
50. Walter Nord, "Improving Attendance Through Rewards," *Personnel Administration* (November–December 1970): 37–41.
51. Edward J. Feeney, John R. Staelin, Richard M. O'Brien, and Alyce M. Dickinson, "Increasing Sales Performance Among Airline Reservation Personnel," in O'Brien, Dickinson, and Rosow, *Industrial Behavior Modification*, pp. 141–158.
52. William L. Crawley, Beverly S. Adler, Richard M. O'Brien, and Elaine M. Duffy, "Making Salesmen: Behavioral Assessment and Intervention," in O'Brien, Dickinson, and Rosow, *Industrial Behavior Modification*, pp. 184–199.
53. Fred L. Fry, "Operant Conditioning in Organizational Settings: Of Mice or Men?" *Personnel* (July–August 1974): 17–24.

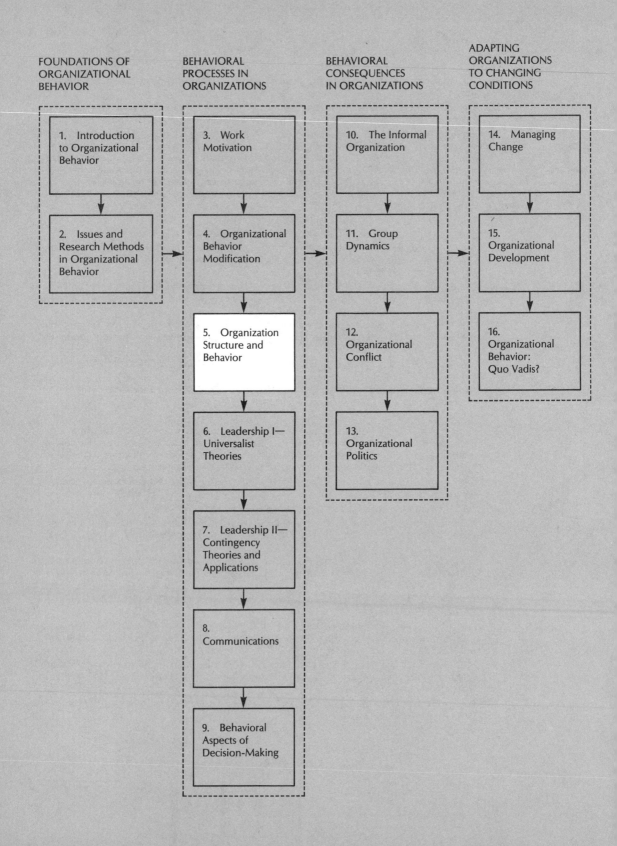

**FOUNDATIONS OF ORGANIZATIONAL BEHAVIOR**

1. Introduction to Organizational Behavior

2. Issues and Research Methods in Organizational Behavior

**BEHAVIORAL PROCESSES IN ORGANIZATIONS**

3. Work Motivation

4. Organizational Behavior Modification

5. Organization Structure and Behavior

6. Leadership I— Universalist Theories

7. Leadership II— Contingency Theories and Applications

8. Communications

9. Behavioral Aspects of Decision-Making

**BEHAVIORAL CONSEQUENCES IN ORGANIZATIONS**

10. The Informal Organization

11. Group Dynamics

12. Organizational Conflict

13. Organizational Politics

**ADAPTING ORGANIZATIONS TO CHANGING CONDITIONS**

14. Managing Change

15. Organizational Development

16. Organizational Behavior: Quo Vadis?

# Organization Structure and Behavior

## ■ Learning Objectives

After you have read and studied the material in this chapter, you should be able to:

☐ Explain the difference between functional and divisional organizational structures.

☐ Describe why staff experts are needed in many organizations.

☐ Show how "tall" organization structures differ from "flat" ones.

☐ Explain the concept of decentralization of authority.

☐ Show how bureaucratic and project structures differ along the flexibility dimension.

☐ Describe how the various aspects of organization structures affect the behavior of people.

# Chapter | 5

# ■ KEY TERMS

**Organization structure**
**Functional structures**
**Divisional structures**
**Line organization**
**Line–staff organization**
**Tall structures**
**Flat structures**
**Mechanistic structures**
**Organic structures**
**Bureaucracy**
**Project structures**
**Centralization of authority**
**Decentralization of authority**

# ■ CHAPTER OUTLINE

I. Two Basic Structural Types
  A. Functional Structures
  B. The Divisional Structure
II. The Use of Staff Experts
  A. Effects on Behavior
  B. Research Evidence
III. Tall and Flat Structures
  A. Effects on Behavior
  B. Research Evidence
IV. Employee Flexibility
  A. Bureaucracy
  B. Project Management
V. Centralization and Decentralization
  A. Effects on Behavior
  B. Research Evidence
  C. Conclusion
VI. The Impact of Structure on Performance
VII. Summary

# *Opening Incident—Alice Marchant*

Alice Marchant was at a crucial decision-making point in her career. After graduating from college with a degree in business administration four years ago, she had joined the auditing department of a large branch of a federal agency. The position had appealed to her because she would be able to use her accounting background right away rather than go through a long company training program as was the case with most other job offers. Also, the job was a new one and appeared to offer considerable scope for making changes and having responsibility. After a brief familiarization period, her title was to be "Chief, Special Projects," and she was to organize and manage a series of auditing programs that were experimental in nature for this particular unit. A staff of junior accountants and trainees reported to her, but she also had to rely on many other people throughout the organization for their help and cooperation in getting these projects off the ground.

After four years with the agency, she was becoming disillusioned. Initially, she found the job especially challenging; most of the problems required a lot of thought and creativity, and she was involved with a wide range of functions within the organization as well as with some pretty important people. But lately she had begun to feel "cramped" as well as frustrated. Most of the more challenging programs had been successfully implemented and evaluated, and most of the work now seemed to be more and more routine. For the few projects that she really felt were worthwhile, she couldn't seem to generate much enthusiasm in other parts of the organization and, in some cases, had met outright hostility. It was becoming more common to hear, "We've done it this way for twenty years now and it's worked fine. Why should we change now?"

A friend of Alice's who had graduated at the same time had recently told her of an opening in his organization. The job was that of a department manager, a first-level managerial job in a large retail chain. While Alice had a desire to get out of the accounting field and into a "firing line" position, she was concerned about several things. First, this job would require a one-year training program in retail operations; second, as far as she could see, the position was a clear drop in status since her present job involved contact with some pretty important people; third, the job had been described as being accountable for the total performance of a given department (sporting goods, men's wear, etc.) and the company had a reputation for having little tolerance for people who couldn't generate the expected results. But the most puzzling thing of all was that this "lower-level, lower status" job paid 20 percent more than she was making now.

In Chapter 1 we mentioned that this book would concentrate on the behavioral, rather than the structural aspects of organizations. Our definition of "structure" includes such organizational design issues as authority and responsibility relationships, organizational policies and procedures, decision-making systems, individual job design, and formal control systems. Although this distinction between behavior and structure is theoretically useful, in practice it is extremely difficult to separate the two, since structure influences behavior and there are frequently structural explanations for the behavior of individuals in organizations.

In the areas of leadership, motivation, communication, and in particular, informal organization, the interaction between the formal structure of the organization and the behavior of those operating within it is significant. For example, the formal authority possessed by leaders influences their style and their effectiveness; employee motivation is affected by the degree of structure present, both in the total organization as well as in the individual's job design; channels of communication and informal relationships are heavily influenced by formal organization structures. Therefore, while it is conceptually useful to separate structural and behavioral considerations, the potential impact that organization structures can have upon behavior (and vice versa) must be considered if a clear understanding of organizational behavior is to be achieved.

The purpose of this chapter is to describe some typical structures that can be observed in many organizations and the potential effect of these structures upon human behavior. In contrast to other chapters, we will not develop a separate applications section because (1) most managers do not have the authority to make sweeping changes in the design of their organization and (2) the discussion of the theories themselves will illustrate the utility of the concepts in the more immediate environment of the manager.

# ■ TWO BASIC STRUCTURAL TYPES

If you look briefly at the organization charts of many different organizations, you will see what appears to be an almost infinite variety of structures. However, if these structures are examined closely, most of them will fit into one of two basic categories: functional or divisional.

## □ Functional Structures

The oldest and most commonly used structure is the functional structure. When it is used, the organization is departmentalized on the basis of the key functions it must perform to reach its objectives. Several examples of functional structures for different kinds of organizations are shown in Figure 5-1.

It is clear from Figure 5-1 that the work of the various functional areas must be coordinated by a higher authority. For example, in a manufacturing firm, the functions of production, marketing, and finance must be coordinated by the president. None of these functions can, by themselves, achieve organizational goals.

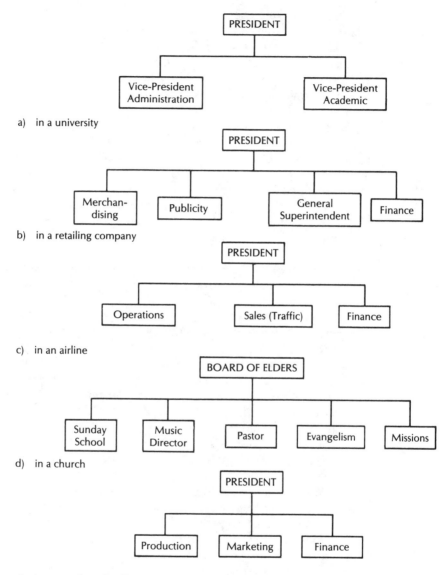

**FIGURE 5-1.  Functional Structures in Various Types of Organizations**

**Advantages of the Functional Structure**    There are several advantages associated with the functional structure:

1. *It encourages specialization of labor.* This normally leads to efficiency in the performance of tasks. A person who is a specialist in marketing, for example, will

do a better marketing job than a person who is a jack-of-all-trades. The functional structure therefore promotes a career path for people with specialized skills.

2. *Employees understand the structure.* It is easy for employees to understand that specialized functional areas exist in the firm and that these specialized areas must work together. As well, employees in each of the areas work with people who have training similar to theirs; this enhances task accomplishment because they see that they have something in common with their co-workers.

3. *It eliminates duplication.* In the functional structure, there is only one marketing department, one production department, and so on. (As we shall see shortly, this is not true in the other basic structure.) With only one department in each of the key functions, there is tight control over the activities that are being performed and little duplication of activities occurs. It is very unlikely that one group would be working on, say, the effects of advertising on sales without being aware that another group was working on the same question. Rather, all work is centrally coordinated so that duplication is kept to a minimum.

**Disadvantages of the Functional Structure**   There are several disadvantages associated with the functional structure:

1. *Employees do not have a systems perspective.* Perhaps the major failing of the functional structure is that employees become overly concerned with activities in their own specialized area and are not concerned enough about coordinating their work with other areas of specialization. The classic example of this problem is the conflict that exists between marketing and production in many firms. Marketing wants a diverse product line and short delivery times in order to maximize sales; production wants a limited product line and long production runs in order to minimize costs.

2. *No one function is accountable for results.* Since no single function can achieve organizational goals by itself, each one can argue that it is blameless if the organization as a whole doesn't perform well. If a company suffers a financial loss, for example, who is to blame? Marketing? Production? Personnel? Finance? The answer is usually not clear, so much argument occurs as each functional area tries to blame the others for the failure.

3. *There is a lack of training for top management.* Since each manager in a functional structure works in a specialized area, they may not be getting good training for truly top management positions (e.g., president). The top person in an organization must be able to see how all parts of the organization work together, but a person who has come up through the ranks in a specialized area may have difficulty seeing this. As a result, certain functions (i.e., those of the person's previous experience) get preferred treatment and the total organization suffers.

## ☐ The Divisional Structure

There are enough problems with the functional structure that many companies have adopted the divisional structure. When this structure is used, the organization is broken down into divisions; each division operates as a semiautonomous unit and as a profit center. The divisions may be formed on the basis of product, customer, or geography (see Figure 5-2). Whatever basis is used, each division operates almost as a separate business. Divisional performance can be assessed each year by the parent company because each division behaves as a separate company. Firms with this structure are often called conglomerates.

**Advantages of the Divisional Structure** There are several advantages associated with the divisional structure:

1. *Expansion is facilitated.* If the parent company wishes to expand into additional lines of work, it can simply add another division which focuses on this new line of work. Since many companies seem very interested in growth per se, this is an important advantage.

2. *Accountability is increased.* Since each of the divisions is responsible for reaching its own profit targets, there is much more discipline than in the functional structure. The manager in each division must constantly think in terms of actions that will generate profits for the division.

3. *Expertise is built within the division.* If a division is organized around products, the managers within that division will have detailed knowledge about those products. If a division is organized around geography, managers in that division will have detailed knowledge about local customs. Knowledge of this type benefits the division and increases the chance of good performance.

4. *Training is received for top management.* Since the head of a division is really acting in the role of president, the divisional structure is a good training

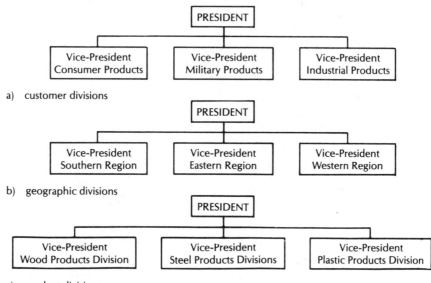

a) customer divisions

b) geographic divisions

c) product divisions

**FIGURE 5-2. Three Bases for Divisionalization**

ground for top managers. A person who successfully headed a division could likely take over an independent company because of his or her previous experience as a top manager.

**Disadvantages of the Divisional Structure**    In spite of these substantial advantages, the divisional structure has some potential problems:

1. *There may be duplication of activities.* It is quite likely that two (or more) divisions in a conglomerate could be working on the same problem. If these different divisions do not communicate with each other about what they are doing (and often they do not), costly duplication can result. For example, if two divisions are working on a new rust-inhibiting paint but they are unaware of each other's work, much less may be accomplished than if their work were coordinated. This type of duplication of effort is probably the most important disadvantage of the divisional structure.

2. *Specialists' communication is limited.* Each division in a conglomerate will have specialists (e.g., chemists, engineers, geologists, etc.) with skills that are relevant for that division. The communication between, say, engineers working in different divisions may be very low. This is a disadvantage because various studies have shown that new ideas often emerge when specialists have face-to-face discussions about problems they are working on.

3. *There is no strategy for adding divisions.* One of the criticisms of the divisional structure is that it can get the parent company involved in such a diverse set of activities that no one has an overview of the entire organization. In the 1970s, for example, many conglomerates were forced to get rid of certain divisions because they were performing badly, but no one in the parent company knew enough about the divisions' activities to take appropriate remedial action.

Whether an organization has a functional or a divisional structure, it must make several important structural decisions. These decisions involve (1) whether or not to use staff experts; (2) what the shape of the organization will be; (3) whether the organization will be structured in a flexible or rigid way; and (4) how authority will be distributed. Because each of these decisions can have a major impact on the behavior of people working in organizations, they are treated in some detail below.

# ■ THE USE OF STAFF EXPERTS

Suppose Bill Smith starts a company and over a period of several years the firm grows and becomes quite successful. Bill (now president) heads an organization that looks like the one shown in Figure 5-3. This is a "line" organization, i.e., all the positions in the organization are in the direct line of authority from the top of the firm down to the bottom. Each level in the organization is subordinate to the ones above it, and there are no advisory specialists. This structure might work

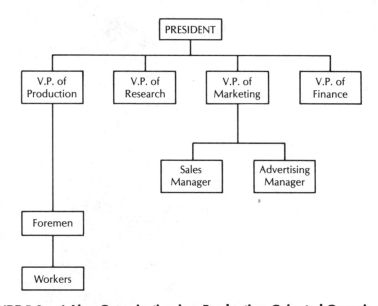

**FIGURE 5-3.　A Line Organization in a Production-Oriented Organization**

very well as long as the company does not get too large. However, with increased growth the need for specialized experts almost surely will emerge. If these experts are added to the organization, the structure is called a "line–staff" structure. Depending on the organization, these experts might be personnel experts, legal advisors, market researchers, accountants, industrial engineers, and so forth (see Figure 5-4).

The line–staff structure emerged as a response to the increasing environmental and functional complexity facing organizations. As firms became larger and more functions were added, it became impossible for managers to keep up with the latest technical developments in their functional area *and* perform their day-to-day duties. Also, it was recognized that certain functions were more directly related to the organization's goals than were others. In the military, for example, the "line" engaged in battles; the "staff" provided support functions for those in battle. It is common today in most organizations to find staff units composed of individuals with a great deal of expertise in narrow areas.

The line–staff structure is a method of preserving the authority relationships in organizations in the face of primary and secondary goals. In the line–staff organization, certain functions are considered central to goal attainment (line functions), and others are considered secondary (staff functions). The principle of line–staff relationships states that line personnel have command *authority* in their functional areas; staff personnel, on the other hand, are said to have the right to provide *advice* to line personnel in their (staff) field of expertise. Strictly speaking, it is incorrect to say that line functions are the "most important" and staff functions are "least important," since there are instances in which staff functions, while secondary in relation to goals, are nevertheless quite important. In these

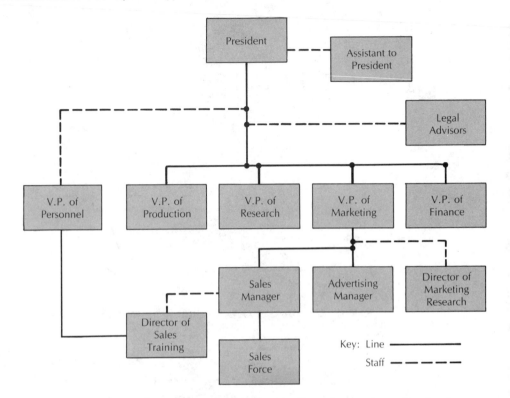

**FIGURE 5-4.   Outline of a Typical Line-Staff Structure in a Production-Oriented Organization**

situations, staff people usually possess "functional authority," which can make them equivalent to the line, although such situations are generally temporary.

An example of staff importance is the "safety" function in a coal mine operation; while safety is not a primary function of the organization (i.e., it is not the organization's *main* objective to produce safe mines), the function is nevertheless so crucial to productivity that the safety engineer is given the equivalent of line authority. This permits the production manager of the mine to retain full authority and accountability over the complete operation of the mine, but should the situation require, also allows the safety engineer to exert influence in matters of mine safety. In this instance, the production manager would likely have a general safety orientation and training, whereas the safety engineer would be highly specialized in the field of safety engineering.

Line–staff theory generally recognizes three types of staff: personal, advisory, and control. *Personal staff* members (e.g., assistant to the President) assist specific line managers but generally do not act for them in their absence. The main function of *advisory staff* (e.g., personnel and marketing research specialists) is to advise line managers in areas where the staff has particular expertise. The term *advisory staff* is actually a misnomer since technically all staff are advisory. *Control staff* (e.g., accounting, quality control) are those with the responsibility of controlling some aspect of organizational performance, although they theoretically still only provide advice. The degree of functional authority held by control staff depends on the organization's objectives. In a bank, for example, the auditor would probably have functional authority within the accounting system; in an aerospace firm, quality control would have functional authority, but probably not in a toy manufacturing company, and so on.

The accountability of line managers is preserved by giving them the right to reject advice provided by staff. If line managers were forced to take the advice of staff, then staff would be making decisions within the line managers' areas of responsibility, meaning that line managers could (or should) not subsequently be

---

## *Organizational Reality 5-1*
## *Line and Staff*

The chairman of one of Japan's most successful electronics manufacturers offers an interesting view: "The U.S. puts its best young minds in staff jobs and has for years. Bright people have gotten the message. They avoid line jobs. Japan, on the other hand, wants its brightest people in line jobs. After all, that is what manufacturing is all about."

Arch Patton, an expert on executive compensation, believes the key line posts—engineering, manufacturing, and marketing—require the best talent available in a competitive world. Yet staff positions have far outstripped line jobs in number and influence with, Patton believes, serious consequences for the ability of U.S. industry to compete.

With the increase in production after World War II, and the increasing cost of penalties for noncompliance with government regulations, came changes that complicated the decision-making process where line and staff were concerned. The twenty-five largest industrial companies had an average of six vice-presidents in 1945, eighteen in 1974, and thirty in 1981. The decision-making process became more fragmented and more people got into the act. Staff jobs were widely designated as "thinking jobs." Line workers were merely "doers." It did not take long for students, especially MBA's, to sense the advantage of staff jobs. They were new, had top management attention, and were as well-paid as line jobs. In addition, performance was hard to assess, while a line job could be judged "by the numbers." And promotion was just as fast or faster. But, Patton asks: Is it really in the national interest for line jobs not to be thinking jobs? Certainly staff is essential in a complex world, but if better people held line jobs, perhaps fewer staff jobs would be necessary. Perhaps the line job's span of control could be broadened. Perhaps this would permit removing some of the very expensive management layering that seems to plague so many companies. Many companies are letting staff go in the current recession. It is not quite as easy or cost effective to wipe out the critical line jobs because they are usually the guts of the business.

---

Source: *Business Week* (15 April 1982): 12–15.

held accountable for the performance of their area. This principle is also based on the belief that staff, being relatively more specialized, are not exposed to the whole picture and would be giving advice based upon a limited perspective. Since it is the line managers who have the broadest perspective, it is they who should make the final decision.

While the distinction between line and staff is relatively easy to make on paper, it can be difficult in practice. It is important to remember that determining what is line and staff is based, not on the functions performed, but on the *goals* of the organization. For example, in a manufacturing firm we generally think of personnel as a staff function because it plays a support role for the primary functions of marketing, finance, and production. However, in an employment agency, personnel activities are of a line nature, since they are directly related to the organization's goals. Similarly, the legal staff of a business firm serves in a staff capacity; in a law firm, however, the legal function is line.

---

## Organizational Reality   5-2
### The Executive Assistant

The executive assistant position exists in many organizations. People who are executive assistants are usually one of three types. First, they can be staff people up from the ranks. For example, Lyn Johnson is the executive assistant to the president of Shell Oil. In her position she organizes most of the president's official encounters with people outside Shell Oil. This involves assisting the president in choosing speaking engagements, helping with speech writing, and keeping him up to date on a variety of issues.

Another kind of executive assistant is the one with a few years of line experience, who is a "comer" in the company but needs some high-level experience. Ben Heineman of Northwest Industries takes bright young executives, makes them his special assistant for a couple of years, and then puts them into top line positions. One former assistant, for example, became president of one of Northwest's chemical subsidiaries and then moved up to vice-president of Northwest.

The third type of executive assistant is one who may be as old or older than the boss. This may be a person who realizes that he or she won't make it to a top line position, but who likes having the power that goes along with reporting to a top executive.

Other people in the organization are often suspicious of executive assistants because they don't know how much power the assistant has or how favorably the boss views the assistant. Another potential problem is that the executive assistant can lose his or her own identity in the shadow of the boss. One executive assistant quit soon after his boss did because he found he had no reputation or identity as an executive in his own right.

---

Source: Walter Kiechel, "The Executive Assistant," *Fortune* (15 November 1982): 177–180.

If goals were clear and relatively stable in terms of number and priority, it would be easy to specify line–staff functions and their relationships. However, since this is rarely the case, it is common for considerable confusion to exist, causing many problems in the areas of authority relationships, influence processes, and status systems, to name a few.

## ☐ Effects on Behavior

The major behavioral implications concerning the line–staff organization result from the lack of clarity of definitions of line and staff and the subsequent confusion of authority relationships. Since few organizations are stable enough to allow complete and clear delineation of primary and secondary objectives, the relationships between line and staff are in a constant state of potential conflict. The formal authority system is further complicated by the informal power and influence systems that arise when formal definitions of authority are unclear (see Chapter 10).

Perhaps the major source of conflict between line and staff is the so-called *principle of staff advice*, stating that line managers may reject staff's advice. This principle causes considerable conflict, since "experts" do not like to have their advice rejected. Line managers also find themselves in a difficult position when faced with advice from staff, particularly highly specialized staff. Imagine the plight of the marketing manager who rejects the "advice" of the corporate patent attorney who believes that the manager's new product may infringe on a competitor's patent! In these situations such "advice" is generally perceived as authority, and staff people exert considerable influence even though it is not formally vested in their positions.

Line managers also resent staff who make proposals with little thought for practical limitations. A common complaint is that staff groups are "ivory tower theoreticians" with little appreciation for problems on the firing line. This resentment can be compounded, since staff personnel generally tend to have more formal education (in their speciality as well as other areas) than line managers. This poses a status problem that may take the form, for example, of a young, college-educated personnel assistant attempting to tell a production foreman how to motivate employees. The fact that staff functions are secondary in the organization seems almost paradoxical to their potential influence, and this serves to increase resentment in line managers.

Staff personnel feel equally frustrated, particularly when line managers ignore their advice. A staff employee may spend many hours developing a new supervisory training program only to have a production manager reject it because "we don't have time for that fancy stuff down here." Ideally, line managers should recognize the expertise that is available to them and seek out the advice of the staff, but often they avoid it.

Other behavioral problems that occur in the line–staff structure can be traced to the *unity-of-command* principle. Theoretically, the line–staff structure is designed to *preserve* this principle in light of the existence of primary and secondary organizational objectives. However, because people do not act as mechanically as the organization chart assumes, the system becomes laden with power struggles, influence systems, politics, and confrontations over authority relationships.

## ☐ Research Evidence

Even though line–staff conflicts are so common, there is surprisingly little empirical research on the topic per se. One of the few studies conducted to verify and specify the nature of line–staff conflicts found that staff officers (who tended to be younger than line officers) were more promotion-conscious, had more formal education, were more concerned about personal appearance than their line counterparts, and measured their success on "selling" programs to line officers.[1] Staff and line belonged to two different social groupings within the organizations, and there was considerable antagonism between the two. Tensions were further increased because staff officers perceived that their promotions were determined

> ### Box 5-1: The Line–Staff Organization and Power Relationships
>
> Classical management theory describes the line–staff organization in quite rational terms, as if the designation of line and staff will automatically solve disagreements over responsibility and authority. Yet, in actual practice, many managers would have difficulty identifying functions as either line or staff, and most would agree that they have many conflicts over who has the authority to make certain decisions. Why would this be so?
>
> The reason is because of a failure to distinguish between authority relationships and power relationships. Although power is discussed in more detail in Chapter 10, it is a useful concept here for understanding what actually goes on between line and staff functions. Power is the *ability* of one person or group to exert influence over another; it goes with the person or group because of a particular set of properties attached to them. For example, a physically strong person may exert influence over a weak person, even though there is no authority relationship present.
>
> In organizational practice, it is not uncommon to find staff functions being very influential, even though they have no formal authority. These people or groups have gained power, usually through expertise in their areas, although the sources could go beyond this. For example, the son of the company president may be the personnel officer and technically exert only advisory influence; however, his influence could be taken as actual authority because of the power attached to him by virtue of his personal relationship to the president. Similarly, a particular staff employee could be so specialized in his/her field (e.g., labor law) that any "advice" is actually taken as authority. Expertise gives him/her considerable power.

by line officers, who were known to resent the higher-status staff officers. Line managers feared staff's innovations would "show them up," and conflicts developed to the point where, in one organization, line officers refused to eat in the same cafeteria as staff. Although this study generally verifies the statements made in the previous section, it can hardly be called conclusive evidence, since the findings are based upon data from only three organizations. Clearly, there is much room for research on line–staff conflicts.

## ■ TALL AND FLAT STRUCTURES

Regardless of whether an organization has a functional or a divisional structure, a decision must be made as to what the "shape" of the organization will be; this involves deciding whether it should be "flat" or "tall." A flat organization has few hierarchical levels and many workers reporting to each boss (wide spans of control). A tall organization has many hierarchical levels and few workers reporting to each boss (narrow spans of control). As indicated in Figure 5-5, two companies with equal numbers of employees may have quite differently shaped structures. Holding the number of employees constant, an increase in the number

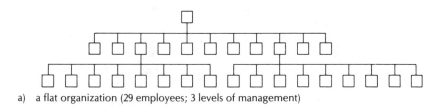

a)    a flat organization (29 employees; 3 levels of management)

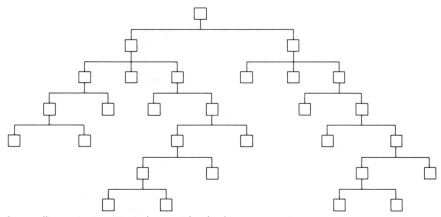

b)    a tall organization (29 employees; 7 levels of management)

**FIGURE 5-5.   Tall and Flat Organizations**

of levels decreases the span of control, while decreasing the number of levels increases the span of control.

## ☐ Effects on Behavior

The shape of an organization has an impact on both employee satisfaction and performance. Theorizing about this issue began in the 1920s, and until the late 1940s it was assumed that narrow spans of management were better than wide spans in terms of both employee satisfaction and performance.[2] The argument was that if a boss had only a few people to supervise, personalized time and attention could be given to each one. This attention would result in better performance because employees would understand the job better; it would also cause higher satisfaction because employees would feel that the boss cared about them.

## ☐ Research Evidence

The first studies appeared after World War II. In one company, a level of management was eliminated while the company was in a growth phase, so the organization became flatter and the span of control increased.[3] No negative effects on morale or productivity were evident. Another study at Sears compared retail stores with flat and tall structures and found that the employees in the flat structures were more satisfied and productive than their counterparts in the tall structures.[4] The researchers concluded that in the flat structure, managers really had no alternative but to delegate authority because they couldn't closely supervise the large number of subordinates they had. Workers like the autonomy and authority they were given by these managers and they responded with high performance. Two other studies—one using teachers and one using salespeople—also found that employee satisfaction was higher in flat structures.[5]

Findings such as those mentioned resulted in the universalist conclusion that flat structures were always more effective than tall ones. However, additional research suggested the contingency conclusion that flat structures were better only under certain conditions. For example, one study showed that employee need structures influenced the conclusion about which structure was superior; tall structures were better for fulfilling employees' safety and security needs, while flat structures were more appropriate for fulfilling self-actualization and autonomy needs.[6] Another study found that employee performance did indeed improve as the organization structure became flatter, but only to a point; beyond that, performance declined.[7]

Overall, the research on tall and flat structures suggests that flatter structures are often associated with higher levels of employee satisfaction; however, the results for employee performance are not as clear-cut. We have previously noted this tendency in both the leadership and motivation areas. In addition to the shape of the organization's structure, other factors, such as the size of the organization, employee needs, and the nature of the job affect employee performance and satisfaction.

# ■ EMPLOYEE FLEXIBILITY

One structural element that is an important determinant of employee behavior is the amount of flexibility that employees have as they do their assigned tasks. In some organizations, rigid rules and procedures must be followed to the letter when tasks are performed; in others, employees are allowed great flexibility while performing tasks. In one organization, secretaries may be required to be at their work stations at all times; in another, they may be allowed freedom to move around, as long as productivity standards are met. As another example, in some organizations expense accounts must be filled out in great detail; in others, only a general statement of expenses is required. The flexibility dimension is composed of two distinct elements: (1) the flexibility evident in the organization's structure which allows it to cope with environmental change, and (2) the flexibility available to individuals within the organization as they perform their respective duties. We will emphasize the latter element.

Labels frequently applied to the extreme variations in structural flexibility are "mechanistic" and "organic," with the former describing the more rigid types of structures and the latter the more flexible types.[8] These extremes can be compared and contrasted on a variety of organizational design dimensions, a number of which are shown in Table 5-1. Some of these factors will be discussed in detail in this chapter.

**TABLE 5-1.  Organizational Characteristics of Organic and Mechanistic Structures**

| Organizational Characteristics Index | Type of Organization Structure | |
|---|---|---|
| | *Organic* | *Mechanistic* |
| Span of control | wide | narrow |
| Number of levels of authority | few | many |
| Ratio of administrative to production personnel | high | low |
| Range of time span over which an employee can commit resources | long | short |
| Degree of centralization in decision making | low | high |
| Proportion of persons in one unit having opportunity to interact with persons in other units | high | low |
| Quantity of formal rules | low | high |
| Specificity of job goals | low | high |
| Specificity of required activities | low | high |
| Content of communications | advice and information | instructions and decisions |
| Range of compensation | narrow | wide |
| Range of skill levels | narrow | wide |
| Knowledge-based authority | high | low |
| Position-based authority | low | high |

Source: Ralph M. Hower and Jay W. Lorsch, "Organizational Inputs," in *Systems Analysis in Organizational Behavior*, ed. John A. Seiler (Homewood, Ill.: Richard D. Irwin and Dorsey Press, 1967), p. 168. Used with permission.

The mechanistic and organic extremes are represented by *bureaucracy* and *project structures,* respectively. Each of these flexibility variations is described in some detail below. These two forms do represent extremes, so employees in most organizations would probably not be as constrained as suggested in the pure bureaucracy, nor would they have as much flexibility as suggested in the project structure. Nevertheless, these two extremes are not uncommon, so you might well experience one type or the other at some point during your career.

## ☐ **Bureaucracy**

Bureaucracy is an emotion-laden term, often used as a synonym for red tape, inefficiency, and ineptness. It is easy to find individuals who can relate a humorous and/or frustrating experience in dealing with a bureaucratic organization or "bureaucrat," as we affectionately label those who work in this type of organization. This negative connotation is unfortunate since the term *bureaucracy* was originally used to denote an efficient organizational form. Max Weber, a German sociologist and political scientist, conceived of the bureaucratic model as an "ideal" organizational structure.[9] In the early 1900s, organizations were in a state of transition due to the influence of the Industrial Revolution and changes in the social structure and processes of society. Weber saw increasing government involvement in administrative activities and believed that the organization structures of the time were inappropriate for the social and political problems that had arisen. The bureaucratic structure was therefore designed to (1) maintain equal treatment for the clientele (customers), (2) process clientele efficiently, and (3) increase the rationality of decision making. Each of these was seen by Weber as an improvement over the organizational practices of that time.

The bureaucratic structure was designed to minimize the personal influence of the individual employee in decision making and to coordinate the large number of decisions with the organization's goals. Weber's characteristics of a bureaucracy illustrate his "legalistic" approach to organizational design.

1. *Specialization of labor*—The goals of the organization are divided into functional specialities. Individuals become "experts" in their own functional areas. Appointments to positions are on the basis of ability, not loyalty.

2. *Well-defined hierarchy of authority*—Officials of the bureaucracy are arranged in a hierarchical order, with each level being controlled by the next higher level.

3. *Clearly defined responsibilities and authority*—The duties of each official are clearly spelled out, and lines of authority and accountability are clear. Job descriptions delineate each official's sphere of responsibility, and he or she is the ultimate authority within those limits.

4. *Systems of rules and procedures*—To assure consistency of decision making, officials are guided by explicit rules and procedures. Decisions are made by first categorizing the "case," then by applying the appropriate rule.

5. *Impersonality of relations*—Attained through specialization of function and the creation of rules and procedures. Emphasis is placed upon logical rather than emotional considerations.

6. *Promotion based on technical qualifications*—Assures that offices (jobs) are always filled with qualified people.

7. *Centralization of authority*—With specialization of labor, problems of coordination are increased. By centralizing authority in the upper levels, coordination problems are minimized.

8. *Written records*—To preserve and maintain uniformity of action, bureaucracies maintain adequate files of previous decisions. This assures equal treatment of clients, since officials can refer to precedent cases and make consistent decisions.[10]

Given the above characteristics of bureaucracy, it is easy to understand why people see them as cumbersome, impersonal organizations. Nevertheless, for certain kinds of activities, bureaucracy has proven to be a viable type of structure. Although public organizations are not the only examples of bureaucratic organizations, they are probably the most typical, since they handle many routine tasks for masses of clients.

**Effects on Behavior**   The implications of the bureaucratic model for the behavior of the organization's members revolve around the centralization of authority and need for control within the organization. Weber's list of bureaucratic characteristics clearly shows the importance of reducing individual discretion in decision-making activities. Historically, the rationale for doing this came from the unfortunate experiences that occurred in organizations where individuals' decision-making powers were not restricted by stated organizational policies. There is little doubt that individuals will perceive decision-making situations differently and, consequently, apply different solutions to the "same" problem. The rigid rules, policies, and procedures of the bureaucracy, as well as its other characteristics, attempt to prevent this and preserve the equality of treatment that is so crucial, particularly in government organizations.

The pure bureaucratic model has both positive and negative implications for behavior. To some degree, value judgments are necessary in labeling specific behaviors as positive or negative, but it is generally agreed that the following behaviors tend to emerge within the bureaucratic structure:

1. *Rigidity of behavior*—Because of the need for control within large organizations and the consequent use of general, impersonal rules, the behavior of bureaucratic officials may become quite rigid. Behavior often becomes rule-oriented, particularly if a decision is challenged by a client or customer. In the extreme, enforcement of the rule may become more important than serving the client.

2. *Impersonality of treatment*—Since bureaucratic rules and procedures are purposely designed to be impersonal to provide equal treatment for all clients, this behavior must be considered a positive result. This same impersonality, however, can cause clients to feel they are not being treated as individuals, and this can cause them to resent the organization.

3. *Identification with subgoals*—Because the organization is divided into functional units and adherence to organizational policies is emphasized within subunits, members of the organization may begin to identify with the goals of the subunit at the expense of the goals of the larger organization. As functionalization becomes highly developed, members are unable to see (or do not care) how their particular function relates to the total system. Client treatment, then, becomes fractionalized, again lead..g to client dissatisfaction.

---

## Organizational Reality   5-3
## Corporate Structure and Growth

A fast-growing high-technology company can easily fall victim to its own success. Explosive expansion can lead to corporate bureaucracy, and sheer overweight can kill the informality and entrepreneurial drive that brought success to the company in the first place. To date, the Hewlett Packard Company has been able to innovate by continuing to nurture small entrepreneurial units in the face of extraordinary growth, but there are signs that Hewlett Packard's growth in computers is colliding with its unique entrepreneurial culture. The decentralized management style that assigns the design and manufacturing of products to the individual divisions and gives sales responsibility to separate marketing groups has resulted in overlapping products, lagging developments in technology, and a piecemeal approach to key markets.

"Becoming a computer company has had a dramatic effect on our company," says John A. Young, chief executive officer and president. His biggest challenge, he adds "is to orchestrate the divisions and provide a strategic glue and direction for the computer effort, while keeping the work units small. Having small divisions . . . that people can run like a small business is highly motivational, especially for professionals. Keeping that spirit of entrepreneurship alive is very important to us."

Industry experts agree, but wonder how to solve the problem. Experts say that Hewlett Packard must recognize that a coordinated marketing program is rapidly becoming more important for success than sheer engineering skill. The founders of the company are now semiretired, but they continue to wield enormous power. The company is still riding on the momentum of older products introduced several years ago and rapidly nearing market saturation in the fast-paced computer business. The company faces a difficult time of catch-up.

Young's efforts to revamp Hewlett Packard have been hindered not only by the conservatism of the founders and the Hewlett Packard board, but also by the background of much of the company's top management. Even those running computer operations got their start on the instrument side. "The remaking of Hewlett Packard won't be complete until the bulk of senior management jobs are filled with people who got their hands dirty in the computer business" says one former manager.

---

Source: "Can John Young Redesign Hewlett Packard?" *Business Week* (6 December 1982): 72–78.

4. *Minimum acceptable behavior*—One of the unanticipated undesirable consequences of managing an organization by impersonal rules is that it induces members to focus on the minimum standard of behavior. In the pure Weberian form, this might not pose a problem since advancement is on the basis of merit and technical qualifications; however, if another promotion criterion is interjected (such as seniority), motivation to perform above the minimum level may disappear.

5. *Operationalization of goals*—The process of making performance goals clear and measurable is known as "goal operationalization." While there is nothing wrong with this in the general sense, undue reliance on operationalization can create misleading impressions about organizational or subunit effectiveness. For example, it might be concluded that if a welfare department distributed four thousand welfare checks last year and six thousand checks this year, its performance has improved and greater efforts might be made to distribute even more checks the following year. However, if the society's goal is to reduce the welfare roll through better treatment of its causes, the activities of the welfare department may be detracting from this overall goal. This type of operationalization can occur in bureaucracy because of the need to measure performance, on the one hand, and the need to reduce individual discretion, on the other.

6. *Resistance to change*—Bureaucracies can be slow to change because (1) their highly specialized functional units are difficult to coordinate during periods of change; (2) the highly structured environment of rules, policies, and procedures is intertwined throughout the system and it requires considerable effort to redesign these policies and procedures for new situations; and (3) existing patterns of behavior become highly internalized because adherence to the bureaucratic system is usually rewarded. Because there is little incentive for the individual to change or innovate, behavior tends only to change through modification of the reward and punishment system.

7. *Narrow development of bureaucrats*—In the bureaucratic structure, work roles are broken down into narrow, specific areas. This allows for the implementation of one of bureaucratic philosophy's major cornerstones—the trained official. Over a period of time, workers can become experts in a very specialized area to the detriment of their overall development. To the extent that workers may be capable of higher levels of work, motivation may decrease as a result of the confining nature of the job. Development may also suffer because of the workers' inability to broaden their base of experience.

8. *Avoidance of responsibility*—The need for control and predictability that causes the bureaucrat to adhere to the policies and rules laid down by the organization can, in the extreme form, cause an avoidance of responsibility. There can be considerable safety and security in using rule-oriented decisions, especially if decision makers face controversy within their sphere of authority. People who are continually vulnerable to conflict and personal attack can thus seek refuge in the organization's impersonal rules.[11]

The above list of bureaucratic behaviors paints a fairly negative picture of this type of structure. This is unfortunate, since bureaucracies have advantages most people overlook. The negative aspects, though often encountered, can be placed in proper perspective after considering the following points. First, it should be noted that most, if not all, of the undesirable consequences are the result of *extremes* in behavior. In other words, adherence to organizational rules and procedures is not undesirable unless it is taken to an extreme; similarly, there is nothing wrong with making goals operational, but the complete substitution of quantitative measures for human judgment can create problems, since behavior is oriented toward the measures rather than organizational effectiveness, and so on.

Second, much of the behavior occurring in a bureaucracy can be traced to a single phenomenon: the need for control. It should be no surprise after reading the chapter on motivation that the use of extreme controls causes extreme, dysfunctional behaviors on the part of workers. March and Simon[12] suggest that the extreme degree of control present in bureaucracies is the result of a "machine" philosophy of organizations that is fundamental to the bureaucratic model. This cause-and-effect model is shown in Figure 5-6. The diagram illustrates, in simplified form, the general bureaucratic model in which *any* behavior—desirable or undesirable—results in more control. The "machine" model of organization becomes continually more mechanistic and depends increasingly on control to attain its objectives.

Third, the adequacy of bureaucratic behavior should be viewed in the light of the available alternatives. While many clients criticize the behavior of bureaucrats, few stop to realize that the alternative (in the extreme) is action taken solely on the basis of an individual's personal discretion. If this occurred, there would be little equality of treatment among clients and inefficiencies would result because of a lack of uniform procedures. Imagine the Internal Revenue Service trying to process 80 million tax returns with no uniform rules or procedures, and IRS employees making decisions about how much tax individuals should pay!

Finally, bureaucracy and the behavior of its members should be evaluated according to the tasks that are typically performed. The routine nature of many bureaucratic tasks is inconsistent with more flexible types of structures. To put the matter another way, it may be the types of jobs that bureaucracies undertake rather than the type of structure or managerial philosophy employed that affects behavior. The servicing of masses of individuals or the processing of large

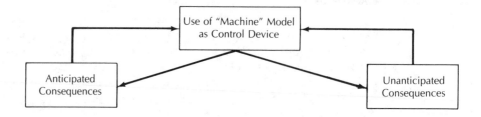

**FIGURE 5-6.    The Basic Machine Model of Organizations**

Source: James G. March and H. A. Simon, *Organizations* (New York: John Wiley, 1958), p. 37. Used with permission.

quantities of similar data simply do not require much individual discretion. It may be more advantageous for antibureaucrats to examine ways of eliminating the tasks bureaucracies perform rather than to attack the concept of bureaucracy itself.

**Research Evidence**    Research on bureaucratic behavior comes from both case studies and survey research. Both approaches tend to confirm the theoretical predictions made earlier. Sociologist Robert Merton[13] developed a model of bureaucratic behavior that described "trained incapacity" (i.e., the inability of bureaucratic members to adapt to different situations). He believed that bureaucrats "learn" that certain responses are appropriate to particular situations, but they then generalize these responses to other situations. Philip Selznick's study

---

### Box 5-2: A Bureaucratic Tale

Consider the following true story of an encounter between a college student and the university bureaucracy.

Clarence Roy was a graduate student about to finish the requirements for graduation. The bureaucracy had three rules that had to be satisfied before a student could graduate: (1) a graduation fee of $25 had to be paid, (2) a "graduation application form" had to be completed, and (3) the thesis had to be turned in by April 25 for a June graduation. Anticipating a June graduation, Roy had paid his fee and completed the form earlier in the term. Only recently did it become evident that, because of his scholarship, it would be financially more beneficial to have an August graduation than the June one. On April 25, Roy took his completed thesis to the graduate school to inform them of this change of plans. The following exchange took place:

ROY:    I've changed my mind and I would like to wait until August to graduate.

CLERK:    Well, I'm very sorry but you have to graduate in June.

ROY:    Why?

CLERK:    Because you've paid your fees, completed the form, and your thesis is done. If you don't show up at the June graduation, everyone past the name "Roy" will receive the wrong diploma. Therefore you have to graduate.

ROY:    But I don't want to graduate.

CLERK:    But you have to.

ROY:    But I don't want to.

CLERK:    But you have to.

How many universities have ever encountered a student who should graduate but didn't want to?

of the Tennessee Vally Authority indicated similar behaviors.[14] He found that bureaucracy resulted in considerable goal displacement (failing to emphasize the organization's goals) and that the subgoals of departments were perceived as major goals. This increased the delegation of authority (i.e., control), causing further goal displacement. Alvin Gouldner analyzed the purpose of bureaucratic rules and found that they served to reduce the interpersonal tension that is present with close supervision.[15] Interestingly, Gouldner concluded that the use of general and impersonal rules did not reduce the need for close supervision in a bureaucracy but only tended to make it more palatable. Michael Crozier, in studying two French bureaucracies, found that control and the use of impersonal rules caused workers to become rule-oriented and that employees followed rules for the sake of the rules themselves. The rules became security for the workers and discouraged them from making decisions. More rules had to be created to handle unique situations. It was found also that power and influence accrued to those who were able to control the remaining areas of uncertainty. This created conflict between the managers in bureaucratized areas and those in the "unknown" areas.[16]

While it is quite clear that bureaucratic structures cause certain behaviors to emerge, it should be pointed out that there are "degrees of bureaucracy" and that no single organization is likely to possess all the characteristics of the pure form. One study found that the degree of bureaucratization varied with the type of organization in question. Organizations concerned with *objects* were more bureaucratic than those concerned with *ideas;* "people-oriented organizations" (e.g., social work agencies) were less bureaucratic than nonpeople-oriented organizations (e.g., a trucking firm).[17]

**Bureaucracy and Professionalism**   Recent research in bureaucratic behavior has concentrated, not on the behavior of the bureaucrat, but on the nonbureaucrats (i.e., professionals) employed by bureaucratic organizations. Most of this research indicates that the highly structured and controlled bureaucratic system can inhibit the professionals' performance. One case study showed that clients needing professional treatment were treated as "routine" because the work systems, policies, and evaluation system were based upon bureaucratic principles.[18] This study advocated a major structural change to allow the professionals to use their professional abilities to treat their clients' special problems. In a survey of structural relationships in various occupations, it was found that bureaucratization was inversely related to professionalism and that increased bureaucratization threatened professional autonomy.[19]

That there is conflict between the requirements of bureaucratic organizations and the requirements of professionalism is not surprising when one compares the characteristics of each. Bureaucracies are best suited to routine types of tasks in which the employee is required to exercise little discretion in carrying out organizational duties. Professional employees, on the other hand, are trained to exercise considerable discretion in their disciplines and are in fact trained to use their unique skills to solve unique problems. Because bureaucracies tend not to recognize problems as "unique," professionally trained employees find the bureaucratic system underutilizes their talents. In addition, bureaucracies tend to be highly functionalized (i.e., division of labor and task according to function) and therefore have a tendency to emphasize functional divisions at the expense of joint problem-solving efforts. Professionals, in contrast, tend to be more suited to joint efforts and collaborative types of activities and thus find the more rigid, mechanistic system of the bureaucracy to be confining. Later in this chapter in the discussion of matrix management, we will find how organizations can adapt to better utilize the talents of their professionals.

**Conclusions** Although the research on bureaucratic behavior tends to confirm the predictions made on the basis of the theoretical model, one should recognize that organizations differ in their degrees of bureaucratization. Moreover, many predictions of behavior are based on sometimes unrecognized assumptions about the individuals occupying the work roles. To say, for example, that a particular bureaucratic job is dehumanizing is to make an implicit assumption about the individual in that role. Or the statement that "too much control breeds discontent

---

### *Organizational Reality  5-4*
### *A Chief Executive's View of Structural Flexibility*

Among other things, Fletcher Byrom is: chairman of the board and chief executive officer of Koppers, chairman of the President's Export Council, chairman of the Committee for Economic Development, trustee of Allegheny College and the Carnegie–Mellon University, and a director of the Mellon National Bank, ASARCO, Continental Group, and the Ralston–Purina Company.

Byrom believes that the key role of any chief executive officer is to act as a role model for the managers in the corporation. The model emerges from Byrom's nine commandments contained in his talk "Hang Loose: A Message to My Successor."

The nine commandments include hanging loose, maintaining a well-lubricated intuition, using growth to get and keep good people, using those same people to achieve further growth, and generating a reasonable number of mistakes.

Part of Byrom's organizational philosophy is the belief that organizational relationships depend on who is in what job at any given time. Like a football coach, Byrom agrees with the game plan of changing the offense on the basis of the players available.

Byrom thinks that an inflexible organization chart which assumes that anyone in a given position will perform exactly the way his predecessor did is ridiculous. People will simply not operate that way, so the organization should shift and adjust to the fact that there is a new person in that spot. Given the choice to adapt, people will do so.

---

Source: *Organizational Dynamics* (Summer 1978): 37–55.

and poor motivation in the bureaucrat" would be wrong if an individual wished to be highly controlled, and so on. It is reasonably clear, however, that over-emphasis on particular bureaucratic characteristics can have undesirable effects upon behavior. It is also clear that bureaucracies are limited in the types of tasks they can perform effectively. Bureaucracies are best at handling routine, on-going types of activities in which efficiency, equity, and consistency are of prime importance. They tend to be less adequate at managing creative, unique, and collaborative types of activities.

## ☐ Project Management

In terms of employee flexibility, the "project organization" represents the oppo-site end of the continuum from the bureaucratic structure. The project organiza-tion is the most recent development in organization structures. Like other structures, it grew out of a specific need, i.e., it was initially created by managers who wanted a structure that could adapt to unique and rapidly changing situa-tions. The project organization idea originated in the aerospace industry, where rapid technological change and new product development were essential for the space program. (It is sometimes said that if the United States had attempted to place a man on the moon by using a traditional bureaucratic structure, Cape Canaveral would still be a swamp with a huge bureaucracy studying the fifty ways it might be drained.)[20] The project organization has since been adopted by many firms in the private sector who face the need to utilize their human resource talent more effectively and to adapt to rapid change in their environments.

The main difference between the project organization and other more mech-anistic types is the focus of the organization. Whereas traditional structures are focused on *functions* in relation to objectives, project structures are organized around *projects*. These projects can be products, services, clients, or activities, depending on the type of work the organization is doing. The projects may range from major commitments of the organization's time and money to very minor, short-term projects. In either case, the organization's efforts are directed toward a specific project.

As an example, a company in the consumer home products business might be organized by function and might be very bureaucratic in its operations (see Figure 5-7). The organization is divided into functional units, and the chain of command passes down through the functions. Even though the firm might deal with many different products, each functional unit makes its individual contribu-tion to the total product mix. The job of the executive in charge of each function is to coordinate the area so that each product line receives adequate attention. This structure is very traditional and is found in many organizations.

The same organization—this time with a project structure—is shown in Figure 5-8. The focus of the organization now is on specific products (i.e., projects) rather than functional areas as was formerly the case. The functional areas exist, but in this case they are secondary to the project structure. In this situation, project managers may have considerable authority over individuals from the

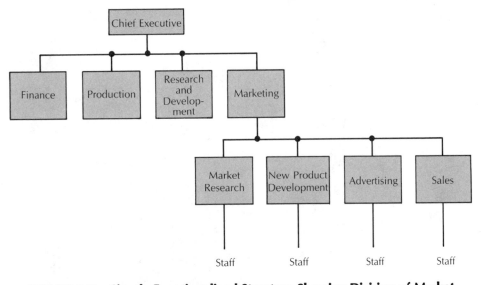

**FIGURE 5-7.　Simple Functionalized Structure Showing Division of Marketing Function**

different functional areas; the project managers have the responsibility of coordinating the people from these diverse areas so that the project is properly completed. While individual employees still have a functional boss (for example, a vice-president of finance), they also report to a project manager.

The project team is of critical importance in the project structure. Whereas in bureacratic structures there is a rigid division of authority and responsibility, the project structure utilizes a much more fluid, informal concept of authority. There may be visible organizational level differences in a project structure, but influence tends to be according to ability rather than formal position in the hierarchy. The project structure requires that employee contributions be maximized, and this is best done using a team approach rather than a manager-subordinate one. In many cases, the team leader is more of a coordinator of effort than a traditional boss.

Each project has a project manager (PM). The amount of authority given to the PM varies widely (see Figure 5-9). At one extreme, the PM may have complete authority over all members of the project team and the functional boss may have none. This is known as the "aggregate" form of project management. Perhaps the best example of this was project Manhatten (the building of the atomic bomb during the second World War). In that project, physicists and other relevant personnel were physically moved from their normal place of employment to an isolated place in the desert where they worked on the development of the atomic bomb under tight security. The PM had complete control over the workers, and their former line bosses (e.g., university department heads) had no control.

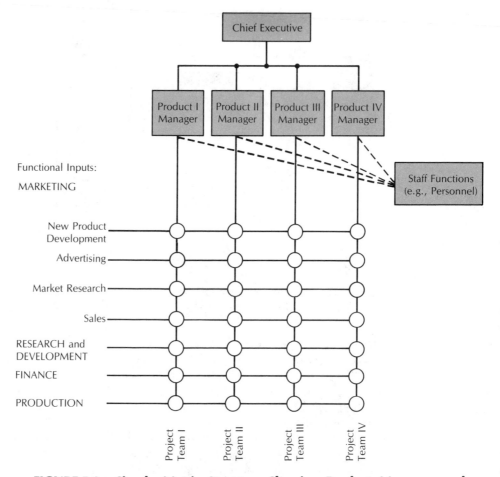

**FIGURE 5-8.    Simple Matrix Structure Showing Product Managers and
Functional Components of Groups**

At the other extreme, a PM may have virtually no formal authority over
members of the project team. This is known as the "staff" form of project
management. When the PM has little or no authority, influence must be used to
get things done. Many minor projects which are undertaken by organizations
give the PM very little authority. For example, if a business school at a university
wanted to develop a professor evaluation form, they might have a project team
do this. Normally the head of the project team would not have authority over the
team members, so he or she would have to use whatever influence was available
to get team members to work on the project and to do the kind of work the PM
wanted. Obviously this requires considerable interpersonal and leadership skills.

The middle area of Figure 5-9 (i.e., where the project manager has some
authority but it may not be clear how much) is called the "matrix" form of project

AMOUNT OF AUTHORITY GIVEN TO THE PROJECT MANAGER

**FIGURE 5-9.   Three Types of Projects**

management. Looking back at Figure 5-8, we can see that the PM has some authority over the people on the project (from advertising, marketing research, finance, production, etc.) but it is also clear that the traditional functional managers (product managers I, II, III, and IV) retain some authority over the people on the project. In the matrix form of project management, therefore, people working on projects have two bosses. This creates the potential for conflict between the project manager and the functional line boss.

---

### Box 5-3: The Matrix Manager: A Manager or a Cheerleader?

Managers in matrix organizations have a difficult life. Although they have responsibility for their projects, often they do not have formal authority over the people on their project teams. This would be even more common in organizations that are highly bureaucratic.

How do they get things done then? Some people have likened them to "organizational cheerleaders." In other words, their job is to generate enthusiasm, increase commitment, and generally maintain morale. They "cheer on" their team but never have any real authority over their team members since that still lies within the functional organization.

But it is at this point that the analogy breaks down. For example, if the Dallas Cowboys lose a football game, nobody blames the cheerleaders. In fact, sometimes the cheerleaders provide the only bright spot in the game! But such is not the case with our organizational cheerleader. If the project is not done on schedule or if there are budget overruns, the project leader takes the blame, even though there was never total authority present in the job.

This, therefore, causes project managers to adopt other roles in addition to the cheerleader one. Some examples are politician, beggar, backstabber, social worker, facilitator, bargainer, compromiser, and "enforcer." Each role, played properly, can increase the influence of the project manager.

**Applications for Project Management**   The project structure is not one that will make all others obsolete, even though it can accomplish things that other structures apparently cannot. The following criteria should be satisfied before a project structure is used:

1. Projects must be unique (work activities must be nonroutine). Routine activities are best managed in conventional functional or divisional structures.
2. Organizational members must be of semiprofessional or professional caliber, not only in terms of qualifications, but in attitudes as well.
3. Projects must have a specific duration. Teams might be organized for the research and development portions of a program, but the ongoing production of the product is transferred to a traditional function or divisionalized structure.
4. Problems must require collaborative efforts from people possessing a wide range of skills and abilities.

Some common examples of the use of project organizations are as follows:

1. Consumer-oriented companies operating in environments in which new-product development is frequent, e.g., soaps and other home products.
2. Unique technological situations in which the development of future projects depends upon the successful completion of existing ones, e.g., aerospace industries, NASA, most research and development activities.
3. "Crash programs" in which speed is very important, cost is secondary, and a wide variety of expertise is needed, e.g., NASA programs, medical and energy research programs.
4. Engineering companies needing the flexibility to move resources as projects are completed, e.g., building a dam. As the dam moves from the development to the maintenance stage, the management system moves from a project structure to a more mechanistic one.

In sum, the project structure is the theoretical opposite of the bureaucratic structure. Each should be viewed as a tendency rather than an absolute, and neither is "better" than the other since each is appropriate for different situations.

**Effects on Behavior**   The use of the project structure is consistent with McGregor's Theory Y concept of human behavior (i.e., external control is not necessary to obtain human performance). In fact, the project organization is premised on the belief that the absence of imposed organizational control increases individual contribution and maximizes the input of the organization's human resources. This orientation is a major reason why project organizations generally utilize professional people. It is suggested that the (assumed) higher level of personal responsibility and "professional" orientation of professionals toward their area of expertise allows them to function well in a relatively less-controlled structure.

A point of contrast between the extreme types is that, while bureaucratic structures are designed to eliminate conflict, project structures (particularly the matrix form) often induce it. This is consistent with the historical change in philosophy regarding the function of conflict in organizations. Classical writers viewed conflict and disagreement as counterproductive; behaviorists, on the other hand, believe that a certain amount of conflict is useful.[21] Project organization, because of its deemphasis of authority relationships, allows influence according to knowledge or expertise, and this increased uncertainty creates conflicts in the organization; these conflicts are generally thought to stimulate creativity.[22]

The project structure is not without its problems. Although the effects of uncertainty on people's behavior should be relatively less (since organizational change tends to be the norm), the climate in the project structure can be psychologically disrupting. This is particularly true if the organization is in a state of decline. For example, there was a decline in morale reported at NASA after the government announced cutbacks in the funding of the space program. Prior to this cutback, the effects of change were small as workers were usually placed in other ongoing projects.

The matrix form of project management violates one of the major cornerstones of classical management theory—the unity of command principle. Because an individual has two superiors—a functional superior and a project superior—difficulties can arise. Again, it is assumed in matrix structures that professionalism and commitment to projects can overcome this problem. Related to this is the

---

## Organizational Reality  5-5
### The Matrix Structure at Texas Instruments

For many years, Texas Instruments managed innovation brilliantly with what observers believed was one of the best and most complex planning systems in the industry. Recently the company has been experiencing financial difficulties, and at the April 1982 shareholders meeting, President J. Fred Bucy laid the blame for the company's problems squarely on its matrix structure, which overlapped strategic and operating managements.

To correct these problems, Texas Instruments is striking at the heart of its lifelong technology orientation by giving new respect to the marketing function and by decentralizing authority. The new structure will create product customer centers, (PCC's) for each operating division, will scale down the large central staff, and will allow the PCC managers to play in the same ball park as Texas Instruments' smaller competitors.

This dramatic change has produced far-reaching changes in senior management, including the election of a new group of executive vice-presidents who have set up a clear mechanism for executive succession for the first time at Texas Instruments.

It is still too early to tell whether the company's new approach will work. Some outsiders question whether top management will ever really give up enough authority to let individual managers run their own businesses.

---

Source: "An About-Face in Texas Instruments Culture," *Business Week* (5 July 1982): 77.

problem of workers' adjustment to the matrix structure. For the individual worker, a change from one type of structure to another may cause problems. Many individuals who have worked in traditional, authority-oriented structures can experience uncertainty and anxiety when placed in a matrix structure.

**Research Evidence**    Analyses of the project structure were initially case studies, but recently there has been an increasing amount of survey research that allows us to judge its effectiveness more confidently. Probably the best examples of project organization in practice are the studies reported at NASA and in the aerospace industries, all of which show how growth in product diversification and problems of integrating technology into current systems caused a change from functional to project organization structures.[23]

Many recent studies have concentrated on the behavioral problems encountered in matrix structures. One study noted that project forms of organization in general produced insecurity about possible unemployment, and fears of retardation of career and personal development, more frequently than functional organizations.[24] As a result, employers can expect less loyalty from employees, and there may be considerable mobility between employers in the same industry as projects are completed.

Other research illustrated the effects of the ambiguous authority structure in the matrix organization.[25] In a survey of forty-six companies, it was found that managers relied heavily on such influence processes as negotiation, personality, and respect for ability. Informal relationships became more important than formal positions. Another study of the introduction of the matrix version into a traditional bureaucratic health and social services organization found that employees were reluctant to drop former behavior patterns learned in the bureaucracy.[26] For example, in the formation of public health teams, the physician still dominated group processes, reflecting the traditional role of the physician. Another study found some ambiguity of authority relationships in the project structure, as one fifth of the managers surveyed did not agree on the decision-making authority of the project manager.[27]

The matrix form of project management often causes role conflict and role ambiguity. Role conflict exists when an individual perceives that significant others (e.g., bosses or coworkers) are making conflicting demands. When a functional boss says one thing and a project manager says another, the employee who is the target of these conflicting demands will normally experience role conflict. Role ambiguity, on the other hand, exists when an employee simply does not know what is expected of a person in the role the employee is currently occupying. A person who moves from a bureaucratic structure to a project structure may experience considerable role ambiguity in the new job because tasks and authority relationships are not as clearly defined in the project structure.

Research on the effects of role conflict and role ambiguity is quite consistent. Generally speaking, the greater the perceived role conflict and role ambiguity, the lower the employee's job satisfaction and the greater the likelihood of employee absenteeism and turnover.[28]

In sum, the research evidence on the project structure indicates that the more complex system of relationships results in some unique behavioral problems not encountered in other types of structures. Many of these problems can be traced to the basic philosophy of project organization, with its emphasis on flexibility and the resulting lack of clarity regarding formal authority relationships. In the view of some critics, these problems are significant enough to warrant abandonment of the project structure. In their view, this type of flexible structure creates such confusion and complexity that it hinders the performance of the organization and the people who work for it.

# ■ CENTRALIZATION AND DECENTRALIZATION

An important structural feature of organizations that influences people's behavior is the decision-making discretion that exists at each level in the management hierarchy. At one extreme (centralization), management might feel that all major decisions (and many minor ones) should be made by top management. Top management might believe that lower-level managers are not capable of, or interested in, making important decisions, so they retain the authority for themselves. At the other extreme (decentralization), top management makes a point of giving lower-level managers the right to make a wide variety of decisions. Top management might do this because they feel that lower-level managers are capable of, and interested in, making important decisions.

The concept of decentralization first gained attention as a result of the reorganization of General Motors and Dupont in the 1920s.[29] Since that time it has become a generally accepted method of increasing the effectiveness of human resources, although the success of it is a function of many factors. Decentralization (and its opposite, centralization) is an authority concept. If an organization is centralized, decisions are made at the upper levels of the organization; if decentralized, the authority to make decisions is pushed down to the lowest level possible.

While the concept of decentralization is simple in theory, there are several complicating factors. First, it is common to equate decentralization and geographic separation of organization units. While authority for decision making *may* be given to branch plants, this need not occur (i.e., it is possible for an organization to have its decision-making authority centralized, yet have geographical separation of units. Most banks operate in this manner, with the central office making the major policy decisions for the branches.)

Second, different organizational functions may exhibit different degrees of decentralization. Thus, it can be misleading to characterize an entire organization as either centralized or decentralized. In a retail organization, for example, some of the buying decisions may be decentralized to the local store level, but some control systems such as inventories are usually centralized to make efficient use of expensive data processing systems.

Finally, there is no simple way to distinguish between centralized and decentralized organizations. Although it is easy to understand that increased delegation of authority is necessary for decentralization to occur, authority—and therefore decentralization—cannot be measured in "units." Organizations are best viewed on a continuum, ranging from total decentralization to total centralization. Where a particular organization falls on the continuum is largely a matter of judgment. It is fairly easy to identify the extremes (e.g., military organizations are generally highly centralized and conglomerates highly decentralized), but most organizations are more difficult to categorize.

Decentralization is considered the more flexible structure since decisions are made at lower levels in the organization. The increased responsibility delegated to employees is designed to overcome the general, impersonal treatment received in more mechanistic structures. It is believed that, by allowing decisions to be made at the point of action, decision makers can consider appropriate variables and provide "special treatment," resulting in better decisions. Decentralization similarly attempts to overcome many of the behavioral limitations of the "machine models" by increasing the decision-making responsibilities of employees. This is consistent with McGregor's Theory Y assumptions about human behavior, and it causes a significant change in the management practices of decentralized organizations.[30]

## ☐ Effects on Behavior

Because the techniques involved in decentralization are designed to make effective use of human resources, it is generally thought to cause increased employee motivation. If we accept the argument that rigid, control-oriented structures stifle human initiative, then a structure that provides for greater individual freedom and opportunity for decision making should be very effective. It is important to point out, however, that this prediction assumes certain human characteristics. It is likely that some individuals will not function well in a decentralized organization since the weight of the responsibility would be too great. Other difficulties might arise as an organization changes from a centralized system to a decentralized one. If workers have been "trained" to accept little responsibility, they may feel uneasy about a change that requires them to make increasingly complex and difficult decisions.

Decentralization is also viewed as an effective training device since, theoretically, workers learn to accept greater amounts of responsibility earlier than they would under more mechanistic (centralized) systems. One approach to learning theory proposes that the most effective learning (i.e., change in behavior) occurs through experience.[31] Decentralization allows for the opportunity to experience responsibility, which presumably assists in developing innate individual decision-making abilities.

Given the nature of decentralization, it follows that decision-making behavior under this system is less predictable than under more rigidly controlled systems. Under the bureaucratic system, for example, the tightly controlled policy structure increases the predictability and reliability of decisions. But in the decentralized organization, the use of individual discretion decreases the predictability of outcomes. This, of course, is not necessarily bad. The philosophy of decentralization holds that, while the predictability of decisions may be lower, the overall quality is better and employees are more satisfied. Predictability of decisions is not a major organizational goal, and too much emphasis upon it can result in suboptimization (decisions in specific functional areas not consistently directed toward the goals of the total organization).

Because decision-making authority is located at the point of action, decentralized organizations tend to be more adaptable to environmental changes. Broad policy decisions can be interpreted at the lower levels and applied with the proper knowledge of local conditions. Should a major environmental factor change at the local level, the decision maker is able to adapt the organization to the situation without first obtaining top-level approval. For example, if a sudden heat wave strikes a certain community, the retail appliance chain store operator cannot afford to wait for head office approval to increase his stock of air conditioners.

---

## *Organizational Reality   5-6*
## *Structure and Performance*

The Federal Mediation and Conciliation Service (FMCS), headed by Kay McMurray, stakes its reputation on mediators who wade into highly visible labor disputes and introduce innovative resolutions to collective bargaining disputes. The service was recently thrust into the limelight because National Football League owners asked FMCS to head off a strike threatened by the NFL Players Association. But the agency's biggest challenge will be how well it handles hundreds of smaller disputes with a budget that was slashed 20 percent last year. Many of the 243 mediators feel that budget cuts have eroded their standing and effectiveness. They no longer have secretaries to answer phones, type reports, or do other chores. The conference rooms that provided neutral turf for settling disputes are gone, and the mediators lost autonomy when their regional offices were cut from eight to four.

McMurray concedes that morale is low. He brought in as a management consultant Duane M. Buckmuster, a retired senior vice-president for industrial relations at United Airlines. "There is going to be more decentralization" says McMurray, who called in his four regional directors twice in the first month for conferences, has begun making field visits, and recently approved installation of an IBM computer, which will connect terminals on most mediators' desks, making report writing and case assignments easier.

"Kay is a better choice than many in this administration" says a top AFL-CIO official. "But," he adds, "he will be able to perform his role only as well as he has resources to do it."

---

Source: "Budget Cuts Are Slicing Labor Mediators' Morale," *Business Week* (13 September 1982).

## *Box 5-4: An Experience with Decentralization*

An organization that practices decentralization gives its operating managers considerable scope to interpret policies. Given this, it will be common to find different managers interpreting policies differently. The authors had an experience several years ago with a decentralized retail chain which has a corporate policy of "Customer Satisfaction Guaranteed or Your Money Refunded." We had purchased an outboard motor at a store located in City A. After a period of about six months, it became apparent that the motor was not going to work properly and likely never would. For various reasons, the motor was returned to a store in City B, where we asked for the manager of the appropriate department and requested that our money be refunded. He apologized for our problems with the motor but said he could not refund our money since the item was purchased at another store and was bought on sale. We reminded him of the corporate policy of customer satisfaction but he wouldn't budge, maintaining that his interpretation of the policy was the correct one.

We then decided to drive to a different store located in City C, found the department manager, and told him the same story. His decision was much different. He refunded the full price of the motor (not the sale price which we had paid), reimbursed us ten cents/mile for having to travel to his store, gave us vouchers for a free lunch at the store, and apologized for having put us to all our trouble.

Which manager made the right decision from the company's point of view? Why?

### ☐   Research Evidence

While it is commonly believed that decentralization has proven to be a more effective form of organization, there is little concrete, scientific evidence to support this contention. The major reason for the lack of evidence is probably because decentralization is a relative concept and is difficult to measure. Until agreement can be reached on what is and what is not decentralization, assessments of its effectiveness will be limited. Because of this measurement problem, the available research tends to be of the case study variety and employs only descriptive, relative measurements. While there is little survey research on decentralization per se, much of the behavioral science literature, particularly on motivation and job satisfaction, is relevant, since decentralization is known to affect job design. Therefore, this research, which was discussed in Chapter 2, should be kept in mind.

One of the most thorough case study reports on decentralization is Peter Drucker's account of the experience of General Motors.[32] He describes the importance of decentralization to General Motors as follows:

There is the sheer size of the business—250,000 workers in peacetime, twice that number during the war. There is a problem of diversity: not only do the finished products—over two hundred in peacetime—range from a diesel-electric locomotive costing $500,000 to a bolt costing a fraction of a cent; the production units required range from gigantic plants with 40,000 employees to machine shops. There is a problem in autonomy: the 500 men of ability, experience, and ambition who are needed in major executive jobs in order to turn out all these different finished products of General Motors could not possibly be organized and managed from the top. . . . Divisional management must be both autonomous and directed; central management must at the same time give effective, unifying leadership and be confined to regulation and advice. . . . General Motors could not function as a centralized organization in which all decisions are made at the top, and in which the divisional managers are but little more than plant superintendents.[33]

Somewhat on the negative side, one study reported on an organization development program that was instituted because an organization was having difficulty making the transition from centralization to decentralization. The following problems had been identified:

1. Communication problems between corporate staff and line top managers
2. Lack of clarity in terms of decision-making authority
3. Interpersonal problems aggravated by the above

Between 1958 and 1964, with the assistance of an outside organizational development consultant, the company learned to adapt to the new structure and profits, which, in a time of stabilized industry profits, were the highest in the company's ten-year history.[34]

---

### *Organizational Reality  5-7*
### *Decentralization at Citibank*

After an Opinion Research Corp. survey of major banks gave Citibank low marks in customer service, the bank decided to investigate. Citibank discovered the root of the trouble lay in their employees' feelings about themselves and their jobs.

Beginning with the belief that "everybody wants to feel like somebody," Citibank introduced a system change to make the customer feel worthwhile. The changes led to other changes, in which the same attitude was directed at the employees.

It was a costly makeover, as Citibank had introduced automatic teller machines. Service representatives were there to help customers with business that couldn't be handled by machines.

The new system meant decentralizing almost everything, so that one person could handle a transaction from start to finish. As well, employees who did the job were put in direct contact with the customers and computers.

There were major technological changes as well as step-by-step education and training in skills and attitudes. Managers had to learn to honor the opinions of the employees and meet commitments to them. Ongoing checks show the program to be quite successful in boosting morale and improving customer service.

---

Source: "Management in Practice," *Management Review* (May 1980): 42.

**Conclusion**   There are a limited number of studies indicating that a decentralized structure is in some ways superior to the more centralized form. At present, measurement problems prevent more rigorous research but, since decentralization is an authority concept, the wealth of literature on decision making, job design, and motivation is relevant and can be, at least in part, generalized to decentralization. Much of this literature indicates that enlarging the scope of the job (job enrichment) can produce increased employee motivation, although the evidence is far from conclusive. Certainly the evidence cited in Chapter 2 which suggested that job enrichment may have no effect on motivation is consistent with our statement that the philosophy of decentralization contains some built-in assumptions about human behavior.[35] When these assumptions are incorrect, the structure will not produce the predicted results.

Depite the popularity of decentralization and its assumed positive effects, it should be remembered that it is a design that is only relevant for certain types of activities. There are many successful firms that have attained their positions through a philosophy of centralization. Aside from the obvious cases such as military and police organizations, there are also many successful "market-oriented" firms that tend to be centralized. Compare, for example, the operating philosophies of two large retail chains: Sears Roebuck and K-Mart. The Sears organization has a reputation for being decentralized, K-Mart for being centralized; yet each is successful in the marketplace. However, because of their different managerial philosophies, one would find them very different organizations to work for, and the types of organizational behavior occurring within each would be very different.

# ■ THE IMPACT OF STRUCTURE ON PERFORMANCE

To this point we have stressed the impact of organizational structure on people's attitudes and behavior. This is important, because it helps us to better understand what is likely to happen when people work in various structures. However, simply focusing on people's attitudes and behaviors gives us an incomplete understanding of the impact structure has on organizations. We must also consider how (or if) an organization's structure affects its performance.

During the past thirty years, many studies have been conducted which analyzed the effects of various structural variables on organizational performance. These variables include organization and subunit size, span of control, flat vs. tall structure, administrative intensity (the number of administrators divided by the number of production workers), specialization (the number of different functional activities in a firm), formalization (the extent to which peoples' required behavior is described in writing), and centralization.

One group of researchers reviewed the empirical evidence on these variables to see what effect they had on organizational performance.[36] For several variables (organization size, span of control, flat vs. tall structures, administrative intensity, and formalization) there are no *consistent* findings. Rather, some studies have found positive effects and some have found negative effects. These differences appear to be caused by methodological differences and by different groups being used as samples (for example professional vs. blue-collar workers).

For the other variables, some rather consistent findings are evident. First, there is an inverse relationship between subunit size and subunit performance, i.e., as subunit size increases, performance declines. Second, there is a tendency for more specialized organizations to be better performers (although hard performance data are often lacking in studies drawing this conclusion). Third, centralization and performance are negatively related, i.e., the greater the degree of centralization, the lower the organization's performance.

The empirical evidence on the effect of structure on attitudes, behavior, and performance is much like the empirical evidence on motivation and leadership, on two counts: (1) conflicting findings are obvious, but some fundamental consistencies are evident, and (2) the connection between the independent variable (structure) and the dependent variable (performance) is often unclear.

The lack of simple relationships between structure and performance is very frustrating to students, managers, and researchers because each group would like to know for certain just what the "right" structure is. The contingency view suggests that what is "right" structurally depends on a host of variables like type of employees, technology used by the organization, the environment facing the organization, the need structure of employees, and so forth. Until these contingency variables are analyzed in more detail, we will continue to see research findings which find little relationship between structure and performance.

For example, consider an organization that has a functional structure; this structure is probably liked by some employees and disliked by others. The performance of this organization may *appear* to be unaffected by structure, but in reality, the structure is facilitating certain people's work and inhibiting others. The *net* effect therefore appears to be zero. Circumstances like this are both important and hard to detect. Nevertheless, this is the type of work that must be done if stronger conclusions are to be forthcoming about the impact of structure on behavior. The complexities of organizations are not likely to be understood by referring to simple-minded rules about which structure is best. The alternative is a systematic study of the structure-performance relationship to determine the circumstances in which each aspect of structure is most useful.

## *Opening Incident Revisited—Alice Marchant*

The pain that Alice Marchant is experiencing, as described in the opening incident, is very common to people contemplating a change in career pattern. The differences in the two jobs can be traced directly to the various theories of organizations discussed in this chapter. Had Marchant had a greater appreciation for these theories back when she graduated she might have made a different choice, although not necessarily so. Marchant took her first job because of the challenge and status it offered. And she was correct. Considering her experience, skills, and abilities at that point, the job offered reasonable challenge and oppor-tunity. But despite its original attractiveness, it was still a bureaucratic job. And it was this part that eventually affected Marchant's satisfaction with it. Over time, Marchant's skills and capacity increased; the scope of the job didn't and wasn't likely to. Although this could happen in any organization, it is more likely in a bureaucracy because of the basic need to keep most jobs highly prescribed. Therefore, Marchant has outgrown her job in a relatively short period of time.

To make matters even worse, her personal attempts at "enlarging" the job through her own efforts have met with resistance, mostly due to the bureaucratic resistance that is often found in this type of organization. It is for reasons such as this that many people search for alternatives at about this stage in their careers.

But we should also understand why Marchant is having difficulty with the other job opportunity. It is unlike what she has experienced to date, both in terms of the duties she is to perform and in the accountability of the position. And, of course, this is why the position pays more money. She would be moving from a staff to a line position, from a centralized organization to a decentralized one, from a position of considerable job security to one of less job security, and from one with little scope for innovation to one with a fairly wide scope for innovation.

In terms of her own career development (and making certain assumptions about her value system), the change of jobs would probably be a wise move. If she doesn't leave her present position soon (either through a promotion or by quitting), the job will eventually start to affect her capacity; in other words, after a period of time, the job can affect—or put a ceiling on—the abilities of the indi-vidual. In terms of future career decisions, Markham would also be better off, since the front-line experience she would receive in the new job would make her attractive to other companies as well.

Is it fair to conclude that one should never work for a bureaucracy—or at least should not stay very long with one? No, not really. It depends upon many factors, not the least of which is an individual's personal value system. But knowledge about the various types of organizations and the effects—both positive and negative—they can have on behavior is important information to have when making these kinds of decisions.

## ■ SUMMARY

In this chapter we have discussed some structural alternatives and their influence on human behavior. Within the context of a functional or a divisional structure, an organization must decide how it will use staff experts, whether the organiza-tion will be flat or tall, whether the organization will be flexible or rigid, and whether it will centralize or decentralize authority.

Generally speaking, the impact of structure on behavior in organizations is reasonably predictable. Based on the research that has been performed on these relationships, and given some assumptions about the people in organizations, it is possible to develop some reliable principles. For example, we are able to predict the general effects of "too much control," a problem encountered in the more mechanistic forms of organization. Or, in matrix forms, we can see that uncertainty of structure can cause adjustment problems, and in some cases we can even predict the specific reaction (e.g., lack of loyalty).

Nevertheless, we should always be aware of our assumptions when we make general statements about the impact of structure on human behavior. For example, we have predicted that mechanistic structures *can* breed certain types of undesirable consequences, but sometimes we fail to realize that, in making this statement, we are making implicit assumptions about those affected by the organization. Part of this problem can be traced back to the classical organizational research that treated the human variable as a "given" in the management process. But even in the current research we often fail to specify (1) what causes individuals to react in one way or another and (2) how the nature of these individuals has affected our conclusions. In most organizational research we tend to account only for the extremes since, as mentioned in Chapter 1, it is in these situations that we can learn the direction and magnitude of the crucial variables. But this is done at the expense of the masses of individuals who account for the majority of organizational members. It is probably this single fact that accounts for much of our (lack of) knowledge regarding the effects of structure on behavior. Consequently, most of our conclusions must be qualified by "assuming that. . . ."

Evidence indicates that, as a society, we are moving toward systems of more complex relationships, an issue we explore more fully in Chapter 16. While structures of the past were satisfactory for their purposes, we must remember that our society was much less complex seventy-five years ago. We have also observed that complex organizational structures result in unique behavioral problems previously not encountered. It would seem reasonable to predict that, assuming our movement toward complex structures continues, we can expect even more complex behavioral problems to develop in the future. It is important that we look upon these situations not only as indicating the fundamental nature of people, but also as natural changes in the development of organizations.

# ■ REVIEW QUESTIONS

1.  In what ways does the structure of an organization affect the behavior of its employees?

2.  Describe the characteristics of "mechanistic" and "organic" organization structures.

3.  What are the advantages and disadvantages of the flexibility allowed for employees in organic organization structures?

4.  What effect do the characteristics of bureaucratic structures have on employee behavior?

5. Review the concept of decentralization. How effective is it?

6. Discuss the essential features of a line–staff organization structure. Why is it considered a middle-ground structure on the mechanistic–organic continuum?

7. What is the major behavioral problem area in the line–staff structure?

8. Discuss the essential features of the matrix form of organization.

9. Under what circumstances is a matrix structure likely to be effective?

10. What are some typical employee reactions to the matrix structure?

# ■ EXERCISE 5-1: THE STATE SOCIAL SERVICES ORGANIZATION

The State Social Services Organization was one of the departments of the state government and was responsible for administering the state's social service programs. These varied from performing welfare activities to organizing senior citizen groups. In the service delivery area of the department (as opposed to the financial, personnel, etc., functions), the majority of employees were professional social workers. Almost all of these possessed some type of college degree, varying from the Bachelor of Social Work to the PhD in Social Service Administration. Those without university degrees all had at least fifteen years' experience in social work and belonged to the social worker's professional association.

The director of the division had become increasingly concerned in the past several years about the morale of the professional staff. He had received two position papers from the local unit of the professional association, both discussing what the association considered to be adverse working conditions for its members. Specifically, the reports stated that

1. Caseloads for social workers were so high that in most instances the social worker responsible only had time to collect the information necessary to satisfy the state's requirements for minimum treatment.
2. Many social workers felt underutilized and not performing professional roles for which they had been trained.
3. State budgeting procedures prohibited the workers from using funds in the manner they thought best.
4. There was little interunit cooperation between the various departments of the State Social Services Organization, thus each department felt it was competing with the others.
5. The association was concerned about the performance of the current director, whose background was in accounting and finance rather than social services.

1. What are the central issues being voiced by the association?

2. What types of structural changes can you suggest that might alleviate these problems?

3. What are some of the limitations of the suggestions you offered for the preceding question?

# ■ EXERCISE 5-2: "ONE BUSINESSMAN'S VIEW OF ORGANIZATIONAL STRUCTURE"

The above title headlined an article in a major eastern newspaper which contained an interview with a local businessman on management. One of the topics discussed in the interview was organization structure. Below is an excerpt of the interview pertaining to that topic:

> Personally, I think we need to redefine our whole perception of organization structure. Most of our organizations now are so highly structured that there is no room for creativity, no opportunity to use initiative or try out one's own ideas. Most people are so confined in organizations that all they do is follow orders and stick to the organization's procedure and policy manuals. If someone took these manuals away from them they'd be lost. How many times have I entered a person's office and seen an organization chart hanging on the wall? Too damn many, I'll tell you. We're almost at the point where we worship the organization chart more than we do the goals of the company itself. I think most companies would be much better off if tomorrow they burned every organization chart in the place and began concentrating on the job to be done.
>
> Take my company, for example. Five years ago we decided to do just that. Not only did we toss out the organization charts, but we also ignored other things in the company such as job descriptions, policy manuals, and previous practices—anything that restricted the freedom of the executives to make decisions. I simply told each of my vice-presidents that they were in charge of their areas and I expected them to do what was necessary to accomplish our goals. Now they all have the flexibility and freedom necessary to utilize their own personal creativity in doing their jobs.

1. What is your opinion of the businessman's message?

2. Has he really done away with structure?

3. What evidence of structure still exists?

4. What response do you think you would get if you interviewed his subordinates?

# ■ EXERCISE 5-3: VERWOLD HARDWARE

Hans Verwold grew up in a suburb of Minneapolis. He exhibited an entrepreneurial attitude early in life, and by the time he graduated from the university in 1964 with a bachelor's degree in marketing, he had already been involved in several small-scale operations. He returned home after graduation to take over his father's hardware store because he felt this would give him a chance to further refine his entrepreneurial skills. It would also be an opportunity to put into practice some ideas he had gotten at the university.

Hans threw himself into work with great vigor. After carefully analyzing the local market, he added some completely new product lines, expanded others, and discontinued some altogether. He also streamlined the record-keeping function by instituting a mechanized data processing system. Within three years profits and sales had increased dramatically. Encouraged by this success, Hans opened two new stores in the Minneapolis area in 1967. These were also very successful, and by 1970 the company employed fifty-one people (see Exhibit I).

Hans decided to expand further in the next few years. Since he felt that the Minneapolis market was getting saturated, he branched out regionally to include such cities as Fargo, North Dakota, Eau Claire, Wisconsin, St. Cloud, Minnesota, and Duluth, Minnesota. By 1980, the company employed 103 people at sixteen different locations. Hans observed that these regionally dispersed stores were also successful, but not as successful as the first new stores he had opened.

Over the next several years the company expanded farther west and south to include the states of Montana, Iowa, South Dakota, and Nebraska. By 1983, the company had twenty-nine stores and 203 employees. It was at this point that difficulties began. The financial statements for 1983 showed that the company was still making a profit, but that it was far below expectations. Hans therefore called a meeting of the three vice-presidents to get their views on what was wrong.

The meeting was not very pleasant. All three complained that in the last several years their jobs had become almost impossible. The vice-president of marketing complained that she was forced to spend promotion money in new markets that she really didn't know much about. She also noted that her travel expenses were up considerably. The merchandising vice-president complained that he was unsure about what product lines to carry in the different regions. He also implied that the marketing vice-president didn't seem very interested in cooperating with merchandising. He noted that several sales ads had recently appeared in local papers for products the company didn't even have in stock. The marketing vice-president retorted that it wasn't her job to coordinate the two functions.

The operations vice-president wasn't happy either. He claimed that store managers in the various regions paid little attention to his suggestions for store operations. The store managers rationalized this behavior by pointing out that the operations vice-president didn't have any knowledge about their local markets and that he shouldn't try to impose unreasonable ideas on them from the Minneapolis head office.

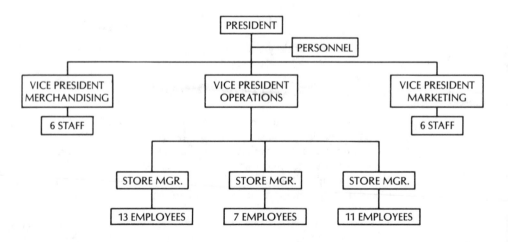

**EXHIBIT 1.    Verwold's Hardware Store**

Hans Verwold listened to these and other complaints for three hours. The general picture that was painted was one of discord among members of the top management team and apathy among employees at the retail outlet. Head office employees in the marketing, operations, and merchandising functions seemed reasonably content, but some couldn't see how their particular job fit into the total scheme of things.

Hans was in a state of considerable anxiety after the meeting ended. He knew the company could not survive financially if it had another couple of years like the last one. He was also concerned about the satisfaction and motivation levels of his employees.

1. What is the problem here? How is the structure of the organization contributing to the problem?

2. Design a structure that will resolve the problems mentioned in the case. Indicate how the structure will solve the problem.

# ■ ENDNOTES

1. Melville Dalton, "Conflict Between Staff and Line Managerial Officers," *American Sociological Review* 15 (June 1950): 342–50; see also George Strauss, "Tactics of the Lateral Relationship: The Purchasing Agent," *Administrative Science Quarterly* 7 (1962): 161–186.

2. See, for example, A. Graicunas, "Relationship in Organization," in L. Gulick and L. Urwick, eds., *Papers on the Science of Administration* (New York: Institute of Public Administration, 1937), pp. 183–187.

3. F. L. Richardson and C. R. Walker, *Human Relations in an Expanding Company* (New Haven: Labor and Management Center, 1948).

4. J. C. Worthy, "Organization Structure and Employee Morale," *American Sociological Review* 15 (1950): 169–179.

5. H. H. Carpenter, "Formal Organizational Structural Factors and Perceived Job Satisfaction of Classroom Teachers," *Administrative Science Quarterly* 16 (1971): 460–465; see also J. M. Ivancevich and J. H. Donnelly, "Relations of Organizational Structure to Job Satisfaction, Anxiety-Stress, and Performance," *Administrative Science Quarterly* 20 (1975): 272–280.

6. L. W. Porter and E. E. Lawler, "Properties of Organization Structure in Relation to Job Attitudes and Behavior," *Psychological Bulletin* (1965): 23–51.

7. H. R. Jones, "A Study of Organization Performance for Experimental Structures of Two, Three, and Four Levels," *Academy of Management Journal* 69 (1969): 26–38.

8. Origin of these terms is credited to T. Burns and G. M. Stalker, *The Management of Innovation* (London: Tavistock, 1961).

9. Max Weber, *The Theory of Social and Economic Organizations*, trans. A. M. Henderson and Talcott Parsons (New York: Oxford University Press, 1947). Recently some doubt has arisen about exactly what Weber was saying about bureaucracy; see R. M. Weiss, "Weber on Bureaucracy: Management Consultant or Political Theorist?" *Academy of Management Review* 8 (1983): 242–248.

10. H. H. Gerth and C. Wright Mills, "Characteristics of a Bureaucracy," in *From Max Weber* (London: Oxford University Press, 1946).

11. The following discussion is abstracted from, but not limited to the following sources: James G. March and Herbert A. Simon, *Organizations* (New York: John Wiley and Sons, 1958), pp. 36–48; Peter M. Blau and W. Richard Scott, *Formal Organizations* (San Francisco: Chandler, 1962), pp. 59–86; and Rolf Rogers, *Organization Theory* (Boston: Allyn & Bacon, 1973), pp. 3–17.

12. March and Simon, *Organizations*, pp. 36–37.

13. Robert K. Merton, "Bureaucratic Structure and Personality," *Social Forces* 18 (1940).

14. Philip Selznick, *TVA and the Grass Roots* (Berkeley: Univ. of Calif. Press, 1953).

15. Alvin Gouldner, "About the Functions of Bureaucratic Rules," in *Organizations: Structure and Behavior,* ed. Joseph A. Litterer, Vol 1, 2nd ed. (New York: John Wiley and Sons, 1969).

16. Michael Crozier, *The Bureaucratic Phenomenon* (Chicago: Univ. of Chicago Press, 1964).

17. Richard N. Hall and Charles R. Tittle, "Bureaucracy and Its Correlates," *American Journal of Sociology* 72 (November 1966): 267–72.

18. Jerry L. Gray, "Matrix Organizational Design As a Vehicle for Effective Delivery of Public Health Care and Social Services," *Management International Review* 14 (1974): 73–87.

19. Richard H. Hall, "Professionalization and Bureaucratization," *American Sociological Review* 33 (February 1968): 92–104.

20. The bureaucrats reply that any organization could have accomplished what NASA did if given a blank check to do the job as was essentially done with the moon project.

21. J. A. Litterer, "Conflict in Organization: A Reexamination," *Academy of Management Journal* 9 (1966).

22. For a discussion of the positive and negative aspects of conflict, see Chapter 12.

23. For a detailed discussion of project management in the aerospace industry, see George A. Steiner and William G. Ryan, *Industrial Project Management* (New York: Macmillan, 1968).

24. Clayton Reeser, "Some Potential Human Problems of the Project Form of Organization," *Academy of Management Journal* 12 (December 1969): 456–67.

25. Richard M. Hodgetts, "Leadership Techniques in the Project Organization," *Academy of Management Journal* 11 (June 1968): 211–19.

26. J. L. Gray, "Matrix Organizational Design."

27. Richard A. Goodman, "Ambiguous Authority Definition in Project Management," *Academy of Management Journal* 10 (December 1967): 395–407.

28. See, for example, R. J. House and T. R. Rizzo, "Role Conflict and Ambiguity As Critical Variables in a Model of Organizational Behavior," *Organizational Behavior and Human Performance* 7 (1972): 467–505; see also R. H. Miles, "An Empirical Test of Causal Inference Between Role Perceptions of Conflict and Ambiguity and Various Personal Outcomes," *Journal of Applied Psychology* 60 (1975): 334–9.

29. Alfred D. Chandler, Jr., "Management Decentralization: An Historical Analysis," *Business History Review* (1956).

30. But interestingly enough, the original impetus for decentralization at General Motors and DuPont came, not out of this behavior principle, but out of sheer necessity due to growth. See Alfred D. Chandler, Jr., "Management Decentralization."

31. This is the concept of "experiential learning" referred to in Chapter 1. One example of this approach to teaching is D. A. Kolb, I. M. Rubin, and J. McIntyre, *Organizational Psychology: An Experiential Approach* (Englewood Cliffs, N.J.: Prentice-Hall, 1979).

32. Peter Drucker, *The Concept of the Corporation* (New York: John Day, 1946).

33. Ibid., p. 43.

34. Richard Beckhard, "An Organizational Improvement Program in a Decentralized Organization," *Journal of Applied Behavioral Science* 3 (1966): 3–25.

35. Job enrichment is discussed from another perspective in Chapter 15, Organizational Development.

36. D. Dalton, W. Todor, M. Spendolini, G. Fielding, and L. Porter, "Organization Structure and Performance: A Critical Review, *Academy of Management Review* 5 (1980), 49–64.

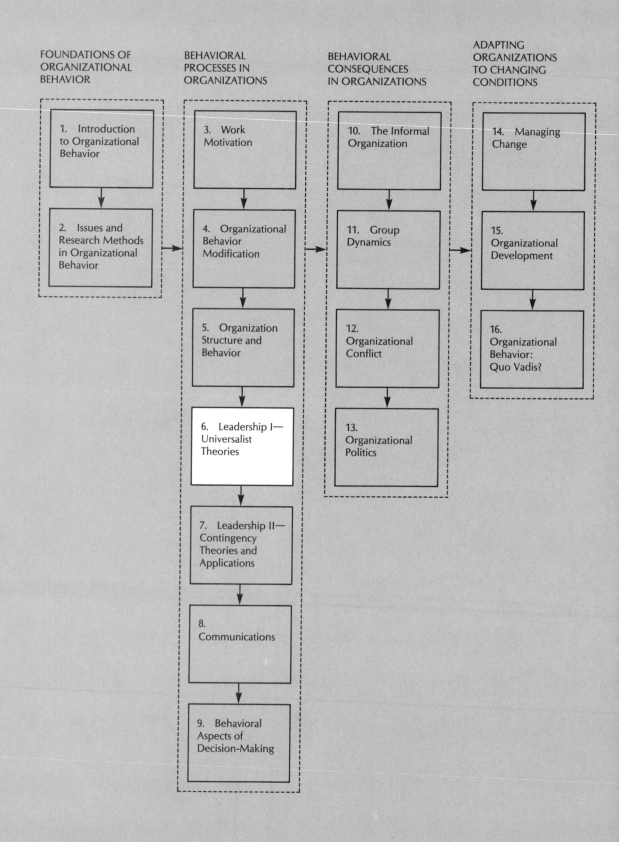

FOUNDATIONS OF
ORGANIZATIONAL
BEHAVIOR

BEHAVIORAL
PROCESSES IN
ORGANIZATIONS

BEHAVIORAL
CONSEQUENCES
IN ORGANIZATIONS

ADAPTING
ORGANIZATIONS
TO CHANGING
CONDITIONS

1. Introduction to Organizational Behavior

2. Issues and Research Methods in Organizational Behavior

3. Work Motivation

4. Organizational Behavior Modification

5. Organization Structure and Behavior

6. Leadership I—Universalist Theories

7. Leadership II—Contingency Theories and Applications

8. Communications

9. Behavioral Aspects of Decision-Making

10. The Informal Organization

11. Group Dynamics

12. Organizational Conflict

13. Organizational Politics

14. Managing Change

15. Organizational Development

16. Organizational Behavior: Quo Vadis?

# Leadership I — Universalist Theories

## ■ Learning Objectives

After reading and studying this chapter you should be able to:

- ☐ Explain how the terms "manager" and "leader" differ.
- ☐ Discuss the differences between the "functions" and "roles" approaches to the description of managers' jobs.
- ☐ Differentiate between the autocratic, democratic, and "abdicratic" leadership styles.
- ☐ Explain the difference between universalist and contingency leadership theories.
- ☐ Describe the main features of six popular universalist leadership theories.

# Chapter  6

## ■ KEY TERMS

Universalist leadership theories

Contingency leadership theories

Leadership

Leader functions

Leader roles

Reciprocal influence

Leadership substitutes

Leadership styles

Autocratic style

Democratic (participative) style

Abdicratic style

Production-centered leadership

People-centered leadership

"Great man" theory

Trait approach

Leader behavior approach

The Managerial Grid

Theory X and Y

System 4 management

Need for power

## ■ CHAPTER OUTLINE

I. Introduction

II. General Leadership Considerations
   A. What Is Leadership?
   B. The Importance of Leadership
   C. Leadership Styles and Their Implications
   D. Environmental Characteristics and the Leader

III. Universalist Theories of Leadership
   A. The "Great Man" Approach
   B. The Trait Approach
   C. The Leader Behavior Approach
      *Ohio State University Studies*
      *University of Michigan Studies*
   D. The Managerial Grid
   E. McGregor's Theory X and Y
   F. Likert's System 4 Management
   G. A Final Thought on Universalist Theories

IV. Summary

## *Opening Incident—Lieutenant Forbes*

On October 12, 1966, Second Lieutenant John Forbes, fresh from West Point, took command of Company B of the 44th Battalion of the First Army in Vietnam. He replaced an experienced first lieutenant who was well-liked and respected by the men in the company. On the very first day of his command, Forbes received information from headquarters that he must immediately evacuate the company from its position because the Viet Cong were rapidly closing in. He was told that there were medical helicopters stationed one-half mile away, and that these would be used for the evacuation. A dirt road ran straight to the helicopters and Forbes ordered the men to march down the road. The men refused, arguing that they had been taught not to march down an open road in an area infested with Viet Cong because they would be easy targets for snipers. The men said that Forbes didn't know anything about jungle warfare and they therefore would not obey his order. Upon hearing this, Forbes took out his revolver, pointed it at the head of the first man in the line and said, "You will march or I will pull the trigger." The men marched.

## ■ INTRODUCTION

Like the topic of work motivation, the study of leadership has received much attention during the past few decades. This emphasis has resulted from the presumed importance of the leadership function at both the organizational and societal level. Many managers believe leadership is *the* major determinant of productivity and organizational success. This belief can be seen in the millions of dollars spent annually by individual companies on leadership training programs. In the broader society, the cry is often heard that "stronger leadership" or "a more dynamic leader" is needed, and the issue is debated from boardrooms to barrooms. Regardless of the setting, leadership is a topic of great concern to managers, workers, organizational researchers, and the general public.

Since few topics have been so extensively researched, making some sense out of the wealth of leadership material available is a formidable task. We have therefore separated leadership into two chapters, one dealing with "universalist" theories of leadership, and one dealing with "contingency" theories.

*Universalist leadership theories* are those arguing that there is one type of leader behavior inherently superior to all others, irrespective of the situation in which the leader operates. These theories are based largely on observations of leader traits and/or behaviors and have resulted in prescriptive statements about what characteristics leaders should possess or how leaders should behave to be effective. They are nonsituational in nature, with each proposal claiming to be universally applicable.

*Contingency theories,* on the other hand, assume that different situations require different leader behaviors, i.e., leader effectiveness is contingent upon situational differences. Emphasis is placed on analyzing situational variables to determine which behaviors are appropriate in which situations. Rather than prescribe one type of leader style, these theories attempt to describe the circumstances in which various leadership styles are effective.

In this chapter we first review some general material that is important in understanding the topic of leadership. We then describe the best-known universalist leadership theories. In the next chapter we examine several contingency theories of leadership and also suggest how leadership theories can be applied in organizational settings.

## ■ GENERAL LEADERSHIP CONSIDERATIONS

Before an analysis of specific leadership theories can be profitable, it is important that one become familiar with some basic terms and concepts that are fundamental to an understanding of leadership. We will consider the following important questions:

1. What is leadership?
2. How important is leadership in terms of employee morale and productivity?
3. What are the different leadership styles and their implications?
4. What is the relationship between leader behavior, environmental variables, and leadership success?

### ☐ What Is Leadership?

To some, "leadership" has an inspirational connotation wherein the leader inspires followers to strive for successively greater heights. Others see the role of the leader as a more supportive one with the leader assisting followers rather than directing them. In practice, leadership is partly each of these. For example, the role of the quarterback on a football team is significantly different from that of the chief surgeon on a surgical team. Exactly how these situations are different and how effective the various types of leaders are is a topic of interest to people in all types of organizations.

Numerous definitions of leadership have been proposed. One that captures two major aspects of leadership is the following:

Leadership is both a process and a property. The *process* of leadership is the use of noncoercive influence to direct and coordinate the activities of the members of an organized group toward the accomplishment of group objectives. As a *property*, leadership is the set of qualities or characteristics attributed to those who are perceived to successfully employ such influence.[1]

**Managers vs. Leaders**   It is important to make a distinction between the terms "manager" and "leader." A manager is one who performs the functions of management (planning, organizing, directing, and controlling) and occupies a formal position in an organization. For example, the sales manager is the individual who manages the sales force of the company. A leader, on the other hand, is anyone who is able to influence others to pursue certain goals.

Is the sales manager both a manager and a leader? Not necessarily. The sales manager is certainly a manager because of the formal position he or she occupies. Whether the sales manager is also a leader depends on the sales manager's ability to inspire sales people to pursue organization goals. This raises the important distinction between formal and informal leaders. The informal leader of a division, department, or group is the person who is able to influence other people's behavior. The formal leader in any of these areas is the individual who has been appointed to head the area.

Can the informal leader also be the formal leader? Yes. There is no reason at all why an informal leader may not also be the formal leader. The important point to keep in mind, however, is that the formal leader is not automatically the informal leader. When managers make a mistaken assumption regarding informal leadership, difficulties often arise. (The issue of formal and informal aspects of organizations is discussed in detail in Chapter 10).

**Functions vs. Roles**   In the formal position of manager (for example, sales manager, vice-president of finance, front-line foreman, president, etc.) individuals must perform certain functions in order to do their job effectively. Traditionally these functions have been described as planning, organizing, directing, and controlling. *Planning* is the forward-looking aspect of the manager's job and involves making decisions about future activities that the organization will get involved in. *Organizing* refers to the task of structuring an organization to accomplish tasks. The manager must organize authority relationships and work flows in order to carry out this function effectively. The *directing* (leading) function involves the human element in organizations. Ideally, it requires that the manager behave in such a way that subordinate performance and satisfaction are kept at high levels. The *controlling* function involves insuring that plans actually are carried out. Both human and mechanical procedures must be used to insure that the controlling function is done properly.

For many years, this "functions" approach to management has been widely accepted and many basic textbooks in management are organized around those functions. Recently, however, critics have argued that this approach is too vague and is not very useful in giving practitioners and students a good understanding of what managers do. They argue that attempting to describe the complexity of management using four basic functions is futile. Thus, learning that there are four basic management functions may not be very helpful to students of management or actual practicing managers. Another problem with the functional approach is that it is very difficult to assess what a given manager is doing at a particular time. For example, when a manager digs the first spadeful of dirt at the ground-breaking ceremony for a new factory, what function is the manager performing?

The arguments of critics have led to the development of an alternate view of what managers do. Mintzberg has proposed that the "roles" approach is a more fruitful way to understand what managers actually do in the dynamics of their day-to-day work.[2] This approach recognizes that managers play a wide variety of roles in an organization rather than perform a short list of functions. In Mintzberg's view, managers perform three basic roles; each of these is sub-divided into further specific roles.

*Interpersonal roles* are those that refer to the relationship between the manager and other individuals, both inside and outside the organization. The interpersonal role is subdivided into the *figurehead* role (the manager acts as a representative of the organization), the *leader* role (the manager motivates workers to achieve organizational goals), and the *liaison* role (the manager develops relationships with other members of the organization).

In the *informational role*, the manager transmits and receives information. This role is subdivided into the *monitor* role (the manager gathers information in order to determine what is going on in the organization), the *disseminator* role (the manager transmits information to relevant individuals within the organization), and the *spokesman* role (the manager transmits information to individuals outside the organization).

The *decisional role* involves the manager in the role of *entrepreneur* (initiating change), *disturbance handler* (managing conflict), *resource allocator* (allocating organizational resources to individuals and groups), and *negotiator* (representing the organization at major negotiations, e.g., contract negotiations with the union or public forums with public-interest groups).

Mintzberg's roles approach gives us a pretty good insight into the dynamic (often frantic) pace of the manager's job in an organization. By indicating the wide variety of roles that managers must perform, as well as suggesting that the manager may or may not have formal authority when performing these roles, we get a much better understanding of the complexity of leadership. Thus, the leader is not a person who simply barks orders; neither are subordinates people who humbly follow those orders.

## ☐ The Importance of Leadership

Most leadership research to date has been designed to develop a more complete understanding of the leadership process; if this is achieved, the knowledge can be used to help leaders become more effective in the situations they face. The measure of leader effectiveness is thus an integral part of leadership research. While the measures of leader effectiveness have varied a great deal (including variables such as output, quality, employee satisfaction, morale, turnover, absenteeism, and sabotage), they fall into essentially two categories—those dealing with employee job performance and those dealing with employee job satisfaction.

Implicit in leadership effectiveness research is the belief that leadership actually has a measurable impact on the measures of effectiveness noted above. How great is the actual impact of leadership on employee performance and satisfaction? The answer to this question depends to a considerable extent on whether leadership is defined in a broad or narrow sense. Examples of broad and narrow definitions are as follows:

1. *Narrow definition*—Leadership is the interaction between the leader and those to be led, the goal being task accomplishment; this must be achieved within the constraints (e.g., task design, size of work force, etc.) imposed by higher management. Leader effort is directed at resolving immediate task and human-relations problems. This definition is often equated with the term "supervision."

2. *Broad definition*—Leadership is the interaction between the leader and those to be led, the goal being the achievement of overall organizational objectives. Leadership is directed at conceptualizing total organizational problems, with primary emphasis on administrative, rather than task or human-relations problems.

If leadership is defined narrowly, its influence on variables such as employee job satisfaction, turnover, absenteeism, and morale tends to be high, while its impact on employee output is normally low. If leadership is broadly defined, the situation is reversed, with output being heavily influenced and morale being only indirectly affected, because large increases in output are normally achieved by investment decisions of top management, not by the additional effort of workers. Similarly, the investments to improve output have only an indirect effect on worker morale.[3]

---

### Organizational Reality 6-1
### The Impact of Leadership

Buckbee-Mears is a small maker of metal stampings and eyeglass lenses (sales $90 million). Recently it hired Ryal Poppa as chairman and chief executive officer. Poppa had become restless at Pertec Corporation after he sold the computer equipment maker to Triumph Adler, the Volkswagen subsidiary. He would like to repeat, if not eclipse, his outstanding performance at Pertec, where he boosted sales from 28 million to 200 million in just eight years.

"I'll be looking for a major growth area in-house that we can exploit," Poppa says, "but then I'll look for a major acquisition that could double the size of the company." Financial analysts seem to feel that the new president is just what the company needs. The company apparently needs a leader who can sense where it should be in the future and can redeploy the company's hodgepodge of assets in a more systematic fashion.

---

Source: *Business Week* (18 January 1982): 102.

## Box 6-1: How Important Is Leadership?

A tremendous amount of time and money has been spent in the twentieth century studying leadership effectiveness and ways to improve it. All of this work is based on the assumption that leadership is important, i.e., that the activities of leaders actually have an effect on employee satisfaction and productivity. There is both good and bad news.

First, the *good* news. There is a fairly strong consensus among researchers that leaders who use a democratic style generally have employees with higher satisfaction levels than leaders who use an autocratic style. The *bad* news is that leadership style is not systematically related to worker productivity. Thus, while democratic leaders may have more satisfied employees, there is no guarantee that the employees will be more productive. Conversely, while an autocratic leader may have less satisfied employees, there is not necessarily a decline in productivity associated with this dissatisfaction. If all this is true, is leadership really important? Perhaps factors outside the organization influence productivity much more than leaders do.

When dealing with the question of a leader's influence on workers we must be careful about the assumptions we make. Traditionally, the study of leadership has focused on the influence and/or authority the leader has over those led. It is easy to get the impression that the flow of influence or authority is always from the leader toward the subordinates (Figure 6-1a). More recently, however, it has been recognized that in any complex organization the flow of influence is not only from the top down but also from the bottom up. Subordinates therefore may have a substantial influence on leaders at the same time that leaders are having a substantial influence on them (Figure 6-1b).

The two-way position is a realistic assessment of what actually happens in organizations. For example, consider the manager of a department that is using mass-production techniques to produce a consumer good. How is this manager's behavior influenced by subordinates? One obvious answer is that the leader will closely supervise employees who are not doing well and will loosely supervise

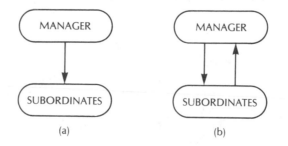

**FIGURE 6-1.  Two Views of Influence in Organizations**

employees who are good producers. Thus, by their performance, employees are influencing the leader. The leader, of course, is also influencing them. As another example, consider the manager who has an employee who is very hot tempered. Although theoretically the manager has authority over this person and can order the person to do many work related activities, in practice the leader may be very fearful of the employee's temper and will change his or her leadership pattern to accommodate this particular employee. The manager will undoubtedly be unhappy about this, but may feel that there is nothing that can be done. In this case, the employee is probably exerting more influence on the leader than the leader is influencing on the employee. Overall then, it is most realistic to view organizations as places where managers and workers interact in a complex fashion, each influencing the other to some degree.[4] All of these influence attempts by both managers and subordinates occur within the context of a certain organizational climate (Figure 6-2).

Several studies support the notion of reciprocal influence between leaders and subordinates. In one laboratory experiment, students were led to believe that they had been hired for supervisory positions.[5] Their "subordinates" (actually confederates of the experimenter) behaved in either a competent or incompetent fashion; the influence of subordinate behavior on leader behavior was then noted. The results supported the hypothesis that subordinate performance affects the leader's behavior. The leaders of low-competence subordinates exhibited closer supervision, prescribed job procedures more vigorously, and were less friendly toward subordinates than the leaders of high-competence subordinates.

In a longitudinal field study involving sixty managers from a manufacturing firm, it was shown that both subordinate performance and compliance with the leader's wishes caused the leader to exhibit more supportive behavior. Subordinate performance and compliance influenced the leader's use of punishment more than the leader's use of punishment influenced subordinate performance and compliance.[6]

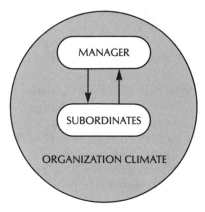

**FIGURE 6-2.** **Influence and Organizational Climate**

**Substitutes for Leadership**    In addition to the fact that influence does not simply flow from the leader to the subordinate is the possibility that there are actually "substitutes" for leadership.[7] These substitutes mean that leadership may not be as important in influencing employee attitudes and performance as previously thought. Some of these substitutes are as follows: (1) the degree of organizational formalization (the extent to which objectives, work schedules, and responsibility of employees are clearly stated); (2) repetitive tasks (for example those found in a mass production situation); and (3) the professional orientation of employees (experience, training, and knowledge in a specific field). It makes intuitive sense that these (and other) factors may give subordinates enough guidance and direction that leadership will have only a minimal effect on them. The preliminary research that has been conducted to test this notion gives some tentative support for the idea that substitutes for leadership do exist. However, since testing of this idea is still in its infancy, much work remains to be done before strong conclusions can be reached.

## ☐  Leadership Styles and Their Implications

The behavior the leader exhibits during supervision of subordinates is known as leadership style. Style can be viewed as being composed of two distinct elements—the leader's *assumptions* about subordinate employees, and the leader's actual *behavior* when interacting with subordinate employees. Although this distinction is often not made in leadership research (emphasis is generally placed on

---

### *Organizational Reality   6-2*
### *European vs. U.S. Management Styles*

European managers have held parochial views of their businesses, focusing on traditional markets, emphasizing engineering and production, and downgrading marketing and managerial skills. Faced with changing technologies, increased competition, shifting world demand, and slow growth at home, they are looking for dynamism abroad, but unlike some U.S. companies that seek to find solutions by emulating Japan's organizational behavior, most European internationals are looking to the United States as their model.

"The old styles worked when the speed of change was not so fast and you had time to correct mistakes," says Robert Schnorr, head of strategic planning for Brown, Boveri and Co. of Switzerland. Younger, more aggressive managers are revamping organization charts, corporate cultures, and management practices. Even though promotion from within remains the rule in most companies, there has been a significant increase in willingness to raid other companies and industries for executives with track records. The hope is that these new managers will have brought with them a global focus, a systematic method for attacking new markets, and the strategic planning techniques largely developed by Americans.

---

Source: "Europe's New Managers: Going Global with a U.S. Style," *Business Week* (24 May 1982): 116–122.

actual leader behavior), it is important to keep in mind, particularly when changes in leader behavior are desired. A change in leader behavior can be achieved by either changing the leader's assumptions about employees or by first forcing behavioral change of the leader and then hoping for attitudinal change later.

The implications of style for leadership training are discussed more fully in the applications section of Chapter 7, as well as in Chapter 15 on Organization Development. For the time being, it is important to note that assumptions about subordinates (or attitudes toward leadership) may not be consistent with actual leader behavior.

There are probably as many different styles of leadership as there are leaders. However, three types are generally recognized: autocratic, democratic (participative), and "abdicratic" (laissez-faire).

**The Autocratic Style**    The autocrat believes that decision-making authority must be retained by the leader. Although the reasons for this belief vary (the leader may assume that subordinate employees are either incompetent, disinterested, or lazy), the superior–subordinate relationship is the same—the leader gives orders and subordinates are expected to follow them. Assuming the leader is competent, the advantage of this type of leadership style is that tasks are efficiently completed, since there is no opportunity for the time-consuming two-way communication associated with more democratic styles.

The primary problem with the autocratic leadership style is that workers are made aware of *what* to do, but not *why*. This often leads to (1) low employee morale, and (2) workers following leader directions to the letter while knowing the directions are wrong. Later, when blame is attached for errors, subordinate workers will take no responsibility since they were merely "following orders."[8] Thus, the autocratic style, while satisfying the leader's needs, may induce employees to avoid responsibility, initiative, and innovative productivity.

We must be careful not to conclude that autocratic leadership invariably leads to low employee productivity and morale because we are then making implicit assumptions about workers. Obviously, individuals who prefer a safe, secure situation in which they are not required to assume any responsibility will find the autocratic style quite satisfying. Perhaps the crucial question then is, "How does an employee learn not to accept responsibility?" One answer was provided in the chapter on motivation: employees learn not to accept responsibility by never being given any.

**The Democratic (Participative) Style**    In contrast to the autocrat, the democratic leader delegates authority to subordinate employees, allowing them discretion to make certain decisions based on their interest and competence in dealing with the situations they face.

The advantages of this style are as follows: First, the employees' feelings of self-worth and satisfaction are increased because the leader conveys a sense of confidence in employee judgment. Second, participation allows employees to satisfy high-level needs such as esteem and self-actualization by letting them take part in important decisions. Third, employee participation in decision making improves the quality of decisions, because when more people think about a problem it is likely that a better solution will be found. Finally, there will be less resistance to change because those who have developed the solution will usually support its implementation.

Those who favor participative management argue that when managers allow subordinate employees a say in decisions that affect them, employee satisfaction and performance improves. The most frequently cited study on this subject is a field experiment that was conducted in a garment factory.[9] Management had decided to implement a change in work procedures and did so in three different ways. One group was simply told what the new procedure would be. A second group was allowed to elect a representative that met with management; this representative then reported to the group about management discussions that were taking place with respect to the proposed change. In two other groups, all members met with management, discussed the problem, and agreed as a group on changes that would be implemented.

The results were fairly dramatic. The output in the "no-participation" group dropped after the new procedure was implemented. In addition, there was considerable evidence that employees were dissatisfied with the change. In the "total participation" groups, however, both performance and satisfaction were higher after the change than before.

---

### Organizational Reality  6-3
### Participative Management at Motorola

Motorola Incorporated recently instituted a participative management program involving about 12,000 employees. A trial project was started at a plant with 1,200 employees, and once the program was successfully operating, it grew and spread to other plants.

At the beginning, several areas that employees could influence were identified (quality of product, delivery of product, housekeeping and safety, etc.). Then manufacturing production teams were organized so that employees could see the results of their efforts.

Constant feedback was essential to the program's success. The "I recommend" device was used, where one bulletin board posted the week's results, and another was used to write suggestions related to quality, costs, machine operation, and in-plant service. Supervisors were required to post an answer to a suggestion within seventy-two hours. Results of the program have been highly positive. The company reports a 25 percent increase in equipment output, increased cooperation between employees and supervisors, improved safety and cleanliness, and reduced turnover because jobs have become more interesting and meaningful.

---

Source: Walter B. Scott, "Participative Management at Motorola—The Results," *Management Review* (July 1981): 26–28.

Studies like this one are used by supporters of participative management to make the universalist argument that this style of leadership is always superior to other styles. Unfortunately, the studies that have been conducted on this subject do not always support this claim. One review of the effects of participative management on employee performance and satisfaction yielded the following results:[10]

|                           | Positive | No Effect | Negative |
|---------------------------|----------|-----------|----------|
| Effects on Productivity   | 10       | 26        | 10       |
| Effects on Satisfaction   | 26       | 13        | 4        |

These findings are quite consistent with other studies that have noted a tendency for leadership behaviors to have an impact on subordinate satisfaction, but not subordinate performance.

Why might these results have occurred, i.e., what are the potential disadvantages of participative management? First, employees may have no interest in participation; if it is implemented, they may be dissatisfied by the extra work that is required of them. They may simply want to do their job and be let alone. Second, the leader may be put under considerable time pressure by superiors. When this happens there simply is not time for adequate participation. Third, the

---

### *Organizational Reality*  6-4
### *Employee Participation*

There is little doubt that employee participation programs are becoming very popular. Yet much doubt remains about the extent to which employee participation benefits organizations. Even seemingly precise measures such as output per employee may be difficult to interpret, because very few companies can account for all the changes besides participation that might affect output in a given plant. Where gains are observed, they might be caused by employees working harder, by threat of a plant closing, or by other factors that have little to do with increased employee participation.

The major problem with most participation schemes is not that the idea is faulty, but that too much is promised too soon. Participation requires a major commitment on the part of management and workers to function in a totally new system of relationships. Supervisors find, for example, that they receive many challenges to traditional work methods once participation is encouraged. This, in turn, causes repercussions further up the hierarchy and middle managers must rethink their ideas about how work should be done. In short, participation causes major changes in organizations, and these must be carefully and vigorously dealt with if participation is going to succeed.

---

Source: Charles G. Burck, "What Happens When Workers Manage Themselves," *Fortune* (27 July 1981): 62–69.

leader may lack the flexibility to behave in a consultative fashion. Finally, employees may see "participation" as "manipulation." If employees feel that participation is a gimmick to allow the leader to present information in such a way that employees will make the decision the manager wanted all along, they will feel manipulated. Few benefits will result from phoney participative management.

One of the most popular management techniques of recent years—quality circles—is very consistent with the idea of democratic management. The idea behind quality circles is that regular formal discussions among workers about how to improve their work will result in improved ways of doing things. Underlying this notion, of course, is the assumption that management has a willingness to implement changes suggested by workers. A democratic manager would obviously welcome these kinds of suggestions.

**The "Abdicratic" Style**    The abdicratic (or laissez-faire) leader chooses not to adopt a leadership role and actually abdicates the leadership position, generally relinquishing it to someone else in the work group. While technically not a leadership style (it is more the absence of one), it does warrant brief mention since the absence of leadership may have a positive or negative effect.

These is a variety of reasons why a leader may exhibit an abdicratic style. Some leaders perceive that the costs associated with leading are greater than the benefits. The specific reason may be lack of self-confidence, fear of failure, or the perceived social cost of ostracization by the work group. We can immediately question why a leader who feels this way is occupying this type of role. On the positive side, a leader may adopt an abdicratic style because he or she feels that subordinates will perform better if they are given a great deal of discretion. As we shall see in Chapter 7, the abdicratic style may be very effective with workers who are highly motivated and experienced. Thus, when we consider different circumstances, it is evident that the autocratic, democratic, or abdicratic styles can have positive or negative effects on subordinate productivity and satisfaction.

**Summary**    The theoretical extremes of "autocratic" and "democratic" are helpful in contrasting the basic leadership styles. While it may be possible to find an

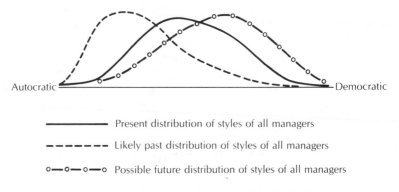

FIGURE 6-3.    **The Range of Leadership Styles**

individual manager who exhibits behavior consistent with one or the other of the "pure" types, the vast majority of managers exhibit behavior that is not at either extreme. Figure 6-3 indicates this important point, and also suggests that as time passes, there may be a tendency for the "average" leadership style of all managers as a group to gradually shift toward the democratic side of the continuum. This does not imply that an individual manager automatically becomes more democratic as time passes, but it does suggest that the probability of encountering democratic management styles in organizations has increased over time. One possible reason for this shift is the impact of behavioral scientists (not to be confused with Behaviorists) and their writings on management thinking. As well, the trend in our society toward more egalitarian institutions may be responsible.

One important observation on leadership styles: As we shall see later in this chapter, research has identified two other styles that leaders may exhibit—task orientation or people orientation (a production-centered or people-centered style, respectively). These specific styles should not be confused with the general issue of autocratic and democratic leadership styles. The autocratic-democratic dichotomy is a single continuum measuring the amount of discretion the leader gives subordinates. Thus, as a leader becomes more autocratic (gives subordinates less discretion), he or she becomes less democratic. The production-centered vs. people-centered dichotomy, however, is not one continuum, but two (see Figure 6-4). Thus, a flexible leader could increase concern for both the task and people at the same time. We will consider this important notion in more detail shortly.

## ☐ Environmental Characteristics and the Leader

One of the most fundamental questions relating to leader success is "Does the leader influence the environment, or does the environment influence the leader?" Or, to put the question another way, "Does the leader make history, or does history make the leader?" Answers to these questions are important because they suggest which leadership theories will most accurately explain and/or predict leader success.

Those who argue that the leader acts on the environment generally attribute great personal strength of will to the leader. Of course, it is possible to observe past successful leaders and argue that their perseverance overcame discouraging environmental constraints. In the political realm, for example, it might be claimed

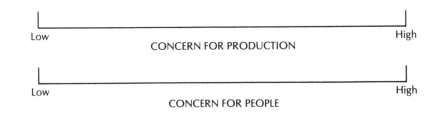

**FIGURE 6-4. Two Leader Behaviors**

that both Richard Nixon and Adolph Hitler rose to power by simply resolving to do so. Although this characteristic undoubtedly influenced their success, attributing their success strictly to personal characteristics is an oversimplification, since crucial environmental factors were also at work in both cases. In Hitler's case, for example, the facilitating environmental circumstances were economic. As the Great Depression worsened, the German people became more amenable to his type of leadership. For Richard Nixon, the increasing American discontent with the Vietnam War in 1968 allowed a certain political strategy (withdrawal of troops) that facilitated getting elected. In both these cases, circumstances beyond the leaders' control helped considerably in their coming to power. The same type of reasoning is appropriate for leaders in business, religious, and educational organizations.

It is unlikely that either extreme position (the leader makes history or history makes the leader) is accurate. In most situations, the characteristics of the leader interact with the characteristics of the environment to determine leader effectiveness. A complicating variable in this question is the potential for interaction between the leader and the environment. For example, other things being equal, owners of small business firms have a greater potential for influencing their immediate environment than managers in very large organizations.

With these general leadership issues in mind, we can now proceed to our examination of the universalist theories of leadership. Remember that these theories prescribe a particular style of leadership as being "best."

## ■ UNIVERSALIST THEORIES OF LEADERSHIP

While many proposals have been offered over the years as the "one best way" to lead subordinates, the following ones are particularly popular:

1. The "great man" approach
2. The trait approach
3. The leader-behavior approach
4. The Managerial Grid
5. Theory X and Theory Y
6. System 4 management

We will briefly review the content of each proposal, and follow this with a critique using available research evidence. We should say up front that the critiques of these theories will sound quite negative. This is because universalist theories argue that a single style of leadership is appropriate across all situations—an idea which appears to have logical problems. However, we present universalist theories so that you can (1) observe the similarities in them, (2) see how ideas developed of what constitutes effective leadership, and (3) detect the problems with these theories. As a result, you will have a more realistic understanding of the complexities of leadership.

## ☐ The "Great Man" Approach

The earliest and simplest view of leadership was the "great man" approach.[11] The approach is aptly named, since it assumed that men and women of great vision, personality, and competence rose to positions of prominence and affected the course of history. Included in this category are individuals such as Alexander the Great, Jesus Christ, Julius Caesar, Joan of Arc, Winston Churchill, and other prominent historical figures.

Proponents of this approach also point out that great men and women can be found in certain families with unusual frequency and that there may be a genetic reason for this. In the twentieth century, the Kennedy family is cited as an example.

**Critique**  There are four major criticisms of the great man approach from an organizational perspective. First, if we accept the argument that leadership ability is inherited, favoritism in promotions is bound to occur as relatives of previously successful leaders enter the organization. In North America at present there is a definite bias against this idea as a basis for promotion.

Second, the selection process becomes crucial for organizations, since the great man approach leans heavily toward the position that "leaders are born, not made." It is therefore essential to staff the organization with born leaders. Given our present knowledge about leadership, it is simply not possible to do this.

Third, organizations that accept the great man theory will place little emphasis on management development programs. If leaders are born, there is no need to develop them. There is also no use trying to develop "nonleaders" since, by definition, that is not possible. It seems unlikely that this view of human learning is reasonable; rather, it appears that most managers can benefit from development programs.

Finally, if the great man approach is accepted, no attempts will be made to design jobs to fit individual managers. This is because the great man approach assumes that true leaders will be able to analyze any situation and effectively cope with it.

**Conclusions**  Although the great man approach is an interesting approach to leadership, the in-depth analysis of a few exceptional individuals does not give us systematic insights into what is generally required for leadership success. A related problem is that many of the analyses of great historical figures have concentrated on political or military types. While individuals in these categories have certainly had a major impact on world history, many other individuals (particularly business leaders) have also shaped history by their actions. In sum, there is no denying that "great people" have significantly affected the course of human events through their leadership qualities. However, the theory is limited to hindsight. That is, we have not yet developed a method of developing "great people," we have only been able to observe them after they have achieved their greatness. It would appear, therefore, that the great man approach to leadership is of limited value.

## ☐ The Trait Approach

The trait approach is based on the "great man" theory, but it is more sophisticated and systematic in its analysis of leaders. Like its predecessor, the trait approach assumes that the leader's personal attributes are the key to leadership success. However, unlike the great man approach, trait theorists do not necessarily assume that leaders are born with these traits, only that certain traits (whether inherited or developed) are necessary for leadership success.

On the surface, the trait approach seems reasonable. From approximately 1900–1945, researchers intensively studied successful executives in an attempt to determine just what the important traits were. It was thought that if these traits could be identified, the personnel of a given company could be tested to determine whether or not they possessed them. Those that did could be groomed for positions of leadership in the firm.

While some traits (e.g., intelligence, initiative, self-confidence, sociability, and dependability) were found to be positively related to leader success, only a few of these appeared with any frequency across different studies.[12] One researcher who reviewed over 100 trait studies found that only 5 percent of the traits appeared in four or more studies.[13] Thus, the hoped-for benefits of the trait approach never materialized.

To demonstrate why this might have happened, consider the following: When students taking organizational behavior courses are asked to list names of people they consider to be famous male leaders, they typically come up with names such as Julius Caesar, Winston Churchill, Adolf Hitler, Abraham Lincoln, Mao Tse Tung, Alexander the Great, Napoleon, Jesus Christ, and John F. Kennedy. If the belief that there are common traits across successful leaders is correct, we should be able to observe great similarities in leaders. However, consider the above list: what are the common traits in these individuals? The answer is not clear. While we might agree that all the leaders were highly motivated, had a lot of perseverance, and were able to motivate their followers, these are very general concepts and do not give us much help. Worse, we can immediately think of major differences in the leaders. Most people would agree, for example, that Jesus Christ and Adolf Hitler do not have much in common. Likewise, there are major differences in the physical features of these leaders (for example, Abraham Lincoln was very tall while Napoleon was very short). Thus we run into difficulties when we attempt to find common traits across leaders. This is true for both physical traits (height, weight, body shape, etc.) and for psychological traits (intelligence, extraversion, verbal fluency, etc.)

**Critique** There are many conceptual and methodological problems with the trait approach to leadership. First, and in the practical sense most important, is the fact that (1) people who fail as leaders and (2) people who never achieve positions of leadership often possess some of the same traits as successful leaders. Thus, for example, although taller people may generally be more successful as leaders, many tall people have neither the inclination nor the capabilities to be leaders. At the same time, many short people have risen to positions of leadership.

Second, both *physical* attributes (height, weight, appearance, etc.) and *psychological* attributes (perseverance, intelligence, initiative, etc.) have been considered "traits." The former are observable while the latter technically are not. For traits which are not directly observable, major problems are evident. For example, if an employee doggedly pursues a certain course of action, what trait (if any) is causing the behavior? Is "perseverance" the cause or is it "obsession"? Since psychological attributes cannot be observed, their existence can only be inferred from behavior. It is during this inference process that questionable conclusions can be made.

Third, the traits possessed by successful leaders are invariably value-judged as positive. Thus, a leader might be seen as decisive, strong, intelligent, and persevering, instead of being seen as a person who leaps to conclusions, is brutal, egg-headed, and obsessed. The reluctance to admit that leaders often demonstrate "negative" qualities may have hindered the development of an accurate portrayal of effective leaders. One study of informal leaders in a prison, for example, showed that they tended to be homosexual, neurotic, and psychopathic.[14]

Fourth, there is little consensus on what words mean that are used to label traits. In a study of executives' leadership qualities, Stryker demonstrated the magnitude of this problem when he asked seventy-five top executives to define the term "dependability," a trait that has often appeared in studies of leadership.[15] The executives defined this trait in 147 different ways! Even after similar definitions had been combined, twenty-five different definitions remained. This finding is discouraging because a lack of consensus on the basic *definition* of a trait makes further research into its *importance* very difficult.

Fifth, it is often difficult to measure traits. "Intelligence," as measured by I.Q. tests, is often a characteristic of successful leaders, but there continues to be a debate about just what I.Q. tests measure. The recent claim that I.Q. tests are inherently biased against minority groups further complicates the measurement problem, especially since many minority group leaders are effective. Even if a positive correlation between intelligence and leadership can be shown, this still may not prove anything. If a company uses the results of intelligence tests to promote people, and then a researcher finds a positive correlation between intelligence and management level, all this proves is that the company has certain promotion criteria, not that intelligence is a prerequisite for leadership.

Sixth, even if a trait can be clearly defined and accurately measured (a tall order!), it is unclear how high a score a person must achieve on a given trait to make it effective. It would seem logical to assume that there is a threshold, but little is known for sure in this area. For example, if a person scores "8" on a 10-point scale that measures "dependability," is that enough?

Seventh, when researchers observe the behavior of an executive and then make some deductions about the traits that are causing that behavior, they may forget that executives often behave in a way they think is appropriate for their job, not in a way that is consistent with their "real" nature. This causes the researcher to ascribe traits to a leader that the leader does not really possess, which in turn leads to faulty conclusions about the traits that are necessary for effective leadership.

Eighth, the fundamental assumption that leaders must have certain traits in order to occupy positions of leadership may be incorrect. Instead, the general population may need a leader and anyone who is *perceived* as having leadership qualities may be followed. If this argument is correct, research should focus on followers, not on leaders as trait research has done.

Finally, the trait approach implicitly assumes that leadership success is determined by qualities internal to the leader and that the leadership environment is not important. This is a very questionable assumption since numerous environmental characteristics have an impact on leadership effectiveness.[16] The research and theory presented in the next chapter indicate the importance of these environmental characteristics.

**Conclusions**    The above comments do not mean that the trait approach is completely invalid. As Stogdill has noted:

> . . . the view that leadership is entirely situational in origin and that no personal characteristics are predictive of leadership . . . seems to overemphasize the situational, and underemphasize the personal, nature of leadership.[17]

It is easy to understand why the trait approach developed. The belief that certain traits could be used to predict leader effectiveness was an intuitively plausible and simple approach. Had it yielded strong evidence that specific traits predicted leader success, the greatest amount of benefit would have been derived from the simplest approach. It may be that a group of traits that cause leaders to be effective actually exists, but current measurement problems prevent such a list from being identified. As our measurement tools become more powerful, perhaps we will develop a list of traits that is useful in identifying and improving leadership talent. In the meantime, we must conclude that the trait approach lacks predictive value except in some narrowly defined situations. These situations are too specific to be of much use to most managers.

## ☐ The Leader Behavior Approach

The inability of the trait approach to consistently define specific traits that would differentiate successful and unsuccessful leaders led to the conclusion that emphasis on the *behavior* of leaders (which could be measured) rather than emphasis on traits (which could not be measured) was an appropriate new research strategy. Beginning in the late 1940s and continuing through the early 1960s, research based on this emphasis was conducted at Ohio State University and the University of Michigan.

**The Ohio State University Studies**    The goal of the research at Ohio State was to (1) identify the behaviors exhibited by leaders, (2) determine what effect these behaviors had on employee satisfaction and performance, and (3) identify the best leadership style. To do this, questionnaires were developed to assess leadership style. The Leader Behavior Description Questionnaire (LBDQ) was designed to tap *subordinate perceptions* of the leader's behavior, while the Leader Opinion Questionnaire (LOQ) measured the *leader's perception* of his own style.

After an analysis of actual leader behavior in a wide variety of situations, two important leadership behaviors were isolated.[18] They were labeled "Initiating Structure" and "Consideration," and were defined as follows:

1. *Initiating Structure (IS)*—the extent to which the leader structures and defines the activities of subordinates so that organizational goals are achieved (sometimes referred to as production- or task-oriented).
2. *Consideration (C)*—the extent to which leaders are concerned with developing mutual trust between themselves and subordinates, as well as respect for subordinates' proposals and concern for their feelings (sometimes referred to as employee- or human-relations orientation).

It was generally assumed that C and IS were independent, i.e., a leader's score on one dimension had no implication for the leader's score on the other dimension. While some studies did find that leaders who were rated high on both dimensions were effective, this was by no means a universal finding. Instead, research—done largely with military and blue-collar personnel—indicated that both leader behaviors were important, but that each had different implications. Leaders who scored high on Initiating Structure generally led high-producing groups and were rated highly by their superiors. However, the subordinates of those leaders tended to have lower morale, higher grievance rates, and higher turnover. Leaders high on Consideration, on the other hand, generally led groups with higher morale but lower productivity. Thus, each of the specific leader behaviors had positive and negative outcomes associated with them. The extension of these findings by some later theorists led to the universalist conclusion that leaders high on both IS and C would simultaneously satisfy their superiors (by achieving high performance) and their subordinates (by improving their morale).[19]

**Critique**   Given the difficulties inherent in the trait approach, the logic behind the leader behavior approach appears quite reasonable. Nevertheless, it has been subject to substantial criticism. First, the assumption that C and IS are independent has been questioned. One study found that it *was* difficult for a given person to be both task-oriented and employee-oriented and that, in fact, these two aspects of leadership were best handled by different individuals.[20] Other researchers, using other lines of reasoning, have concluded that C and IS are *not* independent,[21] and that a leader *can* be both task-oriented and employee-oriented.[22] Perhaps the most realistic view is that it may be possible for some managers to have high scores on both behaviors, but this ability is not widely distributed in the general population. If C and IS are, in fact, distinctly different behaviors, then they require considerable flexibility on the leader's part. Most people are probably not this flexible and will find it difficult to change their style for each situation they encounter.[23] Those who can, however, may make very good leaders.

## Box 6-2: Is Style Flexibility Necessary?

One of the commonsense assumptions that is usually made about leaders is that those who have a flexibile style will be more effective than those who are less flexible. Is this a reasonable assumption? This can be analyzed by asking two questions.

First, is style flexibility really necessary? In our rapidly changing society where managers frequently change jobs, perhaps it is more important to place managers in jobs based on their basic leadership style rather than worry about flexibility that they might need in some future situation. Since there are so many different management jobs in our society, there will always be room for both autocrats and democrats and therefore it may be unnecessary to have leaders who have style flexibility.

Second, are there negative aspects to flexibility? If employees see their boss using one style on Monday and another on Friday, they might see the boss as "inconsistent." Or, a leader with a flexible style might be seen as "unpredictable" because his or her style cannot be predicted ahead of time. This might cause employees considerable anxiety as they wonder how the boss will respond to the next situation. Finally, workers may see a flexible style as "wishy-washy." They may view changes in style as vacillation rather than as a rational response to different situations.

Is style flexibility necessary?

Second, there is some question about the basic findings of the leader-behavior studies. An examination of the research evidence indicates that many studies fail to show a significant relationship between the two leader behaviors and the effectiveness criteria (such as productivity) used in the studies.[24] The possibility therefore exists that C and IS are not as important as previously assumed, at least as far as productivity is concerned.

Third, in many of the research studies, subordinate responses on the LBDQ questionnaires did not agree with leader responses on the LOQ questionnaires. This indicates that leaders saw their behavior in one way and subordinates saw it in another. This raises the important question of how leadership style should be measured: from the subordinate's or the leader's perspective? Obviously each side has a legitimate claim.

Finally, the impact of environmental variables on specific leader behaviors is ignored in these studies. For example, we do not know if, in those situations indicating successful IS leaders, there were other variables that affected the relationship between the leader's behavior and productivity. As mentioned earlier regarding the autocratic leader, there are individuals who prefer to have their work highly structured; consequently, it is not surprising that some leaders who initiate structure will perform effectively. Because the leader behavior theory does not consider situational variables (like employee needs), it is probably an oversimplification of reality.

**Conclusions**   The leader behavior approach is appealing, perhaps because it is easy to understand. Also it is easier to identify with specific behaviors than with personality traits, and this allows managers to "practice" these leader behaviors. (It is generally assumed that specific behaviors can be learned, and this appeals to managers who want to improve their effectiveness.) Thus, while Initiating Structure and Consideration do have an influence on morale and productivity, it is difficult to believe that leadership success can be predicted by examining only two basic leader behaviors.

**The University of Michigan Studies**   The studies were conducted during the same general period as those at Ohio State and resulted in some very similar conclusions. After studying numerous industrial situations, the Michigan researchers concluded that two leadership styles—employee-centered and production-centered—influenced employee performance and satisfaction.[25] Employee-centered leaders were those who were interested in their subordinates as people, showed concern for their well-being, and encouraged worker involvement in goal setting. Production-centered leaders, on the other hand, emphasized the technical aspect of the job, set work standards, and closely supervised workers.

## Box 6-3: Satisfaction and Turnover

Many managers feel that they have two key problems with employees—high turnover and low satisfaction. What they often don't realize is that these problems are interrelated, particularly for employees at lower levels of the organization. Research on this problem indicates that employees with low satisfaction levels are less likely to remain with the organization than are employees who are satisfied with their work. If managers work on improving employee satisfaction, perhaps their turnover problem will be resolved.

Perhaps the most well-known of the Michigan studies was conducted in a large insurance company.[26] A field experiment was designed to test the impact of employee-centered vs. production-centered leadership styles on the output of four divisions in the company. The results of this particular experiment showed that productivity increased under both leadership styles (20 percent under employee-centered and 25 percent under production-centered), but that employee satisfaction and turnover were negatively affected by production-centered leadership.

Generally speaking, the Michigan studies showed that employee-centered leaders supervised groups with higher morale and productivity, while production-centered leaders supervised groups with lower productivity and morale. These findings led to the belief that the employee-centered leadership style was superior to the production-centered leadership style.

**Critique**    The conclusions of the Michigan group are very similar to those reached in the Ohio State studies. Both have been valuable in identifying specific leadership behaviors that influence employee productivity and satisfaction. The similarity between the Michigan and Ohio State studies has led many theorists to argue that these two aspects of leadership—task and people—are elements that should be incorporated into leadership effectiveness studies.

**Conclusions**    The Michigan studies do not demonstrate that one type of leadership style is always superior, nor are they able to specify in advance which style will most effective. The latter point is what researchers are striving to achieve, and to do this a systematic analysis of environmental variables and leadership behavior is required. The Michigan studies, however, do not stress environmental variables.

## ☐  The Managerial Grid

Blake and Mouton have designed an organization development program emphasizing the importance of the two basic leader behaviors (concern for people and concern for production) originally identified in the Ohio State and Michigan studies.[27] Blake and Mouton assume that these two concerns are independent, i.e., increased and decreased concerns for production and people can occur simultaneously. Given this assumption, there are five possible leadership styles that managers can use (see Figure 6-5).

The model is designed to help managers first see their current leadership style and then to help them develop the most desirable style. According to Blake and Mouton, the most desirable style is one in which managers show a high concern for both people and production (the 9,9 style).  (Because Blake and Mouton's program is concerned with developing the total organization, it is discussed in detail in the Organization Development chapter.)

**Critique**    The most fundamental criticism of the Grid is Blake and Mouton's argument that the 9,9 style is superior to all other styles of management. They say, for example:

> Managerial styles based on 9,1 direction with compliance, or 5,5 conformity with compromise, or on 1,9 security and comfort through convenience, or on 1,1 acquiescence and complacency, or the "clever" but corrupt relationships produced by facades or by debilitating paternalism, are, at best, second best. Actually they are quite unacceptable, long term. In comparison with performance contributed under 9,9, with its condition of candid communication based on conviction and commitment which results in creativity, other bases for work relationships seem to fall short.[28]

But as Bernardin and Alvares point out:

> Despite the abundance of contrary evidence, Blake and Mouton asserted that their 9,9 team manager—high on production and high on people—will always be the most

| Style Label | Leader Emphasis on Production | People |
|---|---|---|
| 1,1 | Low | Low |
| 9,1 | High | Low |
| 1,9 | Low | High |
| 5,5 | Moderate | Moderate |
| 9,9 | High | High |

**FIGURE 6-5.  Five Possible Leadership Styles**

effective type of leader regardless of the situation and, in fact, a 9,9 orientation applied to the organization as a whole will foster a kind of corporate Darwinism.[29]

**Conclusions**  The belief that there is one leadership style that is inherently superior to others is clearly contrary to the contingency idea of leadership. It seems unlikely that the 9,9 management style is appropriate for organizations experiencing different growth rates, labor relations, competition, and a host of other differentiating problems.

## ☐  McGregor's Theory X and Theory Y

Douglas McGregor's "Theory X and Theory Y" is perhaps the most widely known of all theories, having received much exposure in textbooks, management training programs, and journal articles.[30] It is difficult to determine if McGregor's theory should be classified as a theory of motivation or a theory of leadership. We have chosen to describe it as a leadership theory because it deals with the assumptions leaders make, but the reader should note that this theory, like many leadership theories, also has important implications for the motivation of workers.

Building on the work of Maslow, McGregor argued that traditional managerial behavior was inappropriate since it was based on questionable assumptions about employees. These assumptions, which he labeled Theory X, were:

1. Employees are inherently lazy and will avoid work unless forced to do it.
2. Employees have no ambition or desire for responsibility; instead they prefer to be directed and controlled.
3. Employees have no motivation to achieve organizational objectives.
4. Employees are motivated only by physiological and safety needs.

McGregor contended that many management practices were based on Theory X assumptions, and pointed to such examples as hierarchical models of organization where one person controls another, or, on a smaller scale, a quality control inspector who checks on the behavior of others. He further believed that Theory X assumptions were outdated and that employees would contribute far more to the organization if a completely different set of assumptions, which he labeled

Theory Y, were the guiding force behind managerial behavior. The Theory Y assumptions are:

1. Employees find work as natural as play if organizational conditions are appropriate. People appear adverse to work only because their past work experiences have been unsatisfactory.
2. Employees can be motivated by higher-order needs such as ego, autonomy, and self-actualization.
3. Employees seek responsibility since it allows them to satisfy higher-order needs.

Again, remember that these classifications illustrate the extremes; most managers make assumptions that fall somewhere in between.

The reader should note the strong similarity between autocratic management, Theory X, Initiating Structure, and production-centered behavior, and between democratic management, Theory Y, Consideration and employee-centered behavior. On the surface, each of the terms is referring to approximately the same thing. However, McGregor's theory is different from the others, since he dealt directly with the important question introduced in Chapter 1, "*Why* do employees behave the way they do?"

McGregor believed that a manager's style of leadership was the determinant of employee behavior; therefore, if a manager treated employees as though they

---

### Organizational Reality 6-5
### Tandem Computers

Tandem Computers is headed by James G. Treybig (pronounce Trybig), an individual with interesting views about management. The "truth according to Treybig" involves acceptance of ideas such as "all people are good" and "people, workers, management, and company are all the same thing." Although many traditional motivational tools like stock options and flexible working hours are used at Tandem, other techniques such as company-boosting propaganda urging hard work and respect for coworkers are pursued with a vigor rarely found in North America. Workers are also allowed a peek at strategic company secrets in order to generate a team feeling.

The purpose of this activity is to get workers pointed in the right direction so that close supervision of workers is not required. Treybig believes that most companies are overmanaged and the corporate objectives can be achieved with less management than is normally assumed. Accordingly, at Tandem, control involves making sure workers understand the company philosophy, rather than requiring periodic reports. This type of management system works well in a company like Tandem that has one basic product and a clearly defined market. It could, however, create serious coordination and control problems in a diversified firm.

---

Source: Myron Magnet, "Managing by Mystique at Tandem Computers," *Fortune* (28 June 1982): 84–91.

were lazy and lacked a sense of responsibility, they would fulfill those expectations. On the other hand, if a manager treated subordinates as though they were mature, responsible individuals, they would respond accordingly. In other words, McGregor believed that the assumptions held by managers were self-fulfilling prophecies.

McGregor's theory also attacked a fundamental metaphysical question: "Is man basically good or bad?" If we accept Theory X and Theory Y, the answer is that people are "bad" (e.g. lazy) because of the way they have been treated.

**Critique**   McGregor's contribution lies in his explicit statement of managerial assumptions and their effect on employee behavior. His conclusion that Theory Y assumptions are superior, is, however, open to question. Numerous practicing managers would argue that employees are, in fact, lazy not because of the kind of supervision they receive but because of characteristics inherent in the employee. In addition, it seems unlikely that the "work is as natural as play" assumption is realistic.[31]

**Conclusions**   There is some disagreement as to whether McGregor's Theory X and Y is a universalist leadership proposal. His writings certainly indicate his belief that Theory Y assumptions are the best ones for a leader to make about employees. On the other hand, he explicitly stated that he labeled the two theories "X" and "Y" to avoid placing any values on each. However, in reading his descriptions of the assumptions, the terms used (e.g., lazy, indolent, etc.) certainly are value-laden. Moreover, McGregor argues that society should strive for a Theory Y climate, since these assumptions on the part of managers will maximize human potential. It is for these reasons that we have classified his theory as universalist, although it could be practiced in a contingency framework. This will be discussed in more detail in the applications section of the next chapter.

## Box 6-4: *Should Leaders Be Trained to Be Autocrats?*

Management and leadership training are very much in vogue at the moment. Most, if not all of this training tells leaders to consult their workers when making decisions, to treat employees as "human beings," and in general to develop a democratic leadership style. Yet leadership theory and research have demonstrated that the autocratic style can be effective in a variety of situations. Why aren't there any training programs that stress the autocratic style?

### ☐ Likert's System 4 Management

Rensis Likert, one of the Michigan research group, has proposed that organizational effectiveness and employee satisfaction are maximized when leaders behave in a participative fashion and involve subordinates in the decision-making process.[32] He is, in essence, arguing that leaders should always use an employee-centered style. His "human resource" approach to leadership identifies four basic styles of managing organizations—referred to as "systems"—ranging from the autocratic to the democratic extremes:

1. *System 1*—management has low confidence in subordinate employees and does not involve them in the decision-making process. Workers are forced to work under threats and punishment. Authority is highly centralized at the top of the organization.

2. *System 2*—management has "condescending confidence" in subordinate employees, with the relationship approximating that of master and servant. A few rewards are used to motivate workers; most decisions continue to be centralized at the top of the organization.

3. *System 3*—management has substantial, but not complete, confidence in employees' abilities. Broad policy decisions are made at the top of the organization with subordinate employees permitted to make specific decisions at lower levels.

4. *System 4*—management has complete confidence in employees' abilities. Decision making is decentralized throughout the organization and there is widespread responsibility on the part of lower-level workers.

Likert believes that System 4 management is the ideal type, and that if management conducts itself in this fashion, the result will be lower grievance rates, reduced turnover and absenteeism, and increased employee job satisfaction and morale. Likert argues that this style of management is always superior to the other three types in terms of both organizational effectiveness and employee satisfaction.

These ideas are shown pictorially in Figure 6-6. In Likert's view, certain causal variables (systems 1–4) yield certain intervening variables (e.g., attitudes toward

---

### Box 6-5: Is Turnover Bad for the Organization?

Conventional wisdom says that high turnover is bad for organizations because it costs money to train new employees when experienced ones leave. It also upsets stability. However, this may be an unnecessarily narrow view. One of the big benefits of turnover is that "new blood" is brought into the organization. If turnover were zero, managers might become very complacent and fall into uncreative ways of doing things, since there would be little reason for changing behavior patterns. This might make the organization less adaptable and threaten its survival.

How should this conflict between stability and adaptability be resolved? Some turnover is necessary to encourage innovation, but beyond certain levels the negative aspects of turnover outweigh the positive ones. This level differs across organizations, with those in rapidly changing environments needing a greater level of turnover than those in stable environments.

superiors, communications, performance levels, etc.) which in turn lead to end-result variables (e.g., absenteeism levels, earnings levels, etc.). For example, a system 1 climate leads to poor communication, low performance goals, and restriction of output; this in turn leads to high productivity, absenteeism, and turnover in the *short run,* but lowered productivity and earnings in the *long run.*

One of the interesting aspects of Likert's proposal is his "human resource" approach. This approach emphasizes the value of the human resources in the organization and attempts to avoid wasting these resources, just as we would encourage the plant superintendent to avoid wasting raw materials. Likert maintains that human resources are often "spent" (through turnover, absenteeism,

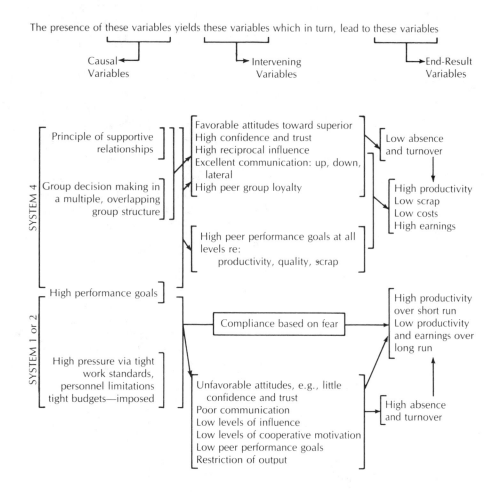

**FIGURE 6-6.  The Effect of Alternative Management Systems on Organizational and Employee Goals**

Source: R. Likert, *The Human Organization* (New York: McGraw-Hill, 1967.) Used with permission.

etc.) by inappropriate styles of leadership. More important, the organization often does not know it is spending these resources since productivity may appear to be satisfactory. But Likert maintains that autocratic styles of leadership generate short-run increases in productivity at the expense of long-term human assets. Since human assets take a long time to develop, this is inefficient management.

A common example of this is when a company experiences a drop in profits; the typical reaction is to "tighten up the ship" (generally through cost-cutting measures) and increase the degree of management control on the assumption that "someone must take charge in these difficult times." But these actions, while solving the immediate problem, may cost the organization considerably in its human assets through turnover, poor morale, etc. Likert maintains that the same short-run results can be obtained without the long-run costs by using the System 4 style of management.

**Critique**     One of the problems with Likert's theory is that empirical support for it has been generated almost exclusively by Likert and his associates.[33] Predictably, numerous criticisms of Likert have arisen regarding his view that System 4 management is always superior. Situational variables are ignored in Likert's model and a substantial amount of research (discussed in the next chapter under contingency theories) indicates that the impact of situational variables can be high.

**Conclusions**     Likert's position that the use of supportive relationships invariably causes the organization to display certain characteristics and thereby always attains certain desirable or undesirable outcomes does not appear viable.

## ☐   A Final Thought on Universalist Theories

Several of the theories presented above stress the importance of leader concern about subordinates as people. This is, in fact, a widespread belief that to be effective, managers must develop good interpersonal relationships between themselves and their subordinates. How accurate is this belief? Although it sounds very logical and reasonable, some research challenges this very fundamental idea. We have already looked at the work of McClelland in Chapter 3, dealing with the needs for achievement, affiliation, and power. McClelland has also conducted research that indicates the situations in which each of these needs is most useful.

McClelland argues that the motivation that makes a good entrepreneur (nAch) does not make a good manager.[34] This is because the internal environment of large organizations is quite different from the environment of the small firms usually run by entrepreneurs. Recall that people high in need for achievement are always looking for ways to do things better themselves, and they also want immediate feedback on how they are doing. However, managers in large organizations cannot do everything by themselves, nor are they likely to have immediate feedback on how they or their subordinates are doing. The manager's job is therefore best done by someone who likes to influence other people. Put another way, the most effective managers are those who have a high need not for achievement or affiliation, but for *power;* this conclusion immediately suggests autocratic, authoritarian management to many people.

McClelland clarifies his basic argument by pointing out that the most successful managers have the following characteristics:

1. *High need for power*—a desire to be strong and influential; this desire is not for personal gain, but to influence employees to achieve organizational goals.

2. *Low need for affiliation*—the manager should not be too concerned about how well he or she is liked by workers; people with a high need for affiliation are too likely to make exceptions to company rules in an attempt to be liked; this does not help the company and may create low morale among the employees who are not given special treatment.

3. *High inhibition in exercising power*—the power the manager has should be exercised in a controlled way; the manager should not threaten subordinates.

4. *High level of maturity*—the manager is not egotistic, is willing to seek expert advice on problems and is not unduly impressed with his or her own self-importance.

5. *A coaching style*—the manager does not try to force people to do things, but tries to help them figure out ways to do a better job for the company.

The most provocative aspect of McClelland's work is his notion that managers should be less concerned about their employees' needs and more concerned about helping them do their job properly. This conclusion is a rather dramatic departure from the usual assumptions about the benefits of "human relations" and "democratic management." Recognizing this might cause objections, McClelland cites evidence from his research that supports his "effective manager profile."

The work of McClelland and others demonstrates that we must be very careful when drawing general conclusions about what constitutes effective leadership. Each situation is unique, and because of this fact it is likely that "one best way" answers will not be satisfactory in many situations. Accordingly, in the next chapter we consider several leadership theories that attempt to deal with this very practical and important problem.

## *Opening Incident Revisited—Lieutenant Forbes*

Lieutenant Forbes and his men reached the helicopter and were safely evacuated. When they reached the main base, the men in the company immediately began spreading the word of the incident. A television reporter and crew happened to be on the base at the time and the following exchange occurred (*live*) on the evening news:

REPORTER:   Lieutenant Forbes, is it true that you threatened to kill one of your men if he did not begin the march?

FORBES:   Yes.

REPORTER:   Why did you do that?

FORBES:   Because I had ordered the men to evacuate the area and they refused. This was a combat condition and I was prepared to use my authority to its fullest in order to get the others to obey me.

REPORTER:   But you're very inexperienced in these matters. It is well known among experienced officers that walking down a road is just not done because of the danger of sniper fire. The men knew this and were therefore perfectly justified in refusing your order, weren't they? You were just lucky that no one was killed!

FORBES:   There was no luck involved, sir. I received information from headquarters telling me that the Viet Cong had us almost completely surrounded and the road to the helicopter was the *only* safe direction to move.

REPORTER:   Well, why didn't you *tell* the men that?

FORBES:   Sir, what am I going to tell them the next time I give an order?

REPORTER:   I never thought of that.

Of course, whether or not Lt. Forbes would have shot one of his own men is difficult to say. We can only surmise that he would have (his men certainly thought so!). In any case, Forbes' analysis of his leadership situation is clear: the only style possible under these conditions was the autocratic style. While few would disagree with this conclusion, Forbes faced a difficult situation because of his new position in the group and lack of experience. Autocrats seldom have much difficulty as long as the subordinates think the leader knows what he is doing. But if for any reason they see their leader as incompetent, then the autocratic style can cause disastrous results.

Forbes had no choice in this situation except to (1) rely heavily on his formal authority as commanding officer of the unit, and (2) convince the men that he would use that authority if he had to. If he had explained the reason for his strange order, the men's confidence in him would have increased slightly. But explanation takes time, and it is unlikely that their confidence in him would have increased enough to eliminate questions the next time he gave an order. Thus, Lt. Forbes did not want to establish the precedent that he would explain every order until the day arrived when the men had sufficient confidence in him. The autocratic style was highly effective in this situation and was probably the only reasonable alternative.

# ■ SUMMARY

While the leadership theories discussed above are diverse in their approach, substance, and conclusions, they all possess one common characteristic—the notion that there is "one best way" to lead subordinates. Whether it be the assumption that leader success is guaranteed by the existence of certain individual traits ("great man" theory, trait theory), by specific leader behaviors (Michigan and Ohio State studies, the Managerial Grid), or by the way the leader views subordinates (Theory X and Y, System 4), all the proposals make rather sweeping claims about their effectiveness.

Although each of the universalist approaches has been popular at one time or another as *the* answer to the leadership effectiveness problem, the empirical support for them is less than convincing. The most deficient theories appear to be the great man and the trait approaches, although they may have potential if used in a contingency framework, i.e., in certain situations, one set of traits is appropriate, while in other situations a different set is needed. The other leadership theories have been criticized because empirical support for them (1) has been generated largely by the developers of the theory, and (2) is based on weak research methodologies.

In general, the critics of the universalist approaches have made a very strong case on both theoretical and practical grounds that the approaches are an oversimplification of the complex reality of leadership. This is not to say that universalist approaches will always fail if used as the basis for managerial action. Rather, it indicates a desire on the part of many leadership researchers to get a better understanding of the way in which situational variables such as technology, work groups, individual differences, payment systems, etc., influence the leadership process. Contingency theories, the subject of the next chapter, are generally accepted as a more realistic (but complex) way of giving the appropriate weight to these important situational variables.

# ■ REVIEW QUESTIONS

1. What are the differences between universalist and contingency theories of leadership?

2. Why is it important to distinguish between the "broad" and "narrow" definitions of leadership?

3. What are the differences between the autocratic, democratic, and abdicratic styles of leadership?

4. What are the major limitations of the trait approach to leadership?

5. How did the "leader-behavior approach" attempt to make up for the shortcomings in the trait approach?

6. How did the Managerial Grid build on the ideas of the leader behavior approach?

7. How did McGregor's Theory X and Theory Y utilize Maslow's hierarchy of needs?

8. What is meant by the statement that McGregor's Theory X and Theory Y are "self-fulfilling prophecies"?

9. How is Likert's "human resource approach" different from the other approaches to leadership?

10. What is the major limitation of the universalist theories of leadership?

# ■ EXERCISE 6-1: A CONFLICT OF LEADERSHIP STYLES

Susan Layton and Jane Bucher each supervised twenty clerks at the head office of a large insurance company. The clerks performed routine tasks such as filing, typing, and general office duties. Layton and Bucher, although good friends, had sharply different ideas about how their clerical staffs should be managed.

Layton felt that jobs of the clerical type resulted in boredom and job dissatisfaction for the people doing them. In her view, it was important to prevent the errors that would invariably occur because of the lack of attention paid to the job. Accordingly, she had instituted numerous checks on the work of the clerks, and had required that each do a carefully designed function.

Bucher agreed that the work caused boredom and dissatisfaction. However, she felt that the way to reduce the negative impact of these things was to increase the decision-making scope of the jobs. Accordingly, she allowed the clerks she supervised to decide among themselves how the total work load was going to be divided. The only specific requirement was that productivity objectives set out by higher management must be achieved.

1. Compare the leadership styles of Layton and Bucher.

2. What assumptions about human nature are each of these managers making?

3. Role-play a conversation between Layton and Bucher about the "best" leadership style.

4. Which of these leaders is most likely to be effective? Why?

# ■ EXERCISE 6-2: ONE OF THE BOYS

Barry Lawton joined the Fairchild Manufacturing Company as a production worker immediately upon graduation from high school. The company manufactured a wide variety of electric switching equipment that was used in industrial settings.

Barry got along well with his coworkers, but not with his foreman. Barry and his coworkers were united against the foreman because they felt he was too autocratic and rule-oriented and treated them like children. Because of this, there were many conflicts between the foreman and the workers. The whole climate of the work group suffered and worker morale was low (although productivity remained at a satisfactory level). As time passed, it became clear that Barry had a knack for smoothing over the work-related conflicts that were caused by the foreman's attitudes. Barry prided himself on this ability, and he worked at refining it further. He felt that it was important for management to treat workers with more respect and dignity and he said this to anyone who would listen. His coworkers enthusiastically agreed with his idea that if management treated workers well, they would be happier and more productive.

Two years after Barry joined Fairchild, the much-despised supervisor was transferred. The plant superintendent approached Barry and offered him the job. Barry immediately accepted, and set out to implement his ideas about managing people. For the first few weeks, things went well. The workers were very happy to be rid of the old autocratic boss and they told Barry that it was nice to have "one of the boys" as their new foreman. For his part, Barry consciously treated his new subordinates in precisely the way he had always said subordinates should be treated.

As time passed, Barry began to be concerned about his section because it was obvious that productivity had not increased under his leadership. In fact, a trend was developing in the opposite direction. Barry knew how this would be viewed by the plant super-intendent, so he started to gently apply pressure for more output. The workers didn't take this pressure too seriously, and joked that Barry shouldn't worry so much. This pattern continued for several months and output continued to decline. By now Barry was deeply concerned and was plagued by doubts about the validity of his leadership ideas. One day as he was passing the ceramic switch line, he saw four workers looking down at the floor and laughing. As he came closer, he saw several switch boxes (each worth $700) lying broken on the floor. He asked what had happened and was told in a lighthearted fashion that the production line had been left unattended for a few minutes and the boxes had simply fallen off. Barry was furious and loudly chewed out the workers who were at fault. He then stormed back into his office. Thirty seconds later Joe Mankiewicz, one of the four workers, charged into Barry's office.

JOE:   What do you think you're doing, Barry?!! You can't talk to me like that in front of all our friends.

BARRY:   You mean *your* friends! You guys are not friends of mine anymore. Ever since I took over as foreman, you've been taking advantage of me and loafing on the job.

JOE:   Aw, come on, Barry don't get upset. It was only three switch boxes that broke. The company can afford it. We've got to stick together.

BARRY:   Don't give me that "we've got to stick together" nonsense! If you guys don't increase your productivity you won't have a job to come to.

JOE:   That sounds like a threat. What happened to all your big talk about treating workers with dignity and respect? Since you got into management, you're a changed person.

BARRY:   Go back to your station, Joe. I don't want to discuss this any more.

Barry sat in his office and wondered how things had gotten so fouled up.

1.   What is the problem here? What mistakes has Barry made?

2.   What do the leadership theories presented in this chapter suggest should be done in this situation?

3.   Discuss the impact of task-oriented and people-oriented behavior in this situation.

4.   What should Barry Lawton do now?

## ■ EXERCISE 6-3: THE RELUCTANT SUBORDINATE

George Buchanan was manager of one of the offices of Credit Investigations, Inc., a firm specializing in reporting on the credit ratings of individuals. Various retail outlets across the country paid for the service whenever they wished further information on a credit card applicant. Buchanan technically supervised five women in his role as office manager; however, he actually dealt with only one—his personal secretary, Joanne Crawley. Buchanan would spend some time at the start of each day explaining what needed to be done; Crawley would then allocate the work among the other workers in the office in what she thought was the most efficient way.

One Monday afternoon, Crawley asked to speak to Buchanan. She was obviously distraught and began by explaining to Buchanan that one of the workers in the office, Sue Masaryk, was refusing to do the work that was being assigned to her, claiming that Crawley was not her superior and had no right giving her orders.

1. What should Buchanan do?

2. How did this problem come into being?

3. Role-play the discussion which might occur between Buchanan and Crawley.

## ■ ENDNOTES

1. Arthur G. Jago, "Leadership: Perspectives in Theory and Research," *Management Science* 28 (1982): 315.

2. Henry Mintzberg, *The Nature of Managerial Work* (New York: Harper and Row, 1973).

3. For a detailed discussion of the impact of leadership on employee productivity and satisfaction, see R. Dubin, et al., *Leadership and Productivity* (San Francisco: Chandler Publishing Company, 1965).

4. For a discussion of this issue, see D. Kipnis and S. Schmidt, "Intraorganizational Influence Tactics: Explorations in Getting One's Way," *Journal of Applied Psychology* 65 (1980): 440–452; also D. Eden and A. Shari, "Pygmalion Goes to Boot Camp: Expectancy, Leadership, and Trainee Performance," *Journal of Applied Psychology* 67 (1982): 194–199.

5. A. Lowin and J. R. Craig, "The Influence of Level of Performance on Managerial Style: An Experimental Object Lesson in the Ambiguity of Correlational Data," *Organizational Behavior and Human Performance* 3 (1968): 440–458.

6. C. N. Greene, "A Longitudinal Investigation of Modification to a Situational Model of Leadership Effectiveness," *Proceedings* of the National Academy of Management Meetings (1979): 54–58.

7. S. Kerr, "Substitutes for Leadership; Some Implications for Organization Design," *Organization and Administrative Sciences* 8 (1977): 135–150; also S. Kerr and J. Jermier, "Substitutes for Leadership: Their Meaning and Measurement," *Organizational Behavior and Human Performance* 22 (1978): 35–403; also J. P. Howell and P. Dorfman, "Substitutes for Leadership: Test of a Construct," *Academy of Management Journal* 24 (1981): 714–728.

8. This problem was particularly evident during the Nuremburg trials of Nazi war criminals, many of whom attempted (unsuccessfully) to use this line of defense.

9. L. Coch and J. French, "Overcoming Resistance to Change," *Human Relations* (Winter 1948): 512–532.

10. E. Locke and D. M. Schweiger, "Participation in Decision Making: One More Look," in B. M. Straw, ed., *Research in Organizational Behavior* Vol. I (Greenwich, Conn.: AI Press, 1978), pp. 265–339.

11. T. Carlyle, *Lectures on Heroes, Hero Worship and the Heroic in History*, ed. P. C. Parr (Oxford: The Clarendon Press, 1910).

12. For example, see R. Stogdill, "Personal Factors Associated with Leadership: A Survey of the Literature," *Journal of Psychology* 25 (1948): 35–72; also C. Gibb, "Leadership," *Handbook of Social Psychology* ed. G. Lindzey (Reading, Mass.: Addison–Wesley, 1954). For a comprehensive analysis of leadership traits, see R. Stogdill, *Handbook of Leadership* (New York: The Free Press, 1974), especially chapters 5 and 6. Strictly speaking, some of these "traits" could be better classified as "characteristics," e.g., height, weight, etc. Nevertheless, the basic theory regarding their predictive value is the same.

13. R. Stogdill, *Handbook of Leadership*, pp. 35–71.

14. C. Schrag, "Leadership Among Prison Inmates," *American Sociological Review* 19 (1954): 37–42.

15. P. Stryker, "On the Meaning of Executive Qualities," *Fortune* 57 (1958): 116–119; 186–189.

16. Several of these environmental characteristics are discussed in Chapter 7.

17. R. Stogdill, *Handbook of Leadership*, p. 72.

18. A. W. Halpin and B. J. Winer, "A Factorial Study of the Leader Behavior Descriptions," in R. M. Stogdill and A. E. Coons, eds., *Leader Behavior: Its Description and Measurement* (Columbus: Ohio State University, Bureau of Business Research, 1957).

19. The value of this assumption has been questioned in L. Larson, J. Hunt, and R. Osborn, "The Great Hi-Hi Leader Behavior Myth," *Academy of Management Journal* 19 (December 1976): 628–641; see also P. Nystrom, "Managers and the Hi-Hi Leader Myth," *Academy of Management Journal* 21 (June 1978): 325–331. At a more fundamental level, the whole idea that the two key dimensions of leadership are "task" and "human" is strongly questioned in B. Karmel, "Leadership: A Challenge to Traditional Research Methods and Assumptions," *Academy of Management Review* 3 (July 1978): 475–482.

20. R. Bales, E. Borgatta, and A. Couch, "Some Findings Relevant to the Great-Man Theory of Leadership," *American Sociological Review* 19 (1954): 755–59.

21. F. Fiedler, "How Do You Make Leaders More Effective? New Answers to an Old Puzzle," *Organizational Dynamics* (Autumn 1972): 3–18.

22. See, for example, W. Schmidt and R. Tannenbaum, "How to Choose a Leadership Pattern," *Harvard Business Review* 36 (1958): 95–101; also W. Hill, "Leadership Style: Flexible or Rigid?" *Organizational Behavior and Human Performance* 9 (1973): 35–47; also R. Likert, *The Human Organization* (New York: McGraw-Hill Book Company, 1967); also P. Weissenburgh and M. Kavanaugh, "The Independence of Initiating Structure and Consideration," *Personnel Psychology* 25 (1972): 119–180.

23. This is illustrated more fully in our discussion in Chapter 1 regarding changing behavior. Further examples are included in the discussion of Fiedler's Leadership Contingency Model in Chapter 9, and in Chapter 17, Organization Development.

24. A. Korman, "Consideration and Initiating Structure: A Review," *Personnel Psychology* 19 (Winter 1966): 119–180.

25. R. Kahn and D. Katz, "Leadership Practices in Relation to Productivity and Morale," in D. Cartwright and A. Zander, eds., *Group Dynamics* (Evanston, Ill.: Row Petersen and Company, 1960).

26. N. C. Morse and E. Reimer, "The Experimental Change of a Major Organizational Variable," *Journal of Abnormal Social Psychology* 51 (1956): 120–129.

27. R. Blake and J. Mouton, *The Managerial Grid* (Houston: Gulf, 1964).

28. Ibid., p. 318.

29. H. J. Bernardin and K. Alvares, "The Managerial Grid As a Predictor of Conflict Resolution and Managerial Effectiveness," *Administrative Science Quarterly* 21 (1976): 84.

30. D. McGregor, *The Human Side of Enterprise* (New York: McGraw-Hill Book Company, 1960).

31. E. Lauck Parke and C. Tauskey, "Need Theory, Reinforcement Theory, and Job Enrichment," Working Paper #74-30, University of Massachusetts.

32. R. Likert, *The Human Organization* (New York: McGraw-Hill Book Company, 1967).

33. The reader will note this was also mentioned in Chapter 4 as a criticism of McClelland and Herzberg, and is also true of other theories mentioned in this chapter.

34. D. C. McClelland and D. H. Burnham, "Power Is the Great Motivator," *Harvard Business Review* (March–April 1976): 100–110.

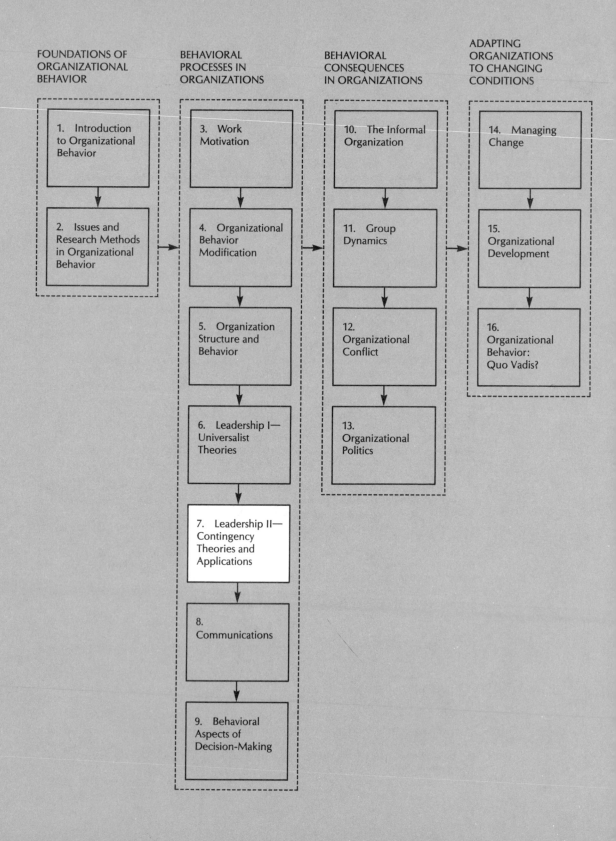

FOUNDATIONS OF
ORGANIZATIONAL
BEHAVIOR

1. Introduction to Organizational Behavior

2. Issues and Research Methods in Organizational Behavior

BEHAVIORAL
PROCESSES IN
ORGANIZATIONS

3. Work Motivation

4. Organizational Behavior Modification

5. Organization Structure and Behavior

6. Leadership I— Universalist Theories

7. Leadership II— Contingency Theories and Applications

8. Communications

9. Behavioral Aspects of Decision-Making

BEHAVIORAL
CONSEQUENCES
IN ORGANIZATIONS

10. The Informal Organization

11. Group Dynamics

12. Organizational Conflict

13. Organizational Politics

ADAPTING
ORGANIZATIONS
TO CHANGING
CONDITIONS

14. Managing Change

15. Organizational Development

16. Organizational Behavior: Quo Vadis?

# Leadership II — Contingency Theories and Applications

## ■ Learning Objectives

After reading and studying this chapter you should be able to:

☐ Explain what is meant by a contingency leadership theory and give several examples of this approach to leadership.

☐ Discuss the issue of style flexibility and the arguments for and against it.

☐ Discuss some of the important practical aspects of leadership in organizations.

☐ Understand how the Situational Leadership model builds on the earlier research dealing with leader behavior.

☐ Describe the key variables in Fiedler's Contingency model and explain how they interact with a leader's style to determine leadership effectiveness.

☐ Understand the important variables in Vroom and Yetton's Decision-Making Model and how the leader must analyze these variables before choosing a style.

☐ Explain how House's Path–Goal Model builds on earlier research and what it says about the impact of situational variables on style.

☐ Explain how each of the contingency leadership theories could be applied in actual organizations.

# Chapter 7

# ■ KEY TERMS

Contingency leadership theories
The situational leadership theory
Task behavior
Relationship behavior
The leadership decision-making
model
The leadership contingency model
LEADER MATCH training
The path–goal model
Leadership training

# ■ CHAPTER OUTLINE

# *Opening Incident—Carolyn Barnes*

The Mission Chapel was a nondenominational church located in the downtown section of a large midwestern city. The Chapel's choir had forty-five volunteers and performed each Sunday from September through June.

There were two distinct types of people in the choir. Approximately ten people were experienced singers, with many years of formal music and voice training. The remaining thirty-five people had little or no musical training but were in the choir simply because they liked to sing. The experienced singers were expected to help the inexperienced ones; in addition, the experienced singers did solo performances on a regular basis.

The choir director, Carolyn Barnes, was known throughout the city as an excellent musician. In addition to directing the chapel choir, she judged the various musical competitions held throughout the year and was also the producer of a popular local T.V. musical show. Barnes was paid a token salary of $5,000 per year for conducting the chapel choir. Practice was held for two hours on Wednesday evenings, at which time the choir worked on a variety of numbers, the goal being a good performance of the music when the time came to sing it in the regular church service.

Barnes ran the choir with a firm hand. She decided which music was to be performed, the date on which it would be performed, who the soloists would be, the nature and timing of special concerts, and the structure of the Wednesday night practices.

In her opinion, she was very effective, since the choir had placed first in all three competitions it had entered in the past eighteen months. Morale of the choir also seemed very high and turnover was fairly low (10 percent).

In spite of this success, Barnes had noticed two things that disturbed her. First, absenteeism was running at 20 percent at both the practice sessions and the regular Sunday services. She had tried to solve this problem by pointing out the importance of regular attendance for every member, but this had been ineffective. Second, certain of the choir members (generally men) were continually talking and cutting up during the practice sessions. This was annoying to Barnes and on several occasions she had made it clear that she was not going to tolerate it. These comments had not had any effect and the problems had continued. Barnes wondered if her leadership style was appropriate for the situation, and whether she should change it in an attempt to solve these two problems.

# ■ INTRODUCTION

Contingency approaches to the study of leadership effectiveness stand in direct contrast to the universalist approaches described in Chapter 6. Contingency theories start from the basic assumption that different situations demand different leadership styles if the leader is going to be effective. This assumption implies that leadership theories must take environmental and individual-difference variables into consideration before the "correct" leadership behavior can be exhibited.

In general, contingency theories of leadership are more complex than universalist theories since they must (1) specify the situational variables influencing the leadership process, and (2) indicate the way in which these situational elements interact to determine the type of leadership behavior that is most appropriate. This is obviously a difficult task. Compared to the universalist approaches (some of which have been in existence for several decades), the contingency approaches are in their infancy; hence, much of the evidence concerning them is still being interpreted and refined. Nevertheless, because they overcome the limitations of the universalist models, they are an important contribution to the understanding of leadership.

## Box 7-1: The Trouble with Contingency Theories

During the last few years contingency theories of leadership have become very popular. While it is generally agreed that contingency theories give a more realistic picture of the complexities of leadership, they are not without their own problems. One problem is that contingency theories often analyze extreme situations and then state the leadership behavior (autocratic or democratic) that will be most effective in those situations. Unfortunately, extreme situations are unusual; "middle ground" situations predominate and neither autocratic nor democratic behavior will be best. Instead, an "average" of these behaviors will probably be most effective.

An additional practical problem concerns costs. It is important that contingency models be tested extensively to see whether their predictions are accurate and reliable. This of course costs money, and managers may be reluctant to use contingency theories for this reason.

Finally, compared to universalist theories, contingency theories are complex and sometimes hard to understand. For practicing managers, this may create real problems. What is probably desired by most managers is a simple, straightforward statement about how to lead, and this is what universalist theories, not contingency theories, offer. However, "ease of use" is a less defensible criterion than "effectiveness."

## *Organizational Reality 7-1*
## *Theory Z*

Several books have been written recently extolling the virtue of Japanese management techniques (often called Theory Z). These books tell of harmonious employee–employer relations, high productivity, and effective human resource management. The usual conclusion is that American firms should adopt these practices in order to achieve what the Japanese have. However, Japanese success may be due not so much to effective management as to disciplined workers. Labor does what it is told, does it right, and does not interfere with changes management introduces to improve productivity. The Japanese society, not management, created this disciplined work force. Hierarchy is a central feature in Japanese society, and each person knows his or her place in the system. Attempting to implement Theory Z in the U.S. would not be feasible because the U.S. culture is not appropriate for it.

Source: B. Bruce Biggs, "The Dangerous Folly Called Theory Z," *Fortune* (17 May 1982): 48–53.

## *Organizational Reality 7-2*
## *The Cultural Contingency in Leadership*

George P. Craighead, a managing partner, New York office of Egon Zehnder International Incorporated, believes that deeply rooted cultural and educational differences are responsible for a lack of real communication between American and European executives.

The most important difference between American and European executives lies in their vastly dissimilar educational experiences. In Europe education is more formal, disciplined, and authority-oriented. American schools are much more liberal in many respects. The European also receives a far broader education, dealing with a wider variety of subjects. The American tends to concentrate on a few subjects that will immediately translate into career assets. In the U.S., schools at all levels give little emphasis to other languages. In contrast, most European senior executives are likely to be fluent in at least three languages.

Americans have developed management systems to measure and select those who stand out, versus those who are just average. In contrast, Europeans are more relaxed about the measurement of human performance.

One other factor must be kept in mind. Tough times in the United States may be seen as prosperous days in other countries. Americans are not used to not being number one in all economic activity. As a result, a new breed of American executive is likely to be much tougher than his predecessor.

Source: George P. Craighead, "Alike But Different: U.S. and European Executives," *Personnel Journal* (June 1982): 456–458.

# ■ CONTINGENCY LEADERSHIP THEORIES

Four of the most widely known contingency theories are the Situational Leadership Model, the Leadership Decision-Making Model, the Leadership Contingency Model, and the Path–Goal Model. Each of these theories is discussed and critiqued below. While reading the critique, keep in mind that although contingency theories are a distinct improvement over universalist theories, they are not perfect. Thus, certain shortcomings are pointed out so that you will get a realistic view of the complexities of leadership.

## □ The Situational Leadership Theory

Hersey and Blanchard have developed a contingency theory of leadership that is based on the Consideration and Initiating Structure dimensions of the Ohio State leadership studies, but places the two sets of behaviors into a contingency framework.[1] Slight modifications in terminology are made, with Consideration described as "relationship behavior" and Structure as "task behavior." Relationship behavior is the extent to which a leader engages in two-way communication with subordinates, provides support and encouragement, and exhibits other facilitating behaviors. Task behaviors are those that provide direction to subordinates such as telling them what to do, how to do it, and when to do it. The two leader behaviors are shown in Figure 7-1.

The Situational Leadership graph shows that the two sets of behaviors can occur in various proportions (a leader can have lots of task behavior and little relationship behavior, or lots of relationship behavior and little task behavior). To simplify the number of combinations, the graph is divided into four quadrants, each describing one of the four basic leadership styles. The styles are as follows:

S(1) High task, low relationship—Telling style
S(2) High task, high relationship—Selling style
S(3) Low task, high relationship—Participating style
S(4) Low task, low relationship—Delegating style

Figure 7-1 shows how a leader's behavior changes as the leader progresses from S(1) to S(4). As the leader changes styles from S(1) to S(2), he or she reduces task behaviors and gradually increases relationship behaviors. Moving from S(2) to S(3) means a further reduction of task behaviors and even more emphasis on relationship behaviors. When proceeding from S(3) to S(4), the leader reduces both task and relationship behaviors.

Hersey and Blanchard propose that each of the four styles is effective in certain situations, and that the maturity (developmental) level of the subordinate is the major factor determining leadership style effectiveness. Maturity level is defined as:

. . . the ability and willingness of people to take responsibility for directing their own behavior. *These variables of maturity should be considered only in relation to a specific task to be performed.* That is to say, an individual or a group is not mature or immature in a *total* sense. All persons tend to be more or less mature in relation to a specific task, function, or objective that a leader is attempting to accomplish through their efforts. Thus, a saleswoman may be very responsible in securing new sales but very casual about completing the paperwork necessary to close a sale. As a result, it is appropriate for her manager to let her alone in terms of closing on sales but to supervise her closely in terms of her paperwork until she can start to do well in that area too.[2]

Maturity is therefore generally defined as worker willingness (motivation or desire) and ability (competence) to perform a specific task. Four levels of maturity are identified and described as follows:[3]

M(1)—worker is unable and unwilling
M(2)—worker is unable but willing (i.e., lacks confidence)
M(3)—worker is able but unwilling (i.e., lacks motivation)
M(4)—worker is able and willing

The most effective leadership occurs when the subordinate's maturity level is matched with the most appropriate leadership style. S(1) is best for managing workers with a low maturity level, S(2) and S(3) for workers with moderate maturity levels, and S(4) for workers with high maturity levels.

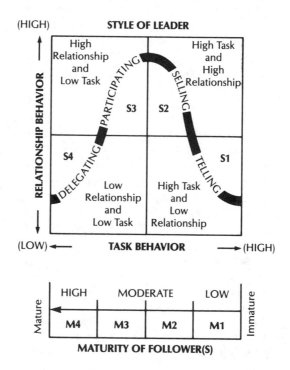

**FIGURE 7-1.   The Situational Leadership Model**

Source: Paul Hersey and Kenneth H. Blanchard, *Management of Organizational Behavior,* 4th ed. (Englewood Cliffs, N.J.: Prentice-Hall, 1982), p. 152. Used with permission.

Hersey and Blanchard illustrate the main points of the Situational Leadership theory by use of a parallel example—the parent–child relationship. When the child is very young, the parents must provide a great deal of structure. As the child enters school, a considerable amount of structure must still be provided but so must a great deal of trust and respect (relationship behavior). As the child moves through high school and into college, he or she accepts more and more responsibility; hence it is appropriate that the parents give less and less structure while continuing to give emotional support. Finally, as the child establishes his or her own family, both types of supportive behavior decline to a very low level.

In addition to being a general leadership theory, Hersey and Blanchard's model also prescribes appropriate leader behaviors for specific situations. The prescriptive statements are couched in behavioral terms so that leaders are aware of the appropriate leader behavior, as opposed to more general statements such as "treat your employees better." As well, the model is useful for planning developmental strategies for workers. The leader can see what specific changes are necessary in order to develop subordinates from an M(1) level to an M(4) level. The model also addresses the issue of a worker whose performance deteriorates over time—regresses, for example, from M(3) to M(2). Again, the model is specific; in this case it tells the leader to adopt more task behavior but to maintain high relationship behavior.

The model has a thorough development history, both as a theory and as a teaching package. Hersey and Blanchard have designed a series of instruments that managers can use to determine the maturity levels of their followers and their personal range of styles. The instruments show mismatches between leader style and subordinate maturity and point out how the appropriate leadership style can be achieved.

**Critique**    The Situational Leadership model is very popular and has received considerable attention in recent years. Most of the attention, however, has been from consultants and trainers rather than academic researchers. This means that there is limited research evidence regarding its effectiveness. In addition to their own work, however, Hersey and Blanchard do cite some research that supports their model. A study by Stinson and Johnson showed that the behaviors of Initiating Structure and Consideration were moderated by the relationship between the individual and the task.[4] Their study showed that task structure was relative to the skills of the subordinate. Another study investigated the Situational Leadership Model in teaching settings and supported its effectiveness.[5] A field study at the Xerox Corporation on the effectiveness of the Situational Leadership training program came to the following conclusions.

1. Highly effective managers indicate greater knowledge and use of Situational Leadership than less effective ones.
2. All managers in the study reported using Situational Leadership at least some of the time (thus indicating that the training had an impact).
3. On the average, managers who applied the model correctly rated their subordinates' job performances higher than managers who did not.

The above findings are limited because the measures of effectiveness were self-report data rather than external evaluations, but they do provide some indication of the perceived usefulness of the model.

In terms of theoretical problems with the model, the following are evident. First, the theory requires that a leader be perceptive enough to determne subordinate maturity levels. The theory also assumes that the subordinate will agree with the superior's assessment. The problems in this area are easily seen when parents and children disagree. The child argues that he or she possesses enough maturity to do something without parental guidance, while the parents wish to control the situation with certain rules which the child does not like. The argument is often resolved by a display of power by the parents.

Second, the theory assumes that the leader possesses enough style flexibility to move from task-oriented to relationship-oriented behavior as subordinate maturity levels change. This issue has come up on other occasions in our analysis of leadership. If the "one basic style" proponents are correct, the leader will often be unable to change style as subordinates mature. Hence the leader may not be able to adopt the most effective behavior.

Third, employee turnover has a big impact on the Situational Leadership theory. Since new employees are constantly coming into an organization and experienced ones are leaving, in an organization with high turnover the theory would imply that a task orientation would be most appropriate since most employees would be new. In any case, the theory requires the manager to assess very carefully the "mix" of maturity of subordinates and to behave accordingly.

Finally, the theory assumes that the nature of the task being supervised is such that the leader can treat each worker in a slightly different way. There is no question that this is a reasonable assumption in many cases. However, there are situations where it is not possible, e.g., the choir circumstance in the opening incident. How does a leader of a group like a choir exhibit different styles when all members of the group must perform the task in a very specific and interdependent way?

Situational Leadership has been well integrated with previous theories of organizational behavior. Its ability to incorporate the "best" of other approaches, such as Theory X and Theory Y, the Ohio State leadership studies, and contingency management, helps to improve its acceptance. Much research needs to be done, however, to gather additional information on the effectiveness of the model.

## ☐ The Leadership Decision-Making Model

Vroom and Yetton have developed a contingency model of leadership style based on the idea that a leader must decide how much participation subordinates should have when making decisions.[7] This participation can range widely. At one extreme, the manager might allow no participation and simply make the decision (an autocratic style). At the other extreme, the manager might stress group problem solving and allow subordinates total freedom to make the decision (a participative style). These extremes, as well as middle-ground positions, are described in Figure 7-2.

1. You solve the problem or make the decision yourself, using information available to you at the time.

2. You obtain the necessary information from your subordinates, then decide the solution to the problem yourself. You may or may not tell your subordinates what the problem is in getting the information from them. The role played by your subordinates in making the decision is clearly one of providing the necessary information to you, rather than generating or evaluating alternative solutions.

3. You share the problem with the relevant subordinates individually, getting their ideas and suggestions without bringing them together as a group. Then *you* make the decision, which may or may not reflect your subordinates' influence.

4. You share the problem with your subordinates as a group, obtaining their collective ideas and suggestions. Then you make the decision, which may or may not reflect your subordinates' influence.

5. You share the problem with your subordinates as a group. Together you generate and evaluate alternatives and attempt to reach agreement (consensus) on a solution. Your role is much like that of a chairman. You do not try to influence the group to adopt "your" solution, and you are willing to accept and implement any solution which has the support of the entire group.

### FIGURE 7-2.   The Range of Leadership Styles

Source: V. Vroom and P. Yetton, *Leadership and Decision Making* (Pittsburgh: University of Pittsburgh Press, 1973), p. 13. Used with permission.

Vroom and Yetton argue that each one of these leadership styles can be effective, depending on the answers to a series of work-related questions that the manager must ask himself or herself (see the top of Figure 7-3). The answers to these questions will indicate the leadership style that will be most effective. To demonstrate how this model works, consider the case of a leader of a group of clerks in an insurance company who is dissatisfied with the present filing system and wants to introduce a new one. The leader doesn't really know much about the alternative filing systems that are available, but he does know that the clerks must be comfortable with the new system or their productivity will decline. His relations with the clerks are good and they identify well with the company, but because of the routine nature of their work, they are quite vocal about how things are done in their department.

What leadership style should be used in this type of situation? If we follow through questions A–F in Figure 7-3 and use the information in the case, we get the following answers:

A. Yes, there is a quality requirement (the system must work)
B. No (the leader doesn't know about filing systems)
C. No (it is not obvious how to go about introducing a new filing system)
D. yes (subordinates are vocal about operations of the department)
E. No (same reason as D)
F. Yes (subordinates identify with the organization)

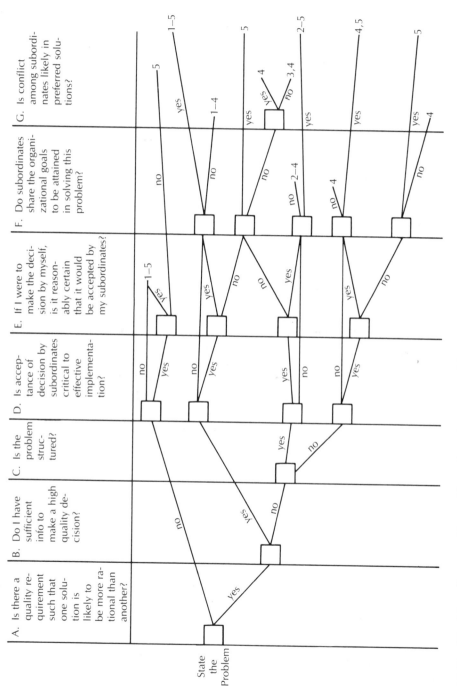

**FIGURE 7-3. Decision-Process Flow Chart for Group Problems (Numbers at the end of the decision tree correspond to those in Figure 7-2.)**

Source: V. Vroom and P. Yetton, *Leadership and Decision Making* (Pittsburgh: University of Pittsburgh Press, 1973), p. 194.

Given this pattern of answers, the model indicates that style #5 (participative) would be most appropriate. If we think about this situation, the model makes good practical sense.

What happens if we change one of the situational features? Suppose subordinates did not identify with the goals of the organization (question F). The best leadership style is now #4. The leader should allow participation in this situation, but the leader must make the final decision because subordinates do not share organizational goals. Allowing them to make a decision in this situation would be unreasonable and an abdication of responsibility on the manager's part.

A key idea in the Vroom–Yetton model is that of the "feasible set." This simply means that more than one of the five leadership styles in Figure 7-2 may be effective, depending on the answers to the questions in Figure 7-3. If the manager views time as a constraint, he or she can use the most autocratic style in the feasible set. If the manager wants to spend time developing his or her subordinates, the most participative style in the feasible set can be used.

**Critique**    The strong point of Vroom and Yetton's approach is their treatment of issues that strongly influence leadership effectiveness (the quality requirement in decisions, information availability, acceptance by subordinates, etc). The model was developed after experimentation with other similar models, so it represents considerable thinking about how leadership styles and problem types interact. While it is a prescriptive model, it does recognize that different leadership styles can be effective in different situations.

There is not a great deal of empirical research evidence on the model, since it was proposed fairly recently. In one study, ninety-six managers reported one successful and one unsuccessful decison they had made.[8] They also indicated (1) the decision method they had used in each problem, and (2) the quality, effectiveness, and acceptance of the decision. Decision processes (leadership styles) within the feasible set were rated as successful significantly more often than decision processes outside the feasible set.

On the negative side, one writer has pointed out a number of methodological problems in the model which may reduce its usefulness.[9] He notes, for example, that the supporting study noted above is based on self-report data from managers. This type of recollection by individuals may or may not be consistent with what (objectively) happened. Thus, there might be social desirability bias: managers might report that their decision style was more participative than it really was because of the current emphasis in organizations on the benefits of participative leadership.

Another criticism is that the Vroom–Yetton model is unnecessarily complex and that simpler models predict effective styles equally well. In response to the latter criticism, a further analysis of ninety-six managers' responses was conducted.[10] This showed that the more complex Vroom–Yetton model predicted effective leadership decision styles better than simpler models. Thus, simpler models could be used, but only at the expense of predictive accuracy. Both positive and negative evidence is very tentative at the moment, and a more informed conclusion will have to await further testing of the model. The theory looks promising because it specifically deals with the question of subordinate involvement in decision making—a topic of great interest to both subordinates and managers.

## ☐ The Leadership Contingency Model

Fiedler has proposed a contingency model of leadership effectiveness that attempts to explain the fact that both autocratic and democratic leaders have been observed to be effective.[11] In Fiedler's model, leadership effectiveness is the result of an interaction between the style of the leader and the characteristics of the environment in which the leader works.

**Leader Style**    The style of the leader is assessed by use of the "Least Preferred Coworker" (LPC) concept. Leaders are first asked to think of the person they were *least* able to work with. The leaders are then asked to describe this person on a series of bipolar scales such as those shown below:

| | | |
|---|---|---|
| Unfriendly | $_____$ <br> 1 2 3 4 5 6 7 8 | Friendly |
| Uncooperative | $_____$ <br> 1 2 3 4 5 6 7 8 | Cooperative |
| Hostile | $_____$ <br> 1 2 3 4 5 6 7 8 | Supportive |
| Guarded | $_____$ <br> 1 2 3 4 5 6 7 8 | Open |

The responses to these scales (usually sixteen in total) are summed and averaged; a high LPC score suggests that the leader has a human relations orientation, while a low LPC score indicates a task orientation. Fiedler's logic is that individuals who rate their least preferred coworker in a relatively favorable light on these scales derive satisfaction out of interpersonal relations; those who rate the coworker in a relatively unfavorable light get satisfaction out of successful task performance.

**Environmental Variables**    Fiedler proposes that three environmental variables interact with leader style to determine leader effectiveness:

1. *Leader–member relations*—the extent to which the leader and subordinates are attracted to one another.
2. *Task structure*—the extent to which task requirements are clearly stated. Task structure can be measured by considering things such as clarity of goals, the degree to which goal attainment can be determined, the number of ways goals can be attained, and the number of goals to be attained.
3. *Leader position power*—the formal organizational authority held by the leader.

Each of these three variables is divided into "high" and "low" categories after they are measured. This division yields eight possible combinations of the three situational variables (see Figure 7-4). Fiedler originally argued that the various combinations of these three variables determined the *favorableness of the situation* for the leader. So, as indicated in Figure 7-4, when leader–member relations are good, task structure is high, and position power is high, the situation is favorable for the leader. As we move from octants 1 through 8, the situation becomes less and less favorable for the leader.

Recently, Fiedler has revised his interpretation of what the horizontal axis measures. He now says the various combinations of the three variables measure the *amount of control and influence* the leader has. Thus, when leader–member relations are good, task structure is high, and position power is high, the leader has high control and influence. As we move from octants 1 through 8, the leader's control and influence declines.

Once the leader and environmental characteristics have been measured, the impact of their interaction can be assessed through observations of leaders in actual situations. Figure 7-4 indicates how the situational and leader style variables interact to determine leadership effectiveness. On the basis of a great deal of

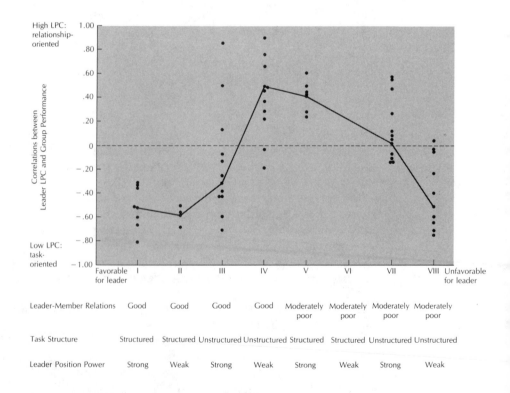

**FIGURE 7-4.  Fiedler's Leadership Contingency Model**

Source: F. Fiedler, *A Theory of Leadership Effectiveness* (New York: McGraw-Hill, 1967). Reprinted by permission.

empirical research in diverse leadership situations (e.g., basketball teams, industrial foremen, cooperative managers, etc.), Fiedler has concluded that in situations that are extremely favorable or extremely unfavorable (i.e., the leader has a great deal or very little control), a task-oriented leader functions best, while in situations intermediate in favorableness (i.e., the leader has an intermediate amount of control), a human-relations-oriented leader is most effective. Thus, in conditions I, II, III, and VIII, the directive leader functions best, while in conditions IV and V, the human-relations-oriented leader is most effective. (No evidence is available in octant VI and the evidence in octant VII is inconclusive.)

Fiedler gives examples to illustrate his theory. He maintains that it would be inappropriate for the captain of an airliner to ask for the opinions of his crew on how the plane should be landed, since the leader has power (by expertise as well as position), the task is well structured, and the captain has the informal backing of the crew. A situation characteristic of condition VIII might be a volunteer committee asked to plan the annual company picnic. The leader of this group, without position power and informal backing, and facing a relatively unstructured task, might "lose" the group unless a directive approach is taken to "get things moving." The human-relations-oriented leader would function best in condition IV, since the leader can use the resources of the group (knowledge about the task and their goodwill) to get the task accomplished. This situation might be characteristic of the newly appointed manager who is less familiar with the task than the subordinates.

One of the practical applications of Fiedler's theory is a training program using the basic ideas of the contingency model. LEADER MATCH is a programmed learning system that trains leaders to modify their leadership situation to fit their personality.[12] This contrasts with most training programs that try to change the leader's personality to fit the situation.

Leaders that are in training read a workbook that requires four to six hours to complete. The workbook includes an LPC scale, brief leadership situations that the trainee must analyze, feedback on how well the trainee did on the exercises, directions on how to measure the amount of situational control the leader has, ways to increase or decrease the amount of control the leader has, and guidance on how to help subordinates improve their performance.

The LEADER MATCH program has been used to train leaders in a wide variety of situations. Training programs have included police sergeants, middle managers, public health managers, navy personnel, military college students, and ROTC leaders.[13] In all of these studies the leaders trained with LEADER MATCH were rated more highly than untrained leaders (although in some cases the results were not statistically significant).

In one study the leadership effectiveness of 114 acting platoon leaders in summer training was assessed.[14] One third of the cadets were randomly assigned to the LEADER MATCH training, one third were simply told they would be evaluated as part of a study, and one third were told nothing. At the end of the summer, their superiors rated these acting platoon leaders (superiors did not know which leaders had been trained). The trained leaders received significantly higher performance ratings than either of the other two groups.

Fiedler argues that LEADER MATCH training works not only in situations where long-standing leader–subordinate relationships exist, but also in short-term leader situations. In a study of ROTC cadets serving in various leadership positions for only one day each, it was found that the performance of trained cadets was significantly higher than that of untrained cadets.[15] As further support for his argument, Fiedler notes that trained and untrained cadets did not differ on their scores for nonleadership items, which indicates that the leadership training positively affected specific leadership variables.

**Critique** Fiedler's contingency model has been widely accepted as an insightful model of leadership effectiveness. Recently, however, there has been growing criticism of a number of important features of the model. First, Graen and his colleagues argue that empirical studies conducted since the model was first proposed (evidential studies) fail to support the model with the force that earlier (antecedent) studies did.[16] Many of the evidential studies have been conducted by researchers other than Fiedler, whereas the antecedent studies were largely conducted by Fiedler.

Second, the meaning of some of the variables included in the model is not clear. For example, it is difficult to classify tasks as "structured" or "unstructured" in an absolute sense, since these are relative concepts. What this means in a practical sense is that a given task could be labeled "unstructured" in one study and "structured" in another study. This obviously introduces error into the measurement of this variable.

Third, use of the LPC score to differentiate task- and human-relations-oriented leaders may be an oversimplification of the concept.[17] In addition, the LPC score is a measure of the internal *attitudes* of the leader, and may not readily translate into task- or people-oriented *behavior*.

Fourth, there is an almost complete absence of studies assessing the effectiveness of "middle" LPC leaders (recall that Fiedler's research examined only high and low LPC leaders).[18] If we accept the argument that many leaders will be neither high nor low, but somewhere in the middle on LPC scores, this criticism is important. Fiedler has argued that middle LPC leaders are not concerned primarily with either the task or with human relations. In his view they will perform poorly in most leadership situations. Is this true? An alternative plausible view of middle LPC leaders is that they are not so rigid in their task orientation (as low LPC leaders are) or relationships orientation (as high LPC leaders are), and they therefore might make *better* leaders than either high or low LPC leaders. One study that tested this idea found that middle LPC leaders performed well in all leadership situations.[19] On average, middle LPCs performed significantly better than high LPCs and as well as low LPCs.

Fifth, Fiedler has been criticized for not using employee satisfaction as a criterion of leader effectiveness.[20] Instead, he focuses strictly on performance. While group performance is certainly important, focusing solely on it gives an incomplete picture of what leadership effectiveness is all about. To address this issue, one study examined the relationship between leader LPC and fifteen measures of subordinate satisfaction; the results showed that followers of high LPC leaders were more satisfied for ten of the measures while followers of low LPC leaders were more satisfied for five of the measures.[21] These mixed results suggested that there is no simple relationship between leader LPC and subordinate satisfaction; other variables are probably interacting with LPC to influence satisfaction.

When these possible interactions were analyzed, it was found that subordinate satisfaction was highest when the LPC scores of the leader and followers were different (e.g., high leader LPC–low follower LPC, and vice versa). When leader and follower LPC scores were similar, subordinate satisfaction was low. We can speculate that in groups where leader and follower LPC are different, both task and human relations functions are being performed (task by the low LPC leader and human relations by high LPC subordinates) and this increases satisfaction. This idea is very consistent with comments made in the preceding chapter on the need for *both* task and human relations functions in organizations.

Finally, and perhaps most damaging, critics claim that the structure of Fiedler's model is such that it is insensitive to disconfirming evidence, i.e., it is capable of incorporating almost any research finding into its framework. As Kelly has noted:

> The ultimate criticism of Fiedler is that he has revealed his genius twice; firstly, in devising the model, which stands like calculus to arithmetic compared to previous leadership models; and secondly, more dangerously, in his ability to integrate new findings into his model.[22]

From a practical standpoint, it might be erroneously concluded that Fiedler's model tells us that managers should be task-oriented more often than human-relations-oriented, since the model specifies task-oriented behavior in four of the six conditions. However, this ignores the possibility that, say, condition IV may represent a significant proportion of all managerial situations.

The Fiedler model serves essentially three useful purposes. First, it provides additional evidence that effective leadership is situational in nature, and this has important implications for leadership training. Second, it is a counterbalance to the human relations theories that dominated organizational behavior theory during the 1950s and 60s. Fiedler's finding that directive leaders are effective in various situations tends to place autocratic managers in a somewhat more favorable light. Finally, Fiedler's analysis has opened up additional possibilities for leadership effectiveness that were not previously considered. This aspect, designing the situation to fit the leader's style, will be discussed in greater detail in the applications section of this chapter.

In sum, despite the criticisms of Fiedler's model, it remains an important breakthrough in the study of leadership. One indication of the model's success is the amount of research effort expended in attempts to verify or refute it. Certainly Fiedler has a realistic view of leadership and, as such, his theory is a major contribution to knowledge in the leadership area.

## □  The Path–Goal Model

The two dimensions of leader behavior called Initiating Structure and Consideration continue to be viewed as important by leadership researchers. Because of the frequency with which these two behaviors appear to be associated with effective leadership, most agree today that they do play an important part in the leadership role. However, the effect that these two behaviors have on employees does not seem to be constant. As noted in Chapter 3, there is general agreement that leaders who initiate structure for their groups are rated higher by their superiors and tend to have higher-producing groups. However, the relationship between initiating structure and employee satisfaction is not clear-cut; in some circumstances initiating structure is positively related to subordinate satisfaction, while in other cases it is not.

Robert House has formulated a model of leadership that helps reconcile the conflicting findings just described.[23] House's proposal draws on expectancy theory (discussed in Chapter 3) and is called a "path–goal model" because it suggests that the leader's job is to increase the payoffs to workers for achieving work goals. The leader does this by clarifying the path to these goals, by reducing blockages that prevent workers from reaching the goals, and by behaving in a way that will increase worker satisfaction on the way to achieving the goals.

The path–goal model assumes that leader behaviors influence subordinate performance and satisfaction, but that subordinate and task characteristics moderate the effects of leader behavior (see Figure 7-5). If workers feel that they are quite capable of accomplishing a task without direction from the boss, directive leadership behavior will cause dissatisfaction. Likewise, if the task requirements are perfectly clear, directive leader behavior is not necessary.

The theory reconciles some of the conflicting research findings on the relationship between leader-initiated structure and employee satisfaction mentioned earlier. An underlying assumption is that higher-level jobs are more ambiguous

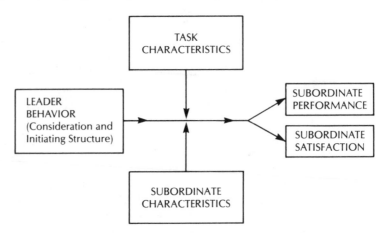

**FIGURE 7-5.   Key Variables in the Path–Goal Model**

than lower-level jobs (i.e., task characteristics and goal behavior are not as apparent to the person occupying the higher-level position). In high-level jobs, therefore, leader-initiated structure clarifies the behavior appropriate for work-goal attainment, thereby reducing the subordinate's uncertainty. Since the clarification is helpful to the high-level employee, the initiation of structure increases employee satisfaction. For routine, low-level jobs, on the other hand, initiating structure is not necessary and subordinates may interpret it as a lack of trust. Initiating structure in this instance may cause dissatisfaction.

With respect to Consideration, if a subordinate has a routine job, consideration may improve job satisfaction, perhaps because it makes the job more bearable. As well, a subordinate with a high need for affiliation would probably prefer the leader to be considerate. If a subordinate has a high need for achievement, however, he or she may prefer the leader to initiate structure because this will enhance task performance.

A number of research studies have tested these ideas in the path–goal model. In one study at a university medical school, it was found that when the leader initiated structure in routine tasks (e.g., janitorial work), subordinate satisfaction declined.[24] When structure was initiated in higher-level administrative jobs, no such effect was evident. This clearly supports the predictions of the path–goal model.

Another study examined path–goal predictions for variables other than task structure. White-collar employees of a manufacturing firm and tellers and loan department clerks in a bank were used to test the moderating influence of task variety, feedback, and the opportunity to work with others when performing tasks.[25] In the manufacturing firm, all three variables were significant, i.e., when the tasks had high variety, low feedback, and little opportunity for interaction, instrumental leader behavior increased subordinate satisfaction. In the bank, the same was true for variety and interaction with others, but not for feedback. This study also supports the basic ideas of the path–goal model, at least for employee satisfaction.

Unfortunately, not all studies are clearly supportive. In a sample of civil servants, project engineers, and military officers, researchers discovered that instrumental leader behavior increased subordinate satisfaction even when tasks were structured.[26] This does not support the theory. In another study of eighty-nine middle- and lower-level managers in a heavy equipment firm, considerate behavior on the part of the leader was associated with higher satisfaction for subordinates with either simple, structured jobs or with ambiguous jobs.[27] This finding supports the path–goal model, but these researchers also found that under conditions of high role ambiguity and job complexity, leader-initiated structure was not positively related to subordinate satisfaction. This is not supportive of the theory.

**Critique**  On the positive side, House's model is helpful because it deals with specific leader behaviors and how they might influence employee satisfaction and performance. The model is an improvement over the universalist models and even attempts to overcome some of the limitations of other contingency models. The path–goal model differs from others because it not only recognizes situational variables as being important, but also allows for individual differences.

On the negative side, the studies testing the model have yielded conflicting findings. Some studies support the model's predictions for employee job satisfaction but not for employee performance; others show that leader consideration is positively related to employee satisfaction (as predicted by the theory), but that initiating structure may also be positively related to employee satisfaction even when tasks are structured (the opposite of that predicted by the theory).

Overall, the empirical evidence to date suggests that the theory (like many others) gives helpful insights into employee *satisfaction,* but has problems predicting employee *performance.* This shortcoming cannot be ignored since it is one of the primary concerns of practicing managers. In the previous chapter we suggested that subordinate performance may cause changes in leader behavior instead of the other way around, as predicted by the theory.[28] These and other

## Box 7-2: What Is the "Truth" About Leadership Effectiveness?

It is evident from the material presented in Chapters 4 and 5 that much time and effort has gone into leadership research. The assumption underlying this research is that the truth about leadership effectiveness will be discovered if we search long enough. Is this a reasonable assumption? The answer to this question depends on which view of "truth" we have.

One view is that truth is unchanging. This view prevails in the physical sciences. For example, the structure of the universe is assumed to be set and research scientists conduct experiments and develop theories in order to determine what that structure is. This "unchanging truth" assumption means that time is not a constraint in research. When scientists arrive at the truth it will still exist because it is unchanging.

The other view is that truth changes over time. This view is likely to be accurate where people are concerned. Perhaps the most obvious example of "changing truth" concerns leadership styles. One hundred years ago the autocratic style was probably practiced with much greater effectiveness than it is today. Why? Because the people subject to leadership in the twentieth century seem to be increasingly motivated by a participative style.

The implication of the "changing truth" assumption is somewhat discouraging. It means that academics and managers will have to modify their theory and practice to adjust to changes in the "truth" about people. It will therefore not be possible to develop the "right" theory and then simply apply it for all time. Changes will have to be made continually as truth changes.

uncertainties about the theory will probably be reduced by additional research, but emphasis needs to be placed on employee performance.

## ☐ Summary of Contingency Proposals

Contingency approaches to leadership effectiveness have been developed to consider environmental variables in leadership situations. The rationale for these proposals is that effective leadership is not an absolute, but rather depends on a number of variables, both human and environmental, that are interacting in every leadership situation. Much of the effort of contingency theorists has been directed at measuring and defining the variables believed to be important. The theories have made significant advances in recent years, but much remains to be done before a complete understanding of leadership is possible.

# ■ SUMMARY AND CONCLUSIONS OF LEADERSHIP THEORIES

At this point you may be slightly confused and perplexed about the current "state of the art" of leadership. This is not surprising in view of the large number of leadership theories and the lack of strong conclusions regarding any particular one. In this section we will try to summarize, interpret, and speculate on the subject of leadership. We hope this will bring the material into perspective and will also provide some background for our discussion in the next section on the application of leadership theories. As a summary effort, Figures 7-6 and 7-7 contain brief explanations of each leadership theory with respect to (1) its substance, (2) the assumptions made about leaders and subordinates, and (3) the impact of environmental variables.

## ☐ Conclusions About Leadership

Despite the conflicting evidence and uncertainty surrounding many of the theories, there are some conclusions that can be drawn which should be helpful in understanding leadership:

1. Understanding the leadership process has increased dramatically during the past four decades, with relatively simplified views of leadership effectiveness having been replaced with more realistic proposals. However, no single proposal yet seems sufficient to account for the success of different leadership styles in different situations. It is hoped that each new proposal is a closer approximation than its predecessors of a more complete understanding of leadership.

2. Numerous leadership studies indicate that there are two important dimensions of leader behavior that consistently appear: concern for people and concern for the task. This has led some people to build theories totally around these two behaviors, which, in the light of more recent evidence, seems to be unrealistic. Nevertheless, these two behaviors are important factors in leadership success.

| Comparison Features | Universalist Approaches to Leadership | | | | |
|---|---|---|---|---|---|
| | *Great Man Theory* | *Trait Theory* | *Leader Behavior* | *Theory X and Theory Y* | *System 4 Management* |
| 1. Substance of the approach | Certain men and women of outstanding character or ability become leaders and have a profound impact on history. These outstanding people may be found in certain families with unusual frequency. | Effective leaders possess certain personality traits necessary for success. Traits commonly cited include initiative, self-confidence, intelligence, dependability, and sociability. Trait theory is a refinement of the "great man" theory. | Two effective leader behaviors are initiating structure (IS) and consideration (C). The former generally results in higher performance, while the latter generally results in higher employee morale. | The traditional (Theory X) assumptions which management makes about employees (they are lazy and prefer to avoid work) are unrealistic; these should be replaced with a new set of assumptions (Theory Y) which presume that employees wish to have a meaningful job and desire to contribute to organizational objectives. | Effective leaders have complete trust in the ability of subordinates and decentralize authority throughout the organization. |
| 2. Assumption(s) about qualities of the leader | The qualities of the leader are the crucial determinant of leader success. These great men and women can be identified only after they have demonstrated their capability. | Individual qualities (traits) are of overriding importance in determining success of the leader. The individual possessing the necessary traits will be successful. | The individual leader influences the environment by his specific behavior. Leader behavior is the main determinant of effectiveness. | Leaders fall into one of two general classes; those who treat subordinates in a Theory X fashion and those who treat subordinates in a Theory Y fashion. | The leader is committed to effective management of the human component. The leader makes the assumption that the participative approach is always best. |
| 3. Assumption(s) about subordinates | Subordinates will enthusiastically follow the leader because of his/her ability to reach goals or because of the leader's ability to control and motivate subordinates. | Subordinates will perform if led by an individual with appropriate traits. | Subordinates have a preference for considerate behavior on the part of the leader, although they will respond to some extent to pressure for production. | Subordinates resist organizational demands only because they have been treated poorly in the past. Subordinates have great capacity for assuming responsibility and directing their behavior toward the achievement of organizational goals. Man is neither "bad" nor "good" but reacts to how he is treated. | Subordinates have needs beyond pay. They have a desire to make a positive contribution to the organization and to have a stake in organizational outcomes. |
| 4. Assumed impact of the environment on the leadership process. | Low; the leader acts on the environment and/or uses it to his/her advantage. | Low; the leader acts on the environment and/or uses it to his/her advantage. | Low; leadership effectiveness is achieved by leader emphasis on IS and C without concern for environmental variation. | Low; Theory Y leadership is more desirable than Theory X leadership regardless of the characteristics of the environment. | Low; participative leadership behavior is assumed superior to other leadership styles in all environments. |

**FIGURE 7-6.    A Summary and Comparison of the Universalist Theories**

| Comparison Features | Contingency Approaches to Leadership | | | |
|---|---|---|---|---|
| | Situational Leadership Model | Leadership Decision-Making Model | Leadership Contingency Model | Path–Goal Model |
| 1. Substance of the approach | Different leadership styles and behavior can be effective, depending on the maturity levels of subordinates. Immature subordinates require considerable task direction, while mature subordinates require little supervision. | Different leadership styles are appropriate in different situations. The most appropriate style is determined by considering key factors (for example, the importance of subordinate acceptance of the decision) before making the decision. | One style is not always best. The effectiveness of a leader is determined by the interaction of environmental and personality variables. | Effective leaders are those who increase employee motivation by clarifying for subordinates the paths to effective performance as well as the connection between performance and rewards. |
| 2. Assumption(s) about qualities of the leader | Leaders can exhibit behaviors that are high or low on task orientation and relationship orientation. Leaders are able to change style as the maturity of subordinates changes. | Leaders are able to determine which key factors are important and which are not. They are also able to use different styles based on their analysis of the key variables. | Leaders are basically autocratic or democratic. The job should be engineered to fit the particular style of the leader. It is difficult to change the style of a leader. | The leader has the interest and ability to increase the effectiveness of his area of responsibility by improving the motivation of his subordinates. |
| 3. Assumption(s) about subordinates | Subordinate preferences for a leadership style change as their maturity on the job changes. Immature subordinates prefer a task orientation on the part of the leader, while more mature subordinates prefer a relationships orientation. | Subordinates want to be involved in decision making in some circumstances but do not want to be involved in others. | Subordinates prefer different leadership styles depending on how task structure, leader-member relations, and position power are interrelated. | Certain things (particularly organizational level) influence both the type of supervision that subordinates desire as well as the leader behaviors which are feasible. Differences between subordinates' needs are assumed. |
| 4. Assumed impact of the environment on the leadership process | Moderate; the only environmental variable is employee maturity levels. | High; factors such as the quality requirement of the decision, information available on the problem, etc., all govern the leadership decision-making style which is most appropriate. | High; the type of leader behavior which is most effective depends on the interaction of environmental and leadership style variables. | Moderate; at present stage, model includes only one environmental variable—leader activities. |

**FIGURE 7-7 A Summary and Comparison of Contingency Leadership Theories**

3. The recognition that situational variables are important implies that contingency theories must be used if understanding and prediction of leadership success is to be achieved. However, it should also be noted that this does not automatically invalidate the universalist approaches. Thus, for example, it is likely that certain traits *are* important for leadership success in certain situations.

4. Leadership theories, like theories of motivation, are moving from the simple to the complex. As we have every reason to expect this trend to continue, we can anticipate even more complex models in the future. This will be viewed with mixed emotions by managers and researchers. On the one hand, it is likely that we are approaching a greater understanding of a very complex process; this feeling, however, will be tempered by the realization that while contingency

theories may be more realistic, they become so at the expense of simplicity. This dilemma is highlighted by the practicing manager who feels a need for simple, easy-to-implement solutions. This "ease of use" dimension should not be underestimated. Some of the universalist proposals that have gained the widest acceptance in management circles seem to be popular not because they are theoretically sound or empirically justified, but because they can be simply stated, neatly presented, and easily put into effect. So, on the one hand, we have the researchers who are developing more complex leadership models, and on the other we have practicing managers who are looking for workable and easily adopted solutions. Both are correct in their own way, but we still must face the fact that the two groups may be moving in opposite directions.

5. Contingency theories are not without problems. An obvious one is the number of situational variables that must be included in a model. It is difficult to determine when one has included enough situational variables. Even assuming that the variables can be specified, the problem of weighting them remains. Is task structure more important than position power? Is technology more important than pay? And so forth. As an interesting aside, note that if contingency theories are carried to their logical extreme, we will have a model of leadership effectiveness for each manager in each situation.

# ■ APPLICATIONS

Research is most useful when it helps us improve our managerial practices. We must now face the question, "How does the wealth of leadership research presented in Chapters 6 and 7 help us improve the practice of management?" While several clues have been presented, these need to be clearly translated into some practical suggestions for the "real world."

There are two basic schools of thought on how to apply leadership knowledge. The first (and most common) assumes that increasing the competence of leaders (through leadership training) will improve their effectiveness by changing their behavior. The other approach assumes that since changing behavior is very difficult, the job should be changed to fit the leader's style and capabilities. Each of these approaches is examined below and the implications for applying leadership knowledge are noted. This section concludes with the presentation of a number of typical leadership situations; suggestions are made (based on leadership research findings) as to the most effective leadership behavior. When reading this section, keep in mind the cautions discussed in Chapter 1 regarding the application of theory. While we will not prescribe leadership behaviors, we will discuss some important considerations that, because of research findings, managers should keep in mind in their day-to-day activities.

## ☐ Leadership Training

One thing is clear from the discussion so far: no single leader behavior is invariably superior to all others. This does not automatically mean that individuals cannot be effective in every situation they encounter, but rather that they must exhibit different behaviors in order to be effective. Whether or not a given individual is capable of exhibiting these different behaviors is therefore an important determinant of leadership success. Some "natural leaders" appear able to adopt an "appropriate" leadership role regardless of the situation, i.e., they have the ability to assess each situation they encounter and act appropriately. More typically, leaders experience some difficulty in adapting to the leadership role in different situations.

Many organizations have concluded that leadership training will improve managers' abilities to demonstrate sound leadership behavior; as a result much time, effort, and money has been expended in the development of leadership-training programs. Although the training methods vary, the purpose is the same: to develop more effective leaders.[29] Some of the factors that should be considered in developing leadership talent are as follows:

**Individual Commitment**   Since training is designed to change the individual's attitudes or behavior, a primary requirement is that the individual *desires* to change. Many managers who attend leadership training courses are satisfied with their present performance and leadership style. Thus, their interest in new approaches to leadership is quite low, as is that of managers whose performance is not up to par. While this is not to say that no changes will occur, attempts at change will meet with more success if some commitment to change is evident in the individual being trained.

**Organizational Climate**   One commonly overlooked factor influencing the success of leadership training is organizational climate (the "atmosphere" of the workplace). It is not unusual for training programs to cause changes in both attitudes and behavior in individuals while they are in the training program; however, these behaviors can be "unlearned" when individuals return to their regular organizational environment, because this environment contains expectations from others—colleagues, subordinates, and superiors—who have not been trained and whose expectations have not changed. Trainees may find that their newly acquired behaviors are inconsistent with the expectations of the untrained personnel with whom they interact.

One study showed that leadership training produced considerable role conflict on the job for the trainees since their subordinates had become accustomed to their previous leadership styles; in addition, the trainees' superiors did not support their new behaviors.[30] Not surprisingly, follow-up studies indicated that most trainees had reverted to their original behavior. Another study showed that the behavior acquired in a leadership training program created so much role conflict for the trainees that within one year after the course, almost 20 percent of them had left their company and a further 25 percent had applied for other jobs.[31]

R. J. House maintains that many attempts at leadership training are ineffective because organizations ignore the structural and social influences that affect behavior on the job.[32] With a viewpoint reminiscent of reinforcement theory discussed in Chapter 4, he maintains that effective change in leadership behavior is a function of the degree to which these influences are perceived as motivators

## Box 7-3: Does Training Improve Leadership Effectiveness?

Leadership training in the form of role playing, seminars, and university degree programs is very popular. What hard evidence is there that this training results in more effective leaders? Fiedler argues that, on balance, it is discouraging. One study compared leadership effectiveness for Belgian military groups led by trained petty officers and by untrained recruits and found that the groups led by the recruits performed as well as those led by the petty officers. Another study at a Canadian military college found the same pattern. In that study, groups led by untrained enlisted men performed as well as those led by captains and majors.

A study of managers in the U.S. Post Office yielded similar results. The performance of postal supervisors was assessed by their superiors and the amount of training these supervisors had received was then compared with their performance ratings. It was found that these two measures were unrelated. The same findings were evident in a study of police sergeants.

These findings are not unusual. After a survey of scores of companies, one researcher concluded that there was little hard evidence that management training had improved management performance.

Source: F. Fiedler, "How Do You Make Leaders More Effective: New Answers to an Old Puzzle," *Organizational Dynamics* (Autumn 1972): 3–18.

by the individual and the degree to which the learned behavior is reinforced on the job.

**Degree of Change Required**    Another factor often overlooked in leadership training is the extent of behavioral change required. Since behavior is a product of many variables interacting over extended periods of time, attempting to induce major changes in behavior over relatively short periods of time may be ineffective. This has implications for both managers and subordinates. From the manager's point of view, it is unrealistic to expect major changes in subordinates' behavior in the short run. If this point is kept in mind, it can reduce the dissatisfaction with training programs that managers and subordinates may feel.

This note of caution is particularly important when universalist theories are applied. For example, subordinates who have consistently been treated in a Theory X fashion will probably learn to react accordingly and exhibit the behavior patterns McGregor predicts. If their manager suddenly adopts a Theory Y philosophy, he or she will more than likely be disappointed in subordinates' short-term reactions. Not being conditioned to expect such treatment, it will probably be perceived as a "soft" approach to management and subordinates may take advantage of the situation. The manager will then erroneously conclude that "Theory Y doesn't work," and revert to the Theory X leadership style.

**What Can Be Taught?**    One of the most significant questions in leadership training is what can actually be taught, either in training courses or on-the-job development. This is an important limiting factor in certain leadership proposals. The limitations of the trait approach are obvious since, by definition, traits cannot be taught. This leaves us with the alternatives of teaching either specific leader behaviors, or of teaching diagnostic skills so that leaders can determine what kind of situation they are facing.

One of the drawbacks of teaching specific leader behaviors (aside from whether or not these behaviors are appropriate) is that the connection between attitude change and behavioral change is often very weak. It is not uncommon for researchers to report that, after being exposed to a leadership training program, participants improved significantly on various attitude scales as measured by questionnaires. However, this is different from stating that participants improved their actual leadership behavior as a result of the program. While behavioral change may be easier to effect if attitudes are positive, there is no reason to believe that they automatically go together. Attitude scales measure only the respondents' ability to answer questions about normative leadership behavior, not how they will actually behave as leaders. In short, whether or not behavioral change can be taught, at least in the short run, is questionable.

The teaching of diagnostic skills seems more realistic than teaching specific behaviors, since emphasis is on the conceptual, rather than the behavioral, level. The difference is similar to the distinction between teaching baseball skills (i.e., how to be a better ballplayer) and how to manage a baseball team. While we may be unable to improve a given individual's prowess at playing baseball (since there are limiting factors beyond our control), we can nevertheless teach someone about baseball so that he can make better decisions in managing a team. The type of teaching in the two situations is clearly different.

The situation is similar for leadership. While we may not be able to improve managers' leadership behavior consistently, we can teach them the diagnostic skills that will allow them to analyze which type of behavior is required in a given situation. Whether or not the person has the specific behavioral skills required to then behave in the appropriate manner is another question. While some would argue that arming an individual with the tools to diagnose but not with the skills with which to implement is a useless exercise, we believe otherwise. First, by analyzing the situation and determining what is required, it is possible for leaders to select another individual whose style fits the situation if theirs does not. Second, leaders are less likely to make the mistake of attempting an oversimplified solution in the light of their knowledge about the situation. (It is better to have a doctor who is a good diagnostician but who has a poor bedside manner, than it is to have a doctor who is a poor diagnostician with a good bedside manner.)

In sum, leadership training must be viewed realistically. While behavioral change is possible, it is likely only if (1) the individual is committed to change, (2) the environment is supportive, (3) the degree of change expected is reasonable, and (4) feasible changes are taught. By expecting too much in too short a time, organizations can nullify positive attitudes that have been developed in training programs. The development of leadership talent is not something to be franchised out at specified times during the year, but ideally is an ongoing process that occurs on the job as well as in specific training programs. Leadership training programs will often induce positive attitudes toward certain types of leadership styles or situations, but the organization has the responsibility of making the transition from attitudes to behavior.

## ☐   Changing the Job Instead of the Leader

The theme of the above discussion was that behavior is difficult to change and that managers and subordinates should not expect large changes over relatively short periods of time. Realizing these difficulties, Fiedler has argued that instead of attempting to induce behavioral changes in the leader, a better strategy is to adapt the situation to take advantage of the leader's present style.[33] Since two of the variables defining the leadership situation—task structure and leader position power—are structural elements rather than behavioral ones, this seems like sound advice.

Fiedler maintains that normal training and experience generally serve to make the situation more favorable for the leader, whereas lack of these same elements generally results in an unfavorable situation. Most training programs attempt to teach managers to behave in a specific fashion, even though the Contingency Model of Leadership Effectiveness indicates that task-oriented leaders function best in favorable and unfavorable situations and human-relations-oriented leaders function best in situations intermediate in favorableness. Therefore, a training program that enhances the human-relations skills of relationship-oriented managers who face an unfavorable situation may make them less effective than before. Similarly, increasing the human-relations orientation of directive leaders facing an unfavorable situation will, according to Fiedler, reduce their effectiveness. Given these problems, Fiedler makes the following observation:

> The luxury of picking "a natural leader" from among a number of equally qualified specialists is rapidly fading into the past. Business must learn how to utilize the available executive talent as effectively as it now utilizes physical plant and machine tools. Your financial expert, your top research scientist, or your production genius may be practically irreplaceable. Their jobs call for leadership and responsibility. Replacements for these men can be neither recruited nor trained overnight and they may not be willing to play second fiddle in their departments. If their leadership style does not fit the job, we must learn how to engineer the job to fit their leadership style.[34]

Critics of Fiedler's approach might argue that proper diagnosis of the situation and an accurate assessment of his or her own leadership style will allow a manager to make style changes to fit the situation. For example, a leader might see that a directive, autocratic style is inappropriate in a situation in which the task is relatively undefined, and therefore change his or her style to a more participative one. While this approach seems promising at first glance, it should be recalled that large changes in behavior are difficult for most people. Another possibility would be for the leader to structure the task more clearly by clarifying objectives, formulating measurement criteria for successful task accomplishment, or prescribing the means by which goals are to be accomplished. However, even though these variables may be within a manager's control, the ability to manipulate them is usually restricted. Similarly, it is unlikely that a leader could make drastic changes in position power over a short period of time.

## Box 7-4: Are Experienced Leaders More Effective Than Inexperienced Leaders?

Does supervisory experience improve leadership performance? There are very few studies which bear directly on this question, yet the belief is widely held that experienced leaders are more effective than inexperienced ones. Fiedler argues that this belief can be seen easily in companies where managers must spend a certain amount of time in a certain job before they can be promoted.

Data relevant to this question were generated from various groups such as directors of research and development teams, foremen of craft shops and heavy machinery shops, managers of meat and grocery markets, post office supervisors, and police sergeants. Experience was correlated with performance ratings and none of the correlations were significant in the positive direction, i.e., none of the sample correlations showed that the more experienced, the more effective a leader was. In fact, the median correlation between leadership experience and performance was —.12.

Source: F. E. Fiedler, "How Do You Make Leaders More Effective? New Answers to an Old Puzzle," *Organizational Dynamics* (Autumn 1973): 3–18.

In Fiedler's view, a more realistic alternative is to allow for the nonadaptive behavior of people and attempt to find a situation in which the present style of the manager is appropriate. This tends to be the least disruptive in terms of behavioral change and is limited only by the fact that situations are not static.

On the basis of his theory, Fiedler suggests several ways in which leadership training, selection, and effectiveness can be increased:

1. Development of a careful program of managerial rotation that moves some individuals from one job to another at a faster rate than it moves others. This allows for individual differences in managerial styles.

2. Management training programs that emphasize the type of training that individuals need. Again, training a task-oriented manager who faces a favorable situation to be relationship-oriented will be ineffective.

3. Management training programs that are devoted to teaching participants how to modify their environment and their own jobs so that they fit their style of leadership.

4. Management training programs that provide the participants with a wide variety of leadership situations so they can experiment with different types of leader behaviors.[35]

**Summary**    There is a very fundamental difference of opinion between the proponents of leadership training and those who question its usefulness. The former argue that training will change managerial behavior and make it more effective, while the latter usually argue that because people are resistant to behavioral change, changing the job instead of the leader is a better way to improve leadership effectiveness. Those who hold the latter view are clearly in the minority. Speaking realistically, it is almost certain that organizations in the public and private sector will continue to accept the view that training is useful. Even Fiedler has developed a training program (LEADER MATCH), although it is designed for use with "changing the job instead of the leader" assumptions. The most important point in this debate is usually missed: Until training programs are more systematically and rigorously assessed, the proponents of each side will be able to marshall data to support their particular view.

## ☐   Some Sample Situations

To the extent that research on leadership allows, we will present some frequently encountered leadership situations to illustrate the types of leadership behavior that might be appropriate. The situations discussed and the conclusions drawn are based upon both universalist and contingency theories of leadership. The reader should recognize that the situations described in this section contain many assumptions, both explicit and implicit. Each of these assumptions should be kept in mind as conclusions are presented.

**Crisis Situations**    Most people generally accept the argument that autocratic leadership is appropriate in crisis situations. By definition, in a crisis there is no time for consultation with subordinates, nor is morale a crucial consideration. Goals tend to be reduced to one—or at least very few—such that performance is of paramount importance and feedback is immediate and concrete. This creates a highly structured situation, allowing the leader a more favorable environment in which to make decisions. (It is assumed that the leader is knowledgeable regarding solutions to the crisis; if not, the leader usually exercises authority by appointing someone who is knowledgeable.) A common example of autocratic leadership is in wartime operations of military organizations. The commanding officer often faces situations in which quick, decisive actions are necessary and subordinates expect directive leadership.

It is not difficult to find other contexts where autocratic leadership is appropriate. For example, when universities face budgetary crises, the previously collegial atmosphere tends to become more autocratic. Obviously, the key to successful use of this style depends upon a consensus that a crisis actually exists.

## Box 7-5: How Do You Measure Leadership Effectiveness?

As we have seen in this chapter, there is much concern for improving leadership performance. Not only have organizations spent millions of dollars on leadership training, but academics have researched the topic for many years. With all of this effort it would seem reasonable to assume that the term "leadership effectiveness" would be well defined. This is true only some of the time.

For some jobs, measuring leadership effectiveness is easy. The managers of professional sports teams, for example, are not paid on the basis of how satisfied their players are, or on how much "character" they build; they are paid on the basis of how many games the team wins. In these and similar cases, leadership effectiveness is clear. However, defining effectiveness for many managerial jobs is not nearly as easy. How do we clearly judge the effectiveness of a university president? Of a vice president of research and development? Of the secretary of Health and Human Services? Performance appraisal of management jobs like these is often a highly political process because precise objective measures of performance do not exist. Instead, we rely on assessments by superiors, peers, or subordinates. Of course these people may not be objective in their assessments, and this distorts reality either in favor of, or against, the manager being assessed. This in turn confounds the measurement of the relationship of leader experience, training, and "effectiveness."

**Situations in Which the Leader Has No Formal Authority**    In most formal organizations, leaders have been delegated authority that gives them certain rights (e.g., the right to reward and punish subordinates). However, certain situations may be encountered in which the leader has no formal authority and must rely on other factors to influence behavior. An example is a group of interested parents who have come together to discuss issues of importance in the local school district. In this situation the leader must generally adopt a more permissive, democratic style of leadership, since a directive style may offend some group members. This statement is based upon certain assumptions about the situation. It could be argued that in the absence of a formal leader, the group may disintegrate for lack of strong direction. Or, if we merely assume that the individuals composing the group need autocratic leadership, then we clearly negate the earlier conclusion that a democratic leadership style would be best. Generally speaking, however, the lack of formal authority increases the likelihood that democratic or participative leadership will be appropriate.

**Situations Requiring Technical Expertise**    There are situations in which the expertise of a particular individual is needed, thus allowing that person to exert unusual influence upon group members. The person could be either the appointed leader or someone in the group who has no formal position. In any event, the demands of the situation allow the individual with the necessary knowledge to influence the behavior of others (see Chapter 10 and the discussion of social power). In these instances an autocratic style can be utilized effectively, since it is clear that participation by those who are not qualified is inappropriate. Participation under these circumstances will probably result in frustration and dissatisfaction for group members, since they expect the leader to be directive because he or she is the only one who knows what to do.

In a manufacturing organization, a foreman may be the only person who knows how to fix a particular machine; or an engineer may be the only person with knowledge of how to correct a manufacturing defect. The crucial point is that the group must perceive that the leader has the necessary expertise. Only if this is true can the leader be directive. If this is not true, regardless of the leader's technical qualifications, the group may resist and/or resent any influence attempts.

**Professional or Collegial Situations**    Professional relationships, such as those existing between engineers, scientists, medical personnel, professors, etc., generally require participative leader behavior. The primary reason is that the tasks facing these groups tend to be relatively unstructured and require the input of more

---

## *Organizational Reality   7-3*
## *The Technical Manager*

Technical managers are usually the people who received top grades in math and science courses, finished their tests before anyone else, and easily solved problems. But once in actual management positions, those same problem solvers have to deal with *people*, whose problems are not always as easy to solve. To a technical person whose self-image rests upon being a problem solver, difficult human relations conflicts can be disturbing because they attack his self-worth. Jim Kutsko, manager of employee relations at Cobe Laboratories Inc., in Lakewood, Colorado, says many technical managers don't manage people well, because if they can't fix a problem, they deny it exists.

Kutsko lists three qualities he looks for when hiring a good technical manager. First, a strong technical background is needed to direct the work of subordinates, but a person whose technical abilities are not as strong as other technicians likely has a better chance to succeed as a manager. This is because the person's self-image is not as strongly tied to problem-solving ability. Second, it's important to have technical managers who have been in a situation where they haven't been able to solve a problem. This way, they won't encounter as much trauma when they come up against a "people" problem. Finally, employers should look for someone who can tolerate ambiguity—one who attempts to solve a problem, but isn't obsessed with a solution.

---

Source: "Developing Technical Managers," *Personnel Journal* (October 1982): 729–30.

than a single individual. But this is not the only reason. Many other groups face unstructured tasks, but because of the nature of the subordinates, the tasks are structured for them; but in professional situations, the individuals are qualified to contribute to the solution of the problem. Their training and experience, while allowing them the background necessary to participate, also makes them realize that there is no one best way to solve the problems they face. The leader must therefore attempt to maximize professional creativity and this is best done through a collaborative, consultative leadership style. Common examples of this are medical research teams, architectural groups designing a new building, or public health teams attempting to improve the quality of life of the disadvantaged. In all of these cases, leadership must take into account the knowledge possessed by various individuals; the importance of formal positions is therefore reduced.

## Box 7-6: *Functional Analysis in Leadership Research*

Many different approaches to the study of leadership have developed during the twentieth century. It is the opinion of two researchers that, in spite of this, the problem of operationalizing leadership has not been solved. One problem is that leadership research has relied too heavily on questionnaires and not enough on leader behavior. Another problem is evident when leadership is defined. Most definitions of leadership stress the importance of "influence." Although the exercise of influence is obviously part of leadership, there are many other elements in the leadership process.

These difficulties do not mean that leadership cannot be usefully studied. What it does mean is that emphasis must be placed on analyzing the relationship between observable behavior and its antecedents and consequences. Less emphasis should be placed on subjective opinion and perception and more on observable events. What is necessary, therefore, is a functional analysis of leadership behaviors.

Source: T. Davis and F. Luthans, "Leadership Reexamined: A Behavioral Approach," *Academy of Management Review* 4 (April 1979): 237–48.

**Routine Task Situations** Participative leadership styles are not particularly effective in situations involving routine tasks. Participation assumes some degree of uncertainty in a situation so that the ideas of group members will contribute to the solution of a problem. However, if there is little uncertainty, then participation tends to be a waste of time. Perhaps the major difficulty here lies in the definition of "routine." We must ask, "routine according to whom?" While a task may appear routine to the leader, it may not appear so to the subordinate. Everything else being equal, if output is the criterion of effectiveness, a more directive style is more effective; however, if morale is the criterion, then a more participative approach is most appropriate.

**Unique Task Situations**   In the course of regular work activities, a work group may encounter a situation unique to them. Depending upon a variety of factors, the leader may wish to change from a directive to a more participative leadership style under these circumstances. The underlying idea here is that group members, through their experiences and knowledge, may be able to contribute to the solution. This, therefore, requires the use of a more participative style. Again, it should be remembered that what is "unique" to a particular group is a relative matter.

It is important to stress once more the point that the comments above are only general conclusions about leadership situations. Since we have concluded that contingency theories of leadership are more likely to be accurate than universalist theories, it follows that sweeping statements about the effectiveness of a given leadership style simply cannot be made. Instead, the leader must analyze the key variables in his or her specific situation before making a decision about which leadership style to adopt.

An indication of how this can be done is presented below in "Carolyn Barnes Revisited." The predictions of each leadership theory are considered by using relevant facts from the opening case; in addition, the predictive consistency of the theories is assessed. You are urged to do the same kind of analysis for exercises 7-1 and 7-2 at the end of this chapter. Once you become comfortable with this kind of analysis, it can be used in any leadership situation that you might encounter.

---

### *Organizational Reality   7-4*
### *Apple Computer, Inc.*

Apple Computer Incorporated, which nearly tripled its sales in 1981 to $335 million, has been growing at a breakneck speed, and faces competition from rivals up to a hundred times its size. The temperamental but never dull Steve Jobs, who started Apple in 1977 in a garage with a friend, Steven Wozniak, has encouraged a creative risk-taking spirit at Apple, where the average age of employees is twenty-eight.

Recently in a major management shake-up, a top-level team of vice-presidents took over the running of the company from Michael M. Scott, who was demoted after he fired forty Apple employees. Scott's management style had been described as "decisive but also authoritarian and insensitive." His demotion (he later resigned) was a clear signal.

Because of Apple's immaturity, however, industry observers continue to be more worried about its management abilities than about the competition it faces. Its style is certainly unusual. Says one executive, "There seems to be so little control and so much chaos that I can't believe the company isn't flying off into space in a thousand pieces. On the other hand, it does seem to keep pulling off its plans." A more seasoned manager in the semiconductor industry calls it "Camp Run Amok."

---

Source: *Business Week* (8 February 1982): 66–71.

## *Opening Incident Revisited—Carolyn Barnes*

You will recall that in the opening incident Carolyn Barnes was concerned about whether her leadership style was appropriate for the situation she faced. What do the leadership theories discussed in this chapter tell us?

The situational leadership theory says that subordinate maturity levels are the key to determining effective leader behavior. Ten members of the choir are mature (i.e., they know what to do technically) while thirty-five are in various stages of immaturity. The theory suggests that different styles are appropriate for these two groups. Unfortunately, it is not feasible for Barnes to treat the high and low maturity people differently because the choir must perform as a group. Perhaps the maturity level of the inexperienced members will improve as time passes and they become technically more capable. Barnes can then use a more participative style. For the moment, however, the theory suggests than an autocratic style is most appropriate.

Vroom and Yetton's Decision Making Model requires managers to answer some very specific suggestions before deciding which style to use. If we look at Figure 7-3 and ask the questions shown there, we observe the following: There is a quality requirement (A), the leader has sufficient information to make a quality decision (B), the problem is structured (C), and acceptance by subordinates is not critical to effective implementation because the majority of them are not technically capable (D). Answers to questions E and F are Yes. Given this information, the decision-making model argues that any of the five leadership styles is feasible. (This is because some of the critical questions are answered "Yes" and some are answered "No.") Which style Barnes decides to use depends on time constraints and her views of developing choir members.

If we use Fiedler's Contingency Model to analyze Barnes' situation, we see the following: Leader–member relations are good, task structure is high (music is very structured), and leader position power is low (the choir members are volunteers). Given this combination, an autocratic style is most appropriate (see Figure 7-4, octant II).

The Path–Goal model says that the leader should help subordinates get to their goals. It seems reasonable to assume that the choir members have good performance as one of their goals. Given this, and given the fact that nonprofessional singers would probably welcome guidance from a professional, Barnes should probably adopt an autocratic style. Presumably, the professional members of the choir will be less satisfied with this style (because they know what to do), but as noted above, the trained and untrained members cannot be treated differently because of the nature of the task.

On balance, the analysis of the situation using these four contingency leadership theories suggests that Barnes continue with her present directive style. The absenteeism may simply be an effect of the volunteer nature of the choir, while the talking problem may be the result of the interest and enthusiasm of the members. In neither of these cases is leadership style causing problems.

# ■ SUMMARY

The material presented in the last two chapters indicates that leadership is a complex phenomenon. Despite the wealth of research available, it remains so complex that we do not yet fully understand all its facets. Still, the human mind is such that we need to organize the available evidence into a framework that facilitates discussion and understanding. We have done this by placing the mass of leadership research into a universalist–contingency framework and then discussing the essence of each theory. This framework allows the reader to observe the variety of approaches to leadership that have developed; it also gives a realistic view of our current understanding of leadership. Since much frustration and disappointment has resulted from unrealistic expectations associated with leadership research in general and leadership training in particular, we feel it is important to create realistic expectations. In an attempt to keep confusion at a minimum, we have condensed some of the theories into a few situational descriptions, with our own interpretations of appropriate leadership styles. As research continues on this important topic, the current uncertainties will surely be reduced.

# ■ REVIEW QUESTIONS

1. What is the key variable affecting leadership effectiveness in the Situational Leadership Theory? How does it affect leader behavior?

2. What are some of the problems with the Situational Leadership Theory?

3. What factors are important in leadership effectiveness in the Leadership Decision-Making Model?

4. Why is the "quality requirement" important when a leader is trying to decide whether to use an autocratic or democratic style?

5. What are the three environmental variables in the Fiedler leadership model?

6. What is the meaning of a "favorable" situation for the leader in Fiedler's model?

7. Why is it difficult to classify tasks as either "structured" or "unstructured"?

8. How is the House "Path–Goal Model" of leadership related to the expectancy model of motivation discussed in Chapter 3?

9. What is the main value of the Path–Goal leadership model?

10. What types of advances have been made in leadership research and knowledge over the past fifty years?

11. What are the implications for managers in the fact that leadership theories are becoming more complex?

12. What are some of the major problems with leadership training?

13. Why is organizational climate an important variable in leadership training?

14. Why may changing the job to fit the leader be a better strategy for change than attempting to change the leader's behavior?

# ■ EXERCISE 7-1: THE SALES MANAGER

Art Cranston was a regional sales manager for a major computer manufacturer. In this position he supervised twenty-two industrial salespeople who sold computers, word processors, and other office equipment to business and educational organizations. Supervising the sales force involved setting sales quotas and targets after discussion with the salespeople, checking on performance levels, developing and monitoring compensation programs, allocating salespeople to different territories, and many other traditional duties performed by sales managers. Salespeople were paid on a salary-plus-commission basis, with the salary portion being small enough that it did not provide an adequate standard of living. Cranston thought that the commission component would motivate the salespeople to sell more aggressively.

On balance, the performance of the sales force was quite good, although there were two definite problem areas. One of these was turnover, which was averaging 23 percent per year. Cranston was concerned about this, but he also knew that high turnover was a common problem in selling occupations where incentive compensation schemes were used. His major concern about turnover was the time and money he had to spend looking for new salespeople and then training them to do the job the right way.

The other problem concerned two salespeople who chronically failed to reach their objectives. In an attempt to overcome this problem, Cranston had instituted a Management by Objectives system. He felt that if goals were mutually decided on by the salesperson and the boss, that the salesperson would be more committed to the goals and would work harder to achieve them. This system improved the performance of salespeople who were already satisfactory, but it had no effect on the two low performers. The other solutions he tried involved clarifying a salesperson's duties. Over a period of several years Cranston had developed a detailed system that all salespeople used when they called on prospects. The feedback he received from salespeople was that the system was very helpful in improving their sales. Cranston also heard comments such as "Art, you're very task-oriented, but we're happy because what you're doing puts more money in our pockets." These views were widely held by the sales staff but not by the two problem employees.

At a sales convention in St. Louis during October, Cranston happened to overhear Jim Brewer (a top salesman) arguing loudly with Mike O'Donnell (one of the poor performers) about the nature of incentive schemes:

BREWER: I think our compensation scheme is really good. It forces a guy to keep moving. If he does that, he makes a lot of money and the company also benefits.

O'DONNELL:   That's easy for you to say! What about me? I can't make big money with the compensation scheme we're using.

BREWER:   That's because you're not working hard enough.

O'DONNELL:   What do you know about how hard I work? We hardly ever see each other except at these conventions!

BREWER:   You must not be working hard enough if you aren't making much money.

O'DONNELL:   I'm working very hard! The problem is that Cranston doesn't have any feeling for people. All he thinks about is sales volume. This incentive scheme just won't work for everyone, because each person is unique.

BREWER:   Are you saying Cranston should develop a unique incentive scheme for each salesperson?

O'DONNELL:   Yes.

BREWER:   That's ridiculous. Then everyone would be running around worrying about whether their deal was better or worse than someone else's. Besides, the paperwork would be outrageous.

O'DONNELL:   Well, the present system isn't working!

BREWER:   That's not what most of the people here would say. You're out in left field on this one!

After hearing this conversation, Cranston was both pleased and disturbed. He felt that most of the salespeople would agree with Brewer, but he also knew that O'Donnell firmly believed what he was saying. He wondered what all this meant for his leadership of the salesforce.

1.   Should Cranston try to use different leadership styles with different salespeople? Is this feasible?

2.   Will O'Donnell's idea of a unique incentive scheme for each salesperson work? What are the benefits? What are the drawbacks?

3.   What can Cranston do to improve the performance of O'Donnell and other low performers?

4.   Use the leadership theories in this chapter to draw some conclusions about the most appropriate style of leadership for Cranston. What are the shortcomings of these schemes?

## ■ EXERCISE 7-2: THE MANAGER

Darrell Porter was the manager of a professional minor-league baseball team. During the past season, the team had posted a 71–60 won–lost record. During the off-season, Porter contemplated the team's strengths and weaknesses and wondered what he could do to improve its record.

The season had been a difficult one for Porter. On top of the standard problem of high turnover (the parent club often moved the team's most promising players up to the major leagues), there had been a number of disruptive personality conflicts among team members. Porter was an easygoing, quiet man who did not interfere in these disputes unless they occurred in the dugout or on the field. He had recently had a long talk with the owner of the team, who suggested that Porter should exercise greater control over the team. The owner felt that the players would "put out" more for a manager who would direct their energies toward winning games instead of fighting.

Porter knew that some of the most successful major league managers were volatile, aggressive managers, but he felt uncomfortable with this advice and wondered if he should change his leadership style.

1. Use the leadership theories in this chapter to reach a conclusion about an appropriate management style for Porter to use.

# ■ ENDNOTES

1. P. Hersey and K. Blanchard, *Management of Organizational Behavior* (Englewood Cliffs, N.J.: Prentice-Hall, 1982).

2. Ibid., p. 151.

3. Maturity levels are depicted as being discrete; like leader behaviors, they actually occur in infinite degrees.

4. J. E. Stinson and T. W. Johnson, "The Path–Goal Theory of Leadership: A Partial Test and Suggested Refinement," *Academy of Management Journal* 18 (1975): 242–252.

5. Arriso L. Angelini, Paul Hersey, and Sofia Caracushansky, "The Situational Leadership Theory Applied to Teaching: A Research on Learning Effectiveness," an unpublished paper cited by Hersey and Blanchard.

6. Raymond A. Gumpert and Ronald K. Hambleton, "Situational Leadership: How Xerox Managers Fine-Tune Managerial Styles to Employee Maturity and Task Needs," *Management Review* (December 1979): 8–12.

7. V. Vroom and P. Yetton, *Leadership and Decision Making* (Pittsburgh: University of Pittsburgh, 1973).

8. V. Vroom and A. Jago, "On the Validity of the Vroom-Yetton Model," *Journal of Applied Psychology* 63 (1978): 151–162.

9. R. Field, "A Critique of the Vroom-Yetton Contingency Model of Leadership Behavior," *Academy of Management Review* 4 (1979): 249–257.

10. A. Jago and V. Vroom, "An Evaluation of Two Alternatives to the Vroom/Yetton Normative Model," *Academy of Management Journal* 23 (1980): 347–355.

11. F. Fiedler, *A Theory of Leadership Effectiveness* (New York: McGraw-Hill Book Company), p. 196.

12. F. E. Fiedler, M. M. Chemers, and L. Mahar, *Improving Leadership Effectiveness: The LEADER MATCH Concept* (New York: Wiley, 1976).

13. Several of these studies are discussed in F. E. Fiedler and L. Mahar, "The Effectiveness of Contingency Model Training: A Review of the Validation of LEADER MATCH," *Personnel Psychology* 32 (1979): 45–62.

14. Ibid., 32: 52–53.

15. F. E. Fiedler and L. Mahar, "A Field Experiment Validating Contingency Model Leadership Training," *Journal of Applied Psychology* 64 (1979): 247–254.

16. G. Graen, et al., "Contingency Model of Leadership Effectiveness: Some Experimental Results," *Journal of Applied Psychology* 55 (1971): 196–201.

17. T. Mitchell, "The Contingency Model: Criticisms and Suggestions," *Academy of Management Journal* 13 (1970): 253–67. For an in-depth analysis of the characteristics of the LPC scale, see R. Rice, "Psychometric Properties of the Esteem for Least Preferred Coworker," *Academy of Management Review* 3 (January 1978): 106–118; see also C. Schriesheim, B. Bannister, and W. Money, "Psychometric Properties of the LPC Scale: An Extension of Rice's Review," *Academy of Management Review* 4 (April 1979): 287–290.

18. C. Schriesheim and S. Kerr, "Theories and Measures of Leadership: A Critical Reappraisal of Current and Future Directions," in J. G. Hunt and L. L. Larson, eds., *Leadership: The Cutting Edge* (Carbondale, Ill.: Southern Illinois University Press, 1977), pp. 9–45.

19. J. W. Kennedy, "Middle LPC Leaders and the Contingency Model of Leadership Effectiveness," *Organizational Behavior and Human Performance* 30 (1982): 1–14.

20. Schriesheim and Kerr, "Theories and Measures of Leadership."

21. R. W. Rice, "Leader LPC and Follower Satisfaction: A Review," *Organizational Behavior and Human Performance* 28 (1981): 1–25.

22. J. Kelly, *Organizational Behavior* (Homewood, Ill.: Richard D. Irwin, Inc. 1974), p. 390.

23. R. House, "A Path–Goal Model of Leader Effectiveness," *Administrative Science Quarterly* 16 (September 1971): 321–38.

24. A. D. Szilagyi and H. P. Sims, "An Exploration of the Path–Goal Theory of Leadership in a Health Care Environment," *Academy of Management Journal* 17 (1974): 622–634.

25. C. A. Schriesheim and A. De Nisi, "Task Dimensions As Moderators of the Effects of Instrumental Leadership: A Two-Sample Replicated Test of Path–Goal Leadership Theory," *Journal of Applied Psychology* 66 (1981): 589–597.

26. Stinson and Johnson, "The Path–Goal Theory of Leadership."

27. A. Abdel-Halim, "Personality and Task Moderators of Subordinate Responses to Perceived Leader Behavior," *Human Relations* 34 (1981): 73–88.

28. For a specific reference to the importance of this idea in the path–goal model, see C. Greene, "Questions of Causality in the Path–Goal Theory of Leadership," *Academy of Management Journal* 22 (1979): 22–41.

29. The reader should also refer to Chapter 15, where some specific programs for modifying organizational behavior are discussed.

30. E. A. Fleishman, E. Harris, and H. Burtt, *Leadership and Supervision in Industry* (Columbus, Ohio: Bureau of Education Research, Ohio State University, 1955).

31. A. J. Sykes, "The Effects of a Supervisory Training Course in Changing Supervisors' Perceptions and Expectations of the Role of Management," *Human Relations* 15 (1962): 227–43.

32. R. J. House, "Leadership Training: Some Dysfunctional Consequences," *Administrative Science Quarterly* 12 (March 1968): 556–71.

33. F. E. Fiedler, "How Do You Make Leaders More Effective? New Answers to an Old Puzzle," *Organizational Dynamics* (1972): 3–18.

34. F. E. Fiedler, "Engineer the Job to Fit the Manager," *Harvard Business Review* 43 (1965): 115.

35. F. E. Fiedler, "How Do You Make Leaders More Effective?"

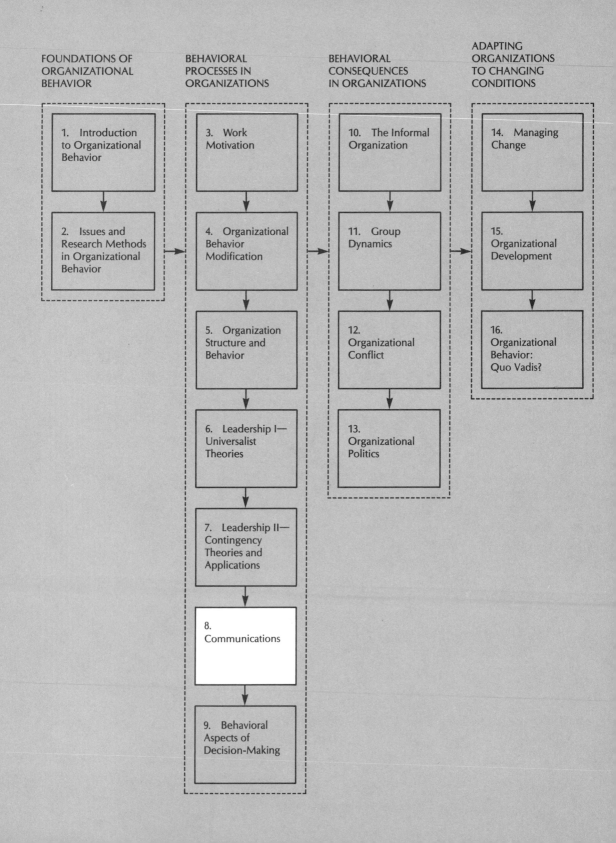

FOUNDATIONS OF
ORGANIZATIONAL
BEHAVIOR

BEHAVIORAL
PROCESSES IN
ORGANIZATIONS

BEHAVIORAL
CONSEQUENCES
IN ORGANIZATIONS

ADAPTING
ORGANIZATIONS
TO CHANGING
CONDITIONS

1. Introduction to Organizational Behavior

2. Issues and Research Methods in Organizational Behavior

3. Work Motivation

4. Organizational Behavior Modification

5. Organization Structure and Behavior

6. Leadership I— Universalist Theories

7. Leadership II— Contingency Theories and Applications

8. Communications

9. Behavioral Aspects of Decision-Making

10. The Informal Organization

11. Group Dynamics

12. Organizational Conflict

13. Organizational Politics

14. Managing Change

15. Organizational Development

16. Organizational Behavior: Quo Vadis?

# Communications

## ■ Learning Objectives

After reading this chapter you should be able to:

☐ Describe the communication models.
☐ Explain the three types of communication flows in organizations
☐ Diagram the four basic communication networks.
☐ Know at least four methods of stimulating upward communications.
☐ Explain how communication content affects the communication process.
☐ Practice effective listening skills.
☐ Engage in nondirective listening behaviors.
☐ Describe at least two specific skill applications.

# Chapter  8

# ■ KEY TERMS

**Encoding**
**Decoding**
**Feedback**
**Noise**
**Communication networks**
**Communication skills**
**Perception**
**Stereotyping**
**Projection**
**Nonverbal communication**
**Nondirective interviewing**
**Directive interviewing**
**Counseling**

# ■ CHAPTER OUTLINE

I. Approaches to the Study of Communication
II. Communication Models
   A. The Simple Communication Model
   B. The General Communication Model
   C. The Superior-Subordinate Communication Model
III. Communication Flows
   A. Downward Flow
   B. Upward Flow
   C. Lateral Flow
IV. Communication Networks
V. Communication Content
   A. One-Sided vs. Two-Sided Communication
   B. The Ordering of Communication Content
   C. Emotional vs. Rational Communication
   D. Summary of Communication Content
VI. Communication Skills
   A. Effective Listening
   B. Perception
   C. Nonverbal Communication

## *Opening Incident—Treeline Manufacturing Company*

Treeline Manufacturing Company employed 300 employees in the wood products industry. The management had always prided itself on the good relations that existed between the company and its employees. There had never been a strike in the company and the relations with the union were considered to be good.

The president of Treeline, Carlos Romero, had formed an "executive committee" that met every Tuesday morning to discuss specific issues facing management. These meetings also served to improve communications between managers since this was the only time they had the opportunity to meet together. At one meeting, the committee was discussing how valuable the meetings had been and suggested that they should examine some way of improving communications with the employees as well. One manager related an experience that seemed to sum up the lack of communications with the employees. Apparently he had been talking with one employee and discovered that the employee did not even know who the president of the company was.

After considerable discussion, it was decided to embark on a program to improve communications with employees. Several ideas were put forth, but it was decided to begin with a simple campaign to inform employees about the company and its operations. This campaign would consist of three graphs describing total sales, inventory levels, and number of employees working in the company, and the graphs would be updated weekly.

After several months, the shapes of the graphs were as follows:

SALES        INVENTORY       # OF EMPLOYEES

About this time Romero had a visit from the president of the union. He was very upset and said that the membership wanted to open up the job security clause of their contract. Several foremen also reported a noticeable drop in the morale of their employees. One day in the cafeteria, several employees confronted Romero and demanded to speak to him about the rumor that the plant was closing.

---

Probably the most overworked of all organizational clichés is, "We have a communication problem." But like most clichés, the fact that it is overworked simply indicates that it probably reflects reality. To illustrate the importance of communication, we will examine in this chapter the relationship between communication and other organizational processes and how communication can affect organizational performance. One useful perspective views communication as the "activating force" behind organizational functions such as planning, organizing, staffing, directing, and controlling.[1] The planning function, for example, provides a road map for individuals to follow in carrying out their responsibilities. But regardless of the quality of the plans, procedures, organization structures, and so on, they are meaningless if the transformation from thought to action breaks down through poor communication. A well-thought-out plan is useless if it cannot be properly communicated to the right people.

Effective communication, however, is not a guarantee of success. Using our example above, poor plans, procedures, or organization structures that are effectively communicated are equally worthless. The manager who effectively communicates something that negatively affects subordinates' motivation is an ineffective manager. This latter point is quite important since often it is not our inability to communicate effectively that hinders our effectiveness, but rather our ability to communicate effectively something which we do not intend to communicate. In sum, effective communication is a necessary but not sufficient condition for managerial effectiveness. To regard effective communication as a substitute for sound management practice is inaccurate and misleading.

# ■ APPROACHES TO THE STUDY OF COMMUNICATION

Depending on one's purpose, communication can be studied from several different perspectives ranging from the very abstract (communication models) to the very concrete (communication skills). One reason for the variety of approaches is that communication is relevant to many disciplines other than management; this breadth of interest has caused various researchers to focus on several different aspects of the subject. The approaches most relevant to our study of communication include communication models, flows, networks, content, and skills. The relationship among these approaches on the abstract–concrete continuum is illustrated in Figure 8-1.

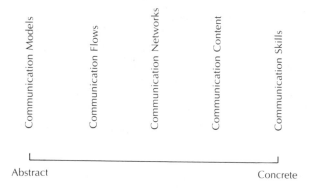

**FIGURE 8-1. The Relationship of the Various Approaches to the Study of Communication**

The most abstract method of studying communication is through the examination of information processing *models* (i.e., studying how information is transmitted from the source to the receiver and what possible factors influence the communication as it is transmitted). The characteristics of all information-processing systems are studied and described, and attempts are made to generalize principles of information processing that are applicable to all systems. Data can be generated from either physical systems (e.g., computers) or behavioral systems (e.g., the grapevine). It is assumed by researchers that a more accurate understanding of information-processing theory will result in more effective utilization of communication processes and channels.

Another approach is to study communication *flows* (i.e., the nature and direction of information movement). This method is concerned with communication needs (i.e., who needs what information) rather than the processes that occur as information is transmitted. Viewing communication from this perspective helps us decide what information is needed where, as well as methods that will facilitate movement in the desired direction.

A derivative of this approach is the study of communication *networks*. Network analysis investigates the mechanics of communication flows and evaluates the relative effectiveness of different types of communication systems. Because networks can be artificially created and controlled, considerable laboratory research has been done in this area.

Communication can also be studied from a *content* perspective. Here it is recognized that certain types of content (e.g., syntax, semantics, symbols, etc.) or ways of presenting the content are more effective than others in influencing behavior. Much of the research in social psychology has used the content approach, since it is useful for studying attitude change and has implications for applications as diverse as advertising and brainwashing. Since employee attitudes are an area of concern to all managers, the study of communication content and related issues warrants our attention.

Yet another approach, and perhaps of most interest to practicing managers, is one that attempts to develop communication *skills* in individuals. Whereas the other approaches do have behavioral implications, the skill approach is almost totally behaviorally oriented and tends to have a strong human relations slant to it. Emphasis is on the identification of those behaviors that will result in more effective communication between, for example, managers and subordinates.

As was indicated in Figure 8-1, all the above approaches are related. The discussion in Chapter 1 of the relationship between theory and practice is descriptive of the relationship between the two extremes of the continuum in Figure 8-1. For example, the communication skills approach is developed from the more abstract and theoretical information-processing models and can be seen as the application of the principles developed in those models. We recognize that some effective communicators have little formal knowledge of information-processing principles and, conversely, ineffective communicators may have extensive knowledge of information-processing principles. However, these cases are unusual, and, as has been suggested several times in previous chapters, we are concerned with what applies to the majority of people, not the exceptions. Accordingly, it is important for the understanding of communication theory and the development of communication skills that we briefly examine each of these approaches to communication. Since the informal communication process (the grapevine) will be discussed in Chapter 10, we restrict the discussion of the various approaches to the formal communication processes that occur in organizations (e.g., manager–subordinate communication, interviewing, etc.).

# ■ COMMUNICATION MODELS

We begin our discussion of communication by examining some general communication models. These models are abstract representations of the actual activities that occur from the time the sender of the message begins communication until the target of the communication acts on it.

## ☐ The Simple Communication Model

In order for the communication process to occur, a minimum of three elements must be present: the source (or sender), message, and receiver (see Figure 8-2). The communication *source* may be either a person or an object (e.g., a book, a piece of paper, or a mechanical device such as a radio or television). The communication *message* can take many forms; it may be an instruction, a question, an appeal, or even a facial expression. The *receiver* is the person to whom the message is directed. The characteristics of the receiver influence the way in which the message is received and interpreted.

**FIGURE 8-2.   A Simplified Communication Model**

The basic model is important because sources, messages, and receivers can take many forms, and these forms influence the acceptance of communications. The message we communicate may have broader implications than we intend, since we normally communicate more than the spoken word. While our words say one thing, our actions may communicate something entirely different. The factory time clock, for example, may communicate to employees that management does not trust them to come to work on time.

While the simple model is useful for understanding the communication process at a very fundamental level, it is not sufficient for understanding the intricacies of most organizational communication. We have expanded the model to include a more complete description of the communication process; we then apply it to communication processes between managers and employees.

## ☐   The General Communication Model

A more complete communication model is represented in Figure 8-3. The model consists of several segments:

**The Source**   As mentioned previously, this is the origin of the communication and can be an individual, group, or inanimate object. The effectiveness of a communication depends to a considerable degree on the characteristics of the source. Aristotle believed that acceptance of the source's message could be increased by a number of tactics, including *pathos* (playing on the emotions of the receiver), *logos* (generating logical arguments), or *ethos* (asking for message acceptance because the source is trustworthy).

Much research has been done on the effect of source credibility. Not surprisingly, the results indicate that high-credibility sources have a greater potential for influencing behavior than low-credibility sources. Experiments have shown that the content of a message is often interpreted according to the source. Consequently, a credible message may be seen as actually having low credibility if the receiver is distrustful of the source. Other research has indicated, interestingly enough, that source credibility has no effect upon *attention* of the receiver;

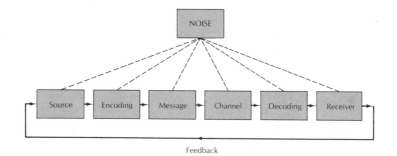

**FIGURE 8-3.   The General Communication Model**

therefore, ineffective communication caused by lack of source credibility is likely due to the lack of acceptance of the communication rather than lack of attention.[2]

An important question here is, "How does the source get credibility?" One way is to use a high-prestige medium to carry the message. Academicians, for example, gain professional credibility by publishing in refereed journals. (Refereed journals are those using scholars to referee manuscripts submitted to the journal that are in their area of expertise. They accept or reject the manuscripts for publication.) Entertainers gain credibility by utilizing the competitive media to contact their audiences. These examples are appropriate for mass communication, but for interpersonal communication the tactic is clearly not feasible. In these circumstances, consistency of behavior with communication (developed over time) is probably the most effective way of increasing source credibility. Another factor in organization communication is whether the source has formal authority over the receiver; if this is the case, the manager will likely have greater "credibility," and the message transmitted will more than likely be accepted and acted upon by the receiver (subordinate).[3]

**Encoding**   Once the source has decided what message to communicate, the content of the message must be put in a form the receiver can understand. The most typical coding process results in written or spoken messages using an accepted language (e.g., English, mathematics, etc.). The message itself is the result of the encoding process. Putting communications in a form that the intended receiver can understand increases the probability that the response desired by the sender will occur.

**The Channel**   The actual means by which the message is transmitted to the receiver (visual, auditory, written, or some combination of these three) is called the *channel*. Some typical communication channels are noted in Table 8-1. Appropriate channel selection is important to avoid problems that may occur in either the understanding or the retention of a message. To explain a complex mathematical problem to students, an instructor may use a variety of methods: auditory (lecture), visual (graphical solution), and written (lecture notes). Similarly, a manager who wants to increase the probability that a message will be retained by subordinates may follow a verbal instruction with a written memorandum.

**Decoding**   The process by which the recipient of the message attaches meaning to it is called *decoding*. The extent to which the decoding by the receiver coincides with the intent of the encoding of the sender depends heavily on the individual characteristics of the sender and receiver. The greater the similarity in the background or status factors of the communicators (i.e., "speaking the same language"), the greater the probability that a message will be perceived accurately. One reason why communication between organizational levels is troublesome is that background differences exist among individuals. The company president may have difficulty communicating with first-line employees, because of decoding problems caused by status differences.

**TABLE 8-1.   The Basic Communication Channels**

| Channel | Required Source Activity | Required Receiver Activity | Some Examples |
|---|---|---|---|
| 1. Auditory | Speaking<br>Use of mechanical<br>  sending device | Listening | Telegraph signals<br>Radio<br>Telephone conversations |
| 2. Visual | Action | Observing | Ship-to-shore visual<br>  signals<br>Hand signals<br>Color emphasis<br>Flag waving |
| 3. Written | Composition | Reading | Reports<br>Company policy manuals<br>Books |
| 4. Auditory–visual<br>  combination | Speaking and<br>  action | Listening and<br>  observing | Television, movies<br>Ballet<br>Students listening to a<br>  lecture |
| 5. Visual–written<br>  combination | Action and<br>  composition | Observing and<br>  reading | Billboard advertising<br>Magazines<br>Newspapers<br>Transit advertising |
| 6. Auditory–<br>  written<br>  combination | Speaking and<br>  composition | Listening and<br>  reading | Students following<br>  handouts provided<br>  by the instructor |

**The Receiver**   The *receiver* is the individual or group for whom the message is intended. Like the sender, the receiver is subject to many influences that can affect the understanding of the message. Most important, the receiver will perceive a communication in a manner that is consistent with previous experiences. Communications that are not consistent with expectations will likely be rejected. The message from management that there will be no employee layoffs this year is not likely to be believed if layoffs occurred last year. Much research has been done on the importance and characteristics of receivers, and we will utilize some of these ideas later in the communication content and skills sections.

**Feedback**   Information flow in the general communication model is not restricted to one direction. The sender of a message will observe one of three reactions to the message: agreement, disagreement, or apathy. On the basis of these observations, changes in the message can be made. Of course, the speed at which feedback occurs varies with the situation. In face-to-face conversation, feedback is practically instantaneous, whereas in the case of mass advertising, many weeks or months may pass before the sender (the advertiser) obtains any feedback about the message from the receiver. Feedback can also take many forms. Verbal feedback is, of course, the most obvious, but feedback can also occur in nonverbal forms such as facial expressions, physical gestures, or written responses. For example, a manager may "chew out" a problem employee about consistent tardiness; the feedback the manager receives could take many forms including any of these:

1. Positive or negative verbal reaction from the employee (immediate).
2. Blank look on the employee's face (immediate).
3. Employee turning his back on the manager later in the day (delayed).
4. Employee comes in late the following day (delayed).

Some of this feedback from the employee indicates that the communication has been effective, some indicates it has no effect, and some is neutral in nature.

**Noise**    In each act of communication there are influences that interfere with the transmission of the message. Although the term *noise* may be taken literally, as in the case of two factory workers trying to communicate over the noise of the machines around them, the term generally refers to conceptual noise (i.e., those personality, perceptual, and attitudinal differences in individuals which confound

## Box 8-1: Communication Problems

There are many things that can go wrong during the communication process as it is represented in Figure 8-3. Some of the most common problems are as follows:

1. *The source does a poor job of encoding the message.* The source may simply be too lazy to clearly develop the message, or the source may purposely encode the message to cause a negative response in the receiver. The source may also be unaware that the message is offensive to the receiver. This is particularly true when cross-cultural communication takes place.
2. *The channel does not properly convey the message.* There may be technical problems that inhibit the message (e.g., radio static), but the human problems are generally more important. Tone of voice when conveying a message can markedly affect the way the message is received. The use of an inappropriate medium also causes problems. Using a form letter to tell the vice-president of finance that his services are no longer required is an example of an inappropriate channel.
3. *The receiver decodes the messages improperly.* The problems here are mirror images of those noted in 1. The receiver may be a "lazy listener" or may read into the message things that are not there. The receiver may also take offense at the message even though it is obvious that the sender intended no such offense.

and complicate to varying degrees the ability of individuals to understand one another). Noise is evident at each stage of the communication process. For example, when the source encodes a message, noise is evident in the form of biases (either positive or negative) about the intended receiver. Or when the message is transmitted through the channel, noise occurs if individuals cannot understand some of the terms used. Some other examples of conceptual noise that affect communications are as follows:

1. The lack of understanding between races because of steretyped images each has about the other.
2. A father attempting to communicate with his son, whom he perceives as lazy.
3. A manager attempting to improve a subordinate's performance at salary review time.
4. Management attempting to inform employees about the current financial condition of the company prior to contract negotiations.

In general, the total communication process functions most effectively when the *field of experience* of the source and the receiver overlap, as shown in Figure 8-4. There is an inverse relationship between the degree of commonality in

---

### *Organizational Reality* 8-1
### *Communications at Kropp Forge*

An extensive communication program has led to much improved labor–management relations at the Kropp Forge Company, an Illinois-based producer of hammer forging equipment. Gordon Jenkins, president of Anadite Inc., Kropp Forge's parent company, was aware that there were significant labor–management problems at the company, since several lengthy strikes had occurred during the mid-seventies. Jenkins felt that this type of difficulty was common in firms that were unionized because management didn't take enough time to talk to workers. In an attempt to overcome problems of this nature, Jenkins developed a number of specific employee communication programs which have virtually eliminated the adversary relationship between labor and management.

For example, Jenkins made personal daily visits to the plant facilities. He also learned the first names of most employees and discussed day to day operations with them. The company also developed "wives at lunch" programs, where workers' wives toured and lunched at the plant. The wives left with a much better understanding of their husbands' jobs.

As a result of these and other communications programs, when labor–management bargaining began in 1981, a new spirit of cooperation was evident. The president of the union noted that management representatives discussed many issues at length and gave the union a great deal of information about important topics. The union was therefore much better able to understand why management had to refuse certain requests and was able to grant others.

---

Source: "Management in Practice," *Management Review* (May 1982): 43–44.

the field of experience and the effort required for effective communication. This is because of the increased psychological energy that is required to overcome the natural barriers to communication. For example, to communicate with someone who does not speak your language requires extreme patience and concentration. But it is important to realize that, while common frames of reference facilitate communication, they do not occur by accident. The fact is that common frames of reference occur through communication; in other words, the causal relationship between the two is mutual (i.e., the systems effect). The effect of this phenomenon can be seen in situations such as the racial legislation in the United States: the theory behind much of the legislation is that forced communication through legislated integration will result in a more common frame of reference for different racial groups.

## ☐  The Superior-Subordinate Communication Model

Although the general communication model is helpful for understanding how the complete communication process operates in an abstract sense, a model that explicitly considers superior-subordinate relationships will give greater insight into the nature and importance of communications in organizations. An organizational model of communication is helpful if it accomplishes the following:

1. Differentiates between superiors and subordinates.
2. Deals with whether communication between the two is accepted or rejected.
3. Deals with behavior which results from the acceptance or rejection of the communication.

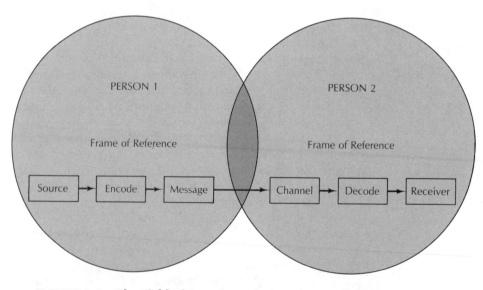

**FIGURE 8-4.   The Field of Experience in Interpersonal Communications**
Source: W. Schramm, *The Process and Effects of Mass Communication* (Urbana, Ill.: University of Illinois Press, 1954), p. 6. Reprinted by permission.

The model illustrated in Figure 8-5 is an attempt to satisfy these requirements. The general framework is similar to that used in Figure 8-3; however, the model is expanded somewhat, and the general terms of the earlier model are replaced with specific organizational ones.

In the normal course of fulfilling their responsibilities, managers (*sources*) must communicate with subordinates (*receivers*). Although managers possess formal organizational authority which allows them to force employees' compliance with orders, managerial effectiveness is more readily achieved if employees agree with and support what is being communicated.

The *channel* through which the message is transmitted depends upon whether the message is oral or written. If oral, the transmission takes place whenever the manager speaks to subordinates. If written, the message will be carried through the formal organizational communication system (which, of course, closely parallels the lines of authority). From an organizational behavior point of view, some of the more interesting outcomes of the communication process occur when the subordinate receives a message.

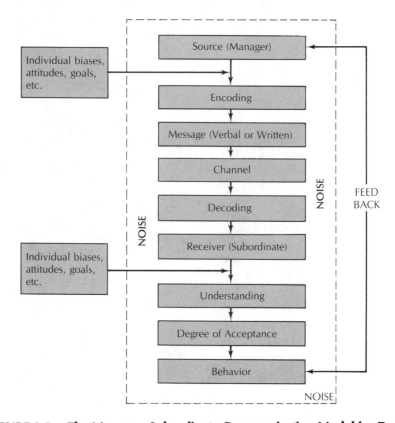

**FIGURE 8-5. The Manager–Subordinate Communication Model for Downward Communication**

As indicated in Figure 8-5, the *decoding* of the message is done by the *receiver* (subordinate); this decoding may or may not imply a proper *understanding* of the message, and understanding is a prerequisite for employee *acceptance* of the message. The breakdown of the decoding-understanding-acceptance chain is the point at which many problems or conflicts arise in organizations. If the communication from the manager is misinterpreted or not properly understood, the resulting *behavior* is unpredictable. While the behavior may coincidentally be in line with what the manager desires, the probability is much higher that actual behavior will deviate from desired behavior if the message is not understood. The situation is worsened when the manager reprimands or criticizes employees for behavior the employees see as consistent with the manager's communication. The observation by management of employee behavior is the *feedback* the manager requires to evaluate the appropriateness of employee behavior in light of the communication. On the basis of feedback received, approval or disapproval of employee behavior is communicated, and the process begins anew.

Although Figure 8-5 emphasizes downward communication, the feedback that occurs indicates that upward communication is also part of the process. In addition, communication can originate at lower levels of the organization and proceed upward. To describe this process we need only reverse the positions of the sender and the receiver in Figure 8-5 and realize that the same processes and principles operate in upward communication. When subordinates communicate upward, they also receive feedback regarding the effectiveness of their message. Since the two directions of communication operate more or less simultaneously,

---

### *Box 8-2: Minimizing Communication Breakdowns*

Listed below are several steps that can be taken to minimize communication breakdowns.

1. *Use face-to-face communication.* The sender is able to receive feedback quickly and is able to determine whether he or she has been understood.
2. *Be empathetic.* It is important to know the needs and feelings of the intended receiver. Failure to do so can result in badly misinterpreted messages.
3. *Avoid credibility gaps.* Words must be consistent with actions. If promises are made, they must be kept or a credibility gap will develop.
4. *Choose the right time for communication.* Your message will be most effective if it is sent when there are few competing messages and when it offers a solution to the receiver's problem.
5. *Be brief.* Get to the point of the message and use words that the receiver will understand.

Source: Stan Kossen, *The Human Side of Organizations* (San Francisco: Canfield, 1975), pp. 66–70.

over time a certain amount of learning occurs in terms of what inhibits and enhances effective communication. This learning process tends to make organizational communication more efficient.

In terms of improving organizational communication, the model tells us that managers should be on guard for the unintentional interjection of biases—either in content or media—that might cause subordinates to misunderstand the message being transmitted. Also, management must be aware of the factors beyond their control that can affect understanding. For example, management may follow the correct procedures and principles of effective communication, but understanding is lost because the receiver is not in the proper frame of mind to understand management's intent. Consequently, the feedback function is important since it tells managers how the communication was received and also gives some clues as to how they might redirect their efforts to achieve greater understanding.

The value of feedback, of course, varies from situation to situation, depending upon the individual's sensitivity. Some feedback is quite obvious—it does not take an overly sensitive person to judge the reaction of an employee who storms out of the office and slams the door. Most feedback, however, is more subtle, and managers must be sensitive to the "real" meaning behind a subordinate's behavior.

# ■ COMMUNICATION FLOWS

Within organizations there are three directions in which communications flow: downward, upward, and laterally. These flows are illustrated in Figure 8-6.

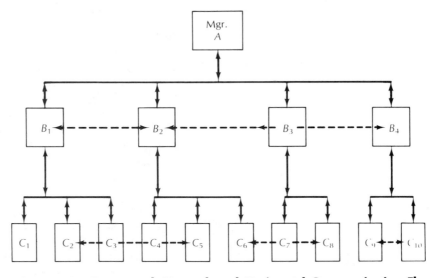

**FIGURE 8-6.   Downward, Upward, and Horizontal Communication Flows in an Organization**

## ☐ Downward Flow

The downward flow of communication generally corresponds to the formal organizational communications system, which is usually synonymous with the chain of command or line of authority. This system has received a great deal of attention from both managers and behavioral scientists since it is crucial to organizational functioning. For example, the study of communication models tells us that there is an inverse relationship between communication clarity and the number of levels in the organization (i.e., the more levels in the organization, the more difficult it is to insure that employees down the chain of command have a clear understanding of, for example, corporate objectives.) This lack of understanding can occur because each level requires additional encoding and decoding, and this increases the probability that error will creep into the communication. These difficulties have led some to conclude that the "top-down" communication system should be replaced with some other type (e.g., the "bottom-up" system discussed below). However, despite its limitations, the top-down system is an important part of the organization because much of the information needed to manage an organization originates at the upper levels and must be transmitted to the appropriate lower levels. While employees may disregard or misinterpret what does come down from the top, they would undoubtedly be worse off if no information were forthcoming. So, while the top-down method may not match other methods for speed, at least it forms the basis for consistent action on a wide variety of organizational issues and problems. The equity achieved by this system—or at least perceived by employees—is also an important factor in operating an effective organization.

## ☐ Upward Flow

The upward flow of communication involves two distinct manager–subordinate activities in addition to feedback: the participation by employees in formal organizational decisions and employee appeals against formal organization decisions. The exact forms these types of communication take vary with the situation. Generally, employee participation is a means of increasing upward communication and can be either formal or informal. Examples of formal upward flows are management by objectives,[4] participative management, regular meetings between managers and their employees, or joint policy-making bodies designed into the organization structure. Informally, upward flows occur in conversations between managers and subordinates or from the feedback a manager receives through observation of employees.

The second form of upward communication, the employee appeal, is a result of the industrial democracy concept that provides for two-way communication in areas of disagreement. In most unionized organizations, the grievance process is actually a formalized structure with explicit rules and procedures. While the type of communication that comes through this channel may be unpleasant as well as biased, it nevertheless is a valuable means for hearing what employees have to say. Perceptive managers will look upon the appeal system as one gauge of organizational health. However, the mere number of grievances filed should not be the only indication considered because the behavioral climate in the organization may be so threatening that employees are afraid to appeal decisions and , instead, leave the organization. In this sense, the use of the appeal mechanism by employees can be viewed as a sign of positive organizational health.

The emphasis on upward communication in many organizations is partly the result of the Theory Y approach to management discussed in Chapter 6. The increasingly common assumption by managers that employees have a desire to grow psychologically and to contribute to the organization's goals is consistent with Theory Y assumptions. Similarly, the techniques of participative management and management by objectives, both of which stimulate upward communications, are based on Theory Y assumptions. In fact, virtually all behavioral theories of organization are based on the need for some kind of upward communication. In many situations the need for upward communication is becoming less of a management prerogative. Many labor unions are demanding more of a voice in the management of the organization, and employees are seeing participation not as a privilege, but a right.[5]

---

## Box 8-3: Is Clear Communication Always Desirable?

Virtually all writing about communication exhorts people to be clear, precise, and succinct when they communicate. It is argued that clarity, precision, and succinctness lead to communication effectiveness. But is this always so? Isn't it sometimes beneficial (and necessary) to be vague in order to be effective?

Consider the manager who is faced with a personality dispute between two subordinates who must work together. Each subordinate will undoubtedly give a somewhat different version of the problem as well as some other comments about the other person in the dispute. Does the manager communicate these comments? NO. Rather, the manager facilitates resolution of the dispute without communicating certain remarks that each person may have made about the other. In this way the problem may be resolved by focusing on the areas of agreement rather than the areas of conflict. The problem may thus be solved by leaving certain things unsaid rather than clarifying them.

---

**Stimulating Upward Communication**    Although most managers agree on the need for upward communication, it is often not clear what actions can be taken to stimulate it. Often, the upward channels are designed only for formal, job-related information; other types of communications about feelings and attitudes are ignored. The problem is even more serious if we recognize that downward communication tends to be the natural order of things, thus placing an unusually heavy burden on the employees to communicate upward. Given this situation, it is important to develop ways to stimulate upward communication. This might be accomplished by satisfying the following criteria.

1. *Coverage must be systematic and balanced.* While spontaneous communication is often useful, efforts at stimulating upward communication must be planned, systematic, and balanced. The planning requirement assures that communication is not left to chance, while the balance requirement attempts to prevent upward communication originating from only a few sources. Many times only the most vocal organizational members are heard, whereas the less vocal may have important things to say as well. In following these principles, management obtains information from a wider variety of sources, and communication is not limited to crisis situations. The old adage "no news is good news" does not hold for upward organizational communication.

2. *The flow of communication must be directed.* Communication that is not directed to the proper receivers becomes rumor and finds its way through the organization according to who will listen. Properly directed communication, however,

---

## Organizational Reality 8-2
### Stimulating Upward Communications at RMI Company

Six years ago, the Niles Ohio RMI Company, producer of titanium, was in real trouble. Labor problems besieged its operations, productivity was dismal, and employee morale was low. Most of all, communications were poor, not only between management and labor, but between the various departments in the firm.

Four years later, RMI was a different company, with a 77 percent increase in productivity and a 600 percent increase in sales. The solution to RMI's plight: a straightforward communication relationship with its employees based on five principles: (1) RMI made each employee feel as if he or she were part of a team working toward a common goal, (2) every employee was convinced that the best way to guarantee job security was to ensure that the company was profitable, (3) every employee understood that the company expected excellence, (4) employees were encouraged to feel that they were members of RMI's family before they were members of a union or a specific department, and (5) RMI encouraged employees to participate in community affairs so that they would feel closer to their community.

The company held regular dinner meetings to bring together front-line supervisors, middle, and top managers to establish a closer relationship between all levels of management. Union officials were also invited to the meetings to discuss specific items or problems. As well, customers were invited to make presentations to employees, and under RMI's open-door policy, every employee has received the right to arrange a meeting to speak to any executive on any serious issue. The company has also launched an "action request" program where more than 500 workers' suggestions have been implemented, dealing with improved service and quality, reduced costs, and improved productivity.

---

Source: Edward R. Toth, Jr., "Little Things Mean a Lot to Workers," *AMA International Forum* (November 1981): 32–33.

reaches those individuals who are in a position to take action. Employees who are dissatisfied and wish to communicate with management must be directed to the correct channels, and these channels should be known to everyone.

3. *Listening must be sensitive.* Because of the fundamental nature of hierarchical systems, employees may be conditioned to tell management what they think management wants to hear rather than what they actually feel. Complaints are often disguised in ways that prevent them from being obvious to the listener. Consequently, management must attempt to respond not only to the spoken word, but to the meaning of the words. To a large degree, the sensitivity of the manager determines the amount and type of communication that is directed upward from subordinates.

4. *Listening must be objective.* Upward communication will be selective and infrequent if employees think their communications are not being perceived in an objective fashion. It is easy for managers to show more interest in favorable communication than unfavorable or to seek out those employees who will agree with them and ignore those who do not. Objectivity in upward communication means that management must make a conscious effort to avoid these biases.

5. *Listening implies action.* Communication is not an end in itself but a means to an end. While listening to employees is certainly important, unless some kind of action is forthcoming, the listening function loses its value. In some cases, listening itself can give the employee the impression that action will be taken, and management must be cautious not to leave the impression that communication efforts guarantee results. If, for example, employees offer suggestions for work improvements that cannot be implemented, they should be told why.[6]

If properly utilized, upward communication is potentially one of the most useful managerial practices. Better decisions can be made if the data from the lower levels of the organization are communicated upward. Though not a panacea for all organizational problems, upward communication can be an important preventive maintenance activity.

## ☐ Lateral Flow

The lateral flow of communication across departments is sometimes the most difficult to observe when technically the formal organization does not recognize it. However, lateral communication is beneficial since it acts as a coordination device for departments that are working toward the same objective but performing different tasks. Lateral communication facilitates a more logical and efficient interaction between departments and in so doing generally facilitates movement toward organizational goals.

Lateral communication is recognized in the more behaviorally oriented types of organization structures. In Chapter 5 the discussion of matrix organization structure highlighted the importance of communication between project members. In this type of structure, lateral communication should be encouraged, since effective task accomplishment depends upon the mutual contribution of all project members.

In sum, the impact of structure on the flow of communication is significant. The basic patterns of communication are initially determined by the relationships between individuals that are spelled out in the formal organization chart. However, because communication is a behavioral process as well as a structural one, the people within the system adapt the formal channels and flows to suit their requirements. The downward flow of communication informs employees of management's expectations and the upward flow completes the circle to let management know how the expectations were received. The lateral flow meets the coordinative needs of functionalized departments, serves to satisfy the social needs of employees, and in some cases is a necessary requirement for task completion.

# ■ COMMUNICATION NETWORKS

A more sophisticated perspective (in the research sense) of communication flows is the study of the relative effectiveness of various communication networks. Whereas in the previous section we were concerned with only the general upward, downward, and lateral movement of communication, there are other specific flows (networks) which exist within these broad categories. Beginning in the early 1950s and continuing to the present, many research studies have been conducted to test the impact of various networks on the effectiveness of communication.[7] The vast majority of these studies have been conducted in the laboratory, where the independent variable is the structure of the network, and the dependent variables are speed and accuracy of communication, and participant morale. Subjects are usually placed in groups of four to six, randomly assigned to one of the several networks, and asked to perform tasks ranging from simple to complex. The networks that are usually examined are the circle, all-channel, wheel, and the chain. These are illustrated in Figure 8-7.

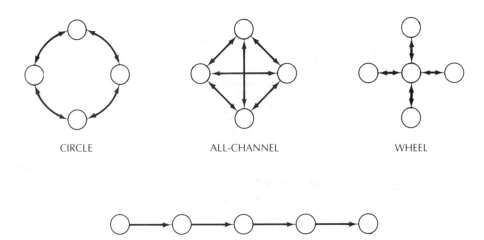

CIRCLE          ALL-CHANNEL          WHEEL

CHAIN

**FIGURE 8-7.   Four Different Networks of Communication**

While these networks have been examined in laboratory experiments, they do have close counterparts in actual organizations. The circle network is analogous to a group working in a physical arrangement such that workers can communicate with their immediate neighbor but not with others in the group. The all-channel network approximates the communication patterns occurring in a task force or functional team employed in a matrix structure. The wheel arrangement describes a manager and the immediate work group in which the subordinates must obtain their information from one source. The chain best decribes the one-way downward communication process that is likely to occur from the chief executive through the organizational ranks.

Although there are some conflicting findings in this area (as usual!), a systematic review of much of the literature done by Burgess indicates that the following general conclusions can be drawn:[8] As far as performance on *simple* tasks is concerned, the wheel and all-channel networks score the best and the circle network the worst. However, the morale of participants in the wheel network is generally low, while in the circle network it tends to be high. When *complex* tasks are performed, the all-channel network is most effective, a fact consistent with our knowledge about matrix organizations. The chain network tends to be useful only for simple tasks; morale tends to be lower at the lower end of the chain because of the lack of feedback in the system. This is again consistent with our knowledge of communication models.

---

## *Organizational Reality   8-3*
### *Facilitating Task Communication*

At Corning Glass Works' engineering headquarters in Corning, New York, a proposed engineering building was researched to accommodate staff communication needs before blueprint entries were considered. Studies by MIT's Sloan School of Management concluded that engineers get more than 80 percent of their ideas through face-to-face contact with their peers. Corning wanted to house its 800 engineers and support staff in a building that would create the most stimulating and productive environment possible.

The Decker Engineering Building includes glass and mirrored walls to extend the degree of visual contact between offices. A broad skyline along the center of the building allows the sun to shine upon lush trees and plants. On the principle that some of the best ideas can emerge over a cup of coffee, discussion areas equipped with wall-size writing surfaces and "work" chairs were placed adjacent to the coffee machines. The 24,000 square-foot building boasts a video-equipped problem-solving room where a TV receiver picks up worldwide transmissions via satellite.

Company officials were hoping for a 15-percent increase in engineering productivity in the new building. Nine months after its completion, efficiency had "significantly risen."

---

Source: David E. Leibson, "How Corning Designed a "Talking" Building to Spur Productivity," *Management Review* (September 1981): 8–13.

These findings must be stated with some caution since evidence also exists that other factors influence the communication process. For example, the establishment of task structure within the group is also important in determining performance.[9] Once this structure is achieved, the task facing the group is more readily accomplished *irrespective* of the basic network the group is using to solve it. Findings of this nature support the contention in Chapter 5 that organizational structure greatly influences many organizational behaviors, including communication activities.

Although laboratory experiments give considerable insight into the importance of communication networks in problem solving, further experiments within actual organizations are needed to generate a more accurate picture of what occurs when additional complicating factors are at work.

# ■ COMMUNICATION CONTENT

One of the primary concerns of managers is the content of communications directed at others. On the surface, at least, it would appear that a given message could be couched in a variety of terms and presented in a variety of ways. The purpose, then, of examining communication from a content perspective is to learn what research has taught us about the potential of various types of content for changing attitudes. Much research has been done in this area, but we will restrict ourselves to examining content from the following perspectives: one-sided versus two-sided communications, the ordering of separate communications, and emotional versus rational communication.

## ☐ One-Sided vs. Two-Sided Communication

It is generally recognized that there are two sides to every argument. In organizations it is not unusual for individuals to be on opposite sides of the fence on a particular issue. From a managerial perspective, this situation requires that the manager know something about the principles of one-sided versus two-sided communication. Suppose, for example, a manager wishes to introduce some type of technological change into a work group; on the assumption that the group resists the change, what is the best approach for the manager to take? Should the manager present both the favorable and unfavorable aspects of the change, or should stress be put only on the benefits the employees will receive as a result of the change?

Much of the research relevant to this question deals with the effects of advertising and propaganda, so we must generalize these findings to communication in organizations. The effect of one-sided versus two-sided communication depends partly upon the level of knowledge possessed by the receiver prior to the communication effort. Given a relatively low knowledge level to begin with, the one-sided and two-sided communication efforts produce about the same degree of attitude change in the receiver. However, if the initial knowledge level is high, the one-sided effort is significantly less successful than the two-sided one. For individuals with low initial knowledge levels, the one-sided communication does not present any conflict with existing attitudes and is therefore more acceptable; however, if the receiver is already aware of the pros and cons of a situation, providing only one side of the issue is less acceptable since more conflict is created. For these individuals, the two-sided communication has more potential for improving attitudes since it is more consistent with existing attitudes.[10]

A similar phenomenon exists for subsequent communication (i.e., attempts to change attitudes at a later date after initial exposure to the knowledge). Again, research has shown that the two-sided communication is more effective than one-sided in maintaining resistance to subsequent attempts to change attitudes.[11] If individuals have been exposed to only one side of the story initially, they are more likely to change their attitude at a later date should someone attempt, by providing the other side, to change their mind.

These findings have important implications for managerial communication. Some obvious areas for application are labor–management negotiations, inducting new employees into the organization, and attempting to overcome the negative consequences of group influence upon the individual. We might tentatively conclude that in labor–management negotiations, attempting to "win" by providing only one side of the issue to the labor negotiating team is likely to be unsuccessful, since labor's level of knowledge about the organization is probably quite high. Admitting to both sides of the issue may decrease their resistance to management's position and vice versa. The new employee is exposed to a variety of communications from management as well as other members of the organization. Assuming that the initial level of knowledge about the organization is low, management is advised to provide information on the positive and negative factors in the organization. When the employee is subsequently socialized into the work group, he will be more likely to resist attempts at "brainwashing" by any disgruntled employees.

## Box 8-4: Why Do Low-Ranking People Want to Communicate with High-Ranking People?

The highest-ranking people (HRPs) in organizations generally find that many lower-ranking people (LRPs) want their attention. Why is this so? There are three main reasons why LRPs want to communicate with HRPs. First, it increases the LRP's status. In much the same way as the president's secretary has higher status than the vice-president's secretary, LRPs who communicate with HRPs generally find their own status enhanced by the contact.

Second, HRPs are usually able to pull strings and LRPs are not. Thus, LRPs may feel that the only way to reach their goals is to somehow get the attention of HRPs.

Third, since information is power, LRPs will be better off if they can somehow be privy to information that other LRPs are not. Since HRPs typically have the information, the calculating LRP will find ways to get this information from the HRPs.

## ☐ **The Ordering of Communication Content**

Given differing points of view, is it most advantageous to give your viewpoint first or last? In the social psychology literature, two distinct views exist, one arguing for primacy (the message received first is the most persuasive) and the other arguing for recency (the message received last is the most persuasive). The primacy effect does occur under certain conditions, but the exact nature of these conditions is uncertain. Some research suggests that, in situations where individuals are not captive audiences to the communication, the initial communicator may have the advantage since people can subsequently decide not to listen to later communications.[12]

Two factors favor recency over primacy. If one's message is the last to be heard, then there is a longer time interval between opposing communications; this serves to reduce the effect of the previous communication. Second, the mere fact of recall works in favor of the recency concept since that which is heard most recently is most likely to be remembered. However, since employees are rarely tested on their recall *per se*, this advantage may be less relevant to organizational communications.

A related issue is the sequencing of pro and con arguments. In other words, whether a person should get the last word may depend in part on the nature of that person's position. Although organizations are not debating institutions, there are nevertheless many instances of interpersonal communication between managers and subordinate employees where opposite positions are taken. An understanding of this process may assist the manager in influencing employee attitudes.

The weight of the laboratory evidence suggests that the pro-con sequence (i.e., presenting the favorable arguments first, followed by the opposing points) is superior to the con-pro sequence in changing attitudes. The logic of this position is that, after hearing the pro arguments, the individual is less likely to feel strongly about the con arguments, since to do so would create dissonance with the previous pro arguments. The same logic holds in reverse for the con-pro sequence. Other factors can also affect this relationship. For example, if the individual or group being communicated to already agrees with the position of the communicator, the sequence is likely to be immaterial.[13]

One important application of these principles is the performance appraisal interview in which the manager wants to communicate the subordinate's strong and weak points (these can be interpreted as being pros and cons). The interview will likely be most successful if the manager begins with the employee's strong points, since it is in this area where agreement is likely to occur. This may result in less resistance to the weak points since the employee has been placed in a more positive frame of mind. This also means that the weak points may be those factors that remain in employees' minds if they are communicated last. Therefore, it may be wise to end the interview on the positive note such as how the manager intends to support employees in their attempts to improve their performance.

## ☐ Emotional vs. Rational Communication

Theoretically speaking, every communication has two inherent appeals: emotional and rational. The emotional part of communication appeals to the *feelings* in the receiver, and the rational part appeals to the logical, *thinking* part. While the distinction in real life is obviously not so clear as proposed here, it is useful for analytical purposes to treat them separately. An additional complicating factor is that definitions of emotional and rational may differ between individuals who are communicating. For example, whereas a message may appear factual to management (e.g., "We have decreased our work force by 10 percent this year"), it may evoke an emotional reaction from employees ("I wonder if I'll be next").

A frequent failure in dealing with resistance to change is the failure on the part of both management and workers to recognize the difference between rational and emotional resistance to change. Management attempts to institute a change in the work system by introducing new equipment, only to find that it is not working as well as the old equipment. What has happened is that workers are resisting the change because it has disrupted social (emotional) relationships that were established under the old system. The normal reaction of management is to try to convince the workers that the new system is superior to the old. But this is premised on the assumption that employees lacked information on this fact. If their resistance is emotional in nature, this additional information will have little, if any, effect on their attitudes. As a general rule we can say that, if resistance to change is rational in origin, additional information will reduce the resistance; however, if the resistance is emotional, it must be dealt with on an emotional level. The specifics on how this can be done are discussed in the communication skills section, and how this can be applied to change strategies is discussed in Chapter 14.

## ☐ Summary of Communication Content

It is not possible to separate entirely the issues of flow and content in communications. In some cases, the successs or failure of the communication flow is largely a function of the communication's content. For example, management may find that a particular communication may be more effective if the information is "leaked" through the grapevine, particularly if there is little trust between management and the employees. Similarly, employees may not believe a communication from colleagues if they perceive the message should come down through the formal channels. Probably the deciding factor in the content/flow issue is the importance and relevance of a communication to the receiver. Information that does not have a direct effect on the receiver, regardless of the content, should be sent through formal channels. For example, announcing to employees that the firm is going to raise prices to its customers probably does not affect the employees directly and will therefore be received and understood via the top-down method. However, if the firm wishes to announce a new vacation plan, it may be best to follow a multichannel approach and provide a mechanism (bottom-up) by which management can receive feedback on how the information was received.

Clearly, the content of communication affects how it is perceived and how much it will cause changes in employee behavior and attitudes. While we have attempted to point out some of the things managers should be concerned with when communicating, perhaps the best lesson to be learned is how complex the communication process is. In this discussion we have only scratched the surface; moreover, much of the evidence available has yet to demonstrate its validity in organizational settings. Perhaps the greatest limitation of our knowledge of communication is that we know very little for certain about the relationship between communication content and *behavior* change since the majority of studies in the area deal only with *attitude* change.

---

## Organizational Reality   8-4
## "Leveling" at ROLM Corporation

Management at ROLM Corporation, a Santa Clara, California, manufacturer of digital computers and telephone equipment, has discovered the value of "leveling" with employees. Going beyond honesty and frankness, leveling means an honest appraisal of an employee's job and performance. It also includes constructive criticism and much preparation for the leveling communication.

At ROLM, there are no established guidelines. Every manager must consider the nature of the problem, the personality of the employee, and the degree to which the facts behind the problem are understood. However, some general procedures do exist. The process is ongoing and deals with both positive and negative feedback. Leveling takes place immediately after a significant event has occurred. In the day-to-day conduct of leveling meetings, guidelines are established both for performance and objectives.

Leveling consists of telling the truth, but the truth must be made acceptable by the proper selection of words and attitudes. "We have a problem," for example, shows an employee that the manager is on his or her side and is ready to communicate. ROLM managers use varied approaches when leveling, since the process must be matched to people and their jobs.

Leveling can backfire if the process turns into a shouting match and closes the lines of communication. At ROLM, management has found that the best way to prevent backfiring is to eliminate the causes. Emotionalism is a primary reason for backfiring, so an ongoing process is recommended to develop realistic expectations and to reduce emotions.

Leveling is a two-way street. Managers need employee feedback for fact gathering and employees should be told of the need for their input and feedback.

---

Source: Frank Stagnaro, "The Benefits of Leveling with Employees: ROLM's Experience," *Management Review* (July 1982): 17–20.

# ■ COMMUNICATION SKILLS

Describing the communication process from a skill perspective is difficult for several reasons. First, because skills are individual in nature, they can be practiced in many different ways. It is difficult, therefore, to generalize about the effectiveness of a particular skill. Second, the list of communication skills is almost infinite. It is impossible to differentiate between separate behaviors or to enumerate a complete list of all the skills observed. Consequently, we can never be sure that we have accounted for all the skills. The upshot of these two problems is that relatively little is known, in the scientific sense, about communication skills. As one might guess, the teaching of communication skills tends to be personalized and inefficient. Since no two people can perfectly copy each other's behavior, a skill taught by the teacher can be completely changed when used by the learner. Moreover, since skill is closely tied to personality, the teaching of skills is limited since it is difficult to teach personality changes. This type of problem is not restricted to the communication skill area. The reader may have noted that, as we progressed from the abstract model stage through the networks and content issues, our statements became increasingly qualified. The reasons for this were detailed in Chapter 2 in the discussion of prescriptive vs. descriptive models and theory vs. practice.

The qualifying of our statements does not minimize the value of communication skills, but only points out that it is difficult to make specific statements about "how to do it," and that communication skills are difficult to teach (behaviorally speaking). With these two cautions in mind, we find it useful to try to interpret communication theory from the manager's perspective. In the sections that follow, we describe some general propositions about communication skills as they relate to effective listening, perception, and nonverbal communication.

## ☐ Effective Listening

In the general communications model (Figure 8-3), it was noted that decoding is crucial for the receiver's understanding of the message. Effective listening in communications is the equivalent of the decoding process and involves more than merely *hearing* the spoken work; it is the *understanding* that must be achieved before the communicator and the listener can relate to each other.

The nature and importance of effective listening has its origin in psychotherapy. In the doctor–patient relationship, the psychotherapist's understanding of the patient's problem can come only through effective listening techniques. It is not until the listener (doctor) fully understands what the communicator (patient) is saying that effective treatment can begin. In fact, the initial treatment the patient usually receives is the listening that is practiced. Having someone else listen— really listen—to your problem can itself have therapeutic value.

Carl Rogers and Fritz Roethlisberger argue that ineffective listening is the greatest barrier to effective communication.[14] They suggest a simple game that illustrates the point. When a husband and wife are having a heated argument, they should stop and make a rule that each person can speak only afer he or she accurately restates or summarizes the *ideas* and *feelings* of the previous speaker. It is easy to see what will occur. One person cannot argue his/her side until the previous statement is properly understood; this forces understanding which, in turn, reduces the need for the argument! While conversations take longer under these conditions, they tend to be less emotional and more effective, since each party must see the situation through the other's eyes. Effective listening thus requires the ability to detect the real meaning in the words and actions of others.

Many times our own egos interfere with effective listening. The words that we use or the positions we adopt become rigid, and much of our communication effort is oriented toward protecting our own position rather than increasing our understanding of the other person's position. While the other person is speaking, we often are not listening at all but are using this time to formulate what we will say if only they will shut up! Effective listeners utilize this time to think in terms of the speaker's goals, to search for hidden meanings in the choice of words or the inflection in the speaker's voice, and to try to see the situation from the speaker's point of view. Table 8-2 summarizes the "Ten Commandments of Effective Listening."

## ☐ **Perception**

Perception is the term used to describe how individuals "see" their environment and the elements operating within it. From a communication perspective, it is part of the decoding process. People's perceptions are determined by their needs. Children raised in relatively poor families, for example, when asked to draw pictures of coins, consistently exaggerate their size as compared to children raised in wealthier households. When we are extremely hungry, we are able to drive down a busy street and pick out only the signs of eating establishments. Perhaps much of the conflicting results in some of the organizational behavior research can be traced to the fundamentals of perception. For example, it has been noted that blue-collar workers tend to rank the importance of pay considerably higher than do white-collar workers, causing some to conclude that blue-collar workers are motivated by money and white-collar workers are not. In fact, the relative perceptions of pay for each group may be influenced by the degree of need satisfaction that is present, with white-collar workers rating the importance of pay lower because they perceive less need for it. Put another way, things become important when we cannot have them.

Within the general heading of perception, there are several aspects which relate to communication skills: selective perception, stereotyping, projection, and the "halo effect."

**Selective Perception**   Selective perception is basically the application of reinforcement theory (discussed in Chapter 4) to the perception process. Selective perception means seeing what one wants to see. In our regular activities, we tend to see those things that please us and to reject or ignore unpleasant things. Selective perception allows us to keep our dissonance (the existence of conflicting elements in our perceptual set) at a tolerable level. If we encounter something that does not fit our current image of reality, we structure the situation to minimize our dissonance. Thus, we manage to overlook many stimuli from the environment that do not fit into our current perception of the world.

This process has significant implications for management activities in general and communications in particular. In one study it was shown that, given a case problem to solve, business executives tended to see the problem in terms of their own organizational functional areas.[15] This type of behavior creates considerable

**TABLE 8-2.   Ten Commandments of Effective Listening**

---

1. *Stop talking!*
   You cannot listen if you are talking.
   Polonius *(Hamlet)*: "Give every man thine ear, but few thy voice."
2. *Put the talker at ease.*
   Help him feel that he is free to talk.
   This is often called a permissive environment.
3. *Show him that you want to listen.*
   Look and act interested. Do not read your mail while he talks.
   Listen to understand rather than to oppose.
4. *Remove distractions.*
   Don't doodle, tap, or shuffle papers.
   Will it be quieter if you shut the door?
5. *Empathize with him.*
   Try to put yourself in his place so that you can see his point of view.
6. *Be patient.*
   Allow plenty of time. Do not interrupt him.
   Don't start for the door or walk away.
7. *Hold your temper.*
   An angry man gets the wrong meaning from words.
8. *Go easy on argument and criticism.*
   This puts him on the defensive. He may "clam up" or get angry.
   Do not argue; even if you win, you lose.
9. *Ask questions.*
   This encourages him and shows you are listening.
   It helps to develop points further.
10. *Stop talking!*
    This is first and last, because all other commandments depend on it.
    You just can't do a good listening job while you are talking.

Nature gave man two ears but only one tongue, which is a gentle hint that he should listen more than he talks.

---

Source: Keith Davis, *Human Behavior at Work* (New York: McGraw-Hill, 1972), p. 396. Reprinted by permission.

conflict within an organization where separate functional units should be cooperating in the attainment of common goals. In an interpersonal sense, selective perception places a barrier between the two parties. One person will hear only those communications that are consistent with his/her perception of the other person and vice versa. Managers who feel they have a problem employee on their hands may see only undesirable behavior and ignore those behaviors that do not fit their perceptions of the employee. No matter what the employee does, the manager will still see only a problem employee. The implication of this is that managers should constantly examine their own behavior for the presence of biases that influence their perceptions of others.

## Box 8-5: Barriers to Effective Communication

There are two major barriers to communication—physical and psychological. Physical barriers are generally quite obvious. The formal structure of the organization is one physical barrier. Formal communication of things like company policy is often distorted as it is transmitted from the top to the bottom of the organization because it must pass through many management levels. Another physical barrier is distance. Organizations often find it difficult and expensive to communicate with far-flung units that are part of the organization.

Psychological barriers are less obvious but are often more important. The most fundamental of these is the fact that, while we rely on words to communicate, a given word may mean different things to different people. Another major barrier is the personality match of the sender and receiver. To the extent that personalities are not compatible, effective communication will not occur.

Lack of a common frame of reference for those communicating is another barrier. The less the parties have in common (in terms of language, values, goals, etc.), the less likely it is that effective communication will occur. Numerous other specific psychological barriers to communication exist. These include poor listening habits, finishing sentences that other people start, talking instead of listening, impatience, and losing one's temper.

**Stereotyping**    Stereotyping is the application of selective perception. When we have preconceived ideas about other people and refuse to discriminate between individual behaviors, we are applying selective perception to our relationships with other people. Perhaps the most common stereotypes are racial; we apply sweeping generalizations we have previously learned to all members of a particular race. But stereotyping is not limited to racial situations, since we can stereotype any behavior. Within organizations, two frequently found stereotypes are "Union members want to get the most money for doing the least amount of work," and "Management wants to get the most out of employees for the least money."

Stereotyping is a barrier to communications because those who stereotype others use selective perception in their communications and tend to hear only those things that confirm their stereotyped images. Consequently, stereotypes become more deeply ingrained as we find more "evidence" to confirm our original opinion. Perhaps even more significant is the fact that we generally treat other people in a manner consistent with our image of them. If a manager perceives that workers are lazy, they will probably be treated as if they actually are lazy; if workers are treated as though they are lazy, the probability is increased that they will react accordingly. Through this process, stereotypes reinforce themselves and may actually *cause* the behavior that was originally assumed. This, of course, is a restatement of McGregor's Theory X and Y discussed in Chapter 6.

Like selective perception, stereotyping has a convenience function in our interpersonal relations. Since people are all different, ideally we should react and interact with each person differently. To do this, however, requires considerable psychological effort. It is much easier to categorize (stereotype) people so that we can interact with them as members of a particular category. Since the number of categories we recognize is relatively small, we end up treating many people the same even though they are quite different. Our communications, then, may be directed at an individual as a member of a category at the sacrifice of the more effective communication on a personal level.

**Projection**    Projection has two meanings—that of projecting one's own motives into others' behavior, and the use of defense mechanisms to avoid placing blame on oneself. Both of these functions are a result of the ego at work. Like stereotyping, projecting one's motives to others' behavior is a convenience function, but it is also a way of improving one's self-image, since attributing others' behavior to our own motives tends to be satisfying. If we recognize the opposite (i.e., that other people engage in certain behaviors for reasons different from ours), this can create dissonance. For example, managers who are motivated by money may assume their subordinates are also motivated by it. If the subordinates' prime motivation is something other than money, serious problems may arise.

As a defense mechanism, the projection phenomenon operates to protect the ego from unpleasant communications. Frequently, individuals who have a particular fault will see the same fault in others, making their own fault seem not so serious. One study, for example, indicated that people scoring high on traits such as stinginess, obstinacy, and disorderliness tended to rate others much higher on those traits than did individuals who did not have the traits.[16] We might generalize and predict that managers who are autocratic may see others as even more autocratic; or a person who is antiunion might see this trait in others, even if it is not there. The entire communication process is affected by this type of "noise."

**The "Halo Effect"**    The term *halo effect* refers to the process of forming opinions based on one element from a group of elements and generalizing that perception to all other elements. For example, if we meet someone for the first time who is driving a particular car we happen to like, we may form particular opinions about his managerial abilities based upon the single factor of agreeing with his choice of cars. In an organization, a good attendance record may cause positive judgments about productivity, attitude, or quality of work. In performance evaluation systems, the halo effect refers to the practice of singling out one trait of an employee (either good or bad) and using this as a basis for judgment of the total employee (e.g., seeing the well-dressed manager as the "good" manager).

The halo effect is important for organizational communication since it tells us that communication is affected by very subtle factors. One study indicated that knowledge that the company was in receivership caused employees to devalue higher pay and good working conditions as compared to employees who believed they were working in a financially secure firm.[17] It is possible, then, that communication to employees will be seriously affected if there is some factor that is coloring their perceptions.

## ☐ Nonverbal Communication

One of the areas of communication that has received considerable attention is nonverbal communication, since messages are transmitted through physical, as well as verbal channels. Porter has defined four aspects of nonverbal communications:

1. *Physical*—pertaining to the personal method, i.e., facial expressions, tone of voice, sense of touch, smell, and body motion.
2. *Esthetics*—creative expressions such as those found in music, dancing, or any of the creative arts.

---

### Organizational Reality   8-5
### Communication at Varian Incorporated

To boost employee education and productivity, many companies are using upward communications to promote good employee relations. At Varian Incorporated, a manufacturer of medical and industrial equipment, management meets each month with blue-collar workers in the "Varian Forum." Employees sign up on a voluntary, rotating basis to voice their concerns and complaints to supervisors and plant managers.

Robert Holtcamp, director of personnel at corporate headquarters in Palo Alto, California, says several changes have come about as a result of the meetings. Varian's vacation policy became more liberal because of workers' complaints. Medical and retirement benefits were improved, based on employees' suggestions. Inventory methods were made more efficient after workers pointed out inaccuracies in the existing system.

The program, initiated in 1979, is not seen by participants as a fixed institution. Holtcamp says the Varian Forum will change as managers and employees see fit.

---

Source: "Management in Practice," *Management Review* (March 1982): 46–47.

3. *Symbolic*—conveying messages through symbolic representations of reality; includes religious, status, or ego-building symbols.
4. *Signs*—mechanical means of conveying messages such as bells, buzzers, locks on doors, etc.[18]

Although all forms are present in most organizational activities, for our purposes the physical means of communicating are the most interesting. As the popular books on the subject have suggested, a person's physical reaction to a communication can be more important than his or her verbal reaction.[19] In the interpersonal communication process, it is important that each communicator be able to "read" the nonverbal cues exhibited by the other party. Because physical reactions are more subtle and subject to interpretation, the reading of these communications is more an art than a science. A few examples illustrate the use of nonverbal communication:

1. A person listening with arms folded indicates a psychological defense to the communication.
2. Facial expressions, generally self-explanatory, communicate reaction to the communicator's message. Examples are a look of surprise, disbelief, questioning, etc.
3. Silence can communicate a variety of things: apathy, listening, boredom, embarrassment, etc., depending upon the circumstances.
4. Leaning forward while conversing indicates interest; leaning backward indicates lack of interest.

The value of nonverbal communication is limited because it is always subject to interpretation and may not be consistent across different people. Nevertheless, through sensitivity and experience in utilizing the nonverbal cues, one can find them a useful tool in interpersonal communication.

# ■ SPECIFIC SKILL APPLICATIONS

We have previously mentioned that the description and teaching of specific skills (especially in a textbook) is a difficult task. We have discussed some general skill considerations that each person should be aware of when communicating, although we recognize that reading about them and practicing them are two different things. To bridge the gap between communication theory and practice, we will discuss some sample communication situations that illustrate some of the principles just presented. These are, of course, only a few of the many situations in organizations that require communication skills. However, we have chosen examples that illustrate cause-and-effect relationships so that the analytical thinker can apply the concepts to a wider variety of real-life situations. The examples we have chosen are interviewing, performance appraisal, and counseling. In this section we are essentially prescribing behavior, and we caution the reader to view this accordingly. All statements and conclusions are based on implicit assumptions about the situation, the people, and their motivations.

## ☐ **Interviewing**

Although interviewing can have many goals in organizations (selection, appraisal, information seeking, etc.), there are two general processes for reaching these goals: nondirective and directive interviewing.

**Nondirective Interviewing**   Also called unstructured or open-ended interviewing, nondirective interviewing has been used for many different purposes. It is fundamental to the process of psychotherapy and is based on the proposition that an interviewee can provide much more useful data without specific direction than if directed along predetermined lines. Nondirective interviewing has its organizational origins in the Hawthorne experiments where the researchers attempted to gather additional data that would assist them in explaining their earlier findings. They discovered that, by providing only very general direction (referred to as "cues"), employees would expound on their thoughts and be much more open than if they were asked leading, structured questions. Data gathered in this way must be interpreted in light of other data the interviewer has available.

While it is true that the nondirective approach can generate much more data than the directive one, much of the information may be either useless or misleading. Consequently, data from nondirective interviews must be interpreted, and this opens up the possibilities for perceptual biases on the part of the interviewer. Obviously, the success of the nondirective approach depends a great deal upon the interviewer's skill in being able to provide the proper cues, to guide when guidance is needed, and to correctly interpret the data gathered.

The relevance of the nondirective approach depends on the situation. If an interview is primarily for fact-finding purposes (such as the initial employment interview), then the nondirective approach is very inefficient and can be frustrating to the prospective employee. If the type of information needed is readily available (e.g., biographical information), then it can be asked for directly. However, if the manager faces a situation in which the nature and/or source of the problem is not known, then the nondirective approach is more effective.

Probably the greatest difficulty in these situations is deciding if the situation dictates a structured or unstructured approach. What the manager may perceive as a relatively straightforward event may in fact be only a small part of a much larger, abstract, personal problem of the employee. For example, if an employee approaches management and states a need for a raise in pay, the management may respond in one of two ways. First, a manager may decide to grant or not to grant the raise, provide the reasons why, and then terminate the interview. Or the manager may ask a question such as, "Tell me why you think you need a raise," which could result in management learning much about the employee's feelings, attitudes, motivations, and so on, that was previously unknown.

Another variable affecting the success of the nondirective approach is the climate in which the interview occurs. A supportive, nonthreatening climate encourages the interviewee to speak freely, much as the patient confides in the therapist. The manager who uses the nondirective technique in a negative, threatening climate will likely find that it generates only blank looks from employees, who are willing to provide only the specific information asked for.

The methods of conducting a nondirective interview are many and vary with personal styles, but they all cue the interviewee that a response is desired (but not the nature of the response). Some techniques commonly used to stimulate the interviewee to respond are as follows:

1. *The echo*—Echoing back a person's statements shows you are interested and would like to hear more. It is also noncommittal. For example, if an employee has just expressed displeasure with a promotion, the echo would be, "You say you're unhappy about your promotion?"

2. *The grunt*—Verbal indications of interest indicate to the interviewee that you are listening. The "uh-huh" type of response is one way of indicating this interest. Note, however, that the inflection of voice can give the grunt different meanings.

3. *The restatement*—This is similar to playing the game suggested by Rogers and Roethlisberger. After an interviewee has responded, the interviewer can add some structure to the situation by interpreting what has been said with a restatement. This shows the interviewee that the interviewer (1) has been listening and (2) has interpreted correctly what has been said. Of course, this technique can communicate to the interviewee that the interviewer has *not* properly understood, a cue for further explanation.

4. *The silent treatment*—In most conversations, silence is taken as a negative sign. Consequently, many interviewers find silence uncomfortable in the interview and, should it occur, they jump in with a remark, question, or comment. In nondirective interviewing, a period of silence is viewed as potentially positive, as the interviewee may be thinking an issue over or waiting to hear the interviewer's reaction to what has just been said. Assuming the situation is appropriate for a nondirective interview, the interviewer may want to wait out the interviewee rather than run the risk of directing the interview along a path not wanted by the interviewee.

There is no one best way to conduct a nondirective interview, since personal styles can affect the communication process. Moreover, few situations will be either-or in nature; this requires the interviewer to be directive on some occasions and nondirective on others. Interviews will be a balance of each with the interviewer (manager) deciding what the proper mixture should be. The intricacies of this decision are explored further in the next section.

**Directive Interviewing**    The nature and methods of the directive approach are opposite to those of the nondirective one (i.e., the manager directs the interview along preplanned lines, and the interviewee responds to specific questions provided by the manager). It is important to remember that directive interviews are neither better nor worse than nondirective ones—they are simply used for different purposes. Directive interviewing techniques are most appropriate for situations in which interviewee perceptions, biases, attitudes, and values are unlikely to affect the information gathered. In combination with the nondirective approach, directive interviewing can be used to explore something in more detail that has been raised in a nondirective setting. This is often referred to as the "funnel approach" in which the interview begins in a very unstructured fashion, but as the interview progresses and specific points are made, the interviewer then directs the discussion along these lines. Again, the sensitivity of the interviewer plays an important role in determining the appropriateness of the structured and unstructured approaches. Perhaps the best way of learning how each technique may be important is to examine several situations requiring interviewing skills.

## ☐ The Performance Appraisal Interview

One of the most difficult communication situations involving subordinates is the performance appraisal interview. One reason for the difficulty is the differing perceptions of the objective of the interview. If the manager sees the interview as an opportunity to pass judgment on the employee and the employee sees the interview as an opportunity to tell the manager what to do differently in the coming weeks or months, then it is unlikely that constructive communication will occur. In the following example we assume that the performance appraisal interview has three objectives which should be accomplished in sequential order:

1. To determine how employees feel about their performance.
2. To inform employees how the manager sees their performance as compared to standards.
3. To discuss and agree upon ways in which good performance can be maintained and poor performance can be corrected.

We should also keep in mind that the purpose of the performance appraisal interview is to increase the future productivity of employees and that, if employee behavior is not influenced in a positive direction as a result of the interview, then the interview has failed.

**Opening the Interview**    The opening of the interview is crucial since this sets the tone for the discussion. We know from our earlier discussion that communications not consistent with the individual's self-perception will likely be rejected. Consequently, before managers can effectively communicate with employees about performance they must *first* learn how employees see their own behavior. This information is best obtained by a relatively nondirective question such as "How do you feel your work has been progressing?" The exact nature of the opening statement, of course, depends on the situation. If the employee knows it is a performance appraisal interview and feels threatened by it (because of some unfortunate past experience), this approach may result in a minimal response as the defenses of the employee are aroused by the situation. We cannot emphasize too much the importance of the individual manager's sensitivity in these situations in deciding what is correct and incorrect. However, the general principle of knowing how employees see themselves still holds; the method by which this is accomplished can vary from situation to situation.

**Communicating Performance**  Assuming the interview has been opened properly, the manager next must communicate to the employee how performance has been judged. Strictly speaking, managers should not form this opinion until they have heard the employees' perceptions of their own performance. Since it is probable that some new information will come forth as a result of the interview, it is unwise to formulate a preconceived opinion before all the data have been acquired. If the two perceptions agree, there is less opportunity for conflict in meeting the third objective (improving performance). However, to be realistic, let us assume that there are some differences in perception. Given this, the manager must again be aware that communications counter to the employee's self-image are likely to be rejected. In this circumstance, the object is to minimize the defensive reactions of the employee. We cited evidence earlier suggesting that favorable communications presented first reduce defenses and increase the probability that later unfavorable comments will be accepted. Using this as our guiding principle in perception of the employee's performance, the manager should probably state the favorable perceptions first and follow up with the less favorable ones. Reversal of this process places employees on the defensive, stimulates their emotions, and decreases the probability that the later favorable comments will have any effect. Employees are then more likely to leave the interview in a poor state of mind, and therefore performance is unlikely to be improved.

**Improving Performance**  The probability that future performance will improve depends on how the first two stages have been carried out. Assuming that the interview is positive up to this point, the next objective is to *help* the employee to improve performance in whatever areas have been discussed and to maintain those behaviors that are desirable. Again, the general principles of communication are useful here. We know that communication directed at performance improvement must be consistent with the employee's self-image. Also, emphasis should be positive, supportive, and a mutual responsibility. Employees must perceive that the manager is not being punitive and wants to help them develop their potential. The communication that the manager uses should be consistent with this objective. If performance goals are set, they should be realistic in that employees must feel they are capable of attaining them. Using the mutual-influence communication process avoids unrealistic goal setting.

An interesting way of avoiding many of the pitfalls mentioned here is for management not to conduct formal performance appraisal interviews. In other words, performance can be appraised, communicated, and improved without a formal interview process. Formalizing the process can increase the defensive reactions of employees and make communication between managers and subordinates much more difficult. Perhaps a better way is to communicate performance when the need (either positive or negative) arises, rather than at a specific time of year. In this way, employees will not be on guard and managers will not be apprehensive, thus eliminating two common barriers to effective performance appraisal.

## ☐ **Counseling**

Counseling is an activity that has become relatively widespread as a result of the nondirective interviewing used in the Hawthorne experiments. Although, technically, any two-way communication between manager and subordinate is counseling, the term is generally used to indicate those situations in which the manager and the subordinate interact because of some personal or work-related problem the employee has. Emphasis tends to be on employees recognizing and understanding their own problem; the counselor serves as a sympathetic listener who may make some suggestions for resolving the problem.

---

### *Organizational Reality  8-6*
### *Performance Appraisal at The Sybron Corporation*

The Sybron Corporation, headquartered in Rochester, New York, decided to take direct action when they were unhappy with their existing performance evaluation system.

A review of the system indicated that the problem was not in the system itself, but in the area of management training. The system was essentially good, but it was so sophisticated that few managers had the skills to use it effectively.

Sybron and its consultants designed a training program to provide managers with the necessary skills and motivation to set objectives and assess performance. The program also trained managers to encourage their employees to work to their full potential through a systematic approach to goal setting.

More than 250 managers have been through the program. The course is held one full day a week for four weeks, with eight to ten managers participating each time. In the first part of the program, managers are taught interpersonal and communication skills for setting reviews, determining goals, and carrying out performance and salary reviews. The managers practice the skills and receive feedback on how they are progressing, including viewing themselves on videotape for nonverbal communication problems.

The second part of the program provides managers with five general principles to help them improve their performance interviews:

1. They are taught to maintain and enhance the employee's self-esteem;
2. They are told to focus on behavior, not personalities or attitudes;
3. They are taught how to reinforce positive aspects of behavior;
4. They are taught basic listening skills so the employees will feel accepted;
5. The managers learn to be confident in the employees' abilities to improve their performances and to be willing to help, if necessary.

---

Source: *AMA International Forum* (January 1981): 32–33.

Because counseling situations are very personal in nature, many managers are reluctant to get involved in them. It is their belief that it is unwise for the manager to "get too close" to employees. Others believe that the employee's personal life is none of the manager's business and are afraid they will be accused of prying if they get involved. For those problems that are extremely personal, it is probably unwise for the line manager to take an active role in trying to help or advise the employee. However, the manager can develop a climate in the work setting such that employees will feel free to come to the manager with their concerns, particularly if the concerns are affecting performance.

**Handling Problems When Emotions Are High**    Although there are many situations in which a counseling attitude is useful, the nature of the process can best be illustrated by an extreme example. Assume the manager is confronted by a subordinate who is emotionally upset about something. This might be the result of a heated argument between the employee and a colleague, dissatisfaction with a recent job assignment, or a conflict just experienced with a customer or client. What do communications principles tell us we should do?

Before the manager can respond, he must first learn how the employee perceives the situation. This can be accomplished by following some of the counseling responses listed earlier. If emotions are high, the manager will likely be required to do a considerable amount of interpreting of the employee's responses since they may be disjointed and confused.

The initial response of the manager will be to *listen* to the employee. This serves to draw off emotions affecting the employee's ability to communicate. We learned earlier that simply providing facts in emotional situations is ineffective and, in this case, can even make the situation worse if the employee feels that no one really understands the problem. A good rule-of-thumb is that the manager should not get *actively* involved in the conversation until the emotional state of the employee has been improved. At this point, the manager can take a more directive approach and begin to assist the employee in solving or dealing with the problem; or the employee may be referred to someone more qualified to deal with the problem.

The value of effective listening when emotions are high cannot be overemphasized. The therapeutic value of releasing emotions is very great, although this in itself does not guarantee a solution will be reached. Many times the reason that employees cannot deal with a problem is *because* of emotional factors; by allowing people a mechanism through which they can release emotional tensions, a solution may be found without the direct involvement of the manager.

Since our natural reactions in these types of situations may be opposite to the kinds of behaviors that should be exhibited, effective counseling must begin with the manager making a conscious effort to use a nondirective and supportive approach. One reason why counseling situations are so unpleasant for many managers is because their directive approach and inability to listen effectively to the employee has resulted in some unfortunate experience in the past. Effective listening should never be left to habit. It results from conscious effort.

## Opening Incident Revisited— Treeline Manufacturing Company

The problems revealed in this incident illustrate several issues regarding the communication process. The major one, perhaps is whether Romero would have been better off not communicating the information about the company. This is a difficult question to answer, since the information communicated (i.e., content) cannot be separated from the channels, the methods, the networks, and perceptual processes.

It would appear that part of the problem with the information itself was the manner in which it was communicated. Merely posting information on a bulletin board with no explanation of its meaning invites different interpretations of the message. In this case, the perceptions of the information have been affected by the previous experiences of the employees. Each employee will interpret the information in the light of what it means for himself or herself personally. Clearly, with the graphs showing a deteriorating company situation, there are important implications for each worker's job in the company.

Romero has also failed to realize that information has both a logical and emotional side to it. Even though the information may have a perfectly logical explanation to it, from the employee's point of view it will evoke strong emotions. The only way to deal with the problem here is to provide more information which might overcome any fears the employees have. So Romero's mistake was not in communicating the information, but in communicating *only* this information.

The incident also shows the result of not communicating enough information. Rumors are generated when employees try to "fill the gap" of missing information that is important to them. Although some information may be largely ignored by employees, information that has a personal meaning will be considered carefully.

It is to be hoped that Romero will learn some lessons about effective communications. This program of downward communication should be continued, but it should also be reexamined to improve its effectiveness. Most importantly, the executive committee should review all information before it is passed down and ask the question, "How will the receivers (employees) perceive this information?" If it is anticipated that the perceptions will be wrong or negative, then the communications process—including content, networks, methods, and channels—should be reviewed carefully. The major lesson to be learned from this incident might be that communicating information wrongly is as bad as communicating the wrong information!

# ■ SUMMARY

Communication is the force through which action is introduced into the structure of the organization. But, valuable as it may be, it cannot make up for poor management decisions or inappropriate managerial strategies. Too often we tend to view communication as a sterile process demanding only that we make our message clear and direct it to those intended. It is to be hoped that we have made the point in this chapter that communication is a very complex process and that behavioral variables make effective communication much more difficult than is usually realized.

Knowledge *about* communication is distinctly different from skill *with* communication. Accordingly, we have attempted to illustrate how some generally accepted communication principles can be applied to some common organizational problems. But in the final analysis, because communication is a skill, the effectiveness of any given communication theory will vary from individual to individual. To improve these skills it is necessary to practice them consciously as often as possible and to seek feedback so that personal skills can continually be upgraded.

# ■ REVIEW QUESTIONS

1. What is the general role of communication in determining organizational performance?

2. What is the relationship between communication models and communication skills?

3. What is the function of encoding? Decoding?

4. Why is channel selection important in communication?

5. What function does feedback serve in the communication process?

6. What are some common barriers to understanding in communications?

7. Why is the upward flow of communication important for management?

8. How does lateral communication serve as a means of social satisfaction?

9. Why is the study of communication networks important?

10. What purpose would a company newsletter serve? What might be some dangers?

11. How can the content of communication affect its influence on behavior?

12. Why are communication skills difficult to teach?

13. What is the main function of "effective listening"? What are some common organizational situations in which this technique might be useful?

14. How does perception affect the communication process?

15. What would be some reasonable measures of the degree of success of a performance appraisal?

16. When should nondirective interviewing be used? Directive interviewing?

17. Why should managers learn counseling skills?

# ■ EXERCISE 8-1: THE ASSUMED TAKEOVER

Slater Engineering, Ltd. employed sixty mechanical and industrial engineers. Its main work was drawing up specifications for various projects that were going to be completed by different manufacturing firms. Slater itself did no manufacturing. The business was quite cyclical, with a flurry of activity occuring just prior to the time of the government's awarding contracts to different manufacturers. Once these contracts had been awarded, the demand for the services provided by Slater fell off sharply, although generally the engineers were not laid off.

Recently, the employees of Slater began to hear rumors that the firm was going to be taken over by Broadleaf Manufacturing, a company interested in developing in-house expertise in the engineering area so that it would not have to contract out the engineering work. An article to this effect has also appeared in one of the financial papers. Alfred Slater, the president, has not commented on either of these rumors.

Should the president comment on the rumors? Why or why not?

# ■ EXERCISE 8-2: SHEILA ROBINSON

"What a good idea!" Sheila thought to herself as the plane drifted downward on its glide path. She had spent the last twenty minutes reading an article in the airline magazine entitled "Where Good Ideas Really Come From," and was thinking about how the message of the article might apply to her company. The major theme of the article was that the best ideas for improvement were most likely to come from the rank-and-file employees, not the managers of the company, because the rank-and-file are in the position to see where most things go wrong. The article went on to describe the various ways of getting these ideas flowing upward so they could be used to improve the organization and its profits.

One idea that appealed to Sheila was the idea of an employee suggestion system. The article proposed that special "suggestion boxes" be placed in strategic places around the organization with blank forms for employees to fill out describing their ideas for improvement. Since this seemed to be an easy way to start, she decided to implement it when she got back to her company.

After discussing the idea with several of her senior managers, it was agreed to put the program in place. Several specially designed boxes were placed in various areas around the company and the following memorandum was sent to all employees:

TO: All Employees
FROM: Sheila Robinson, President
All of you will no doubt notice the special "suggestion boxes" that have been placed around the building. This is a new campaign we have started to solicit ideas for improvement from the employees. I would like each of you to think of ways that our operations can be improved, write them on the form provided, and drop them into the box. The boxes will be emptied once each week and the ideas reviewed. Those that appear to warrant further study will be passed on to the appropriate department. I know that all of you have ideas for improvement and I look forward to reading about them. With your help, this can be a better place to work for all.

Sheila anxiously awaited the first batch of suggestions. After the first week, the personnel manager brought them in. There were two: one was an obscene note to Sheila, and the other suggested that the suggestion boxes be scrapped.

1.   Why has the system not worked the way Sheila hoped?

2.   Do you think the system can be salvaged?

3.   How should the system have been implemented?

# ■ ENDNOTES

1.   We are indebted to Dr. Earl Planty for this perspective.
2.   As mentioned previously, much of the research in communication theory has come from the literature on social psychology. Rather than review the many studies that have been done on each subject, we prefer to provide summary statements based upon reviews of the literature by others. For those interested in reading further in the area of communicatory credibility, we recommend Paul F. Secord and Carl W. Backman, *Social Psychology* (New York: McGraw-Hill, 1964), pp. 130–31. We use this format throughout this chapter.
3.   Some caution must be used in defining "credibility of the source." Since we are concerned with potential influence, not the "correctness" of the communication, a manager could possess credibility because, regardless of whether an instruction to a subordinate is right or wrong, the subordinate perceives that obedience is appropriate. In other words, managerial authority and the perception that it will be exerted make management more "credible."
4.   See Chapter 15 for a detailed discussion of M.B.O.
5.   For example, legislation in the Netherlands requires most public corporations to have a specific amount of employee representation on the board of directors, and many firms in North America are moving toward this concept.
6.   Earl G. Planty and William Machaver, "Stimulating Upward Communication," in *Effective Communication on the Job* (American Management Association, 1956).
7.   As examples, see H. J. Levitt, "Some Effects of Certain Communication Patterns on Group Performance," *Journal of Abnormal Social Psychology* 46 (1951): 38–50; M. E. Shaw, "Some Effects of Problem Solution Efficiency in Different Communications Nets," *Journal of Experimental Psychology* 48 (1954): 211–17; Alex Bavelas, "Communication Patterns in Task-Oriented Groups," *Journal of the Acoustical Society of America* 22 (1950): 725–30; Harold Guetzkow and

Herbert A. Simon, "The Impact of Certain Communication Nets Upon Organization and Performance in Task-Oriented Groups," in Albert H. Rubenstein and Chadwick J. Haberstroh, eds., *Some Theories of Organization* (Homewood, Ill.: Dorsey Press, 1960), pp. 259–77.

8. Robert L. Burgess, "Communication Networks: An Experimental Reevaluation," *Journal of Experimental Social Psychology* 4 (July 1968): 235.

9. Harold Guetzkow and Herbert A. Simon, "The Impact of Certain Communication Nets."

10. A. Lumsdaine and I. L. Janis, "Resistance of 'Counterpropaganda' Produced by One-Sided and Two-Sided 'Propaganda' Presentations," *Public Opinion Quarterly* 17 (1953): 311–18.

11. Secord and Backman, *Social Psychology*, pp. 138–39.

12. Ibid., pp. 144–45.

13. Ibid., pp. 144–45.

14. Carl R. Rogers and F. J. Roethlisberger, "Barriers and Gateways to Communication," *Harvard Business Review* 30 (July-August 1952): 44–49.

15. Dewitt C. Dearborn and Herbert A. Simon, "Selective Perception," *Sociometry* 21 (1958): 140–43.

16. R. R. Sears, "Experimental Studies in Perception, 1. Attribution of Traits," *Journal of Social Psychology* 7 (1936): 151–63.

17. B. A. Grove and W. A. Kerr, "Specific Evidence on Origin of Halo Effect in Measurement of Morale," *Journal of Social Psychology* 34 (1951): 165–70.

18. George W. Porter, "Nonverbal Communications," *Training and Development Journal* 23 (June 1969): 3–8.

19. For example, see Gail E. Myers and Michele T. Myers, *The Dynamics of Human Communication* (New York: McGraw-Hill, 1973), Chapter 12.

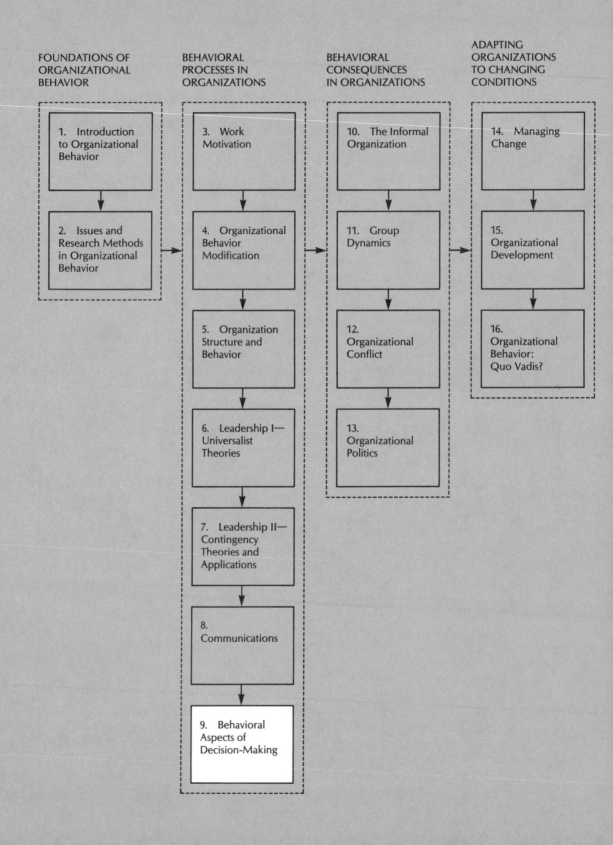

FOUNDATIONS OF
ORGANIZATIONAL
BEHAVIOR

1. Introduction to Organizational Behavior

2. Issues and Research Methods in Organizational Behavior

BEHAVIORAL
PROCESSES IN
ORGANIZATIONS

3. Work Motivation

4. Organizational Behavior Modification

5. Organization Structure and Behavior

6. Leadership I— Universalist Theories

7. Leadership II— Contingency Theories and Applications

8. Communications

9. Behavioral Aspects of Decision-Making

BEHAVIORAL
CONSEQUENCES
IN ORGANIZATIONS

10. The Informal Organization

11. Group Dynamics

12. Organizational Conflict

13. Organizational Politics

ADAPTING
ORGANIZATIONS
TO CHANGING
CONDITIONS

14. Managing Change

15. Organizational Development

16. Organizational Behavior: Quo Vadis?

# Behavioral Aspects of Decision Making

## ■ Learning Objectives

After reading this chapter carefully you should be able to:

- ☐ Describe the organizational context in which decision making takes place.
- ☐ Distinguish between the various models of decision making.
- ☐ Describe the decision-making environments of certainty, risk, and uncertainty.
- ☐ Explain the basic decision-making strategies that can be used and the situations in which they are appropriate.
- ☐ Describe the rational decision-making process and indicate how the idiosyncracies of human behavior can alter this process.
- ☐ Explain several widely used decision-making techniques.
- ☐ Describe the strong and weak points of group and individual decision making.
- ☐ Recognize the importance of creativity in decision making.

# Chapter  9

# ■ KEY TERMS

**Problem and opportunity decisions**

**Programmed and nonprogrammed decisions**

**Rational decision making**

**Certainty**

**Risk**

**Uncertainty**

**Problem analysis**

**Decision making**

**Weights and criteria method**

**Decision trees**

**Delphi technique**

**Nominal grouping**

**Brainstorming**

**Groupthink**

**Creativity**

# ■ CHAPTER OUTLINE

I. General Observations About Decision Making

II. The Decision-Making Environment
   A. The Predictability of Decision Outcomes
   B. Individual Decision-Making Models
   C. Management Styles in Decision Making
   D. Organizational Models of Decision-Making Behavior
   E. General Decision-Making Strategies

III. The Decision-Making Process
   A. The Problem-Analysis Phase
   B. The Decision-Making Phase
   C. The Implementation Phase

IV. Decision-Making Techniques
   A. The Weights and Criteria Method
   B. Decision Trees

## *Opening Incident—Franklin Real Estate*

Franklin Real Estate, Inc. is a small but rapidly growing firm in a midwestern city. The company is managed by four members of the Franklin family. The father, John, is the president and his three sons, Art, Bill, and Mark, occupy the other management positions. The company has two main areas of activity: traditional residential real estate sales, and speculative buying and selling of commercial property. With respect to the latter, the four managers meet once a month to determine if any good opportunities exist. At the last meeting, the following discussion took place:

JOHN:   Well boys, I'll get right to the point. I've heard through my contact downtown that the government has decided to start construction on a nuclear power plant on the western edge of the city within six months. I wasn't able to find out exactly where they're planning to build, but since they don't hold any land in the area now, they'll have to buy property soon. Once word gets out, the land in question will really jump in value. If we buy now, we could make a large profit when we sell the land in six months. Of course, if we buy land they don't want, we'll have to sell it for whatever we can get six months from now, after their decision is known.

ART:   What land is currently available that the government might want?

JOHN:   Since Mark is our expert in this area, I mentioned this to him yesterday and asked him to analyze the situation. What's your opinion, Mark?

MARK:   I feel there are really only three blocks of land that are feasible for what the government wants to do. (Mark then presented the following information regarding the three properties.)

| Block | Cost | Probability That Nuclear Plant Will Be Built On Block | Value of Land If Government Decides To Buy It For The Power Plant | Value of Land If Government Decides Not To Buy It For The Power Plant |
|-------|------|------|------|------|
| 1 | $ 40,000 | .2 | $ 80,000 | $45,000 |
| 2 | 60,000 | .5 | 110,000 | 35,000 |
| 3 | 100,000 | .3 | 220,000 | 65,000 |

JOHN:   Well, the fact that there are only three blocks makes our decision easier. What other information should we have?

BILL:   How much money is available?

ART:   A maximum of $100,000. If we decide on a block that doesn't require a $100,000 outlay, we'll put the excess in certificates of deposit at 15 percent for six months. We can't get our hands on more than $100,000 because we're already committed in other areas.

JOHN:   I think we have all the relevant facts now. Any opinions on what we should do?

BILL:   Well, I think we should buy block . . .

ART:   (interrupting) Now wait a minute! Every month we go through this routine of trying to make investment decisions based on everyone's off-the-cuff opinion. This is too time-consuming. What we need is some sort of procedure to make these decisions. Once we've developed the procedure, we just apply it every month and save ourselves a lot of time.

MARK:   What kind of procedure do you have in mind?

ART:   I'm not really sure. But we've got to do something.

At this point a lengthy discussion took place about whether or not it was feasible to develop a procedure for making decisions like this. The meeting ended with nothing resolved.

---

The process by which a problem is recognized and alternatives are developed and analyzed to resolve it forms the focus of this chapter. From both an individual and an organizational perspective, decision making is an important activity. The outcome of a decision, for both individuals and organizations, is the investment of time and money. For example, for the individual it might mean pursuit of a university degree, while for a corporation it might mean acceptance of a major research project. Since the outcome of the decision-making process often has major implications, it is important to study how people make decisions, both at the individual and group level. At the very minimum, a person's frustration level will be reduced if that person has some understanding of the nature of decision making. At maximum, much better decisions will be made, with the accompanying individual and organizational benefits.

In this chapter we first make some important general observations about decision making. Several aspects of the decision-making environment are then noted. The actual decision-making process is discussed in detail, and a comparison of ideal and actual behavior in each phase of the process is presented. Several specific decision-making techniques are then analyzed; the chapter concludes with a comparison of individual and group decision making and a discussion of creativity in decision making. We have not included a separate applications section because the application of the ideas is presented at the time they are introduced.

# ■ GENERAL OBSERVATIONS ABOUT DECISION MAKING

Before we look in detail at the topic of decision making, it is necessary to make some general observations about it. First, decision making is the essence of management because it is required when carrying out the key functions of management: planning, organizing, directing, and controlling. For example, when the planning function is going on, decisions must be made about what the firm will do with respect to new products, employee-compensation programs, and a host of other activities. Likewise, when the directing function is performed, the manager must decide whether to use an autocratic or a democratic style, how to motivate employees, and so on. Decision making is therefore the essence of management because it is the central focus of what managers do when they perform the functions of management.

Second, managers encounter both problem decisions and opportunity decisions. *Problem decisions* are necessary when something has gone wrong, while *opportunity decisions* are appropriate when there is no pressing problem but an opportunity exists to do something that will benefit the organization or the people in it. Not surprisingly, people tend to be preoccupied with problem decisions in spite of the fact that opportunity decisions may have larger benefits.

Third, before problem decisions are necessary, several conditions must exist:

1. *There must be a deviation between what was planned and what has actually occurred.* This demonstrates the importance of setting measurable organizational objectives.

2. *The decision maker(s) must be aware of the deviation.* If objectives have been stated so crudely that results can be interpreted in a variety of ways, there will be difficulty getting agreement that a deviation exists.

3. *The decision maker(s) must have a desire to resolve the problem.* If a student receives a lower grade than expected on an examination, but is in the

process of dropping out of school, there is obviously going to be no desire to do better on the next exam.

4. *There must be resources available to resolve the problem.* An organization in which sales have fallen far short of those that were projected may have a perfectly clear understanding of the problem. In addition, everyone may agree that it exists, and there may be tremendous desire to improve the situation. Yet, if resources are not available to do so, nothing of substance will happen.

Fourth, decision making is the process of choosing from among potential solutions to problems. The point at which the actual decision is made is an event, but people often place too much emphasis on the event and not enough on the process. As we shall see later in the chapter, the process of making decisions is a very lengthy one, and while the event of choosing an alternative is often dramatic, it is only one step in the long process of analysis. We will stress the process aspect of decision making in this chapter.

Fifth, it is difficult to judge managerial effectiveness in decision making except over a period of time. At any one point a manager may make a very good or a very bad decision, but managerial effectiveness should be judged on the basis of multiple decisions. Realistically, we must admit that careers may turn on a single

## Box 9-1: Programmed Decisions

Programmed decisions can be observed in all types of organizations. In a bottling plant, for example, that part of quality control dealing with whether the bottle is filled to the proper level follows a programmed decision. A simple procedure like having a chalk line behind the line of bottles is used in some plants. If the level in a bottle is above or below the line, the bottle is rejected.

The credit-granting function in banks is another example of programmed decision making. Typically, the bank has a formula for combining variables such as the applicant's current monthly payments, total assets, yearly income, etc. The applicant's score determines whether a loan will be granted. In this case, only a minimum level is set and any score above the minimum means the loan will be approved.

As another example, consider a store's policy on merchandise returns. If you purchase a shirt that does not fit and you want to return it, what happens? You will probably be allowed to exchange it for a shirt that does fit, or get a credit voucher that can be used for future purchases. Many stores will not allow the sales clerk to return your money; rather, they require you to go to a special returns office.

In all of these cases the decision is programmed, but many different "programs" are evident. In all cases the programs reduce the use of worker discretion.

decision; thus, the political realities of organizations often overshadow rationality. Ideally, however, a manager's track record over a large number of decisions should be the basis for judging managerial effectiveness in decision making.

Sixth, while there are infinitely many decisions that can be made, they really can be placed into one of two categories:

> 1. *Programmed decisions*—These are decisions for which a routine (either physical or conceptual) has been established. For example, when salespeople turn in their expense accounts at the end of each month, there is a specified procedure in most firms for handling this situation. Every individual who is involved in this activity knows exactly what to do, and the procedure is used regularly. In all organizations there are many programmed decisions that must be made.
>
> 2. *Nonprogrammed decisions*—As the term implies, these are decisions that do not recur frequently and therefore no routine has been established for making them. For example, if a firm wishes to build a new plant but has never done so before, this activity is clearly a nonprogrammed decision. Many decisions will have to be made in areas where management has no precedents to follow. Nonprogrammed decisions can have a much greater impact on the organization than programmed decisions.[1]

Seventh, programmed and nonprogrammed decisions can be found at all levels in the organization, but generally speaking, the former should be made near the bottom while the latter should be made near the top of the organization (see Figure 9-1). This balance is usually upset when top management becomes overinvolved in programmed decision making (represented by the dotted line in Figure 9-1). When this happens, lower-level employees may be demotivated because top management is continually interfering and making decisions within the employees' area of expertise. If top managers are too heavily involved in

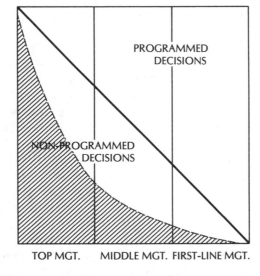

TOP MGT.    MIDDLE MGT.  FIRST-LINE MGT.

**FIGURE 9-1.   Decision Types and Management Levels**

programmed decisions, it is also likely that they will give too little emphasis to nonprogrammed decisions such as corporate strategy. If these crucial nonprogrammed decisions are not made, the organization may find itself in deep trouble. Since the situation represented by the dotted line in the figure is not unusual, managers must continually strive to see that decisions are made at the most appropriate level in the hierarchy. This is accomplished by pushing as many decisions as possible downward and as few decisions as possible upward. When this is done, lower-level employees are given opportunities to make decisions and managers are not burdened with detailed decisions that can be made by someone else. Each level in the hierarchy will then be contributing effectively to overall organizational objectives.

Finally, there is considerable debate about what the term "rational decision making" means. Individuals frequently accuse each other of being "irrational." In

---

## Organizational Reality   9-1
### Sharing Decision-Making Authority

Two years ago at the annual meeting of Data General Corporation, the world's number three minicomputer maker, belligerent shareholders pressed management to explain why revenues had suddenly flattened out and why profits had plunged 30 percent.

Much of the criticism had centered on the management of Edson de Castro, president and founder, who had maintained absolute control over a company that had grown too large for such one-man rule. A group of senior executives recruited over the past two years from larger computer makers—most notably IBM—have now settled in and have brought with them their own brand of decentralized, more disciplined management. The company no longer has the line functions of engineering, marketing, sales and service reporting to de Castro. "I'm no longer the initiator (of company actions), but the review agency," de Castro says of his new role.

Three business divisions reporting to Robert C. Miller handle strategic marketing, coordinate the design and manufacture of products, and sell them in specific markets. The changes were perhaps hardest for de Castro to accept. He did not remove himself from the day-to-day decisions, insiders report, until he appointed Miller, a veteran of fifteen years at IBM, to head the company's three business divisions.

Miller is more willing to stand up to de Castro than other managers in the company, insiders say. As a result, one manager reports "Miller has more latitude and authority than any of the former heads of the business division."

The management overhaul is paying off for the company but it illustrates the problems of centralized power and what may be required to share that power effectively—subordinates who are just as comfortable using it.

---

Source: "Data General Tries for Its Second Wind," *Business Week* (7 March 1983): 75–83.

most of these cases, the term simply means that one person does not agree with the other person's viewpoint. It is therefore important to define what a rational decision is. For our purposes, a *rational decision* is one in which the decision maker has a specific goal that he or she is trying to reach and is using his or her mental faculties in an attempt to reach this goal.[2] The term "irrational" therefore implies that the individual has suspended his or her mental capability to pursue an objective.

Note that the definition of a rational decision does not deal with the question of whether the goal the individual is pursuing is a "reasonable" goal. It is practically impossible to deal with goals and their "goodness," given the tremendous diversity in value judgments that people make about almost any goal. The definition does recognize the tremendous number of individual differences that exist in a given population of people. Since these differences are typically found even among members of the same organization, it would appear that this is the only realistic definition of the term "rational" that could be adopted. However, it does suffer from the shortcoming that almost anything that is decided by any person could be considered a rational decision.

These introductory observations should be kept in mind as we proceed through the various aspects of decision making. This is a complex subject, and much remains to be learned about it. However, some general guidance of this nature should be helpful as we next look at the environment in which decisions are made and at the actual decision-making process.

# ■ THE DECISION-MAKING ENVIRONMENT

As noted in Chapter 3, no two organizations have exactly the same internal environment. Since decision-making activity takes place within specific organizations, we might conclude that different organizations have little in common with respect to the basic activity called decision making. However, this is not true. There are several major elements of the internal environment that influence decision making in all organizations: (1) the predictability of decision outcomes, (2) individual decision-making models, (3) management styles in decision making, (4) organizational decision-making models, and (5) general decision-making strategies which can be used in organizations.

## □ The Predictability of Decision Outcomes

When managers make decisions, they find that the quality of information about the alternatives, the payoffs, the risks, etc., varies widely. As indicated in Figure 9-2, the information environment that managers face ranges all the way from complete uncertainty to complete certainty. While there are an infinite number of circumstances in which decisions are made, we can divide the continuum into three basic parts.

| SUBJECTIVE PROBABILITIES | OBJECTIVE PROBABILITIES |
|---|---|

UNCERTAINTY                    RISK                    CERTAINTY

**FIGURE 9-2.  Certainty, Risk, and Uncertainty**

**Certainty**   At one extreme, managers can have very exact information about the relevant aspects of the problem facing them. When certainty exists, the manager knows exactly how many alternatives are available, the nature of each alternative, the payoff from each alternative, and the likelihood of chance events associated with each alternative. This situation is not very likely to occur often in managerial decision making, although there are certain types of management decisions where virtual certainty exists. Generally speaking, the lower the organizational level, the greater the degree of certainty. At upper levels, uncertainty exists about which alternatives are available, what their payoffs will be, the probabilities of success,

---

### Organizational Reality   9-2
### Decision Making in Hollywood

Decision making at its simplest is a consideration of clearly defined alternatives using clear-cut criteria in a well-known future. This is an increasingly deceptive picture. The complexity may be seen by considering the major Hollywood studios' filmmakers.

Today most of the studios are bankers who finance films, and more importantly, distribute them. Five years ago, 80 percent of a film's revenues came from its box-office performance, but by 1990, domestic theater attendance could drop by more than 50 percent. For the film companies, that is bad news: they split the box-office gross with theaters almost 50-50. They take a smaller percentage in the expanding pay TV and cable markets—typically only about 20 percent.

Pay TV is not the only problem. The industry is losing an estimated $1 billion in annual revenues to professional pirates who sell illegal tapes. Independent filmmakers also find it easier to get financing from several sources in the newer markets, rather than relying on studios (e.g., Bruce Gilbert and Jane Fonda produced "On Golden Pond"; the same film had its TV rights presold as part of a package deal to Home Box Office and NBC).

Besieged on all sides, movie companies are leaping on the technology bandwagon, fighting piracy and taping, while forming joint ventures for pay TV and advertiser-supported cable TV at a breakneck pace. Decision makers must not only predict their own costs and products, but the future directions of several entertainment-related industries and the future lifestyles of their customers. This type of activity more accurately reflects what is required in strategic decisions today. Many interrelated factors must be considered, each of which impacts differently and with varying degrees of risk in an emerging and ill-defined future.

---

Source: "How TV is Revolutionizing Hollywood," *Business Week* (21 February 1983): 78–89.

and so on. Using our earlier distinction, programmed decisions are made in an atmosphere of relative certainty, while unprogrammed decisions are made in an environment of relative uncertainty.

**Risk**  Under conditions of risk, the manager is able to define the problem clearly, to list many (but not all) of the alternatives, and to make an assessment of the likelihood of payoffs, given a certain alternative. However, the manager cannot guarantee that a certain payoff will occur once a given alternative is chosen. If a retail chain decides to open a new outlet, there is no guarantee that this new outlet will be economically viable. There is also no way to know for certain whether the location that has been chosen is better or worse than some other location. However, managers can do various analyses to assess more accurately the likelihood that a particular location will be successful.

Situations of risk require the use of probability analysis. In order to use probability in making decisions, managers must have some basis for assesssing the likelihood that a given alternative will result in a certain outcome. In the store example above, managers would need to determine (among other things) the probability that sales would be above a certain minimum level. Normally they would do this on the basis of sales data from many other store locations. What is involved here is the use of *objective probabilities,* i.e., probabilities that are based on quantifiable past experience. (If we flip a coin, the probability that a head will turn up is 0.5. This can be determined objectively because a coin has only two sides.)

While some business decisions can be based on objective probabilities, many must be based on *subjective probabilities.* In this circumstance, management does not have objective data on the likelihood of certain events occurring. Therefore, other bases for assessing outcomes must be used; these include intuition, group discussions, or any other technique that gives managers a better handle on the likelihood of a given outcome occurring. When a personnel manager decides to hire a certain person for a marketing research position, the personnel manager decides on the basis of the best available information. However, there is no guarantee that the person will perform well in the job. Although the personnel manager probably gave a series of tests designed to reveal certain things about the applicant, the personnel manager knows that these tests are not foolproof. Thus, there is no way to predict objectively that the person will be a good employee.

The majority of managerial decisions are made under conditions of risk. Whether objective or subjective probabilities are used, these situations require that data be gathered and analyzed. Specific techniques for doing this are discussed later in this chapter.

**Uncertainty**  Uncertain conditions exist when managers cannot assign probabilities (subjective or objective) to chance outcomes for the alternatives that they develop. At the extreme, the manager cannot even define clearly what the problem is or the possible alternative solutions. This is because the decision maker has virtually no information about the problem, or because the problem is one that has never been faced before. Uncertainty is most likely to arise in top management decisions, particularly those that are a major departure from the organization's current practices.

The obvious thing to do in conditions of uncertainty is to gather more information. If probabilities are not known, a task force might be assigned to assess the experience of other firms who have faced this problem. Or, a brainstorming session might be conducted where alternative solutions to the problem can be proposed. There are numerous ways to gather additional information, but they all cost money. In some cases there is no additional information to gather. If a new production process is being tested and no one else has ever used this process, there is little available in the way of additional information.

---

## Organizational Reality   9-3
### Information As the Basis for Decision Making

When Amp Incorporated ran a sales contest in the fall of 1980, executives could not declare a winner. The reason: they did not have the necessary information. Although headquarters received the sales reports, it did not have the breakdown by product line needed to find the best salesperson.

Amp's problem is not unique. By the very nature of their jobs, executives cannot anticipate their information needs. Now, more and more companies are setting up information centers where executives can get help in finding the facts they need and tools for analyzing them quickly. Although most of these centers operate as adjuncts to existing data processing departments, they differ in that managers retrieve and manipulate data on their own. They can thus target the information they want and are not deluged with irrelevant raw data.

In 1980, Country Mutual Insurance company found that an unusually large number of commercial customers were cancelling their accounts. James Ely, manager of underwriting, found it hard to call on the company's computer files, since each request had to be specifically programmed by the data processing department. He therefore turned to the company's information center, which has been in operation since 1979. The staff consultant analyzed his problem, got him his own computer copy of the files and appropriate analysis tools. Thus equipped, Ely says, he examined nearly 100 aspects of the files and found that some of Country Mutual's prices were uncompetitive. Some rate adjustments were made and the problem was resolved. Ely says that the information center is a real time saver and that using traditional means might have taken a year. He found his answer in a month.

The information center lets the manager control the direction of the inquiry and switch in midstream if need be. The easy access to centralized files sets information centers apart from the personal computers used by so many executives. Information centers can be security problems, but they can also point out weaknesses in a company's data-collection strategy.

---

Source: "Helping Decision Makers Get at Data," *Business Week* (13 September 1982): 118–123.

## ☐ Individual Decision-Making Models

During the last decade, research on individual decision making has concentrated on determining how individual decision makers use information. More specifically, when confronted with various pieces of information, how do individuals combine them? To demonstrate the conclusions in this area, consider the following example: A sales manager wishes to hire a salesperson. The manager has information about five different candidates' education and experience, letters of recommendation from their previous employers, and interview ratings with the sales manager. How would the manager combine these diverse pieces of information during the process of making a choice among the five candidates? There are at least three general approaches that the manager could use.[3]

**The Compensatory Approach**    A candidate scoring below average on, say, the experience criterion, might still be considered for the job because he or she has a great deal of education (the additional education that the candidate has compensates for the lack of experience).

**The Conjunctive Approach**    The manager may set minimum levels of acceptability on *all* the criteria. For example, the manager might decide that all candidates must have at least a university degree, three years experience, a good letter of recommendation, and a positive interview rating. If a candidate falls below the minimum acceptable level in any of these areas, he or she will not be considered further. In this model, a good score on one criterion *cannot* offset a low score on another criterion.

**The Disjunctive Approach**    The manager may look at the characteristics of the five candidates and if one outstanding attribute is observed in an applicant, that applicant may be given the job.[4] This approach is typically used by decision makers who have strong beliefs in the value of certain things. Experience might be considered by some managers to be the only relevant criterion; if an individual has a great deal of experience, that alone will be enough to convince the manager that the person should be hired.

These three approaches are commonly used even though decision makers may not realize that they are using them. It is not clear which best describes what the typical manager in an organization does.[5] Assessment of an individual manager's decisions over time will help determine which approach that manager favors.

## ☐ Management Styles in Decision Making

When managers make decisions, they must first gather information and then evaluate it. In terms of information gathering, the decision maker can concentrate on either getting the "big picture" or just the details. The former strategy is called the *preceptive style* while the latter strategy is called the *receptive style*.[6] A quality control inspector, for example, assesses the overall pattern of output of a production line to determine if quality control standards are being met (a preceptive

---

### *Organizational Reality   9-4*
### *Japanese Decision Styles*

Although it is unusual, there are some Westerners working for major Japanese companies. In their positions, they can observe decision-making styles in Japanese companies. Thomas Cappiello, a public relations man for the trading company Nissho Iwai, feels that a good leader in Japan is one who doesn't make decisions; instead, he finds out what the decision is. In a similar view, Geoffrey Tudor of Japan Air Lines points out that if a manager tried to make an important decision unilaterally, he would be removed from his job in a face-saving way. John Macklin, an executive for Fujitsu, observes that if a company president wants a certain decision made, he may first plant the idea with a few subordinates, then let them do the analysis on the problem and make the decision. He will then compliment them on a good idea and decision.

Apparently these practices are widespread. In terms of individual participation in decisions, this type of environment can be very motivating. Ronald McFarland, a supervisor at Isuzu Motors, says that one nice thing about Japanese companies is that the ideas of even new employees are listened to.

---

Source: "Outsiders in Japanese Companies," *Fortune* (12 July 1982): 114–128.

style); an auditor or accountant, on the other hand, considers detailed information (a receptive style).

Once the information has been gathered, it can be analyzed either *systematically* or *intuitively*.[7] Intuitive decision makers use a trial and error approach, i.e., they briefly examine many alternatives and they have many stops and starts in the process. They are not bound to a particular technique or a rigid structure in their analysis of the problem. Intuitive decision makers often rely on hunches and they defend their solution on the basis of whether or not it works. Systematic decision makers, on the other hand, stick to a highly structured way of looking at the problem. They define specific constraints early in the decision process and they conduct an orderly search for additional information. They stress the method of solving the problem and defend their solution on the basis of their use of a systematic, rational procedure for making the decision.

The two dimensions of information gathering and information evaluation are combined in Figure 9-3; several occupations that might be found in each quadrant are also noted. Whether intuition or systematic decision making is better is a question that is presently subject to great debate. With the increasingly complex situations in which managers find themselves, it might be argued that systematic decision making is absolutely necessary. However, it is also true that some individuals have a knack for using unstructured approaches to reach a good decision. As indicated in Figure 9-3, the decision maker's occupation is important in influencing whether systematic or intuitive decision making is used.

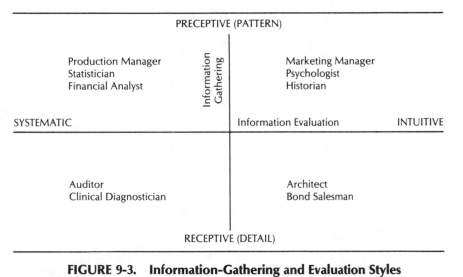

**FIGURE 9-3.   Information-Gathering and Evaluation Styles**

Source: J. McKenny and P. Keen, "How Managers' Minds Work," *Harvard Business Review* (May–June 1974): 79–95.

---

## Box 9-2: Seat-of-the-Pants Decision Making

When people are faced with a complex problem, they have two basic ways to deal with it: they can (1) gather the relevant data and systematically analyze it, or (2) make a seat-of-the-pants decision and hope for the best. Many people seem to feel that the latter approach is not only more interesting than the former, but that it also works better.

Consider, for example, the recollections of famous people on how they became wealthy. When the late Jean Paul Getty, the oil billionaire, was recalling his early days in the Texas oil fields (in a *Playboy* interview), he told how he sent geologists to gather core samples in order to assess systematically the chance of striking oil. The geologists told him the samples did not look promising, but Getty said he just *knew* there was oil there. And sure enough, he was right!

People reading this interview probably thought, "My, isn't that great! Here is a man who was unimpressed with technical reports and jargon; instead he went out and followed his instincts and made millions." Unfortunately, few people ever stop to consider the fact that for every Jean Paul Getty, there are a hundred others who also *knew* there was oil somewhere, went out and drilled for it, and struck a dry hole. These people are never interviewed because nobody wants to hear from them.

Overall, systematic decision making will lead to better decisions. Pointing out successful seat-of-the-pants decisions is a popular pastime because these exceptions are so interesting. Unfortunately, these kinds of decision makers can never tell others how to make good seat-of-the-pants decisions.

## ☐   **Organizational Models of Decision-Making Behavior**

Research on decision-making behavior at the organizational level has resulted in several ideas about how decisions are made. These ideas are: (1) the economic model; (2) the administrative model; (3) the political model, and (4) the garbage can model.

**The Economic Model**   The economic (rational) model of decision making comes from classical economics and involves a number of simplifying assumptions. Decision makers are assumed to recognize all possible alternatives that might solve the problem as well as the consequences of each of these alternatives. Further, decision makers are assumed to possess perfect information and are able to prioritize the alternatives so as to *maximize* organizational objectives. These are far-reaching assumptions and few people would argue seriously that they actually describe organizational decision making. However, they do form a starting point. The major problem with these assumptions is that numerous studies show that managers are either incapable of making or are not motivated to make the kinds of maximizing decisions that are assumed by this model.

**The Administrative Model**   The administrative model has been proposed as an alternative to the assumptions of the economic model.[8] In the administrative model, decision makers are assumed to be forced by mental and motivational limitations to "satisfice." When satisficing, decision makers choose alternatives that meet or exceed a predetermined minimum criterion, but they do not expend the energy necessary to find the very best alternative. This model has very strong implications for the amount of search managers are willing to do as they seek to develop a list of alternatives.

The administrative model is generally accepted as a realistic description of how organizational decisions are made. To demonstrate this model, think of the important decisions you have made in the last year and ask yourself this question: Did you examine all the possible alternatives to determine which one would give you the very best solution to your problem? The answer is that you probably did not; rather, you developed a less-than-complete list of alternatives and, after some sort of analysis, you chose an alternative that you felt would basically satisfy your needs.

**The Political Model**   In the political model, the individual's pursuit of his or her own self-interest is considered to be the dominant rationale for making decisions. The model often portrays organizational decision makers in an unfavorable light and suggests that they are willing to do whatever is necessary to get their way. Hence, the use of unethical practices, threats, influence, etc., is a significant feature of this model. This model differs from both the economic and the administrative models, because it assumes that all members of the organization are pursuing their own self-interest, even if it is at the expense of the organization or the people in it.

## *Organizational Reality* 9-5
## *The Politics of Decision Making*

Not all the actions or reasons related to decisions are consistent. Consider President Reagan's decision to place sanctions on European firms selling products—with U.S. technology built in—for the Soviet Union's Urengoi gas pipe line. These sanctions were proposed at the same time that the President decided to extend the 1976 grain agreement with the Soviets in order to improve export sales in a sagging U.S. agricultural sector.

To comply with the sanctions, European companies must sacrifice export sales and jobs by abandoning $1 billion worth of contracts. But if the firms defy the U.S. ban, U.S. administration reprisals could be even more painful.

Germany's Allgemeine Elektricitäts–Geselschaft (AEG) could lose a $270 million contract to build turbines for the pipeline through its AEG–Kanis Turbinenfabrik. However, it is a leading maker of electrical equipment and electronic products, with technological links with the U.S. that include a network of licenses from General Electric and other U.S. companies (such as Texas Instruments). It has also negotiated a joint venture with United Technologies Corporation and Mostek Corporation that would give AEG access to advanced integrated circuit technology. In strictly business terms, the risk of U.S. retaliation against these links would outweigh AEG's stake in the pipeline. "We have other interests besides Kanis and the pipeline," says AEG Legal Advisor Dieter Reichert. "Blacklisting would freeze all our U.S. license agreements and other cooperation."

For decision makers in multinational companies, U.S.–European relations are a two-edged sword, and their ongoing strategy–decision-making systems must monitor more than the typical "immediate action" environments.

Source: "Sanctions Whipsaw the Alliance," *Business Week* (9 August 1982): 20–21; "Why Reagan Is Willing to Sell Russia Grain," *Business Week* (9 August 1982): 21.

To demonstrate the dynamics of the political model, consider the following: Suppose you are a member of a committee in an organization and you are listening to a presentation by one of the other committee members. You detect a major logical flaw in that person's presentation. Suppose also that this other person and you are both in line for promotion. Would you publicly point out the logical flaw in the presentation in an attempt to publicly discredit the person and improve your own promotability?

In the most general sense, the political model assumes that people are "looking out for #1" and that cooperation between groups and individuals is not likely unless they are given some incentive to cooperate. In this model it is assumed that the various parts of an organization are not well coordinated, and the relationship between an organization and its external environment is not as "tight" as usually assumed. In this circumstance, it is easy to see how decision making could depart from the economic ideal. (The political model is discussed in detail in Chapter 13).

**The "Garbage Can" Model**   The most pessimistic (or perhaps realistic!) view of organizational decision making is the "garbage can" model.[9] The premise of the model is that the decision-making environment in organizations has become so complex it is impossible to describe accurately how managers make decisions. In this complex environment, problems, solutions, decision makers, and decision-making techniques all exist in a state of flux. Decisions get made when (1) a problem arises for which a solution is available, (2) the solution does not require excessive amounts of organizational resources, and (3) the problem and its solution are known to a decision maker who has the time, energy, and power needed to get the solution implemented.

The garbage can view of the decision-making environment in organizations is hard for many people to accept. However, the discussion of organizational politics in Chapter 13 supports the idea that the rational model of organizations leaves much decision-making behavior unexplained. The garbage can model attempts to account for some of these "irrationalities" in organizational life.

## ☐ General Decision-Making Strategies

Two dimensions are important in influencing how managers go about making decisions.[10] One dimension involves individual beliefs about cause and effect, a concept treated in Chapter 2. Two individuals may be in complete agreement that X causes Y or they may be in complete disagreement as to what will happen if X occurs. The notion about cause and effect relationships is a crucial one in decision making because a logical decision cannot be made unless something specific is known about "what causes what to happen."

The other major dimension is the amount of agreement that exists between individuals on the goals the organization should pursue. Once again, there may be a range from complete agreement to complete disagreement. For example, the marketing department might wish to pursue the goal of a broad product line in hopes of attracting customers; production, however, may want a narrow product line in the interest of efficiency.

The two major dimensions can be combined into a matrix (see Figure 9-4) which indicates four general decision-making strategies. In cell one, the relevant individuals or groups agree about cause and effect and the goals that the company should pursue. The strategy for making a decision in this circumstance is *computational,* and is most appropriate for programmed decisions.

In cell two, there is disagreement about cause and effect relationships, but there is agreement about the goals that the organization should pursue. In this circumstance, a *judgment* strategy is most appropriate; this involves discovering an acceptable way to get to the already agreed-upon goal. There may, of course, be considerable conflict in this situation, since various individuals or groups will probably have differing ideas about the best way to get to the goal.

In cell three, there is agreement about cause and effect relationships but disagreement about the goals the organization should be pursuing. The most appropriate decision-making strategy in this case is *compromise.* Here, each party

GOAL PREFERENCES

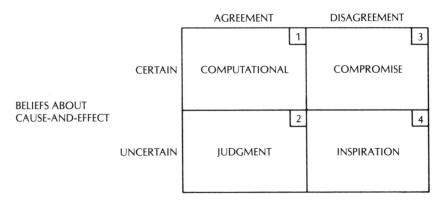

**FIGURE 9-4. Decision Strategies**

bargains with other parties in the organization about the goals that will be pursued. Obviously, considerable conflict may also develop in this situation. If two marketing executives cannot agree on the market objective for a new product, they will have considerable difficulty reaching an agreement about what price should be charged. If a high-price strategy is proposed by one manager, and the other manager feels that a low-price strategy is better, some compromise will have to be worked out.

In cell four, there is neither agreement about cause and effect relationships nor which goals should be pursued. The best decision strategy here is appropriately called the *inspirational* strategy. In this circumstance, decision techniques such as intuition, experience, creativity, gut feel, etc. are all appropriate strategies as the parties attempt to discover some sort of common ground that they can agree upon. While this circumstance does cause difficulties, it is also one which presents many opportunities for creative decision making.

# ■ THE DECISION-MAKING PROCESS

The five internal characteristics of the decision-making environment have a strong, *general* influence on the way managers make decisions. We now turn to an analysis of the *specific* processes that may be observed when managers actually make decisions.

From the time that a person first recognizes a problem to the time that a solution is implemented may be very short or very long, with the time requirement being largely determined by the complexity of the problem. For example, when a student decides which route to take to class, very little thought is given to the problem. However, when writing a major term paper, that same student will devote considerably more conscious mental effort to the problem. In the discussion below, the assumption is made that relatively complex decisions are being made. The decision-making process is divided into three main stages and each of these stages is analyzed. For each step in the process, the ideal behavior is stated and then compared to what may actually happen instead. The overall process is indicated in Figure 9-5.[11]

## ☐ The Problem-Analysis Phase

In this stage the decision maker's only goal is to come to a clear understanding of what the problem is. The importance and difficulty of doing this should not be underestimated. Countless examples exist of organizations or individuals who wasted time and money pursuing inappropriate solutions based on faulty problem analysis. To minimize the chance of this type of mistake, decision makers should proceed through the steps indicated below.

1. *Develop standards.* Before a manager can assess whether or not a problem exists, a standard must be in place. Standards are relevant for all kinds of organizations—public or private, profit-pursuing or nonprofit, manufacturing or service. The standards may be stated qualitatively or quantitatively (preferably the latter), and individuals in the organization must have a clear idea of what the standards are. So, for example, a manufacturing firm may set a standard by stipulating the units per hour that are to be produced of a certain product; a hospital may set a standard in terms of occupancy rates; an airline will probably have a standard relating to the percentage of seats that are filled; a government agency may have a standard about the number of clients that should be served in a particular time period. Overall, the standard indicates to members of the organization what their required performance is.

Unfortunately the development of standards can be a highly controversial and political activity. Much has been written, for example, about the disputes that the United Auto Workers union has had with General Motors at its Lordstown Vega plant.[12] The workers argued that the standard of production was set too high and that excessive work was required to maintain that standard. Management, on the other hand, argued that engineering studies showed that the standard was reasonable, given the manpower and machine power in the plant.

Why are conflicts over standards so common? First, the individuals affected (either workers or management) may fear that they will be allowed no input into setting the standards. They may therefore fear being confronted with an unreasonable job. Second, even if they are involved in setting the standard, they may feel that the way in which the standard is measured is inappropriate and will make their performance seem inadequate. Third, they may feel that measurement occurs at an inappropriate time. For example, if performance is measured on a day when many regular workers are off sick, it may appear that productivity in a particular department is not up to par. Fourth, workers may object to specific standards because they feel that management will use performance statistics against them. Whatever the reason, the setting of standards is a very difficult activity in many organizations; it should not be approached as a simple job that must be done quickly in order to "get on with more important things." If the standards are not realistic and/or have no support, any kind of productivity measurements will be met with great resistance.

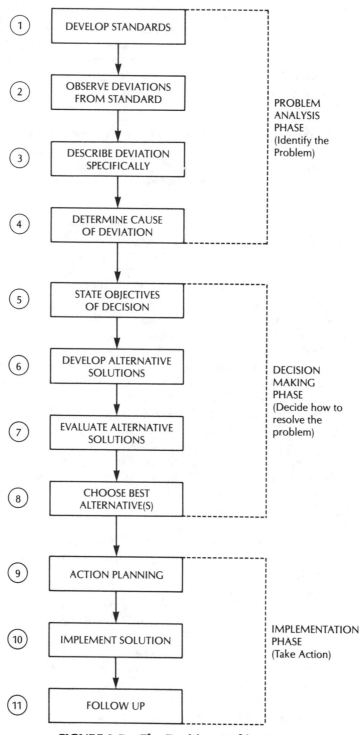

**FIGURE 9-5. The Decision-Making Process**

2. *Observe deviations from standard.* The next logical step in the problem-analysis phase is to observe performance (either machine or human) and determine whether there is any deviation from standard. The deviation may, of course, be on the high side or on the low side; the idea is to determine whether organizational performance is close to what was predicted when standards were originally set. Several questions must be answered in this phase:

a) Is there agreement among managers and employees that a deviation exists?
b) How bad is the deviation, i.e., is it significant enough to cause a major disruption in progress toward the goal originally set?
c) Is there a trend in the deviation, i.e., is it a random thing or is there a pattern?

There are several practical problems that can arise when these questions are asked. With respect to a), getting agreement on whether or not a deviation exists may be difficult even when a clear standard exists. Although this sounds strange, we must remember that people see the world through their own particular biases and they can easily distort reality. This is particularly true if reality threatens strongly held beliefs or reflects negatively on a person's self-worth. If a sales manager assumes that Joe Smith's sales of ninety-one units last month (standard = 100) constitutes a deviation, the sales manager may find that Joe does not agree with that conclusion. Joe may have many reasons why ninety-one units were sold and may not even perceive a deviation. This problem of failure to recognize deviations must not be underestimated. Objective observers of various stiuations are often astounded at how the parties in the situation are unable to clearly see reality. Yet, it is indisputable that individuals distort reality, so this problem cannot be ignored. Failure to accept that a deviation exists also means that there will be little desire to change behavior.

With respect to b), a different problem arises. Although Joe may agree that sales of ninety-one units constitutes a deviation, he may argue that it is an insignificant deviation. The point at which a deviation becomes "significant" may be almost impossible to pin down.

With respect to c), trend analysis may be helpful in answering the question, but here again individual idiosyncracies play a large role. If Joe's sales are ninety-one, eighty-three, and seventy-two units for the last three months, the sales manager may conclude that a negative trend has developed. Joe, however, may argue that a host of one-time occurrences deflated sales, and once these adjustments are taken into account his sales actually went up.

3. *Describe the deviation specifically.*[13] The old saying, "a problem that is well-defined is a problem that is already half-solved" is an oversimplification, but its point is well taken: we cannot proceed to a solution until it is clear what the problem is. This step requires that the observed deviation be described in detail, which involves stipulating the location, magnitude, and timing of the deviation. Any additional information that gives the decision maker a better understanding of the deviation should be gathered at this point.

The major practical problem with this step is that people avoid it altogether. Typically, what happens is this: an individual makes a cursory observation of a situation, observes a deviation from standard, and then immediately leaps to a conclusion about what caused the deviation. This very fundamental error is the major pitfall that must be avoided in the problem-analysis phase. In our society, where decisive action is admired, it is not surprising that individuals try to determine immediately the cause of a deviation rather than first carefully describe the deviation. Failure to describe the deviation accurately, however, often results in failure to find the cause of the problem.

4. *Determine the cause of the deviation.* If steps 1, 2, and 3 have been handled properly, a successful conclusion to the problem-analysis phase is very likely. If clear standards are set, if the deviation from standard is observed, and if this deviation is well understood, the cause can be much more easily determined. Step 4, therefore, requires the use of the information that has been gathered in the previous three steps.

The most fundamental practical problem at this point is the tendency to draw a conclusion and then to search for data that support the conclusion. A person may appear to be proceeding logically through the problem-analysis phase but, deep down, has already decided what the problem is and is now merely going through the motions of finding data to support that problem definition. This tendency may be very difficult to detect, since some individuals speak as if they are proceeding very rationally. Consider, for example, the manager faced with a subordinate who has fallen short of certain production goals. The manager may appear to be developing the information in steps 1, 2, and 3, to deduce rationally what the problem is, but in fact may already have decided that the problem is that the subordinate is simply lazy. If some other sequence of events is really causing the deviation, this manager will probably never find it out. Because individuals become attached to pet solutions, they may be unwilling to disprove a possible cause; therefore they will fail to successfully complete the problem-analysis phase.

Another practical problem in step 4 is sloppy statement of the problem that has been uncovered. For example, when a manager says, "We have a morale problem," or "We have a communication problem," or "We have got to get organized," it is usually not clear what he or she means. Each subordinate will interpret the manager's statement of the problem in a slightly different fashion and this diversity of interpretations means that very little progress can be made toward really getting at a solution.

A final problem is the tendency of some managers to define problems in a way that allows their particular expertise to be brought to bear. For example, a marketing manager will define a deviation in marketing terms since he or she will feel most comfortable with a marketing-based problem. The same is true for other individuals with other functional biases. Technical training is also a problem. An accountant will feel very comfortable dealing with accounting problems and may therefore attempt to define many problems in accounting terms.

*Summary.* Steps 1–4 of the Decision-Making Process (Figure 9-5) must be conducted only when there is a problem confronting management. Steps 5–11, however, must be done in all circumstances, whether or not a problem presents itself to management. Thus, the earlier distinction between problem decisions and opportunity decisions must be kept in mind at this juncture. For problem decisions, we must start at step 1 and proceed through the entire model; for opportunity decisions, we need not start at box 1 but instead start at box 5 and proceed through the model.

## ☐ The Decision-Making Phase

Once the cause of the problem is known, the decision maker must decide how to resolve it. Deciding upon the specific solution to the problem is the goal of this phase. To do this, several steps are required.

5. *State objectives of the decision.* For problem decisions, the objective is to solve the problem that has just been defined in step 4. For opportunity decisions, the objectives must first be stated. These objectives deal with things like maximizing profit, maximizing productivity, reducing rejects, improving customer service, etc.

Once again, human idiosyncracies can cause serious problems in stating objectives. To start with, there may be little agreement on the objectives that the organization should pursue. A manufacturing firm may wish to do some state-of-the-art manufacturing, but the finance people in the firm may feel that this is inadvisable and that production should continue to work in areas that it is familiar with. This will no doubt cause a disagreement and no objectives can be set until this disagreement is resolved. Even with specific issues resolved, the general objectives of one segment of the firm may be in disagreement with the objectives of the other segments. The classic example of this is the dispute that routinely occurs between production and marketing people, with the former wanting long production runs and standardized products while the latter want speedy delivery and a wide variety of products. Each of these areas has a perfectly legitimate goal, yet conflicts of this nature mean that objective setting is difficult. Organizational politics also plays a role in the setting of objectives. If the corporation president wants to pursue a certain goal it may be difficult for organizational members to object successfully. Stated more generally, any powerful individual in an organization may be able to stipulate objectives that push the organization in a certain direction.

6. *Develop alternative solutions.* At this step, the decision maker develops as many possible solutions to the problem as can be generated. The greater the length and diversity of the list of alternatives, the greater the likelihood that a workable solution will be found. Creativity is important in this step, since innovative solutions often resolve problems when traditional solutions will not.

The practical problems in this step are two-fold: First when individuals attempt to develop alternative solutions, they typically suggest those that have worked for similar problems they have encountered in the past.[14] While these suggestions can be useful, they often lead to the implementation of solutions that really do not confront the problem at hand. The major reason this happens is that individuals do not expend the effort needed to develop a long list of alternative solutions. Rather, they develop a couple of alternatives that look feasible and then spend considerable time arguing about the relative merits of those solutions. Second, the conservative nature of most decision makers means that innovative alternatives are dismissed because "we've never done it that way." Thus, people are either unwilling or unable to seriously consider innovative alternatives.

7. *Evaluate alternative solutions.* Once the list of potential alternatives has been developed, they must be analyzed systematically to determine which one is best. To do this, some sort of criterion must be developed so that the alternatives can be compared with each other. Some of the techniques for accomplishing this are discussed later in this chapter.

The major problem with this step is that (like step 3 in the problem-analysis phase) individuals often avoid it altogether. Although it appears strange that a crucial step like this would be avoided, this is precisely what occurs. Why is this so? First, the proper analysis and evaluation of alternative solutions requires much time and effort and people are often not motivated to take the time, or expend the effort, to make a decision properly. Second, the decision maker may feel that the analysis required is beyond his or her capability. So, a shallow analysis is done and a decision is made on that basis. Third, there may be disagreements among individuals working on a problem about the proper method that should be used to evaluate the alternatives. These difficulties constitute a formidable list and it is not surprising that step 7 is so often avoided by decision makers. Once again, it cannot be overemphasized that the consequences of failing to do this step properly are significant. Individuals who avoid the evaluation of alternatives will often find that the alternatives they pick will have many unexpected negative features. Proper evaluation increases the likelihood that the negative features will be recognized before the decision is made.

8. *Choose the best alternative.* Once steps 1–7 (for problem decisions) or steps 5–7 (for opportunity decisions) have been completed, the decision maker can choose the best alternative. The alternative that is best will, of course, depend on the criterion that the decision maker has chosen. Once a particular alternative has been chosen, the decision-making phase has been completed.

The problems that are encountered in step 8 are largely the result of failure to adequately conduct steps 1–7. For example, if objectives have not been stated clearly in step 5, the decision maker will be unable to tell whether the alternative chosen is the best one. Likewise, if a proper analysis has not been done in step 7, there will probably be numerous disputes about what the best alternative is. Or, if the deviation from standard has not been described adequately, the decision maker cannot be sure that the solution chosen is solving the actual problem.

One final caution: even if the decision maker has done an excellent job in steps 1–7, he or she should be prepared for disagreements. As noted above, certain individuals already have their minds made up before step 1 begins and a logical analysis of a problem will have no influence on them. When this happens,

## Box 9-3: Values and Decision Making

In one sense it is naive to believe that "rational decision making" is possible or that people will agree on an issue if only they will use a rational process. This is because people's values influence which alternative solutions they will prefer. For example, is interschool busing a good idea? The answers people give to this question are heavily influenced by their values. Making a rational decision in this case is very difficult because of these strongly held views. To make matters worse, the whole problem is so complex that evaluation studies of busing have come to contradictory conclusions about its usefulness. The problem is further complicated by the fact that people's values influence the criteria they feel should be used to judge busing's effectiveness.

   Although the busing issue is a complex and highly visible one, the comments above hold for any decision. Since values are so strongly held by people, they must be dealt with when going through the steps in the decision-making process. Ignoring values or telling people that their values are wrong will simply cause resentment and will slow down the process.

the decision maker must deal with the emotional issues that are causing resistance. Ways in which this can be done are indicated in Chapter 8.

Steps 5–8 should be used for both problem and opportunity decisions. Once these steps have been completed, the decision maker is in a position actually to implement the solution that has been chosen.

## ☐   The Implementation Phase

In this phase the decision maker must convert thoughts into action. This really requires the decision maker to consider how to most effectively introduce change (this topic is discussed in detail in Chapter 14). Three steps are required in this phase.

9. *Action planning.* Once the problem has been defined and a solution has been developed to resolve it (the "problem analysis" and "decision-making" phases, respectively) a specific plan of action must be developed. This implementation of decisions is of crucial importance, so considerable care must be taken when this step is carried out. Action planning requires that the decision maker develop a systematic plan for actually implementing the decision. This requires the decision maker to think about issues such as: (1) should employees participate in the implementation plan or should they simply be required to implement the decision? (2) what kind of coordination is required between the decision maker and those who will implement the decision? (3) who will monitor the implementation to see if it is working properly? and (4) what criteria will be used to determine if the proposed solution really solves the problem?

10. *Implement the solution.* Two key concepts must be kept in mind in this phase: the quality of the decision and the acceptance of the decision. A high-

quality decision that is not accepted by those who must live with it is useless. Suppose a manager decides that resolution of a certain problem requires the implementation of a new requisition system. No matter how quality-oriented this system is, if subordinates will not acccept it, it will not succeed. Likewise, if a solution is implemented strictly because the employees will accept it, yet the decision itself is of low quality, it is unlikely that it will resolve the problem. These quality and acceptance aspects appear to be multiplicatively related—a low score on either of the variables results in a fairly low overall effectiveness score.[15]

The practical problems with step 10 can be a nightmare of frustration for the decision maker. The literature of organizational behavior is full of examples of attempts by managers to implement changes, only to find that those affected have vigorous objections. Problems like this can be avoided by allowing those who will be affected by the change to participate in the actual decision-making phase, but this process takes considerable time and money.

11. *Follow up.* Once the proposed solution has been implemented, management must monitor the extent to which that solution really resolves the problem. Often a solution that appears to be perfect runs into considerable technical or human difficulty once it is implemented. A control system must therefore be in place to detect whether or not the solution really has resolved the problem.

The greatest practical difficulty with steps 9–11 is bridging the gap between thinking and action. Steps 1–8 are largely mental while steps 9–11 require both mental and physical action. While many individuals are very strong at steps 1–8, they may not have the interest, inclination, or ability to make the leap successfully from thinking to action. In addition, the particular manner in which the solution is implemented and follow-up is gathered is critical.

As the above discussion shows, the decision-making process is long and complicated, and many things can (and do!) go wrong at each step of the way. Knowledge about both the technical and human elements in the orgnization is important if the decision maker is to successfully make and implement decisions.

## ■ DECISION-MAKING TECHNIQUES

There are many decision-making techniques available for use by managers. Before we discuss these, it is important that we make a distinction between decision-making techniques, strategies, and processes. Decision *techniques* are designed to solve specific problems, using well-defined step-by-step directions. Although this sounds very specific and rigid, these techniques can be used on many different problems. Decision *strategies* are much broader than techniques and involve ways of approaching problems. For example, the judgment strategy discussed earlier is a general approach to making a decision when there is agreement about organizational goals, but not about cause-and-effect relationships. Once the general judgment strategy is decided upon, specific techniques that are consistent with it can be used. Decision *processes* occur within the context of general decision-making strategies and specific decision-making techniques. For example, if one member of a group becomes upset with the direction the group is taking, and an argument ensues, this is indicative of the dynamic process within the group as it seeks to make a decision.

In this section, we will discuss five of the most popular and/or heavily researched decision-making techniques: (1) the weights and criteria method, (2) decision trees, (3) the Delphi technique, (4) the nominal-grouping technique, and (5) brainstorming. The first two can be used in either a group or individual setting, while the last three require a group setting.

## ☐ The Weights and Criteria Method

Managers are often faced with problems in which the alternatives are known but the criteria for making the decision and the weights for these criteria are disputed. In these situations, a system called the weights and criteria method is very useful. Consider the following problem:

> A manager who has been transferred from New York to Chicago must decide which of two houses to buy. One is a ranch-style located in the suburbs, while the other is a two-story located close to downtown. The manager feels that about 80 percent of the reason for buying a house is its style, but location is also a consideration. The manager likes a two-story twice as much as a ranch style, and suburban locations four times as much as downtown locations. Which house should be purchased?

Figure 9-6 indicates a very systematic approach for resolving problems like this. In order to use the weights and criteria method, the following steps are necessary:

1. List the alternatives (houses) that are to be analyzed. These form the *rows* of the matrix. In this case there are two alternatives.
2. Develop the criteria that are to be used to make the decision. These form the *columns* of the matrix. In this case there are two criteria.

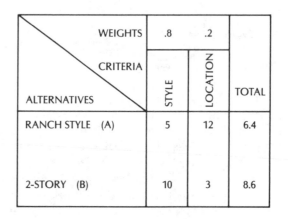

| WEIGHTS | .8 | .2 | |
|---|---|---|---|
| CRITERIA ALTERNATIVES | STYLE | LOCATION | TOTAL |
| RANCH STYLE (A) | 5 | 12 | 6.4 |
| 2-STORY (B) | 10 | 3 | 8.6 |

**FIGURE 9-6.   Solution to the Manager's Problem**

3. Weight the criteria. The total of the weights should equal 1 or 100 or some other convenient number. Note the weight for each criterion above the criterion. In this case the criteria have been weighted based on the manager's preferences noted above.

4. Start with the first criterion and assess each alternative (house) on that criterion. In this case, the first criterion is house style, so each house should be assessed on that criterion. Go to the second criterion and assess each alternative on that criterion. In this case the manager has used a scale 1–15 for each criterion.

5. For each alternative, multiply the *weight* for each criterion times the *value* for each criterion to get a total score for each alternative. For example, house A's total score is (.8)(5) + (.2)(12) = 6.4. Each alternative is totaled in this way.

6. Choose the alternative (house) with the highest score. In this case, house B should be chosen. If the scores had been close, the manager could have refined the analysis further before picking one of the houses.

The weights and criteria method may be used in either an individual or a group setting. In the former, the manager simply decides on the criteria that will be used to assess the problem, and the weights that should be given to each criterion. In a group setting, there may be major disagreements about the criteria that should be used and/or the weights that should be attached. Considerable group discussion may therefore be necessary to determine what the criteria and the weights should be. This is an excellent way of getting people to think about the problem and this activity increases the likelihood that a better decision will be made.

## ☐ Decision Trees

The method described above is useful for making decisions on a one-time basis. Many other managerial decisions require that a series of events in the future be taken into account before a decision is made. When this situation exists, and when managers have enough information to assign at least subjective probabilities to outcomes, decision trees are an excellent systematic technique for making decisions. To demonstrate this technique, consider the following problem:

A company has developed two products that have market potential; however, only one product can be developed because of resource limitations. After conducting appropriate market tests the company developed the following information: There are two possible levels of sales for each product—high (probability = .6) or low (probability = .4). The profits (in $000,000s) for the two products under high and low demand are as follows:

| Product | High Demand | Low Demand |
|---------|-------------|------------|
| 1 | 25 | –5 |
| 2 | 10 | 3 |

Which product should the company market?

The solution for this problem is indicated in Figure 9-7. In decision-tree analysis, two basic steps are necessary. First, the problem must be conceptualized, i.e., the tree must be drawn. Second, a mathematical analysis must be performed in order to determine the best alternative.

**Conceptualizing the Problem**   This is the crucial step and is undoubtedly the most difficult part of the process. If difficulty is encountered in drawing the tree, this is clear evidence that the problem is not understood. If the problem is not understood, the manager cannot make a rational decision. The goal of this step is to represent pictorially the decision problem and the sequence of events that can occur. This is done from left to right. To draw the tree, the decision maker must first determine how many alternatives there are. In the simplified case shown in Figure 9-7, there are only two alternatives. Once these alternatives are noted, the implications of each must be developed. In both alternatives the implications are relatively simple, and are taken directly from the description of the problem. For each alternative, the probabilities must be indicated; the payoffs for each alternative are also shown at the extreme right of the tree.

**Mathematical Analysis**   Once the problem has been conceptualized, it is necessary to determine which alternative is best. To do this, we work from right to left. Assume the manager has decided to use the criterion of expected value to make the choice. This criterion is based on the notion that because we cannot predict the future, we should take a weighted average of possible future outcomes and choose the alternative with the best "expected value." The expected value for the two alternatives is:

$$EV_1 = .6(25) + (.4)(-5)$$
$$= 15 - 2$$
$$= 13$$

$$EV_2 = (.6)(10) + (.4)(3)$$
$$= 6 + 1.2$$
$$= 7.2$$

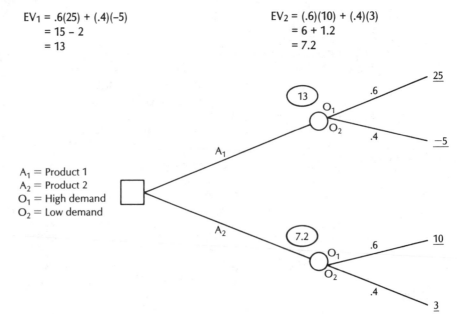

$A_1$ = Product 1
$A_2$ = Product 2
$O_1$ = High demand
$O_2$ = Low demand

**FIGURE 9-7.   Solution to the Two-Product Problem**

# Box 9-4: But You Can't Quantify That!

One of the most controversial aspects of decision making concerns the ability of decision makers to quantify key variables in a problem. It is important to be able to do this, because many decision-making techniques require numerical values. Most people agree that there are many variables that can be quantified. Things such as profits, costs, sales revenue, and so forth are all things we are used to seeing stated in numerical terms. No one seems to object to this; in fact, people seem to feel it is useful to quantify these kinds of things.

The difficulty arises when attempts are made to quantify variables like the value of a park to local residents, the value of preserving a vanishing species of animal, or ultimately, the value of a human life. Can these things be quantified? Perhaps this is the wrong question. A more significant question might be: "Do we *want* to quantify these things?"

To demonstrate the significance of this latter question, consider this example: Suppose an automobile manufacturer discovers a design flaw that is dangerous to human life. Should the company correct the flaw? To make this decision, certain information is needed. Assume that the company concludes that (1) the flaw will cost $20 million to fix, (2) twenty-three people will die if it is not fixed, and (3) class-action suits against the company by relatives of those killed will amount to $10 million.

In purely quantitative terms, the company should not fix the flaw because at most it will cost them $10 million. However, this decision implies something about the company's view of human life. Stated quantitatively, the value of human life is $434,782 ($10 million divided by twenty-three people). This sounds terribly mercenary and no one in the company would be willing to say that the company made the decision on this basis. But the fact remains that the value of a human life can be quantified in a given situation. The problem is that the person doing the quantifying looks very heartless. So, most people prefer to talk in generalities about issues like this and everyone feels good when someone says "You can't quantify that!"

So, in this case the manager should choose alternative one because it promises (but does not guarantee) the best return.

A manager can do a problem like that in Figure 9-7 individually or a group can be formed to do the problem. The strength of the group approach is that subjective probabilities can be discussed much more vigorously than if an individual makes the decision. Group discussions will also bring out other areas of disagreement and points that need to be refined. Whether decision trees are used on an individual or group basis, they force decision makers to conceptualize the problem in its entirety. When this is done, a much better groundwork has been laid for a successful decision.[16]

---

*Organizational Reality    9-6*
*Expected Utility*

One of the concepts that university students are exposed to is expected utility (EU). The basic issue that EU addresses is how to help people make optimal decisions under conditions of risk. The concept is applicable to both monetary and nonmonetary problems. For example, a person who suffers from severe headaches might find that an operation is available to reduce the pain, but there is also a risk of blindness from the operation. Before making a decision, the person would want to know such things as the probability of the operation's success, the probability that the operation would cause blindness, the value of getting rid of headaches, etc. Clearly, there is no answer that will be satisfactory to everyone, as each person must subjectively assess the important elements in the problem; EU can then be used to make the decision.

Suppose an investor assigns numerical preference values to three stocks as follows: IBM, 20; A.T.&T., 15; and GM, 10. If given a choice of an outright gift of A.T.&T. stock vs. a 75 percent chance of winning both IBM and GM stock (assuming the value of each stock is $10,000) which should be chosen? The expected utility is as follows:

Gift of A.T.&T. stock = 1.0(15) = 15
75% chance of IBM and GM stock = .75(20) + .75(10) = 22.5

The best decision, based on EU, is to choose the 75 percent alternative.

Whether EU actually *describes* the way people make decisions, or whether it simply indicates how they *should* make decisions is a question that is hotly debated. There is considerable evidence that people do not use EU when making many business or personal decisions, but when faced with problems that will have a big impact on them personally, people may be more likely to make the effort to do an EU-type analysis.

---

Source: Ira Horawitz, "How To Think Straight," *Fortune* (19 April 1982): 201–204.

## ☐ The Delphi Technique

This technique, named after the ancient oracle at Delphi, was developed at the Rand corporation, and is mainly used for forecasting future events. In order to use Delphi, it is necessary to get a panel of experts to give their opinions. For example, a group of biologists might be asked their opinions on the likelihood that 50 percent of the world's food will be harvested from the sea by the year 2000. Or, a group of oil experts might be asked how likely it is that the U.S. will develop an oil substitute by 1995.

The Delphi technique can be used on a wide variety of topics of interest to both society in general and to business firms in particular.[17] For business firms, Delphi can be used to predict things like technological breakthroughs in production processes, new product types, and the economic outlook. For government organizations, Delphi can be used to predict political coalitions, weapons developments by foreign powers, and the supply of critical natural resources like oil.

The Delphi procedure works as follows:

1. Experts on the questions the organization is asking are identified and are engaged to give their opinion. Usually fifteen to twenty experts are involved. The experts are not brought together, nor do they talk to each other.

2. A structured questionnaire is sent to these experts. This questionnaire asks them to give numerical estimates to questions the organization is interested in. For example, if a public utility wishes to predict electrical consumption in an energy-conscious environment, experts might be asked the question "What will the annual percentage increase of electrical usage be over the next five years?" Experts might also be asked questions that require them to assess the probability of a certain event occurring. For example, experts in the tire industry might be asked "What is the probability that there will be a major breakthrough in the construction of tires such that car owners will never have to buy replacement tires?"

3. The results of the estimates by each of the individual experts are tabulated and a summary of these results is fed back to all of them. The summary typically shows the average, the median, and the range of responses on the questions. The experts are asked to look over this summary and then to make another estimate based on the summary.

4. A second summary is prepared, giving exactly the same information as the first one. This summary typically draws some conclusions about what the emerging consensus is on the issue under examination. Experts who have given responses that are not close to the emerging consensus may be asked to justify their opinions.

5. The experts are then asked to make a third estimate. A final summary is developed from these answers and is presented to the top management of the organization doing the study.

The Delphi technique has one major advantage over other group decision-making techniques: there is no face-to-face interaction of the participants. When there is face-to-face interaction in groups, certain individuals inevitably dominate the discussion and inhibit the useful ideas of the less aggressive members of the group. This problem does not exist in Delphi because members do not talk to one another. Rather, the experts simply fill out the questionnaires referred to above. Yet each respondent realizes that other experts are involved in the project; hence, each respondent will probably take very seriously the other views that are made known when the summaries are fed back. Thus, the advantage of expert opinion is preserved in Delphi and the disadvantage of personality clashes and dominant individuals in a face-to-face setting is avoided.

Delphi is difficult to classify in terms of its appropriateness for group or individual decision making. In fact, it is neither. In one sense, the Delphi technique is a group technique, but in another sense it is simply a group of individuals giving opinions.

Although the Delphi technique has demonstrated its utility in a variety of circumstances, not all people view it favorably. This may be due to the somewhat mystical nature of the process. We have previously seen that people may resist certain techniques or ideas simply because they do not understand how they work (an obvious example is the computer). This may be a drawback with respect to the Delphi technique. Other problems include difficulties in stating the questions in such a way that the respondents will interpret them the same way, determining who is an expert, and deciding how many rounds of questionnaires to administer.[18]

## ☐ The Nominal-Grouping Technique

A technique for group decision making that is in some respects similar to the Delphi is the nominal-grouping technique.[19] Five to ten individuals are assembled in a room and are asked to write their solutions to a problem given to the group. A group might be asked things like how to improve morale in their particular organization, how they might improve upward communication, how to develop employee skills, or a host of other problems.

The procedure for using the nominal technique is as follows:

1. Individuals write down their solutions to the problem without discussing them with other members of the group. This is the "listing" phase of the process.

2. After approximately twenty minutes have passed, the "recording" phase begins. The individuals are asked to give the solutions that they have written down to the group leader; the leader then writes each individual's solutions on a flip chart that all members can see. All individual solutions to the problem are listed on the flip chart but the solutions are not matched with the individuals who suggested them.

3. The final stage in the process is the "voting" phase. Ballots are distributed to members of the group and they are asked to rank order (in terms of importance) the solutions that are on the flip chart. The ballots are then tabulated and the alternative with the highest score is designated as the choice of the group.

Like the Delphi method, the nominal-grouping method is premised on the notion that allowing group discussion may inhibit creativity. Note that in each of the three phases above no discussion is allowed among group members. However, great encouragement is given to individual members to get their solutions in front of the group so that an extensive list of possible solutions to the problem can be considered by the group. How well does this idea work?

A review of studies comparing nominal grouping with other techniques revealed that nominal grouping was superior to, or as good as, other techniques in areas such as decision quality and participant satisfaction.[20] However, the technique may not be superior to all other group decision-making methods. One study, testing the ability of subjects to predict the order of finishing in selected horse races, compared the effectiveness of the nominal-grouping technique with that of social-judgment analysis (SJA).[21] The latter involves giving subjects in a group information about each other's preferences before decision making begins. It was found that the methods were equal in terms of the quality of the group decisions, but that SJA was better at developing consensus in the group.[22]

As noted earlier, implementing decisions that have been made is an important part of the total decision-making process. There is evidence that the specific technique used to *make* the decision influences whether or not attempts are made to *implement* it. In one study, sixty-five registered nurses in a problem-solving workshop made problem-solving decisions using the nominal-grouping technique, structured discussion (groups used the rational decision-making process), and open discussion (groups discussed one alternative at a time).[23] Problems that the groups dealt with were categorized as simple, moderately complex, and complex. After the nurses returned to their home organizations, an assessment was made of how many attempts they made to implement the changes that had been developed in the workshop. For all levels of problem complexity, nurses in the nominal groups made more implementation attempts than nurses in the open-discussion groups. For simple problems, they also made more implementation attempts than nurses in the structured-discussion groups.

## ☐ Brainstorming

The brainstorming technique was developed by Alex Osborn, a partner in an advertising agency.[24] The technique was used originally to develop an advertising program, but it can be used any time an organization wants to develop creative or free-wheeling ideas. These ideas may depart drastically from generally accepted practice. Procedurally, the technique involves getting six to ten people together to come up with a creative solution to a problem. The idea in brainstorming is to create an atmosphere of enthusiasm and nonjudgment in terms of the usefulness of an idea. To facilitate this, the following guidelines are used in brainstorming:

1. Criticism of ideas that are developed is not allowed. It is felt that criticism inhibits creativity and not allowing group members to make a judgment on the value of someone else's suggestion is thought to encourage creativity.

2. No idea is considered too far out. The idea in brainstorming is to encourage people to state publicly any idea that comes to mind.

3. Participants are encouraged to build on the suggestions of other group members. The stress is on group development and ownership of solutions, not on individual development and ownership.

4. As many ideas as possible are encouraged. The greater the number of ideas, the greater the probability that a useful one will be found.

The brainstorming technique has been used by many firms in both the public and private sector.[25] Interestingly, the shortcomings of brainstorming are usually not mentioned. A few years after Osborn published his book on brainstorming, an experiment was conducted to determine if brainstorming actually resulted in more ideas being generated than in traditional group decision-making systems.[26]

The findings were not encouraging for brainstorming. Four men worked individually on three different problems; when their performance was compared with that of a four-man group on the same three problems, it was found that the people working individually generated significantly more (and superior) ideas than did the four-man brainstorming group. Other studies have found the same tendencies.[27]

As we have noted on several occasions in this book, the hard evidence often is at odds with the claims made by the developers of certain techniques or programs. The disconfirming studies cited above suggest that group decision making actually does inhibit creativity, in spite of the best efforts to avoid it. We must therefore be careful about accepting the claims of the benefits of brainstorming.

## ☐ Advantages of Systematic Decision-Making Methods

There are several important advantages associated with the five systematic decision-making techniques discussed above:

1. They require the individual or group to use a system when making a decision; this is an improvement over the unstructured "what do we do now" approach. Even brainstorming—a technique that many people see as freewheeling and disorganized—has rules and regulations that are to be followed.

2. They all require decision makers to think about their assumptions and biases. These procedures generally cannot be used unless this is done, and although some people might prefer to ignore their biases and assumptions, confronting them can be very useful. The weights and criteria method and decision trees force decision makers to explicitly state their biases and assumptions, while the nominal grouping, Delphi, and brainstorming techniques require only an implicit consideration of biases and assumptions.

3. They all force the decision maker to deal with payoffs. Whether these are stated qualitatively or quantitatively, the advantage of systematic methods is that the decision maker must give some conscious thought to the kinds of gains that will be made if a certain decision is made.

4. They all require the decision maker to think clearly about the problem. This is perhaps the most important advantage of systematic methods. This should enhance the quality of the decision that is eventually made.

## ☐ Disadvantages of Systematic Decision-Making Methods

Various objections have been raised to the use of systematic decision-making methods. These methods are criticized as:

1. *Too time-consuming.* This is certainly true, but whether or not this is a disadvantage is debatable. If an individual uses systematic methods on simple problems, perhaps time is indeed wasted; however, if these methods are used for major problems, it would seem to be time well spent.

2. *Too difficult to use.* Some decision makers say they do not understand a certain method and hence they cannot use it. Again, this is not really a disadvantage but simply a situation that can be corrected. Once the decision maker is

taught how to use the method, this objection will disappear. In practice, however, this "reason" may really be an excuse for not doing a systematic analysis of a problem.

3. *Too rigid.* Practicing managers often argue, "You can't slot this problem into a rigid procedure." The response to this objection is fairly straightforward—if the procedure is not appropriate for the problem, don't use it. However, the objection about rigidity is often but another excuse for not using systematic analysis.

4. *Insensitive to the "people element."* Often considerable emphasis is placed on quantitative analysis in systematic decision-making methods and critics argue that the human element is ignored. This is, however, an illusion. While it may be uncomfortable for the decision maker to quantify the "people" element in a problem, it can be done. What critics are really saying here is that they don't feel right about quantifying certain things because it will make the decision maker appear to be "heartless."

5. *Used to rationalize the decision after the fact rather than to make the decision.* Once again, this is not a fault of the systematic method, but of the bias that the individual or group is imposing upon the system. Systematic methods should be used to make the decision, not to rationalize it.

# ■ INDIVIDUAL VS. GROUP DECISION MAKING

In the previous section we noted that certain systematic decision-making techniques can be used on either an individual or group basis, while others are designed specifically to be used in groups. The fundamental question then is, "Do groups or individuals make better decisions?" It is important to answer this question since there are so many work groups and committees in decision-making roles in organizations.

Before addressing the question, however, we must define what "better" means. The criteria normally used to define a "better" decision are (1) quality of the decision, (2) individual satisfaction with and acceptance of the decision, and (3) the time required to make the decision. The research findings on these criteria are quite clear: (1) the quality of group decisions is higher than the quality of the average individual decision, but lower than the best individual decisions, (2) individual satisfaction and acceptance is enhanced when decision-making authority is delegated to groups, and (3) groups require more time to reach a decision than do individuals.[28]

## ☐ Advantages of Group Decision Making

There are several advantages inherent in group decision making. First, groups usually have a greater knowledge base that can be brought to bear on the problem. This is an almost automatic outcome, since more than one person is involved.

Second, the number of approaches to resolving the problem is usually greater in groups because each group member thinks along somewhat different lines.

Individuals can get into ruts thinking about a problem in isolation, but in the group situation, approaches that group members perceive as unfruitful will be challenged.

Third, the group format allows increased participation by a variety of individuals. Although participation per se does not guarantee a high-quality decision, it does increase member satisfaction. If we accept the idea noted earlier that the effectiveness of a decision is a function of both quality and acceptance, member satisfaction is an important goal to pursue. Consider the following equation:[29]

$$ED = Q \times A$$
where ED = effectiveness of the decision
Q = quality of the decision
A = acceptance of the decision

---

## *Organizational Reality   9-7*
### *Decision-Making Teams at Ford Motor Company*

At the Ford Motor Company, more than 250 problem-solving teams are tackling work-related problems in the Ford-United Auto Workers Employee Involvement (EI) Program. The program is a major step in a cooperative effort to invite employee participation in decisions affecting their work and overall work environment. In its early stages, the program showed positive results in improved employee-supervisor and union–management relations. There was significant improvement in product quality and operational efficiency, as well. The EI program is not a substitute for the grievance procedure or collective bargaining, but both company and union officals point out that the number of shop floor complaints has declined due to improved relations.

There are three types of approaches to EI within Ford. The first type emphasizes problem-solving groups, where a small number of employees with similar positions meet periodically to solve work-related problems. In the second type, EI quality circles are used to stress the use of more formal quality control and statistical techniques. In the third type, EI team-building groups work at improving group functions to achieve group objectives. The groups focus on interpersonal and analytical aspects of problem solving.

The first step for an EI project involves setting up a local union–management steering committee. The committee identifies potential projects and objectives. Once an EI project is under way, it is monitored by the committee. Employee groups report their progress, make recommendations to management, and publish their results.

"Awareness" conferences are held to brief management and supervisors on the concepts and principles of EI. Cooperation between supervisors and employees is reportedly much higher due to the increased open and meaningful communication that is part of the EI program.

---

Source: Gerard Tavernier, "Awakening a Sleeping Giant: Ford's Employee Involvement Program," *Management Review* (June 1981): 15–20.

# Box 9-5: Committees and Their Effectiveness

IS A CAMEL A HORSE THAT WAS DESIGNED BY A COMMITTEE? The question reflects a common perception about committees and their effectiveness. Many people see committees as taking up more time, being less efficient, being less willing to confront crucial issues, and generally making ineffective decisions, as compared to individuals. When someone says, "I have to take that decision to my committee," there are usually a lot of groans, and snide remarks like, "Well, that kills that idea!"

While all of the above may be true to some degree, the fact is that committees generally make better decisions than the average individual. Try this for yourself. Below is a "problem" that you can solve individually and within a group. Given in random order is a list of fifteen occupations. Study the list and rank the occcupations in order of occupational prestige (i.e., from the highest status to the lowest). The highest status occupation will be 1 and on down to 15, the lowest. Once you have done this by yourself, gather about five or six of your friends and decide in your group (committee) on the ranking. To increase your effectiveness as a group, you should follow these rules:

1. Do not vote on the answers.
2. Do not "horse-trade" (i.e., trade one of your answers for another one).
3. Make an effort to draw out every group member and listen to what each has to say.
4. Each group member has the right to veto (i.e., if one person does not agree, then the group has not reached a decision).

After the group has reached a decision on all fifteen occupations, compare group and individual answers with the correct list, which can be obtained from your instructor. For a proper comparison, you should compute the average individual score and compare that to your group score. And remember, the lower the score, the better the answer.

The fifteen occupations are as follows:

1. Insurance agent
2. Undertaker
3. Barber
4. Airline pilot
5. Priest
6. Janitor
7. Dentist
8. Mail carrier
9. Policeman
10. Taxi driver
11. Garbage collector
12. University professor
13. Physician
14. Plumber
15. Author of novels

The practical implications of this simplified equation are straightforward: if either decision quality or acceptance is low, decision effectiveness drops sharply. Thus, concern must be shown for both quality and acceptance. Participation clearly deals with the acceptance issue; if individuals have participated in making a decision, they are more likely to support its implementation than if the decision is simply imposed on them. On an organizational level, group members can be appointed to decision-making groups that represent various areas of the organization, and this can enhance the implementation of changes that affect more than one area. The recent trend toward appointing employees to Boards of Directors is an example of this idea.

## ☐ Disadvantages of Group Decision Making

The most practical disadvantage of group decision making is the time required to make decisions. In one sense, this may not be a disadvantage because the extra time that is taken usually results in a better decision. However, in most organizations there is a sense of urgency about decisions, and groups or committees have a reputation for being slow. Thus, decisive individuals can experience frustration as they await the decision of a group, or participate in the group process. The old saying, "If you don't want any action taken on an important issue, give it to a committee" represents the frustration many managers have experienced with committees.

A second problem with group decision making is that certain individuals invariably dominate the discussion; as a result, the dominant individuals' preferences may be accepted and other (perhaps better) ideas will never be discussed.[30] This is one of the most significant problems in group decision making. As one writer has noted:

> . . . groups fail to reach their full potential because of problems associated with the interaction process . . . groups perform at a level generally better than the competence of their average member, but rarely as well as their most proficient member.[31]

The Delphi technique, nominal grouping, and social-judgment analysis are all techniques that have been developed to overcome these problems with interactions among people in groups.

A third problem with groups is the potential for "groupthink," the tendency for group members to suppress critical comments in the interest of maintaining group solidarity and a feeling of togetherness.[32] Because individuals fear being labeled as "uncooperative" by other group members, they do not voice concerns about the direction the group is taking, even if there are logical grounds for being concerned. (The issue of groupthink is discussed in detail in Chapter 11.)

Finally, groups may make decisions that are simply a compromise between the various views held by individual members. This is particularly likely when a group must make a decision on a controversial issue. By definition, on controversial issues there will be opposing views. After a brief discussion, the group may conclude that a decision favoring either side is unacceptable, so a compromise solution is chosen. Unfortunately, this kind of decision has several shortcomings: First, it may please no one. By definition, in a compromise no one gets exactly what he wants, so everyone in the group may be unhappy. Second, a compromise simply avoids the issue that was causing the controversy. Good decisions are not made when important issues are ignored. Third, a compromise may result in a low-quality decision. If people cannot agree on something and a compromise is quickly accepted to get the problem solved, other possible solutions to the problem are not even analyzed to see if they are superior.

## ■ CREATIVITY AND DECISION MAKING

We often hear exhortations for managers to "think creatively" when they make decisions, because this will help organizations that are trying to survive in a harsh economic environment. To be successful in this kind of environment, it is argued, requires that strategic and operational decisions be made creatively; if this is

---

### *Organizational Reality  9-8*
### *Involving the Union in Management Decision Making*

United Auto Workers President Douglas A. Fraser joined the Chrysler Corporation Board in May, 1980. His primary interest in taking a board seat was not to increase the union's bargaining clout but to inject worker thinking into management decision making. "I can't represent my members if I'm always reacting to management decisions," Fraser says. "We have to be there when the decisions are made. And we can bring an important resource to the board. People in the plants will tell me things they won't tell management."

So far Fraser's main role has been to raise points the other seventeen directors ordinarily do not consider. He prevailed on the board to set up a committee to study the impact of plant closings on workers and the community. In one case, this resulted in a decision to keep a glass plant open by bringing more work into the plant. Fraser also used his insider's knowledge of Chrysler's financial condition to argue strongly, in letters to Chrysler workers, that a prolonged strike would cripple the company and cost them their jobs. Nevertheless, workers rejected a tentative agreement in the U.S., partly because of a lack of trust in management—the very thing Fraser hopes to correct by giving workers a voice in management.

Fraser foresaw some of the problems involved in the concept—suspicion of labor's voice on the board, and conflict of interest. He has stayed away from meetings at which bargaining issues were discussed and has stepped down when a strike occurred. But adopting this "on again, off again" procedure certainly shows that board representation for labor will not be easily institutionalized. There are also formidable legal barriers. Courts have held that a U.S. director must represent all shareholders equally—an untenable position for a union representative during bargaining or a strike.

---

Source: "A Union Seat on the Board: The Test Isn't Over," *Business Week* (22 November 1982): 30.

done, the organization can then effectively meet the demands of the external environment.

This is a sound idea, but these kinds of statements are often made without ever defining creativity. What is creativity and what constitutes a creative decision? Creativity is the generation of *new* and *useful* ways of doing things. A creative decision therefore, is one that solves a problem or exploits an opportunity in a new and useful way. Stated in this way, it is easy to see why creative decisions are so important to organizations. Creative decisions are a major aid in helping organizations cope with change.

Can people learn to be more creative? At present the answer is a tentative "Yes," but considerable research needs to be done on two issues: (1) how to train people, and (2) how creativity training works to improve the likelihood of creative decisions. Since it is often very difficult to determine if training (creativity or otherwise) actually has an impact on people's behavior, these are important questions to answer. One field experiment that developed data on both these issues found that creativity training actually did result in measurable improvements in the creative behavior of engineers and technicians in an industrial company.[33] The authors stressed that the total creative process (dealing with problem finding, problem solving, and solution implementation) must be dealt with in creativity training.

## ☐ The Creative Process

The exercise of creativity can take place in any one of the three aforementioned phases of the total creative process. In each of these phases, both ideation (idea generation) and evaluation (judgment as to the utility of the idea) must occur if creativity is to be achieved.[34]

Within this general context, certain specific things take place. These things are difficult to describe exactly because we do not yet fully understand all the things that go on in the human mind. Nevertheless, there are several basic steps that have been identified:[35]

1. *Preparation.* If the word "creativity" is used in everyday conversation, many people seem to feel that it is something that just happens. Research on what constitutes a creative decision or a creative discovery decisively refutes this common belief. The preparation stage involves a great deal of hard work and a high level of motivation in order to assemble or develop relevant information on the problem to be solved. This step also involves organizing the data in such a way that the decision maker can get a thorough understanding of the problem.

2. *Incubation.* The incubation stage is difficult to describe, but what apparently happens is that the decision maker lets the information that has been gathered in the preparation stage "simmer on the back burner." In other words, the decision maker stops thinking intensively about the problem and simply allows it to exist in the background. At this juncture, he or she may appear to be doing virtually no work on the problem but, because the incubation period takes place in the mind, this is a misleading conclusion. Work *is* continuing on the problem.

3. *Inspiration.* The point at which the creative solution first enters the decision maker's mind is the point of inspiration. This may be either a flash of insight (the "Eureka" phenomenon) or it may be a gradual and growing awareness that the problem has a solution. This is probably the most satisfying stage to the decision maker because the conceptual logjam has finally been broken. Once again, however, we must remember that without the work in the preparation and incubation stages, the inspiration stage would not occur.

4. *Validation.* In the validation stage, the creative solution is tested to see if it is workable and useful for either the organization or for other individuals. Years of testing may be required to determine whether the solution really works. A manager who has developed a new structural arrangement that he or she feels is a creative solution to a long-standing organizational problem may find in the validation stage that the solution is not workable. This can be a very depressing state of affairs; the manager must return to the preparation stage and begin to work through the process again.

## ☐ Characteristics of Creative Individuals

Numerous research studies have examined the issue of whether creative individuals have personality characteristics that distinguish them from less creative individuals. These studies reveal several general characteristics that creative individuals seem to possess.[36]

1. *They are nonconformists.* This is not meant as a negative remark but simply to indicate that creative individuals do not seem overly concerned about whether or not they do things the way other people do, or dress the way other people dress, or think the way other people think. They simply have their own view of the world and they pursue it. As part of this nonconformist behavior, highly creative people prefer a great deal of autonomy and freedom, i.e., they like to have the right to do what they wish and to pursue what interests them in a fashion that is comfortable for them.

2. *They value the use of their mental faculties.* Creative individuals get a great deal of satisfaction out of using their mental abilities to solve knotty problems. This is particularly evident when a problem exists that has defied resolution despite the efforts of many others to solve it. Creative individuals seem attracted to these kinds of problems because they can use their intellectual abilities in a way that will not only resolve the problem, but will also bring them some recognition and satisfaction along the way.

3. *They resist making judgments until the relevant facts in the problem have been reviewed.* One of the notable characteristics about creative individuals is their reluctance to say "It can't be done." Interestingly, creative individuals may say "It can't be done" for one problem but not for another. They therefore may be very creative with respect to one problem but be closed-minded with respect to another.

4. *They are relatively young.* Large numbers of studies have been conducted to determine whether age has any significant effect on creative abilities. By far the

most creative ages for individuals are the years from thirty to forty. This is true of a wide variety of occupations both in the sciences and in the arts. We could speculate that the most creative years fall between thirty and forty because the individual needs some time to prepare for the career in which he or she is going to be creative, yet must be young enough to have some sort of "youthful vigor" to achieve the high effort level required in creative decision making. The works of famous composers, sculptors, painters, etc. all did not come about easily. Years of hard work and learning were necessary before these things could be done. The same is true of managerial decisions in organizations, even if the examples do not seem so dramatic or are not so well-known. The fact that students train for four years in business schools is another example of training. Only after this training are they given the opportunity to make creative managerial decisions. The finding that the most creative period is between thirty and forty should not lead us to conclude that little creative behavior occurs outside these years. There are many examples of people engaging in creative behavior prior to and after the thirty-forty span. Nevertheless, the evidence indicates that for most people the thirty to forty age bracket is the peak time for creative behavior.

5. *They are unsympathetic to authoritarian environments.* This may pose great practical difficulties for the creative individual, because many managers are more concerned about subordinates following orders than they are about goal achievement. When creative individuals find themselves in this kind of circumstance, their creative output declines and/or they leave the particular organization. The loyalty of creative people is often perceived by managers to be quite low and their turnover in organizations may be quite high.

## □ Developing a Climate That Encourages Creativity

If organizations hope to gain the benefits of creative decision making, some concern must be shown for creating a climate in which people will feel free to be creative. This need for creativity in decision making must, of course, be balanced with a concern for some sort of organizational order. This balance may be very difficult to achieve because not enough is known about individual creativity to specify exactly when there is too much freedom (leading to chaos) and when there is too little freedom (leading to a decline in creativity). Nevertheless, research in this area suggests that the following internal organizational climate features should be present to maximize creative decision making:[37]

1. *Positive reinforcement for creative decisions.* As we saw in the chapter on performance management, rewarding desirable behaviors increases the probability that they will recur in the future. Applying this logic to the issue of creativity and decision making, it is clear that creative decisions must be rewarded if management hopes to induce people to continue to make them. If creative decisions are continually suppressed by management, if proper credit is not given for creative ideas, or if creative people are treated in a negative fashion, less and less creativity can be expected in the future decisions of these people. If, on the other hand,

appropriate awards are given for creative decisions that benefit the organization, the creative abilities of people will be stimulated.

The rewards for creative behavior need not be restricted to monetary rewards. If we analyze the world around us we see immediately that creative works always have an author. This is true for artists, composers, sculptors, and other individuals (including managers) who are engaged in creative work. These examples demonstrate the importance of reinforcing creative behavior and the resources available to management beyond monetary reinforcement for encouraging creative behavior. Recognition often costs management very little, yet the impact it has upon the person who did the creating may be substantial.

2. *Appropriate resource support.* If the organization expects creative decisions from various groups or individuals, it must provide resources to facilitate creative decision making. The obvious example is resources being allocated to a research lab, but every position in an organization has some creative potential, whether the environment is a traditionally research-oriented one or not. If individuals in an organization are not given proper resources to do their job, management can expect less than an optimal amount of creative decision-making behavior.

Some people argue that more creativity is evident when resources are scarce ("necessity is the mother of invention") than when resources are plentiful. There is certainly some truth to this notion, but there must be a minimum level of support or all the enthusiasm in the world will not lead to creativity. A research lab, for example, must have certain equipment or the basic activities of the lab cannot be carried out. Likewise, a manager must have certain minimum facilities to do the job properly.

We must admit that it is difficult to determine what is an "appropriate" resource support level. Given the human tendency to pursue ever larger amounts of resources, we can expect to find people asking for more than they really need. Nevertheless, the basic principle of adequate resource support stands. When the level of support is appropriate, it conveys to the individual that the organization has confidence in what that individual is doing. This may aid creative decision making.

3. *Realistic deadlines.* In return for the organization providing adequate resource support, it is not unreasonable for the organization to ask decision makers to meet certain deadlines. While many people feel that this goes against the notion of freewheeling creativity (the individual should be given as much time as possible to make creative decisions), the establishment of realistic deadlines actually facilitates creative decision making. This happens because most individuals probably are not highly motivated to complete a task until the deadline nears. As an example, consider the goal set by President Kennedy in the early sixties to put a man on the moon by 1970. The goal was achieved in July of 1969. Apparently a realistic deadline motivates managers and researchers to complete the creative decision making process.

4. *A balance between freedom and conformity.* If an organization hopes to foster creative decision making, the extent to which decision makers must conform to organization rules and regulations must be tempered with the knowledge

that creative decisions may not emerge from highly structured environments. By the same token, it must be kept in mind that the desire for creative decisions is based upon the belief that these decisions will benefit the organization. Therefore, there must also be guidelines within which the decision makers must operate so that they can simultaneously be creative and also contribute positively to organization goals.

If we accept McGregor's assumption that employees are enthusiastic about work, that they desire additional responsibility, and so forth, we can trust employees to exhibit the balance between freedom and conformity. However, as noted earlier, such assumptions do not fit all employees, so guidelines will have to be developed to ensure a balance.

## *Opening Incident Revisited—Franklin Real Estate*

In the opening incident the managers of Franklin Real Estate were having difficulty making an investment decision. Art Franklin was particularly adamant that they use a decision-making technique that would (1) result in good investment decisions, and (2) cut down on the time required to make decisions.

What kind of technique should Franklin Real Estate use? Because all the key variables are quantified (and everyone seems to agree on the figures), decision-tree analysis is a good starting point. The solution to the problem is shown in Figure 9-8. Based on the probabilities and payoffs, alternative #4 (buy blocks 2 and 3) is the best because it has the greatest expected value.

Several additional observations can be made about this problem. First, what if the probabilities are in error? In order to deal with this potential problem, the decision-tree analysis should be redone to see if a higher or lower probability in each alternative will change the answer. If major changes in probabilities are necessary before a different alternative becomes better, the brothers can be confident that they have made a good decision.

Second, some creativity is necessary to arrive at the decision of buying blocks 2 and 3. Had the brothers had their normal disjointed discussion about investments, they might simply have decided to invest in block 1 *or* 2 *or* 3.

Third, the risk preferences of the brothers must be taken into consideration before a decision is made. If one of them is very risk-averse, he would prefer alternative #1 because the worst that could happen is a $5,000 gain. In alternatives 2 and 3, a substantial loss could be incurred if the government bought block 1. If another brother was very risk-oriented, he would probably prefer alternative #3 because it might result in a big gain (or loss).

Other techniques that were discussed in this chapter could be used to analyze this problem. For example, if the weights and criteria method were used, it would be necessary to develop the criteria (e.g., profit, risk, etc.) that were important in making the decision. These criteria would then be weighted and each alternative

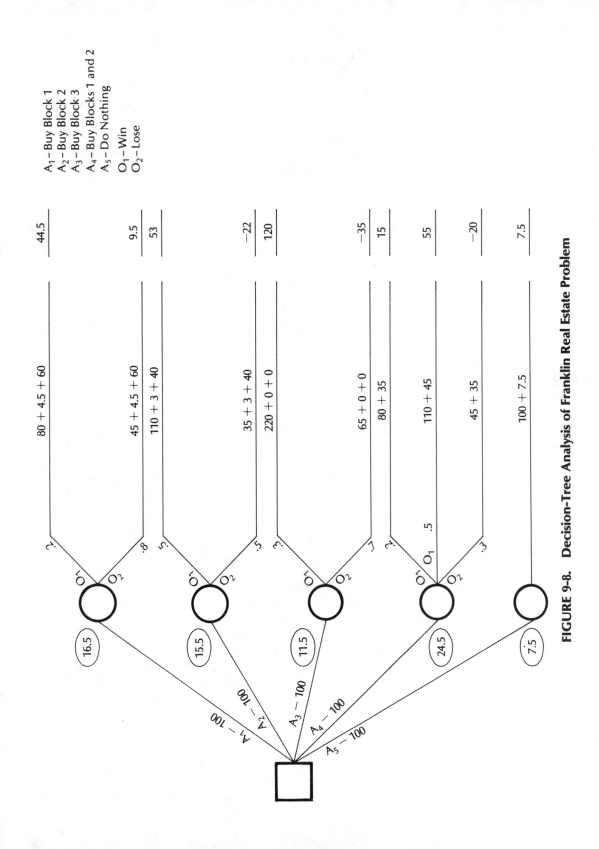

**FIGURE 9-8. Decision-Tree Analysis of Franklin Real Estate Problem**

$A_1$ – Buy Block 1
$A_2$ – Buy Block 2
$A_3$ – Buy Block 3
$A_4$ – Buy Blocks 1 and 2
$A_5$ – Do Nothing

$O_1$ – Win
$O_2$ – Lose

would be scored. Each alternative would then be totaled, using the procedure described in the chapter. The alternative with the highest score would then be chosen.

The nominal grouping procedure, brainstorming, and Delphi could also be used, but it appears that, given the nature of the problem, decision-tree analysis is the most straightforward technique. An interesting exercise is to make the decision using a variety of techniques, and then observe the extent of agreement between the techniques as to what the best alternative is.

To make a good decision in a reasonable amount of time, the managers at Franklin Real Estate need to discuss what kind of decision-making system they feel is most useful. During this discussion, important issues like risk preferences will emerge and these can be resolved. Once the important concerns are dealt with, the company can adopt the method that best suits them. Future decisions will therefore be easier to make and will take less time.

## ■ SUMMARY

In this chapter we discussed the subject of organizational decision making. Several observations were made about this topic. The relationship between decision making and the functions of management was noted, as well as the fact that before it is necessary to make a decision several conditions must exist. A central point is that decision making is the process of choosing from among potential solutions to a problem. The point at which the actual decision is made is an event, but the process is the part of decision-making that is stressed. The distinction was also made between problem and opportunity decisions and between programmed and nonprogrammed decisions.

Each organization has a unique decision-making environment. Some similarities across organizations can be observed, however. These observations involve *models* of decision-making behavior (the economic, administrative, political, and garbage can models), the *predictability* of decision outcomes (certainty, risk, and uncertainty), and general decision-making *strategies* (computational, judgment, compromise, and inspiration). These three general areas are relevant for all organizations, but the specifics in each will differ.

The actual decision-making process can be broken down into three major steps: the problem-analysis phase, the decision-making phase, and the implementation phase. Several substeps in each of these phases were presented, first from the rational perspective (i.e., how the process should work), and then from the behavioral perspective (i.e., how human idiosyncracies influence the rational process).

Several decision-making techniques were presented, including the weights and criteria method, decision trees, the Delphi technique, the nominal-grouping technique, and brainstorming. These are all systematic techniques requiring that certain procedures be followed. The advantages and some perceived disadvantages of these systematic techniques were also noted.

Group and individual decision making were contrasted. Generally speaking, groups make higher-quality decisions than individuals, but they take more time to make a decision. The quality of group decisions is not always better than that of individuals, particularly when "groupthink" (the suspension of critical judgment in the interest of group solidarity) develops.

The rapidly changing environment in which most organizations find themselves means that creativity in decision making is becoming increasingly important. The generation of new and useful ways of doing things will help organizations cope with this increasingly rapid change. The creative process consists of four steps: (1) preparation, (2) incubation, (3) inspiration, and (4) validation. The characteristics of creative individuals were noted and suggestions were made for developing a climate that encourages organizational members to be creative.

# ■ REVIEW QUESTIONS

1.  What is the difference between programmed and nonprogrammed decisions? Give two examples from your own work experience.

2.  What are the four basic decision strategies that are available when decision makers consider cause and effect beliefs and goal preferences?

3.  What is a rational decision? An irrational decision?

4.  What kinds of problems might arise in the use of the conjunctive, disjunctive, and compensatory approaches?

5.  What kinds of nonrational things happen during the problem-analysis stage of decision making? The decision-making stage? The implementation stage?

6.  Which steps are typically the least well carried out in the decision making process?

7.  What are the basic advantages of the weights and criteria method? How can these advantages be undermined by decision makers?

8.  In what kinds of situations are decision trees useful? The Delphi technique? Nominal-group technique?

9.  What advantages are claimed for brainstorming? What does the empirical evidence on brainstorming show?

10.  Compare and contrast group and individual decision making. What are the major problems with group decision making?

11.  What kind of organizational climate should exist to encourage creativity?

# ■ EXERCISE 9-1: THE PRINCIPAL'S PROBLEM

The principal of a high school needs a teacher to replace one who has resigned. Five candidates apply for the job. The principal has certain general guidelines he follows in picking candidates. In his view, teaching experience is the most important consideration. However, the amount of formal education the candidate has is also important, as is the principal's assessment of the candidate after a personal interview, and letters of recommendation from the candidate's past employer. Ratings of the teacher from previous students is least important. The brief descriptions below indicate what the principal knows about each candidate.

Candidate A—Master's Degree in Education; six years teaching experience; fair letter of recommendation; good ratings from previous students; fair interview rating.

Candidate B—Three years at university; six years teaching experience; excellent letter of recommendation; excellent ratings from previous students; fair interview rating.

Candidate C—One year of university; six years teaching experience; fair letter of recommendation; excellent rating from previous students; fair interview rating.

Candidate D—Master's Degree in education; five years teaching experience; good letter of recommendation; excellent ratings from previous students; excellent interview rating.

Candidate E—B.A. in Education; ten years teaching experience; poor letter of recommendation, fair ratings from previous students; poor interview rating.

The principal is having difficulty deciding which candidate to pick.

1. Assuming that you must use the criteria the principal has stated, which candidate would you pick? Which technique would you use to pick a candidate?

2. What would you do if the principal disagrees with your choice?

# ■ EXERCISE 9-2: THE USURY BANK

On September 5, the board of directors of the Usury Bank decided that expansion of the bank's business was desirable and that one additional branch should be opened by the following June. After this fundamental decision had been made, the board was faced with picking a specific location. A search committee was formed to review site availability and on January 5 the committee reported to the board that it had found three sites that looked promising.

Site 1 is in a shopping center in a rapidly expanding residential area. Because of this, the branch will likely be very profitable and growth will be rapid. However, other banks will reason the same way, so it is probable (80 percent chance) that a competitor will enter this market. There is another influence on profit and that is the state of the economy. Other things being equal, the greater the expansion of the economy, the greater the profit the bank will make. The table below shows the total expected profit from the branch for the first five years of operation, given various states of the economy and various states of competition.

|  | State of Economy | | |
|---|---|---|---|
|  | *Expansion* | *Stability* | *Recession* |
| Competitor Enters Market | $500,000 | 400,000 | 150,000 |
| Competitor Does Not Enter Market | 750,000 | 550,000 | 300,000 |

The bank officers believe that there is a 0.5 probability of expansion, 0.3 of stability, and 0.2 of recession.

Site 2 is in an established residential sector where competition has existed for many years. Profit over five years will be $200,000, $150,000, and $50,000 for "Expansion," "Stability," and "Recession," respectively.

Site 3 is at the edge of an urban renewal project. Many new commercial buildings are being built, but the site where the branch would be is still zoned residential (as it has been for the past eighty-five years). A zoning change request is currently before the zoning board but the decision will not be known until September of next year. However, the bank officers have heard via the grapevine that there is a fairly good chance (0.7) that the zoning change to "commercial" will go through. However, if it does not, the bank will not be able to purchase either site 1 or 2 because they will have been sold by that time. The bank will, however, be able to sell off site 3 for approximately $400,000. The site is very favorable in terms of potential profit, since the business will be with large-scale manufacturing firms. The bank officers must decide whether they are going to try to get a large share of this business or not, i.e., they must decide to either "build big" (in terms of both physical branch size and personnel) or "build small." The table below indicates the projected revenues over the first five years of operation for both options, given various economic outcomes.

|  | State of Economy | | |
|---|---|---|---|
|  | *Expansion* | *Stability* | *Recession* |
| Build "Big" | $2,400,000 | 1,500,000 | 500,000 |
| Build "Small" | 1,400,000 | 1,100,000 | 600,000 |

What should the bank development committee do?

# ■ ENDNOTES

1. James March and Herbert Simon, *Organizations* (New York: Wiley, 1958).
2. E. Frank Harrison, *The Managerial Decision Making Process* (Boston: Houghton-Mifflin, 1975).
3. M. J. Wallace and D. P. Schwab, "A Cross-Validated Comparison of Five Models Used to Predict Graduate Admission Committee Decision," *Journal of Applied Psychology* (1976): 559–563.
4. R. M. Dawis and B. Corrigan, "Linear Models of Decision Making," *Psychological Bulletin* (1974): 95–106.
5. See H. Einhorn, "The Use of Non-Linear, Non-Compensatory Models As a Function of Task and Amount of Information," *Organizational Behavior and Human Performance* (1971): 1–27; also H. Einhorn and R. M. Hogarth, "Unit Weighting Schemes for Decision Making," *Organizational Behavior and Human Performance* (1975): 171–192.
6. J. L. McKenny and P. G. W. Keen, "How Managers' Minds Work," *Harvard Business Review* (1979): 79–90.
7. McKenny and Keen, "How Managers' Minds Work"; see also E. Sanford and H. Adelman, *Management Decisions: A Behavioral Approach* (Cambridge, Mass.: Winthrop Publishing, 1977), p. 135.

8. H. A. Simon, *Models of Man* (New York: Wiley, 1957).

9. M. D. Cohen, J. G. March, and J. P. Olsen, "A Garbage Can Model of Organizational Choice," *Administrative Sciences Quarterly* 17 (1972): 1–25.

10. J. Thompson and A. Tuden, "Strategies, Structures, and Processes of Organizational Decision," *Comparative Studies in Administration*, ed. J. Thompson et al., (Pittsburgh: University of Pittsburgh Press, 1959).

11. The model of the decision making presented here is a composite of numerous models that have appeared during the last several decades.

12. "Sabotage at Lordstown," *Time* (7 February 1972): 76.

13. The most impressive analysis of this phase of the process appears in C. Kepner and B. Tregoe, *The Rational Manager: A Systematic Approach to Problem Solving and Decision Making* (Princeton: Kepner-Tregoe, Inc., 1976).

14. R. Cyert and J. March, *A Behavioral Theory of the Firm* (Englewood Cliffs, N.J.: Prentice-Hall, 1963).

15. See the discussion of individual and group decision making later in this chapter for a formal statement of this idea.

16. For a more detailed treatment of decision trees, see F. Magee, "Decision Trees for Decision Making," *Harvard Business Review* (July–August 1964); also J. F. Magee, "How to Use Decision Trees in Capital Investment," *Harvard Business Review* (1964): 79–96.

17. See, for example, M. Jolson and G. Rossow, "The Delphi Process in Marketing Decision Making," *Journal of Marketing Research* (1971): 443–448.

18. For a critical analysis of the Delphi technique, see H. Sackman, *Delphi Critique: Expert Opinion, Forecasting, and Group Process* (Lexington, Mass.: D. C. Heath and Co., Lexington Books, 1975).

19. A. H. van de Ven and Andre Delbecq, "The Effectiveness of Nominal, Delphi, and Interacting Group Decision Making Processes," *Academy of Management Journal* 17 (1974): 605–632; also A. L. Delbecq, A. H. van de Ven, and D. H. Gustafson, *Group Techniques for Program Planning: A Guide to Nominal and Delphi Processes* (Glenview, Ill: Scott Foresman and Co., 1975).

20. J. J. Sullivan, "An Experimental Study of a Method for Improving the Effectiveness of the Nominal Group Technique" (Ph.D. dis., University of Florida, 1978). For specific applications of nominal grouping, see the following: G. D. Burton, D. S. Pathak, and R. M. Zigli, "Using Group Size to Improve the Decision Making Ability of Nominal Groups," *Proceedings of the 37th Annual Meeting of the Academy of Management* (1977): 53–56; Thad B. Green and Paul H. Pietri, "Using Nominal Grouping to Improve Upward Communication," *MSU Business Topics* (Autumn 1974): 37–43; W. M. Colley, "Size and Performance of Nominal Groups As Related to Problem Identification in a Management Environment," *Dissertation Abstract International* 38 (1978): 4251A.

21. J. Rohrbaugh, "Improving the Quality of Group Judgment: Social Judgment Analysis and the Nominal Group Technique," *Organizational Behavior and Human Performance* 28 (1981): 22–288.

22. For a more detailed description of Social Judgment Analysis, see K. R. Hammond, J. Rohrbaugh, J. Mumpower, and L. Adelman, "Social Judgment Theory Applications in Policy Formation," *Human Judgment and Decision Processes in Applied Settings*, ed. M. F. Kaplan and S. Schwartz (New York: Academic Press, 1977).

23. S. E. White, J. E. Dittrich, and J. R. Lang, "The Effects of Group Decision Making Process and Problem-Situation Complexity on Implementation Attempts," *Administrative Science Quarterly* 25 (1980): 428–440.

24. A. F. Osborn, *Applied Imagination* (New York: Scribner's, 1974).

25. C. Gregory, *The Management of Intelligence: Scientific Problem Solving and Creativity* (New York: McGraw-Hill, 1967).

26. D. Taylor, C. Block, and P. Berry, "Does Group Participation When Using Brainstorming Facilitate or Inhibit Creative Thinking?" *Administrative Science Quarterly* 3 (1958): 23–47.

27. T. J. Bouchard, "Personality, Problem Solving Procedure, and Performance in Small Groups," *Journal of Applied Psychology Monograph* 53 (1969) 1, part 2; see also T. J. Bouchard, "Training, Motivation, and Personality As Determinants of the Effectiveness of Brainstorming Groups and Individuals," *Journal of Applied Psychology* 59 (1974): 226–227; also P. C. Dillion, V. K.

Graham, and A. Aidells, "Brainstorming on a Hot Problem," *Journal of Applied Psychology* 56 (1972): 487–490.

28. C. R. Holloman and H. W. Hendrick, "Adequacy of Group Decisions As a Function of the Decision Making Process," *Academy of Management Journal* 15 (1972): 175–184; also H. H. Kelley and J. W. Thibaut, "Group Problem Solving," *The Handbook of Social Psychology,* ed. G. Lindzey and E. Aronson (Reading, Mass: Addison-Wesley, 1969), ch. 29.

29. Norman R. F. Maier, "Assets and Liabilities in Group Problem Solving: The Need for an Integrative Function," *Psychological Review* 74 (1967): 239–249.

30. For a review of this problem, see I. D. Steiner, *Group Process and Productivity* (New York: Academic Press, 1971); also J. Rohrbaugh, "Improving the Quality of Group Judgment; Social Judgment Analysis and the Delphi Technique," *Organizational Behavior and Human Performance* 24 (1979): 73–92.

31. J. Rohrbaugh, "Improving the Quality of Group Judgment."

32. Irving L. Janis, *Victims of Groupthink* (Boston: Houghton-Mifflin, 1972).

33. M. Basadur, G. Graen, and S. Green, "Training in Creative Problem Solving: Effects on Ideation and Problem Finding and Solving in an Industrial Research Organization," *Organizational Behavior and Human Performance* 30 (1982): 41–70.

34. Ibid, p. 44.

35. A. Oxenfeldt, D. Miller, and R. Dickinson, *A Basic Approach to Executive Decision Making* (New York, AMACON, 1978), p. 157; also C. Patrick, *What Is Creative Thinking?* (New York: Philosophical Library, Inc., 1955).

36. D. W. MacKinnon, "The Nature and Nurture of Creative Talent," *Readings in Managerial Psychology,* ed. H. J. Leavitt (Chicago: University of Chicago Press, 1964); also G. A. Steiner, *The Creative Organization* (Chicago: University of Chicago Press, 1965); also D. W. MacKinnon, "Assessing Creative Persons," *Journal of Creative Behavior* (Summer 1967): 303–304. For a review of research which attempts to identify creative individuals, see A. Roe, "Psychological Approaches to Creativity in Science," *The Creativity Question,* ed. A. Rothenberg and C. R. Hausman, 1976.

37. G. A. Steiner, *The Creative Organization;* also D. G. Pelz, "Freedom in Research," *International Science and Technology* (February 1964): 54–66; also G. Zaltman, R. Duncan, and J. Holbek, *Innovations and Organizations* (New York: Wiley, 1973); also J. D. Femina and C. Sopkin, *From Those Wonderful Folks Who Brought You Pearl Harbor* (New York: Simon and Schuster, 1970); also N. R. Baker, E. Winofsky, L. Langmeyer, and D. J. Sweeney, *Idea Generation* (Cincinnati: College of Business Administration, Univ. of Cincinnati, 1976).

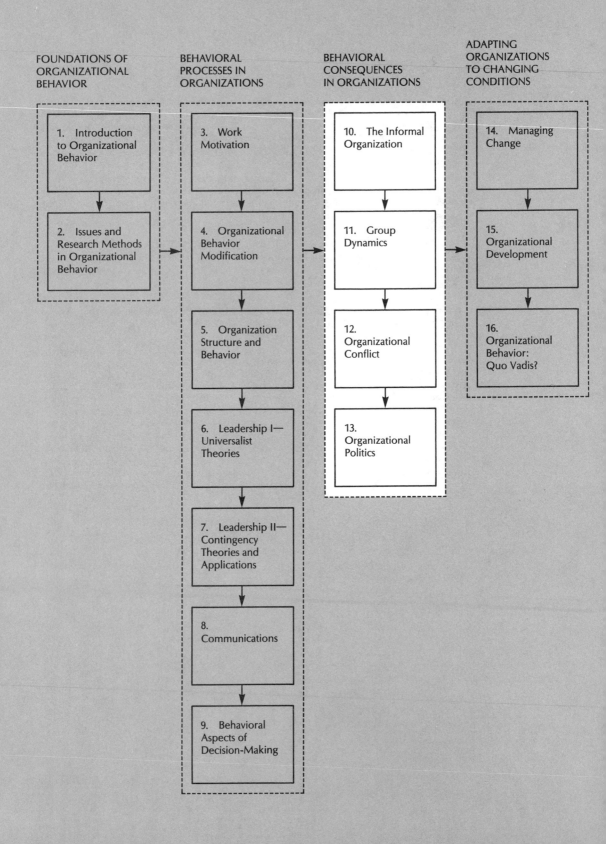

**FOUNDATIONS OF ORGANIZATIONAL BEHAVIOR**

1. Introduction to Organizational Behavior

2. Issues and Research Methods in Organizational Behavior

**BEHAVIORAL PROCESSES IN ORGANIZATIONS**

3. Work Motivation

4. Organizational Behavior Modification

5. Organization Structure and Behavior

6. Leadership I—Universalist Theories

7. Leadership II—Contingency Theories and Applications

8. Communications

9. Behavioral Aspects of Decision-Making

**BEHAVIORAL CONSEQUENCES IN ORGANIZATIONS**

10. The Informal Organization

11. Group Dynamics

12. Organizational Conflict

13. Organizational Politics

**ADAPTING ORGANIZATIONS TO CHANGING CONDITIONS**

14. Managing Change

15. Organizational Development

16. Organizational Behavior: Quo Vadis?

# Behavioral Consequences in Organizations

# SECTION III

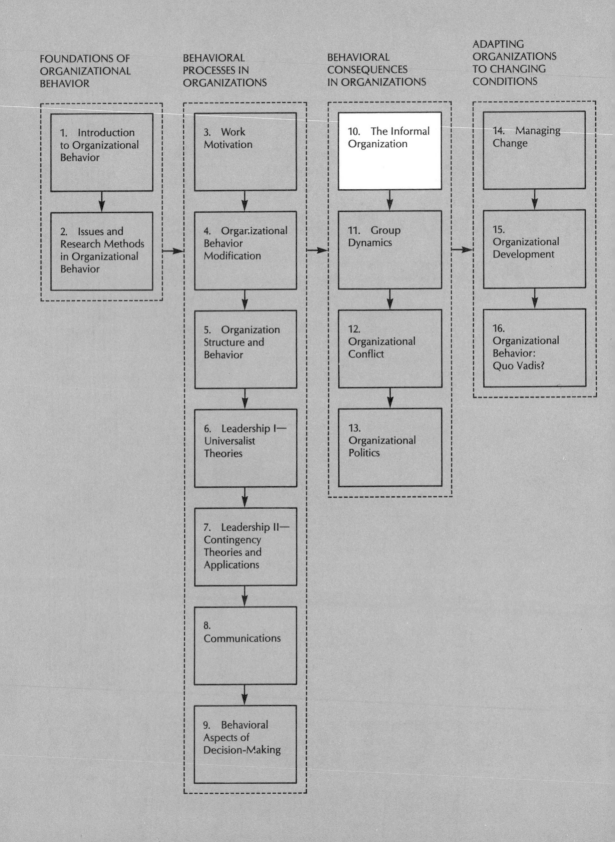

FOUNDATIONS OF ORGANIZATIONAL BEHAVIOR

1. Introduction to Organizational Behavior

2. Issues and Research Methods in Organizational Behavior

BEHAVIORAL PROCESSES IN ORGANIZATIONS

3. Work Motivation

4. Organizational Behavior Modification

5. Organization Structure and Behavior

6. Leadership I—Universalist Theories

7. Leadership II—Contingency Theories and Applications

8. Communications

9. Behavioral Aspects of Decision-Making

BEHAVIORAL CONSEQUENCES IN ORGANIZATIONS

10. The Informal Organization

11. Group Dynamics

12. Organizational Conflict

13. Organizational Politics

ADAPTING ORGANIZATIONS TO CHANGING CONDITIONS

14. Managing Change

15. Organizational Development

16. Organizational Behavior: Quo Vadis?

# The Informal Organization

## ■ Learning Objectives

After reading this chapter carefully you should be able to:

☐ Describe the basic nature of the informal organization and its fundamental properties.

☐ Compare and contrast the formal and informal organizations.

☐ Diagram the informal organization.

☐ Describe how managers can use the concept of status to improve organizational and individual effectiveness.

☐ Explain the advantages and disadvantages of the "grapevine."

☐ Recognize the problems that arise out of the informal organization.

☐ Name some specific strategies for dealing with the informal organization.

☐ List the sources of power available to a manager and explain how they might be used.

# Chapter 10

# ■ KEY TERMS

**Informal structure**
**Organizational role**
**Norms**
**Grapevine**
**Sociogram**
**Status**
**Scalar status**
**Functional status**
**Ascribed status**
**Achieved status**
**Status symbols**
**Social power**
**Reward power**
**Punishment power**
**Expert power**
**Referent power**
**Legitimate power**
**Suboptimization**

# ■ CHAPTER OUTLINE

I. Formal and Informal Organizations Compared and Contrasted
   A. Origin of Structure
   B. Position Terminology
   C. Goals of the Organization
   D. Influence Processes
   E. Control Mechanisms
   F. Communication Processes
   G. Charting the Organization

II. Functions of the Informal Organization
   A. Security
   B. Social Satisfaction
   C. Communication Channel
   D. Balancing Device
   E. Source of Motivation

## *Opening Incident—Ralph Wilson*

Ralph Wilson sat looking at his questionnaires in amazement. What on earth was he going to do with this obviously worthless information?

Upon nearing completion of his master's degree in management at State University, Ralph had elected to do a research thesis instead of the usual course work. He had been working closely with one of the professors during his stint at State, and between the two of them a satisfactory thesis topic had been agreed upon. The topic of pay had always interested him and he had pretty well decided to enter the compensation field after graduation. He was especially curious about the relationship between organizational level and satisfaction with pay. From his reading and general knowledge of the area, he had hypothesized that satisfaction with pay should relate closely to organizational level. That is, given certain conditions, people at higher levels should be more satisfied with their pay than people at lower levels.

To test this theory, Ralph and his professor had made contact with a relatively small data processing company employing about 250 people. In addition to the managerial personnel, the firm employed mostly programmers, computer operators, clerical workers, and the usual staff of maintenance people. The president of the company agreed to let Ralph administer his questionnaires on the company site in groups of about twenty-five.

Since measurement of organizational level was crucial to his study, he took great pains to design a questionnaire which would measure this accurately. He examined the company organization chart, but he couldn't use this because he would be unable to attach names to positions, since the questionnaire was to be completed anonymously. He thought of asking for job titles, but he knew that in most companies job titles could be misleading and would therefore be inaccurate. He finally decided upon a simple measure—a sketch of a hierarchy divided into four discrete levels, upon which the respondents were to circle the number which best described their level in the organization. Wilson's chart on the questionnaire looked like this:

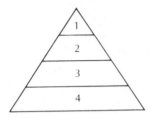

After tabulating the responses, he summarized the results of the organization chart and drew a sketch to approximate its shape. Based on the information from the questionnaire, the organization chart looked like this:

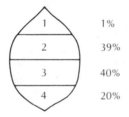

Wilson had a sinking feeling that his precious study was about to go down the tubes.

In Chapter 5 we examined some types of formal organization structures and discussed their potential impact upon employee behavior. In addition to the *formal* structure as set out in the organization chart, there exists another "structure" which is also important in determining employee behavior. This structure is called the *informal* organization and refers to the patterns of behavior and influence that arise out of the human interaction occurring within the formal structure. While formal and informal organizations are similar along some dimensions, there are also important differences. Because the informal organization can exert a strong influence on employee behavior, it is important to understand its nature, how it works, in what ways it affects behavior, and how it can be used in the management of organizations.

Examples of behavior in the informal organization are many and varied:

1. A production worker may restrict output to conform to the norm of the work group.
2. Management may plan an important announcement for employees, only to find out that the message was leaked earlier through the grapevine.
3. The manager of a department may find that the leader of the company baseball team appears to exert more influence during the baseball season than the line managers.
4. A potentially conflict-laden meeting may proceed very rationally since most of the disagreements on issues were worked out the night before over a few drinks.

In other words, any behavior that occurs "above and beyond" that prescribed by the formal organization is a result of the informal organization.

In general, the informal organization emerges because the formal structure does not satisfy all employee and organizational needs. The exact form the informal organization will take thus depends on the specific deficiencies in the formal structure and in employee need satisfaction. It is important to remember that managers do not have a choice as to whether or not the informal organization will develop; informal relationships *will* be formed within any formal structure. It is important for the manager to understand (rather than to attempt to suppress) the informal organization and to channel its energies toward organizational goals.

Another reason for the existence of the informal organization is the employees' need for predictability and stability in interpersonal relationships and social processes. The formal organization is unable to provide this, since formal structures are generally designed from a mechanical, rational perspective, not a behavioral one.[1] The informal relationships that develop from on-the-job interaction provide the necessary security and predictability that individuals need, and this results in another structure parallel to the formal one.

The concept of informal relationships within formal organizations can be viewed from two perspectives: a macro one that describes the broader, informal relationships that pervade the entire structure, and a micro one that examines individual behavior within the confines of smaller, well-defined groups. The former perspective usually bears the label "informal organization," whereas the latter is often called "group dynamics" or "small group behavior." In this chapter we will discuss the informal organization in detail; Chapter 11 treats the subject of group dynamics. Since each of the perspectives is related to interpersonal relationships on the job, we will reserve our discussion of applications for the end of Chapter 11.

We begin this chapter by comparing the characteristics of the informal and formal organizations and then describing the basic functions of the informal organization. Next, some central concepts important for an understanding of the informal organization are presented, and we conclude this chapter with a discussion of some potential problems associated with the informal organization.

# Box 10-1: The Function of "Work to Rule"

Lest we ever forget that the informal organization exists or underestimate its significance, we are often reminded of both of these when workers decide to "work to rule." While management sometimes sarcastically comments, "Well, at least they've decided at last to work!" everyone well knows the main effect of working to rule: a major slowdown and breakdown of the "normal" way of doing things. While the negative effects of a work-to-rule campaign can be partly attributed to working at a slower pace, the majority of the effects are due to the workers' refusal to do anything but abide by the rules of the formal organization. Strictly speaking, of course, rules preclude any type of decision-making activity by workers. The informal organization often supplants some of these rules by "better" ways of doing things, and these "better" ways always involve the use of discretion by workers. A work-to-rule campaign, therefore, eliminates this flexibility, and workers do exactly as they have been told—no more, no less. Here are some common examples of how work-to-rule behavior can cause problems:

1. Air traffic controllers often violate federal regulations (such as distances between aircraft, numbers of aircraft in a specific area, etc.), in situations in which they feel it is safe to do so, in order to increase the efficiency of airlines and minimize passenger delays. In a work-to-rule program, aircraft are often stacked up for long periods of time (resulting in missed connections, flight delays, etc).

2. A city bus driver will often wait for brief periods, particularly in bad weather, for people who have not yet arrived at the bus stop. This pleases the customers and the lost time can usually be made up in the remainder of the route. In a work-to-rule program, the driver would leave the bus stop on schedule, regardless of how many people were running to catch the bus.

3. Customs officers are generally quite selective in searching travelers' luggage. For example, if several flights arrive at the same time, officers will sometimes minimize the inspection times to get the people through faster. In a work-to-rule effort, every passenger is searched thoroughly since everyone is a potential smuggler. This results in long waiting lines, exhaustive searches, and short tempers.

But note the differences between a "work slowdown" and a "work-to-rule" program. In a work slowdown, workers perform at the minimum pace necessary to do the job, but they do the job in the same manner as they did before. In a work-to-rule campaign, workers actually do their jobs differently—the way prescribed by the formal organization. Of course, the two can be used in conjunction with each other.

# ■ FORMAL AND INFORMAL ORGANIZATIONS COMPARED AND CONTRASTED

In the fifth chapter we studied some characteristics of formal organizations. We will use some of the concepts presented there to compare and contrast formal and informal organizations. As will be seen, they have both similarities and differences.

## ☐ Origin of Structure

Formal organizations are goal-oriented and designed around general principles of organization, which are presumed to be consistent with the desired objectives of management. Formal structures are the result of conscious thought processes and are designed to be rational in relation to organizational goals. Changes in the formal structure can be made by administrative decree. In contrast, the informal organization develops spontaneously. Individuals adopt behavior patterns which are caused by a wide variety of social and personal factors, and the resulting informal structure reflects these different individual goals rather than the organization's goals. Consequently, the informal organization is a function more of emotion than of logical thought processes. When changes occur in the informal structure, they are the result of a collective (though sometimes subconscious) agreement on the part of the members, not a result of the imposed authority of the administrative system.

## ☐ Position Terminology

In the theoretical concept of formal organization, the relationship between the individual and the organization tends to be mechanical and impersonal. The responsibilities and behaviors required of individuals are specified in job descriptions, which are generally designed without regard for who will be performing the job. The informal organization equivalent of the "job" is the organizational *role*. However, the concept of organizational role is more complex than that of a job since it includes not only individuals' formal responsibilities and expectations, but also other people's expectations of the role occupant. It is not unusual to find that the formal job description's requirements and the role expectations of an individual's colleagues are in conflict. For example, the formal organization may require a certain level of productivity but, because of fears of rate cutting, the informal organization may place pressure on its members not to exceed a certain quota.

Because role expectations come from many different sources, they make greater demands on workers than do the formal job descriptions. Technically, formal job descriptions can prescribe behavior only within the organization, but role expectations can come not only from the person's job but also from family, friends, colleagues, and so on. Since each person sees a given role from his or her own perspective, there are frequently conflicting expectations confronting the

---

### Organizational Reality   10-1
### Informal Organization at J. C. Penney Company

The J. C. Penney Company understands that job descriptions do not tell the whole story about relationships on the job. Seldom do job descriptions specify that an employee must be able to get along with coworkers or bosses, although everyone knows that this is a very important concern. Probably nowhere is this more critical than the relationship between a secretary and the boss.

At J. C. Penney Company, every effort is made to match secretary and boss. Several times a year, Penney hires high school graduates with business training but no experience. In classes of about twelve, they receive a three-week orientation and training course. They are then assigned to work in several departments and for several managers before deciding where they would like to work.

If a secretary doesn't like a particular job or a boss doesn't like the secretary's work, the individual is reassigned. When both secretary and boss agree, the position then becomes permanent.

Penney reports the system has dramatically reduced secretary turnover.

---

Source: *Management Review* (February 1980): 49.

role occupant. A worker may have to choose between an evening with family and bowling with the company team. This situation is likely to present considerable conflict for a worker attempting to sort out the costs and rewards associated with each alternative.

### ☐  Goals of the Organization

Goals of the formal organization are created by the owners (or managers representing the owners) and are generally described in profitability or efficiency terms for most organizations. Subgoals may relate to market share, return on investment, cost per unit, or other quantifiable measures. In contrast, the informal organization's major goal can be broadly defined as the social satisfaction of its members. This does not mean that the informal organization cannot contribute to formal organizational goals (in fact, as will be illustrated later, the informal organization can contribute significantly to formal organization goals); rather, the social needs of its members must be satisfied in the process. Ideally, the goals of the informal organization are in perfect agreement with those of the formal organization. In actual practice this is almost never the case, partly due to the fact that workers have individual goals that are seldom in complete agreement with formal organization goals.

### ☐  Influence Processes

We will explore the influence concept in more detail later in the chapter, but at this point it is a useful criterion to employ in comparing the two types of organizations. Influence within the formal structure is by formal position and is determined by the authority allocated to that position. Job descriptions generally detail the extent of the authority vested in the position, including its quality (degree of authority) and quantity (number of individuals over whom authority is exercised). The formal organization equates authority with influence; in other words, if individuals have been given authority, they are assumed to have influence. In contrast, influence processes in the informal organization occur by approval from the relevant group, not by organizational decree. Generally, the individual with the most influence is the person who is most able to satisfy the needs of the group. This may or may not be the appointed (formal) leader. Because informal leaders emerge as the result of social processes, social factors determine influence in the informal organization with formal factors having a secondary influence. Thus, influence in the informal organization is attached to the *person,* whereas in the formal organization it is attached to the *position.*

## ☐ Control Mechanisms

In Chapter 5 we discussed how controls (e.g., rules, policies, procedures, etc.) are inherent in the design of formal organizations. While the degree of formal control varies from organization to organization (e.g., from bureaucracy to matrix), some form of control is always present to constrain the behavior of organizational members. In the informal organization, standards of behavior, referred to as *norms,* are similarly communicated to members through social processes. Because the informal organization is a social organization, norms are oriented toward controlling social behaviors, and sanctions are directed at those who violate them. The primary function of norms is to increase the probability that socially desirable behavior will occur on a predictable basis. As mentioned earlier, informal organizations tend to satisfy employee needs for structure and predictability, and the enforcement of norms provides some assurance that only acceptable behaviors will be exhibited.

## ☐ Communication Processes

One of the major functions of hierarchical lines of authority in formal structures is to identify the correct channels of communication. Therefore, lines of authority can also be viewed as lines of communication (we examined this in Chapter 8). If taken literally these lines would indicate that two individuals working under different superiors would have to follow the chain of command through their respective bosses in order to communicate with each other. Informally, however, this seldom happens. The informal organization devises it own channel of communication (the *grapevine*) for both social and organizational communication purposes. The grapevine carries whatever information the informal organization needs and, although it is selective and often carries inaccurate or distorted information, it is generally faster than formal channels of communication.

## ☐ Charting the Organization

Organization charts are pictorial representations of authority relationships in the formal organization. Should a job description change or a reorganization of the company occur, the boxes and lines on the chart can easily be redrawn to reflect the design of the new organization. The purpose of these charts is to indicate who has authority over whom, how communication should travel, how each job relates to each other job, and the objectives of the organization. The equivalent charting of the informal organization is referred to as a *sociogram,* an example of which is shown in Figure 10-1. The sociogram illustrates interaction relationships between members of a particular group and is developed by observing the actual behavior of members in an organization or work group. Through observation it is possible to determine such factors as (1) who has the most influence, (2) which members do not conform to the group norms, and (3) which members have been excluded from the group.

The entire informal organization may also be charted; this would show interaction patterns within the group as well as those up and down the total hierarchy.

Formal chart showing Manager A and Subordinates B, C, D, E, and F

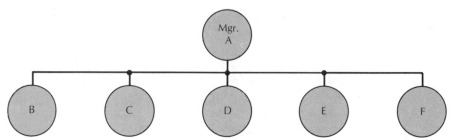

Informal chart (sociogram) showing Manager A and Subordinates B, C, D, E, and F

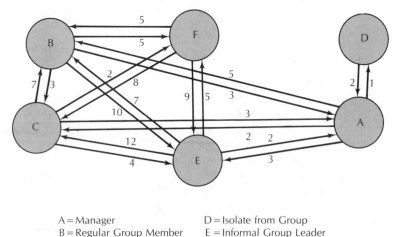

| A = Manager | D = Isolate from Group |
| B = Regular Group Member | E = Informal Group Leader |
| C = New Employee | F = Regular Group Member |

Numbers indicate number of social interactions initiated

**FIGURE 10-1.   Charts Showing Comparisons of Formal and Informal Organizations**

A humorous, yet perhaps realistic chart of an informal organization is shown in Figure 10-2.

In sum, both the formal and informal organizations have common attributes, but the manifestations of these attributes differ significantly along a number of dimensions. Informal organizations represent the human side of organizations and are thus dependent on the nature of individuals in the organization; formal organizations, since they are consciously thought out, are usually highly structured and give less emphasis to human considerations. In one sense, it may be useful to view the formal organization as "how it should be" and the informal organization

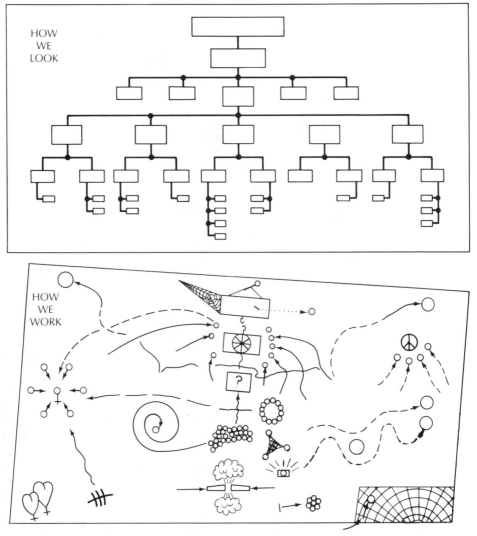

**FIGURE 10-2.   How It Should Be Compared to How It Actually Is**

as "how it actually is." Table 10-1 summarizes many of the differences between formal and informal structures that were discussed above, as well as some additional differences which follow from our discussion.

# ■ FUNCTIONS OF THE INFORMAL ORGANIZATION

A better understanding of a phenomenon can be achieved if it is known what function it performs. If we analyze the reasons behind the existence of the informal organization, we can improve our understanding of how it can be managed.

**TABLE 10-1.   A Comparison of Formal and Informal Organization Characteristics**

| Characteristic | Informal Organization | Formal Organization |
|---|---|---|
| 1. Structure | | |
| A. Origin | Spontaneous | Planned |
| B. Rationale | Emotional | Rational |
| C. Characteristics | Dynamic | Stable |
| 2. Position terminology | Role | Job |
| 3. Goals | Member satisfaction | Profitability or service to society |
| 4. Influence | | |
| A. Base | Personality | Position |
| B. Type | Power | Authority |
| C. Flow | Bottom up | Top down |
| 5. Control mechanisms | Physical or social sanctions (norms) | Threat of firing, demotion |
| 6. Communication | | |
| A. Channels | Grapevine | Formal channels |
| B. Networks | Poorly defined, cut across regular channels | Well defined, follow formal lines |
| C. Speed | Fast | Slow |
| D. Accuracy | Low | High |
| 7. Charting the organization | Sociogram | Organization chart |
| 8. Miscellaneous | | |
| A. Individuals included | Only those "acceptable" | All individuals in work group |
| B. Interpersonal relations | Arise spontaneously | Prescribed by job description |
| C. Leadership role | Result of membership agreement | Assigned by organization |
| D. Basis for interaction | Personal characteristics, ethnic background, status | Functional duties or position |
| E. Basis for attachment | Cohesiveness | Loyalty |

While all of the reasons (or functions) discussed below are interrelated, we treat them separately to sharpen our understanding of the behavior patterns operating in informal structures.

## ☐ Security

One of the major functions of the informal organization is to increase the feeling of security of its members. We have already mentioned that individuals prefer some degree of stability in their working lives, and the informal organization performs this function by exerting influence and control over the behavior of those in it. Deviant or abnormal behavior is not tolerated, and this assures members a reasonable degree of stability in their interpersonal relationships. The informal organization also increases member security by protecting members from outside influences such as management or other work groups. For example, management may wish to release or transfer a particular individual but, because the person is an important member of the informal group, management may find itself faced with strong resistance to the transfer.

In the Hawthorne studies (see Chapter 1), one of the experiments indicated that production was held to a group-approved norm because the workers believed that any deviation from what was normal—either above or below—would result in changes in work methods and work relationships.[2] Since workers valued their group relationships, they saw rate restriction as one way of preserving their social stability. A major reason workers find security in the informal organization is that the rules for behavior are set by the workers, not by management.

## ☐ Social Satisfaction

We learned from the motivation chapter that people have social needs that are manifested in social contact (e.g., the formation of significant interpersonal relations and the striving to be accepted by other people). The informal organization facilitates satisfaction of these needs. For example, the interactions required by the formal organization tend to initiate the social contacts made, resulting in the formation of attitudes, feelings, and beliefs about other people. On the basis of these required interactions, individuals then form close-knit groups that provide maximum satisfaction and security.

The need for social interaction on the job is the motivation behind many behaviors. Activities such as coffee and group lunch breaks, idle conversation, baseball pools, and going-away parties illustrate some of the more common forms. To the extent that an individual becomes more accepted in the informal organization than the formal, the social gratification received may be more meaningful than rewards such as pay or job security offered by the formal organization. Moreover, it is easier to develop a social identity in a small, informal group than a large, formal one. In many cases, employees become only numbers to the formal organization; they therefore seek personal identity, recognition, and acceptance in their informal groups.

## ☐ Communication Channel

As mentioned earlier, the informal organization provides an additional channel of communication for the organization, called the *grapevine*. Information that is deemed important by the informal organization is sought out and quickly communicated to interested group members. Because the information is seen as important (if it weren't, the informal organization wouldn't bother with it), it tends to be transmitted rather quickly, the exact speed depending partly upon the degree of importance of the communication. In some instances, the perceived need for information is so great that the grapevine actually creates its own information (rumors) to satisfy its own needs. For example, if employees are expecting to be laid off because of a downturn in demand for the company's product, in the absence of an official company statement, rumors will invariably begin to circulate regarding layoffs. Depending on the nature of management-employee relations, even the facts on the issue may not squelch the rumor, should this

---

### *Organizational Reality* 10-2
### *Rumors and Corporate Image*

When ridiculous rumors and gossip extend beyond the backyard fence to include corporations and their products, executives don't find them the least bit funny. Corporate rumors over the past few years have included McDonald's adding earthworms to their hamburger meat and Rev. Sun Myung Moon's Unification Church controlling Procter and Gamble.

Professor Frederick Koening of Tulane University suggests that hard times are partly responsible for the rise of rumor mongering. For example, if one person isn't as successful as others, the contention may be, "If I'm not making it, everyone who is has got to be playing dirty."

Corporate solutions to rumors vary with the circumstances. McDonald's hoped the earthworm story would be considered so outlandish that it would fade away on its own. When it didn't, Douglas Timberlake, McDonald's public relations director, decided to get at the source of the rumor. Eventually, press attention, induced by a company-called press conference, as well as a letter from the U.S. Secretary of Agriculture confirming McDonald's compliance with DOA standards, dispelled the rumor.

Procter and Gamble realized the enormity of the Moonie rumors after a substantial number of phone calls were made to its consumer service department. The company took direct action and, in letters to seven newspaper editors, P & G acknowledged the rumor and pointed out, "(Our) moon and stars logo originated in 1880, when the little soap company used it to market its Star brand candles." The denial worked to some extent, although company officials say they still receive about 300 calls a month about possible Moonie connections.

---

Source: *Management Review* (November 1981): 7.

information as offered by management not coincide with the employees' perception of management's intentions.

Unfortunately, what the grapevine possesses in speed it usually lacks in accuracy. Because information is transmitted through many different sources in the informal organization (see Chapter 8), it tends to become distorted from source to source. For issues that are particularly important to the informal organization, such as potential layoffs, the degree of distortion generally increases as the emotional investment in the information increases. But regardless of the accuracy of the information, the mere act of communicating necessary information tends to satisfy the needs of the informal organization. This is because the need for information is consistent with both of the previously identified functions of the informal organization—security and social satisfaction. Security for employees can be defined as having information that is relevant to the work situation; therefore, efforts are directed toward gathering the information necessary to increase worker security. Also, in order to transmit information, social interaction must occur; thus, rumors can be created and transmitted because the act of doing so increases perceived security in the group and increases the degree of social acceptance of the person transmitting the rumor.

## □ Balancing Device

The informal organization serves as a balancing device in several ways. First, it has the capacity (although not always the motivation) to overcome deficiencies built into the formal structure. Since it is impossible for formal systems to prescribe every type of decision and behavior that is necessary for effective work accomplishment, the formal organization often relies on the informal organization to take up any "slack" that may be present or to compensate for important areas that are not specifically covered in job descriptions. Union "work-to-rule" decisions illustrate the importance of the balancing function of the informal organization; when workers refuse to do things not specifically called for in their job descriptions, and adhere strictly to their written job requirements, they are essentially refusing to allow the informal organization to compensate for deficiencies in the formal structures and procedures. The result is usually a noticeably slower pace of work and decreased customer satisfaction.

Second, the informal organization serves a balancing function by giving satisfactions to individual members that the formal structure cannot give. A production worker receiving little respect from management can derive considerable satisfaction from being an informal group leader, by being held in high esteem by coworkers, or by having workmates laugh at his or her jokes. As noted earlier, the psychic rewards that one can obtain by belonging to a social group may be as important as the material rewards provided by the formal organization. These types of satisfactions can be a significant influence on behavior since, unlike many interactions with management, feedback about behavior in the small group is almost invariably quick and specific. This creates a potential for greater individual satisfaction from both a psychological and a security standpoint.

### ☐ Source of Motivation

The informal organization is often a source of motivation for individuals. In addition to the example presented above regarding group acceptance (which may motivate some individuals), there are other opportunities that allow the informal organization to perform the motivation function. When workers are involved in tedious, boring jobs, for example, the opportunity for social interaction on the job can provide them with the diversions necessary to tolerate such a task. Another potential source of motivation is the status that can be achieved by individuals because of certain attributes they possess or the position they occupy in the informal group. Increased status can be ego-satisfying and therefore a source of motivation. Because the concept of status is so important in informal organizations, much of the next section is devoted to it.

## ■ CENTRAL CONCEPTS OF THE INFORMAL ORGANIZATION

The significance of the informal organization for the day-to-day management of the total organization lies in understanding the major social processes that occur in it. Two concepts that are particularly important in understanding behavior in organizations are *status* and *influence*. These are referred to as social processes since the sources of status and influence tend to be behavioral rather than structural in nature. Because influence is in part determined by status, we begin by discussing the nature and functions of status in organizations.

### ☐ Status

Status is the rank or relative position of an individual in a group. From a practical point of view, it is useful to view status as an individual's *social* position within a group. This position is determined by *status attributes* (i.e., those factors that cause one individual to be ranked or placed differently from another in a social system). Characteristics such as age, sex, race, education, and religion are common status attributes used to place individuals in a status hierarchy. These combine with other types of attributes (e.g., job skills) to determine an individual's position in the informal group.

A certain status attribute is valued if two conditions are met: the attribute must be perceived by the relevant group as being *scarce* and *desirable*. Given that these two conditions have been met, it is possible to define what is "high" and "low" status in a particular group. For example, individuals with large incomes and/or wealth are commonly perceived as having high status because money is perceived as both scarce and desirable by many people. Theoretically, however, any attribute may have value *if the relevant group perceives that the attribute is both scarce and desirable.* Thus, what is high status to one group may be totally meaningless to another. In a group where education is a desired attribute, an individual with a PhD would probably have a high status, but in a group where education was not desirable, having a PhD might result in low status.

Status itself can be of two varieties, *ascribed* and *achieved*. Ascribed status is that social position occupied because of attributes inherent in the individual, such as race, sex, and age, while achieved status is the position a person attains through personal choice, such as education, skills, or marital status. In both formal and informal organizations, the actual status of a person is the result of an interaction of ascribed and achieved status, with the effect of each determined by the relative weight given each by the group. Acceptance of an individual in one group may depend largely upon race and little upon other status attributes. In another group, actual accomplishments (perhaps being able to play football well) may be the primary factor that determines group acceptance.

Within organizations, two additional types of status can be identified: *scalar* and *functional*. Scalar status pertains to a person's formal position within the hierarchy. A vice-president of marketing, for example, possesses higher scalar status than a salesperson. Functional status, however, relates to an individual's function within the organization. It recognizes that some jobs have higher desirability than others. For example, even though the janitor and a clerk may have the same scalar status (i.e., they are both on the same organizational level), the clerk may have higher functional status if the work of the janitor is perceived as being less desirable. Generally there is a strong relationship between functional and scalar status but this is not always the case. A common exception might be the secretary to the president of an organization. The secretarial position has relatively low scalar status, since the job probably lacks any formal authority; but in terms of functional status, the job may be perceived as prestigious because the

---

## *Organizational Reality* 10-3
### *Status in Organizations*

To date, the "message" communicated by the size and decor of executive offices has been one of rank and authority. The Buffalo Organization for Social and Technological Innovation (Bosti) surveyed 4,000 white-collar workers in the public and private sectors and found the following indicators of prestige (in order of importance): size of office, location, amount of furniture, controllable access, quality of furniture, and number of "devices" such as telephones and computer terminals.

Some observers of the corporate scene feel this may be changing, and that offices and their contents should be more functional, i.e., facilitate the work that the occupant does. A number of companies are going to the standard-size office concept, i.e., a philosophy that everyone at the same level gets the same size office. Also, some companies now use the choice corner locations (previously reserved for high-ranking executives) for conference rooms. The most extreme moves away from status-oriented offices are likely to be seen in the offices of design firms. Salespeople in these firms point out that once the top executive in a firm accepts a certain concept, other executives will quickly follow suit.

---

Source: Walter Kiechel III, "What Your Office Says About You," *Fortune* (31 May 1982).

secretary reports directly to a position with high functional and scalar authority. The opposite condition (low functional status but high scalar status) may occur when an individual has been "kicked upstairs," (i.e., has been promoted to a high-ranking position where there is nothing to do).

An important qualification of status involves the definition of the term *relevant group*. We have already noted that in the informal organization, the values placed upon status attributes are determined by the specific group in question. Strictly speaking, then, it is incorrect to refer to something as "high status" until one qualifies it with a definition of the group. In the secretary example above, this job would have high (functional) status primarily for those who aspire to be secretaries to presidents. In this case the relevant group might include all the other secretaries in the organization. While in everyday conversation this qualification does not present major problems, it becomes important in the managing of work groups, since smaller groups are more apt to have definitive (and perhaps different) opinions about status and social position within the group. If this fact is not considered, managers run the risk of incorrectly assuming that their own status preferences are identical to those of the group they supervise.

**Status Symbols**    Since status is a social concept, groups find it convenient to be able to identify an individual's status quickly and efficiently, so that decisions can be made regarding appropriate behavior. To accomplish this, *status symbols* are devised which serve to visually communicate a person's status. Although these symbols are not foolproof indicators of status, they are useful guidelines in making preliminary judgments. More precise judgments are possible only after more prolonged social interaction.

Status symbols in organizations can take any form. Position in the formal hierarchy can usually be judged by such status symbols as size of office, type of decor, size of desk, and similar items that are usually provided by the organization. Even though the use of the term *status* here pertains to position in the formal hierarchy, it is nevertheless important to note that the symbols have been designated as desirable by the informal organization, not the formal.

Status symbols are also created by the informal organization. Even though the formal organization considers the members of a particular work group as "equals," a status hierarchy can emerge based on behaviors and attributes that the group considers desirable. Thus, in some groups, skill at a certain task will differentiate the members such that the highest producer in the group is accorded the highest status. Another group may have a status hierarchy similar to that of the formal organization and attribute high status to those having a desk by a window or to those having a physical location closest to the boss.

**Why Is Status Important?**    Status is important in organizations because it satisfies the basic human need for personal identification. The tendency for individuals to differentiate themselves from others is a constant social process that occurs in every type of organization. Knowledge about status assists us in our everyday relationships since we are better able to structure, understand, and predict the

## Box 10-2: Status Symbols and the Formal Organization

We have stated that status is an informal concept (i.e., one which is defined by the informal organization through its social processes). However, there is usually a strong relationship between the official organizational hierarchy and the informal status system. In some cases, the relationship is so close it is difficult to tell the difference. To illustrate this, below is a policy statement from a university outlining precisely what status symbols each organizational level is entitled to:

DEAN: 1 desk 72 × 36 × 29, 1 armchair (tilter), 2 armchairs (desk height), 1 couch (3 seater), 1 occasional table, 2 side files, 1 wastebasket, 1 desk tray (2 tier, legal size), 2 ashtrays (ceramic, 5½" dia.), 2 planters, 2 plants.

ASSOCIATE DEAN: 1 desk 72 × 36 × 29, 1 armchair (tilter), 3 armchairs (desk height), 1 occasional table, 1 side file, 1 wastebasket, 1 desk tray (2 tier, legal size), 2 ashtrays (5½" dia.), 1 planter, 1 plant.

DEPARTMENT HEADS: 1 desk 66 × 36 × 29, 1 armchair (tilter), 2 armchairs (desk height), 1 side file, 1 wastebasket, 1 desk tray (2 tier, legal size), 1 ashtray (ceramic, 5½" dia.), 1 planter, 1 plant.

FACULTY: 1 desk 60 × 36 × 29, 1 armchair (tilter) 2 armless chairs (desk height), 1 side file, 1 wastebasket, 1 desk tray (2 tier, legal size), 1 ashtray (ceramic, 5½" dia.)

GRADUATE ASSISTANTS (two students per carrel): 2 armless side chairs (desk height), 1 side file, 2 wastebaskets, 2 desk trays (regular size), 2 ashtrays (4" dia., glass).

social interactions that are important to us. Knowledge about another's status allows us to behave in an appropriate manner, and this reduces the uncertainty and anxiety associated with some interpersonal contacts. We learn, for example, to behave in certain ways when interacting with a clergyman. We also learn to expect certain behaviors from individuals of a given status level, since our experience teaches us to associate certain behaviors with certain roles. When individuals behave in a manner significantly different from what is expected, social sanctions may be used to bring behavior in line with expectations; or, if the behavior does not change, social interactions may cease.

Status also streamlines communication in both a structural and a behavioral sense. Structurally speaking, status symbols allow identification of the relative position of an individual in a hierarchy, making communication more efficient. Perhaps the best example of this principle is military organizations in which the status hierarchy is quite visible. Each formal position has officially designed symbols, such as the number of stripes or insignia design. Symbols of this type make it possible for members to identify formal position immediately, therefore requiring a minimum of social interaction to determine organization status. Communications are very efficient under such conditions since they can be primarily task-oriented.

Behaviorally speaking, status allows us to develop communications appropriate for the type (i.e., status) of individual with whom we are communicating. We know, for example, that we can speak frankly with a member of our own status group, but perhaps we should choose our words carefully when communicating with someone of significantly different status. When status levels are not clear, difficulties may arise. For example, at one time college students were able to identify professors easily, since professors were the only individuals close to a classroom who wore neckties. Recently, dress expectations for professors have changed somewhat, and the students who have not become accustomed to the new dress codes occasionally experience anxiety when they find in an informal gathering that they are speaking to a professor whom they believed to be a student!

## Box 10-3: Open Mouth, Insert Foot . . .

Status and status symbols are important concepts in our everyday lives. We need these concepts to help us cope with the variety of interpersonal situations that we encounter. Our perceptions of status, status symbols, and the roles attached to them serve as "efficiency devices" which allow us to interact and communicate without having to think out each situation separately. The following illustration, taken from a student's written assignment, illustrates how this can be embarrassing:

As a graduate student I was employed as a research assistant to one of the professors. Because I needed easy access to the professor's office, I was given a key which not only fitted his office but the front door to the general office area. One day I was leaving for lunch and, since the front door was always locked during lunch hour, I was beginning to lock it. As I turned away from the door, a man, wearing a sweatshirt, blue jeans, and work boots and carrying a box of books approached me and asked if I would unlock the door so he could go in. Since there was no one else in the office area and there were many valuable items lying around (typewriters, calculators, etc.), I was extremely reluctant to let him in. In fact, I told him that the office was closed during lunch hour, but if he waited another twenty or thirty minutes, one of the secretaries would return and let him in. In very polite terms, he then informed me that he was Professor X who was just arriving on campus to assume his position as assistant professor, having just finished his PhD at Harvard University, and he only wanted to put his books in his office. Needless to say, I felt very sheepish. In an attempt to make up for my indescretion, I proceeded to carry the rest of his books in for him. My embarrassment continued during the next term, as I found myself in Professor X's course. Fortunately for me, Professor X did not hold the same prejudices I did, as I received an "A" in his course.

Finally, status is important because increased status can be ego-satisfying and therefore can serve as a motivational device. We indicated in Chapter 3 that many individuals have a need to increase their perceptions of their own worth through the satisfaction of their ego needs. Increasing the perceived status of an individual is one method of accomplishing this. Some possible ways of using status as a motivational tool, as well as some potential pitfalls in so doing, will be discussed in the applications section of the next chapter.

## ☐ Influence Systems

In the comparison of informal and formal organizations discussed earlier, it was mentioned that, whereas the formal organization describes formal rights and authority relationships, in the informal organization no formal authority exists. Instead, individuals exert *influence* upon one another. In other words, while the formal organization is concerned with the *right* to influence behavior, the informal organization involves the *ability* to influence behavior. This distinction suggests that the holder of a formal position may not necessarily be able to influence others and also that individuals without authority may have influence. Since the actual systems and processes of influence may be at variance with the formal organizational structure, it is important that we understand the nature and sources of organizational influence.

**Influence As a Social Process**   To possess influence means to be able to determine or affect the behavior of others. In contrast to authority, which is vested in the position an individual occupies, influence arises out of the social contract that exists between individuals. Strictly speaking, authority does not exist if individuals do not allow themselves to be influenced by the person with authority. In the informal organization, influence can exist independently of the formal relationships because certain individuals or groups allow themselves to be influenced by others. Therefore, influence in the informal organization is based upon this acceptance principle and is the result of social rather than organizational factors.

**Power and Influence Systems**   Influence in the informal organization is called *power* (as distinguished from authority). The exercise of power involves the exerting of influence over others without the formal right of authority. We can therefore identify two distinct influence systems in organizations: the formal system, based upon the authority structure, and the power structure, based upon *actual* influence relationships. The power structure describes the ongoing influence systems that occur outside the formal hierarchy. For example, the secretary to the president, while having little or no formal authority, may be quite powerful (i.e., influential), because of the formal relationship with the president. Conversely, a manager who has formal authority but never uses it will most likely be perceived as having little influence.

To understand how power operates in organizations, it is necessary to understand the potential sources of power. What is it that allows one person to influence another, even though no formal right to do so exists? While several lists suggesting different sources of power have been developed, the following one is widely accepted.

1. *Reward power* exists when person A has the ability to control the rewards that person B receives. For example, if a poor boy marries a rich girl, he may readily behave in the way demanded by her parents, even though they have no formal authority over him, if he believes that acceding to their wishes will result in monetary and/or social gains for himself.

2. *Punishment power* is the opposite of reward power in that person A can exert influence over person B if A has the ability to determine punishments for B. Within a social group, for example, one individual can influence the behavior of another if the first individual can inflict social punishments, such as ostracism from the group. Therefore, influence is present without the existence of a formal authority relationship.

3. *Referent power* exists when person B is influenced by person A because B admires A and wishes to be like A. This form of power tends to be very effective since it involves a psychological commitment on B's part. The followers of Hitler (before he became leader) avidly accepted and were influenced by his extreme viewpoints, even though they were not required to do so. At the other extreme, the disciples of Jesus Christ exhibited the same type of enthusiastic commitment, but to goals that most people agree were more beneficial to society. It is important to note that neither of these individuals had formal organizational authority behind them, yet both had little difficulty in influencing the behavior of people who identified with them.

4. *Expert power* exists when person B is influenced by person A because A possesses some special or expert knowledge that B needs. For example, dentists and doctors can influence the behavior of their patients in health care matters even though they do not have formal authority over them. While in most cases the influence is exerted only so long as B needs A's expertise, there are situations in which the influence goes beyond the immediate relationship. For example, many doctors tend to exert influence beyond the doctor-patient relationship, and we see many sports heroes and other public figures on television attempting to influence us to buy various products. In these cases, influence is possible because expert power becomes transformed into referent power (i.e., we tend to identify with people who have expert power).

5. *Legitimate power* exists when person B believes that person A has the "right" to influence him and that, because of shared norms and values, B feels an obligation to accept this influence. "Legitimate power" is actually a synonym for formal authority, since the most common examples of shared norms and values are those held by formal organizations. A subordinate will allow the manager to influence him or her because it is part of the norms or values necessary for continued employment in the organization.[3]

In all of the above categories except the last, A's ability to influence B is not related to formal hierarchical position. In fact, we have purposely chosen examples external to organizations to illustrate how power can function separately from a formal authority structure. Some examples of how power can operate independently within formal organizations are as follows:

1. The informal group leader communicates to a new group member that the group prefers certain ways of doing things and that violation of these accepted ways might lead to "problems." (Reward or punishment power)

## Box 10-4: How Much Power Does a Manager Have?

All companies want managers who are powerful. That is, the only managers that are useful to a company are those that can exert influence over others. We might even view the process of management as one of influence. Probably the main reason the reader is reading this book is to increase his or her influence in certain matters. So, if power is that important to a manager, how much power might a manager have and how can it be increased?

Using the model presented in this chapter we can outline the potential power that most managers should have. By virtue of their position, most managers would have reward and punishment *authority* (i.e., the right to mediate rewards and punishments for subordinates). But if a manager does not exercise that right (i.e., if people do not perceive that manager as having the *ability* to reward and punish), the manager will not be very influential on this dimension. In other words, authority must be exercised before it can be transferred into reward or punishment power, particularly over the long run.

Every manager should have some expert power. In some cases, this may mean that the manager has to be the "best" worker in order to justify the manager's position of authority. In other cases, it may mean simply that the manager must have the respect of the subordinate group. But in general terms, we can say that the manager should be seen as someone who can solve problems for the subordinates. This takes on the connotation of expertise and therefore increases the influence of the manager.

Ideally, every manager should aim for referent power since this is the most intensive and long-lasting of the lot. This concept basically means that one person (the subordinate) desires to be like the other person (manager) and will therefore imitate the behaviors of the manager. Unfortunately, there is no specific method for getting someone to identify with you. We generally say that when one person sees another being rewarded for certain kinds of behaviors and if the first person desires those rewards as well, then there will be a propensity to imitate (model) the behavior of the person receiving the rewards. Assuming that subordinates desire to have better positions in the company, if they see their boss promoted for certain behaviors, they will tend to imitate those behaviors.

And finally, legitimate power recognizes the underlying value systems of organizations (i.e., that it is "right and reasonable" that one person influence another in the interests of both the individual and the organization). As long as the manager does not go beyond the bounds of "reasonable," most subordinates will allow themselves to be influenced strictly as a normal course of events. Managers can increase their legitimate power most easily by obtaining more formal authority from the organization, but they can also increase it by consistently making good, sound decisions; this will show people that the manager can use authority properly, thus increasing their zone of tolerance for authority.

2. An ambitious young executive admires the behaviors of a senior executive and the rewards that accrue to that person. This identification becomes so strong that the young executive begins to imitate the behavior of the senior executive in the hope that similar rewards will be forthcoming. (Referent power)

3. The production manager relies on the advice of a junior industrial engineer when questions of machine design and workflow come up. (Expert power)

4. The manager instructs a subordinate to carry out an instruction, and the subordinate automatically responds accordingly. (Legitimate power)

Each of these types of power can be observed in any organization. In practice, however, the distinction between the various categories is less clear, not only because the categories can be overlapping, but also because power structures and formal authority structures are not completely independent of each other. For example, if a manager gives a subordinate an instruction and the instruction is carried out, has the subordinate allowed his or her behavior to be influenced (1) by the perceived possibilities of rewards and/or punishments, (2) because the manager is perceived as an "expert" in the problem area, or (3) because the manager is the official leader. In most cases, the answer is that each of these is partially responsible for the influence. Nevertheless, the categories are useful, since through an understanding of the basic sources of influence in organizations, we are better able to understand how informal organizations function and whether the influence is counter to or consistent with the goals of the formal organization. Because there is overlap between the power structure and the authority structure, it is best to view power and authority as *independent,* although not *exclusive,* of each other.[4]

**Status and Influence Systems**   By now it should be clear that there is a strong relationship between organizational status and organizational influence. In the formal organization, scalar status and formal authority are associated with influence; in the informal organization, achieved status and social power are the major determinants of influence. In general, we can say that status is associated with influence because (high) status is accorded to those individuals who possess one or more sources of social power. However, we must be careful when specifying cause and effect, since it is equally true that those who have the ability to exert influence are accorded (high) status by groups. The important fact is that the two are strongly related.

## ☐ Communication Systems

We have previously described the informal communication system known as the grapevine. It is important to view this system within the context of power and status systems, as the three together constitute the major social processes that are characteristic of informal organizations.

The general principles of informal communication systems closely parallel the concepts discussed in power and status systems. In other words, interpersonal communication tends to follow established status hierarchies, and communication content is influenced by power relationships. Although power and status systems are first established through communication as the social system evolves, once the system is in operation, communication tends to be the result of status differences rather than the cause of them. Subordinates, for example, communicate differently to managers than to peers, both because the manager is in a position to exercise authority and power and because the manager has higher status than the subordinate. In the informal organization, quantity of communication is affected by status relationships, and the type of communication can be determined by the social power one person can exercise over another. Thus, if a member of a work group is perceived as being highly competent in a particular task area but this is the only reason that person is included in the social group, most of the communication directed at that individual will probably be task-oriented. Communication that is not consistent with the individual's status will be minimal.

One of the most important concepts in the study of informal organizations is the idea of *mutual causality*. We have already encountered several examples in this section. Status, power, and communication are so closely related that each is thought of as both a determinant and a consequence of the others. As will be discussed in the next chapter, it is important for the manager to understand how the three are interrelated so that the motivational forces at work in the informal organization can be used to further the goals of the formal organization.

# ■ POTENTIAL PROBLEMS WITH THE INFORMAL ORGANIZATION

To complete our understanding of the workings of the informal organization, it is important that we discuss some potential problems associated with it. We will use the concepts already explained and show how these can work against the goals of the formal organization.

## ☐ Social Costs

Since the informal organization is a social organization, it is to be expected that considerable social interaction will occur. To the extent that some of this interaction is not directly related to work activities, there may be a "cost" attached to maintaining the informal organization. Activities such as horseplay or idle conversation are nonproductive in the strictest sense of the term. However, it should be remembered that employees have social needs that must be satisfied, and if the satisfaction of these needs is prevented, other costs, such as lowered motivational levels, may be incurred. Studies have noted that social interaction can be a means of relieving boredom on the job or it may provide an additional challenge if the employee knows that socializing is frowned upon.[5]

Evidence of the importance of social interaction on the job can be illustrated by the behaviors that result when social interaction is eliminated. While workers may cease socializing as ordered, they may also reduce their output. In other words, a manager may achieve the goal of eliminating nonproductive activity at

## Box 10-5: Clothes Make the Manager

One of the most important (but subtle) aspects of management positions is the informal consensus that exists about appropriate managerial dress. From a strictly rational point of view, we could argue that manner of dress shouldn't make any difference; what should count is how well the person does his or her job. In practice, however, how an executive dresses does make a difference.

Perhaps the most important point about dress codes is that managers are very reluctant to admit that they exist. Thus, the aspiring manager must be on the alert to subtle hints about the appropriate way to dress.

Is there a generally safe way for upwardly mobile managers to dress? Yes. It is generally agreed that for men, a blue or gray two-piece suit with a white shirt and dark tie is pretty safe. For women, the most popular attire is a two-piece suit (not of the swimming variety) with a blouse and stylish—but conservative —tie.

One company we know of placed considerable importance on the appearance of their executives. To make sure that they were appropriately dressed, the company instituted a fringe benefit that allowed each executive to obtain a certain amount of clothing free of charge at a prestigious clothing store.

the expense of the productivity goal. This is known as *suboptimization*. It seems almost paradoxical to state that, in order to increase productivity, the manager may have to allow—or even encourage—seemingly nonproductive behaviors! In practice, social interaction probably contributes to productivity up to a certain point, but an excess is obviously detrimental. One of the manager's responsibilities is to determine where "contribution" ends and "excess" begins.

## ☐ Resistance to Change

The development of a social structure within the formal organization results in a certain rigidity, since the norms of behavior that develop over time influence and control the behavior of group members. Because norms satisfy the need for security and predictability, there is considerable resistance to making changes that will affect the norms. This relationship between the technical and social side of organizations is often ignored in planning organizational changes. For example, managers may fail to realize that technical changes in manufacturing methods can affect the social structure of a plant and therefore cause resistance to the change. Many studies have shown the sensitivity of the relationship between the technical (rational) and social (emotional) side of organizations.[6]

## ☐ Staffing Inflexibility

The existence of the informal organization tends to decrease the organization's flexibility in staffing decisions. There is a loss in the interchangeability of personnel since the informal organization adds unofficial criteria to the selection process. While technical qualifications such as education or training are necessary requirements for good job performance as far as the formal organization is concerned, they may be seen as only partly relevant by the informal organization. The requirements of the informal organization are factors such as personality, social background, or other status attributes. If a particular individual does not fit into the existing social organization, productivity will likely suffer. In short, there are two types of requirements for effective staffing: technical and social. Although this division is an oversimplification, it is basically true that the formal organization decides on the technical aspects and the informal organization dictates the social requirements.

## *Opening Incident Revisited—Ralph Wilson*

Pity poor Ralph Wilson! His master's thesis is at stake and his organizational data look more like a tulip bulb than a regular organization. What happened? Ralph, of course, had failed to understand the significance of the differences between the formal and informal structures of organizations. Although he thought his little diagram was perfectly clear, it meant something entirely different to the people completing the questionnaire. If Ralph had wanted a "perfect" diagram or ranking within the formal structure, there is only one source for this information—the formal organization. That is, he would have to spend time with a senior person in the organization, examine job descriptions and organization charts, and then construct a chart accordingly.

In asking the people in the organization the same question, he will receive different answers because their perceptions of the organization will be influenced by many variables, a majority of which are ignored by the formal structure. One example of how the chart can become distorted is the following: two computer programmers are seated at a table completing the questionnaire; they each look at the diagram and then at each other. One programmer who has been with the company for three years looks at the other one, who has only been there six months, and says to himself, "Hmmmm . . . if I've been here that long, and he's only been here six months, and if I trained him on his job, and if I still continually help him in his work, then he must be a level 4, which makes me a level 3." In a similar fashion, the secretary of the president of the company is completing the questionnaire. She knows that her boss is level 1, she works under him, therefore she must be level 2! And so it goes throughout the whole company.

What Ralph Wilson got on his questionnaire was not the organization structure but the *influence structure* (i.e., patterns of influence throughout the organization). In terms of influence, the secretary probably is level 2 and the senior programmer level 3, even though each would technically be level 4 on the formal chart, since they would not have authority over subordinates.

So where does this leave Ralph Wilson on his thesis? Well, he probably has two choices: he can revise his questionnaire and ask the company for permission to administer it once again, something they probably wouldn't be too keen on doing. Or he can change the focus of the thesis to study the relationship between influence in organizations and satisfaction with pay. Oddly enough, this is probably a more useful research study than his original one! So, having learned a very valuable lesson, Ralph Wilson will likely graduate after all.

## ■ SUMMARY

This chapter introduced the concept of the informal organization and contrasted it with formal organization structures. The informal organization is made up of the social processes that occur within an organization as employees go about their jobs. The informal organization is characterized by (1) different goals from the formal structure, (2) influence processes that are based upon power rather than authority, (3) norms that are control mechanisms operating within informal groups, (4) a commmunication channel that is quick but sometimes inaccurate, (5) and a status hierarchy often illustrated by status symbols. The informal organization performs various functions for its members: offers security and social satisfaction, serves as a channel of communication, a balancing device, and a source of individual and group motivation. The major social processes that operate in informal groups are status systems, influence systems, and communication systems. Influence in the informal organization is based upon power rather than authority, and power can originate from reward, punishment, referent, expert, or legitimate sources. Although informal organizations can contribute to organizational effectiveness, they can cause problems in the form of increased socialization on the job, resistance to change, and staffing inflexibility.

## ■ REVIEW QUESTIONS

1.  What is the "informal organization"? What is its function?

2.  Compare and contrast the features of the formal and informal organization.

3.  In what ways does the informal organization benefit the formal organization? In what ways does it work to its detriment?

4.  What is *status?* How are status and influence related?

5.  How does the informal organization motivate those in it?

6. How is "power" different from "authority"? Describe the sources of power available to individuals.

7. Describe the functions of communication in the informal organization.

8. What are the "costs" associated with the informal organization?

9. Define the terms *scalar status* and *functional status*. Give examples of each from your own experience. How are these two types of status related?

10. Why is status generally important in organizations?

11. Why are status symbols important?

# ■ EXERCISE 10-1: THE EASTERN MUTUAL INSURANCE COMPANY

For some time the head office of the Eastern Mutual Insurance Company had been experiencing space shortages in their headquarters building and had been planning to relocate, since the present building could not be expanded. The board of directors decided that a committee of senior executives should be formed to examine the space requirements of the company in terms of both quantity and quality. The board also directed the committee to minimize costs wherever possible, since the physical appearance of the building was not seen to be crucial in influencing sales and profits.

After several months of examining various alternatives in building construction, the committee reported to the board. One of their major recommendations to minimize costs was to eliminate many of the costly "fringe benefits" of design that generally were associated with the different levels of organizational status. They viewed the new building mainly from a functional point of view, and their recommendations included the following:

1. Construction of offices only for those who had need of the privacy.
2. All offices should be of equal size.
3. All offices should have the same decor and furnishings to take advantage of quantity discounts in purchases.
4. Rather than assign personal secretaries to executives, all would share a secretarial pool to maximize efficiency. Telephone messages would be taken by a central switchboard operator.
5. Costs should be cut by eliminating such extras as carpeted offices, decorative plants, bookshelves (except where specifically needed), and luxurious furnishings.

1. What is your opinion of the proposal?

2. What advantages do you see in it? What disadvantages?

3. What do you think will happen if the plan is implemented?

# ■ EXERCISE 10-2: MEMORIAL COUNTY HOSPITAL

The Memorial County Hospital was the only hospital in a small rural town and employed 150 persons, seventy-five of whom were nurses. The nursing organization of the hospital was managed by a director of nurses who, in turn, was assisted by five head nurses in the various wards. Each of the head nurses supervised from five to twenty registered nurses (RNs), licensed practical nurses (LPNs), and nurse's aides. Head nurses were responsible for supervising their staff, shift scheduling, maintenance of supplies, training new employees, and completing necessary hospital reports; they were also expected to perform regular nursing duties. Head nurses were usually the more senior nurses in their groups and had considerable experience in their areas of specialty.

Upon the resignation of one head nurse, the director was faced with the problem of selecting a replacement. Because of that ward's highly specialized function, it was decided that the new head nurse should come from that group rather than be transferred from another area. There were ten nurses in the group and their seniority ranged from six months to seven years. One nurse, with seniority of five years, was well-known as the informal leader of the group. She had served as spokesperson for the group on several occasions in the past, and the other nurses tended to follow her advice in most matters. Most everyone agreed she exerted considerable influence within the group.

1. Make a case for selecting this person as the new head nurse.

2. Make a case for *not* selecting this person as the new head nurse.

3. What would be the deciding variable(s) if you had to choose the logic in either 1 or 2 above?

# ■ ENDNOTES

1. This does not mean that the theory of organizational design does not consider behavioral factors, but rather that specific individual features (e.g., personality) cannot be considered. There are also "behavioral theories of organizations," but they do not consider individual relationships.

2. F. J. Roethlisberger and W. J. Dickson, *Management and the Worker* (Cambridge: Harvard University Press, 1939).

3. J. P. French and B. Raven, "The Bases of Social Power," in *Studies in Social Power,* ed. Dorwin Cartwright (Ann Arbor: University of Michigan Institute for Social Research, 1959), pp. 150–67.

4. As one example of the relationship between the two, see Anthony T. Cobb, "Informal Influences in the Formal Organization: Perceived Sources of Power Among Work Unit Peers," *Academy of Management Journal* 23, no. 1 (1980): 155–161.

5. See, for example, "The Case of the Changing Cage," in P. R. Lawrence and J. A. Seiler, *Organizational Behavior and Administration* (Homewood, Ill.: Richard D. Irwin, 1965), pp. 124–31.

6. See, for example, E. L. Trist and K. W. Bamforth, "Some Social and Psychological Consequences of the Longwall Method of Coal Getting," *Human Relations* 4 (1951): 3–38; William F. Whyte, *Human Relations in the Restaurant Industry* (New York: McGraw-Hill, 1948); A. K. Rice, "Productivity and Social Organization in an Indian Weaving Shed," *Human Relations* 6 (1953): 297–329.

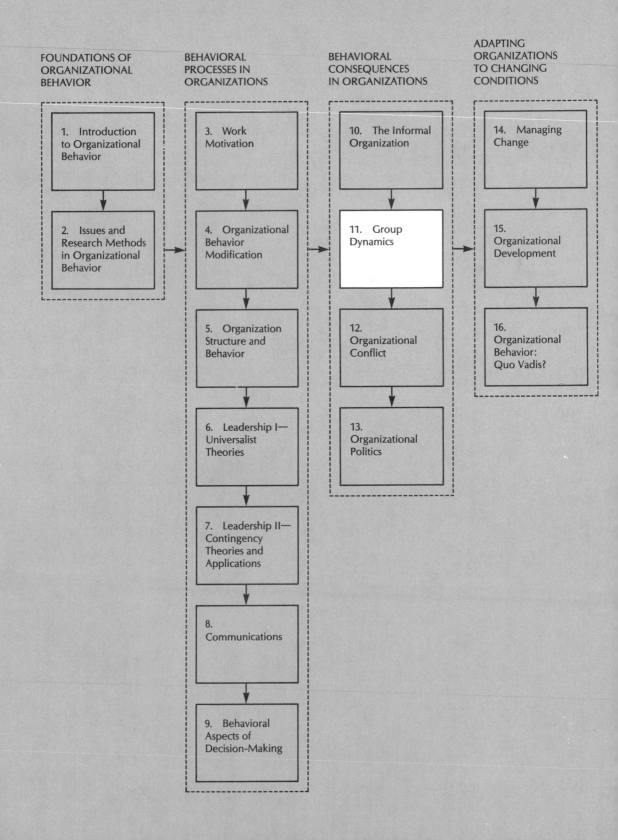

FOUNDATIONS OF
ORGANIZATIONAL
BEHAVIOR

1. Introduction to Organizational Behavior

2. Issues and Research Methods in Organizational Behavior

BEHAVIORAL
PROCESSES IN
ORGANIZATIONS

3. Work Motivation

4. Organizational Behavior Modification

5. Organization Structure and Behavior

6. Leadership I— Universalist Theories

7. Leadership II— Contingency Theories and Applications

8. Communications

9. Behavioral Aspects of Decision-Making

BEHAVIORAL
CONSEQUENCES
IN ORGANIZATIONS

10. The Informal Organization

11. Group Dynamics

12. Organizational Conflict

13. Organizational Politics

ADAPTING
ORGANIZATIONS
TO CHANGING
CONDITIONS

14. Managing Change

15. Organizational Development

16. Organizational Behavior: Quo Vadis?

# Group Dynamics

## ■ Learning Objectives

After careful study of this chapter you should be able to:

☐ Describe and identify group norms operating in a group.

☐ Describe and observe the social structure of small groups.

☐ Explain the relationships between group cohesiveness and productivity, and between cohesiveness and leadership of a group.

☐ Explain why group cohesiveness is important for managers to understand.

☐ List the stages of group development.

☐ Describe the nature of intergroup conflict and how it can affect the performance of groups.

☐ Use the Homans and Bales models of group behavior to analyze the behavior of small groups in action.

☐ Describe several applications of small-group theory to management problems.

# Chapter 11

# ■ KEY TERMS

**Interacting groups**
**Coacting groups**
**Counteracting groups**
**Group norms**
**Zone of acceptance**
**Production norm**
**Informal group leader**
**Regular members**
**Deviates**
**Isolates**
**Group cohesiveness**
**Status congruence**
**Status attributes**
**Intergroup competition**
**Intragroup competition**
**Homans model**
**Bales model**
**Role overload**
**Role conflict**
**Role ambiguity**
**Status**
**Grapevine**
**Groupthink**

# ■ CHAPTER OUTLINE

I. Central Concepts in Group Dynamics
   A. Types of Groups
   B. Group Norms
   C. The Social Structure of Groups
   D. Group Development
   E. Group Cohesiveness
   F. Intergroup Behavior and Conflict
II. Models of Small Group Behavior
   A. The Homans Model
   B. The Bales System

## *Opening Incident—Dennis Calhoun*

"What's wrong with me?" Dennis Calhoun thought to himself on his way home after eight hours at the bank. This was only his second week at work, but he was already disillusioned about his job and was seriously considering quitting, once he could find a position that paid at least as much and offered a fairly secure future.

Since the first day on the job, he had experienced nothing but trouble. The trouble was not with the job itself but with the other people working there. Although he thought he got along well with some of the older employees, there was a group of young male employees that seemed to have something against him. He had tried to be friendly and listen to their instructions as they taught him the various jobs, but they seemed to exclude him from their social activities— such as going to lunch, having a beer after work, and idle chit-chat. Although he didn't know everyone very well, it appeared that this group consisted mostly of the male part-time college students that worked at the bank during their free time. They didn't seem to be very committed to their job although their work was generally satisfactory as far as Dennis could tell. Most of their conversation was about activities at college, such as football games, fraternity parties, and school work.

In a way, Dennis kind of envied them. After finishing high school he had decided not to go on to college since his high-school grades were not especially good and his family could not take the financial burden of a college education. After working two years at a local supermarket, then taking a brief fling at selling insurance, he was particularly pleased at being offered a job as a management trainee with the bank. The bank planned to put him on a program that would allow him to rotate through the various departments over a five-year period, after which time he would be in a better position to decide in which area he wished to make his career. He thought this to be an excellent opportunity and was determined to make a good impression on the bank management.

In thinking now about his job, he recalled how unpleasant the last two weeks had been. Not long after he started to work, someone loosened the casters on his chair so that when he sat down the chair collapsed to the floor. Later, while on an errand to another bank after banking hours, one of the fellows was supposed to telephone the other bank to inform them that Dennis was on his way; when Dennis arrived, the front door was locked and no one was around, forcing him to pound on the front door until someone inside heard him. When he came back to the bank, the rear entrance was locked and he had to find a pay telephone to call inside for someone to let him in. And today was the crowning blow. In the middle of trying to balance a deposit containing over two hundred checks, he left briefly to go to the restroom. When he returned and finished the task, his total didn't balance with the deposit slip. When he rechecked his figures, he discovered that someone had added in a few numbers on the calculator while he was out.

---

In the last chapter, we noted that the term *informal organization* described the large-scale (macro) social relationships that occur within the formal organization structure. In this chapter, we narrow our focus and consider the smaller scale (micro) relationships among workers in small groups. We do this in recognition of the fact that workers cannot interact with all other workers in the informal organization. Instead, each person deals with only a few others in the social structure because workers differ in their desires and opportunities to interact with others, and physical separation and time limitations prevent workers from forming social relationships with just anyone. The relationships formed are often with coworkers, but they need not be. The tendency of workers to form a few strong relationships rather than many weak ones makes the study of small-group behavior an important part of organizational behavior.

Researchers of small-group theory point out that there are actually two approaches to the study of management. One approach—that based on the study of individuals—constitutes the major part of the research available on behavior in organizations. The second approach studies these same phenomena in relation to groups and attempts to analyze how individual theories are modified by group processes. For the most part, theories of organization stress individual concepts and ignore the effects of groups. For example, one assumption made by job enrichment theorists is that individuals will be more motivated to perform if given opportunities to attain satisfaction through more challenging jobs.[1] Our discussion of norms in the last chapter suggests that increased responsibility may not have a motivating effect on the individual if the group has a norm preventing it. Problems of this sort are not uncommon, since all groups have norms regarding various aspects of their work.

This does not mean that individual theories about management are incorrect; rather, it implies that the effects of the group on individual behavior must be considered when attempting to apply individual theories. Considering the possible effects of groups also provides us with additional information regarding the validity of certain research findings. Perhaps research studies reporting "failures" of management theories have actually been reporting the effects of group processes on individual behavior.[2]

In this chapter we analyze the topic of group dynamics as follows: First, the central concepts and terminology of group dynamics are presented. Second, some models of group activity are discussed. Finally, the applications section contains some practical suggestions for using the knowledge about informal organizations and group dynamics to make organizations run more smoothly and effectively.

# ■ CENTRAL CONCEPTS IN GROUP DYNAMICS

Much of group theory strongly resembles the theory related to the informal organization, since one is a part of the other. In this section we point out the areas that are important for an understanding of group theory and how it is differentiated from informal organization. This discussion includes (1) the types of groups that exist in organizations, (2) the concept of group norms, (3) the social structure of groups, (4) group cohesiveness, (5) intergroup behavior and conflict, and (6) group decision making.

## □ Types of Groups

In the broadest sense, a group is any collection of individuals who have mutually dependent relationships. This includes individuals who are in close physical proximity as well as those who have only a psychological attachment. While each group will exhibit different behaviors, they do have much in common. The American Rifle Association, for example, exhibits tendencies similar to a five-man work group that travels together to repair railroad tracks. But generally speaking, smaller, face-to-face groups exhibit clearer patterns of behavior than groups having only a psychological attachment

Groups can be categorized in a number of ways. One very useful scheme stresses the type of interactions that occur in the group as a result of its role in the formal organization. Fiedler[3] has identified three types of groups in organizations: interacting, coacting, and counteracting. In an *interacting* group, the work of one group member is contingent upon that of the others, such as assembly line workers performing separate operations in a prescribed sequence. In *coacting* groups, the work of individual group members is independent, such as a bowling team or a job-shop operation. *Counteracting* groups are those who interact to reconcile mutual differences, such as labor-management negotiating teams. Fiedler's research indicates that these groups differ with respect to the degree of coordination necessary, the amount of aggression and competition present, and the degree to which group goals are shared by members. These differences are schematically represented in Figure 11-1.

## □ Group Norms

As noted in Chapter 10, norms are *standards of behavior* resulting from the interaction that occurs among individuals. Over time, the group's social processes define desirable and undesirable behavior such that each member of the group is

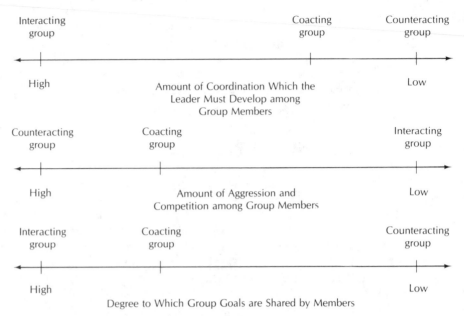

**FIGURE 11-1. Schematic Representation of Interacting, Coacting, and Counteracting Groups Compared Along Three Criteria**

Source: Fred E. Fiedler, *A Theory of Leadership Effectiveness* (New York: McGraw-Hill, 1967), p. 21. Reproduced with permission.

aware of the group's expectations. Norms in the small group perform a function similar to that in the larger informal organization—they control behavior. The major difference between the two is the degree to which norms can be identified and enforced. In smaller, face-to-face groups, norms tend to be clearer and role expectations more concrete than in larger groups.

While norms do change over time, they generally do not change significantly over short periods. Norms are the result of complex social processes that take considerable time to evolve. It is therefore unlikely that they would change greatly in the short run unless the group were affected by a force of considerable magnitude from the outside. For example, a group may have a norm regarding output quotas, but this might change if the group perceived that layoffs were imminent.

While many work and nonwork norms exist in small groups, the one most often referred to is the production norm (the group's perception of "acceptable" production behavior), which is often different from management expectations. Although the reasons for production norms are varied, some common ones are these:

1. Fear of rate-cutting if production gets too high.
2. Fear of reprisal against workers if production gets too low.
3. Fear of production changes if there is too great a deviation among individuals.

Much of our current knowledge about work group behavior began with the Hawthorne experiments. Although earlier management writers such as Taylor had recognized the existence of production norms, their impact was not really assessed until Elton Mayo and his associates conducted their detailed studies. Figure 11-2 indicates the types of production behavior observed in those studies and the terms workers used to identify those who did not adhere to the group's production norms.

Figure 11-2 also indicates that the group norm need not be the average of the group's production. The norm indicates which level of production from each individual is considered *acceptable* by the group, whereas the average may be higher or lower, depending upon the number of workers who deviate from the norm. It is possible to have more than one production norm operating in a group, although this tends to divide the group according to the different norms.

## ☐  The Social Structure of Groups

The process of assigning roles in the small group is similar in concept to that found in the larger, formal organization, except that the processes are behavioral rather than technical in nature. The result of the interaction that occurs between members of a group is a social stratification in which each member occupies a role that contains certain expectations. Within this general social structure, we can identify specific roles as follows:

**Group Leader**  The informal group leader is that person who best satisfies the needs of the group. If a major need is security, for example, the individual who can best serve this function will be the most influential in the group. However, should a need arise for a particular type of technical expertise, the individual who

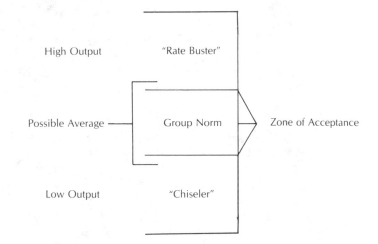

**FIGURE 11-2.  Diagram of the Production Norm and Its Zone of Acceptance**

is technically skilled would adopt the role of group leader until that function is no longer needed. Thus, it is not difficult to imagine situations in which leadership roles can change because of changes in group needs.

The work of Robert Bales indicates that there are generally two types of leaders in groups: a *task leader* who exercises influence relating to task accomplishment and a *social leader* who occupies the role of the human relations specialist and promotes the social processes that increase group harmony and satisfaction.[4]

---

## Box 11-1: What Would Happen to a Group of Isolates?

We know that in any work group a social structure will emerge consisting of an informal group leader, regular members, deviates, and isolates. The category that any given group member will be in depends upon the degree to which he or she adheres to the group norms. But assume that we have eight or ten different groups, all with a well-defined social structure; we then take all the isolates from each group (most likely only one or two individuals per group) and put them into a group by themselves. Would another social structure develop?

Logic dictates that it would. Once all the deviates are placed in the same face-to-face group, they constitute a new social system which will engage in all the group processes that the previous groups went through. This new group will develop norms, although they will probably be different from the norms of the previous groups. When these new norms emerge, then a new group structure will be formed around these norms complete with an informal leader, regular members, deviates, and—after a time—isolates. As only one example, note that convicts—people who have legally been declared deviates in our normal society—form informal structures within the confines of the prison. Groups form around accepted patterns of behavior and new social structures form. It is generally known, for example, that sex offenders are considered the deviates within the informal prison hierarchy and therefore often have to be protected from the rest of the prison population. But even here, it is possible that all the sex offenders will form their informal group.

In other words, any individual's role in a group will be relative to the norms of that particular group and can therefore change, depending upon the group in question. From a managerial perspective, this means that organizations should not view deviates and isolates as lost causes. Just because people may not fit into one group does not mean that they cannot function well in any group. In fact, often significant changes can be made in an employee's behavior simply by changing the group he or she belongs to. This can often be accomplished through interdepartmental transfers of personnel or other types of geographical relocation.

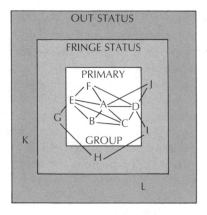

**FIGURE 11-3.   The Orbit of Small-Group Relationships**

Source: William G. Scott, *Organization Theory* (Homewood, Ill.: Richard R. Irwin, 1967), p. 93. Used with permission.

Since the types of skills necessary to perform these two functions are very different, they are seldom found in a single person. Consequently, dual-leadership roles tend to arise and are often filled by different people.

**Regular Members**   Individuals who are neither group leaders nor excluded from the group are called *regular members,* although there will be some variation even within this category since not all members will be accepted to the same degree. They differ from group leaders in that they exert less influence; their behaviors remain in the zone of acceptance of group norms, and they are therefore included in the group.

**Deviates**   Group members who violate group norms are called *deviates* and are excluded from normal group functions. Communications and interactions with deviates are intended to increase their conformity to group norms. Deviates pose a threat to the group's security since their unusual behavior may attract the attention of higher management. A group of salesmen, for example, may resent one individual performing at a significantly higher rate than the others, since this may cause management to put pressure on the rest of the group for more productivity. The reasons for individuals being deviates are quite varied. Broadly speaking, deviates' goals are different from the group's, and this causes them to behave differently. A common example is the individual who wants to get ahead and sees unusually high performance as a method of attaining that goal. This may be in conflict with the group's goal of member security. Although our examples here have pertained only to productivity norms, deviant behavior can violate any type of group norm.

**Isolates**   If a group fails in its efforts to induce a deviate to conform to the group norms, the individual is then psychologically, socially, and possibly physically isolated from the group. This extreme exclusion—similar to solitary confinement—can be interpreted as a further attempt to induce deviates to change their behavior and as a means of protecting the group from the influence of the unacceptable behavior.

Another way of examining group structure relates social structure to *social distance*. Using the sociometric method discussed in Chapter 10, group structure can be diagrammed according to the primary group, those on the fringes of the primary group, and those who are outside the fringes.[5] An example of this method is illustrated in Figure 11-3.

## □   Group Development

Groups do not form overnight. The process of developing from a group of strangers to a unit of cohesive, well-coordinated team members requires time and a great deal of interaction between group members. It follows, of course, that if group members have only limited opportunity to interact, they may never develop into a coordinated unit. This, for example, might explain why some university classes seldom move beyond the initial stages of development. Since interaction is confined to only several hours per week (and even then the interaction between members is limited), the group will not progress much beyond casual acquaintances. In other classes, however, there could be a strong group spirit if different conditions operated.

In the following discussion of group development, we will assume that the group is relatively small and has ample opportunity to interact on a continuing basis. Such is the case with most work groups. Under these conditions, groups usually follow the following stages of development: (1) mutual acceptance, (2) communication and decision making, (3) motivation and productivity, and (4) control.[6]

**Mutual Acceptance**   The initial strategy for establishing trust between group members is the mutual acceptance stage. As the group comes together, communications will be guarded and members will be reluctant to express their true attitudes and feelings. No doubt some will decide at this stage that the group is not for them as they progressively learn more about the other members. This first stage is a "trying out" stage in which each person attempts to find out as much as possible about the rest of the group without exposing too much of himself or herself.

**Communication and Decision Making**   Once mutual acceptance is reached, the group members begin to communicate more openly with each other. Not only does the quantity of communication increase, but communication tends to be more open and honest about feelings and issues that are now seen to be important to the group. Once this stage is reached, the group can begin proposing solutions to common problems and analyzing alternatives.

**Motivation and Productivity**   With fewer interpersonal conflicts affecting the group, and a focus on important issues or problems, the group then begins concentrating on the task. Whatever efforts are needed to achieve objectives are now expended in a group atmosphere. Communication may be less at this stage than at the initial stages, since interpersonal concerns have now been sorted out.

**Control and Organization**   The control and organization stage recognizes the final step in group formation. The collection of individuals is now truly a "group" in the sense that the group dominates the individuals. Group norms have now been established to control individual behavior and the social structure of the group is now firmly established.

While the stages just described are typical of most groups, there are factors that can either change the process or prolong any specific stage. For example, if new group members are constantly entering the group, it will be more difficult to reach the final stage. However, if relatively few individuals enter an established group, the group norms will have less of a chance of being changed. Notice also that if, at the third stage (motivation and productivity) the group is unable to agree upon the problem at hand, then group norms and a stable organization will be not as likely to occur.

From a managerial perspective, groups at the fourth stage can be both a liability and an asset. The liability side will be illustrated later in this chapter in the section on "groupthink," a phenomenon characteristic of strong informal groups. Also, groups that have reached the final stage may be limited in their ability to cope with novel situations, since that is a part of the earlier stages of group development. On the asset side, stable groups spend less time in sorting out interpersonal difficulties and can devote much of their time to task-related activities. The net effect of these types of groups is covered in more detail in the following section on group cohesiveness.

## ☐   Group Cohesiveness

Much of the research on group dynamics has investigated the nature of *group cohesiveness* (i.e., the degree of attraction the group has for the members). The major thrust of this research has been an attempt to understand the relationship between group cohesiveness and productivity. Before we can examine this relationship, however, we must first understand how cohesiveness affects the activities of the small group. The research findings relevant to group cohesiveness are summarized as follows:

## Box 11-2: Why Would Anyone Want to Be a Deviate?

The life of a deviate is difficult, indeed. Deviates are the receivers of much attention, most of it negative in nature. They are often the butt of jokes, scapegoats for a group's inability to meet its objectives, and, in extreme cases, the subject of ridicule by the group itself. Given all the grief that deviates experience, why would anyone be a deviate? The following reasons explain some possibilities:

(1) First of all, some people are not aware they are deviates, at least initially. In some cases, once one is aware of the deviant behavior, efforts are made to conform to group norms. It is obviously impossible for a new group member to be aware of all the group norms, so it is expected that every new group member will be a deviate for at least a brief period until the norms are understood. So excluding this understandable reason, the remainder deal with individuals who consciously or unconsciously continue to deviate.

(2) In some cases, it may not be possible for the person to change his or her deviant behavior. Thus, if the norm of a group is to be physically strong, the 90-lb. weakling will have no choice but to be a deviate. Membership in a group such as this would be very uncomfortable for our weakling, since there is almost no hope for change. In organizations this could be true of job skills, particularly for those that are physical in nature. A person who simply could not develop the level of skill the group believed to be desirable could never be fully accepted by the group.

(3) Deviant behavior is, of course, defined in terms of the relevant group. A person who is deviating from the norms of one group may be, in fact, adhering to the norms of another group. Since we are all members of more than one group, this is actually a very common phenomenon. Being members of different groups, our preferences for membership (and therefore willingness to conform to group norms) must be prioritized, such that membership in one group is more important than membership in others. For example, a person may choose not to wear a coat and tie to work, which violates the norms of his work group; but in so doing, the person may be conforming to the norms of his primary reference group outside the organization. Of course, if the sanctions for not conforming to the norms of the work group become intolerable, the person may either change behavior (begin wearing a coat and tie) or leave the group.

(4) And finally, some people find the attention received as a deviate to be quite rewarding. We learned in the chapter on behavior modification that punishment is often preferred to being ignored, and deviant behavior is one way of making that choice. But this requires a careful strategy because we know that isolates are simply deviates who have been given up on by the group. Therefore, anyone who satisfies the need for attention by being deviant must take care not to be too deviant lest she or he be totally excluded from the group.

1. *The greater the congruence of the status attributes of group members, the greater the cohesiveness of the group.* Individuals with similar status attributes are more likely to be attracted to one another. Groups that lack status congruence find that members do not share the same interests, attitudes, or values, and are therefore less cohesive.[7] For example, if members of a work group are from different ethnic backgrounds, cohesiveness will likely be less than in a group where all members have the same ethnic background, everything else being equal.

2. *Higher status congruence in a group leads to improved social relationships and improved personal emotional states.*[8] Because of the elements of interpersonal attraction, congruence with respect to status attributes leads to less anxiety in interpersonal relations. Using the ethnic background example above, those individuals in the congruent group would be more open and less anxious in their interpersonal relationships since they have a common background which facilitates predictability and understanding of other persons' behaviors.

3. *Cohesiveness of a group is greater if membership changes are infrequent or do not occur at all.*[9] It may require considerable time for groups to sort out desirable and undesirable behaviors. New group members tend to disrupt this process, thus affecting the cohesiveness of the group.

4. *The more cohesive the group, the more communications will be directed at deviates.*[10] In other words, the stronger the perceived need for conformity, the more effort will be directed at those who do not conform. Cohesive groups are better able to mobilize their energies toward deviates, and they are more likely to see deviates as a threat.

5. *Cohesive groups have a higher level of intermember communication than noncohesive groups.*[11] This is a by-product of the increased attraction between members that is characteristic of cohesive groups. Persons similar in status attributes have more things in common than those who are dissimilar; this increases the amount of communication among members.

6. *The greater the cohesiveness of a group, the greater the influence the group will exert upon its members.*[12] This statement might also be used as a definition of cohesiveness. A cohesive group will, by definition, exert influence upon regular members.

7. *Small groups have a greater probability of being cohesive than large ones, other things being equal.* Large groups have a higher probability of containing elements that work counter to cohesiveness. Also, cohesiveness is partly a function of a group's ability to interact, and large groups inhibit the necessary interactions.

8. *The more dependent an individual is on the group, the more cohesive it will be perceived by him.*[13] The extent to which successful task performance depends on total group effort also affects the individual's perception of attractiveness.

9. *Competition within a group (intragroup conflict) has a negative influence on group cohesiveness.*[14] The competition for scarce resources or rewards within the group can overcome the properties of attractiveness.

10. *Competition between groups increases the cohesion within the competing groups.*[15] This is the "in-group" or the "we-they" attitude groups often experience in sporting events or other competitive situations.

**Group Cohesiveness and Productivity**   The above statements suggest certain characteristics of cohesive groups. These characteristics can be related to concepts discussed earlier such as status, power and influence, and communication in informal organizations. While it is obvious that status and power structures affect group productivity, the research available does not yet specify precisely how these variables interact to determine productivity. Nevertheless, we can summarize the research findings regarding the relationship between group cohesiveness and productivity (or indicators of productivity), recognizing that we must necessarily oversimplify the causes and effects. The propositions above suggest the following relationships between group cohesiveness, productivity, and indicators of productive attitudes.

1. *People in highly cohesive groups generally experience fewer work-related anxieties.*[16] Friction and conflict in interpersonal relationships is psychologically upsetting to people. Cohesive work groups are those in which interpersonal problems have been sorted out and anxieties have been minimized. Therefore, to the extent that the productivity of individual workers is reduced by work-related anxieties, a highly cohesive work group can facilitate productivity.[17]

2. *Highly cohesive groups tend to have lower absenteeism and turnover.*[18] Interpersonal anxieties in the work place can be dealt with by group members in

---

## Organizational Reality   11-1
## Using Small Groups at Work

Many U.S. firms now use quality circles. The idea of quality circles originated in Japan where the focus was on statistical quality control. In North America the programs are broader, covering not only the technical aspect of work but also dealing with factors such as work place lighting, work schedules, and basic production processes. In these circles, worker ingenuity is brought to bear on a wide variety of operating and quality problems.

Many companies have found that there are no easy shortcuts in the use of quality circles. A survey conducted by the International Association of Quality Circles found that many circles really are nothing more than meetings set up to deal with problems identified by management. Unless the effort is well organized, a circle meeting may end up being nothing but meandering discussions.

In a well-organized circle, members get training in basic problem solving up front. They also learn how to work as a team in attacking problems. Once in place, the program needs continuous support by both management and workers. A product assurance manager at Hewlett-Packard notes that a program cannot be set up and then be left to run by itself. It will take a lot of work for a long time to make it successful.

---

Source: Charles G. Burck, "What Happens When Workers Manage Themselves," *Fortune* (27 July 1981): 62–69.

a variety of ways. One way is to reduce output, another is to withdraw from the work situation. Since a prerequisite for productivity is employee presence at work, the groups with high cohesion can provide one of the fundamental requirements for productivity.

3. *Workers who have been sociometrically assigned to work groups generally have higher job satisfaction, lower turnover rates, lower indices of labor costs, and lower indices of material costs.*[19] By sociometrically selecting work groups, the probability that individuals with significantly different attitudes, values, and behaviors will be placed together is greatly reduced. There is no guarantee that sociometrically selected groups will always have higher productivity, however, since factors other than interpersonal feelings and conflicts can affect productivity. For example, wartime experiences with air combat crews illustrated situations in which poor interpersonal relations could be put aside in the face of extreme danger.

4. *The effect of cohesiveness upon productivity varies with the source of cohesiveness.*[20] If a group is cohesive only because of its members' strong interpersonal attractions for each other, there may be very little effect on productivity. In the extreme, interpersonal attractiveness could even detract from productivity; group members might be so busy interacting socially that work is neglected. If, however, the group is cohesive because of a common task, productivity may be positively affected.

5. *The effect of cohesiveness upon productivity varies with the type of leadership received.*[21] One study found that, if supportive leadership was used with a highly cohesive group, the group's productivity was very high; however, a highly cohesive group given nonsupportive leadership showed very low productivity. Luthans interprets this to mean that the highly cohesive group is a "time bomb" in the hands of management since its potential is so great—on both the high and low side. The low-cohesive group is a much lower risk since there is less variation in productivity.[22] More recent research has investigated the relationship between specific leader behaviors of I. S. (initiating structure) and C. (consideration) and found that for low-cohesive groups, leader-initiating structure was positively related to role clarity, self-reported performance, and satisfaction. For high-cohesive groups, the same variables were positively related to leader consideration.[23] All this suggests that management should attempt to match leadership styles with the cohesive characteristics of the work group.

**Conclusion** The above comments suggest that it is impossible—and inappropriate—to make sweeping statements about the relationship between group cohesiveness and productivity. However, it should be clear that cohesiveness is a major input into productivity and that, because of the synergistic[24] effects of group behavior, the cohesive group has inherently more "energy" than the uncohesive one. Whether or not this increased energy translates into increased productivity depends upon several factors, some of which can be beyond the control of management. For example, if a worker divorces his wife, who is the sister of a co-worker, the cohesiveness of the group—and their productivity—may be affected.

Also, group cohesiveness may be a function of attitudes or activities that are outside the organization's domain. A group attaining cohesiveness through a company bowling team may not demonstrate increased productivity back at the work place.

It should be apparent that the most dysfunctional type of group (from the organization's point of view) is the one that is highly cohesive but does not identify with the goals of the organization. The most functional type is the highly cohesive group that has internalized the goals of the formal organization and meets no obstacles, either technical or social, in meeting those goals. This relationship between cohesiveness and goal identification is illustrated in Figure 11-4. Note that we have made no assumptions about the appropriateness or desirability of the organization's goals; we are concerned here only with whether group activity facilitates or inhibits achievement of goals that have been set.

## ☐ Intergroup Behavior and Conflict

Thus far we have concentrated primarily on the behaviors and processes that occur *within* work groups. Since organizations divide the work to be done among different groups, it is also important to examine the relationships that can occur *between* groups. Groups must work together to achieve the organization's goals and therefore the intergroup processes that occur warrant our attention.

Because competition between groups is a common occurrence in organizations, much of the study of intergroup behavior has concentrated on counter-

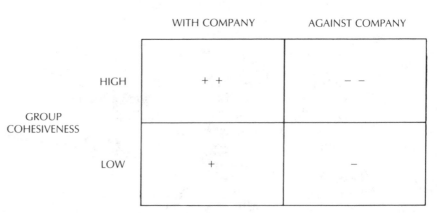

**FIGURE 11-4.   Interaction Effects Between Group Cohesiveness and Goal Identification**

acting groups. Although all groups in a given organization theoretically have a common goal, various organizational systems such as productivity reports, performance appraisals, and resource allocation techniques, serve to increase subgoal identification, thereby jeopardizing cooperation between units.

One of the major sources of intergroup conflict is the organization structure. The typical hierarchical form of organization functionalizes the necessary activities into different operating units, thus emphasizing the division between subunit goals. We would therefore expect different types of intergroup behaviors in organizations that do not functionalize their structures, such as matrix organizations. Group formation in matrix organizations would likely be around professional groups, and conflict would ideally be creative.[25] In any event, the existence of the intergroup conflict can be dysfunctional for organizational performance, although this is not necessarily always the case.

As a general rule, the degree of intergroup competition increases as resources become more scarce. While groups may be working against each other in many situations, if resources are plentiful the behavior of one group tends to have little effect on the other. However, when each group's survival depends on obtaining scarce resources, in-group identification increases and the "us vs. them" mentality develops. Research on group behavior under these conditions indicates that the following patterns of behavior can be expected.

1. Competition for scarce resources breeds mutual mistrust.
2. Each group tends to distort its own position and, on occasion, even falsifies it.
3. Each group sees the other as the enemy and forms its own stereotypes of opposing groups.
4. As conflict increases, individual groups become more cohesive as they band together to defeat the enemy.
5. Groups tend to be more tolerant of autocratic leadership under threatening conditions.
6. Emphasis is on strategy, gamesmanship, politics, and power plays, rather than on common organizational objectives.[26]

It is not difficult to think of many real-life illustrations of these phenomena. In universities, for example, as budgets become tighter, competition for scarce resources is intensified. Various forms of behavior, consistent with the above list, can be observed: faculties bringing courses "in-house" in the belief that other (competing) faculties are not conducting them properly; decreasing the amount of intergroup contact such as interdisciplinary courses; or attempting to find allies in external groups (such as business or professional groups) who can bring pressure to bear at the right places in the university budgeting process.

The effects of competition on groups should be assessed both during and after the competition. The overall effects of competition are often misjudged because this distinction is not made. During competition, we can observe increased cohesiveness, greater in-group identification, and less intragroup bickering and conflict. All of these can occur as the group prepares for battle. Equally important, however, are the post-competition effects. For the winning group, research indicates that cohesiveness is generally increased, group tensions and feelings of competitiveness decrease, and the group becomes "fat and sassy." Losers, on the other hand, exhibit feelings of tension and competitiveness, and attitudes toward cooperation drop dramatically as the group becomes "lean and hungry."[27] Both of these descriptions fit our everyday experiences in competitive situations, although most of our reference points may be outside the context of normal organizational life. In sports competition, for example, this research partially explains why, despite obvious differences in talent, a consistent loser can on occasion upset the leading team.

The above lessons for organizations are significant, inasmuch as competition between groups is often encouraged. While considerable attention has been given to the motivating effects of competitive behavior, its implications for the losers have frequently been ignored. This becomes increasingly important when we remember there are always more losers than winners! One aspect of behavior that is of particular concern is the losers' attitudes toward cooperation. Consider the situation in which two subgroups of an organization are asked to competitively submit plans for a proposed change, with a substantial reward being given to the winning group. Once a winning plan is selected, the losing group must help implement the plan if it is to be successful. Research findings suggest that the losing group will have little motivation to make their opponents' plan work and may even try to sabotage it, depending upon the magnitude of their feelings. Some possible ways of avoiding the negative effects of intergroup conflict are discussed in the applications section of this chapter and in Chapter 12, Organization Conflict.

## ■ MODELS OF SMALL-GROUP BEHAVIOR

Having explored some of the central concepts in small-group behavior, we can now proceed to general schemes of group behavior that allow us to analyze or predict the behavior of a given work group. The reader may have noted up to now that we have been minimizing the causal aspect of group behavior, except in those instances in which causal relationships are obvious. This leaves us with a host of unanswered questions:

1. What causes a group to select a particular norm?
2. How are deviates and isolates determined?
3. What are the major factors that determine group productivity?
4. How do groups reach a steady state?

To answer these questions requires a general model of small group behavior. Two of the most widely used models for analyzing causal relationships in small groups are discussed below.

## ☐ The Homans Model

The model developed by George Homans is a conceptual scheme that describes the central processes that occur in small groups.[28] The model, shown in Figure 11-5, can be used either in the predictive or descriptive sense, although its predictive value is less, given our knowledge about some of the data required.

The model is best viewed in four stages. The first stage describes the *background factors* that affect group behavior. These background factors consist of (1) the physical aspects of the work to be done, (2) the organizational policies and practices that have been designed into the system, (3) the external environment, and (4) personal background factors of group members. These background factors interact to influence the second stage, *required and given behavior*.

*Required activities* are those that group members must perform (i.e., they are prescribed by the organization). They are the result of such factors as leadership styles, the type of job being performed, the level of technology in the organization, and external constraints such as the economic and social environment.

*Required interactions* are those required to complete the task successfully. A job description, for example, may require a personnel manager to regularly interview department managers to determine their training needs. Sometimes the type of work being done determines the required interactions, as would be the case of two dock workers having to cooperate to lift a large container.

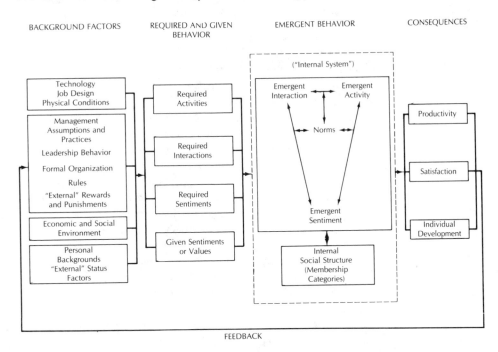

**FIGURE 11-5.   The Homans Model of Work Group Behavior**

Source: Paul R. Lawrence and John A. Seiler, *Organizational Behavior and Administration* (Homewood, Ill.: Richard D. Irwin, 1965), p. 158. Reprinted with permission.

*Required sentiments* are those feelings and attitudes individuals must have in order to perform their jobs in a minimally acceptable fashion. At the broadest level, the work ethic is a required sentiment if a person is to be expected to work steadily. On a more specific level, however, different occupations require different sentiments, which tend to serve as self-selection devices. For example, the nursing profession requires a sentiment about caring for sick people; prison correctional officers require a different type of sentiment, and so on.

*Given sentiments* are those that employees bring to their jobs that are not specifically required or prohibited. These may be attitudes about other workers, political beliefs, or personal beliefs, to name but a few. Ideally, these should be consistent with the required sentiments.

These required and given behaviors interact to cause *emergent behavior,* the third stage of the model. It is here we see the central role that norms play in influencing behavior. For example, research indicates that, other things being equal, emergent sentiments and emergent interaction are positively related. Among other things, this means that the more individuals like each other, the more they will interact. As another example, the relationship between emergent sentiments and emergent activity is influenced by group norms. If an individual is

---

### Organizational Reality   11-2
### Using Small Groups As Study Circles to Improve Productivity

Study circles, popular in Scandinavia, are just now catching on in North America. The circles go beyond plant concerns and deal with the workers' own educational and social needs, along with those of the employer.

DeRidder-Thurston, Inc., of Rochester, New York, manufactures graphic arts materials. It was one of the first American companies to adopt study circles. Participants decide what they will discuss with no set body of knowledge to cover. Most companies allocate time for circles to meet during working hours. There are no instructors, but companies provide individuals to organize meetings, set up speakers, and locate materials requested by the group. At DeRidder, the circle coordinator is a full-time staff member of the personnel department.

DeRidder participants are challenged to uncover problems and present recommendations. One study circle analyzed the company's annual employee review process. Eight sessions later, a revision was recommended. Another study circle suggested an employee evaluation form with five categories to evaluate performance. The form allowed supervisors to evaluate employees using a standardized scale and helped them in designing training programs.

At DeRidder, the first study circle was set up using only supervisors as participants so they would understand the process. Now these groups exist throughout the organization. The management believes that study circles improve communications between employees and bring about a greater awareness of their common objectives.

---

Source: Karen Osborne and Renee Shavat, "Study Circles," *Management Review* (June 1982): 37–42.

not adhering to the group norm, group members will attempt to correct this situation by engaging in physical or psychological sanctions.

The consequences of emergent behavior in organizational effectiveness are indicated in the fourth stage of the model. The emergent behavior affects (or is manifested as) productivity, individual satisfaction, and individual development. These results, then, feed back into stage 1 to affect the background factors.

While it is useful to examine the model in separate stages, in practice the processes described in the model are continually in operation. In a relatively new work group there would be considerable variation in the different stages of the model; however, over time, groups develop a stable social structure, and it becomes more difficult to institute or observe changes in behavior. Once a group reaches a steady state, the addition or deletion of an individual will not significantly affect group structure unless the deleted individual is the dominant one.

The model also illustrates how management decisions can affect small-group behavior. If, for example, management examines the output of the system (stage 4) and decides that more productivity is needed, one or more of several alternatives can be used. First, management can introduce technological advances which, according to the model, will affect the group's social structure and output. Alternatively, management can change the style or method of supervision, institute a new payment scheme, or attempt to improve the work environment. Regardless of the decision, the model indicates that it will have an effect on the emergent social structure of the work group. Of course, the net interaction of all the variables is very complex. But despite this complexity and the lack of data that often characterize the manager's situation, the Homans model can be of great help in analyzing the behavior of small work groups.

## ☐ The Bales System

Another model that is useful for analyzing group behavior is one designed by R. F. Bales (see Figure 11-6).[29] Whereas the Homans model analyzes the total environment and its effect on group formation and productivity, the Bales model concentrates on the types of interactions that occur as a group goes about its tasks. This system would be useful, for example, in analyzing the behavior of committee members in the process of making a difficult decision or in the identification of task and social leaders in the work group.

The model is based upon the two-dimensional theory of group leadership and divides behaviors into two areas: social-emotional and task. These in turn are subdivided into two additional areas: (1) questions and answers and (2) positive and negative reactions. The model is based on the theory that groups proceed through distinct steps (a–f in Figure 11-6) when reaching a decision, and that different individuals in the group occupy certain roles which facilitate the process. Feedback of the data to groups can assist them in evaluating their performance and discussing any improvements they think necessary. For example, if a group is having difficulty arriving at a decision, an evaluation using the Bales system may show that certain individuals in the group are consistently negative in their behaviors or that much of the group's behavior is not task-oriented.

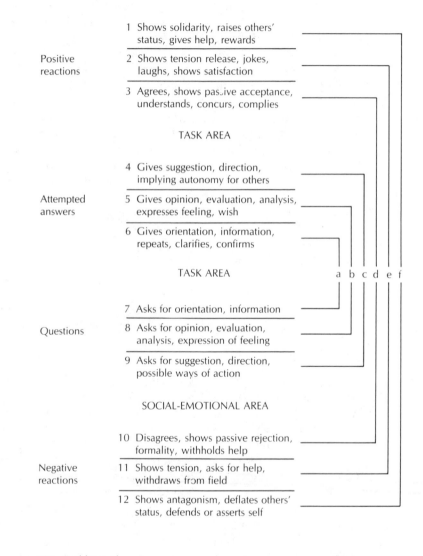

Interaction Process Analysis

SOCIAL-EMOTIONAL AREA

**Positive reactions**

1 Shows solidarity, raises others' status, gives help, rewards

2 Shows tension release, jokes, laughs, shows satisfaction

3 Agrees, shows passive acceptance, understands, concurs, complies

TASK AREA

**Attempted answers**

4 Gives suggestion, direction, implying autonomy for others

5 Gives opinion, evaluation, analysis, expresses feeling, wish

6 Gives orientation, information, repeats, clarifies, confirms

TASK AREA

a b c d e f

**Questions**

7 Asks for orientation, information

8 Asks for opinion, evaluation, analysis, expression of feeling

9 Asks for suggestion, direction, possible ways of action

SOCIAL-EMOTIONAL AREA

**Negative reactions**

10 Disagrees, shows passive rejection, formality, withholds help

11 Shows tension, asks for help, withdraws from field

12 Shows antagonism, deflates others' status, defends or asserts self

KEY: Problems of

a) Orientation          c) Control          e) Tension-management

b) Evaluation          d) Decision          f) Integration

## FIGURE 11-6.   Bales' Group Interaction Model

Source: R. F. Bales, "A Set of Categories for the Analysis of Small Group Interaction," *American Sociological Review* 15 (1950): 257–63. Reprinted with permission.

# ■ APPLICATIONS

Application of the theory presented in the last two chapters involves understanding how to utilize the natural forces and processes that are inherent in every group, formal or informal. Given that the informal organization exists, it is the manager's responsibility to use it in achieving organizational goals. This section describes some of the many opportunities to use the informal organization and small groups to benefit the total organization. Rather than detail specific problems, we have chosen several important aspects of organizational life and elaborated on these with application suggestions.

## ☐ Work-Flow Considerations

Knowledge of the informal group allows us to identify particular areas of concern in work design and work-flow systems. We know that group structure is in part dependent on the design of work and that changes in this design will have an effect on the functioning and structure of the informal group. Through the study of group behavior in work situations, principles can be derived that apply generally to the relationship between group and formal organizational needs.

**Initiation of Action**  In the work-flow process, one individual usually initiates action for another. For example, managers give orders to subordinates, senior workers exert influence over junior workers, and so on. In both the cases just noted, the influence process is consistent with the natural order of other events (i.e., status systems), and therefore the potential for conflict is reduced. It is possible, however, to have a work system in which a lower status worker initiates actions for a higher status worker. This type of situation has been described in William H. Whyte's work in the restaurant industry where he observed lower status waitresses telling the higher status cooks what to cook.[30] This work flow process was counter to the natural order of social processes and was the source of much conflict and frustration. Several solutions can be suggested for problems of this type:

1. Change the initiator from a low-status person to one of equal or greater status.
2. Change the system so that face-to-face contact is avoided by individuals of different status (physical separation tends to reduce status awareness).
3. Place a neutral intermediary between the different status individuals. In the restaurant industry, the spindle is used as the neutral intermediary. Waitresses place orders on the spindle and cooks then process them as they see fit.[31]

Any of the above actions would likely reduce the problem of status conflict in the work design of the situation described.

**Role Overload**  The duties and responsibilities of each individual are generally spelled out in a formal job description. This may not, however, be the actual job the person performs. When informal relationships arise, expectations that are different from formal requirements arise also, thus changing what the worker is expected to do. Although this change in expectations can take many forms, a common one is *role overload* (i.e., experiencing more expectations than one is able to fulfill). Role overload can exist regardless of the formal job description and places considerable strain on the worker. A common example of this is the secretary who is shared by more than one executive. Each may be unaware of the demands placed upon the secretary by the others, and the net effect may be role overload. Rigid, highly formal structures may be able to avoid role overload since duties are clearly spelled out. In less formalized structures, however, it may be difficult to avoid excessive expectations. Informally, the same thing can happen if group members transfer some of their responsibilities to another group member on the basis that "he is better able to do the job." In any event, whether the source of the role overload is structural or behavioral, it increases the pressures on individuals and therefore may reduce organizational performance.

Similar results may occur for *role conflict* (i.e., different role expectations that conflict with one another) and *role ambiguity* (i.e., lack of clear expectations in a role). Effective managers will be on the lookout for problems of this type that may be built into the work design or work-flow system and attempt to eliminate these potential trouble spots.

**Individual Social Needs**    We have mentioned on several occasions the importance of the social needs of employees. The desire to satisfy social needs should be viewed as a natural human tendency, which means that work design systems ideally should take these needs into account. Many jobs are perceived as undesirable by workers because socialization on the job is not possible. Common barriers to socialization include noise, physical separation of workers, lack of adequate facilities in which to socialize, poor design of work groups (i.e., lack of status congruence), or a leadership style that prevents socialization.

**Job Design**    Even though functional status is derived from one's position in the formal organization, it is the informal organization that actually assigns the relative status to a job. A portion of the status in a job can be derived from the perceived level of difficulty, which is determined by the design of the job itself. The redesign of a job may cause serious problems if the status of that job is not consistent with the worker's self-image or if it reduces the status of the job. In either case, changes in the job design should not be implemented without first considering the implication of the change for the informal group.

## ☐  Motivational Considerations

As we have already noted, a great deal of energy exists in any informal group. Some of this energy is already spoken for and is used for things such as group maintenance needs, cohesiveness, or enforcing norms. But beyond this, informal groups have potential for increasing organizational effectiveness.

The most obvious potential for motivation is the use of status symbols to communicate an individual's status in the organization. The only assumption that needs to be made by management is that individuals will change their behavior

# *Box 11-3: The Value of a Window*

On the one hand, the importance of status is so well-known that it appears to be almost common sense. On the other hand, organizations so often overlook status factors—or at least appear to—that another example is probably worth examining.

In this situation, there were three individuals in the purchasing department working in a single room. There were three desks but only one window. The overall layout of the room was like this:

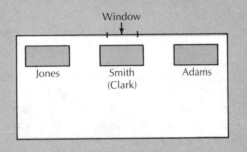

Smith, whose desk was directly in front of the window, had been with the company for thirty-five years and was due to retire. Jones had been with the company for fifteen, and Adams only five years. Upon Smith's retirement, a new person, Clark, was hired to fill the vacancy. Job duties were rearranged to take advantage of each person's previous experience. The manager of the three decided that there would be less disruption if Clark took over Smith's desk. And so he did.

After about a week on the job, Clark approached the manager and said he felt that Jones and Adams were extremely "cold" toward him, didn't appear to be very cooperative and helpful, and that he felt there was considerable resentment toward him. After discussing the matter, they concluded that the resentment might be a result of Clark's taking the desk previously occupied by the senior member of the work group, which was also the only one by a window and therefore the high-status desk.

Having decided upon this, they agreed that if Jones were approached and offered the window, he would probably refuse since he might think the others would consider him childish to put so much weight on having a window. They therefore agreed that it would take a planned strategy to get Jones by the window that he felt he rightfully deserved. The plan was that Clark would start to remark each day about how he left the office with a headache and that he thought it was due to the glare of the light on his desk.

After four or five days of this, Jones finally offered to trade desks with Clark, "even though he preferred to be in the corner." Subsequent to the move, relations among the three improved dramatically, and Clark expressed a feeling of being an accepted member of the group.

for the potential of (or the result of) receiving recognition in the informal organization. Actually, in some cases even this assumption may not be needed, since status is a type of self-fulfilling prophecy (individuals who seek recognition through status are attracted to those organizations that emphasize it). Status symbols can take many forms as long as the two conditions specified in Chapter 10—scarcity and desirability—are met. This means that managers must make judgments about what the group perceives as being scarce and desirable; otherwise they make the mistake of imposing their own values upon others. For example, a particular manager may be motivated by overt symbols of status such as a large office, assigned parking stall, and private secretary. Other workers, however, may be motivated by factors such as freedom on the job, being able to wear whatever clothes they please to work, or being considered the best workers of the group.

Another potential pitfall in using status as a motivator concerns the important role that the informal group plays in defining status. One company decided to give additional status to their best workers by creating an "employee of the month" program, which featured a biographical sketch of the month's best worker—as measured by productivity. Unfortunately, management failed to realize that high productivity was not a norm in many of the work groups, and their act of recognition proved embarrassing to those who were selected. Groups tended to chide those who were chosen, thus adding to their embarrassment. Before long, this "motivator" was actually working against the company, since employees tried to avoid being chosen "employee of the month!"

Using status to motivate must also be done cautiously because items that are scarce are, by definition, not available to everyone. To give status to some workers as a reward for desirable behavior implicitly means that it must also be withheld from others. We are constantly reminded that organizations, being hierarchical in nature, have competition as a major philosophical cornerstone, and this suggests that there must be differences between individuals at all levels. If these differences are removed, the satisfying aspects of status are likewise removed. For example, having a carpeted office is a status symbol only if relatively few others have it. Large pay increases lose much of their impact when the employee discovers everyone else received the same increase. Thus, the ability to use status as a motivator is limited because it cannot be applied to everyone; the very act of doing so reduces its effect significantly.

This limitation is not characteristic of all informal motivators, however. We discussed earlier how people can derive social satisfactoin from joining informal groups and interacting on a social basis. To the extent that a person or group is motivated by social considerations, providing opportunities for interaction would also serve as a motivational tool. Assuming that the right (or opportunity) to socialize is not a status symbol, allowing everyone to engage in it would not reduce its effectiveness.

## ☐ Leadership Considerations

An important aspect of informal organization and small-group theory that has implications for leadership is the informal leader. The informal organization forces us to recognize that the formally appointed leader may not be the most influential person in the work group. This means that, while the appointed leader can issue orders, the orders may not be carried out until the informal leader "approves" them. In most situations there is likely no detectable process that occurs for this approval, and the concept is only apparent in the rare instances in which the informal group decides not to follow the order. Still, the formal leader must recognize that the informal group leader may hold the power of veto because of the influence he or she has in the group.

The understanding of group dynamics and the role of the informal leader can be a valuable tool for management. The formal leader knows that to influence the behavior of the group itself, the informal leader must first be influenced. The manager knows, for example, that if a new procedure is to be accepted by the group, the acceptance of the group leader must first be gained. The manager can also rely on the group to absorb any slack in the system and to make up for deficiencies that are built into the system. But this will occur only if the informal group identifies with management's goals. The informal leader plays an important role in goal identification, since group norms are heavily influenced by the informal leader.

While we discussed earlier the virtues of creating cohesive work groups, management must be cautious lest it create a monster it cannot control. It is possible to create groups that are so cohesive and inner-directed that they cannot be influenced from the outside. The informal group leader is then able to control practically all behavior, and management is helpless to change the situation. Attempts to weaken the group merely serve to strengthen it as the group perceives it is being unfairly attacked.

## ☐ Communication Considerations

The grapevine meets the needs of the work group and in that sense performs a positive function. Certainly, management cannot hope to provide through formal channels all the information that workers would like to have. The grapevine supplements regular channels and provides members of the system with the information and social contacts that satisfy their needs.

Management's major concern about the grapevine is the accuracy of the information it transmits. Because the system is laden with emotional biases, information is often inaccurate. What is more, because management is not a "member" of the grapevine, false information can be freely transmitted without management's knowledge. By examining the source of the grapevine, it is possible to make some suggestions for solving the problems associated with it. If we assume that the grapevine satisfies workers' needs for security and predictability through the transmission of relevant information, then it follows that the disadvantages of the grapevine can be partly overcome by providing the important information through formal channels. The degree to which this will be helpful depends partly on the nature of the organizational climate. If the organization has a history of mistrust and poor employee relations, formal communications may be perceived simply as propaganda and another attempt to hoodwink the employees. In a positive climate, however, the mere act of providing needed information can reduce the problems associated with the grapevine.

To complete our understanding of how the grapevine can be used, it is necessary to discuss the meaning of "important" as it relates to informal communication. The grapevine exists because it provides information that is perceived as important by the members of the informal organization; consequently, when management decides to provide the correct information, the perceptions of what is important to the employees must be kept in mind. The data that are important to management may be totally immaterial to the employee—and vice versa.

The emotional needs of people bias their perceptions of communications (a concept explained in greater detail in the next chapter). What management intends to communicate and what is actually communicated may be quite different. One company, for example, attempted to show its appreciation to its employees and spent $16,000 in refurbishing the physical plant. Subsequent investigation indicated the following perceptions of management's motivation:

1. "They haven't painted this place in twenty years. I'll bet they're going to sell the company and then I'll be out of a job."
2. "They must have painted the building just to provide work for some employees. I'll bet layoffs are just around the corner and I'll be out of a job."
3. "They must have had some paint left over from the shop. I guess management is going to cut back on production, then I'll be out of a job."

What management failed to realize was that at the very time they were planning to paint the building, rumors were circulating in the plant that business was not good (a stockboy had observed a larger than normal inventory which was later explained by a short-term shipping strike), and every subsequent action of management was interpreted according to this bias.

One way of avoiding these problems is for management to consciously keep its "ear to the ground" and try to discover the feelings and fears that employees are experiencing. The stimulation of upward communication in organizations is another method of gathering data on how people feel. In the final analysis, management must be sensitive in its reading of employee behavior to determine the real motivation behind it.

## ☐ Organizational Change Considerations

Although the topic of managing change is the subject of a more detailed discussion in Chapter 14, the impact of change on the informal organization is potentially so great that it deserves special treatment here. Generally speaking, the discussion in this chapter has indicated that group structures and group processes are of paramount importance when implementing changes of any type in an organization. The social structure of groups is highly complex, and the smallest change in the external environment can disrupt established relationships. Since this can be psychologically disruptive, workers tend to resist many changes that are designed to "improve" their environment. The obvious way of overcoming this is to give ample consideration to the social structure and behavior patterns of the work group. This is not to say that good ideas should not be implemented just because the work group resists, but attempts should be made to minimize these disruptions if at all possible. If, however, management decides that a particular work group should be broken up, plans will have to be made for dealing with the problems that will undoubtedly arise.

When planning for change, knowledge of the informal organization can assist in developing new work systems. We have already commented on the informal organization's ability to improve existing practices, short-cut prescribed relationships, and perform tasks more efficiently than is allowed for in the formal system. These may be looked upon as built-in improvements and incorporated into formal systems, although this act itself may invalidate them as improvements. Still, the innate human ability to change the surroundings to suit individual and group needs offers some possibilities for organization change.

## □ Organizational Conflict Considerations

Although solutions to organizational conflict problems are dealt with in greater detail in Chapter 12, in this section we will present some specific methods for dealing with intergroup conflict caused by the hierarchical structure of organizations. Since hierarchical structures have many advantages, methods have been devised to overcome, or at least minimize, the competitive effects of the functionalized structure. Huse and Bowditch offer several suggestions that have proven effective:

1. Ensure that data for problem solving are generated in common.
2. Rotate people among different groups.
3. Recognize the interdependence of groups and establish methods to bring them into closer contact.
4. Locate a common enemy.
5. Develop a common set of goals and objectives.[32]

The sensitive reader will note that all of the above methods are means of reducing the separate group identities and making members of the group feel as though they have more in common than they have differences.

## □ The "Groupthink" Problem

One of the problems that can arise out of a cohesive work group is the phenomenon known as "groupthink."[33] It occurs in a group whose cohesiveness is such that it represses conflict and disagreement that could challenge the decisions of the group. Seeing groupthink as a problem recognizes that deviates, minority opinions, or unpopular views can serve a positive purpose in groups, since they cause the group to re-examine the problem and its alternatives. As noted in Chapter 12, conflict can be a creative force if managed properly, but the groupthink phenomenon prevents this from happening, since the conflict is never allowed to occur.

Irving Janis, who has done considerable research on the groupthink problem, notes several occasions in which groupthink caused poor decisions to be made because no one would speak out against the apparent consensus of the group.[34] For example, his research concluded that such disasters as The Bay of Pigs invasion, the U.S. invasion of North Korea, and the unpreparedness of Pearl Harbor were all due to groupthink. In each case, it was documented that members of the group were not in agreement with the decision, but failed to speak up for fear of being considered a nuisance or ostracized by the group. It was more pleasant for them to agree with the group than to be a dissident.[35]

To help guard against groupthink, Janis offers the following symptoms of the problem:

1. Group members rationalize any resistance encountered that challenges their assumptions about the problem. No matter how much evidence is presented, perceptual filters operate to either exclude or misinterpret the information.
2. Members of the group quickly apply pressure to anyone who appears to challenge the group's decision.
3. Members who do disagree with the consensus avoid disrupting the group by keeping silent about their opinions. In some cases, they may even question their own opinions as a method of rationalizing their role in the group.
4. There often appears to be the illusion of consensus. Even in a relatively large group, there may not be anyone who questions the decision. This silence is often mistaken for agreement.[36]

Applying these concepts to the jobs of managers, it would appear that a useful strategy would be to encourage disagreement when the groupthink phenonemon appears to occur. This might be accomplished by actually appointing an individual to serve as the deviate in case one does not arise by natural causes.

---

### Organizational Reality   11-3
### Avoiding Groupthink

In one of his training films, the famous management philosopher and historian Peter Drucker recounts a story of Alfred Sloan in his days as president of General Motors. A proposal came to the board of directors from one of the executives of the company. After a brief discussion of the proposal, it became obvious that everyone was in favor of it. Sloan asked if anyone had anything negative to say about it. No one did. At this point he said, "If everyone thinks this is a good idea, then something must be wrong. No idea is perfect." He then withdrew the item from the agenda.

A month later the same idea was proposed again and the board voted it down.

---

# ■ CONCLUSIONS

From a practical point of view, the existence of informal groups in organizations must be viewed with mixed emotions. While they can give considerable assistance to the organization (mostly because informal relationships provide for different satisfactions than can be derived from the formal organization), there is little doubt that the informal organization reduces the flexibility of management by placing some constraints upon decision making.

Given that the informal organization exists, managment really has no choice but to try to understand its processes and behaviors and attempt to integrate these into the formal organizational systems. Probably the most difficult part in this is the actual understanding of informal behavior. While observation is a useful tool, it is far from foolproof, and many managers and academicians have been misled by their own values and assumptions while observing others. Having been burned, they then shy away from trying again, only to sit back and curse the organization that is apparently working against them. This is unfortunate, since group influence may well be the most powerful force operating in an organization.

The informal structure is perhaps the best way to reach the difficult goal of maximizing both organizational and employee welfare. This single fact makes the subject of informal organization and work groups a critical area of study for all students and managers. Whatever insights the reader has gained from this chapter, we are certain that this knowledge will have to be sharpened by experience in working with informal groups.

## *Opening Incident Revisited—Dennis Calhoun*

To understand this situation properly, we have to look at it from the point of view of both parties—Dennis and the group.

It is tempting to blame the group and criticize them for being so cruel to a new employee. However, looked at from their point of view, what they are doing is an important activity. Clearly, their group has different objectives from the other group that Dennis represents. The other group—all the management trainees in the bank—come to the organization with different values, sentiments, job skills, and objectives. This means they are a threat to the norms of the college group.

To understand why the trainees are a threat, we must first try to understand what the objectives of the college group are. Since they are part-time college students, they probably place a high value on their wages and job security (for a given period of time). It would be reasonable to suppose that this group might attempt to maximize their earnings through various types of job behaviors that would not be totally accepted by the bank such as changing work procedures, and spreading work out for all group members. In addition, they have different backgrounds and life styles from Dennis' group. "Different" people are usually seen as a threat, which explains why this group is behaving the way it is toward

Dennis. The harassment is likely to continue until either Dennis conforms to their norms (which is unlikely, given the situation), or the group is convinced that Dennis is actually not a threat.

Dennis's concern is equally understandable. Through no particular fault of his own, he has violated the norms of this group. Because of the differences in his background factors, work experience, and career aspirations, there is likely to be no way he can become an accepted member of this group. In fact, should Dennis attempt to become a member, their suspicions would be aroused even more, because the behaviors accepted by this group are not typical of the management trainees. In other words, he might be seen as a spy for management!

Given this situation which has so many "givens" in it, Dennis's options are probably as follows:

1. Actually act as a spy, find out exactly how the group is working against management, inform management accordingly, and hope this makes him look good in the eyes of management. In so doing, he will pay a very heavy social cost (if you think what they're doing to him now is bad . . . !), but it might be worth it, depending upon how management views it.

2. Put up with the harassment for a while longer while trying to show the group that, even though he is a member of a different group, he is not a threat to them. This alternative may have the most promise since the initial harassment is a sort of "test" to see what Dennis will do. If he passes the test, they may let him alone after a while. (Recall that, as young children, there was little fun in picking on someone who didn't fight back.)

3. Retaliation is always a possibility. But Dennis would be at a significant disadvantage here since his own group is loose and members are geographically separated from one another, thus detracting from their cohesiveness. The group in the department, on the other hand, is quite cohesive. Therefore, retaliation may result in even worse treatment. On the other hand, it all depends upon the group's norms. Let us assume that one of the group's norms pertains to "horseplay." If Dennis responds with horseplay, then this may show that he is *capable* of behaving like a group member, which may reduce their antagonism toward him.

4. Compensate by trying to find group acceptance elsewhere. One of the reasons why Dennis is so upset is that he feels he is being ostracized and picked on—*and that he has no other group in which he is accepted.* If he were to seek out other management trainees and try to get closer to them, then at least he would have a group to identify with. They might possibly share stories of harassment and find solace in knowing that all the trainees experience the same thing. With such support Dennis would find the harassment much more bearable.

In any case, the correct approach will depend upon Dennis doing a proper analysis of this group (i.e., what their norms are, who is the informal group leader, etc.) and then planning his strategy accordingly. About the only thing that is concrete here is that Dennis will probably not be able to become a regular member of the college group, and his strategy will have to take that into consideration.

# ■ SUMMARY

This chapter has described the nature and behavior of small groups in the work place. It was noted that there are three types of groups in organizations: interacting, coacting, and counteracting. All groups will develop a social structure that consists of an informal leader, regular members, deviates, and isolates. To form a social structure, groups will progress through the stages of mutual acceptance, communication and decision making, motivaton and productivity, and control and organization. Groups in the final stage of development become cohesive. Cohesive groups can be an asset or liability to the organization, depending upon whether or not they identify with the organization's goals. One of the major factors that determines whether cohesive groups will benefit the organization is the type of leadership they receive. Two models were presented which can be used to analyze cause-and-effect relationships in small groups. Small-group theory can also be used to more effectively manage workflow problems, motivation problems, communication and change problems, and to deal with conflict between groups. The concept of "groupthink" can also be a problem in decision making and managers should be careful about developing this phenomenon in a cohesive work group.

# ■ REVIEW QUESTIONS

1. Why may the distinction between the individual approach and group approach to studying organizational behavior be important?

2. What are the differences between interacting, counteracting, and coacting groups?

3. What are the primary functions of group norms?

4. How is it possible for a group's production average to be above the group's production norms?

5. What are the major functions of the informal group leader?

6. How do deviates and isolates differ from regular members?

7. What are the stages of group development?

8. What are the ways group cohesiveness can be important in affecting productivity?

9. How is it possible for a cohesive group to be detrimental to the organization?

10. What are the limitations of intergroup competition in organizations?

11. How can the Homans model of small-group behavior be useful in organizations?

12. What are some ways the Bales system might be used?

13. What are some common organizational problems that could be better managed using small-group theory?

14. What are the problems associated with "groupthink"?

# ■ EXERCISE 11-1: JOHN BERKELY

John Berkely was a production worker at Universal Manufacturers, Inc., which made components and accessories for the automotive industry. He had worked at Universal for almost six years as a welder, along with twelve other men in the crew. All had received training in welding, both on the job and through external courses. The members of the work group got along very well with one another. There was a lot of kidding around, the usual baseball and football pools, and the group always ate together in the company cafeteria. Most of the fellows had been there for some length of time, except for two men who had been hired in the last two months.

Berkely was generally considered to be the informal leader of the group, so it was no surprise that when the foreman of their crew was transferred and his job was posted, Berkely applied for the job and got it. There were only three other applicants for the job, one from another department and two from the outside. When the appointment was announced on a Friday afternoon, everyone in the group congratulated Berkely, took him out to a bar, and bought him several beers to celebrate.

On Monday morning, Berkely came to work a foreman. It was company practice for all the foremen to wear blue work coats, a white shirt, and tie. Each man's coat had his name badge sewn onto the left-hand pocket. The company had supplied Berkely with his coat which he proudly wore to work on Monday.

Upon entering the work area, all the men crowded around "admiring" his new blue coat. There was a lot of kidding such as, "Hey, John, yer ole' lady go out and buy ya a new wardrobe?" or "Good grief! Mama's little boy got all dressed up to come work!" One of the guys went back to his locker and returned with a can of shoe polish and acted as though he were polishing Berkely's shoes. After about five minutes of horseplay, all of the men went back to work and Berkely went to his office to get more familiar with his new job.

At noon, all the men broke for lunch and went to the cafeteria to eat and talk as usual. Berkely was busy when they left but followed after them a few minutes later. As he came through the food line and paid the cashier, he turned to face the open cafeteria. Back in the far right-hand corner of the room was his old work group; on the left-hand side of the cafeteria sat all the other foremen in the plant, all dressed in their blue coats.

A hush fell over the cafeteria as both groups looked at Berkely, waiting to see which group he would eat with.

1. Whom do you think Berkely will eat with? Why?

2. If you were one of the other foremen, what could you do to make Berkely's transition easier?

3. What would you have done if you were in Berkely's shoes? Why?

# ■ EXERCISE 11-2: TO GROUP OR NOT TO GROUP

The Churchill Manufacturing Company produced several types of recreational products, such as small pleasure boats, campers, and related accessories. Most of the operations were divided into two activities—manufacturing the various component parts and assembling these parts into finished products. There were eight different assembly lines in the plant, which assembled the twenty-seven different products that Churchill produced. However, only eight different products could be produced at the same time. As seasonal demand for the various products changed, assembly lines were reconstituted and reorganized to produce the products needed. There tended to be little change in the staffing of these lines, since most of the work was of an assembly type and the skills were transferable among practically all products.

The general manager of Churchill had recently attended some production management seminars in which the speakers made frequent reference to the "Volvo concept." This concept referred to Volvo's move in one of its plants from an assembly-line operation to one designed around small work teams. Each of these teams was responsible for a significant portion of the final automobile (such as assembling an entire engine), and the groups were given considerable freedom to choose their own work methods and perform their own quality-control function. The work groups were also segregated from each other to increase the group feeling. The general manager was seriously considering implementing the "Volvo concept" in his plant.

1.   What factors should he consider in deciding whether or not the idea should be used?

2.   What problems would likely be encountered in implementing the "Volvo concept"?

# ■ ENDNOTES

1.   See the discussion in Chapter 15 on job enrichment for a more detailed explanation of these assumptions.
2.   For this thought we are indebted to our colleague, Professor G. A. Nuttall, who constantly reminds us of the importance of groups.
3.   Fred E. Fiedler, *A Theory of Leadership Effectiveness* (New York: McGraw-Hill, 1967), pp. 18–21.
4.   Robert R. Bales, *Personality and Interpersonal Behavior* (New York: Holt, Rinehart, & Winston, 1970).
5.   William G. Scott, *Organization Theory* (Homewood, Ill.: Richard D. Irwin, 1967), p. 93.
6.   Bernard Bass, *Organizational Psychology* (Boston: Allyn & Bacon, 1965), pp. 197–198.
7.   Stuart Adams, "Status Congruency As a Variable in Small Group Performance," *Social Forces* 32 (1953): 16–22.
8.   Ibid.
9.   H. Lasswell and A. Kaplan, *Power and Society: A Framework for Political Inquiry* (New Haven: Yale Univ. Press, 1950).
10.  L. Festinger and J. Thibault, "Interpersonal Communication in Small Groups," *Journal of Abnormal and Social Psychology* 46 (1951): 92–99.
11.  B. Lott, "Group Cohesiveness: A Learning Phenomenon," *Journal of Social Psychology* 55 (1961): 275–286.
12.  L. Festinger, "Laboratory Experiments: The Role of Group Belongingness," in *Experiments in Social Process*, ed. J. Miller (New York: McGraw-Hill, 1950), pp. 31–46.

13. J. Litterer, *The Analysis of Organizations* (New York: John Wiley & Sons, 1973), p. 219.

14. Ibid, p. 222.

15. Robert R. Blake and Jane S. Mouton, "Reactions to Intergroup Competition Under Win–Lose Conditions," *Management Science* 4 (July 1961).

16. Stanley Seashore, *Group Cohesiveness in the Industrial Work Group* (Ann Arbor: Survey Research Center, Univ. of Michigan, 1954).

17. A word of caution is in order here. In Chapter 5 we noted that project teams in matrix organizations are formed on the assumption that conflict can lead to more innovative and productive behavior. Yet, here we appear to be saying that conflict in a group can be nonproductive. The solution to this apparent dilemma lies in the type of conflict in question. Group cohesiveness is based largely upon interpersonal considerations, and any type of interpersonal conflict can be counter to group cohesiveness. Project groups, on the other hand, are oriented around task conflict, i.e., different types of people with a variety of ideas on task accomplishment. Particularly for professional people, this would not affect group cohesiveness, although interpersonal conflict still could.

18. J. Litterer, *The Analysis of Organizations*, p. 213.

19. R. H. Van Zelst, "Sociometrically Selected Work Teams Increase Productivity," *Personnel Psychology* 5 (1952): 175–185.

20. J. Litterer, *The Analysis of Organizations*, p. 216.

21. Stanley Schacter et al., "An Experimental Study of Cohesiveness and Productivity," *Human Relations* 4 (1951): 229–239.

22. Fred Luthans, *Organizational Behavior* (New York: McGraw-Hill, 1973), p. 448.

23. Janet Fulk Schriesheim, "The Social Context of Leader–Subordinate Relations: An Investigation of the Effects of Group Cohesiveness," *Journal of Applied Psychology*, 65, no. 2 (1980): 183–194.

24. Derived from the term "synergy," meaning the whole is greater than the sum of the individual parts. Therefore, four individuals working together can do more than the same four working independently.

25. See Chapter 12 for a discussion of the functions of conflict in organizations.

26. The list here is a compilation of principles generalized from the following sources: E. F. Huse and J. L. Bowditch, *Behavior in Organizations* (Reading, Mass.: Addison-Wesley, 1973); D. A. Kolb, I. M. Rubin, and J. McIntyre, *Organizational Psychology: An Experimental Approach*, 2nd ed (Englewood Cliffs, N. J.: Prentice-Hall, 1974); and J. G. March and H. A. Simon, *Organizations* (New York: John Wiley & Sons, 1958).

27. D. A. Kolb et al., *Organizational Psychology* pp. 257–275.

28. G. C. Homans, *The Human Group* (New York: Harcourt Brace & World, 1950).

29. R. F. Bales, "A Set of Categories for the Analysis of Small Group Interaction," *American Sociological Review* 15 (1950): 257–263.

30. William F. Whyte, *Human Relations in the Restaurant Industry* (New York: McGraw-Hill, 1948).

31. For an interesting account of this solution, see Elias H. Porter, "The Parable of the Spindle," *Harvard Business Review* 40 (May–June 1962): 58–66.

32. Huse and Bowditch, *Behavior in Organizations*, pp. 129–131.

33. Irving L. Janis, *Victims of Groupthink* (Boston: Houghton Mifflin, 1972).

34. Ibid.

35. Ibid.

36. Ibid.

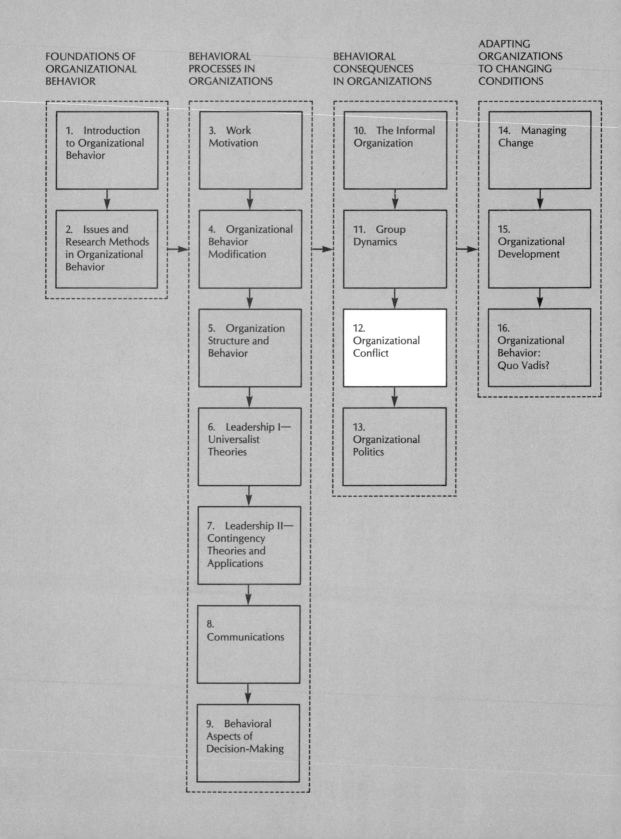

FOUNDATIONS OF
ORGANIZATIONAL
BEHAVIOR

BEHAVIORAL
PROCESSES IN
ORGANIZATIONS

BEHAVIORAL
CONSEQUENCES
IN ORGANIZATIONS

ADAPTING
ORGANIZATIONS
TO CHANGING
CONDITIONS

1. Introduction to Organizational Behavior

2. Issues and Research Methods in Organizational Behavior

3. Work Motivation

4. Organizational Behavior Modification

5. Organization Structure and Behavior

6. Leadership I—Universalist Theories

7. Leadership II—Contingency Theories and Applications

8. Communications

9. Behavioral Aspects of Decision-Making

10. The Informal Organization

11. Group Dynamics

12. Organizational Conflict

13. Organizational Politics

14. Managing Change

15. Organizational Development

16. Organizational Behavior: Quo Vadis?

# Organizational Conflict

## ■ Learning Objectives

After reading and studying the material in this chapter, you should be able to:

☐ Define the term *conflict* and distinguish it from the term *competition*.

☐ Describe how researchers' views of conflict have changed during the twentieth century.

☐ Discuss the alternative ways that conflict might be studied.

☐ Explain the conflict process, including the antecedents of conflict, behavior during conflict, and the consequences of conflict.

☐ Indicate the various ways that conflict can be managed to improve organizational effectiveness.

☐ Explain the nature of intergroup conflict in organizations and why it needs to be managed.

# Chapter 12

# ■ KEY TERMS

**Conflict**

**Competition**

**Intra-individual conflict**

**Inter-individual conflict**

**Individual–group conflict**

**Intergroup conflict**

**Conflict outcomes**

**Conflict management**

**Conflict stimulation**

**Conflict resolution**

**Forcing**

**Smoothing**

**Majority rule**

**Compromise**

**Consensus**

**Confrontation**

**Integration**

# ■ CHAPTER OUTLINE

I.  What Is Conflict?
   A.  The Definition of Conflict
   B.  The Difference Between Conflict and Competition
   C.  Perspectives in Conflict Analysis

II.  The Changing View of Conflict
   A.  The Traditional View
   B.  The Current View

III.  Sources of Conflict
   A.  Limited Resources
   B.  Interdependent Work Activities
   C.  Differentiation of Activities
   D.  Communication Problems
   E.  Differences in Perceptions
   F.  The Environment of the Organization
   G.  Other Sources of Conflict

IV.  A Conflict Model

## *Opening Incident—The Bridger Post Office*

The U.S. Post Office in Bridger, Ohio, employed fourteen people. The office had two main functions: (1) providing service to walk-in customers, and (2) delivering mail door-to-door. These two functions were carried out by clerks and mail carriers, respectively. The office also had a postmaster and an assistant postmaster.

There were six clerks in the post office. Their daily work included sorting incoming mail to the appropriate carrier routes, waiting on customers, sorting outgoing mail, and balancing the cash from their daily sales of money orders and stamps.

There were six mail routes in Bridger, each handled by one carrier. The carriers (all male) spent part of their day taking mail sorted to them by the clerks and sorting it into a "case" that contained the address of each stop on the route in the order that the route was walked. The remainder of the time was spent actually walking the route and delivering the mail.

The job requirements in the post office had resulted in noticeable differences between clerks and carriers. The carriers were physically separated from the clerks, and this sharpened the distinction. The social and work relations between the clerks and carriers were not good, and during the last few months had become particularly bad because the carriers claimed that the clerks were continually sorting mail to the wrong routes. When errors were found (mail sorted to the wrong carrier), the carriers stacked up the letters on their case until a pile of some height was evident. The carriers would then take this pile back to the sorting case, throw it down in front of the sorting clerk, and make some snide remark about the "poor quality of the help." Clerks made no secret of the fact that they did not like to sort mail to the carriers. Not only did they resent the verbal insults from the carriers when errors were found, they also felt the work of sorting was low-status. They much preferred waiting on customers and doing other office activities. The only retaliation clerks engaged in, however, was showing mock sympathy for carriers on cold or rainy days.

The problem reached crisis proportions one day when the sorting errors and the resulting disputes between clerks and carriers got so bad that the carriers were late getting started on their routes. As a result, they did not return at their normal time and had to be paid overtime. When the postmistress heard of this, she hit the ceiling and demanded to know what was going on.

Conflict between individuals and between groups is a universal phenomenon. A better understanding of the important areas of conflict will help managers to use the people in the organization more effectively to reach the organization's objectives. Failure to be concerned about conflict is very costly, since ignoring it will almost guarantee that work and interpersonal relations will deteriorate. If this occurs, employees will have little motivation to work together and organizational effectiveness will suffer.

We begin this chapter by defining *conflict* and differentiating it from *competition*. Several perspectives from which conflict can be analyzed are also examined. Second, the two views of conflict that have been expressed are discussed. Third, the potential sources of organizational conflict are examined. Fourth, a conflict model is developed which indicates how the potential sources of conflict lead to actual conflict and how this conflict may be functional or dysfunctional for the organization. Fifth, some techniques of conflict management are discussed. Finally, intergroup conflict is examined as it relates to the important organizational activity of setting budgets and allocating resources among groups.

## ■ WHAT IS CONFLICT?

One of the problems in organizational conflict is that the term has been defined in many different ways by academics and managers.[1] In addition, the definitions are often value-laden or too broad to be useful.[2] There are also problems in confusing conflict with other terms and failing to state whether conflict is being examined on the micro (individual) or macro (organization) level. These important issues are clarified in this section where we (1) define conflict, (2) show how it differs from competition, and (3) indicate the various perspectives from which we can analyze conflict.

### ☐ The Definition of Conflict

Conflict is behavior by a person or group that is purposely designed to inhibit the attainment of goals by another person or group. This "purposeful inhibition" may be active or passive. For example, in a sequential production line, if one group does not do its job and its output is the input for another department, the other department will be blocked from reaching its goal of, say, producing at standard. Alternatively, the blocking behavior may be active, as in the case of two fighters trying to knock each other out. The key issue in defining conflict is that of incompatible goals. When one person or group deliberately interferes with another person or group with the purpose of denying the other goal achievement, conflict exists.[3]

This blocking of someone else's goal achievement can take place in one of three ways, as indicated in Figure 12-1. Type I conflict (Figure 12-1a) exists when Unit *B* blocks Unit *A*'s attempts to get the resources *A* needs to meet its goals. For

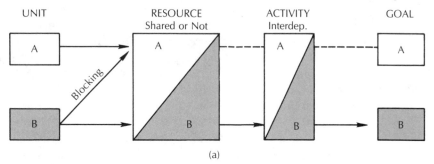

(a)

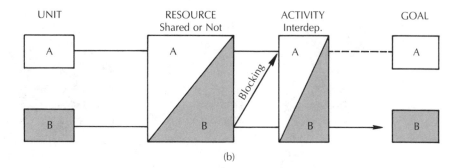

(b)

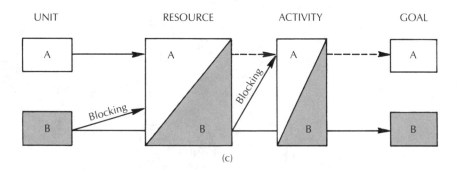

(c)

**FIGURE 12-1.  Three Types of Conflict**

Source: S. Schmidt and T. Kochan, "Conflict: Toward Conceptual Clarity," *Administrative Science Quarterly* 17 (1972): 364–365. Copyright 1972 by Cornell University. Used by permission.

example, in the annual budget process the marketing department (Unit *B*) may have a powerful representative on the board of directors who is able to get funds diverted to marketing and away from production (Unit *A*). This would allow Unit *B* to reach its goal of a certain sales level, but it may well block Unit *A* from reaching its goal of adequate production to meet demand (this is certainly irrational behavior from the organization's point of view, but this kind of thing happens all the time).

Type II conflict develops when the blocking behavior occurs at the activity stage instead of the resource-attainment stage (see Figure 12-1b). Here, Unit *B* blocks Unit *A* in *A*'s actual job activity. For example, if Unit *B* (a construction crew that pours foundations) does its job so poorly that Unit *A* cannot build on the foundation, conflict results. Here again, the conflict is undesirable from the organization's point of view.

Type III conflict occurs when Unit *B* interferes with Unit *A* at both the resource-attainment and activity stages (see Figure 12-1c). The example cited under Type I conflict could be expanded to include Unit *B* (marketing) interfering with Unit *A* (production) by demanding that production alter its schedule to accommodate a special order.

## Box 12-1: An Example of Activity Blocking

A department head in a large business school was receiving complaints from department secretaries that faculty members were often unreasonable in their requests for typing to be completed on short notice. The department head decided that the way to solve this problem was to establish a system of priorities for work. Accordingly, she instituted a system of green slips and pink slips. The department head sent out a memo to all faculty members explaining the system and informing them that the system would take effect immediately. When faculty members had typing to be done, they would fill out one of the slips (green for normal jobs, pink for rush jobs) and attach it to the job.

The faculty members simply ignored the system. They were able to do this largely because the secretaries continued to accept typing jobs that did not have green or pink slips attached.

In behaving this way, faculty members were passively blocking the department head's goal-achievement plans at the activity level. The department head initially responded to this defiance with strong efforts to make the system work, but when she saw that the secretaries didn't seem upset that the old system was continuing to operate, she quietly let the "slip system" fade away.

This incident demonstrates the concept of blocking behavior and also demonstrates the power of groups when they are in conflict with an individual, even if that individual is the boss.

## ☐ The Difference Between Conflict and Competition

The terms *conflict* and *competition* are often mistakenly used interchangeably. Perhaps the most widely accepted view at present is that competition takes place when individuals or groups have incompatible goals but do not interfere with each other as they both try to attain their respective goals. Conflict, on the other hand, occurs when individuals or groups have incompatible goals and they interfere with each other as they try to attain their respective goals. These definitions suggest that the key behavioral difference in conflict and competition is analogous to the behavioral differences evident in a race and a fight.[4] In the former, the goals are incompatible (only one runner can win), but the runners do not interfere with one another. In the latter, the goals are also incompatible (only one fighter can win), but interference is an obvious part of conflict.

Using these two definitions allows us to clearly categorize many of the familiar activities in our society. One of the things that becomes apparent immediately is that certain activities which are typically viewed as homogeneous must be further broken down. For example, certain sports (boxing, tennis, football, hockey, etc.) are characterized by obvious blocking behavior at the activity level (playing the game). There is also blocking behavior at the resource-attainment level.

In the past, the New York Yankees have been accused of "buying the pennant." In making this claim, other team owners are really arguing that they have been blocked at the resource attainment stage (they can't get good players), so their goal (winning the pennant) cannot be realized. Sports contests in which any of the three types of blocking behavior occurs are therefore conflict situations. Other sports, however, show little or no blocking at any level. Swimming,

---

### Box 12-2: Conflict and Competition in Sports

If we use the definitions of conflict and competition developed in this chapter, we see an interesting phenomenon when comparing "conflict" sports with "competition" sports. Football, boxing, baseball, hockey, and basketball are conflict sports where direct interference with the other team or individual is a key part of the sport. These are also the sports in which the participants are paid large sums of money. Other sports (such as swimming, track and field, weightlifting, speed skating, rowing, etc.) are competition sports where no interference is allowed. In these sports, participants make very little money. Why is this?

We can speculate that sports fans are willing to pay more to see conflict than to see competition. Much concern has been expressed over violence in sport, and lawsuits have been filed by players who have been injured during the course of a game. Yet the general public seems to like violence in sports. (Observe the behavior of fans at a hockey game when both benches are empty!) Although this doesn't speak too highly of people's behavior on these occasions, it is a fact that cannot be ignored.

horse racing, gymnastics, bowling, and others are classified as competition since blocking behavior is not part of the game.

The same kind of analysis holds if we analyze business activities. While the general public usually refers to what businesses do to each other in the market-place as competition, this is an oversimplification. At one extreme, business firms vigorously block one another's attempts to achieve goals, and this is conflict. For example, in an industry where consumer demand is low and industry production capacity is high, conflict is almost certain to result as each firm attempts to reach its goals at the expense of the other firms. Blocking activity in these cases often takes place at the activity level. A different situation exists in industries where government contracts are the rule. Here, competition is more likely. Each firm submits bids and strives to reach its goal of getting the contract. Blocking behavior is not evident, even though there can be only one winner and the goals of the firms are incompatible.[5]

## ☐ Perspectives in Conflict Analysis

We can analyze the effects of conflict from four different perspectives, beginning at the individual level and ending at the organization level. These four perspectives are discussed below.

**Intra-individual Conflict**   This refers to conflict within an individual about which work activities to perform. There may be internal conflict because (1) the individual does not feel that it is morally "right" to do a certain thing, (2) two different bosses are making contradictory demands, or (3) doing a certain job in a certain way will help the individual at the expense of his or her coworkers.[6] Analyzing this type of conflict is difficult because "inner states" of the individual must be assessed.[7]

**Inter-individual Conflict**   This refers to conflict between two individuals and is the subject of much research in psychology. Research on this type of conflict (e.g., marriage counseling) often focuses on personality differences and *why* individuals feel obliged to block the goal attainment of the other person. Within organizations, it appears that tendencies toward inter-individual conflict are exaggerated by the environment of the job. For example, if a person who places a great deal of emphasis on "doing his own thing" is subordinate to a rigid, conservative boss, it is likely that some sort of inter-individual conflict will develop.

**Individual-Group Conflict**   In organizations, there are two important situations where individuals find themselves in conflict with groups. The first situation is one in which an individual is violating group norms. This problem was examined in Chapters 10 and 11 where it was noted that groups have a powerful influence on individuals. The reason for this conflict is that groups have a greater ability to block an individual's goal achievement than the other way around. Only in unusual cases will an individual be able to mobilize the resources to block the group's movement toward its goals. This is clearly seen when groups force indi-viduals producing above the group norm to reduce their output. The group does this by threatening to block the attainment of the individual's psychic goals (the desire to belong) and physical goals (the desire to stay healthy!).

The second case of individual-group conflict is one in which subordinates of one boss collectively disagree with a course of action the boss wants to take. A conflict exists here because the subordinates are blocking the goal achievement plans of the boss (the desire to run an effective department, for example).

---

## *Box 12-3: Is Competition Good or Bad?*

Generally speaking, competition is good if the following conditions are met:

1. *The competitors are from different organizations.* A good example of this is athletic competitions. If thirty golfers compete in a match, they are better off because people like to see who wins and will pay for the privilege of watching. Who would pay to watch them collaborate?
2. *Each party to the competition has a relatively equal chance of winning.* No one wants to enter a competition in which he or she feels doomed before starting. Motivation is low in such situations. If a company conducts a sales contest but most of the salesmen feel that Johnny Gladhand, the "superstar salesman," is almost certain to win, the contest will have little effect on the behavior of the other salesmen.
3. *Each party must see winning as a rewarding experience.* Although a company president may be able to develop the skills necessary to mop the floors better and faster than the janitor, there would be little incentive to compete because the president's skills are better used elsewhere.
4. *Competing parties must not subsequently be required to collaborate.* Competition always creates losers, and losers are not too keen on helping out the winners later on. Therefore, while the competition may serve as an incentive in one situation, it may be at an extremely high price to be paid later because there is no desire for cooperation and collaboration.

The modern view is that competition is basically healthy but that its focus needs to be changed in most organizations. For example, we now recognize that "win-win" competition (i.e., those situations in which both parties can have what they want) are usually better than "win-lose" competitions (i.e., those situations in which one party gets what it wants at the expense of the other party). A sales contest in which anyone who sells over a certain quota receives a bonus can be better than one in which only one person can win.

Some organizations inadvertently create competition under the guise of trying to reward their employees. For example, a salary-increase pool allocated to a given department can actually detract from productivity, since members will be reluctant to help others for fear that it might cost them part of their salary increase. This would be particularly dysfunctional if the productivity of the unit heavily depends upon intermember cooperation.

Although the boss can exercise formal authority to suppress this type of conflict, this is generally an unwise course, since subordinates often find a way to retaliate.

**Intergroup Conflict**   This involves conflict between groups of people, irrespective of the size of the group. Included in this category, therefore, is interdepartmental conflict *within* organizations and conflict *between* organizations. Specific examples of intergroup conflict are labor–management conflict, United Nations debates, wars, marketplace conflict by firms attempting to outsell each other, conflict between departments in a firm as each fights for a bigger share of the organization's budget, and so on. This perspective on conflict has been widely researched, and it will be the focus of discussion in several places in this chapter.

# ■ THE CHANGING VIEW OF CONFLICT

If we look back over this century, it becomes obvious that assumptions about whether conflict is good or bad for organizations have changed substantially. There are two distinct phases of thinking about conflict: the traditional view and the current view.

## ☐ The Traditional View

This view of conflict, which was popular until the early 1940s, assumed that conflict was bad for organizations. In the view of the traditionalists, organizational conflict was proof that there was something "wrong" with the organization. The Hawthorne studies (discussed in Chapter 1) were probably important in shaping the traditional view because in those studies the dysfunctional consequences of conflict were noted. Another likely factor in the traditional view was the development of labor unions and the often violent conflict between labor and management. During the early twentieth century labor unions were struggling for the legal right to bargain collectively. It was not until the 1930s that this goal was reached. Along the way, many confrontations occurred between labor and management. These were almost always viewed as bad for both the organization and the individual, and it is therefore not surprising that the traditionalists viewed conflict as undesirable. Overall, the traditional view assumed that organizational performance declined steadily as conflict increased (see Figure 12-2).

Because conflict was viewed as bad, considerable attention was given to reducing or eliminating it. Perhaps the most general reaction was to suppress it. This was done in an obvious way by simply demanding that people in conflicting situations change their behavior for the good of the company. It was also done indirectly by rigidly prescribing the limits of authority of each job so that individuals would be less likely to be in conflict. While these tactics sometimes worked, they were largely ineffective because (1) they did not get at the exact cause of the conflict and (2) suppressing the conflict did not allow any of the positive aspects of conflict to come out.

The traditional view of conflict appears to be losing ground as time passes, yet it still describes the views of many people. Why should this view be so wide-

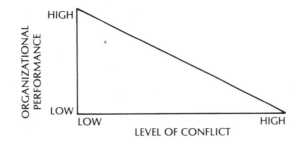

**FIGURE 12-2.   The Traditional View of Conflict**

spread, given that some conflict has been shown to be beneficial? One researcher answers this question by saying that the important institutions in our society—the home, church, and school—are founded on the traditional view of conflict, and these institutions have a powerful influence on society.[8] Since these institutions are very influential when we are young, we are subtly influenced to have a particular view of conflict. In the home, for example, parents suppress conflict by telling their children to stop fighting. In schools, teachers are assumed to have the correct answers, and exams are a check to see whether students are deviating from these. Most churches stress brotherhood and peace, not conflict. If this argument is correct, the change in the view of conflict from traditional to current will take many years.

## ☐  The Current View

The view which prevails among researchers at present (and is gaining ground in the rest of society) is that organizational conflict is neither good nor bad per se, but is inevitable. Thus, conflict will occur even if organizations have taken great pains to prevent it. This situation is similar to that for the informal organization discussed in Chapter 10, where it was noted that the informal organization will emerge and be active irrespective of management's attempts to suppress it. Thus, organizations will experience conflict even if they have carefully defined employee jobs and their managers are reasonable people who treat employees well. (The reasons for this are discussed later in this chapter.) There are even some instances in which conflict is purposely created, such as the project management structure discussed in Chapter 5.

The current view of conflict is shown in Figure 12-3. When the amount of conflict (low to high) is related to organizational performance (low to high), we see that there is an optimum level of conflict which maximizes organizational performance. This optimum level is neither low nor high. The argument is as follows: In an organization where there is too little conflict, little impetus for innovation and creativity exists. Employees are comfortable and not concerned about improving performance. As a result, things which might improve performance get very little attention. At the other extreme, organizational conflict is so disruptive that employees cannot give proper attention to performance goals because interpersonal or intergroup conflict saps employee energy. Here again, performance suffers. At moderate levels of conflict, however, employees are

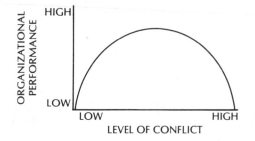

**FIGURE 12-3.   The Current View of Conflict**

motivated to resolve conflicts, but these conflicts do not disrupt the normal work activities.

There are two important implications of the current view. First, much of the conflict in organizations may be good because it stimulates people to find new ways of doing things. If two employees are in conflict about the best way to do a job, the manager might be advised to encourage the conflict to see which individual is correct. The best technique can then be used in doing the job in the future. (This approach should be used sparingly because it usually results in a winner and a loser and this has implications for the organization.) As another example, consider two departments that are in conflict. Each department tries to get its own way and engages in whatever blocking behavior it feels is necessary to prevent the other department from attaining its goals. Top management may see this as dysfunctional; but instead of trying to suppress the conflict (the traditional

---

### *Organizational Reality*   12-1
### *A Consultant's View of Conflict*

Part and parcel of any organization is the presence of conflict. Kenneth Sole, president of Kenneth Sole and Associates, a training and consulting firm, believes that since conflict is inevitable, his task is to reduce its adverse impact on corporations.

Sole says every conflict can be turned into a positive or negative situation, depending upon the attitudes participants bring to it. The worst mistake is to suppress conflict once it has been perceived. Sole says if people were better able to allow conflict to surface naturally, there would be more battles, but less costly ones.

Sole argues that it is better to react initially than to let trouble brew over time. By suppressing conflict, misattribution may arise and the conflict is taken out on innocent bystanders.

Talking around the issue is another problem resulting from suppressed conflict. Sole says this situation damages the people and the organization until someone realizes it rests on one basic conflict.

---

Source: *Management Review* (January 1982): 5.

approach), management might try to induce the departments to find a solution which allows each to get what they want.

Second, *management* of conflict, not suppression, becomes a key activity. If we assume that conflict can be good or bad, it is important that constructive conflict be encouraged and destructive conflict be resolved. But what criterion should we use to make this decision? Robbins suggests that the most practical and important criterion is group performance.[9] Organizations exist to achieve goals, and high performance by groups in the organization increases the likelihood that organizational goals will be reached. Thus, if the criterion of group performance is used, managers must view conflict in terms of its effect on group performance before they move to resolve it or encourage it. Specific methods for encouraging and discouraging conflict are discussed later in the chapter.

# ■ SOURCES OF CONFLICT

There are numerous sources of conflict within formal organizations. Those discussed below have been analyzed extensively by researchers and are instrumental in determining how much conflict there will be.[10]

## ☐ Limited Resources

Perhaps the most fundamental fact of organizational life is that resources are finite. Even the most successful companies have found that they are limited in what they can accomplish.[11] With this realization groups and individuals see that there will be times when they will have to fight for what they want. The most obvious manifestation of this problem comes when the annual budget is set. Each department typically submits a request for its needs during the next fiscal year, and top management adjusts the request based on its knowledge of the total organization. Department heads often see their requests cut back because the resources for the total organization are limited. When cutbacks occur, however, the potential for conflict increases because the heads of various departments begin making value judgments about why management decided to cut back one department but not another. As a general rule, *the greater the scarcity of resources, the greater the potential for conflict.*

## ☐ Interdependent Work Activities

Added to the basic problem of finite resources is the problem of organizational units having to work together. It is bad enough to get less than you wanted for your department because of some other department, but then to have to work with the other department may be more than some managers can take. Suppose you are the head of department *A*, and in the yearly budget just approved by top management, you received considerably less money for operations than you thought was minimally necessary to run your department. Suppose also that you see that department *B* got most of what it asked for. If the work activities of your department are interdependent with those of department *B*, you might well consider purposely slowing down your department's work in an attempt to convince top management that they made a mistake in their allocation of funds.

This is a particularly salient cause of conflict because there is so much interdependence of work activities in organizations. On a grander scale, interorganizational conflict is often caused because the activities of many separate organizations must be coordinated. In May 1979, California motorists found themselves in long lines waiting for gasoline. The oil companies, the oil producers, consumer groups, and the government spent considerable time arguing about who was to blame. The problem was most likely caused by the tight interdependence of work activities needed to get oil from the wellhead to the consumer. Any purposeful disruption by one of the organizations in the system (e.g., the Iranian government's decision to reduce output) would cause conflict among the other parties in the system. As a general rule, *the more interdependent the work activities, the greater the potential for conflict.*[12]

It is important for managements to know the nature of work interdependence so systems of work can be implemented that will reduce the potential for dysfunctional conflict.

## ☐ Differentiation of Activities

We noted above that interdependence of work activities is an important source of conflict in organizations. Backing up one step further, we can see that the mere *existence* of groups doing different functions creates the potential for conflict. As groups become familiar with how they perform their own jobs, they may turn inward and become uninterested in (1) how their work fits in with other groups or (2) the importance of other groups' work. As a result, when difficult issues between the groups must be dealt with, each group behaves in a way that increases the potential for harmful conflict.

This differentiation in work activities leads to differentiation in goals. Production's goals may be to have long production runs with few changes in product styles, because this allows the production facilities to operate at peak efficiency. Marketing's goal, on the other hand, may be to give customers what they want when they want it. This means rush orders, special orders, and other demands that directly conflict with production's goals.

## ☐ Communication Problems

Both the interdependence and differentiation of work activities demand that communication between individuals and groups be effective. As we saw in Chapter 8, however, this often does not occur. At the broadest level, communication problems develop because not all groups have the same information. Each group therefore takes a position based on its view of the world and the information it has. The obvious solution to this problem is to give all groups equal information. However, this is generally not feasible because individuals with important information may want to use it for their own advantage and not share it.

Communication problems are also caused by technical jargon that is so frequently used in organizations. Over time, each group develops its own language,

---

### *Organizational Reality  12-2*
### *Conflict at Rath Packing*

Since 1979, Rath Packing Co. in Waterloo, Iowa, has been kept alive by its 2500 workers who have granted contract concessions and spent $1500 each to buy 60 percent of Rath's common stock. But the depression in the meat-packing industry is pushing the company toward insolvency, prompting management to demand an 18 percent cut in wages and benefits. The United Food & Commercial Workers (UFCW) is resisting, setting the stage for an unusual showdown between the workers and the company they own.

Rath illustrates the problems facing companies that are handed over to Employee Stock Ownership Plans (ESOPs). Most of the 5000 ESOPs in the U.S. were set up to let companies use tax breaks available under federal law, but they gave workers little voice in management. However, employees elect 60 percent of Rath's board and the dual role required of union officials on the board in such cases presents problems.

Local UFCW officials at Rath want to keep the firm viable, but also want to make as few concessions as possible, and are under pressure from the international union to avoid undercutting agreements made with companies that are not worker-owned. Many Rath workers say they would accept a sizeable wage cut. The UFCW is offering to give Rath the same three-year wage freeze that it recently gave major meat packers. For the moment at least, Local 46's president, although a director of Rath, backs this demand. To the UFCW, the question is whether even major concessions would save the firm.

---

Source: "An Acid Test for Worker–Owners," *Business Week* (2 August 1982): 67–70.

---

which may mean nothing to another group. When the two groups must deal with a contentious issue, the "us vs. them" mentality more easily develops because of the meanings each group attaches to words.

## ☐  Differences in Perceptions

We all "see" the world slightly differently because we have all had different experiences. These different views of the world can be a major source of conflict in organizations because value judgments flow from these views. One of the classic differences in perception involves the value of experience vs. the value of education (this was discussed in Chapter 1). Older, more experienced managers often are in conflict with younger, inexperienced managers about the way in which work should be done. The experienced person usually points out how knowledgeable he or she has become over the years, whereas the inexperienced person argues for "new ways" of doing things. Often this conflict is resolved by the older person exercising his or her authority.

It is hard to make unequivocal statements about how differences in perception will influence conflict. It is also difficult to deduce exactly how a person views the world, unless the person is well-known to the manager. Nevertheless, a realization that differences in perception (by groups or individuals) is crucial to conflict means that it must be included in any discussion of the sources of conflict.

### ☐   The Environment of the Organization

Thus far we have been concerned with factors inside organizations that cause conflict. However, changes in the firm's environment (which it usually has no control over) can cause major conflict within the organization. In the 1970s, for example, college enrollment in liberal arts declined as students began entering disciplines that were more job-oriented. This shift in demand meant that there were pressures to reallocate resources within universities. These pressures caused real problems as the different faculties were in conflict as to how this reallocation should be done. As another example, consider a conglomerate that finds that the demand for the output of one of its divisions is rapidly declining. The obvious thing to do is to cut back activities in that division and channel corporate resources into more profitable divisions. However, if the division having difficulties is an important one and its head is a powerful person, tremendous conflict may develop as other division heads argue for a redistribution of resources within the company.

### ☐   Other Sources of Conflict

Numerous other sources of conflict exist in organizations. They include (1) individual differences (some people enjoy conflict while others don't); (2) unclear authority structures (conflict develops because people don't know how far their authority extends); (3) differences in attitudes (members of different groups have different attitudes); (4) task asymmetries[13] (one group is more powerful than another and the weaker group tries to change the situation); and (5) differences in time horizons[14] (some departments have a long-run view and others a short-run view).

## ■   A CONFLICT MODEL

The model in Figure 12-4 indicates the three important dimensions of conflict: sources (antecedents) of conflict, the actual conflict behavior, and the outcomes of the conflict.[15] The sources of conflict (Box 1) were discussed in the preceding section. They do not always lead to perceived goal incompatibility (Box 2), but when they do, the likelihood for open conflict (Box 4) increases. Before that can happen, however, at least one of the parties must see that there is an opportunity to interfere with the other party (Box 3). If there is no opportunity to interfere, no conflict can take place. Once the conflict is out in the open, any one of several conflict resolution techniques (Box 5) can be used. These techniques are discussed later in the chapter. How the conflict-resolution techniques are used influences whether the conflict will be resolved in a functional or dysfunctional way (Boxes 6 and 7, respectively). The resolution leads either to immediate further conflict (because the resolution is ineffective) or to a change in the sources of conflict or

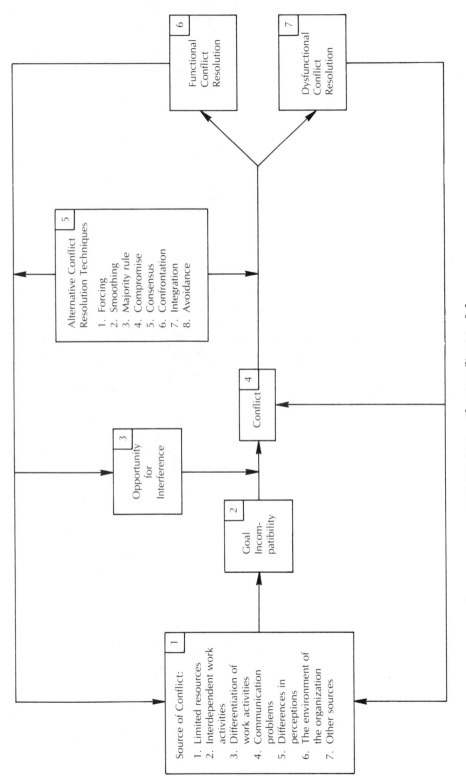

**FIGURE 12-4. The Conflict Model**

perceived opportunity for interference. For example, if the resolution of an inter-group conflict is that the groups are physically separated, the opportunity for interference is altered. Or if the cause of the conflict centers on interdependent work activities and this problem is resolved by consensus decision making, one source of conflict is changed.

The key point in this model is that actual conflict is not an isolated event. It is caused by certain recognizable factors and its resolution is either functional or dysfunctional. The resolution has implications for further conflict in the future.

# ■ CONFLICT OUTCOMES

Earlier in the chapter we argued that conflict can be good or bad. We now should consider the specific positive and negative outcomes that conflict can cause.

## ☐ Positive Outcomes

The positive outcomes of conflict are as follows (Box 6 in Figure 12-4):

1. *The energy level of groups or individuals increases with conflict.* This increased energy level can be seen when people talk louder, listen more closely to what is being said, or work harder. Two of the benefits organizations get from increased energy levels are increased output and innovative ideas for doing the work better.[16]

2. *Group cohesion increases.* Research has shown that, when groups are engaged in a conflict, their internal cohesion increases.[17] The other group is seen as the "enemy," and group resources are mobilized to meet the threat from the "outside." To do this, disagreements within the group must be suppressed and all energies diverted toward the enemy. This process can be seen in the Mideast. Arab nations have trouble getting along with one another except when a common threat (Israel) dominates their relationship. The reason that increased cohesion is considered a positive outcome of conflict is that highly cohesive groups can have high productivity, particularly if they support management's goals.

3. *Problems are made known during conflict.* When conflict develops, management can readily see that something is amiss and can embark on a program to resolve the conflict. If two groups are in disagreement about something but never make it known, they may work at a reduced level of effectiveness without management's being able to determine why. This is particularly likely to happen if the problem between the groups is caused by some system of work that management has set up. Group members may be reluctant to criticize management about the system, and the conflict will not be made known.

4. *Conflict motivates groups to clarify their objectives, and this increases the group's awareness of its purpose.* Groups are quite often apathetic about their particular function until an external threat emerges. When a threat becomes evident, group members begin thinking seriously about the purpose of their group. This type of analysis can lead to better ways of doing things, making the

group more effective. In an organization where two groups are having a conflict, if each group is motivated to think about its objectives, the organization as a whole may benefit. On a day-to-day basis, it may also be easier for management to deal with conflicting groups because the conflict has caused a coherence and stability to emerge in the groups. Conflict may also promote a more efficient division of labor.

5. *Conflict encourages groups to protect values they think are important.* Various groups see themselves as the "protector" of certain values. For example, both "pro-choice" and "pro-life" groups vigorously defend certain values concerning family-size management. Right-wing political groups defend one set of values, and left-wing groups defend another. Within a specific organization, marketing people may stress high quality while production people may stress low unit cost. Although these values are somewhat contradictory, the attempt to resolve a conflict like this might result in a solution that will benefit the entire organization.

6. *Individuals or groups are motivated to mobilize information that is relevant to the conflict.* Although this information is biased by the subjective perceptions of the parties involved in the conflict, additional information is usually developed that can be helpful in resolving the problem. If no conflict exists, there may be no motivation to gather additional information or to look for better ways of doing a job.

7. *Conflict can increase an organization's overall effectiveness because it forces groups or individuals to adapt to the changing external environment that the organization faces.* Conflict serves to point out that the environment is constantly changing, and the organization may have to change the way it does certain things if it is going to adapt to this environment. As we shall see in the next chapter, much conflict is politically motivated, as individuals attempt to get a larger share of the organization's resources for themselves. It is not surprising that conflict occurs in this circumstance; we cannot expect people to simply accept a reduction in the resources they have historically received. The outcome of this type of conflict is, however, an organization that is more capable of coping with rapid change in its environment.

## ☐ Negative Outcomes

The negative outcomes of conflict (Box 7 in Figure 12-4) are as follows:

1. *A decline in communication between the conflicting parties.* When individuals or groups are upset with each other, a common development is that they stop speaking. As we have seen, this is very dysfunctional because conflict is often worsened when there is little information passing between the conflicting parties.

2. *Hostility and aggression development.* It is a typical human reaction to feel hostility toward someone who is blocking one's attempts to reach a goal. Aggression (either physical or verbal) is also a common behavior associated with hostility. While this may satisfy the person's urges to attack the person doing the blocking, from the organization's point of view it is undesirable

because it channels behavior into nonproductive areas. For example, if two groups are in conflict about something, they may spend much of the work day devising schemes to block the other group's goal attainment. Obviously a point is reached where the work of each group is not accomplished.

3. *Overconformity to group demands.* We noted above that conflict could cause groups to become more cohesive and this might result in higher productivity. We must also recognize that members of a group faced with an outside threat may *overconform* to the group demands. This involves blind acceptance of the leaders' interpretation of the opposing group and no thinking about solutions by anyone in the group. This prolongs the conflict and makes it more intense. As time passes, the group is unable to view its opposition with any objectivity and perceptions become very distorted.

---

## Organizational Reality    12-3
## Reducing the Cost of Conflict

More and more business executives are concluding that civil disputes have become too complex and expensive to be left to lawyers alone. Former IBM chairman Frank T. Cary is said to have remarked "My lawyers have an unlimited budget, and every year they exceed it." In response, a quiet revolution in the way corporations handle lawsuits has recently been unfolding. Disputes are being managed rather than instantly litigated.

"The search for alternatives has sprung from delay and frustration with conventional arbitration" says Washington lawyer Homer E. Moyer, "and a desire to build strategies and methods of reducing the high cost of litigation." The search has led to so-called "alternative dispute resolution" (ADR) involving a host of foundations and other bodies, including the Center for Public Resources Inc., the Association of Corporate Counsel of America, and the newly created National Institute for Dispute Resolution.

One of the most talked-about ADR methods is the minitrial, pioneered by TRW, Inc. and Telecredit Inc. in the late 1970s. Although it has no fixed form, the underlying theory is that the parties can settle the case themselves if business executives high enough are forced to consider the merits of their opponents' cases. To educate them, the lawyers present an abbreviated version of their case during only one or two days. In some versions a neutral third party is present. In all cases senior executives can play judge and juror, asking questions of the lawyers and cross-examining any witnesses.

The minitrial is only one of many techniques. Others range from loose negotiation to trial by reference (essentially a formal trial by private judges). Many cases in which facts are hotly disputed or where the legal precedent or principle is fundamental to a company's future will continue to go to litigation. However, corporations are becoming more sophisticated and aware of the cost effectiveness of alternative methods of resolving disputes.

---

Source: "Managing Company Lawsuits to Stay Out of Court," *Business Week* (23 August 1982): 54–65.

An examination of the positive and negative outcomes associated with conflict reveals that obviously, both good and bad things can happen. On balance, what can we say about conflict? The most general statement is this: At low levels of conflict there is little incentive for individuals or groups in an organization to perform well. At high levels of conflict, there is too much incentive and people experience anxiety, fear, and reduced performance. But at moderate levels of conflict, the increased incentive to perform causes the positive outcomes of conflict to outweigh the negative outcomes.

As we saw in Figure 12-3, there is an optimum level of conflict that results in maximum organizational performance. Thus, if a manager observes that organizational performance is not up to standard, it could be that conflict levels are either too high or too low. The material in the following section addresses this very practical issue of what a manager can do to insure that the level of conflict is maintained at a level where organizational performance is maximized.

# ■ CONFLICT MANAGEMENT

If we accept the argument that conflict can have either positive or negative effects on organizations, then it follows that managers have considerable flexibility in dealing with conflict. While there are many specific techniques for managing conflict, there are only two broad approaches: (1) stimulate the conflict or (2) resolve it.[18] The specific techniques that can be used in each of these cases are discussed below.

## ☐ Conflict Stimulation

If groups or individuals in an organization are too set in their ways or too willing to accept unquestioningly the views of a powerful individual, management may benefit from stimulating conflict among them. The fact that groups and individuals may come up with inferior decisions because there is too little disagreement has been demonstrated on many occasions. In fact, one of the major reasons for antitrust legislation is that the government assumes consumers will be better off if vigorous competition and conflict exist among firms supplying consumer goods. Without this conflict, the impetus for new product development and technological breakthroughs would be very low.

One laboratory experiment demonstrates this point very clearly.[19] Groups were formed to solve a problem. As in the typical experiment, there were experimental and control groups. The experimental group had a "planted" member whose job it was to challenge the majority view; the control groups had no such member. In all cases, the experimental groups came up with better solutions to the problem than did the control groups.[20]

What can management do to stimulate conflict? First, it can openly state that it feels conflict to be desirable on certain occasions.[21] For example, departments managed by individuals who are feared by their subordinates may benefit considerably if conflict with the boss is encouraged when a new department head takes over. Although the goals of the boss may be blocked in the process, if these goals were not reasonable or functional in the first place, the organization will be better off. The same thing is possible on the interdepartmental level. If the sales department succeeds in blocking the production department's goal of smooth production scheduling and in the process better serves the consumer, the firm will probably be better off than if strictly internal considerations (like scheduling) had dictated the decision.

Second, new individuals can be brought into the existing situation. These individuals may know little or nothing about the problems and opportunities facing the organization, but their thoughtful questions and comments may force the long-time members to see new ways of doing things. This is readily seen when "outside" members are asked to join the boards of directors of certain firms. These outsiders may severely question accepted industry practices. In the process, long-time board members may get very upset with challenges to the normal way of doing things, but in the end new approaches often result.

Third, the organization can be restructured. When this is done, new reporting relationships develop, and during this development enough uncertainty usually exists that conflict arises. As this conflict is worked out, better ways are sometimes found to do the important tasks of the organization.

Finally, management can implement programs that are specifically designed to induce conflict or competition. The most obvious example of this is sales contests where the winner receives a substantial prize. In many cases these contests are simply competition and not true conflict (salesmen do not interfere with one another), but in others (e.g., selling cars), dealers are in conflict with one another as they each try to reach the goal. Blocking behavior such as advertising and price dealing is necessary because the dealers know that there is a limit on the number of cars that can be sold in a given time period.

## ☐  Conflict Resolution

A variety of conflict-resolution techniques have been used in conflict situations. We will discuss only those that seem to have gained fairly wide acceptance.[22]

**Forcing**    If two workers are in conflict and the boss says, "You two stop arguing; *I* will decide which course of action is reasonable," the two workers can no longer disagree about the issue. The manager has "forced" a resolution of the conflict. Obviously, this method leads to quick resolution, but the aftermath of the conflict may be very negative. The one who loses (i.e., the boss agrees with the other's argument) will often try to get revenge for the incident. This behavior may involve refusal to help out the fellow worker or trying to make the boss look bad.

**Smoothing**    As the term suggests, this conflict-resolution technique involves considerable use of tact by the party doing the smoothing. Smoothing can be an effective strategy in many instances. A manager who is confronted by employees who are in disagreement may find that they are in conflict simply because of a lack of information. Once the manager supplies the relevant information, the conflict may disappear. Suppose that worker *A* and worker *B* are having a dispute

---

### *Organizational Reality   12-4*
### *Reducing Conflict at Iron Ore Company Ltd.*

Almost from its founding in 1949, Iron Ore Company, Ltd. (Canada) was at war with its workers. Len Leyte, former president of Steelworkers Local 5795 in Labrador City, recalls that top managers told the supervisors not to associate with the hourly paid people. That bred contempt from the top of the company to the bottom. The company had endured three major strikes and fifty-two separate work stoppages from 1949 to 1979. Under its new president, Brian Mulroney, there has not been a single work stoppage related to a labor–management disagreement. How was this achieved?

The company devised a formal communications program with outside help: thank you notes from supervisors, informational brochures, plant tours for employees' families, and ads in local papers backpatting employee community involvement, were all used. But these tactics would have been worthless if they had not been accompanied by substantive changes in policy, and by the changes in attitude Mulroney tried to instill. Human relations committees (separate from the bargaining committees) were established, and brown-bag programs were instituted where the "ordinary" worker had lunch with the superintendent and foreman. Mulroney fought to discourage the dictatorial style that was at the root of much employee frustration, and got serious about industrial safety.

Although not all union leaders are enchanted with Mulroney's regime, profits have improved dramatically—much beyond competitors'. The major difference, Mulroney says, is that IOC's management discovered that in the 1980s, no one works *for* you anymore. They with work *with* you or they don't work at all.

---

Source: "Brian Mulroney and the Iron Ore Co.," *Canadian Business* (September 1982): 55–57; 144–151.

---

about work procedures. Worker *A* argues that *B* should change the way *B* does a particular task so that *A*'s work will be easier. Worker *B* says that the method can't be changed because that is the way *B* was told to do it by the foreman. If the foreman simply tells *A* and *B* why *B*'s job has to be done in a certain way, the conflict is more likely to be easily resolved.

Smoothing is usually an ineffective resolution technique if the employees think that there is an unreasonable rationale for the decision (e.g., favoritism). In the example above, if the foreman resolves the conflict in favor of worker *B* and *A* thinks this is only because the foreman likes *B*, worker *A* is hardly going to be happy with the decision. On balance, smoothing works most effectively when the parties in conflict are not aware of important information relevant to the conflict. Individuals who have this information and can bring it to the attention of the conflicting parties can often resolve the conflict.

**Majority Rule**   Many disputes which drag on for a long time tempt participants to resolve them by a simple vote. For example, in committees discussing a contro-versial point where there are reasonable arguments on both sides, we often hear the sentiment, "We've heard enough talk on this issue—let's vote!" (This sentiment is usually expressed by those who feel they have the votes to win!) Although voting and majority rule are important in our democratic society, research has shown that a quick vote on issues usually suppresses thoughtful consideration.

The other problem with majority rule (in the minority's eyes) is that one group always wins and another group always loses. The losing side hardly feels that the voting system is fair, hence they will agitate for changes that favor them. In many companies, for example, one department of the business usually has more status than another. People who work in the lower-status department get fed up over a period of years as they see resources going to the higher-status department when the rational thing to do (from their viewpoint) would be to shift the resource allocation to a more equitable basis.

**Compromise**   Perhaps the most widely used of all techniques, compromise involves giving each of the parties in the conflict *some* of what they want. This is most easily seen in labor–management conflicts. Labor usually begins bargaining by asking for much more than it actually hopes to get, while management begins by offering less than it actually expects to have to give. Even if an arbitrator is used to settle the dispute, the parties will probably behave this way as they attempt to convince the arbitrator that their position is right.[23]

The main advantage of compromise is that it allows a solution to *major* conflicts. In many instances it is almost impossible to resolve a conflict unless each party sees that the other is giving up something. The motivation to reciprocate ("you give–I give") may be the only motivation operating to move the parties toward a solution.

---

### Organizational Reality   12-5
### Productivity and Labor–Management Conflict

In the construction industry there are often jurisdictional strikes caused by disagreements between on-site laborers such as carpenters, bricklayers, glaziers, ironworkers, etc. These disputes often lead to walkouts, which can shut down work on a construction project. In St. Louis this problem had become particularly acute in the late 1960s, so the construction companies got together with the various unions and formed PRIDE (Productivity and Responsibility Increase Development and Employment). This organization is designed to solve jurisdictional disputes and facilitates more efficient operations.

An illustration of how PRIDE works: In 1975, there was a dispute between the ironworkers and the millwrights about who should install forty-foot-high metal doors at the St. Louis Convention Center. After several sessions with people from both unions, PRIDE representatives were able to get a compromise agreement. The ironworkers installed the tracks for the doors and the millwrights hung the actual doors. Before the existence of PRIDE, there probably would have been a shutdown due to a jurisdictional dispute.

---

Source: Irwin Ross, "The New Work Spirit in St. Louis," *Fortune* (16 November 1981): 92–106.

The tendency of people to exaggerate their demands in the hope of getting what they really wanted all along is one of the big problems with compromise as a conflict-resolution technique. Consider a conglomerate where the head of each division must submit a proposed budget for next year's operations. These proposals are considered by the board of directors, who adjust the amount as they see fit. It would not be surprising (and in fact is very common) to find the division heads asking for more than they need. They reason that, even if their request is cut back, they should still get enough to carry on their division's activities. The division heads therefore find themselves in something of a game with the board of directors, precisely because the board has developed a reputation for cutting back requests.

The other major disadvantage of compromise is that neither of the conflicting parties is enthusiastic about the solution. They may both feel they lost because they did not get what they wanted.[24] Their only solace is that the opposing party did not get what it wanted either.

**Consensus**   In Chapter 11 we discussed consensus as a means of improving group effectiveness. As a conflict-resolution technique, consensus requires the conflicting parties to work together to find the best solution to their problem. While this may sound impractical, there are situations where consensus will be appropriate. When an issue (e.g., organizational survival) is so important that the conflicting parties can easily see that their conflict must be resolved, consensus decision making is useful. The laboratory parallel of this real world situation is found in the "arctic and desert survival games" (see Box 12-4). In both these cases, the parties can clearly see that their differences must be resolved if they and/or the organization are to survive.

---

### Box 12-4: Consensus and Conflict Resolution

Two of the more popular experiential exercises in organizational behavior courses are the arctic and desert survival games. In these games, individuals are told to imagine that they have crash-landed in the Arctic or in a remote desert and they have fifteen or so items that they have salvaged from the wreck. They are then asked to rank these items in order of importance.

Once this is done, groups are formed and the group, using consensus problem solving, develops its own ranking of the fifteen items. With few exceptions, the group decision is superior to the individuals' decisions. (The "best" ranking is based on opinions expressed by Arctic or desert search-and-rescue teams.) Although major conflict sometimes develops over the ranking of certain items, the consensus problem-solving system resolves these conflicts and the end result is a better decision.

Source: J. Lafferty, P. Eady, and A. Pond, *The Desert Survival Problem.* Copyright by Human Synergistics, 1970; the Subarctic Survival Problem is available from Experiential Learning Methods, Plymouth, Michigan.

As discussed in Chapter 11, certain ground rules should be observed when using consensus as a conflict-resolution technique. These are as follows:

1. *Do not vote.* As noted above, voting tends to suppress analysis of the problem and generally results in poorer decisions. It also creates a win–lose atmosphere.
2. *Do not "horse trade."* One of the tendencies people have when trying to settle a conflict is to say things like, "I'll accept your view on point *X* if you'll accept mine on point *Y*." In consensus decision making this is discouraged. Instead, each party is required to decide what the most reasonable position on both *X* and *Y* is.
3. *Each person is encouraged to speak.* Some of the most helpful comments are made by individuals who are not aggressive. It is important to create an environment where everyone feels free to contribute to the resolution of the conflict.
4. *Reach a consensus.* It is not necessary to have unanimity. It is important, however, that each party to the conflict feels that he or she can live with the decision that is reached.

Overall, consensus is a positive conflict-resolution technique because (1) it moves the parties away from the win/lose mentality and (2) it takes advantage of the diverse resources available within the group.

**Confrontation**   The confrontation technique requires the opposing parties to openly state their views to each other. While it may seem that this would happen in the normal course of a conflict episode, the fact is that the conflicting parties may often not state the real problem. Husband-wife arguments, for example, are often characterized by beating around the bush and refusing to state the real problem. While this is often the case because one person doesn't want to hurt the other's feelings, the fact is that the problem cannot be solved until it is known. The same is true in organizational conflict. If two departments are in conflict over an apparently trivial point, we might suspect that something far more fundamental is at stake but the parties are unwilling to admit it.

Once the real reason for the conflict has been brought out, the reasons it came into being and the ways it can be resolved are analyzed. The solution is often a fairly simple one, and this is further support for the argument that the reason the conflict wasn't solved sooner was because no one was willing to state the real cause of the conflict.

**Integration**   The integration technique requires the conflicting parties to collaborate in order to resolve the conflict. It requires both parties to have the attitude that, although they may be in conflict, they will strive to develop collaboratively a solution that satisfies the needs of both parties. Thus, the needs of the parties will be integrated by the solution.

That this is a desirable route is often difficult for the conflicting parties to see. The win–lose mentality is often so strong that the opposing groups *assume* an

## Box 12-5: An Example of Integrative Conflict Resolution

One text on conflict resolution gives an example of integrative conflict resolution. A college student returned home for Easter vacation to find his mother and father in a conflict about how to finish the new cabinets in the kitchen. The father (a carpenter) had built the cabinets and wanted them stained a light color while the mother wanted to paint them a much darker color.

The student persuaded the parents to back off from the conflict and write down their goals about how they wanted the cabinets to look. The father wanted the beautiful wood grain to show through and also wanted his workmanship to be seen. The mother's goal was to have cabinets that would coordinate with the color of the floor and would be as stylish as some she had seen in *Better Homes and Gardens*.

Once these goals became clear, it was possible to point out to the parents that a stain could be used that would satisfy both of them. The one that was chosen (a medium-dark oil wood stain) allowed the grain to show through, showed off the workmanship, matched the floor, and looked stylish.

Source: A. Filley, *Interpersonal Conflict Resolution* (Glenview, Ill.: Scott Foresman, 1975), pp. 123–125. The story was related to the author by one of his students.

integrative solution is impossible. What is needed, therefore, is for the conflicting parties to develop the ability to rise above the usual "we–they" view and assume that integration is feasible. A systematic search for these win–win solutions can then be instituted.

# ■ RESOURCE ALLOCATIONS AND INTERGROUP CONFLICT

To this point, we have looked at several facets of conflict. We close this chapter with an examination of intergroup conflict because it represents such a crucial and highly visible part of organizational life. All organizations are broken down into formal departments or divisions, and conflict between these groups is very common. We have already seen in Chapters 9 and 11 how group decisions may be dramatically different from individual decisions, and we will see in Chapter 13 how organizational politics can generate tremendous intergroup conflict. Since intergroup conflict can have such a powerful effect (either positive or negative) on total organizational performance, it is important to analyze what happens during intergroup conflict, and then to consider what management might do to increase the chance that the conflict will be functional.[25]

# Box 12-6: Line-Staff Conflict

The most visible intergroup conflict in many organizations is the conflict between line and staff. It was noted in Chapter 5 that, as organizations become more complex, staff groups (such as marketing research, industrial engineering, legal, etc.) develop because line managers cannot handle their day-to-day duties and keep up with technological, legal, and other changes that have an impact on their work. Staff groups are supposed to solve this problem by giving line managers expert advice; line managers can use this advice to improve the way they run their departments. For example, marketing research develops data on consumers, and marketing managers should be able to use these data to plan new products.

The line-staff system works well in many companies, but in many others there are frequent clashes between line and staff. Why do these conflicts take place? There are three major factors that cause conflict:

1. *Authority*—Many line–staff conflicts are caused by ambiguous authority relationships. Staff may try to make a decision in an area, only to have the line manager say, "You have no authority to make that decision!" Line managers often feel that staff are trying to build an empire at the expense of the line people. A clear statement of authority relationships is necessary to prevent conflict in this area.
2. *The value of ideas*—Staff departments often come forward with ideas to improve the way line managers do their work. The legal department may suggest that, to avoid consumer complaints, certain procedures should be followed when making a product. The people actually making the product, however, may claim these procedures are unworkable because they were thought up by "ivory tower theoreticians" who have had little practical experience with the product. Staff departments do not like to be told that their ideas are no good because they are supposed to be the experts, and experts do not like to have their advice rejected.
3. *Responsibility*—When line management does adopt an idea proposed by staff and it doesn't work, who takes the blame? A classic reaction in these situations is for line management to argue that the idea was no good in the first place, so line managers shouldn't have to take the blame. Staff usually counters with the argument that the idea was perfectly good but it was ineptly carried out.

In all of these problem areas, blocking activity is going on. Staff units feel they are blocked from reaching their goal of having line utilize their skills and from feeling satisfaction that they have contributed to the organization. Line executives' goals are blocked when staff is given functional authority over them and are thereby allowed to keep line from doing what it wants.

## ☐ Resource Scarcity and Intergroup Conflict

With the recent economic problems that have been experienced in our society, the issue of intergroup conflict has become even more important. This is because the economic downturn has caused the environment facing both public and private sector organizations to become much harsher. Because organizations have been forced to cut back, resources available to the various groups in each organization have declined. This almost guarantees conflict between groups, because each of them will fight for a share of the decreased resource pie.

Intergroup conflict can be seen in many organizational activities, but it is particularly evident in the following areas:

1. *Goal setting*—conflicts erupt as various groups in the organization attempt to have their particular goals adopted as the official goals of the organization.
2. *Budgeting*—various groups in the organization fight over the relative share of the budget that each will get.
3. *Organizational effectiveness*—each group attempts to have organizational effectiveness criteria adopted that will make them look the best.

We will examine here only the conflict that develops in the setting of budgets, because this activity has such important implications for the organization as a whole, and because the intergroup conflict follows such a clear pattern.

## ☐ Resource Allocation Procedures in Organizations

Before an organization can rationally develop a budget, it must have previously made some basic decisions about the goals that it will pursue. Once the budget is adopted, resources are channelled to various parts of the firm in an attempt to reach these goals. When resources are unlimited, there are no problems about where resources should go; since the organization does not need to resolve the merits of each particular group's claims, it simply gives each group everything it wants. Once a group is given resources, it is able to pursue all sorts of new and different activities. Over time, these new activities come to be an accepted part of "normal" operations. So, as long as times are good and resources are abundant, there are few problems. However, when the organization must retrench, these new activities must be curtailed to some degree (or canceled altogether) and it is here that conflict develops. Deciding which group will get fewer resources is a highly political and conflict-generating decision.

Because the conflict over resource allocations can have such a dramatic effect on an organization, it is important that the conflict be properly managed. In most organizations, the process is not managed very well. Instead, when conflicts arise between groups they are usually resolved by the common superior of these two areas imposing a decision. For example, suppose a company has three manufacturing plants. As the annual budget setting deadline approaches, each of the plant managers will make a case to their common boss (the vice-president of production) about the resources they need. The boss will have to resolve these

---

### Organizational Reality 12-6
### Compromise at the White House

In an attempt to reduce budget deficits, David Stockman, director of the Office of Management and Budget, proposed cuts in spending in various areas, including military spending. Caspar Weinberger, secretary of defense, naturally opposed cuts in his area. After several weeks of negotiation, the two were unable to reach an agreement on what the cuts should be. As a result, President Reagan asked them to have a "showdown session" to reach an agreement.

During this session, Stockman argued for a $30 billion-dollar reduction in defense spending; Weinberger strongly disagreed, and said that $7 or $8 billion was the maximum reduction that should be allowed. After further questioning from the President, Stockman reduced his figure to $26 billion, but Weinberger stuck to $7 billion. Reagan then told them to "split the difference." After another one-hour meeting with Reagan, they agreed on a reduction of $11 billion.

---

Source: "Rolling Back on Defense," *Time* (21 September 1981): 15.

conflicting claims and make a decision about how resources should be distributed among the three manufacturing plants. The boss will usually make some sort of compromise decision, i.e., because the total requests of the three plant managers probably will exceed the amount available, the vice-president will probably cut all the requests by a certain amount.

When the boss makes decisions like this, he or she is actually behaving like an arbitrator and imposing a binding settlement on the conflicting parties. The conflicting parties will probably exaggerate their demands in the hope of offsetting the expected compromise of the manager–arbitrator. So, the plant managers will ask for a larger share of the budget initially, hoping that after the vice-president imposes a compromise they will get what they wanted in the first place. Unfortunately, this leads to budget demands that are extremely high and the organization is continually faced with cutting back on budget demands. This causes all sorts of ill will and increases the conflict between the parties.

### ☐ Managing Intergroup Conflict

How can intergroup conflict like this be resolved? As a general principle, what is needed is a budgeting system that motivates conflicting groups to reach a decision on their own, rather than having the manager–arbitrator impose a settlement on them. This, of course, is a rather dramatic departure from the normal way of allocating resources in most organizations. However, it is consistent with a more democratic, participative management system.

One specific technique that might be tried in this context (it has already been used in labor–management conflict) is final-offer arbitration. If this system is used, each of the parties submitting a budget request would be required to indicate what they felt each group or department should receive in the way of resources.

The manager-arbitrator would then pick one of the proposed budget packages in its entirety and impose it on all departments. Labor relations research shows that this kind of conflict-resolution technique motivates the conflicting groups to reach an agreement on their own, because they want to avoid the situation where the arbitrator imposes an unacceptable all-or-nothing decision.[26] If the conflicting parties reach an agreement on their own, they will feel more responsibility for the budget allocations and they will have more motivation to stick to its provisions. In one exploratory lab study that analyzed the possibility of using final-offer arbitration for budget conflicts, it was found that members of various departments who bargained over budget allocations were closer together at the conclusion of bargaining under the threat of final-offer arbitration than they were under the threat of the typical compromise arbitration that is found in most organizations.[27]

Final-offer arbitration is only one of many techniques that might be used to manage intergroup conflict. The important goal in any of these conflict-management techniques is motivating the conflicting groups to move voluntarily to a resolution that will benefit the total organization. Until groups can be creatively motivated to pursue organizational rather than departmental goals, intergroup conflict will often have negative consequences for individuals, groups, and organizations.

## *Opening Incident Revisited—The Bridger Post Office*

In the opening incident of this chapter, we saw that a long-standing antagonism between the clerks and carriers in the Bridger Post Office finally developed into open conflict that was severe enough to reduce productivity. What should be done to resolve this conflict? If we keep in mind that the conflict is just one stage in the process, we can develop an effective resolution based on the model in Figure 12-4.

The conflict between the clerks and carriers is caused primarily by the interdependence and differentiation of work activities. Although clerks are inside workers and carriers are outside workers, their work is very interdependent. Also, their work is very different. The goal of the clerks is to get mail sorted to the carriers as quickly as possible so they can get on with what they considered more "desirable" work. Because they did their work quickly, they made numerous errors. When the carriers returned these errors, they blocked the goal achievement of the clerks, because many letters had to be sorted two or three times. Clerks also blocked the carriers' goals of having mail correctly sorted to them and of finishing their routes on time.

There was obvious opportunity for interference for each group, as indicated above. Therefore, it is not surprising that open conflict developed. The question now is, "How should the conflict be resolved?" The forcing or smoothing techniques are probably unworkable in this case because there are some deep-seated differences in the groups. Some form of integrative problem solving is necessary, with the goal being an understanding by both groups of how interdependence of tasks has led to the problem. Confrontation can also be used to make sure that all facets of the problem are examined.

If the conflict resolution is successful, the conflict will have had a functional outcome as far as the long-run effectiveness of the organization is concerned. Figure 12-4 indicates that a functional resolution will affect the likelihood of future conflict by either altering the opportunity for interference or by changing the way the sources of conflict operate. For example, suppose that the two groups in the post office decided simply to avoid verbal exchanges. When carriers found errors in sorting, they would place them on the clerks' sorting table without comment. This would reduce the interference and would be a small move in the direction of resolving the conflict. On a wider scale, a functional conflict resolution would mean that the interdependence and differentiation of work activities (points 2 and 3 in Box 1) would no longer be contributors to conflict. Thus, conflict would be less likely in the future.

# ■ SUMMARY

In this chapter we considered conflict and its effect on organizations and the people in them. Conflict occurs when the goal striving of one group or individual is deliberately blocked by another group or individual. Conflict is distinct from competition in that the latter involves no interference between the parties as they strive for the goal.

We briefly examined conflict from a variety of perspectives—within one individual (role conflict), between individuals, and between groups—and noted that inter-individual and intergroup conflict would be stressed. We also observed that the view of conflict has changed over the years. Originally, managers and researchers felt that conflict was something to be avoided, but recently they have come to realize that conflict may be useful to organizations and society.

The sources of conflict were examined, and a model of conflict incorporating these sources as well as resolution techniques were discussed, and the advantages and disadvantages were noted. On balance, management should take the view that conflict is inevitable but that it will have a positive effect on the organization if managed properly.

# ■ REVIEW QUESTIONS

1. What is meant by "conflict"? How is conflict different from competition? Give an example.

2. Distinguish among Type I, II, and III conflict. Which is likely to cause the most trouble? Why?

3. Which organizational factors typically cause conflict? Given an example of how each factor can cause conflict.

4. What techniques are available for resolving conflict? Give an example of a situation where each technique could be used.

5. Describe how the sources of conflict, actual conflict, and the resolution of conflict fit together to form a process.

6. What disadvantages are there with the forcing and smoothing conflict resolution techniques? In what circumstances are they workable?

7. What problems might be encountered when using the confrontation technique for conflict resolution?

8. Why should managers occasionally induce conflict in their area of responsibility? How is conflict encouraged?

9. What are the functional outcomes of conflict? The dysfunctional outcomes?

10. Why has the traditional view that conflict is bad prevailed for so long?

11. What is blocking behavior? Why is it important in conflict?

# ■ EXERCISE 12-1: JAMES FARRIS

James Farris was a college student who, during the summer, worked in the Denver plant of Western Gypsum Company, a manufacturer of drywall material, various ready-mix patching compounds, and other assorted home-improvement products. The plant was a small one and employed only twenty-five people. Farris worked on the second floor and mixed raw materials (diatomaceous earth, dolomite, limestone, sand, etc.) together in specified proportions to make the ready-mix compounds. Consumers needed only to add water in the right amount to use the product. Because of this, quality control was a key function in the production process.

Farris hated his job but felt it was necessary to pay his way through college. On several occasions he had argued with his foreman about the level of work demanded, but to no avail. One hot afternoon the foreman approached Farris and the following discussion took place:

FOREMAN: Farris, you've got to be more careful when mixing the compound. Walters (the quality control inspector) tells me that six of the last eight batches you mixed were no good. All that stuff has to be remixed and that's going to cost the company a lot of money. We're paying you to mix those batches right! And another thing, you're not mixing the required seventeen batches a day. What's the problem?

FARRIS: I'm making mistakes because you're too demanding. I'm doing only four-teen batches a day instead of seventeen because I physically can't do seventeen. I'm not about to kill myself running around up here in this heat just so I can mix seventeen batches a day. Look, I'm the fifth guy to have this job in the last seven months, right?

FOREMAN:   Right.

FARRIS:   Doesn't that tell you something?

FOREMAN:   Yeah, it tells me that most people today don't want to do an honest day's work!

FARRIS:   Don't give me that! To do this job right, I can only do eleven batches a day. Besides, I'm not so sure those batches were actually bad. I've heard that Walters is very picky when checking batches because it gives him a sense of power over the other workers. Besides, he's just trying to get me because he thinks I scraped his new car in the parking lot the other day.

FOREMAN:   You college guys are all alike! I used to do this job and I never had any trouble. You're just too lazy. And stop blaming Walters; he's been here for twenty-three years and knows a lot more about ready-mix compounds than you'll ever know! Now get back to work and start pulling your weight around here.

One week later, the foreman was told by the personnel manager that Farris had quit.

1.   Analyze this conflict, using the model in Figure 12-4.

2.   How might this conflict have been resolved?

# ■ EXERCISE 12-2: CLINTON MACHINERY, INC.

Clinton Machinery, Inc., manufactured a wide range of industrial machines. The industrial engineering (IE) department at Clinton was made up of seven engineers, all of whom were under forty and all of whom had university degrees in mechanical, electrical, or industrial engineering. The department's main functions were to (1) advise factory line managers about the latest developments in production techniques and machine design and (2) monitor plant design to ensure that peak efficiency was maintained during production.

The IE department had been set up four years ago, but most of the engineers felt that their talents were not being utilized. The main complaint was that the factory managers were set in their ways and were not interested in improving the production operations in the factory. They therefore ignored suggestions from the IE department about improvements that could be made. The situation had deteriorated to the point that Ralph Bryce, the head of the IE department, had requested a meeting with the plant superintendent to make the department's views known.

At the meeting, Bryce expressed the concern of the engineers in his department and pointed out that some excellent ideas had been generated but were ignored by the line managers. Bryce concluded by saying that the best solution to the problem would be to give the IE department authority to force the line managers to implement some of their proposed changes. The plant superintendent said that he didn't think it was wise to do that unless he felt the line managers were in agreement. Accordingly, he called a meeting of both groups to see if the problem could be resolved.

At the meeting, members of the IE department and the line managers were both present. The plant superintendent chaired the meeting and began by noting that IE had some concerns about their good ideas being rejected. The line managers (most of whom had many years of experience but little formal education) immediately objected and said the ideas were not workable. The engineers replied that the line managers were so set in their ways that they wouldn't recognize a good idea if they saw one.

1. Use the model in Figure 12-4 to analyze this situation.

2. What is likely to happen as the meeting progresses?

3. What steps can be taken to resolve the conflict?

# ■ ENDNOTES

1. For an in-depth treatment of these differences, see C. Fink, "Some Conceptual Difficulties in the Theory of Social Conflict," *Journal of Conflict Resolution* 4 (1968): 413–58.

2. S. Schmidt and T. Kochan, "Conflict: Toward Conceptual Clarity," *Administrative Science Quarterly* 17 (1972): 359–70.

3. This view of conflict was proposed in S. Schmidt and T. Kochan, "Conflict: Toward Conceptual Clarity." The three types of conflict discussed in subsequent paragraphs were also proposed by these authors.

4. E. Ross, *Principles of Sociology* (New York: Century, 1930).

5. Throughout the remainder of this chapter the terms *conflict* and *competition* are used in the sense developed above.

6. This type of conflict does not fit in with the definition of conflict that we have adopted, simply because there is only one individual involved. It is nevertheless an important issue, since the stress felt by individuals complicates the management of conflict.

7. For an analysis of some of the organizational implications of intra-individual conflict, see L. Roos and F. Starke, "Roles in Organizations," in W. Starbuck and P. Nystrom, *Handbook of Organization Design* (Oxford: Oxford University Press, 1982).

8. S. Robbins, *Organizational Behavior* (Englewood Cliffs, N.J.: Prentice-Hall, 1979), p. 289.

9. Ibid., p. 288.

10. For a detailed discussion of these sources of conflict, see R. Walton and J. Dutton, "The Management of Interdepartmental Conflict: A Model and Review," *Administrative Science Quarterly* 14 (1969): 73–84; also A. Filley, *Interpersonal Conflict Resolution* (Glenview, Ill.: Scott Foresman, 1975), pp. 9–12.

11. W. Fruhan, "Pyrrhic Victories in Fights for Market Share," *Harvard Business Review* 50 (1972): 100–107.

12. R. Walton and J. Dutton, "The Management of Interdepartmental Conflict: A Model and Review."

13. Ibid.

14. H. Reitz, *Behavior in Organizations* (Homewood, Ill.: Richard D. Irwin, 1977), chap. 17.

15. The basic elements in the model are a combination of ideas proposed by various authors. See footnote 10 for reference to the sources of conflict. The idea of goal incompatibility and the opportunity for interference was proposed in Schmidt and Kochan, "Conflict: Toward Conceptual Clarity." The idea of functional and dysfunctional outcomes was suggested in Robbins, *Organizational Behavior,* although he explicitly deals with group performance as the outcome.

16. D. Nadler, J. Hackman, and E. Lawler, *Managing Organizational Behavior* (Boston: Little, Brown, 1979), chap. 12.

17. See Chapter 11 on Group Dynamics for a more detailed discussion of the effects of cohesiveness.

18. Ignoring the conflict is not included here because "conflict management" implies action on the part of the manager involved.

19. E. Boulding, "Further Reflections on Conflict Management," in R. Kahn and E. Boulding (eds.), *Power and Conflict in Organizations* (New York: Basic Books, 1964), pp. 146–50.

20. When the experimental groups were told to name a member they would like to see dropped from the group, they all chose the planted conflict stimulator. This happened in spite of the fact that the conflict stimulator had been instrumental in developing a better decision.

21. The techniques discussed here are based on those described in S. Robbins, *Managing Organizational Conflict* (Englewood Cliffs, N.J.: Prentice-Hall, 1974), chap. 9.

22. Many of the techniques described here were first systematically analyzed in R. Blake and J. Mouton, *The Managerial Grid* (Houston: Gulf, 1964).

23. For an analysis of the disadvantages of compromise, see W. Notz and F. Starke, "Final Offer vs. Conventional Arbitration As Means of Conflict Management," *Administrative Science Quarterly* 23 (1978): 189–203.

24. This is labeled a lose/lose resolution by one researcher. See A. Filley, *Interpersonal Conflict Resolution* (Glenview, Ill.: Scott Foresman, 1975).

25. Part of the discussion in this section is based on W. Notz, F. Starke, and J. Atwell, "The Manager As Arbitrator: Resource Allocation Conflicts in an Environment of Scarcity," in M. Bazerman and R. Lewicki (eds.), *Bargaining Inside Organizations* (Beverly Hills, California: Sage Publications, Inc., 1983).

26. See, for example, P. Staudohar, "Results of Final Offer Arbitration of Bargaining Disputes," *California Management Review* 18 (1975): 57–61.

27. W. Notz, F. Starke, R. Sproule, and B. Gibbs, "The Manager As Arbitrator: Budgets, Bargaining, and Power," *Proceedings,* American Institute for Decision Sciences, Nov. 22–24, 1982.

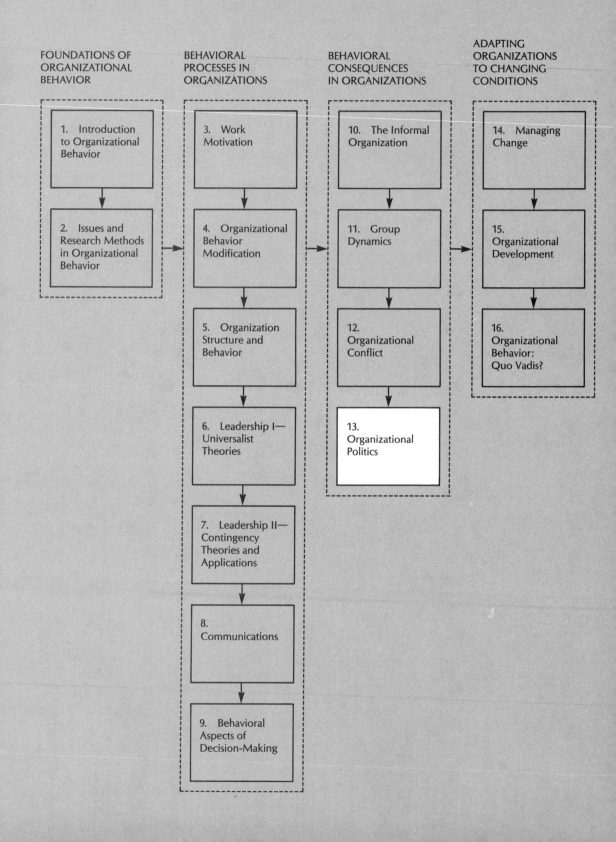

FOUNDATIONS OF
ORGANIZATIONAL
BEHAVIOR

1. Introduction to Organizational Behavior

2. Issues and Research Methods in Organizational Behavior

BEHAVIORAL
PROCESSES IN
ORGANIZATIONS

3. Work Motivation

4. Organizational Behavior Modification

5. Organization Structure and Behavior

6. Leadership I— Universalist Theories

7. Leadership II— Contingency Theories and Applications

8. Communications

9. Behavioral Aspects of Decision-Making

BEHAVIORAL
CONSEQUENCES
IN ORGANIZATIONS

10. The Informal Organization

11. Group Dynamics

12. Organizational Conflict

13. Organizational Politics

ADAPTING
ORGANIZATIONS
TO CHANGING
CONDITIONS

14. Managing Change

15. Organizational Development

16. Organizational Behavior: Quo Vadis?

# Organizational Politics

## ■ Learning Objectives

After carefully studying the material in this chapter, you should be able to:

☐ Explain the difference between the "rational" and "political" perspectives on organizations.

☐ Define organizational politics and show why it exists in all types of organizations.

☐ Understand the concept of "power" and how it is related to political behavior.

☐ Summarize the empirical evidence dealing with political behavior in organizations.

☐ Draw a conclusion about whether political behavior is good or bad for organizations and the people working in them.

# Chapter 13

# ■ KEY TERMS

**Organizational politics**
**Influence**
**Intents and means**
**Political tactics**
**Rational model of organization**
**Political model of organization**
**Power**
**Subunit power**
**Strategic contingencies theory**
    **of power**
**Budget politics**
**Career politics**

# ■ CHAPTER OUTLINE

I. Two Views of Organizations
II. What Is Organizational Politics?
   A. The Definition of Organizational Politics
   B. The Universality of Political Behavior
   C. Political Behavior: Intents and Means
III. The Concept of Power
   A. The Definition of Power
   B. The Relationship Between Power and Politics
   C. Power Differences Across Subunits
IV. Studies of Organizational Politics
   A. Individual Political Behavior
   B. Subunit Political Behavior
   C. The Politics of Budgets and Careers
   D. How Managers View Political Behavior
V. Politics, Conflict, and Decision Making
VI. Organizational Politics: Good or Bad?
VII. Summary

# *Opening Incident—Susan James*

Susan James is one of forty-six employees in one department of a large government agency. She has been on the job for three years. While having coffee with several colleagues one afternoon, she learns that the head of her department is being promoted to a new job in another agency. Not surprisingly, there is much discussion and rumor about who the new head will be.

The department is presently composed of two distinct groups of people—the young "climbers" and the older, less enthusiastic workers. There is animosity between the two groups on several issues, including the criteria for promotion. The young workers feel that performance should be the criterion, while the older workers argue that seniority should be used. Susan is a member of the younger group and would like to be the new head. She also knows that Carl Krause, the informal leader of the older group, assumes he will get the job because he has been in the department for eleven years.

Several years ago, the department adopted the practice of using a four-person selection committee to recommend to the agency director who the new department head should be. Members are elected to the selection committee at a meeting of the entire department. The director is very reluctant to ignore the committee's recommendation because he really believes in participative management.

In the month prior to the election of the selection committee members, Susan makes a point of cultivating friendships. In one-on-one meetings with various members of the department, she determines their likes, dislikes, fears, and hopes. She makes a point of going to lunch with various groups in the department, and she also becomes involved (discreetly) in ongoing discussions about the qualities the new head should possess. Before long, she finds that all the members in the "young" group (and even some of the older workers) are quietly urging her to apply for the head's job.

Given this support, Susan becomes more open in her strategy. In the week prior to the meeting, Susan consults with many of the younger members in the group; they agree to nominate four members from their group and then concentrate all their votes on those four members. They also agree to nominate seven or eight members from the older group in order to split the other group's votes over a larger number of nominees.

At the meeting, four candidates favorable to Susan are elected. Various supporters come by her office after the meeting to congratulate her and to say the important activity in choosing a new head has already been done. All that remains is the formality of the selection committee going through the motions of selecting the new head.

One month later, it is announced that Susan is the new head.

Organizational politics is one of the most important, yet elusive, concepts in organizational behavior. An understanding of this subject is crucial for anyone who has serious career aspirations about being in top management. In today's complex organizations, individuals simply do not move rapidly up the hierarchy unless they have a good grasp of the political aspects of their work environment.

Consider the results of one study which analyzed 149 managers in a manufacturing firm over a five-year interval.[1] During the period, 47 percent were promoted, 14 percent were given a lateral transfer, 22 percent stayed in their jobs, and 17 percent were demoted. The individuals who were promoted exhibited the following characteristics: (1) they understood the complex nature of the organization and the overlapping responsibility that resulted, (2) they recognized that it was more important to get along with their peers than with their subordinates if they wanted to get ahead in the company, (3) they felt they had great freedom on the job, (4) they recognized that good performance was not automatically rewarded, and (5) they recognized that it was more important to seize the opportunity to become known than to simply do a good job and hope for the best.

These comments by successful practicing managers may appear extreme, but they are probably not unusual. To demonstrate the diversity of situations in which political activity is important, consider the following examples from actual organizations:

☐ Bill A. reports to the vice-president of marketing for a public utility. He is aggressive and considers himself top-management material. By ingratiating himself with the vice-president's secretary, Bill is able to gather considerable evidence that the vice-president is frequently out of the office on nonbusiness activities. Bill informally presents this information to certain key members of the board of directors who belong to the same country club that Bill's father does. Two months later the vice-president is fired and Bill is chosen as his replacement.

☐ Mary S. is a sales representative with a major computer manufacturer. One Thursday afternoon her boss informs her that an important customer is arriving at the airport and that she is to pick him up. Mary is complimented that her boss has chosen her for the job. Moment's later, however, Mary's boss says "By the way, don't take your car. It isn't good enough for the customer. I think it's time you bought a new one." Mary feels threatened by this comment, since she can't afford a new car.

☐ Bob G. is a freshman majoring in business. Last Friday he cut his Principles of Management class to play in an important intramural basketball game. After class on Monday he went to the professor's office and said, "I missed class last Friday—did we do anything important?" Bob wondered why the professor looked so disgusted.

☐ Joan R. and John K. are management trainees for a major food marketing company. They do not particularly like each other. They are both in line for a promotion and they are both members of the new-product committee. At a meeting of the committee, John makes what appears to be an impressive presentation. However, Joan observes that there is a major logical flaw in his argument and she makes this flaw known to the committee. Although no decision is made at that time, Joan notices that John's proposal is quietly dropped from the agenda for the committee's next meeting. When the next promotion is announced, Joan gets it.

☐  Louis G. is a finance professor in a large business school in the midwest. He has very strong views about nearly everything and he expresses them vigorously at faculty meetings. When Louis first came to the university he felt that his comments had some impact, but as time passed people paid less and less attention to him. A recent faculty meeting was typical. The Strategic Planning Committee chairman was presenting a report that proposed a new administrative position for the faculty. With the best of intentions, Louis asked what experience other universities had had with this type of position. Several faculty members gave vague responses, and it was clear that the Strategic Planning Committee had not analyzed the issue in much depth. Louis therefore suggested that this analysis be done before a person was hired for the proposed position. He was amazed and infuriated when his suggestion was rejected and the Committee's recommendation was approved instead.

☐  Ron W. is the top regional sales manager of a major food products company. He is also an excellent golfer. Last week he was asked to join a foursome composed of his boss (the national sales manager), the vice-president of marketing (his boss's boss), and the president of the firm. Ron knew that these people were critical to his career, and he wanted to make a good impression. So he played his best and shot a 71, the lowest score by far in the group. He left the golf course in great spirits. When Ron entered his Boss's office the next morning he was greeted by "Ron, what in the world were you trying to prove yesterday? *Nobody* beats the president of this company at golf!" His boss then curtly dismissed him. Ron felt depressed about the incident for several days.

Incidents like those described above happen every day in organizations. They demonstrate that some individuals (e.g., Bill and Joan) are able to assess the realities of organizational life and then act in a way that is beneficial to their careers. Other individuals (e.g., Mary, Bob, John, Louis, and Ron) seem to have difficulty doing so. As a result, their careers are impeded and they don't get what they want.

As we proceed through our analysis of organizational politics, we must recognize several facts: First, though the amount of rigorous empirical research which explicitly analyzes organizational politics is increasing, the field is still in its infancy. Thus, at present it is not possible to predict exactly what will happen when people behave in a political fashion, nor is it possible to state a step-by-step procedure that can be used by people who want to engage in political behavior.

Second, many people in organizations seem to have difficulty understanding what "politics" is and the fact that people they interact with will often behave politically. Whether some people's consciousness can be raised about the importance of organizational politics seems doubtful. They will therefore be in a continual state of frustration and anxiety, and will not understand why things happen the way they do. Often, they will speak out against the "unfairness" of the system in an attempt to get their own way. Other political actors around them will see this as a threat and will take whatever counter measures they feel are necessary.

Third, the very basic question of whether political behavior is "reasonable" arises. Some people are very aware of what political behavior is, but they feel that it is an undesirable part of organizational life and should be avoided. We will address this question in some depth later in this chapter.

In order to discuss effectively the complex issue of organizational politics, in this chapter we will:

1. Examine two opposing views of how organizations function;
2. Define the term "organizational politics" and note the universality of political behavior;
3. Examine the role of power in organizational politics;
4. Report the findings of several studies that have examined organizational politics;
5. Analyze whether politics is good or bad.

## ■ TWO VIEWS OF ORGANIZATIONS

If we examine the study of organizations during the twentieth century, we find that there are two fundamentally different views about how organizations operate. One view—the *rational model*—sees organizations as places where organizational objectives are pursued in the most rational manner possible. In this environment, decisions are made on the basis of hard data, there is no place for individual idiosyncracies or biases, and groups and individuals cooperate to reach organizational goals. The opposing view—the *political model*—sees organizations as arenas where people with different values and biases confront each other on various issues. In this environment, goals are often not pursued in a rational manner, individual biases influence decisions, and groups and individuals are often in conflict.

Which of these two views most accurately describes organizations? Until very recently, most students and practicing managers accepted the idea that people working for organizations behaved rationally in the pursuit of *organizational goals*. By the 1970s, however, writers increasingly argued that people actually spend their time and energy pursuing *individual goals*, often at the expense of organizational goals. Their behavior ranges all the way from blatant stealing from the organization to the more subtle behavior of simply not doing the job in the way management intends.

These opposing views of how people behave in organizations have caused considerable controversy in the last few years. In order to clarify this debate it is necessary to consider the rational and political models in some depth. In the discussion below, five key rational model assumptions are stated and contrasted with the opposing political model assumptions. The assumptions are as follows:[2]

**1. Organizational-Effectiveness Criteria Are Clearly Defined and Measured.**   The rational model assumes that organizations measure how effective they are in reaching their goals, and that the various parts of each organization will be able to agree on the criteria used to determine whether or not the organization is effective.

In contrast, the political model assumes that it is very difficult to get consensus on organizational-effectiveness criteria. It recognizes that people have certain things they wish to pursue and that they will attempt to get organizational-effectiveness criteria stated in such a way that they will look good. For example, a salesperson who is good at sales but has no interest in follow-up service will try to get sales established as the criterion of effectiveness. Because organizations are full of people with diverse interests, in practice it is difficult to get agreement on what organizational-effectiveness criteria should be.

**2. Information Is Available About Contingencies That Will Affect the Organization.** Much of the literature on complex organizations deals with questions about how contingencies such as organizational size, technology, and environment affect the people and the structure of an organization. The rational model assumes that people first generate information about how these various contingencies will affect the organization, and then act in a rational way to deal with them.

The political model assumes that information is indeed available about these contingencies, but that it is subject to distortion and bias, i.e., people interpret information in light of their own biases. Thus, for any piece of supposedly "objective" information, there will be numerous subjective interpretations about what the information means. For example, if sales have declined for the past three months, someone in the organization who feels that marketing has too much power might argue that marketing is not assessing the external environment properly. Marketing, on the other hand, might argue that production is causing the problem because quality control has not been done properly. The important point about arguments like these is that it may be very difficult to decide who is correct.

**3. Rational Structural Planning Takes Place in Organizations.**   In the rational model, it is assumed that before the structure of an organization is decided upon, some sort of structural planning takes place. This planning takes into account the kind of business the firm is in, the types of products it is making, the environment it faces, and so forth. Only after these things have been done is an appropriate organization structure developed.

The political model argues that in most cases structure is not planned, but simply emerges in response to various pressures. The impact of individual personalities on organization structures is a prime example of this. If a powerful individual wishes an organization to be structured in a certain way, it will probably be structured in that way, regardless of whether that is really an appropriate structure. Structural variations can also be imposed by powerful external groups such as consumers. For example, some organizations have established consumer departments to deal with consumer complaints.

**4. Organizations Are Tightly Linked to Their Environments.** This rational model assumption means that bad corporate planning, or an inappropriate structure, or a host of other failures will result in poor organizational performance. The rational model assumes that there is a close relationship between an organization and its environments and that if the organization's internal structure is not set up to cope with its external environment, organizational performance will suffer.

The political model assumes the opposite, i.e., that organizations are loosely linked to their environments, and poor structure or bad corporate planning may not even be noticed either internally or externally. Even if it is noticed, the data that are available to determine who is at fault are often so vague that no one is able to pin down exactly what went wrong or who caused it. The practical outcome of this problem is that people can get away with all sorts of behavior that is dysfunctional for the organization but which may be very functional for them as individuals.

**5. Individuals and Groups Will Work Together to Reach Organizational Goals.** One of the outcomes of the human relations school of management is the widespread belief that if people are treated properly by management they will work together to reach organizational goals. In the rational model, it is assumed that people are cooperative, not competitive.

The political model rejects this notion and assumes that because people pursue their own self-interest, individuals and groups will frequently find themselves in conflict with each other over what goals should be pursued. Conflict between superiors and subordinates, line and staff, and labor and management are examples of this tendency.

**Conclusion** Although there is evidence supporting each of the models, the political model seems most descriptive of modern organizations. An inescapable feature of human behavior is that people look out for "number one"; given this fact, the outcomes as portrayed in the political model are almost inevitable in organizations. If we continually keep in mind the self-interest phenomenon, we will get a much greater appreciation of the role that political behavior plays in organizational life.

# ■ WHAT IS ORGANIZATIONAL POLITICS?

## ☐ The Definition of Organizational Politics

Although it is difficult to define concisely the term "organizational politics," the following definition conveys the key points about the concept:

> Organizational politics involves those activities taken within organizations to acquire, develop, and use power and other resources to obtain one's preferred outcomes in a situation in which there is uncertainty or dissensus about choices.[3]

This definition stresses power, not authority. Recall from Chapter 12 that authority is the *right* to command another person to do something, while power is the *ability* to do so. Authority is attached to a formal position (e.g., vice-president of marketing), while power is attached to a person (e.g., Joe Smith). Thus, political behavior occurs when people use power or some other resource beyond the formal limits of their job to get their preferred outcomes. Note also that this definition argues that political behavior is particularly likely when it is not clear what the best course of action is. In these situations, people will often say to themselves, "Since nobody can prove which alternative is best, I might as well push for my preferences."

We have not emphasized definitions in this book, but it is important to clearly define organizational politics. Consider another definition of politics that has been proposed:

> Organizational politics is the management of influence to obtain ends not sanctioned by the organization or to obtain sanctioned ends through nonsanctioned influence means.[4]

As one writer has noted, this definition has two problems.[5] First, the means and ends that organizations sanction are the *result* of political activity, so including these in the definition of politics is not appropriate. If we accept the above definition, it would mean that powerful people in organizations would not need to behave politically because they determine what is sanctioned; powerless

---

### Organizational Reality   13-1
### Politics at First Chicago Corporation

For the past decade or so, First Chicago Corporation (parent company of the First National Bank of Chicago) has been the scene of a considerable number of internal political battles. Political squabbling has been evident since as far back as 1972, when Chairman Gaylor Freeman stated that four bank officers were in the running for the bank's top management job. A. Robert Abboud won the race in 1975, but this did not stop the infighting.

One employee says people in the bank seem to take sides and then fight with each other. People are tagged as being on one side or the other, and there is much hostility between groups. There is such a lack of trust between people that it is affecting operations.

Insiders say that Abboud (who was later fired) played executives off against one another and this caused the bank's officers to become so preoccupied with organizational politics that they were not effective in their work. He also criticized officers in public and this made them reluctant to discuss problems openly (either political or work-related).

---

Source:   L. Rout, "First Chicago, With or Without Abboud, Is a Place of Tension," *The Wall Street Journal* 65 94 (1980): 1, 20.

people, on the other hand, would frequently have to engage in political behavior. In reality, both weak and powerful individuals can be observed acting politically.

Second, this definition conveys the idea that political behavior is undesirable or "wrong." This is a value judgment, and before accepting it we need to analyze the issue in much more depth.

## ☐  The Universality of Political Behavior

Political behavior is both universal and inevitable. It can be observed in all kinds of organizations—manufacturing firms, government agencies, service organizations, churches, the military, universities, etc. In this sense it is like the informal organization; any attempt to suppress it is certain to fail because the forces that encourage it are so powerful.

What are these forces? Perhaps the most fundamental one is self-interest, i.e., people do things that promise to improve their own financial situation, status, ego, or some other aspect of their lives that is important to them. While we can understand that people will do these things, the fact is that since organizations are made up of many different people, there will almost always be a clash of interests. When people observe that what they are pursuing may be thwarted by someone else—and this happens frequently—political behaviors are more likely to be used.

Another reason political behavior is so widespread is that organizations have limited resources. Organizations must therefore decide which of many possible goals they will pursue. Various groups or individuals will normally be in conflict with one another over whose goals are going to be pursued, and in the process of trying to win these battles, political behavior is commonly observed. This is particularly likely if there is little objective evidence about the goals the organization should pursue.

Self-interest and limited resources guarantee that political behavior will be evident in *all* organizations. Some individuals believe that if they could just get into a certain kind of organization they would not have to cope with the political behavior of others. For example, some people feel that in a charitable organization, which is pursuing a goal that society values, there would be no political behavior because everyone would use their energies to pursue the organization's goals. Unfortunately, this view ignores the two realities noted above: individuals pursue their own self-interests, and organizational resources are limited. Individuals who ignore these realities will often be surprised, shocked, and dismayed at the behavior of others they interact with. Conversely, those who take these realities into account will find that they are much more able to predict the behavior of others.

## ☐  Political Behavior: Intents and Means

When considering political behavior, it is useful to make a distinction between the *intent* of the individual who is trying to influence someone, and the *means* that person uses to do the influencing.[6] With respect to *intent*, the individual is usually trying to achieve personal goals; these may be either congruent or incongruent with organizational goals. If the person's intent is to pursue organizational goals, the person may find that doing so requires suppression of personal goals.

The *means* (specific behaviors) that an individual exhibits while acting politically are called political tactics. These vary across different situations and are determined by a complex mix of (1) the characteristics of the individual, (2) the intent of the person, and (3) the situational characteristics in which the political behavior occurs.

> If the intent is to increase productivity (organizational goal), for example, one may use the reward power base and the strategic maneuver or means of openly promising incentive pay. If the intent is to take over an opposing peer group (personal goal), one may use the informational base and the strategic maneuver of withholding relevant information.[7]

Table 13-1 describes several commonly used political tactics. Note that some of these involve the use of power and some do not.

These tactics (means) can be overt or covert, i.e., the person can be open or secretive about practicing political behavior. When pursuing personal goals that coincidentally happen to be congruent with organizational goals, it is likely the person will use overt means. If challenged by anyone, the person can say he or she is doing it for the good of the organization. However, when pursuing personal

**TABLE 13-1.   Some Commonly Used Political Tactics**

---

**Image building**   Engaging in activities designed to create and maintain a good image. Includes dressing appropriately, drawing attention to one's successes, being enthusiastic about the organization, adhering to group norms, and having an air of confidence about work activities.

**Selective use of information**   Using information selectively to further one's career. Includes withholding unfavorable information from superiors, keeping useful information from competitors, interpreting information in a way that is favorable to oneself, and overwhelming people with technical information they don't understand.

**Scapegoating**   Insuring that someone else is blamed for a failure. Individuals who are skillful organizational politicians make sure that they will not be blamed when something goes wrong and that they will get credit when something goes right.

**Forming alliances**   Agreeing with several key people that a certain course of action will be taken. If a conflict develops, the people in the coalition will get their way because they are strong enough as a group to impose their will on others.

**Networking**   Insuring that one has many friends in positions of influence.

**Compromise**   Giving in on an unimportant issue in order to gain an ally who will be on your side when an issue of importance to you arises at a later date.

**Rule manipulation**   Refusing an opponent's request on the grounds that it is against company policy, but granting an identical request from an ally on the grounds that it is a "special circumstance."

---

---

### *Organizational Reality   13-2*
### *Overt and Covert Intents and Means*

John G. is the assistant personnel director in a firm that has been prosecuted recently for violating Equal Employment Opportunity laws. He proposes a training program for minorities that ostensibly is designed to help them find employment and to improve the firm's image (overt intent). Actually, John is trying to get the personnel director's job by showing initiative that the director never showed (covert intent).

John argues that a training program must be put in place to resolve the firm's image problem (overt means). Of course, a large staff will be necessary to do this properly since so little minority training has been done in the past (covert means). As a result of all this, John's status and power are increased because he is in charge of a large, highly visible program.

---

goals that are incongruent with organization goals, the person will likely use covert means.

## ■ THE CONCEPT OF POWER

If we examine organizations in an attempt to get some idea of what power (influence) really is, we typically find that managers have little trouble understanding its role and importance, but they may not be able to neatly define the term. In one study, ten department managers were asked to rank themselves and twenty other department managers in terms of how much influence each had.[8] Only one manager asked the researchers what they meant by "influence." In spite of this, there were virtually no disagreements in their rankings of the top five and bottom five people on the list, even though ranking twenty-one people is not an easy task. In a similar study of twenty-nine department heads at the University of Illinois, only one respondent asked what was meant by the term "power."[9] The researchers noted that they had found this same phenomenon in several other studies they had conducted. Thus, it appears that practicing managers in organizations have a good idea of the practical meaning of power and how it manifests itself.

Historically, there has been little systematic analysis of power in organizations. One writer argues that this has happened because the three main groups that read management writings—students, practicing managers, and the general public—all want to believe that the rational approach is the way things are done in organizations, and therefore the importance of power is ignored.[10]

For *students*, management education attempts to socialize and prepare them for a career in organizations. From their point of view, it may be better to believe that they are entering a career where they will allocate resources rationally for the good of society than to believe that their career will involve them in nasty power

### *Organizational Reality   13-3*
### *The Quest for Power*

Consider the struggle for the chairmanship of the empire that controls Anglo-American Corporation of South Africa, Limited, and its affiliate, De Beers Consolidated Mines, Limited. The company is currently ruled by Harry Oppenheimer, 73, the son of company founder Sir Ernest Oppenheimer.

Some of the top people at the head office in Johannesburg, South Africa, are putting their money on Julian Ogilvie-Thompson, joint deputy chairman of both Anglo and De Beers. He is undoubetdly brilliant, an icy decision maker who operates as *de facto* chief executive of Diamond Operations. He managed to reach $521 million in pre-tax profits for De Beers in 1982, down 30 percent from 1980 but an extraordinary performance considering the worldwide slump in diamond prices. "He has never been known to make a mistake," says one observer.

The second contender is Nicholas Oppenheimer, 37, scion of the South African family, who was appointed by his father to be joint deputy chairman of Anglo with Ogilvie-Thompson. Harry Oppenheimer appointed a longtime confidant to the chair of Anglo and held on to the chairmanship of De Beers himself.

As if to scuttle any further ambition by Ogilvie-Thompson, Harry genially added almost as an afterthought, "My son will provide the continuity of family."

"Nicky" is now mastering the intricacies of E. Oppenheimer and Sons, Limited, a holding company that has an estimated 8.2 percent stake in Anglo and is the largest single shareholder. Clearly, what is being matched is the stockholder wallop at Anglo of Nicky with the expertise of operations of Ogilvie-Thompson. Although both sit on the fifteen-man executive committee that decides group policy for all companies, Nicky lacks the managerial expertise of the older Ogilvie-Thompson. But watchers in Johannesburg and London note that Nicky is devoting more and more of his time nowadays to the diamond business, very likely to try to head off any ultimate challenge.

Source: "Nicky Oppenheimer: A Very Private Quest for Power," *Business Week* (2 May 1983): 58–59.

struggles with other people over goals and ways to reach those goals. *Practicing managers* presumably find it reassuring to believe that their career progress is based on rational (merit) considerations, not political ones. Similarly, the *general public* takes comfort in the belief that the resources of society are being allocated in an efficient and rational way.

## ☐  The Definition of Power

Perhaps because of this widespread belief in the rational approach, no generally accepted definition of power has emerged. To facilitate the discussion below, we suggest the following simple definition:

Power is the ability of person (or group) *A* to induce person (or group) *B* to behave in a way that *A* desires.

## ☐ The Relationship Between Power and Politics

As we have already noted in the definition of politics, people behave politically in order to acquire and maintain power. In this model political behavior is the independent variable and power is the dependent variable. Once an individual has achieved a certain amount of power, he or she can use it to obtain desired personal outcomes.

However, this does not always happen. While power is often used to get one's way, an individual can achieve desired personal goals without ever using power. Recall the incident at the start of this chapter, where Joan got a promotion at the expense of John because she made him look bad in a committee setting. As management trainees, neither Joan nor John had any real power in the organization, yet Joan was able to further her career at the expense of John. Because the use of power is only one way to further one's personal goals, political behavior can be exhibited by *anyone* in an organization, and can be demonstrated in very diverse ways. Figure 13-1 illustrates two possible routes to achieving desired personal outcomes.

## ☐ Power Differences Across Subunits

In the rational model of organization, it is assumed that subunits at the same level in the hierarchy have equal power. In practice, this is not true, i.e., when the dynamics of influence are closely examined, it is clear that some subunits have more "clout" than others. Why does this happen?

---

### *Organizational Reality   13-4*
### *Sharing Power at the Top*

Edward Hennessy, Jr., chairman of Allied Corporation, professed confidence in executives of Bendix Corporation on January 31, 1983, when the merger of Bendix and Allied became effective. But within days, Bendix Chairman William Agee and President A.L. McDonald both left, gently but firmly pushed by Hennessy, who said he could find no suitable job for either man in the new company. Further, the top executives at three other big companies that Hennessy has acquired since taking over Allied in 1979 all found it unrewarding to remain. Richard D. Loynd, former president of Eltra Corporation, for example, left after it was obvious that Hennessy was not going to share executive power with him.

Reorganizing Bendix while keeping morale up at its headquarters in Southfield, Michigan is only one of many challenges. Merging Bendix will force Hennessy to alter his executive suite to accommodate delegation of power and he is searching for a chief operating officer to be his number-two man.

To develop successfully and to operate the firm, Hennessy will have to decide how much power to give up, how much to keep, and how to go about doing that.

---

Source:   "No Room at the Top for Bill Agee," *Business Week* (21 February 1983): 37.

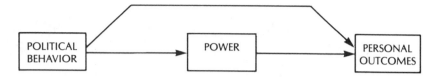

**FIGURE 13-1.  The Relationship Between Power, Politics, and Personal Outcomes**

There are two variables that cause differences in power across subunits: personal and structural. The former refers to the case where the personality of the leaders (or members) of a department is such that they are able to exert an unusual amount of influence in the organization. The latter refers to the fact that power differences are created whenever an organization is broken down into departments. Because of the people and tasks involved in different departments, as time passes judgments are made about which departments are most powerful. As we have already seen, in a given organization there is considerable agreement about who the powerful individuals and departments are.

Hickson and his associates have developed a strategic-contingencies theory of why certain subunits in organizations are more powerful than others.[11] They argue that there are three variables that influence the degree of power a department has. First, and most important, is the department's ability or opportunity to cope with strategic contingencies that face the organization. These strategic contingencies (e.g., dramatic shifts in consumer preferences, restrictive government legislation, shortages of raw materials, etc.) are things that can disrupt the smooth functioning of the organization. A subunit will acquire power if it is able to cope with uncertainty that negatively affects the work of other subunits in the firm. For example, marketing research might have considerable power if it can detect changes in consumer tastes that will require changes in the mix of products produced. Production departments in the firm would then have to rely on the marketing research department for the information necessary to do product planning.

Second, a department will be powerful if its activities are not substitutable. This is simply another way of saying that when a subunit has a monopoly, it will have a lot of power. If only the personnel department has the expertise to recruit a certain kind of specialized engineer, the personnel department will have considerable influence in the department that needs this type of person.

Third, a subunit will have power if its activities are central to the organization, i.e., its activities are important to many other units. The finance department is powerful in many firms because its activities reach everywhere through the budget mechanism.

# ■ STUDIES OF ORGANIZATIONAL POLITICS

Several studies have been conducted which analyze various aspects of organizational politics. These studies have relied on questionnaire and interview data, so the conclusions coming from them must be viewed with some caution. A more complete understanding of organizational politics must await field and laboratory experiments where cause and effect can be more closely assessed.

## ☐ Individual Political Behavior

An early study analyzed the tactics used by 142 purchasing agents to expand their influence in their respective organizations. [12] From the rational perspective, purchasing agents are supposed to negotiate, place, and expedite orders. Politically, however, many of these agents viewed these functions as a bare minimum; they also felt that they should be keeping management informed about market developments, new sources of supply, price trends, ways to save money in purchasing, etc. In most of the firms studied, purchasing agents had disagreements with engineering (the ordering department) and their influence attempts were therefore directed at engineering.

The agents used a variety of influence tactics, most of which were political. These included:

1. *Rule-oriented tactics*—Using the formal rules of the organization to increase one's influence (e.g., the purchasing department might tell engineering that it could not order on short notice and that the purchasing agent must be given more lead time).
2. *Rule-evading tactics*—Evading the formal rules of the organization (e.g., a purchasing agent might appear to comply with a purchase request, but pursue it only half-heartedly because the agent did not believe the parts should have been ordered from the specified vendor).
3. *Personal-political tactics*—Using interpersonal connections to either facilitate or inhibit an order (e.g., expediting an order in spite of the fact that it is late, because the order is from a close friend).
4. *Educational tactics*—Trying to persuade engineering to think in purchasing terms (e.g., presenting the facts in such a way that engineering did what purchasing wanted).
5. *Organizational-interactional tactics*—Attempting to change the formal or informal interaction patterns between purchasing and engineering (e.g., trying to get engineering to ask purchasing for help rather than deciding whom to order from and then getting in an argument if purchasing suggested someone else).

With the possible exception of number 1, all these tactics are political, i.e., the purchasing agents used their influence to get their own way. In many of these cases, the interests of the agent and the organization were actually congruent, so the political behavior was useful for both the purchasing agents and their companies.

A case study of how a person in a newly created management position attempted to increase his influence (see Figure 13-2) gives further insight into the practice of organizational politics. [13] The man in question (Moss) was formally

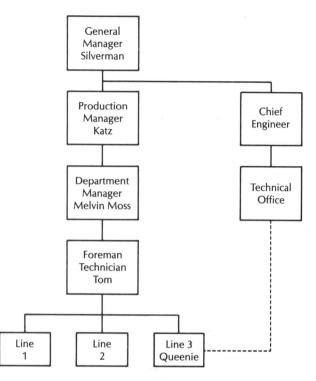

**FIGURE 13-2.  Formal Organization Chart**

Source: D. Izraeli, "The Middle Manager and Tactics of Power Expansion," *Sloan Management Review* (Winter 1975): 57–70.

appointed to head a department, but found that (1) his boss (Katz) delegated very little authority, and (2) one of his foremen (Tom) was perceived by other employees to informally be in charge of the department.

Moss decided that this situation would have to change if he were going to be effective, so he began using the following political tactics to expand his influence:

1. *Neutralization of his boss's supporters*—Moss was able, by various actions, to convey to Tom that he (Moss) was a force to be reckoned with. Tom was reluctant to continue relying totally on his old boss (Katz) because Tom thought Moss might eventually succeed in getting additional authority delegated to him by Katz. If that happened, Tom would be in jeopardy (Moss thought Tom could be doing a better job). As a result, Tom became more amenable to influence attempts by Moss.
2. *Replacing supporters of his boss that he could do without*—Moss felt that a quality control inspector (Queenie), who was not well-liked by her peers, but who was highly regarded by Katz, should be removed because she continually held up production at a time when top management wanted higher output. Moss questioned if her high quality standards were functional and implied that she was a liability to the company. Since Katz was under pressure to increase

production, he finally agreed to remove her. Moss then installed a quality control inspector who was loyal to him.

3. *Getting commitment from those not yet committed to his boss*—By using various tactics, Moss was able to mobilize the support of (1) new career workers that Katz had not yet influenced, (2) older workers who felt that they had been treated badly in the past, and (3) young workers who didn't intend to make factory work their career.

4. *Mobilizing support from higher up*—Moss was able to convince Katz's boss (Silverman) that Katz should be less involved in the day-to-day operations of the department. Katz agreed because he was afraid of falling out of favor with Silverman.

The two studies cited above focus on political behavior at the *individual* level. It is also important to analyze political behavior at the *group* level. Four such studies are analyzed below.

## ☐ Subunit Political Behavior

A study conducted independently of the Hickson *et al.* strategic-contingencies theory gives some support to it.[14] Maintenance engineers in a factory producing cigarettes had an unusual amount of power. An analysis of the situation showed that the engineers were the only ones able to cope with a crucial problem in the factory—machine breakdowns. The plant manager was able to deal with absenteeism and turnover of production workers, production scheduling, changes in demand, and raw material difficulties, but he was unable to cope with what were essentially random machine breakdowns. As a result, the maintenance engineers became a strategic subunit, because the problem they were able to cope with was crucial to the organization. They were therefore consulted on a wide variety of plant decisions, some of which had little to do with machine breakdowns.

Another exploratory study was conducted by the researchers who developed the strategic-contingencies model.[15] Using questionnaires and interviewing, they analyzed the power relationships between the engineering, marketing, production, and accounting departments in seven manufacturing firms (five breweries and two container companies). They found that the three variables noted earlier (coping with uncertainty, absence of substitutability, and centrality) were indeed important in determining how much power a department had. The most powerful departments were those that scored high on all three variables. Departments that scored high on only one or two variables had less power.

Two replication studies tested whether the results originally found by Hickson and his associates could be repeated.[16] In the first, a questionnaire which operationalized various aspects of the strategic contingencies model was given to sixty-two university administrators. In the second, questionnaires were given to department heads in several functional areas of four oil companies. The university study was most supportive of the theory. The researchers found, for example, that absence of substitutability was, in fact, an important determinant of subunit power. The findings from the oil companies were less supportive.

# Box 13-1: Principles of Political Behavior

Hall has proposed the following principles of political behavior in organizations:

**Principle 1.** Groups (coalitions) within organizations vie with one another for status and power. When individuals enter organizations they immediately begin looking for others who share their particular view of the world. For example, engineers, accountants, and other people with specialized training identify with one another and often form very cohesive groups. As we saw in Chapter 13, cohesive groups can be a positive force in organizations, but they can also make narrow-minded decisions which do not take the total organization into consideration. Since organizations are composed of many such groups it is virtually inevitable that these groups will vie with one another for status and power.

**Principle 2.** Change in the external environment of the organization will favor one coalition over the other. The continually changing external environment of the organization presents both problems and opportunities. A given change will be either a problem or an opportunity, depending on the coalition's capabilities. As long as a coalition has the skill to cope with problems that the environment presents, the coalition or group will have considerable status and power. The coalitions that do not have a valued skill will attempt to define environmental changes in such a way that their skills do become important.

**Principle 3.** Power considerations are as important, if not more so, than economic or rational considerations in making organizational decisions. Coalitions in an organization attempt to influence decisions in their own favor. If they are successful, their relative status and power will be enhanced.

**Principle 4.** The dominant coalition will use political means to stay in power. The coalition that dominates the organization will often be challenged by other coalitions for the right to make major decisions. When faced with such a challenge, the dominant coalition will engage in all sorts of political tactics to maintain its position. They may, for example, distort data about a problem. As one staff expert in a city department put it, "The chief calls me in, tells me what's been decided, and sends me off to gather facts and data to justify it."

Source: Roger I. Hall, "Some Emerging Principles of the Politics of Organizational Decision Making." Paper presented at the 1980 *ASAC* Conference.

**Conclusion**  The overall conclusion from these studies is that the sources of power probably vary from industry to industry. In a manufacturing firm, for example, the sources of power would be different from those in a service firm. What would be strategic in each of these cases would be somewhat different, so power would develop in different ways. This conclusion is consistent with the

## Box 13-2: Politics at Manitoba Hydro

Manitoba Hydro is a provincially owned and operated utility whose mandate is to promote efficiency and economy in the supply and use of electric power. In 1979, the Tritschler Commission conducted hearings about alleged mismanagement of the organization. Among other things, the Commission concluded that Manitoba Hydro had:

1. Predicted power shortages (which rationalized expansion decisions), but the shortages never materialized.
2. Underestimated construction costs of new generating plants.
3. Expanded when its financial position was weak.

The principles of political power behavior noted in Box 13-1 give some insight into why these things happened:

**Principle 1.**    The formation of a powerful group. In a province where 90 percent of the electricity is generated by water power, it is not surprising that hydraulic construction engineers were a powerful group. This power was based on technical expertise.

**Principle 2.**    Environmental changes favor one coalition in the organization. The rapid growth in demand for electricity in the 1960s, Manitoba Hydro's previous experience in building hydro plants, and the abundance of rivers in the province that could be harnessed, were all environmental features that increased the power of the engineers' coalition.

**Principle 3.**    Power strategies. In Manitoba Hydro, the hydraulic engineers produced the demand forecast *and* did the planning for future generating stations. Thus there was no separation of responsibilities, and impartial decisions were not likely to be made. The hydraulic engineers were therefore able to push through expansion proposals based on the pretext that there would be an energy shortfall.

**Principle 4.**    Politicking to stay in power. When the predicted demand for electricity did not materialize, the coalition in power attempted to manipulate the environment to increase demand. For example, rates were kept artificially low and deals were made to sell power to the United States and Ontario. By these tactics, Manitoba Hydro was able to maintain (to some degree) an environment that was favorable to increased hydroelectric generation.

Source: Roger I. Hall, "Some Emerging Principles of the Politics of Organizational Decision Making.

position we have taken throughout this book that different situations require different behavior. This situational perspective was particularly noticeable in the chapters on leadership and motivation.

## □ The Politics of Budgets and Careers

Two areas that are consistently significant in organizations are those concerned with (1) setting organizational budgets, and (2) tracking individual careers. Studies of the impact of political behavior in each of these areas give some important insights.

**Budgets and Politics**    Pfeffer and Salancik studied budget allocations at a major university over a thirteen-year period.[17] They used the average proportion of the general funds budget that was given to each of twenty-nine departments as the dependent variable. Independent variables were credit hours taught by each department, departmental representation on the University Research Board committee, and departmental representation on other university-wide committees.

They found that power measures (committee representation) and rational measures (credit hours taught) affected budget allocations. One interesting finding was the −.60 correlation in one department between the proportion of the budget it received and the proportion of credit hours it taught. In this powerful department (which was well-represented on university committees), as the number of credit hours taught declined, the department's proportion of the general budget increased. By contrast, less powerful departments showed a positive correlation between the two variables, i.e., the only way they could get a larger proportion of the budget was to teach more students. Two other studies focusing on universities came to similar conclusions.[18]

A study of budget allocations in the United Fund further demonstrates how politics affect the budgeting process.[19] The researchers hypothesized that the power of groups within the United Fund (e.g., the YMCA, the Boy Scouts, etc.) would be determined by two things: (1) the proportion of the group's budget received from the United Fund versus other sources (the greater the proportion, the less the group's power), and (2) the proportion of the United Fund's total budget that went to the group (the greater the proportion, the greater the power of the group.)

The budget allocations of sixty-six United Funds during 1962, 1967, and 1972 were examined to test these hypotheses. Support was found for both of them. There was rarely any significant association between important demographic variables (rational criteria) and actual budget allocations to social service agencies. For example, there was no relationship between budget allocations for agencies serving blacks and the proportion of blacks in the area they served. Nor was there any relationship between allocations to agencies serving young people and the age distribution in the area served. Another study which analyzed a single United Fund showed the same kinds of results.[20] Both of these studies support the view that political behavior plays an important role in budget allocations.

**Careers and Politics**    The assessment of how politics affect careers can be done from two vantage points: (1) how politics influence who gets a job in the first place, and (2) once on the job, how politics influence who gets promoted.

---

### *Organizational Reality   13-5*
### *Women and Management*

United States Trust Co. and its holding company, UST Corp., looked long and hard for women after announcing a policy to market specifically to professional women. The commitment would be worth little without some women on the bank's board of directors.

The bank's new marketing effort began with special financial planning seminars. In spring of 1982, the bank found three women who fit its director profile; women who, among other things, were "accomplished and visible in their fields."

One of the three women chosen was none other than Barbara C. Sidell, wife of James Sidell, president and director of the company. Mrs. Sidell maintains she was chosen because of her banking knowledge and because she is a lawyer. Mr. Sidell also found nothing unusual about his wife being on the board. He firmly believes that it is because his wife is "anything but a housewife," but rather a seasoned professional, that she was invited to sit on the board.

---

Source: *Wall Street Journal* (December 82): 31.

---

### *Organizational Reality   13-6*
### *Luck and Careers*

Nate Cummings is the man who put together Consolidated Foods (sales over $5 billion). A chance meeting in a dining car on a Baltimore-to-Chicago train between Cummings and a man named Henry Crown had a decisive impact on Cummings' career. Cummings, who owned a small food wholesaling company, was traveling to Chicago to try to acquire the much-larger Sprague Warner and Co. He was only one of several bidders for that firm. When Crown and Cummings began talking it came out that Crown was a close friend of the founders of Sprague-Warner. Crown spoke highly of Cummings to the founder, the shareholders were then convinced, and Cummings acquired the company. This transaction allowed Cummings to work from a much larger capital base in his future acquisitions. Would Consolidated Foods exist in its present form if these two men hadn't met by chance on a train?

In his career, Carter Burgess has been chairman of American Machine and Foundry and president of TWA. In 1941, he was a second lieutenant stationed near Washington, D.C. As Burgess was passing by, the post adjutant stuck his head out of a window and asked Burgess if he had a pressed uniform. Burgess said yes, and was told to go immediately to the Federal Reserve Building. The reason: Roosevelt, Churchill, and their aides were meeting there and needed well-dressed soldiers for various duties. The people at the meeting were impressed by Burgess, and his career took a sharp turn upward. After the war his military contacts led to several executive jobs; he was also assistant secretary of defense for manpower. How would his career have progressed if he had not had a pressed uniform?

---

Source: Daniel Seligman, "Luck and Careers," *Fortune* (16 November 1981): 72

With respect to (1), various studies have demonstrated the importance of personal contacts in getting a job. One study analyzed the importance of formal applications vs. personal contacts in finding a job for three occupations—technical, professional, and managerial.[21] Personal contacts were more important than formal applications for professional and managerial jobs; the reverse was true for technical jobs. Since technical jobs can usually be evaluated quite objectively, these findings are consistent with the theory that political behavior is more likely to be found in areas where procedures or criteria are not explicitly stated.

With respect to promotion, politics appears to play a major role in determining who will get promoted. The pyramidal shape of organizations means that as a person moves up the hierarchy, competition for the restricted number of positions becomes more and more intense. In this competitive environment, factors other than technical expertise or meritorious service become critical because each person probably has similar merit or expertise. The only way to distinguish between people is to develop additional criteria (e.g., how well does the candidate "fit in") when making promotion choices.

---

## *Organizational Reality* 13-7
## *Networking*

The emergence of networking as an aid to career development as well as a support system, has become a force to be reckoned with. Many corporations have formal and informal women's networks to help their female employees at all levels.

At Ralston-Purina in St. Louis, about 10 percent of all female employees are members of Women in Business (WIB). WIB's purpose is threefold: to encourage and develop programs to enhance professional skills and provide understanding of the company; to extend the company's objective of self-renewal and maximize use of its human resources; and to act as a support system for sharing experiences and insights.

Since 1975, WIB has operated with the total approval of corporate executives. At WIB's monthly meetings, corporate officers are often included to explain their jobs and functions, as well as to discuss planning, development, and company performance. WIB also holds bimonthly evening meetings, geared more towards members' individual career development than to furthering the goals of the company.

Another women's network, the Women's Employment Network in Seattle, Washington, is designed to open doors to nontraditional work. The Employment Network is partly a response to Seattle's affirmative action guidelines, which require that 20 percent of workers on any publicly funded project be women.

The Network teaches women about the industrial world, with a two-week crash course on what is available, how to use the tools of the trade, and how to deal with sexual harassment. The women are then given ninety days to consult with employment counselors to find jobs. After twelve training sessions, placement is about 60 percent.

---

Source: "Management in Practice," *Management Review* (August 1981): 43–5.

What characteristics does an aspiring manager have to demonstrate to get promoted? A detailed answer to this question is beyond the scope of this book, but the most important characteristic appears to be the ill-defined one of "fitting in."[22] As one author notes:

> . . . job performance is not a sufficient condition for career advancement in many organizational contexts and may not even be necessary. Social similarities, social background, and social contacts *are* necessary and in many instances sufficient[23] (emphasis added).

The obvious implication of this view is that successful executives are those who are able to get along with their peers and who are seen as fitting in to the organization's internal environment. Once again, the importance of nontask capabilities to career success emerges.

## ☐ How Managers View Political Behavior

The studies cited above deal with a variety of situations (both individual and group) where political behavior appears to play an important role. How do practicing managers view the issue of politics within organizations?

In one study, 428 managers in public- and private-sector organizations were given a series of statements and asked to agree or disagree with them.[24] There were several interesting findings. First, 60 percent of the respondents felt that most casual talk at work was political in nature, and 70 percent agreed that politics was common in their organizations.

Second, a majority of the respondents agreed that political behavior is self-serving and detrimental to the organization in which it occurs. Overall, political behavior was viewed as bad, unfair, unnecessary and conflict-oriented. When respondents were asked to write a brief story demonstrating political behavior in action, 84 percent of the stories portrayed it as being nonrational.

Third, people at lower levels in organizations perceived more politics than people at higher levels. People at lower levels apparently saw themselves as "victims" of political behavior. We can speculate that people at upper levels saw less politics because they felt that they achieved their position not through political behavior, but through meritorious service.

Fourth, there was no difference in the perceived level of political behavior in public- and private-sector organizations. If we recall our earlier notion that individuals pursue their own self-interests regardless of the setting, this finding is not surprising.

Fifth, over 70 percent of the respondents agreed that successful and powerful executives act in a political fashion. They also felt that a person *must* be a good politician to get ahead in organizations.

Finally, political behavior was most frequently perceived in areas where there were no explicit policies or procedures to guide people. Political behavior was easy to observe in the areas of promotions and transfers, delegation of authority, and interdepartmental coordination. Although it may appear that objective criteria exist for issues such as promotion, most of the incidents written by the respondents mentioned that people got promoted because of "pull" rather than because they met the objective criteria for promotion.

This study indicates once again the universality of political behavior in organizations and the fact that most people have reservations about it. It suggests that individual managers face a real dilemma: they must either "join the parade" and behave in a political fashion in order to further their career, or they must decide to opt out of such behavior, realizing that in so doing they may be seriously reducing their chances of getting ahead. This is, of course, a decision that each individual must make, given his personal value system and beliefs about what is right.

# ■ POLITICS, CONFLICT, AND DECISION MAKING

For purposes of simplicity, and to facilitate detailed analysis, we have considered the topics of politics, conflict, and decision making in separate chapters. These topics are, however, closely intertwined. Now that all three topics have been presented, it is possible to consider the interrelationships among them. We first present a conceptual analysis of these relationships and then give an example demonstrating the relationships.

We can start from the most fundamental fact about human behavior that we have noted in this chapter: people in organizations pursue their own personal goals. The pursuit of these personal goals is not *automatically* detrimental to other individuals or to the organization. However, when many individuals are pursuing their own diverse goals, it is very likely that disagreements (conflict) will arise as to whose goals will become the formal, stated goals of the organization. When individuals see that there is conflict about goals, they will engage in a variety of political behaviors (including using biased information which supports what they want to do). At this point severe conflict often develops as each individual or group tries to counteract the political behavior of the opposing individual or group. In these situations, management is often forced to resolve the conflict by acting in an arbitrator role. However, managers who act as arbitrators are themselves subject to political motives, and this will further influence what decision eventually is made.

As a practical example of how politics, conflict, and decision making are related, consider the following situation: A company is involved in the design and manufacturing of military and space components for the U.S. government (for NASA and the Pentagon). This company has been successful at getting government contracts during the last decade because it has concentrated on the more "mundane" products where relatively well-understood technologies are used (e.g., jet engines).

Recently, several members of the marketing department have been stressing the need for the company to pursue more state-of-the-art contracts (e.g., equipment for deep space exploration and new military weapons systems for use in space). The marketing people argue that successful bidding on these contracts will give a trememdous boost to the company's reputation and will also increase its profits. (It will also increase marketing's status, but this is not mentioned.)

The research and development (R & D) people argue that it is unwise to pursue state-of-the-art contracts. They point out that the company has built up a good reputation in one area, and it is very risky to move into something completely new. (They also feel that their present high status will decline if marketing pursues glamorous new projects, but they don't mention this.)

The result is a conflict between marketing and R & D which is at least partly (and perhaps substantially) caused by each group pursuing its own goals. As the conflict escalates, each group engages in various political behaviors to try to get its way. For example, marketing mobilizes information favorable to its point of view. It develops probabilities that the new contracts will be obtained, and probabilities of the profits that will be generated from these new projects. R & D uses various tactics to show that these figures are too optimistic, and points out that if the company pursues these new contracts and fails, it will jeopardize the profitability of the entire company.

As more and more information is generated, and as more political behavior comes to the fore, the situation becomes increasingly confused. Finally a decision is made to pursue new, high-technology contracts. (This decision is made because the president and two influential vice-presidents like the idea.)

Thus, individual preferences initially caused a conflict to develop within two important groups in the company. Once the *conflict* became clear, *political behavior* was evident as each side mobilized biased information designed to insure that a certain *decision* was made. Top management then made a decision based on a combination of factors, including how it saw the information, and how the decision would affect its own goals and desires.

This example is only one of many that could be cited. The important point is that three key concepts—politics, conflict, and decision making—are closely related in the day-to-day dynamics of organizational life. An understanding of these relationships is necessary before we can accurately analyze why things happen as they do in organizations.

# ■ ORGANIZATIONAL POLITICS—GOOD OR BAD?

Until very recently, the majority of people who analyzed organizations or worked in them assumed that political behavior was "bad." However, many researchers and managers are now accepting the idea that political behavior has positive aspects. At the very least, it is now accepted that political behavior is a *fact* of organizational life, and that an improved understanding of it can lead to better results for both organizations and individuals. However, many people still see it as undesirable, so in this section, the major arguments made by the opponents of political behavior are examined. For each of these arguments, the counter arguments made by the supporters of political behavior are presented.

1. *People are treated unfairly when political decisions are made.* Ethnic minority groups argue, for example, that employment decisions are made not on the basis of competence, but on the basis of ethnic origin. (This is, of course, illegal,

but that doesn't stop it from happening.) Opponents of political behavior also argue that it causes decisions to be made on mysterious criteria by an "in-group" that does not really have to answer to anyone. The existence of this in-group (frequently called the "old-boy" network) is often considered unreasonable in a democratic society. The implication of the argument is that the old-boy network will make decisions based on something other than "rational" or "merit" grounds and that competent people may not be given a chance to show their merit; thus, organizational performance will suffer.

The supporters of political behavior reject this line of reasoning. They argue that the old-boy network benefits organizations because it is very efficient. It is efficient because (1) decisions can be made quickly and accurately on the basis of personal contacts, and (2) the organization benefits because the decision maker feels confident about the results when a decision is made on this basis. Information is crucial in making good decisions, and supporters argue that "political" decision making gives better results than decision making on a "traditional" basis.

2. *Political behavior distorts the decision-making process such that decisions are made that are bad for the organization or for society as a whole.* Opponents of political behavior feel that the political maneuvering that goes on in organizations is caused by individuals' desires to improve their career prospects. While this is not bad *per se*, it is often carried to extremes.

---

### *Organizational Reality* 13-8
### *The "Old-Boy" Network*

Ralph S. is the head of the Midwest Foundation, a philanthropic organization that gives money to deserving charitable organizations. At a recent dinner honoring individuals who had contributed money to the local business school, Ralph ran into George R., a young friend of his. The following discussion took place:

**George:** You know, as I look out over this group, I see all kinds of people who are very influential in this city. But these "old boys" form a closed group and they often make unfair decisions.

**Ralph:** What do you mean "unfair"?

**George:** Well, people are treated unfairly by them. Take your foundation, for example. Before you give money to charitable organizations, you consult your old buddies about which organizations to give it to. That means that charities that are not plugged into the old-boy network lose out. That's not right; you should use a more rational system.

**Ralph:** The system I use *is* rational and efficient. I can trust my friends to give me good information on organizations that ask for money. If I simply examined applications for money without ever getting the "inside story" on the applicant, I wouldn't be doing my job. But my friends will give me the *real* story. Trust is the name of the game in this business.

# Box 13-3: Politics and Decision Making

People who engage in political behavior use a variety of tactics to get what they want. The bottom line, however, is that these *informal* political tactics are designed to get *formal* decisions made which will legitimize what the person wants.

Because political behavior influences decisions, it is both controversial and commonly found in organizations. The most typical manifestation of political behavior in organizational decision making concerns the interpretation of information. Suppose a company is considering the manufacture and sale of a new product. Marketing people will provide data on market potential, competition, and so on, but if executives from other areas do not want to go ahead (e.g., because their status is threatened by the new project), they will interpret the data in a way that will justify their opposition. If the marketing people cannot get agreement to go ahead, they will reinterpret the data to make their view look more rational. And so it goes.

Eventually a decision will be reached, but some people will invariably be unhappy. Whether the decision was based on rational grounds or not may be impossible to determine, but each side will claim that its view was the rational one.

The motivation to "look out for number one" is very strong in most people, often strong enough to induce them to do things that further their own career without regard to the harm they may cause to other individuals, the organization, and society as a whole. The most widely cited example of this is the executive who comes to "shape up" a weak division. Typically, some very dramatic actions are taken in the short run, and performance often does improve noticeably. After a couple of years, the executive is promoted to another position on the basis of his successful past performance. But what happens after the executive leaves the division? Sometimes productivity declines and it appears that the executive is really missed. However, performance might have declined even if he had stayed, because the executive generated increased profits in the short run only by reducing training, maintenance, and other such expenditures. Thus, the executive's pursuit of his own personal goals (promotion) induced him to do things that were bad for the organization.

Supporters of political behavior agree that things like this happen, but they respond by pointing out that in a free society, individuals should be allowed to pursue their self-interest as long as they are not breaking the law. The supporters of political behavior also point out that there will always be conflicts between individuals about what goals an organization should pursue and the behavior that is acceptable in the pursuit of these goals. When disagreements arise, there must be some way to resolve them. Supporters of political behavior argue that the most effective and efficient mechanism for resolving these conflicts is the use of power. Hence, political behavior is functional for individuals and organizations because it provides a mechanism for resolving conflicts that might otherwise be unresolvable.

3. *Political behavior and the use of power allows an organization to ignore internal and external groups that may be unhappy with what the organization is doing.* The essence of the criticism is that certain individuals and groups inside and outside organizations are prevented from getting their way because the people in power simply ignore them. What's worse, the people in power stay there by using all sorts of unfair tactics. The most obvious example of this is the refusal of corporations to do voluntarily many of the things (e.g., seat belts, pollution control) that consumer groups believe corporations should do. Consumer advocates respond by attempting to get laws passed requiring that these things be done.

Supporters of political behavior reject this line of reasoning and argue that just the reverse is true—political behavior *forces* an organization to behave realistically (both internally and in its relations with external environment). Supporters agree that in every organization there is a tendency for people at the top to try to retain their positions. At the same time, however, many pressures for change are at work, both internally and externally. If the organization does not deal with these changes, it will find itself in deep trouble. (For example, many of the traditional manufacturing industries in the U.S. find themselves unable to compete with foreign firms because they are unwilling or unable to adapt to fundamental changes in their industry.) Often, political behavior on the part of certain managers in the firm is the only way to move the organization in a direction that will ensure survival.

4. *Organizational politics is very inefficient and time-consuming.* Opponents of political behavior argue that the negotiation, bargaining, conflict, and strategy development that is so evident in political behavior takes up people's time unduly. They express concern that people in organizations will expend so much effort on

---

### *Organizational Reality* 13-9
### *Politics and Environmental Responsiveness*

In one organization a coalition of managers engaged in a variety of political tactics to persuade the board of directors to get rid of a certain low-performing division. For example, they leaked rumors to the division's customers that the future of the division was uncertain. They did this so that orders would decline and divisional performance would decline even more. Had more "rational" tactics been used (e.g., providing objective data on the division's performance) it is doubtful if the board would have agreed, because the division had formerly been very profitable. However, if this division had not been disposed of, the performance of the total organization would have suffered.

---

Source: R. H. Miles, *Macro Organizational Behavior* (Santa Monica, California: Goodyear Publishing Co., 1980) p. 155.

## Box 13-4: Politics and Time Management

One of the most popular management seminars on time management is William Oncken's "Managing Management Time." Oncken is a consultant who teaches thousands of executives each year how to manage their time more effectively. His program is based on an article in *Harvard Business Review* called "Management Time: Who's Got the Monkey?" (coauthored by Donald Wass).

Oncken maintains that the major purpose of bureaucracy is to provide excuses why one department or person is unable to do something for someone else. If another person will not do what you ask, you waste your time by being forced to go through the bureaucracy to get it done.

Oncken believes it is possible to "short-circuit" the bureaucracy (which saves time) through a planned strategy. The strategy involves building up what Oncken calls a "good organizational credit rating." He recommends that every manager select the people in the organization who "can make or break you" (usually no more than ten people). These people should be cultivated in every sense of the word so that a "credit rating" is built up. Then, when you call on these people for help, they recall your credit balance, and repay you by ignoring the bureaucratic red tape. As would be expected, people with poor credit ratings get held up with procedures, forms, rules, regulations, and other bureaucratic hurdles that take time.

political behavior that they will have little time or energy left for pursuing organizational goals. As a result, organizational performance will suffer.

Supporters of politics argue that political decisions are made as quickly as "rational" decisions. They argue that rational processes take a great deal of time because information must be formally gathered and analyzed, and its meaning debated by many people. Political processes, on the other hand, are more informal and tend toward private rather than public discussions of various issues. Therefore, political decisions may be made even quicker than those made on a "rational" basis.

5. *Political processes allow certain individuals to have too much power while other individuals have too little.* This is perhaps the most fundamental criticism of political behavior. Central to this argument is the idea that power corrupts people and that power differences between people should therefore be minimized. The best way to do this is to eliminate political behavior.

In response to this criticism, supporters of political behavior make three points: First, it is not possible to minimize power differences between people because of the pyramidal structure of organizations, and because people differ in their abilities and inclinations to behave politically. Second, the most powerful individuals and departments in organizations are usually those that cope with important uncertainties the organization is facing. Power is therefore a way of inducing people to do those things (e.g., coping with uncertainty) which increase organiza-

## Box 13-5: Eliminating Politics in Government

As noted in the text, organizational politics is considered by many people as something that must be stopped. Nowhere is this feeling more evident than in large, bureaucratic organizations—especially government. Public service organizations, as noted in Chapter 7, are based on the rational model of organizations and are particularly sensitive to any decision or event that appears to be "suspicious" (read political). Consequently, considerable effort is expended insuring that no influence processes occur outside of the rational, bureaucratic system.

One area which has been particularly affected by this trend is promotion decisions. Most government organizations now have "selection boards" which screen applicants and make a recommendation to a commission. The purpose of the board is to make sure that no candidate is treated more favorably than any other, and that no manager makes a hiring decision based on anything other than rational criteria.

The extreme concern about these types of decisions (perhaps as a backlash to Watergate) has caused some interesting outcomes. In at least one government department, it is now policy that *before* the promotion interview, candidates be given the questions they will be asked during the interview. No member on the committee may ask a question that has not been asked of every other candidate.

Where will all this stop? It is difficult to tell, but even the current system has not eliminated the *perception* that politics determines who gets promoted. Unsuccessful candidates still see the decision as being "fixed." Wouldn't it be interesting if attempts to eliminate politics actually increased it?

tional effectiveness. Third, individuals who are able to solve key organizational problems rise to positions of power. This further increases organizational effectiveness. At a society-wide level, an interesting trend is evident regarding the kinds of individuals who become chief executives. In the early twentieth century, the major problem facing organizations was how to satisfy rapidly increasing demand. In this environment, production-oriented people often became presidents of corporations. By the 1930s and 1940s, production problems had been largely resolved and the main problem was how to sell what was being produced. Thus, sales-oriented people rose to positions of power. More recently, the unsettled financial environment has given finance- and accounting-oriented people more power.

At a more specific level, this idea was demonstrated in a study of fifty-seven hospital administrators.[25] These administrators headed two different kinds of hospitals in terms of the funding they received: patient billings (usually paid for by insurance companies), or government subsidies. The administrative talent necessary in these two kinds of hospitals was apparently quite different. In the

## Box 13-6: Politics or Rationality—Which Do You Prefer?

As you proceed through your studies you will take many different courses that are designed to give you a better understanding of complex organizations. Courses like quantitative methods, principles of marketing, accounting, capital budgeting, principles of management, etc., all emphasize systematic and rational approaches to organizational decision making. Many students never question the accuracy or utility of this view of organizational life.

Now that you have been exposed to another point of view—the political one—you have several questions to answer. Do you think that the political view of organizations is a realistic one? If so, are you disappointed that organizations are not places where strictly rational criteria are always used to make decisions? What does this imply about the rational and systematic management techniques you will learn during your school years? Will they be helpful in furthering your career in an actual organization? How do you feel about engaging in some of the political tactics mentioned in this chapter?

These are interesting (and difficult) questions, but you will benefit by asking them and then carefully considering how and why you answered them the way you did.

hospitals where a large portion of revenue was obtained from patient billings, the top administrators were much more likely to have backgrounds in accounting. Subsidized hospitals, on the other hand, were much more likely to have administrators with professional backgrounds (e.g., medicine). When citing studies like this, supporters of political behavior point out that powerful people in organizations often have appropriate training for their positions as well as having good political sense. Surely this combination of talent is better than simply having good training.

**Conclusion**   It is the authors' view that, managed properly, political behavior and the use of power can be very helpful to an organization. Unfortunately, our current understanding of organizational politics does not allow us to state simple rules for effectively managing politics and the use of power. We must also keep in mind that any attempt to closely regulate political behavior may be doomed to failure. Somehow, people always find ways to get around the rules that someone else makes. Before getting too depressed about all this, consider the following quote which indicates that things aren't all that bad:

> . . . Power—because of the way it develops and the way it is used—will always result in the organization suboptimizing its performance. However, to this grim absolute, we add a comforting caveat: If any criteria other than power were the basis for determining an organization's decisions, the result would be even worse.[26]

## *Susan James Revisited*

In the opening incident, Susan James was faced with the problem of how to get promoted ahead of an older, more experienced person who was an informal leader of an important group. Susan's success was due, in part, to her sensitivity about organizational politics.

Recall that Susan's tactics consisted of cultivating friendships prior to the time when these friendships could be used to secure important votes. In the situation facing Susan, the selection committee decision was obviously important, but the crucial decision was the election of members to the selection committee. As we have seen in both Chapters 9 and 13, decisions made within organizations may be based on a variety of criteria, including how well a person is liked. In this situation, Susan realized that having four sympathetic members on the selection committee was very likely to result in her being chosen as the new head.

Susan's behavior in the opening incident is quite consistent with the definition of politics presented in the chapter, i.e., she engaged in various activities (cultivating friendships) to gain power (be chosen department head) so that she could obtain her preferred outcome (career advancement). We can assume that Carl Krause was unhappy with the outcome because he wanted the job. It is also probable that he was unhappy with the voting tactics Susan's supporters used; he would probably say they were "unfair."

Whether the political activities behind Susan's appointment as head of the department are good or bad is difficult to say. At the individual level, some people are hurt and some people are helped by political behavior. At the organizational level, if political behavior results in a more capable individual being promoted, the organization benefits and the net effect is positive. Of course, the definition of "capable" is of crucial importance. In this case, some would argue that Susan was more "capable" than Carl because she saw what was necessary to get the job. Individuals who aspire to positions of authority must be sensitive to important organizational characteristics, and Susan certainly was sensitive. On the negative side, this definition of "capable" might allow a person to rationalize doing whatever is necessary to get his or her preferred outcomes, and this could be very undesirable.

In the end, all individuals must make their own decisions about how involved they will be in organizational politics. It is clear, however, that all sorts of people are prepared to become heavily involved in an attempt to further their careers. Their activities will have an impact on other members of the organization as well as people in the society at large.

## ■ SUMMARY

In this chapter we analyzed the issue of organizational politics. We noted that the subject is difficult to deal with because (1) little empirical work has been done to date, and (2) few people are willing to admit that politics plays an important role in organizations.

We compared the "rational" and "political" perspectives of organizations, and defined organizational politics as the tactics people use to get power or other resources which can be used to achieve what they want. Political behavior is found in all types of organizations, and is not confined to profit-oriented companies.

The term "power" was also defined and its relationship to politics was noted. Different departments in organizations have different amounts of power even if they appear to be equal on the organization chart. If a department is able to cope with strategic contingencies facing the organization and if its activities are non-substitutable, it will have more power.

Several studies which examined organizational politics were presented. These studies demonstrated the diversity of political behaviors that are possible in areas such as interdepartmental conflict, career advancement, and budget setting. It was also shown that while practicing managers do not view political behavior favorably, they see it as very common in organizations.

The chapter concluded with an analysis of the good and bad points of political behavior. Although many people feel that politics and the use of power is undesirable, the individual and organizational outcomes in this kind of system may be more positive than if some other basis were used to make organizational decisions.

# ■ REVIEW QUESTIONS

1. Compare the "rational" and "political" models of organization.

2. Define organizational politics. Why is it so widespread in organizations?

3. Describe some tactics that are commonly used when people behave politically.

4. How are power and politics related?

5. Why do some sub-units in an organization have more power than others?

6. How are politics, conflict, and decision making interrelated?

7. How do practicing managers view political behavior?

8. What is power? How is it related to political behavior?

# ■ EXERCISE 13-1: WELCOME BACK, CLARENCE

Clarence Washington graduated from high school in June and immediately began working as a clerk in the audit section of a social service agency in a large eastern state. The agency's main function was to administer federal government money that had been

After two years, Clarence decided to return to school to work on a degree in management at the state university. Before he left, the director, Marcia Keller, called him in and indicated that she was very pleased with his work and that he should consider returning to the agency in a management capacity when he had completed his studies. Clarence enthusiastically agreed, since he had enjoyed his work up to that point.

Four years later Clarence returned to the agency and was welcomed by Keller. She and Clarence met in her office, where, after exchanging pleasantries, the following conversation took place:

**Keller:** Clarence, I think I've got just the job for you.
**Clarence:** Well, I'm ready to put into practice some of the things I've learned.
**Keller:** Good. I'd like you to supervise an internal audit team that will examine the management efficiency of our agency. As you know, the public is becoming very critical of inefficiency in government agencies. The word has come down from top management that they want this study done to insure that all departments in our agency are performing up to standard. With your management training, you are the logical person for this job.
**Clarence:** (enthusiastically): I took two courses where I learned a procedure to do an internal management audit. I'm sure the procedure can be applied here. I'm anxious to get started on this project.
**Keller:** Excellent. I know you'll do a good job.

After the meeting ended, Clarence went back to his new office and began to plan his strategy for conducting the internal management audit.

1.  What problems is Clarence Washington likely to encounter as he does the management audit? Why?

2.  What can he do to increase the chances that he will be successful in conducting the audit?

## ■ EXERCISE 13-2:   POWER PLAY

Robert Hendrick grew up on a farm in central Indiana. His parents were very strict and conservative in their views, and over the years he developed a strong sense of right and wrong. He had a very happy childhood because his parents had very strong feelings about the importance of the family unit.

After Hendrick graduated with an engineering degree from Purdue University, he went to work for Latimer Hydraulics, a firm which specialized in the custom manufacture of liquid pumping systems for agricultural and industrial uses. Customers would approach the company with a specific problem and the hydraulic engineers would design a system to meet the customer's need. Since the systems were custom-made, testing was an important function.

Hendrick was a first-rate engineer, and it became clear to his boss (Charles Toland) that he was a valuable addition to the company. Hendrick was given increased responsibility in a variety of areas and he always performed well. Four years after Hendrick joined the firm, a major contract was landed by Latimer Hydraulics. The contract involved building a state-of-the-art system for Creighton Manufacturing, and Hendrick was made the chief engineer on the project. In that role he had the responsibility of overseeing all aspects of the contract, including final testing of the system.

Things went well for the first four months. The work was proceeding on time, and preliminary test results were positive. However, three weeks before the new system was to be ready, Hendrick received the results of a test on a major component of the system, indicating that it did not work. The tests were repeated, but the results were the same. Hendrick therefore began redesign work in order to remedy the defect. He also informed Toland that additional time would be needed to complete the project. At that point the following conversation took place:

**Toland:** I'm sorry, but I can't give you any additional time to complete the project. The customer needs it in three weeks. Just sign the test report saying that the system works and we'll get it working later. We've done that before when we had problems.
**Hendrick:** I can't do that. The system doesn't work! It wouldn't be right.
**Toland:** As the chief engineer, you've got to sign the test report.
**Hendrick:** I won't sign it until the system is working.
**Toland:** Now, Bob, listen to reason. This contract is going to put Latimer on the map! You want to be part of that, don't you? Now sign the report.
**Hendrick:** You can sign it if you want. I won't be part of a deception like that. It's unethical.
**Toland:** Well, I'm going to have to sign it. I'm sorry to say this, but I'm going to remove you as chief engineer, effective immediately.
**Hendrick:** That's a rotten deal. I don't think I want to work for a company that does stuff like this. I quit!

Several months later, Hendrick read in the paper of a problem that had developed between Latimer Hydraulics and Creighton Manufacturing involving a pumping system that didn't work. The paper noted that after some negotiations between Latimer and Creighton, a satisfactory arrangement had been worked out. It also noted that Charles Toland had been promoted to executive vice-president of Latimer Hydraulics.

1. What caused the problem for Robert Hendrick?

2. What could Hendrick have done to avoid a situation like this?

3. What would you have done in this situation?

# ■ ENDNOTES

1. F. H. Goldner, "Success vs. Failure: Prior Managerial Perspective," *Industrial Relations* (October, 1970): 457–474.
2. J. Pfeffer and G. Salancik, "Organization Design: The Case for a Coalitional Model of Organization," *Organization Dynamics* (Autumn, 1977): 15–29.

3. J. Pfeffer, *Power in Organizations* (Boston: Pitman, 1980): p. 7.
4. Bronston, T. Mayes and Robert W. Allen, "Toward A Definition of Organizational Politics," *Academy of Management Review* 2 (1977): 675.
5. J. Pfeffer, *Power in Organizations*, pp. 7–8.
6. V. S. Schein, "Individual Power and Political Behaviors in Organizations: An Inadequately Explored Reality," *Academy of Management Review* 2 (1977): 64–72.
7. V. S. Schein, "Individual Power and Political Behavior in Organizations," 67.
8. G. R. Salancik and J. Pfeffer, "Who Gets Power—And How They Hold On To It: A Strategic Contingency Model of Power," *Organizational Dynamics* 5 (1977): 3.
9. Pfeffer, *Power in Organizations*, p. 9. For a similar finding regarding the definition of politics, see R. W. Allen, D. L. Madison, L. W. Porter, P. A. Renwick, and B. T. Mayes, "Organizational Politics," *California Management Review* 22 (Fall, 1979): 77–83.
10. Ibid., 10–14.
11. David Hickson, C. R. Hinings, C. A. Lee, R. E. Schneck, and J. M. Pennings, "A Strategic Contingencies Theory of Intraorganizational Power," *Administrative Science Quarterly* 16 (1971): 216–229.
12. George Strauss, "Tactics of the Lateral Relationship: The Purchasing Agent," *Administrative Science Quarterly* 7 (1962): 161–186.
13. Dafna Izraeli, "The Middle Manager and the Tactics of Power Expansion: A Case Study," *Sloan Management Review* (Winter, 1975): 57–70.
14. Michael Crozier, *The Bureaucratic Phonomenon* (Chicago: University of Chicago Press, 1964).
15. C. R. Hinings, D. J. Hickson, J. M. Pennings, and R. E. Schneck, "Structural Conditions of Intraorganizational Power," *Administrative Science Quarterly* 18 (1974): 22–44.
16. C. S. Saunders and R. Scamell, "Intraorganizational Distributions of Power: Replication Research," *Academy of Management Journal*, 25 (1982): 192–200.
17. Jeffrey Pfeffer and Gerald Salancik, "Organizational Decision Making as a Political Process: the Case of a University Budget," *Administrative Science Quarterly* 19 (1974): 135–151.
18. Jeffrey Pfeffer and William L. Moore, "Power in University Budgeting: A Replication and Extension," *Administrative Science Quarterly* 25 (1980): 637–653; also Frederick Hills and Thomas Mahoney, "University Budgets and Organizational Decision Making," *Administrative Science Quarterly* 23 (1978): 454–465.
19. Jeffrey Pfeffer and Anthony Leong, "Resource Allocations in United Funds: Examination of Power and Dependence," *Social Forces* 55 (1977): 775–790.
20. Keith Provan, Janice Beyer, and Carlos Kruytbosch, "Environmental Linkages and Power in Resource—Dependent Relations Between Organizations," *Administrative Science Quarterly* 25 (1980): 200–225.
21. Mark Granovetter, *Getting A Job: A Study of Contacts and Careers* (Cambridge, Massachusetts: Harvard University Press, 1974).
22. Rosabeth M. Kantes, *Men and Women of the Corporation* (New York: Basic Books, 1977).
23. Pfeffer, *Power in Organizations*, 252.
24. J. Gandz and V. V. Murray, "The Experience of Workplace Politics," *Academy of Management Journal* 23 (1980): 237–251.
25. Jeffrey Pfeffer and Gerald Salancik, "Organizational Context and the Characteristics and Tenure of Hospital Administrators," *Academy of Management Journal* 20 (1977): 74–88.
26. G. R. Salancik and J. Pfeffer, "Who Gets Power—And How They Hold On To It: A Strategic Contingency Model of Power," *Organizational Dynamics* 5 (1977): 20.

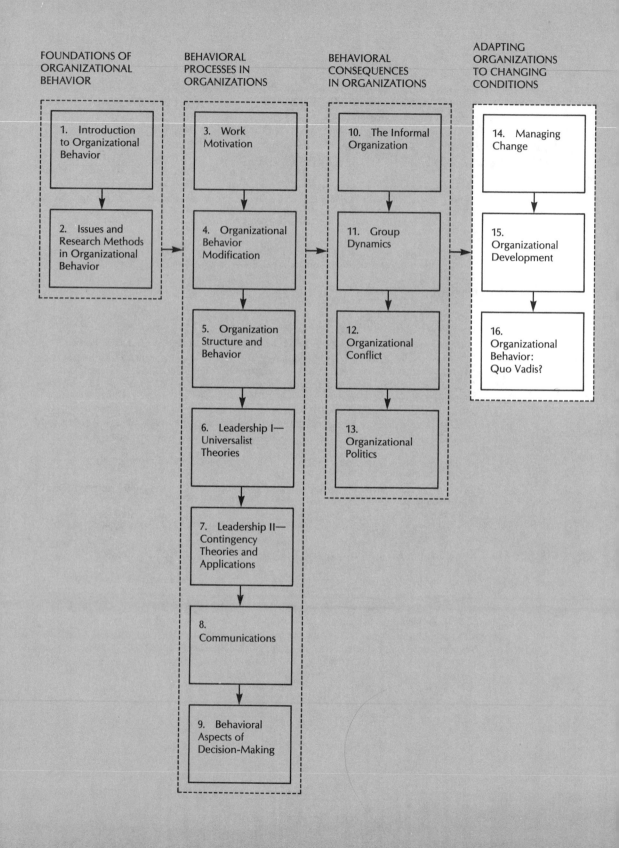

**FOUNDATIONS OF ORGANIZATIONAL BEHAVIOR**

1. Introduction to Organizational Behavior

2. Issues and Research Methods in Organizational Behavior

**BEHAVIORAL PROCESSES IN ORGANIZATIONS**

3. Work Motivation

4. Organizational Behavior Modification

5. Organization Structure and Behavior

6. Leadership I—Universalist Theories

7. Leadership II—Contingency Theories and Applications

8. Communications

9. Behavioral Aspects of Decision-Making

**BEHAVIORAL CONSEQUENCES IN ORGANIZATIONS**

10. The Informal Organization

11. Group Dynamics

12. Organizational Conflict

13. Organizational Politics

**ADAPTING ORGANIZATIONS TO CHANGING CONDITIONS**

14. Managing Change

15. Organizational Development

16. Organizational Behavior: Quo Vadis?

# Adapting Organizations to Changing Conditions

# SECTION IV

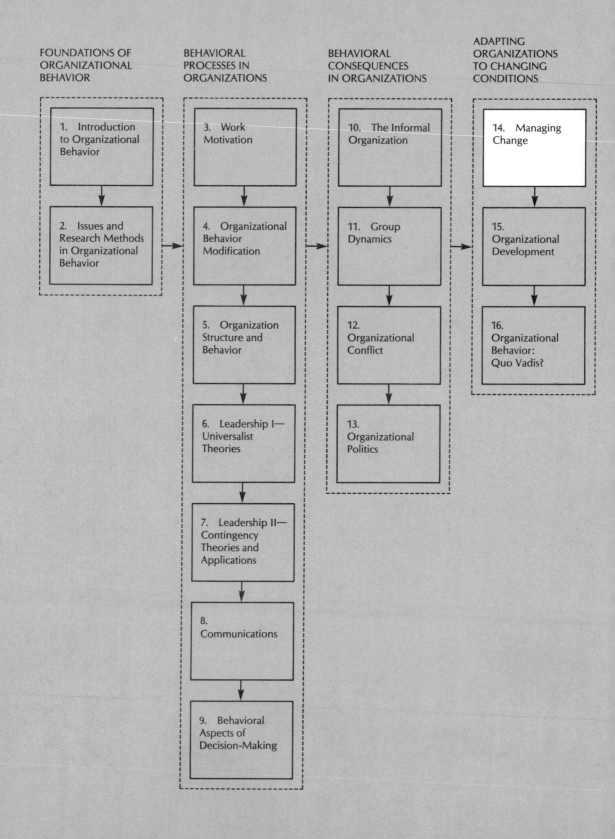

FOUNDATIONS OF
ORGANIZATIONAL
BEHAVIOR

BEHAVIORAL
PROCESSES IN
ORGANIZATIONS

BEHAVIORAL
CONSEQUENCES
IN ORGANIZATIONS

ADAPTING
ORGANIZATIONS
TO CHANGING
CONDITIONS

1. Introduction to Organizational Behavior

2. Issues and Research Methods in Organizational Behavior

3. Work Motivation

4. Organizational Behavior Modification

5. Organization Structure and Behavior

6. Leadership I—Universalist Theories

7. Leadership II—Contingency Theories and Applications

8. Communications

9. Behavioral Aspects of Decision-Making

10. The Informal Organization

11. Group Dynamics

12. Organizational Conflict

13. Organizational Politics

14. Managing Change

15. Organizational Development

16. Organizational Behavior: Quo Vadis?

# Managing Change

## ■ Learning Objectives

After a thorough reading of this chapter you should be able to:

☐ Describe the three levels of change in organizations and the implications these have for managers.

☐ Explain and give examples of different degrees of organizational change.

☐ List and explain the eight most common reasons for resistance to change.

☐ Diagram the force-field analysis method of examining change situations and explain how the model works.

☐ Describe the contingency model of analyzing change situations and give examples of each situation.

☐ Explain the advantages and limitations of using participation to introduce change.

☐ List and explain the six other methods of introducing change.

# Chapter  14

# ■ KEY TERMS

**Cognitive change**
**Rational resistance to change**
**Perception**
**Emotional resistance to change**
**Restraining forces**
**Driving forces**
**"Quid pro quo" approach**
**Contingency change strategies**

# ■ CHAPTER OUTLINE

## *Opening Incident*

Professor Grastark was really excited about this assignment. The dean had asked him to spearhead the renovations project for the faculty's building so that the new, improved space would be ready for the fall term. The project had special appeal since one of the outcomes of the project was a new office for Professor Grastark, who had just been promoted to associate dean. Also, Professor Grastark felt this would be a good opportunity to practice the principles of managing change he had been teaching all these years.

It seemed to be a perfect case study: there were all the usual potential problems associated with change such as status implications, social system problems, and workflow considerations. The nature of the problem appeared to be obvious in that the faculty was short of space and the renovations were intended to make better use of the present space. Budget limitations prevented any new space from being added.

Professor Grastark planned his strategy carefully. The fact that a change must occur meant that his job was to insure that it occurred quickly (classes would begin in two months) and with a minimum of disruption of the daily work. Being a self-proclaimed expert in managing change, he also knew it was important for those affected by the change to have a voice in it, to increase their acceptance.

After reviewing the situation with several other faculty members, it was agreed that the basic problem was lack of adequate space to effectively perform the administrative functions of the faculty. Professor Grastark examined all the possibilities with the campus architect and it was decided that administrative efficiency could best be improved by moving all the administrative functions to the space presently occupied by the graduate student carrels. Since the graduate students needed study space, Grastark decided that a portion of the undergraduate student study hall (which the faculty agreed was poorly used since the students used it primarily as a lunchroom) would be partitioned off, and graduate students would have their own area, secured by locks, available for them. The architect noted that the carrels could not be moved economically and the cost of building new ones was quite large, so Grastark thought it best to consult the graduate students before deciding how their new space would be constructed.

The move also meant that several secretaries would be displaced from their present work stations and moved into smaller quarters which, unfortunately, were a greater distance from their friends and the faculty who assigned them work. Noting the potential problems with this, Grastark decided to let the secretaries have total control over how their new work area would be laid out and decorated. With these basic plans in mind, Professor Grastark instructed the architect to begin preparing the working drawings, with the final touches added after the participation process was finished.

To keep people informed about the change, Professor Grastark sent a memo to everyone describing the general nature of the changes and the proposed construction schedule. Reaction to the memo was quick. First in line was the president of the graduate students association with a petition from the students demanding that the change be stopped. They resented their carrels being taken away and didn't like the idea of being "stuffed in with the crummy undergraduates." Grastark explained carefully that they would be better off in the new situation since they would have more room, the space would be more secure than the open carrels, and more graduate students would have access to the space. The graduate student representative remained unconvinced and left after threatening to lead the student body in a boycott of all classes.

Next in line was the president of the undergraduate students. Obviously annoyed because if a secretary had not shown him the memo he would have had no idea the change was happening, his major annoyance centered on losing so much study space to the graduate students. Again Grastark pointed out the fact that the study hall was not used primarily for studying and therefore could not possibly be a great loss to the students. Grastark also pointed out that everyone must suffer in times of restraint for the common good of the faculty, a point lost on the student representative since he had stormed out of the office before Grastark could finish.

The peak of frustration for Grastark was the secretaries, who complained that the new arrangement would make them inefficient, an interesting fact, Grastark thought, given that the major purpose of the change was to increase efficiency. Several of the secretaries had gotten together the previous evening and drawn up a sketch of a floor plan which, in their opinion, was better than what had been proposed. They requested that Grastark postpone the starting date for the project to give the architect time to incorporate their new plan.

As Professor Grastark stared at the new office layout diagram left by the secretaries, he reflected on the value of the participation process. Of the many thoughts crossing his mind, the most frequent one was why autocratic management was so popular with managers.

# MANAGING CHANGE

The topic of managing change is one that comes closest to describing the totality of a manager's job. Practically everything a manager does is in some way concerned with implementing change. Hiring a new employee (changing the work group), purchasing a new piece of equipment (changing work methods), and rearranging work stations (changing work flows), all require knowledge of how to manage change effectively. Virtually every time a manager makes a decision some type of change occurs.

Change is a fact of life in all organizations. One study showed that most companies or divisions of major corporations find they must undertake moderate organizational changes at least once a year and major changes every four or five years.[1] There are different levels of change, which range all the way from a minor change in a work procedure to a major revamping of the organization structure.

Managing change is a subject that utilizes many of the concepts developed in previous chapters. Knowledge about motivation, leadership, group dynamics, organizational politics, conflict, determinants of behavior, and communications are all important in understanding how change processes can be managed effectively. It is useful, therefore, to view this chapter as the integration and application of the previous chapters.

Our study of managing change begins with an analysis of the levels of change (individual, group, and organizational), and the degrees of change that can occur within these levels. Next we explore why people resist change, and conclude with models for analyzing change strategies and applications of the strategies.

# LEVELS OF ORGANIZATIONAL CHANGE

There are two methods of analyzing levels of organizational change. One method is to examine individual, group, and organizational levels, and the other is to examine the degree of change required of those affected by the change. The combination of level and degree of change produces a matrix for analyzing the relationships, as shown in Figure 14-1.

The effect upon each level in the system is partially determined by the magnitude of the change. For example, individual changes usually do not affect the total organization, but large changes at the individual level can have an effect, such as a change in the chief executive. The information in Figure 14-1 gives examples of the various degrees and levels of changes.

**Individual Level**    Changes at the individual level seldom have significant implications for the total organization, although there is the occasional exception. Examples of changes at the individual level are changes in a job assignment, a physical move to a different location, or the change in maturity of a person which occurs naturally over time. According to social systems theory (see Chapter 2), *any* change in the system will affect other parts of the system, but the effects are often so small they are undetectable except to the trained observer or to the individuals themselves. If a major change occurred in an individual, the ramifications would be such that changes would also occur on the group level. This, in turn, might influence the wider organization.

From an applications perspective, it is useful to understand that only the smallest of changes would have an effect at the individual level only. As noted earlier, although such changes only rarely affect the total organization, a manager who wished to implement a major change at the individual level should understand that the change will likely have repercussions beyond the individual. For

LEVELS OF CHANGE

|  | INDIVIDUAL | GROUP | ORGANIZATION |
|---|---|---|---|
| SMALL | PROMOTION OF INDIVIDUALS | ADD NEW EMPLOYEE TO GROUP | CREATE NEW STAFF DEPARTMENT |
| MEDIUM | TRAINING PROGRAM FOR MANAGERS | MERGE GROUPS | REDUCTION OF WORKFORCE |
| LARGE | CHANGE C.E.O. | DISBAND WORK GROUP | MAJOR RESTRUCTURING OF ORGANIZATION |

DEGREES OF CHANGE

**FIGURE 14-1.    Examples of Interactions Between Levels and Degrees of Change**

example, if a manager decides to transfer an employee, this may disrupt the social functioning of the work group.

**Group Level**   Most organizational changes have their major effects at the group level. This is because most activities in organizations are organized on a group basis. The groups could be departments, project teams, functional units within departments, or informal work groups. Or, as noted in Chapters 10 and 11, changes at this level can affect work flows, job design, social organization, influence and status systems, and communication patterns.

As will be seen later in this chapter, managers must consider group factors when implementing change. Informal groups can pose a major barrier to change because of the inherent strength they contain. Formal groups can also resist change, as exemplified by the resistance shown by unions to the changes proposed by management. Because of the powerful influence that groups can have on individuals, effective implementation of change at the group level can frequently overcome resistance at the individual level.

**Organizational Level**   Change at the organizational level is generally referred to as "organization development."[2] Since the next chapter discusses this topic in depth, we will minimize our discussion here. Changes at this level involve major programs that affect both individuals and groups. Decisions regarding these changes are generally made by senior management and are seldom implemented by only a single manager. Frequently they occur over long periods of time and require considerable planning for implementation. Examples of these changes would be reorganization of the organization structure and responsibilities, revamping of company compensation systems, or major shifts in an organization's objectives.

The relationship between the three levels of change is pictured in Figure 14-2. It suggests that changes at any level affect the other levels, with the dominant effect being from the total organizational level down to the individual level. The strength of the effect will vary with the source; for example, organizational changes will tend to have major impacts on individuals, but individuals will have

|  |  | SOURCE | | |
|---|---|---|---|---|
|  |  | INDIVIDUAL | GROUP | ORGANIZATION |
| EFFECT | INDIVIDUAL | — | L | L |
|  | GROUP | M | — | L |
|  | ORGAN-IZATION | S | M | — |

S = SMALL, M = MEDIUM, L = LARGE

**FIGURE 14-2.   Interaction Effects of Different Levels of Organizational Change**

minimal impacts on organizations. The group, or intermediate level, tends to have moderate effects on both individuals and the organization. The major focus in this chapter will be on managing change at the individual and group levels, since it is here that most managers will experience problems. In Chapter 15, Organizational Development, we will discuss the various approaches to managing change at the organizational level.

# ■ DEGREES OF ORGANIZATIONAL CHANGE

Changes can also occur in various degrees at any level. There can be large changes at the individual level or, at the other extreme, small changes at the organizational level. As illustrated in Figure 14-3, the range of changes varies according to the degree of change required, the length of time required to implement the change, and the level of cognitive versus emotional content of the change. Slight behavioral changes such as changes in budgets, work schedules, and communication systems generally cause only changes in patterns of interaction between organizational members. Such changes, because they involve relatively logical information and reasons, cause little emotional involvement of those affected and thus

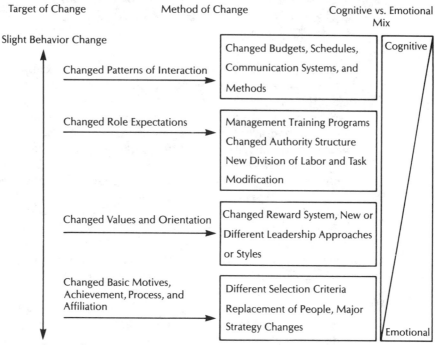

**FIGURE 14-3.   Elements of an Organizational Development Program**

Source: Adapted from P. Lawrence and J. Lorsch, *Developing Organization Diagnosis and Actions* (Reading, Mass.: Addison-Wesley, 1969), p. 87. Used with permission.

## Box 14-1: Oops! Let's Do That Again!

One of the reasons why managing change is so difficult is because change is so final. That is, once a change is made one cannot go back to the original conditions. The reason for this can be explained by the diagram below.

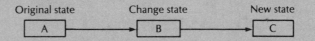

Each of the boxes describes a state of nature. State A is the situation as it exists prior to a change. State B is the state after change. Assume that after state B it is decided that the change was a poor idea and we wish to go back to state A. This is impossible because state A did not include having experienced state B. Therefore, the only possibility is to move on to state C, a new state of nature. The lessons here are: (1) when a change is made it should be thought out carefully because the conditions before the change will never exist again; and (2) to overcome a mistake in managing change usually means that new changes must be made (state C) rather than trying to go back to where everything started.

can occur over relatively short periods of time. For example, if the budget of a department is reduced because of fewer funds available, it is clear why the change is occurring and resistance is likely to be less, despite the fact that members may resent the budget reduction. In these situations, adequate information is usually the only requirement for successfully implementing change.

As we move into areas of greater behavioral change, the cognitive (or rational) aspects of change give way to the emotional aspects. Changes in role expectations or in basic values and orientation affect people differently, since they challenge their previous experiences and accepted ways of doing things. Resistance is encountered because people are reluctant to give up behavioral patterns that were comfortable and psychologically satisfying. Since there is sometimes little concrete data to justify such changes, logical approaches to change lose their effectiveness in these situations. These change situations encounter resistance not only because of the large amount of behavioral change required, but also because the need for change is not usually a matter of accepted fact.

According to Figure 14-3, the largest behavioral changes are those that require changes in the fundamental motives of people. For example, an organization may decide that the historical confrontation between labor and management is destructive and should be changed to a climate of mutual trust and cooperation. As Figure 14-3 illustrates, this might best be accomplished by removing contentious members and replacing them with people who have different values and objectives. A change of this magnitude, which actually is a change in the culture of the entire organization, would take years to accomplish because of the major attitudinal and behavioral changes required.

A similar analysis by Hersey and Blanchard[3] illustrates how different levels of change compare on the basis of difficulty and time involved. Figure 14-4 shows that change progressively affects four different levels: knowledge, attitudes, individual behavior, and group behavior. Changes in knowledge (which are the same as the cognitive changes in Figure 14-3) can occur over short periods of time with little difficulty. Changes in group behavior require more time and are more difficult because they require attitudinal and individual behavior changes. These changes, as we discussed in Chapter 4, require changes in experience through positive reinforcement of behavior over extended periods of time.

In addition to analyzing the different levels of change in organizations, Figures 14-3 and 14-4 also suggest possible solutions to resistance to change. In the "Applications" section of this chapter, we will use these models to illustrate various strategies for dealing with resistance to change. Before we do that, however, it is important to analyze why resistance to change develops.

# ■ ANALYZING RESISTANCE TO CHANGE

Although resistance to change is a common phenomenon in organizations, it must be noted that not all changes are resisted. In fact, if we look at any organization closely we would probably find that far more changes are accepted than resisted. Because resistance to change can result in bizarre types of behavior and can cause managers great difficulty, it gets much more attention in the literature than changes that are accepted. So we tend to characterize people as "antichange" whereas, in fact, they are the most adaptable creatures on earth. In a review of the literature on managing change, Powell and Posner note that much of the writing in the area assumes that employees naturally resist change. However,

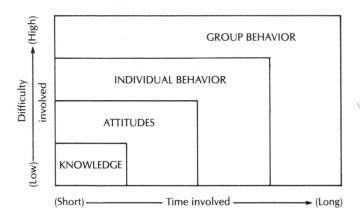

**FIGURE 14-4.  Time and Difficulty Involved in Making Various Changes**

Source: Paul Hersey and Kenneth Blanchard, "The Management of Change," *Training and Development Journal* (January 1972). Used with permission.

it is their contention that there is little empirical evidence to support the existence of widespread resistance, and any resistance that is documented can usually be explained by the self-fulfilling assumptions of managers.[4] Our analysis of resistance to change will similarly suggest that this is an unnatural phenomenon.

---

### Box 14-2: A Change Readily Accepted

As noted in the text, not all changes are resisted. If we examine a change readily accepted, we can learn some important principles of how to manage change effectively. The authors' place of residence is not noted for its mild winters. In fact, it can get downright miserable, notwithstanding the many days of sunshine we get and the many winter activities available. Temperatures can reach 40 below zero and if the wind blows, the wind-chill factor can hit 60 or 70 below. Any winter day will see hundreds, perhaps thousands of Winnipeggers at the airport boarding flights to various places such as Mexico, Florida, the Bahamas, or California. All of these people are going through a major change process: change of physical location (which often means a major cultural change as well), change in daily habits, manner of dress, and social contacts. By any measure, these are major changes. Yet, not only are they not resisting the change, they are even paying large sums for the privilege!

A simple analysis of this change shows the following reasons why there is no resistance:

1. It is their choice to experience the change.
2. Each agrees the change is for the better.
3. The change satisfies an important need for them.
4. Each person is fully informed about the change.
5. The change is planned in advance.
6. Each person anticipates having a positive experience with the change.

If these principles could be incorporated into organizational changes, perhaps resistance to change would be reduced.

---

Accepting the fact that people have a natural instinct to adapt to their environment is the first step toward effective management of change. It not only has the advantage of placing people in a more positive light, but it also suggests that resistance to change is an *unnatural* behavior and therefore the *result* of the situation rather than a built-in response to a change. If managers accept this principle, then they can proceed to analyze the situation to find the (unnatural) cause of resistance. Failure to understand this characteristic of resistance can cause many managers to attempt to ram changes through rather than try to understand the source of the resistance.

**Emotional Versus Rational Resistance**   Figure 14-3 pointed out that changes have both emotional and rational implications for managers. Similarly, resistance to change can have both emotional and rational sources. Various studies have documented the fact that the psychological and sociological factors operating in organizations produce resistance that cannot be understood in reference to objective data.[5] As an initial step toward dealing with resistance, a clear understanding of the differences between emotional and rational resistance is necessary. Depending upon the type of resistance, different strategies are required.

Rational resistance to change occurs when people do not have the proper level of knowledge or information to evaluate the change. The type of resistance is such that providing the necessary information about the change (which usually consists of data, facts, or other types of concrete information) reduces the resistance. For example, an employee may resist being transferred to a different city because he or she may not want to incur the expense of moving; if informed that the firm will pay moving expenses, the employee's resistance will disappear (assuming, of course, that moving expenses were the real reason for resisting the move).

Emotional resistance to change involves the psychological problems of fear, anxiety, suspicion, insecurity, etc. These feelings are evoked because of people's *perception* of how the change will affect them. Because of the personal nature of perception, emotional resistance is often difficult for others to understand. Management can see how a proposed change will benefit an employee, but these "benefits" are often not understood by the employee because of emotional blocks. Change is always viewed from an individual's or group's frame of reference, and dealing with emotional resistance requires that this frame of reference be understood by those proposing the change. For example, management's purchase of a new piece of equipment may, from management's perspective, improve an individual's job. The employees, however, may see the new equipment as one more step towards being replaced by a machine, thus threatening their job security.

The distinction between emotional and rational resistance is admittedly sometimes difficult to make in practice. Management cannot ask people if their resistance is emotional or rational, since people generally see themselves as rational. Some employees would be upset if it was suggested that their reactions were strictly emotional. Only by understanding *why* people resist change can this judgment be made.

Given this understanding, then it is useful to remember that emotional resistance cannot be overcome with rational solutions. In fact, the clue that emotional resistance is being encountered is the failure of logic and reason to reduce resistance. In the example above of management purchasing new equipment to improve work methods, the company may provide facts to prove that no employees have been laid off because of technological improvements; but if the facts are contrary to employees' perceptions, then the resistance will still be present.

Following are some common reasons why employees resist change, although there will be individual differences operating in every situation. Some of these reasons will appear to be rational, but our discussion highlights the emotional side.

**Economic Reasons**    Many people see change as a threat to their economic well-being and security. Technological changes can have this effect since they are perceived as displacing people from jobs. For example, post office workers have traditionally resisted technological changes such as automated letter sorting, since they are a threat to job security. Resistance to change can also occur simply because employees do not know what effects a change will have on their economic position. Uncertainty associated with economic effects is usually perceived as negative.

As is the case with all sources of resistance, the important factor is the *perception* of the individual. There may not be any actual threat to economic security in a proposed change, but if people perceive that there is, then this perception will govern their behavior. To put it another way, economic resistance might be construed as rational resistance, since it is logical that people will resist changes that will negatively affect their economic position. However, economic facts tend to be distorted and perceived according to individual experiences, meaning that resistance often cannot be dealt with by rational means.

**Social Reasons**    In Chapters 10 and 11 we discussed the problems that can arise in small, informal groups, and noted that the social relationships established within groups can be important determinants of behavior. For these same reasons, groups will often resist change if the change is perceived as threatening to the group structure. For example, many changes proposed by management change the flow of work in the unit, which therefore affects the established social relationships. Rearranging desks in an office may have severe repercussions on the way the group is used to conducting its business. Changes that violate group norms may also be resisted, since the norms determine acceptable forms of behavior for the group.

Resistance to change for social reasons was illustrated in the study of coal mining groups by Trist and Bamforth.[6] Production of coal had traditionally been done in small groups of about three people, in which each person was highly dependent upon the others for production and safety. In an attempt to increase productivity, management changed this to the "longwall" system, in which coal was obtained through specialization of individual tasks performed by groups of thirty to forty men. Existing interpersonal relationships were disrupted and productivity dropped following the introduction of the new method, even though it was technologically and organizationally superior to the small-group method. The new norm of low productivity, according to the researchers, was the employees' way of coping with the emotional stress caused by the new work system.

**Status Reasons**    Changes in social systems almost always affect the status of people. As discussed in Chapter 10, status systems within groups become firmly established and any change that reduces the status of the group or individual members will likely meet with resistance. As before, technological changes can be a frequent cause of status problems, since job skill requirements and responsibility levels are often affected. A common example is the introduction of word-processing equipment in offices. Some individuals who previously were typists suddenly become operators of high-technology equipment. While their status is increased, the status of those who remain typists is decreased. To the extent that the word-processor operator controls information needed by others, the status of that job will affect all the jobs that must interact with the operator. Executives, for example, may feel a loss in status since they do not understand the technology of the word processor. Other employees may be shifted from a personal secretary job to a word-processing pool, which would likely be a drop in status. In general, mechanization reduces the skill level in jobs, which reduces the status of those occupying the jobs.[7] As a result, many employees experience severe emotional problems on the job which affect their productivity.

It is difficult to conceive of any organizational change that will not affect the status of someone. A physical change in a unit's layout or space allocation, an implementation of a new work procedure, the insertion of a new employee in the work group, or the purchase of a new piece of equipment will have an effect, not only upon the specific employee, but also upon others in the system.

**Security Reasons**  Previously we noted economic reasons as one source of resistance to change, and pointed out that economic security was important to many workers.[8] In addition to economic security, however, is the need for psychological security, i.e., the need for a degree of predictability in our lives. Predictability of our environment allows us to concentrate on other matters and reduces the anxiety associated with uncertainty. Although some researchers have suggested that some personality types have more difficulty than others in dealing with uncertainty, everyone has some need for structure and predictability.[9] The preservation of this "security blanket" causes us to resist changes because of the uncertainty associated with the outcomes of the change. Since most changes originate at higher levels of the organization and are passed down to lower levels, a degree of uncertainty is almost always the result. It is only those changes that we control ourselves that minimize the negative effects of uncertainty.

**Skill and Competence Reasons**  Changes that reduce the skill and competence required of employees are often resisted. Resistance is caused by the ego need, the satisfaction of which is jeopardized when required skills are reduced. More generally, any change that attacks the ego will be resisted, such as the status examples previously noted.

Often there is a more subtle reason for resistance in this category. Some of the changes implemented in organizations result in employees feeling incompetent. For example, if an employee has been performing a job for a long time, he or she has likely developed a feeling of competence in the job; if the job is changed, the employee will feel less competent and will likely resist the change. Again, technological changes seem to fit this category most often, although it is not limited to these. Computers, for example, are resisted by many people who don't understand them and feel inadequate around those who do.[10]

**The "Path of Least Resistance" Reason**   As a final and more general source of resistance, we will examine the "path of least resistance" reason. This is an expression describing the fact that change is often resisted simply because there is no incentive for people to go along with it and it is easier to remain with the status quo. In the discussion of performance management in Chapter 4, it was noted that changes in performance can be induced if reward systems are structured to reinforce such changes. The same principle applies to managing change. For people to go along with a change, they must have a reason (i.e., an incentive). Later in this chapter we will show how this important principle can provide a strategy for dealing with resistance.

## Box 14-3: Sixteen Things Often Resisted by Employees

We have presented some general reasons why people resist change but it is possible to be more specific. Probably our greatest error in implementing change is forgetting to think about how the change will affect others and, in particular, subordinates. If we do remember this step, then our second error is forgetting to see the change from the subordinates' point of view.

Below is a list of changes that are often resisted. The mere fact that they are resisted does not mean that managers should avoid them, but forewarned is forearmed. It should also be understood that these changes generally are resisted but, consistent with the concept of individual differences, by no means are they always resisted.

CHANGES FREQUENTLY RESISTED ARE CHANGES THAT:

1. Reduce the skill required in jobs
2. Reduce status of people
3. Disrupt established social relationships
4. Threaten psychological or job security
5. Are not fully understood
6. Violate norms of behavior
7. Affect accepted ways of doing things
8. Are forced upon people
9. Reduce the information flowing to people
10. Reduce social-interaction opportunities
11. Make people feel ineffective or incompetent
12. Reduce the power and influence of people
13. Reduce personal privacy
14. Reduce personal authority
15. Expose personal weaknesses
16. Cost employees more than benefit

**Conclusions**   Although we have neatly categorized the various sources of resistance to change, in practice there is seldom a single source. A change in work systems, for example, may be resisted for economic, social, status, and ego reasons. Therefore, solutions to change problems must allow for a variety of sources.

Change processes are also complicated by individual differences. A certain change may evoke different types of resistance from different people. Notice, for example, that the sources discussed closely parallel the need hierarchy discussed in Chapter 3, and in that discussion we pointed out that the hierarchy is affected by individual differences.

Effective change strategies depend upon accurate diagnosis of the source of resistance. To assist in deciding which change strategy is most effective, we will present two models that describe approaches to dealing with resistance to change, one a general model and the other a more specific one.

# ◼ MODELS FOR ANALYZING RESISTANCE TO CHANGE

Models are useful tools for examining relationships between important variables in a system. With managing change, the important variables are those factors that cause resistance and those factors that can be used to reduce resistance. The following two models show which types of strategy can be utilized to increase the effectiveness of change strategies.

**Force-Field Analysis**   A useful technique for analyzing change situations is Kurt Lewin's force-field analysis method.[11] This technique describes and analyzes the various forces that operate in social systems to keep the system either in balance or in a state of change. Lewin's method proposes that two sets of forces operate in any system: forces that operate for change (the driving forces) and forces that operate against change (the resisting forces). If the two sets of forces are equal in strength, then the system is in equilibrium.

The diagrams in Figure 14-5 show how various situations might be represented. The length of the arrows for driving and resisting forces indicates their relative strength, and the numbers along the horizontal axis represent the relative degrees of change. Figure 14-5(a) shows a system in equilibrium, with the dotted line indicating the desired situation. Figures 14-5(b) and 14-5(c) show how the desired situation can be achieved by either increasing the driving forces or decreasing the resisting forces. The significance of the two different forces is to emphasize that driving forces are not just the opposite of resisting forces, i.e., they are qualitatively different forces. For example, a driving force for change might be high cost per unit of output, but the resisting force would not likely be workers' desire to keep cost per unit high. Instead, their resistance would likely be from a fear of losing their jobs because of new technology designed to reduce output cost.

One of the more risky change strategies is merely to increase the driving forces. Herbert[12] refers to the "coiled spring effect" in this strategy, using the analogy of encountering the increased resistance when pushing downward on a

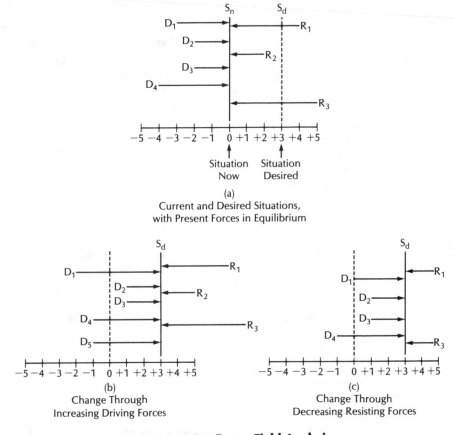

(a)
Current and Desired Situations,
with Present Forces in Equilibrium

(b)
Change Through
Increasing Driving Forces

(c)
Change Through
Decreasing Resisting Forces

**FIGURE 14-5.   Force-Field Analysis**

Source: Kurt Lewin, "Frontiers in Group Dynamics," *Human Relations* 1 (1947). Used with permission.

coiled spring. As more pressure is applied, the resistance increases, which means that more pressure is required just to keep the system in equilibrium. Unfortunately, this is often the response of many managers when faced with resistance to change, and Lewin's analysis shows why these approaches are often ineffective.

Generally speaking, a more effective approach is to concentrate on reducing the resisting forces rather than increasing the driving forces. This serves to keep the pressure off the situation by focusing efforts on the source of resistance rather than trying to overpower it with driving force. At worst, if efforts to reduce resisting forces fail there is less chance for resentment by employees, i.e., the "coiled spring effect."

Force-field analysis provides some general insights into how change might be implemented more effectively. However, the most difficult part of the method is coming up with specific ideas regarding how resisting forces can be reduced. This is best described as an exercise in creativity and would lend itself to the group

## *Organizational Reality*   14-1
### *Using Force-Field Analysis*

A good example of how force-field analysis can be used is described by Lewin. During World War II, female factory workers objected to the requirement that safety glasses be worn in a plant. Many strategies were tried, most of which were increases in the driving forces, but no consistent change occurred. Force-field analysis was then used to diagnose the situation.

Driving forces were identified as being:

1. The necessity to protect one's eyes.
2. Desire to cooperate with the company.
3. Willingness to follow rules.

Resisting forces were identified as being:

1. Feelings that the glasses were too heavy.
2. Feelings that the glasses were unattractive.
3. Feelings that compliance infringed on the individual's freedom of choice.

By concentrating on the resisting forces, the company decided to substitute lighter and more comfortable frames for the glasses. Then each employee was encouraged to decorate her glasses and a contest was held to determine the most attractive glasses, and this individual expression removed the feelings of loss of freedom.

---

decision-making or brainstorming methods described in Chapter 9. Since each situation is unique there will seldom be "pat" answers to these problems.

**A Contingency Model of Analyzing Change**   As has been noted in previous chapters, recent developments in the field of organizational behavior have moved away from universalist approaches to dealing with behavioral problems and have concentrated on situational approaches. Effective management of organizational change benefits from this movement because change is a situational problem. In the applications section of this chapter we will describe some useful change strategies, but these strategies must be used carefully and with full knowledge of their situational effectiveness. The model presented below will assist in diagnosing the situations correctly.

Kotter and Schlesinger[13] have proposed a contingency framework for matching methods with situations of organizational change. Their proposal, shown in Table 14-1, presents six possible methods of dealing with resistance to change, and the situations in which these methods are most effective. The various approaches in the model are described as follows:

1. Education and communication—providing of facts and information; increased communication about the change.

2. Participation and involvement—letting those affected have a voice in how the change will occur.
3. Facilitation and support—providing training for change, effective listening, counseling, and understanding of emotional reactions to change.
4. Negotiation and agreement—bargaining over various aspects of change, making trade-offs to accommodate concerns of those affected.
5. Manipulation and co-optation—using information about change selectively, or seconding a representative (or informal leader) from the group to participate in the design of the change.
6. Explicit and implicit coercion—using power position and threats to force compliance.

As explained in Table 14-1, each of these methods is appropriate in certain situations, though all will have drawbacks. Management must decide the nature of the resistance and then examine the possible approaches to fit the situation. These and other methods of overcoming resistance to change will be explained in the next section.

---

## Organizational Reality 14-2
## Implementing the Metric System

One of the best examples of change and change strategies, presently in progress in Canada, has to do with implementation of the metric system. As expected, resistance (both logical and emotional) was strong, but the government insisted that the program would go through. The change strategy, however, was carefully designed to reduce resistance. The following change policies were adopted:

1. Rather than occurring all at once, the total changeover would occur over ten years.
2. The change would begin with the easiest items, followed by the more difficult changes. Weather and highway measures, for example, were the initial changes.
3. For weather information, the government allowed both metric and standard measures to be used for one year, and then the standard measures were dropped.
4. Advertisements were created which publicized the move (i.e., why it was necessary) and helped to explain some of the new measures.
5. Changes that were expected to encounter the strongest resistance (e.g., supermarket pricing) were pretested in select areas to improve the change process.
6. Government grants were made available to help those firms that would encounter substantial costs in the changeover (e.g., purchasing new scales, etc.).

Since the initiation of the program, resistance has steadily declined. Part of the decline, no doubt, is simply due to a feeling of helplessness resulting from the law, but the support, information, and overall change strategy of the government has helped as well.

---

**TABLE 14-1.  Methods for Dealing with Resistance to Change**

| Approach | Commonly Used in Situations | Advantages | Drawbacks |
|---|---|---|---|
| Education + communication | Where there is a lack of information or inaccurate information and analysis. | Once persuaded, people will often help with the implementation of the change. | Can be very time-consuming if lots of people are involved. |
| Participation + involvement | Where the initiators do not have all the information they need to design the change, and where others have considerable power to resist. | People who participate will be committed to implementing change, and any relevant information they have will be integrated into the change plan. | Can be very time-consuming if participators design an inappropriate change. |
| Facilitation + support | Where people are resisting because of adjustment problems. | No other approach works as well with adjustment problems. | Can be time-consuming, expensive, and still fail. |
| Negotiation + agreement | Where someone or some group will clearly lose out in a change, and where that group has considerable power to resist. | Sometimes it is a relatively easy way to avoid major resistance. | Can be too expensive in many cases if it alerts others to negotiate for compliance. |
| Manipulation + co-optation | Where other tactics will not work, or are too expensive. | It can be a relatively quick and inexpensive solution to resistance problems. | Can lead to future problems if people feel manipulated. |
| Explicit + implicit coercion | Where speed is essential, and the change initiators possess considerable power. | It is speedy, and can overcome any kind of resistance. | Can be risky if it leaves people mad at the initiators. |

Source: John P. Kotter and Leonard A. Schlesinger, "Choosing Strategies for Change," *Harvard Business Review* (March-April 1979): 111. Copyright 1979 by the President and Fellows of Harvard College; all rights reserved.

# ■ APPLICATIONS

Unlike previous chapters in which we presented applications for various theories, we will concentrate on a single phenomenon here—overcoming resistance to change. There are other issues that are mentioned in this section but all have this common theme. Since so many managers have difficulty with managing change, our time on this topic should be well-spent.

Overcoming resistance to change is seldom a matter of a single strategy. Because change itself is a complex process, managers must usually employ several strategies simultaneously. Even this strategy is sometimes insufficient to overcome extreme resistance to change.

As in other types of managerial problem-solving situations, anticipation of the problem is superior to dealing with it after it has occurred. The major purpose of the previous sections was to provide a flavor for the frequency and types of resistance that can be expected in organizations. A clear understanding of the sources of the problem can assist tremendously in deciding on appropriate change strategies. Even if proper diagnosis and preventive measures are taken, there will always be situations in which resistance will still be present. Therefore, this section will also include strategies for dealing with resistance after it occurs.

**Participation in Change**    One of the most frequently recommended strategies for dealing with resistance to change is to allow those affected by the change to participate in its design and implementation. Or, as the old saying goes, "The people in the boat with you never bore a hole in it." Through participation and involvement, people are provided with more information about the change and have the opportunity to influence the change with their ideas. Participation can serve to reduce (though not eliminate) some of the anxiety associated with change and can give participants some ownership of the change itself. Participation can also increase commitment so that implementation tends to be easier.

Participation, however, is not without potential problems. When people are involved in the change process their role will be meaningless if some of their ideas are not accepted and implemented. If participation is used as a manipulative process simply to get employees to agree with the proposals of management, then resentment will be created. When participation is used, management must be prepared to compromise their objectives; otherwise, they would probably be better off not inviting participation.

There is also a strategic question: at what stage in the process should participation begin? If people are involved too early in the planning stages, they not only would not have the necessary information to make adequate suggestions, but they also may resist the idea of change itself. For example, management might want to implement a new production process that will affect many of the jobs in the work unit; if presented with the initial desire for change the employees may question the need for change. However, if the fact of change is decided by management, then the employees' participation could be invited at the level of determining how the change could be implemented and in what form.

### *Organizational Reality*   14-3
### *Managing Change at Glacier Metal Company*

The Glacier Metal Company, Ltd., in London, England is noted for its Works Council, which functions as a participative mechanism for all employees. The council is composed of representatives from each level in the organization and meets once each month. Instead of a majority voting system, the council operates using a unanimous voting system, meaning that every member of council must agree before a decision is reached. The council exists on the theory that employees have considerable power to resist change. If that power is not recognized in a positive sense, then it will be mobilized in some negative way, usually a strike. Instead of a strike, any member of council can stop an unwanted change simply by using his or her veto. The role of the council is to deal with any issue that affects the general working conditions of the employees.

There have been many instances in which the council assisted in implementing a change, but one particular one is illustrative. Because of outdated machinery, the company was becoming uncompetitive in its markets and needed to buy new machinery. However, the new machinery was so much more efficient that it would make about 100 employees redundant, and the unions threatened to strike if the new machines were brought in. The matter came to Works Council since it affected the working conditions of employees. After considerable debate, the council gave its unanimous approval to the new machines on the condition that no employees would lose their jobs, and that the company would let normal turnover take care of the excess employees. Without this participation, there would have been considerable resistance and the new equipment would not have been as efficient.

Although participation is generally useful for implementing change, it does not in itself guarantee that change will be accepted. One research study has noted that participation has positive results only when the outcomes of the process are perceived as important by employees.[14] Therefore, we would not expect that participation would be of value if those participating do not see that the outcomes of the change are important to them.

**The *Quid Pro Quo* Approach**   *Quid pro quo* (a Latin phrase meaning "this for that") provides a useful method for dealing with resistance to change. Most changes, it must be remembered, originate at the higher levels of the organization but have their major impact at lower levels. This generally means that the benefits of the change accrue to the planners and the costs of change are borne by those who must implement it. This fact alone is enough to cause resistance to even the most carefully thought-out change.

To overcome the inequity, changes should have built-in incentives for everyone. Positive reinforcers must be present to offset the resistance that is anticipated. Management can view the situation as one of trade-offs. If something important (i.e., reinforcing) is taken away from employees, it must be replaced with something else. For example, assume that a department is being physically moved from one location to another. The move is such that people who had private offices before will now be in an open office area. Assuming the people valued their offices (i.e., status symbols), then they will likely resist the change. To counter the resistance, management might offer them some positive things they did not have before so that as a result of the move they would be at least no worse off than before. For example, they might be given better furniture than they had before, more work space, or other improvements that will be reinforcing to them.

The "quid pro quo" approach requires compromise in that incentives for change must be built-in that would not otherwise be included. Some might view

---

## Box 14-4: Gaining Acceptance for the "Double Nickel"

A change that has seen considerable resistance in the United States is the implementation of the nationwide 55-mph speed limit. Anticipating that resistance would be widespread, the government forced the change by threatening to withhold federal highway funds from any state that did not enforce the federal speed law. This was a strong incentive, but a negative one that forced compliance and caused bad feelings in those who preferred driving faster.

The "quid pro quo" approach offers an alternative solution that likely would achieve the same objective with less resistance. Much of the resistance was caused by the fact that so many negative things were happening at once and, other than a lower highway death rate, drivers received no benefit. The key to gaining acceptance of the change is to build in an alternative benefit for drivers. At the time the law was imposed, the government had two goals: to save energy and to encourage people to buy smaller cars (which would also save energy). In other words, the speed limit was only a means to an end, not an end in itself. Once this important fact is realized, the "quid pro quo" approach offers possibilities.

Our solution is this: the government could pass a law that regulates speed by the gas mileage rating of the car. The law might read: "Drivers may drive at any speed up to 80 mph, provided that at that speed their car is consuming no more than (say) 30 miles per gallon. For a Volkswagen Rabbit this would be no problem; Lincoln Continentals, on the other hand, would be limited to about 30 mph.

Those who now resist the change would quickly change over to smaller cars in order to enjoy the privilege of driving at higher speeds. The public will give up one thing (larger cars) to get something else (drive at faster speeds).

Write your congressman today.

## Organizational Reality 14-4
## Using "Quid Pro Quo"

The quid pro quo approach to change in industry is illustrated by the approach unions and management are taking to changes being instigated in many manufacturing firms.

In Japan, the change to robotics has been significant. By 1982, 100,000 robots were in place and working in Japan. The Japan Council of Metal Workers Union developed an action plan to study the long-term effects that this influx of robots will have on employment. In a contract settlement, Sanyo Electronics Company in Osaka agreed to a stipulation whereby employees forty-five years old or older would not be transferred to outside locales (which had been the previous practice) due to the replacement of labor by robots. Thus, the Council obtained a degree of stability for its older membership in return for Sanyo's introduction of robotics into its industrial production of electronics.

The use of quid pro quo is also evident in North America. The United Auto Workers and General Motors agreed to several conditions when bargaining the 1982 contract. The company agreed to keep open four of the seven scheduled plant closures and agreed to income protection for workers with ten years or more seniority. The UAW agreed to tighten up on absenteeism and productivity through the use of penalties for absenteeism, such as loss of vacation pay and supplemental employment benefits. The use of the quid pro quo approach allows both management and labor to benefit through harmonious agreement and ratification of the 1982 union contract.

Source: *Business Week* 29 March 1982: 46.

this as "buying off" employees, but in reality it is simply making sure that the change benefits everyone. In other words, under this system employees are given a (positive) reason to accept change.

**Open Communications about Change**  The open communication strategy has two major benefits, one that is obvious and one that is more subtle. For the former, we know that providing information about change may reduce the anxieties of those affected and the resistance to change caused by lack of awareness. As a general rule, the more negative the organizational climate, the greater the importance of keeping people up-to-date about the change. If necessary information is not forthcoming, employees frequently create their own.

On the more subtle level, using open communications affects the secrecy aspect of change. To understand the importance of this strategy we must first realize (and this is difficult for many people to accept) that very few things are truly secret in any organization. Our discussion of informal groups and the grapevine in Chapter 10 noted that the transmission of information, especially the really important stuff, is widespread. This suggests that any changes contemplated by

> ## Box 14-5: Overcoming Resistance to Stability
>
> With a point of view contrary to the theme of this chapter, Robert Albanese suggests that organizations often change for the sake of change and that resistance to change should be taken as a sign that change should be questioned. He maintains that people need a certain amount of stability and predictability in their lives and that too much change threatens this basic need. Albanese writes of the need for "intelligent" resistance to change, which can be used to offset the tendency to change (which is also needed). Intelligent resistance to change can be a useful management tool to improve changes that have been poorly thought out. Rather than overcome resistance to change, Albanese believes management should make use of it.

Source: Robert Albanese, "Overcoming Resistance to Stability," *Business Horizons* 13 No. 1 (April 1970): 35–42.

management (at least those of any significance) are likely not confidential. Assuming this is true, then withholding information about change will only increase anxiety and resistance. At an early point in the planning stage, employees should be informed of what is "in the mill" for they will likely find out anyway.

This is a difficult situation to deal with. On the one hand, management does not like to create anxiety in employees needlessly, and on the other hand there is a good chance they will find out anyway. For example, if a manager is contemplating major changes in the work schedule for employees, at what stage in the planning process should they be informed? In one case with which the authors are familiar, the manager decided not to tell people until he had fully formulated his plan. Unfortunately, the janitor found a worksheet in the trash with a sketch of the new schedule and every employee knew about the change by the next morning!

**Making Change the Norm**   One of the reasons employees resist change is simply because they aren't used to it. However, if change is an accepted practice, then the unusual can become the norm. If the changes are well-managed, this builds trust with employees so that subsequent changes might be accepted more readily.

This is not to say that organizations should change simply for the sake of making changes, but a conscious effort to keep social systems from becoming stale will generally help reduce resistance. Frequent changes also give people practice in adapting and this reduces their fear of new situations. Of course, for this strategy to work, the changes must still be properly implemented.

**Introducing Multiple Changes**   The logic of the multiple-change strategy is: since resistance to change occurs in incremental units, the marginal resistance encountered from introducing several changes is only slightly greater than from a single change. The reasons why multiple-change strategies can be effective are as follows: First, a part of all resistance is due to the initial shock of the change. If many changes are proposed, this shock is spread over the lot. Second, when multiple changes are introduced, emotional resistance can be less because potential negative effects are spread over other positive effects. And finally, multiple-change strategies allow more opportunity for the "quid pro quo" strategy discussed earlier.

**Working Through Informal Leaders**    In Chapter 11 we discussed the importance of informal work groups and their leaders. Because of the influence informal leaders can have, they play an important role in implementing change. If the cooperation of the informal leaders can be gained, resistance to change can be reduced.

Of course the important issue is how to get the cooperation of the informal leaders. One way is to co-opt (see Figure 14-1) the informal leader into the planning process. Getting the informal leader involved in the change itself can increase his or her commitment, which can then have a positive effect upon the group.

**Using Natural Motivators in People**    As noted at the outset of this chapter, people do not naturally resist change. When they do it is because something within them is being threatened by the change. This "something within them" can be called their natural motivators, natural in that they are the result of experiences and therefore are deeply ingrained as determinants of behavior (see Chapter 4). It stands to reason that anything that challenges these natural motivators will be resisted. For example, if an employee has a natural desire to feel important, then he or she will resist any change that is perceived to result in reduced importance. A better strategy would be to design change such that it increases the feelings of importance or, at worst, doesn't reduce them.

**Forcing Change**    Sooner or later every manager will encounter a situation in which change must be forced upon employees. This could be because of deep-seated emotional resistance that cannot be dealt with, or because the pressure of time does not permit more communication and involvement. In any case, forcing change can be difficult at the best of times so we will examine some principles that will assist in the application.

First, employees should be told why the change is occurring and if possible, why the change is being forced. Of course this is appealing to the rational side of people and therefore may not have much effect if their resistance is emotional— which it likely is. Nevertheless, the step is usually necessary.

To force the change itself, managers must rely on the authority and power of their positions. It's mostly a "do it or else" situation. Note carefully in Table 14-1 the situations in which coercion is recommended and the advantages and disadvantages associated with each. Once the change has occurred, it becomes important for people to have a good experience with the change. If people have only bad experiences (such as being criticized for making mistakes) then coercion will only reinforce their original feelings. For example, if the change is a change in job

# Box 14-6: The Fast vs. Slow Issue

One of the thorniest issues in managing change is the question of whether change should be implemented quickly or slowly. Proponents of the fast side inevitably point to the problems Sweden would have had if their change from driving on the left side of the road to the right had been implemented slowly. The advocates of the slow approach point to changes such as implementing the metric system in North America over a period of years as an indication of how effective the slow approach can be. In general, the case for fast change is as follows:

1. The shock of change only occurs once.
2. People are forced to give up the old ways, so results are quick.
3. Implementing change quickly does not preclude using the accepted change processes prior to the change.

The case for slow change can be summarized:

1. It gives people time to adapt and therefore creates less resistance.
2. The familiar is still present, so the new does not seem as threatening.
3. It gives greater opportunity to make additional changes as feedback on initial changes is received.
4. It allows management to "test the waters" to see how much resistance will be encountered.

As might be expected, which of these is the better strategy will depend upon the situation. Making the usual set of assumptions (especially "all things being equal"), the prescriptive statements would be as follows:
Change can be implemented quickly when:

1. The change is a small one;
2. There is agreement on the need for change;
3. Resistance is only a matter of knowledge;
4. The cost of implementing slowly could negate the value of the change itself;
5. No one affected by the change cares one way or the other.

Change can be implemented slowly when:

1. The change requires major adjustments in attitudes and behaviors;
2. Resistance to the change is expected to be high;
3. A high probability exists that the original plan will be changed;
4. There is little agreement on the need for change;
5. The initiators have a weak power base.

design, the employee may feel insecure and inadequate in the new job. Understanding (the supportive role), training (the coaching role) and involvement (the participative role), can all help employees to adapt to a forced change.

The forcing strategy as described here is a variation of the "try it—you'll like it!" technique. People often refuse to do a thing because they think they won't like it, but once they do it, they discover it wasn't so bad after all. Management's job in forcing change is to make sure that people have a good experience with it. This is true of any change, but it becomes especially important when change is forced.

## ■ SUMMARY

Managing change is a part of every manager's job. It requires understanding of all the theories and concepts developed in this book. Change can occur at the individual, group, or organizational level. Change also occurs in various degrees: some changes only affect the cognitive (rational) part of people, others have more emotional implications. Each of these requires different strategies for implementation.

The common problem encountered by managers is resistance to change. Sources of resistance can be economic, social, status, security, competence, or merely because people cannot see the benefits of the change. Implementing change requires that the manager understand the sources and deal with them. Rather than increase the pressure in favor of the change, it is frequently more effective to concentrate on reducing the forces that resist the change.

Dealing with resistance to change is also a situational phenomenon. Some changes can be dealt with through improved information flow, others must be forced upon employees. Other methods of overcoming resistance are participation, the "quid pro quo" approach, making more frequent changes, working through informal leaders, and using the natural motivations of employees.

## *Opening Incident Revisited*

Professor Grastark's frustration is both understandable and predictable. Thinking that he had managed the change properly, he encountered unforeseen resistance both in magnitude and in level. Because he had seen the change as necessary, he assumed that everyone else would see the same need and therefore did not involve them at that level of the change. Although he was not naive enough to believe that everyone affected would agree wholeheartedly with the change, he did predict (wrongly) that by letting them decide on the things that affected them directly, any dissatisfaction with the change itself would be forgotten.

Hindsight reveals several errors in judgment by Professor Grastark: First, he failed to understand the emotional attachment the graduate students had toward their carrels. Grastark attempted to deal with this problem with the "facts" (such as better security, more room, etc.), not realizing that he was, in effect, taking their personal territory away from the students, which reduced their status. Secondly, Grastark failed to recognize that the resistance was a sign that perhaps the change was not handled properly. In other words, perhaps the students were using the loss of their carrels as a manifestation of their dissatisfaction with not being involved from the start. Since Grastark dealt only with the problem of the carrels, he may have been missing the primary reason for their resistance.

Grastark made essentially the same error with the undergraduate students. He could not understand their resistance, since they did not use the study hall much anyway. What he failed to realize was that the study hall also served a major social function for the students, usually at lunch time. Partitioning the space for the graduate students seriously jeopardized this important function. His neglect in informing them of the change (an act which in itself showed them how much he respected their opinions) insured that he would learn of their concerns only through their resistance.

The secretaries represented a different type of problem. They apparently agreed with the need for change, which is not surprising since they could benefit from it. However, Grastark's failure to involve them in the overall planning meant that their personal and social needs would not be reflected in the reorganization. What made their reaction even more frustrating for Professor Grastark was that after examining their plan, it was apparent that it was superior to his own. He, like most people, found it difficult to accept that someone lower in the hierarchy could come up with a better idea than his, although it is not surprising, given that they work in the area every day.

Another factor here, though not a major cause, is a contributing factor to the resistance. Notice that the only party in this change process who will suffer no losses and gain a major benefit is Professor Grastark himself! It is understandable for the others affected to resent having to give up space if they see this space benefiting primarily the initiator of the change. Grastark has been insensitive to the perceptions and feelings of those who are losing something of importance to them.

At this point Professor Grastark has two possible strategies. The first would be to use the authority and power of his position and force the change. Given the relatively low power base of students and secretaries, eventually the change would go through, although each group could make Grastark's life difficult in the process. The second and perhaps preferable alternative is to stop the renovations for the time being and regroup the participation process. For example, Grastark may want to form a committee composed of faculty, students, and support staff to explore the alternatives available and decide on the best. This will no doubt result in Grastark having to compromise his original plans, but the more open communications and involvement of all parties will likely reduce the resistance. The major price Professor Grastark will pay is the time the participative process will take. However, if a more effective decision is the result, the time is well-spent. Besides, the extra benefit associated with the change is the lessons Professor Grastark has learned, which he can pass on in the organizational behavior textbook he is writing.

# ■ EXERCISE 14-1: GENERAL MANUFACTURING COMPANY

Claude Grate was the newly hired manager of the purchasing department at General Manufacturing Company. He had several years of experience as a purchasing agent with another company and was hired by General to reorganize the purchasing function in accordance with an overall corporate plan to improve efficiency and reduce costs.

After several weeks, Claude recognized that the purchasing department had performed little more than a clerical function. There were no purchasing policies, no central buying, and no control over who was buying what. The first step he took was to centralize certain purchases into his department. He decided to start with a dollar amount first, and wrote up a procedure that required all purchase requisitions over $500 to be approved by him before they could be sent to suppliers. He submitted his plan to his manager, who approved it.

Claude drafted a memo to all the other managers which read as follows:

TO: All management personnel

FROM: Claude Grate, Purchasing Manager

I'm sure all of you understand the value of getting the most value from our purchasing dollar. In the past the company has been very inefficient in its purchasing activities, and I am beginning a strategy to improve the purchasing function.

As an initial change, I am creating a new procedure whereby every purchase over $500 must come to the purchasing department first for approval. This will provide us with the opportunity to review the purchase and see if we are getting the most for our dollar. Attached is a copy of the new form to be used for this purpose.

I am sure all of you agree on the necessity for getting the most for our money, and I look forward to your cooperation on this matter.

During the next several weeks, Claude received only two completed forms, yet there was every indication that the company was operating at its usual level of activity.

Questions for discussion:

1. Comment on Grate's method of implementing this change.

2. Is his new system working?

3. How should the change have been handled?

# ■ EXERCISE 14-2: ACME DELIVERY COMPANY

The Acme Delivery Company was primarily engaged in the delivery of small parcels and letters in a major urban setting. It was started by Ralph Ledbetter as a one-man operation, and had since grown into the largest independent delivery service in the city. Ralph employed over 50 full-time drivers, plus several dispatchers that worked in the central office.

The drivers had little in common in terms of their background. Ralph found that both men and women, older and younger people made good drivers. The main ingredient seemed to be a strong dislike for "inside" work. Most of the drivers had been with Acme for five years or more, and some had been with the company since its inception.

Ralph had recently engaged a public relations firm to consult with him on the company's image. They made several recommendations, one of which was that he purchase new uniforms for the drivers. The consultants' studies had indicated that the public perceived Acme as a stable organization, but one that lacked flash and innovation. Since competition in the private delivery business was increasing, Ralph wanted to project a new image of the company in an attempt to retain his share of the market.

The public relations firm presented Ralph with three new designs for the uniforms. Each was radically different from the relatively staid and plain uniforms the drivers were wearing now. Of particular concern to Ralph was that he knew many of the employees, especially the long-service ones, were quite attached to their present uniforms.

1. How would you recommend that Ralph implement this change?

# ■ ENDNOTES

1. Stephen A. Allen, "Organizational Choice and General Influence Networks for Diversified Companies," *Academy of Management Journal* (September, 1978): 341.

2. Technically, the term *organization development* applies to any planned change occurring in an organization. Popular usage of the term, however, is generally to describe OD programs which attempt to make major changes in the organization, although such changes can occur at the individual and group level. Our focus in this chapter is oriented toward the changes implemented by managers rather than external consultants.

3. Paul Hersey and Kenneth H. Blanchard, "The Management of Change," *Training and Development Journal* (January, February, and March, 1972).

4. Gary Powell and Barry Posner, "Resistance to Change Reconsidered: Implications for Managers," *Human Resource Management* (Spring, 1978): 29–34.

5. See, for example, E. L. Trist and K. W. Bamforth, "Some Social and Psychological Consequences of the Longwall Method of Coal Getting," *Human Relations* 4 (1951): 3–38; William F. Whyte, *Human Relations in the Restaurant Industry* (New York: McGraw-Hill, 1948); and A. K. Rice, "Productivity and Social Organization in an Indian Weaving Shed," *Human Relations* 6 (1953): 297–329.

6. E. L. Trist and K. W. Bamforth, "Some Social and Psychological Consequences of the Longwall Method of Coal-Getting," *Human Relations* 4 (1951): 1–38.

7. It might appear that our example of the word processor contradicts this statement. However, it must be remembered that when word processors are used, the tasks performed by typists change. Whereas previously they would have typed, edited, composed, and produced the final copy, under a word-processor system their tasks are usually changed to performing only the most basic tasks. Therefore, introduction of word-processing equipment increases the status of the word-processor operator and reduces the status of those left to do the run-of-the-mill typing.

8. Just how important security is to any particular employee is difficult to specify; some have greater needs than others. See the discussion of Maslow's Hierarchy of Needs in Chapter 3.

9. See, for example, T. W. Adorno, E. Frenkel-Brunswik, D. J. Levinson, and R. N. Sanford, *The Authoritarian Personality* (New York: Harper and Row, 1950).

10. There is a valuable lesson here for those who work with computers. Computer "jocks" are famous for the intimidating techniques used with novices. They talk a language only the experts understand and frequently try to "snow" users who have much less expertise. What they don't understand is that most people resent being made to feel inferior and this resentment is frequently manifested in total resistance to the expert's ideas. Even more interesting, the novice will overtly express total understanding of the computer jock's ideas, thus leaving the impression that he or she is in no way inferior to the jock.

11. Kurt Lewin, "Frontiers in Group Dynamics," *Human Relations* 1 (1947): 5–42.

12. Theodore T. Herbert, *Dimensions of Organizational Behavior* (New York: The MacMillan Company), 1976, p. 345.

13. John P. Kotter and Leonard A. Schlesinger, "Choosing Strategies for Change," *Harvard Business Review* (March-April, 1979): 102–121.

14. Linda L. Neider, "An Experimental Field Investigation Utilizing an Expectancy Theory View of Participation," *Organizational Behavior and Human Performance* 26 (1980): 425–442.

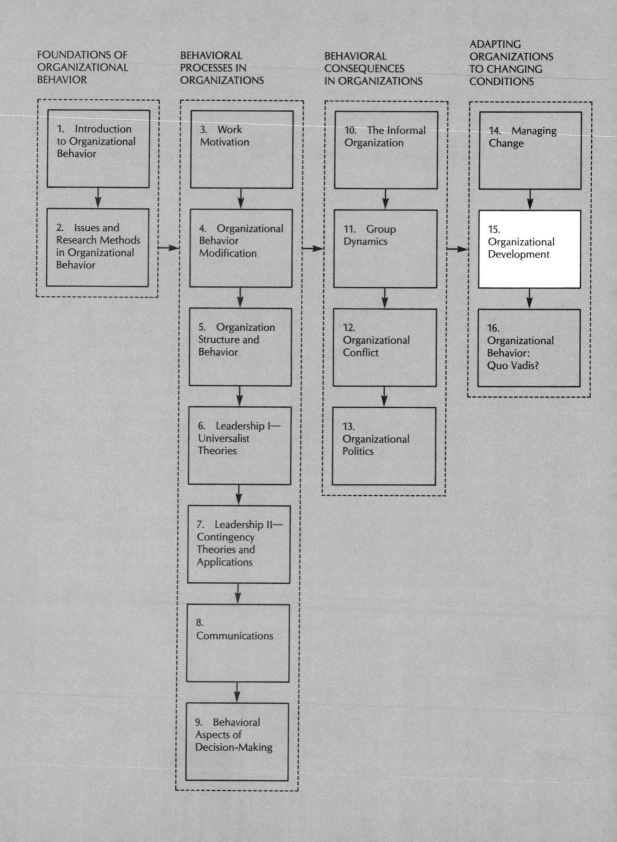

FOUNDATIONS OF
ORGANIZATIONAL
BEHAVIOR

1. Introduction to Organizational Behavior

2. Issues and Research Methods in Organizational Behavior

BEHAVIORAL
PROCESSES IN
ORGANIZATIONS

3. Work Motivation

4. Organizational Behavior Modification

5. Organization Structure and Behavior

6. Leadership I— Universalist Theories

7. Leadership II— Contingency Theories and Applications

8. Communications

9. Behavioral Aspects of Decision-Making

BEHAVIORAL
CONSEQUENCES
IN ORGANIZATIONS

10. The Informal Organization

11. Group Dynamics

12. Organizational Conflict

13. Organizational Politics

ADAPTING
ORGANIZATIONS
TO CHANGING
CONDITIONS

14. Managing Change

15. Organizational Development

16. Organizational Behavior: Quo Vadis?

# Organization Development

## ■ Learning Objectives

After reading and studying this chapter you should be able to:

☐ Explain the micro and macro approaches to organization development.

☐ List and explain the prerequisites that should be met before an organization development program is instituted.

☐ Describe examples of the micro and macro approaches to organization development.

☐ Describe how jobs can be enriched.

☐ Discuss why MBO programs are often ineffective.

☐ Explain the advantages and disadvantages of sensitivity training.

☐ Describe "process consultation."

☐ Discuss the factors that should be considered when evaluating an organization development program.

# Chapter 15

# ■ KEY TERMS

**Organization development (OD)**
**Micro approaches to OD**
**Job enrichment**
**Management by objectives**
**Action research**
**Sensitivity training**
**Macro approaches to OD**
**Process consultation**
**The Managerial Grid**

# ■ CHAPTER OUTLINE

## *Opening Incident—Nina Friesen*

Nina Friesen, manager of training and development for Pacific Western Insurance Company, didn't know whether to be pleased or scared. Her meeting with the president of Pacific Western had certainly been a surprise, and the last thing she expected was to be given a $250,000 budget for the coming year to be used for training and development.

Her pleasure was due to the size of the budget. It was almost four times what it had been the previous year. Her fear was caused by the vagueness of the President's statements about how the money was to be used and what he expected to get out of it. Her recollection of the conversation brought out almost his exact words:

> Nina, I've really noticed some serious problems around here the last year or two. I realize we have almost totally neglected any kind of developmental effort for our people, and that's not good for the company. Some day we may wake up and it'll be too late. Therefore, I'm giving your department $250,000 this year to mount a major development program that will take our managers out of the dark ages and bring them into the twentieth century. Spend the money any way you like, and if you show some tangible results by next year, I'll look favorably upon giving you more money for the following year. One more thing—you know that my vice-presidents and I will be very busy next year setting up that new product line out west so we won't be around very much. However, I want you to tell everyone that I am behind this program 100 percent and that should get you whatever cooperation you need. If you run into any flack, you just let me know. Some of these people will probably resist this type of program, and I want to know who they are.

As Nina mulled over how she might profitably spend $250,000, she also wondered about the probabilities of meeting the president's expectations.

---

As the environment in which organizations operate has become more complex and dynamic, the organization's ability to adapt its resources—both human and technical—to the demands of the environment becomes extremely important. In the previous chapters, we concentrated on topics such as motivation, leadership, and communication, which dealt largely with specific aspects of organizational behavior. While an understanding of each part of organizational behavior is important, some analysis of the relationship between these areas and the overall development of the organization is necessary. Accordingly, in this chapter we describe and analyze some of the proposals to develop the total organization so that it may more effectively (1) satisfy the requirements of profit, service, employee welfare, and so on, and (2) cope with complex, rapidly changing environments. Since these goals are interdependent, this is an important area of study.

Although the term *organization development* (OD) has come into use only recently, it has become very popular, and many organizations have spent large sums of money implementing various types of OD programs. It should be pointed out, however, that both academicians and practitioners have been trying to improve organizations for many decades. In this sense, OD is not a new activity but rather an extension, refinement, and improvement of the many suggestions which have been made during the long history of organizations.

Organization development has also developed a specific focus which concerns the relationship between employees and the organization. This focus—called "quality of work life" (QWL)—emphasizes the changes that are necessary in organizations to better adapt them to the needs and satisfactions of employees. Since many of these QWL programs are quite innovative and have implications for the future of organizational behavior, this topic is discussed in detail in Chapter 16.

In this chapter, we will treat the topic of organization development as follows: First, to clarify our basic understanding of OD, the term will be defined and the important elements in the definition will be analyzed briefly. Second, since the success of OD programs is contingent upon various organizational prerequisites being satisfied, we will discuss the nature of these requirements. Third, some typical organizational problems that might be solved by OD programs are noted. Fourth, a number of representative OD programs are described in detail. This discussion will indicate the tremendous diversity of approaches included under the heading of "OD." Finally, we will evaluate the effectiveness of OD programs by analyzing some of the representative programs to determine what their impact has been on organizations. We have not included an applications section in this chapter since OD by definition, *is* an application of knowledge in an organization with the goal of improving its effectiveness.

## ■ WHAT IS ORGANIZATION DEVELOPMENT?

In the most general sense, OD is the attempt to improve the overall effectiveness of an organization. Since it is such a broad concept in practice, many different definitions have been proposed. However, the following one conveys the essential features of OD:

> Organization development is a *long-range* effort to improve an organization's *problem-solving and renewal processes,* particularly through a more effective and *collaborative management* of *organization culture*—with special emphasis on the culture of *formal work teams*—with the assistance of a *change agent* or catalyst and the use of the theory and technology of applied behavioral science, including *action research.*[1] (Emphasis ours)

An understanding of OD requires that we elaborate on the following key terms:

1. *Long-range effort*—Since the entire organization is the focus for change, improvements cannot be expected overnight. Some OD programs explicitly assume that a minimum of one year (and perhaps three to five years) will be required to achieve the desired changes. In some instances, it may be possible to institute significant behavior changes in the short run. However, for this to occur either (1) the change effort must be directed at a very small part of the organiza-

tion or (2) the influence of an external factor must be so great that it overcomes any normal resistance to change. For example, a firm experiencing a drastic decline in sales will probably be more agreeable to change than a firm not experiencing such a problem.

2. *Problem-solving and renewal processes*—The processes by which organizations adapt to and capitalize on internal and external changes can be either problem-solving or renewal processes. In the former, decisions are made to resolve specific problems facing the organization. In the latter, specific decisions are also made, but the emphasis is on generating the appropriate mix of personnel, money, and materials for organizational survival. Renewal processes, therefore, are the ways in which "life" is injected into the organization.

Since problem-solving and renewal processes are important determinants of organizational success, analysis and improvement of them is emphasized in OD programs. The development process is distinct from the "solution-finding" process. In other words, OD is an attempt to provide the organization with a *means* of coping with its own problems rather than having someone (generally from the outside) prescribe *solutions* to particular problems. The situation is analogous to the educational (i.e., development) process where, ideally, emphasis is placed on developing the child's ability to think, analyze problems, and cope with the environment rather than learning specific solutions to specific problems. A similar philosophy applies to OD: emphasis is on improving the processses by which organizations cope with internal and external problems confronting them.

3. *Collaborative management*—In contrast to the traditional management structure in which orders are issued at upper levels and simply carried out by lower levels, OD stresses collaboration between levels prior to decision making. This approach recognizes that problems and solutions are complex and that no particular group is "the problem," nor is there generally a single, simple solution to any problem. Organizations are viewed in a systems context that recognizes multiple causality and the interrelationships between organizational subsystems.

4. *Organization culture*—The culture of an organization includes the following: accepted patterns of behavior, norms, organizational objectives, value systems, the technology used to produce goods and services—in short, all factors that allow us to differentiate one organization from another. OD recognizes that each organization is different from all others and that problem-solving processes vary across organizations. The assumption that a particular solution can be applied to numerous organizations is thus generally not made. Instead, the culture of each organization must be understood and solutions consistent with that culture developed.

5. *Formal work teams*—OD emphasizes team development. The importance of the small work group is stressed, and attempts are made to capitalize on the energy inherent in these groups. This emphasis is consistent with the collaborative principle mentioned above, as well as the discussion of work groups in Chapter 11 (particularly those comments about the influence the work group has on individual behavior). If the total organization is to be improved, the effort may have to begin on some smaller scale; however, if the *individual* is the focus, we

face the problems that were discussed in leadership training and individual behavior modification. But if the effort begins with *group development,* not only is it possible to utilize the energy in these groups, but individual resistance to change that is so common is more easily overcome. (As we will see shortly, some OD approaches are not consistent with this part of the definition.)

6. *Change agent*—An important aspect of many OD programs is the use of an internal or external consultant—the *change agent*—to aid the organization. The role of the change agent varies considerably, depending on the type of program being utilized. If the program is diagnostic in nature, the change agent may take an active decision-making role as data are gathered, interpreted, and fed back to the organization. However, if the organization is attempting to develop a process through which it can solve its own problems, the change agent usually adopts a very passive role, serving more as a counselor or sounding board for ideas without making substantive proposals. The latter situation is most consistent with the OD philosophy of organizations helping themselves, since the change agent avoids prescribing a specific solution for the organization's problem.

7. *Action research*—The process of identifying the organization's specific problems, gathering and analyzing organizational data, and taking action to resolve the problems, constitutes "action research." It is in sharp contrast to "hypothesis testing research," which deals with problems or situations that are of interest to organizations generally but which may or may not be relevant to a specific organization. An example of the processes that occur from beginning to end in action research are illustrated in Figure 15-1.

---

### Organizational Reality   15-1
### Internal Consultants in a Hospital

In poor economic times, organizational development activities are often the first thing to be cut back. Lutheran General Hospital in Park Ridge, Illinois, however, has found a way around the problem which not only reduces costs but has resulted in more effective training and development of its employees.

The hospital employs 4,000 people, and development of managerial talent is a critical activity. To reduce the reliance on external change agents, the hospital has developed a group of internal change agents that do most of the training for nonmedical personnel. The training ranges all the way from general management training to the more "hard" types of training such as computer skills, shorthand, and speed-reading. The added advantage, according to Anita J. Brown, director of the training and development department, is that internal change agents are able to do follow-up work with employees, whereas the external agents generally "do their thing" and leave. In 1982, 99 percent of the training was delivered by in-house personnel.

---

Source: Chris Lee, "Lutheran General Makes the Most of Human Resources," *Training* (February 1983): 50–52.

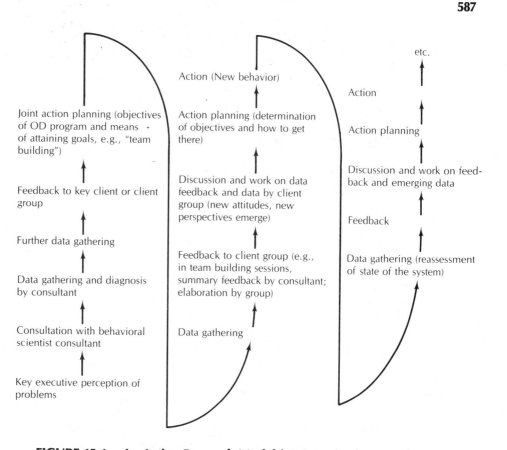

**FIGURE 15-1.   An Action Research Model for Organization Development**
Source: Wendell French, "Organization Development: Objectives, Assumptions, and
Strategies." © 1976 by the Regents of the University of California. Reprinted from *California
Management Review* 12, no. 2 (1976): 23–46, by permission of the Regents.

OD programs generally concentrate on improving two important organizational dimensions—the human element and the task element. The most fundamental *human* goal of OD is the changing of beliefs and attitudes of individuals in the organization. Before these changes can occur, however, it is important that people learn to trust each other. To achieve trust, certain procedures (e.g., open confrontation of conflict) are used. The outcome of these activities can be an increased awareness of and trust in others; this allows individuals to devote more time to goal accomplishment and less to worrying about the nontask activities of others. The most basic *task* goal of OD is the improvement of "hard" data (such as costs, profits, turnover rates, etc.). Improvement in these areas increases the likelihood that the organization will contribute more to the society at large and will also be able to obtain and utilize the scarce resources needed to insure its future existence.

# ■ PREREQUISITES FOR EFFECTIVE USE OF ORGANIZATION DEVELOPMENT

Generally, OD programs will not be successful unless a number of environmental criteria are satisfied. Many OD programs have failed or had only limited success because management and/or the organization administering the OD programs did not fully comprehend either the nature or the importance of these criteria. While meeting these criteria does not guarantee success of OD programs, it does provide a favorable environment, conducive to organizational change. To reduce the probability that an OD program will have a negative (or no) effect on the organization, the following general criteria should be met:

1. *The organization must recognize that a problem exists and must desire to move toward a resolution of that problem*—OD is not a gimmick to be used to "see what happens" in an organization. All too often organizations become aware of a new program and feel that it would be a good thing to try, even though no specific organizational problem is evident. Development programs must have change objectives which serve to increase commitment to the program and allow for effective monitoring of their effects. Development objectives must also be made clear to everyone affected by them; companies that do not clearly communicate OD objectives to those involved will likely be disappointed with the results.

2. *Support for any OD program should begin with top management*—Many managers have participated in OD programs only to find that they are unable to put what they have learned into practice because their superiors have not been exposed to the same learning. Since OD is a systemwide concept, it is unlikely that it will generate positive results if all parts of the system are not involved, at least psychologically. In some cases, damage can result if an OD program has not received the support of top management. As the program progresses, expectations are raised and new commitments are made; if the program dies because of lack of top-management support, morale and motivation decrease because the new expectations are not met. To overcome this problem, some OD programs are designed using a vertical slice of the organization to ensure that all members in the chain of command are exposed to the development process. When these individuals return to their regular jobs, they are better able to put into practice what they have learned because they are interacting with others who have had the same training.

3. *Sufficient time must be allowed for the effects of an OD program to be realized*—Organizations that implement an OD program in the hope that a major organizational problem will quickly be solved are almost invariably disappointed. It is becoming increasingly apparent that many months and, in some cases, several years are required to make noticeable changes in an organization. The reason for this is that conditioned behavior does not change quickly, even at the individual level. Also, the OD program is only one of many variables influencing behavior in the total organization. It is unlikely that a single force will overcome the effects of

## Box 15:1: Action Research vs. Hypothesis-Testing Research

For many years there has been disagreement between practicing managers and academics about the approach that should be used to solve organizational problems. Many academics lean toward the "hypothesis testing" approach. This involves gathering and analyzing data about common organizational problems (e.g., turnover, motivation, conflict, etc.). Once this has been done in many companies and in many settings, general guidelines and conclusions are developed which are then applied to specific companies.

Many managers object to this approach, arguing that "our company is unique and what worked at another company won't work here." These managers are really arguing for the "action research" approach. This involves analyzing a specific company's problems and then taking action to correct them. By focusing on only one company, actions can be taken which presumably will directly solve its problems.

This disagreement about approaches may be unnecessary, since each of these approaches has merit. The hypothesis-testing approach is beneficial because it discovers patterns of human behavior across organizations and then proposes ways to solve problems that may arise from this behavior. The action research approach is beneficial because it tailors solutions to specific problems being experienced by a given company. Thus, the approaches can be complementary, not contradictory (i.e., specific-action research builds on the general knowledge of people in organizations that has been generated through the hypothesis-testing approach). Likewise, the hypothesis-testing approach can utilize the data generated during action research for further analysis of typical organizational problems.

all the others in a short period of time. Organizations, like the broader culture in which they are embedded, do not change drastically over brief periods of time.

4. *The outside consultant's role must be understood*—The purpose of OD is to assist the organization in learning to employ its resources more effectively. If the outside consultant diagnoses the organization's problem(s) and then prescribes a solution, the organization is not likely to be in any better position to deal with future problems, except to bring in the consultant again. (This is lucrative for the consultant but not very helpful to the organization.) Moreover, solutions imposed by consultants may not be optimal since they cannot possibly have the knowledge and information possessed by organizational members. The imposed solution may also be resisted simply because it is externally imposed. However, if the consultant's efforts are focused on the problem-solving process, the organization has been developed in the sense that its problem-solving capacity has been increased.

The failure of OD programs to improve organizational effectiveness can be attributed to either a poor OD program (a program inappropriate for the organization's needs or an appropriate program conducted poorly) or a failure to insure that the important prerequisites for success have been satisfied prior to the start of the program. Since it is difficult to demonstrate that a specific OD program is poor, increasing the likelihood of a program's success is probably best accomplished by paying careful attention to these prerequisites.

# ■ SITUATIONS APPROPRIATE FOR ORGANIZATION DEVELOPMENT

Since OD is a process rather than a solution, it is difficult to specify precisely what kinds of situations may be appropriate for OD programs. However, by viewing organizational problems in general terms, we can suggest several areas for use. Beckard,[2] for example, believes that OD programs can be helpful when organizational features such as the following are in need of improvement:

1. The organization's managerial strategy (e.g., communication patterns, location of decision making)
2. The culture of the organization (e.g., norms, values, power structure)
3. Structure and roles in the organization
4. Intergroup collaboration
5. Motivational levels of employees

In detailing some common objectives of OD programs, French[3] suggests additional areas of application for OD:

1. To increase the level of trust and support among organization members
2. To increase the incidence of confrontation of organizational problems both within groups and among groups, in contrast to sweeping problems under the rug
3. To create an environment in which authority of assigned role is augmented by authority based on knowledge and skill
4. To increase the openness of communications laterally, vertically, and diagonally
5. To increase the level of personal enthusiasm and satisfaction in the organization
6. To find synergistic solutions to problems (synergistic solutions are those in which 2 + 2 equals more than 4 and through which all parties gain more through cooperation than through conflict)
7. To increase the level of self and group responsibility in planning and implementation

Clearly, both lists cover a wide variety of organizational problems and situations. If the value of OD in situations as diverse as these is accepted, the applicability of OD is indeed quite wide. At present, there is evidence to support the argument that the list is feasible; however, the degree of success in each area can vary considerably. We will explore this important concern later in this chapter.

## *Organizational Reality    15-2*
### *Developing a Quality Consciousness in Industry*

More and more companies are struggling to imbue their corporate cultures with a sense of quality, not only on the factory floor but also in the executive suite. This movement is due to the mounting evidence that increased profits and market share are due less to improved research and development efforts and more to increased emphasis upon the quality of the finished product.

The approaches to changing this aspect of corporate culture vary tremendously. At Texas Instruments the change has been instituted by ranking its top 100 executives by the quality of the products their operations turn out, and using incentive bonuses to reward accordingly. At CBS Inc., a computer issues quarterly report cards on the quality of audio records produced at the company's seventeen plants. At Chrysler, any plant manager whose operations miss a prescribed quality target must answer to a committee of senior executives.

However, according to William F. Conway, chief executive of Nashua Corporation, "A program hasn't the slightest chance of success without the support of the chief executive." Many companies who are serious about improving product quality are taking the "top down" approach and training line executives in quality management. Texas Instruments sent 300 top executives to an outside training program and is now putting another 20,000 managers through a sixteen-hour in-house training course. Other companies are using the group approach and forming multifunctional teams to make sure that quality concerns are addressed before new products are introduced. At Carrier Corporation, one team even delayed the introduction of a residential heat pump because of potential quality problems.

Source: "Quality: The U.S. Drives to Catch Up," *Business Week* (1 November 1982): 66–80.

## ☐ Framework for Describing and Analyzing OD Programs

Many OD programs have been proposed, each with slightly different assumptions, methodologies, and effectiveness claims. As we have done in previous chapters when faced with a large number of theories, we have categorized them on the basis of some criterion so that they can be more easily compared and contrasted. For organization development, an analysis of the various theories indicates that there are basically two different approaches used: micro and macro.

1. *The micro approach*—This approach assumes that an organization can be developed effectively by improving the competence of its individual members. As individuals become more administratively and interpersonally competent, they will be more effective in performing their respective jobs. Since many individuals can be developed simultaneously, eventually the organization becomes staffed with "developed" individuals. The micro approach assumes that the organization

will benefit from the development that these individuals have received and will consequently become more effective. A typical example of this approach is an individual manager receiving leadership training in an executive development program containing managers from many different companies or an "in-house" training program for supervisors that focuses on the individual behavior of the participants, not their collective behaviors.

2. *The macro approach*—The assumptions underlying this approach are generally the opposite of those just noted. The macro approach stresses the development of groups, not individuals. In addition, organized support from top management is considered desirable, since changes are anticipated to have wider implications than just the individual. When top management support is evident, the development process can more easily be transmitted downward through the entire organization. Top management support also encourages more systematic development efforts.

As is the case with many analytical frameworks, the micro/macro one can be somewhat confusing if not clearly understood. It is important to keep in mind that micro approaches can be used on a larger scale, thus giving them the appearance of being a macro approach. For example, job enrichment—a micro approach—can be utilized to change many jobs. But it is still an individual approach, since the focus of the change effort is on the jobs *individually* rather than collectively. Therefore, in using the micro/macro framework we are not necessarily speaking of the numbers of people involved but rather the focus of the change effort. So, while these two categories do not perfectly distinguish one OD approach from another, they are nevertheless helpful in categorizing the large number of theories evident in OD. They also help give a more orderly picture of a very diverse field of research.

# ■ MICRO APPROACHES TO ORGANIZATION DEVELOPMENT

A large number of OD programs focus on individual employees and how to increase their effectiveness. More specifically, the goal of these programs is to help the individual grow psychologically which, in turn, presumably assists the person in both task and interpersonal skills. At present the most popular micro approaches to OD are job enrichment, management by objectives (MBO), and sensitivity training. While this group is not exhaustive of the field, it is indicative. Through the description and analysis of these three programs, we can learn much about changing individual behavior in organizations.

## ☐ Job Enrichment

In the highly industrialized countries of the western world, specialization of labor is a very visible feature of society. From an organizational and societal standpoint, specialization of labor is very desirable, resulting in tremendous productivity on the part of individual workers and an abundance of goods for consumers. From the worker's viewpoint, however, the extreme simplification and standardization of jobs may result in adaptive behaviors such as absenteeism, turnover, boredom, and apathy—all indicators of a loss in motivation.

These undesirable consequences of specialization have led many business managers and academicians to propose that the trend toward specialization be reversed and jobs changed to include more variety and challenge. The variety in a worker's job can be increased through *job rotation, job enlargement,* or *job enrichment.* In job rotation, a worker is rotated through a series of different jobs to enhance the variety of tasks performed. Job enlargement extends the worker's present job to include more tasks performed on the same job. Neither of these methods necessarily changes the *level* of responsibility in the job. Job rotation has limited value if a worker is simply rotated through a variety of boring tasks. Washing the fenders of an automobile is not significantly different from washing the wheels. Similarly, job enlargement is limited if it simply extends the job to include more tasks of the same nature. If a person is bored soldering together eight connections on an electrical assembly, to that person it will likely be just as boring (and possibly more frustrating) if the job is extended to include soldering twelve connections.

The technique that is significantly different from the previous two is job enrichment (i.e., increasing the *level* of responsibility in a work role). This type of change means adding tasks that require the worker to make *higher level decisions.* While all workers will make some decisions in their jobs, boredom often occurs when the discretion allowed is below the capacity of the individual. Job enrichment involves changing the job to fit the worker's capacity to make decisions.

It should be noted that both job rotation and job enlargement *can* increase discretion, but they need not necessarily do so. No doubt the lack of success of some so-called job enrichment programs has been caused by a failure to distinguish among these three methods of changing jobs. All of the methods assume that increased responsibility in a work role will increase worker job satisfaction and motivation. Since job enrichment carries this argument the furthest, we will examine it in some detail.

Although we have discussed the general concept of responsibility that workers have in any job (noting that enriched ones have more of it), it is useful to describe more fully the characteristics of an enriched job. There are three features that should be clearly evident:

1. *Workers must feel that the job is meaningful*—Individual employees should feel that the job they are performing is valuable to them, given their particular preferences. This very general definition of the word *meaningful* is typically manifested in one of two ways: First, a job may be meaningful if it requires the worker to use a set of skills that are possessed by a relatively small segment of the person's *reference group.* Thus, the jobs of professionals (e.g., doctors, lawyers, architects, etc.) are generally considered very motivating because the skills that are used are not normally possessed by everyone. It is still possible, however, for tool-and-die makers to feel their job is meaningful since they probably do not

aspire to be doctors or lawyers. Second, a job may be meaningful if the worker can do the complete job. In the typical mass production factory, workers see only a small portion of the total product and have little sense of completeness in their tasks. If the job is changed so that workers produce all or a substantial portion of the product, the job may be more meaningful and motivating to them.

Even though these are separate factors, their interaction is quite important. It is unlikely, for example, that a worker completing a whole task that consists of a series of socially undesirable skills will find a high degree of satisfaction in the job.

2. *Workers must receive feedback on how well they are performing the job*—If workers can clearly see how their work is helping or hindering the organization, they may have an increased desire to perform their jobs. Many unenriched jobs do not allow for this since those who do the work do not inspect it or judge its quality. Rather, the inspection function, which carries more responsibility, is handled by different individuals. As a result, workers who produce the product have no idea whether it works properly or if the customer is satisfied with it. Some firms have attempted to overcome this problem by requiring workers to perform their own inspections, attach their names to the finished product, and answer quality defect or service requests themselves. The reasons why feedback is important were discussed in greater detail in Chapter 4.

3. *The job should allow the worker discretion in deciding how to complete it*—If workers are told what criteria the finished product or service must satisfy and are then allowed to set up their own procedures to reach these goals, they may experience increased motivation to perform the task. Worker discretion can be increased in any of the following three areas:

A. *Pace of work*—workers are allowed more discretion about how fast a job is completed and in what sequence the totality of tasks is completed.
B. *Quality of work*—workers are allowed to judge the quality of completed work and to balance quality with pace.
C. *Selection of resources*—workers are allowed to decide which resources are necessary to perform the required tasks and how these resources should be allocated among the tasks.

There are many instances of job enrichment being used by organizations that want to cut costs, improve employee morale, and reduce turnover and absenteeism. The target jobs for enrichment are usually low-level white- or blue-collar ones; middle- and upper-level jobs are, by definition, already enriched, or at least they have a lesser need for enrichment. The typical procedure for deciding the specific jobs that can be enriched is for management and those with intimate knowledge of the jobs to sit down and generate ideas on specific ways that increased responsibility can be put into a job that, through observation, appears to be lacking it. David Whitsett observes that there are many clues available to management to aid in this process.[4] For example, if there are numerous jobs with the title of "inspector" or "checker," this may be an indication that the inspection function has been removed from workers' jobs. If this is so, the job has lost a

## Box 15-2: Are Boring Jobs Really a Problem?

While no one would deny that there are many boring jobs around in all types of organizations, there is less agreement on whether or not this is a problem. Clearly, the job enrichment proponents believe it is. However, there is another school of thought that maintains that the problem is not nearly as serious as we might think.

For example, a report from the University of Michigan's Institute for Social Research, based on interviews with over 2,000 workers, concluded that boring jobs attract workers temperamentally suited to them. In other words, there are certain types of people who are able to manage the adjustment to a boring job better than others. Another study conducted over a six-year period at a General Motors plant in Baltimore reported that 95 percent of the workers at the plant were satisfied with their jobs. The report further noted that the employees tended to stay in their jobs because of the job security and fringe benefits, and never mentioned job enrichment as a factor in their decision to stay with the company.

Source: Kenneth Jenkins, "Do We Really Need Job Enrichment?" *Management World* (January 1981): 39.

great deal of its responsibility, and building the inspection function back into the job may have positive benefits.

The outcome of this process is often substantial change in a job. In one company, for example, the job of manufacturing a pump for a washing machine was enriched.[5] Prior to the change, the job was done in the traditional assembly-line fashion with the pump, containing twenty-seven parts, assembled by six workers, each with a small part of the pump as his job. Each pump required approximately one and three-quarter minutes to complete. In a two-step process, the job was enriched so that eventually one worker assembled the entire pump, inspected it, and placed his identifying mark on it. After the change, the company reported that (1) assembly time dropped to one and one-half minutes per pump, (2) product quality increased, and (3) cost savings were evident. This example demonstrates the three characteristics of an enriched job noted above. First, by assembling the entire pump, the worker did a complete job. Second, because the inspection function remained with the worker, the worker received feedback on how well the job had been performed. And third, the worker was allowed to determine individual work pace and procedures for completing the job, thus increasing discretion.

**Some Cautions About Job Enrichment**   Since job enrichment has been so well publicized in recent years as a method of increasing worker motivation, one can easily be misled by its possibilities. Although job enrichment can cause increased employee motivation, there are some other factors that should be considered.

1. *Job enrichment is not a substitute for good management*—Regardless of how enriched jobs might be in an organization, if other environmental factors in the organization are not adequate, job enrichment will have little or no effect. Job enrichment is not a substitute for good supervisory practices, wages, and company policies.

2. *"Enriched" is a relative term*—As a general rule, job enrichment proposes that jobs with little responsibility should be improved to provide more responsibility for the incumbent. However, we must remember that describing a job as one with "little responsibility" carries an implicit assumption about the person occupying that role. While the job may appear to be boring to the observer, the person actually performing the job may find it quite challenging.

3. *Enriching jobs may create a "snowball" effect*—Given that organizations have a fixed amount of authority to distribute among the members, enriching one person's job means taking authority away from another (most likely the manager). This not only presents systems design problems (for example, rewriting job descriptions), but it can also present a practical barrier, since labor unions may resist a scheme that eliminates jobs.[6]

4. *Job enrichment assumes workers want more responsibility*—Clearly, if we take the extreme case of a worker who is motivated by *lack* of responsibility, then job enrichment for this person would be a disaster. For workers who, for a variety of reasons, are satisfied with their current level of responsibility, job enrichment may cause more problems than it cures. Although the "try it—you'll like it!" approach mentioned in the previous chapter could be used, there still can be considerable resistance.

5. *Job enrichment may have negative short-run effects*—We have already mentioned in Chapter 4 that behavior usually does not change significantly in the short run, barring an extreme force operating on the individual. This fact has important implications for job-enrichment programs. For a short time after an increase in job responsibility, it is not unusual for organizations to experience a drop in productivity, as workers become accustomed to the work systems. After this initial drop, however, many firms report the increased productivity that job enrichment is supposed to produce. If an evaluation of a job enrichment program is made too early, management may erroneously conclude that the program is not working.

6. *Job enrichment is not a static process*—People become bored in their jobs because their capacity to make decisions is not fully utilized. Even though the job is changed to utilize this capacity, there is ample evidence to suggest that personal capacity is a dynamic, developing attribute.[7] It is likely, therefore, that after a period of time (the exact amount varies from person to person) the worker will outgrow the enriched job. If this occurs, additional enrichment will be required to fully utilize the individual's increased capacity. If jobs cannot be changed over time to use this capacity, the worker could be transferred to another job at a higher level of work (promoted).

7. *Workers should not be involved in the enrichment process*—Strange as it may seem, it is generally recommended that the workers not be involved in the

actual determination of how a job is to be enriched. The logic of this argument is as follows: Workers are sometimes conditioned to seeing their jobs in terms of "hygiene" factors and are unable to respond to the job content beyond their own experiences. The lower the level of the job, the more likely this would be true. Workers are so close to their job that they often cannot see beyond or above it. It is precisely *because* their jobs have no responsibility that they are unable to see the areas in which their responsibility can be increased. In short, the persons best equipped to create ways of enriching jobs are those who design them. This is not to say that workers should not be involved in the *implementation* of the program; most workers can make a positive contribution in this area.

8. *Change is difficult to implement*—The previous chapter discussed the difficulties often encountered in implementing change in an organization, and all the principles of resistance to change apply to job enrichment. In fact, job enrichment theory is a paradox: on the one hand we have a theory telling us that changing jobs through increasing the level of responsibility will result in increased motivation. On the other hand, our knowledge about change processes tells us that this type of change is one of the most difficult things to implement in a work situation. The initiation of a job enrichment program must take this factor into account. In other words, do not expect employees to jump for joy at the announcement of a job enrichment program.

**Summary and Evaluation**    Job enrichment received its major boost from Frederick Herzberg, although the concept had been around prior to his two-factor theory (see Chapter 3). It also gained popularity because it was consistent with the theoretical foundations of organizational behavior at that time, e.g., Maslow's need hierarchy, McGregor's Theory X and Y, etc. Unfortunately, much of the evidence about job enrichment was anecdotal rather than scientific, although there are a few studies that illustrate the benefits of job enrichment.[8] For example, a study at A.T.&T. with clerical and other telephone company employees showed a positive improvement in job performance and satisfaction after job enrichment.[9] Another study with technicians, engineers, and sales representatives showed similar results.[10]

If we assume that individual employees wish to have more variety, complexity, and responsibility in their jobs, job enrichment looks like a very promising way to make individual workers and the total organization more effective. However, it is clear that some employees do not want enriched jobs. Some research has been conducted to determine the individual characteristics that are compatible with job enrichment and those that are not.[11] The tentative findings indicate that workers who do not have the "work ethic" are generally not motivated by enriched jobs, whereas those who do possess it are. When additional, more refined research is conducted, managers will be better able to predict when job enrichment will be effective and when it will not. For the time being, we must consider it to be a useful tool when utilized with the cautions discussed above.

## ☐ **Management by Objectives**

In the early 1950s, Peter Drucker started something of a revolution in management theory by formulating management by objectives (MBO).[12] Although earlier writers had expounded some aspects of MBO in their writings, Drucker's proposal differed in that he believed that involvement in goal setting should be evident at the lower levels of the organization. Drucker argued that one of the major problems confronting large organizations was a lack of identification by the individual employee with the goals of the organization. With functionalization and specialization so highly developed, many workers were very much divorced from the direction and purpose of the larger system.

Drucker's scheme is a method of coordinating individual employee efforts toward overall organizational goals. Mindful of the writings of the behavioral scientists, Drucker feels that getting employees to work toward corporate goals is not just a matter of informing them what the goals are. Rather, employees' support for organizational goals is increased if they participate in the goal-setting process. When goal setting is a mutual influence process between managers and subordinates, the needs of subordinates are considered. Employees are allowed to influence their own work objectives, thus giving them some control over their work environment.

In practice, MBO requires the manager and the employee to discuss the personal and organizational objectives the employee wishes to reach during a specific time period, usually six months or one year. At the end of that time period, the manager and subordinate meet once again to determine how much progress has been made toward the objectives that were previously set. A crucial part of the MBO process is the feedback employees receive on how objectives were (or were not) accomplished. This feedback allows the managers and subordinates to engage in communication that influences employee behavior. The emphasis is upon the personal development of employees and the relationship of that development to corporate objectives.

Although not specifically a part of the original MBO emphasis, the feedback process often tends toward a quantitative assessment. For example, in consultation with superiors, a personnel manager may set an objective of reducing turnover in the organization by 10 percent over the next year; or a quality control supervisor may set the objective of reducing rejects by 5 percent over the next six months. In subsequent meetings, the manager and the subordinate determine how well this objective has been reached.

Two assumptions are made by the theory of MBO:

1. Participation in goal setting increases employees' motivation because of the ego involvement.
2. Participation in goal setting induces employees to exercise internal control over their own behavior; this reduces the need for external control over them.

To the extent that MBO can be implemented in its ideal state, the cause-and-effect relationship suggested in these assumptions should make for a better organizational climate and more effective attainment of organizational objectives. Unfortunately, departure from the ideal state often occurs and causes serious problems. With MBO, one of the major difficulties is that it can be treated strictly as a structural process, with the behavioral foundations of the system ignored. If this occurs, then it is merely a new wrinkle on an age-old philosophy known as "control from above." Applied inappropriately, workers see it as nothing more than a management gimmick to get them to do more for less. When used strictly as a structural process, MBO tends to be reduced to a system of shuffling papers. There is little communication between managers and subordinates, resulting in subordinates setting only goals they know their managers will approve.

The quantitative orientation of MBO performance measures causes two potential problems: First, not all organizational goals can be quantified; attempting to quantify all goals can detract from organizational performance. For example, some staff functions do not lend themselves to precise measurement. Second, once the quantification is made, performance tends to be oriented strictly toward those numbers at the expense of other goals which may have been overlooked or put aside because of their difficulty of measurement. In short, MBO can lead to *goal displacement*. It may be possible, then, to have a system that is designed to enhance goal attainment but that actually detracts from it.

The behavioral side of MBO has its hazards as well. It must be remembered that MBO is designed to be a process of mutual influence between managers and subordinates and that emphasis is upon employee development. In one sense, it is unfortunate that MBO has a built-in performance appraisal system, for it is here that many problems can occur. Even though the system is designed to encourage employee self-control, employees are nevertheless aware that at some point in the future their manager will compare their performance to the objectives previously set. Because the manager still has authority over the subordinate and controls rewards and punishments, the ideal communication process for the purpose of employee development may be contaminated with the traditional concept of organizational control. It should be obvious that if an employee perceives that "today's objectives will be tomorrow's clubs [weapons]," then the MBO system will not accomplish what it is designed to do.

Feedback, however, is crucial in MBO. How is this dilemma resolved? It is here that the subtle differences between structure and style become important. While the structure system—MBO—provides the format for superior-subordinate interaction, how well that interaction works depends largely on the personal style of the manager as perceived by the subordinate. If the manager has a history of autocratic rule and employees feel that threats and punishments will be used to influence behavior, the MBO system will likely be doomed to failure. If, instead, the manager has established a behavioral climate based upon mutual trust and support, the MBO system is more likely to be perceived as something that will assist in the development and progression of employees. One of the authors was witness to a situation in which a manager attempted to implement MBO in the work group but received no response. Subsequent investigation revealed that employees, through observing his past managerial behavior, believed he was trying to collect evidence on their lack of performance.

## Box 15-3: Some Common Errors in Goal Setting

Goal setting is done improperly when the manager

1. Doesn't clarify common objectives for the whole unit.
2. Sets goals too low to challenge the individual employee.
3. Doesn't clearly shape the unit's common objectives to fit those of the larger unit of which it is a part.
4. Emphasizes tacitly that it is pleasing the manager that counts, rather than achieving the job objective.
5. Makes no policies as guides to action but waits for results, then issues ad hoc judgments in correction.
6. Ignores the proposed new goals or ideas of subordinates and imposes only those which the manager deems suitable.
7. Fails to set intermediate target dates (milestones) by which to measure progress of subordinates.
8. Doesn't introduce new ideas from outside the organization nor permit nor encourage subordinates to do so, thereby freezing the status quo.
9. Is rigid in not allowing the knockout of previously agreed-upon goals which have subsequently proven unfeasible, irrelevant, or impossible.
10. Doesn't reinforce successful behavior or unsuccessful behavior when goals are achieved or missed.

Source: Adapted from George S. Odiorne, *Management by Objectives* (New York: Pitman Publishing, 1965), pp. 125–26.

## ☐ Sensitivity Training

One of the most controversial OD approaches, sensitivity training is designed to increase the awareness of individuals with respect to their own motivations and behavior patterns as well as those of others. This is accomplished through the use of training groups (T-groups). In the extreme, the technique uses the group confrontation method to achieve its fundamental goal of increased awareness by individuals of their own behavior.

In an attempt to achieve its objectives, the T-group operates as follows: individuals who volunteer for (or are sent to) the T-group meet at a predetermined location away from the normal place of work. These individuals may be complete strangers coming from many different organizations (stranger groups) or they may all come from the same organization (family groups). The groups, usually composed of ten to fifteen individuals, meet for approximately one week to ten days. There is no set agenda or required material to cover as there is in the typical structured seminar. Instead, the members are faced with a very unstructured environment in which the decision as to what direction to take must be made by the group. The sessions are moderated by a "trainer," whose function is to clarify the basic goal of the session and to assist the group in their functioning. The trainer generally assumes no leadership role, although this varies somewhat, depending on who the trainer is.

In an environment like this, it is not surprising that high anxiety levels develop in the group as some members attempt to impose structure on the others. Conflicts of this sort are ideal for increasing members' awareness of their own feelings and behaviors during conflict or consensus situations. Although the actual conduct of a T-group varies considerably because of the lack of structure, it generally involves group discussions of individual behavior patterns as they relate to particular problems. For example, a group of executives who work together may decide to engage in a T-group session to improve their effectiveness as a team. Each individual might describe how he sees the behavior of others, and the group might suggest possible improvements. After this is done, group members diagnose their own feelings and pursue ways of changing interpersonal relationships.

Certain assumptions underlie the use of T-groups. Campbell and Dunnette suggest the following:[13]

1. When faced with the behavior of others in an atmosphere of psychological safety, individuals who initially lack interpersonal competence can quickly learn to give clear, constructive, and complete feedback dealing with important aspects of group members' behavior.
2. A substantial proportion of group members can agree on the major aspects of each individual's behavior in the group.
3. Behavior within the T-group is not drastically different from behavior outside of it; transfer of learning from the isolation of the T-group to the "back-at-work" situation is thus feasible.
4. Anxiety created by the unstructured T-group facilitates learning.

The extent to which these assumptions are reasonable varies a great deal in practice. Two particularly troublesome issues are psychological safety (T-group members are reluctant to express themselves truthfully for fear of ridicule or hostility) and the difficulties of transferring T-group learning back to the regular job. In those instances where the assumptions noted above are realistic, T-group training probably results in more open, honest, and productive interpersonal relationships.

Perhaps the greatest limitation of T-group training is the theoretical base. The belief that "when all is known, all will be well" traces its roots back to the fundamentals of psychotherapy in which individuals are led to confront their emotions, values, and experiences. The belief is that recognition and understanding of barriers to personal development is a major step toward removing those barriers. However, individuals vary in their capacity to face themselves. Although the role of the T-group leader is to provide support where it is needed and to keep groups from going "too far," this is more an art than a science. Since groups may be more concerned with accomplishing their objectives (e.g., being open with each other) than with individual capacities for confrontation, it is possible that psychological damage can occur. It is for this reason that only trained, experienced leaders should conduct T-group sessions. In addition, the assumption that knowledge *about* behavior is sufficient for behavioral change can be questioned; many factors must be considered before a change in behavior can occur.

# ■ MACRO APPROACHES TO ORGANIZATION DEVELOPMENT

In contrast to the micro, or individual, approaches just discussed, macro OD approaches stress the importance of group involvement in improving the organization. The macro philosophy is broader than the mere idea that a group is a collection of individuals; its philosophy is based on the assumption that organizational change occurs most effectively when the change effort is focused on the larger social system. Since all parts of the system are interrelated, the change effort is oriented toward the larger subsystems of the organization, not the individuals themselves. The macro approach also assumes that major changes are more likely to occur in an organization if change efforts follow a "top-down" pattern rather than a "bottom-up" one. Two of the most widely used macro approaches—process consultation and the Managerial Grid—are discussed in this section.

## □ Process Consultation

Edgar Schein defines process consultation as ". . . a set of activities on the part of the consultant which help the client to perceive, understand, and act upon process events which occur in the client's environment."[14] As the definition suggests, this particular OD program starts from the assumption that the outside consultant does *not* merely conduct an analysis of the organization and then suggest a remedy for the problem that is identified. Rather, the consultant and management *jointly* discuss and diagnose organizational processes (both structural and human) and decide what problems need to be solved. According to Schein, this approach to problem solving is based on the following assumptions:[15]

1. Management often has difficulty deciding what is wrong with the organization. Special diagnostic help is therefore needed.
2. While most managers honestly wish to improve organizational effectiveness, they may need help in deciding how to achieve it.
3. When organizations learn to diagnose their own strengths and weaknesses, they can be more effective.
4. The outside consultant cannot hope to get a clear understanding of the organization's culture in a short period of time; therefore, joint consultation with management (which does know the culture) is necessary.
5. The client, not the consultant, must come to a conclusion regarding the problem, its causes, and its remedy. Decision-making authority about organizational changes remains with the client.

6. The consultant must be an expert at (1) diagnosis and (2) establishing effective helping relationships.

Schein points out that process consultation differs sharply from two other typical consultant models—the "purchase" model and the "doctor-patient" model. When the purchase model is used, the organization defines its problems without outside help and then hires an expert to solve them (e.g., how to design a new plant, how to improve employee morale, how to determine if consumers are satisfied with company products, etc.). This approach is often less than optimal because (1) the organization may have incorrectly defined its needs and/or (2) the consultant chosen is not technically competent. When the doctor-patient model is used, the consultant (doctor) diagnoses the organization (the patient) and then suggests a cure for the problem. The major difficulties here are that the unit that is diagnosed as having problems may reject the diagnosis and/or the unit in question may resist implementing the solutions proposed by the consultant. These limitations are overcome by the use of process consultation, since the consultant's main role is not to suggest solutions but instead to help management understand its organizational problems as clearly as possible. Once this is achieved, management can develop solutions that solve the problems facing the organization.

---

### Organizational Reality 15-3
### Corporate Commitments to Training

Although there are many ways of developing an organization, one of the most common methods is training. Training can take many forms (e.g., technical or supervisory) and is conducted by a wide variety of people. The price tag is high— it is estimated that in 1982 U.S. corporations spent over $1 billion on training programs alone.

While some of this training is contracted out to external consultants, much of it is done by "in-house" trainers, i.e., individuals whose major responsibility is training other individuals in the same organization. As one would expect, the number of trainers in each organization varies widely. However, the following data will give you some idea regarding the commitment that many major corporations have to this phase of organization development.

American Telephone and Telegraph has 10,000 employees engaged in training activities, out of a workforce of one million. Honeywell Corporation employs 97,000 people and has 150 people doing management training alone. There are about 500 professional trainers at Honeywell, but the number grows to almost 4,000 if you include all those performing training activities. New York's Citibank has 300 trainers world-wide for its 56,000 employees, and Sherson/American Express has 345 full-time trainers for 42,000 employees. Apparently, one of the most training-conscious organizations is the U.S. Navy, with 26,000 full-time trainers for its 565,000 enlisted personnel. This ratio of 21:1 is one of the highest in the business.

---

Source: *Training* (October 1982): 23–24.

Schein has found that process consultation normally proceeds through the following sequence:[16]

1. *Initial contact with the organization*—Someone in the organization contacts the process consultant after hearing about the concept and concluding that it may be helpful for the organization.
2. *Defining the formal and psychological contract*—This step involves discussing the nature of its problem(s) with the potential client organization and the extent to which the process consultant can be helpful in solving them. Once these issues have been resolved, the *formal* contract is drawn up, stating such things as which services will be performed, how much the consultant will be paid, etc. In addition, the *psychological* contract establishes other expectations that may not be in the formal contract but which are important for a smooth working relationship between client and consultant.
3. *Selecting a setting and method of work*—The client and the consultant agree on the level of the organization (preferably near the top) that will serve as the focus for analysis. The setting should be one in which "real work" is going on and also one in which observation of group and interpersonal processes is possible. The method the consultant will use to gather data (e.g., observation, informal interviewing) must be decided upon and should be consistent with process consultation goals. This means, for example, that individuals in the client organization should be aware of who the consultant is while data is being gathered.
4. *Data gathering and diagnosis*—Once information is generated (basically by informal interviewing and observation), it is analyzed to reveal specific problems which may be in need of resolution. This phase requires a great deal of time because the consultant must get an in-depth picture of the way employees feel about organizational processes.
5. *Intervention*—In process consultation, as opposed to other models, data gathering and intervention occur simultaneously and continuously throughout the process. Various interventions by the consultant are possible, including agenda setting (making the group aware of its internal processes), feedback of observations (to groups or individuals), counseling (of groups or individuals), or structural suggestions (creating awareness of advantages and disadvantages of various structural attributes of the organization).
6. *Reducing involvement*—The decision to reduce the consultant's involvement is generally made jointly with the client. This occurs after the client and the consultant agree that the basic purpose of the intervention has been largely achieved.
7. *Termination*—In the event that (1) the client and consultant become convinced that productive working together is no longer possible or (2) they agree that the basic goals of the OD intervention have been fully achieved, the involvement of the consultant ceases.

The major limitation of the process consultation technique is, of course, the skill possessed by the consultant. If the consultant possesses a high level of diagnostic skill and is able to adhere to the spirit of the points mentioned above, the likelihood of positive impact on the client organization is increased. Unfortunately, it is impossible at present to determine how well process consultation works because the research evidence that is available is largely in the form of case studies. This type of evidence often exists in new research areas like OD. Unfortunately, as noted in Chapter 2, case studies do not allow us to draw firm cause-and-effect conclusions.

## ☐  The Managerial Grid®

Blake and Mouton[17] have designed an OD program emphasizing the importance of the two basic leader behaviors (concern for people and concern for production). In this sense, their OD program is a logical development from the OSU leadership research (see Chapter 6). An important assumption made by Blake and Mouton is that the two concerns are independent (i.e., increased or decreased concern for production and people can occur simultaneously. Given this assumption, there are five basic leadership styles that managers can use (see Figure 15-2).

The model has gained substantial acceptance as an OD program that helps managers first to see their current leadership style and then to help them develop the most desirable style. According to Blake and Mouton, the most desirable style is one in which managers show a high concern for both people and production (the 9,9 style). In Blake and Mouton's view, leadership styles other than 9,9 are second best, particularly in the long run.[18]

There are six overlapping phases in the program; the first two stress the development of individuals, and the last four emphasize improvements in the total organization. The phases described below generally require three to five years to complete.[19]

1. *Laboratory-seminar training*—In this phase, problem-solving teams composed of approximately twelve to forty-eight managers are introduced to basic Grid conceptions. Diagonal slices of management are used so that no one is in a group with his or her immediate line superior or peers. Problem solving and evaluation of individual and team results are stressed. This phase is not intended to produce drastic organizational changes, but rather to create an environment in which "human problems of production" can effectively be solved. In this and all other phases, the desirability of the 9,9 management style is stressed.

| | Leader Emphasis on | |
|---|---|---|
| Style Label | Production | People |
| 1,1 | Low | Low |
| 9,1 | High | Low |
| 1,9 | Low | High |
| 5,5 | Moderate | Moderate |
| 9,9 | High | High |

**FIGURE 15-2.  Five Possible Leadership Styles**

2. *Team development*—This begins when superiors and subordinates begin analyzing their actual management styles and operating methods. Phases 1 and 2 are designed to increase the individual manager's self-awareness, willingness to listen to others, ability to analyze problem situations critically, and ability to function effectively in group situations.

3. *Intergroup development*—This phase attempts to change the typical win-lose mentality in intergroup relations to one in which joint problem solving is achieved in an atmosphere of problem confrontation. The 9,9 managerial style is used as the basic ground rule in discussions of appropriate problem resolution techniques.

4. *Organizational goal setting*—Once the above issues have been confronted, problems requiring major commitment on the part of employees (e.g., cost control, promotion policies, labor relations) are identified. It is felt that managers who will later be required to implement the organization's goals should help define them in the initial stages.

5. *Goal attainment*—The teams formed early in the program are given "task paragraphs" (designed by special task groups) which indicate a specific problem to be solved as well as an organization goal related to the problem. Information about the problem is also available to the group. After studying this information, the teams answer true-false questions designed by the formulators of the task paragraphs. The team then checks its responses against the answer key; in this way, insights are gained as to what the problem is and what its important aspects are.

6. *Stabilization*—This phase is designed to insure that changes which have occurred during steps one through five will not be lost due to regression to old behaviors. In addition, management can assess the strong and weak points of the activities and the outcomes in the first five phases.

Although Blake and Mouton cite some evidence in support of their program,[20] various critics have pointed out that methodological weaknesses make acceptance of their claims extremely difficult. While individuals may show changes in *attitudes* toward styles of management, changes in actual *behavior* have been difficult to prove. The most fundamental criticism, however, involves their view of the 9,9 leadership style. Through their writings, Blake and Mouton have given the impression that the 9,9 style is superior to all other styles of management. For example,

Managerial styles based on 9,1 (direction with compliance), or 5,5 (conformity with compromise), or on 1,9 (security and comfort through convenience), or on 1,1 (acquiescence and complacency), or the "clever" but corrupt relationships produced by facades or by debilitating paternalism, are, at best, second best. Actually they are quite unacceptable, long term. In comparison with performance contributed under 9,9 with its condition of candid communication based on conviction and commitment which results in creativity, other bases for work relationships seem to fall short.[21]

But as Bernardin and Alvares point out,

Despite the abundance of contrary evidence, Blake and Mouton asserted that their 9,9 team manager—high on production and high on people—will always be the most effective type of leader regardless of the situation and, in fact, a 9,9 orientation applied to the organization as a whole will foster a kind of corporate Darwinism.[22]

The belief that there is one leadership style that is inherently superior to others is clearly contrary to the theory described in the contingency approaches to leadership in Chapter 7. It seems unlikely that the 9,9 management style is appropriate for organizations experiencing different growth rates, labor relations, competition, and a host of other differentiating problems and situations.

# ■ THE EFFECTIVENESS OF ORGANIZATION DEVELOPMENT PROGRAMS

In any organization there are numerous factors to be considered before action is taken to resolve a specific problem. To determine whether an action taken was effective is therefore difficult. As far as OD is concerned, it is generally not possible at this time to accurately trace changes in organizational effectiveness back to specific OD programs. There are several reasons for this:

1. *It is difficult to measure the number, nature, and magnitude of confounding variables*—While an OD program is being implemented, there are numerous other influences operating internally and externally to the firm which influence its effectiveness. Assuming there is a change in the organization, it is difficult to detect which of the influences was the primary cause. For example, if an OD program had been implemented in an automobile manufacturing firm prior to the oil crisis in 1973–74, some might have concluded that the program harmed rather than helped the firm, since sales dropped after the program was implemented. While this conclusion would obviously not be warranted, neither could it be concluded that the OD intervention had kept sales from dropping even further.

2. *Preintervention measures of behavior are not taken*—In order to judge whether an OD program is effective, it is first necessary to have knowledge of the situation prior to the intervention. It is impossible to state that a training program "helped" a particular manager unless we first have some specific measures of the person's behavior prior to the training. Similarly, to state that an MBO program increased an organization's total effectiveness, specific measures before and after the change must be available.

3. *Those doing the evaluations of OD programs have a vested interest in proving success*—Many OD programs have become commercial ventures with companies paying large sums of money for consultants to come in and "develop" the organization. These same consultants then report specific successes of the programs which, of course, serve to generate more clients. This is certainly not to say that paid consultants are dishonest or misrepresent their findings, but it does point to a definite conflict of interest situation and, unfortunately, may contaminate the findings.

All this is not to say that OD programs are not useful in increasing organizational effectiveness; rather, it emphasizes that the data typically gathered in OD programs do not allow us to measure precisely either the nature or the extent of the change. To illustrate this point more clearly, we will analyze three of the OD strategies discussed earlier in this chapter (MBO, sensitivity training, and the managerial grid).

---

### Box 15-4: Prisoners, Vacationers, and the Needy

Each year hundreds of management development seminars are conducted across Canada and the United States. Although there is tremendous diversity in the kinds of people who attend, in our experience three distinct types emerge:

1. *The prisoner*—These individuals attend the seminar because they have been told to go by their boss. Not surprisingly, their attitude is one of indifference or hostility. The views they express during the seminar are generally negative, and they don't believe they will learn anything useful (a self-fulfilling prophecy).
2. *The vacationer*—These people attend seminars to have a good time. They are sociable and spend their time drinking and whooping it up. They often miss seminar sessions because of their social activity. Although they may have a positive attitude toward the subject matter, they often do not learn much because learning is not their top priority. These types can easily be identified by their golf clubs and poker chips.
3. *The needy*—These individuals attend the seminars because they feel they have a need to learn about some particular area. They are attentive, serious, and hard-working. They are often looked down upon by prisoners and vacationers because they are so work-oriented.

The seminar leader, of course, prefers the needy type, although prisoners and vacationers do present an interesting challenge. The real issue is, however, "How do you convert prisoners and vacationers into needy participants?" If anyone has the answer, please let us know.

---

### ☐ Evaluation of MBO

MBO has received a great deal of attention, and there have been many instances of its installation, or at least attempts to install it. Therefore, a substantial body of research exists that allows us to estimate its effectiveness in actual application.

On the positive side, several studies show the results predicted by MBO supporters. Huse and Bowditch report on a successful MBO program in which participants reported (1) significantly greater goal involvement, (2) greater agreement between boss and subordinate about the job to be done, and (3) ways of improving their current job performance.[23] Other researchers found that MBO programs resulted in improved communications, increased mutual understanding, improved planning, and improved attitudes toward evaluation systems.[24]

On the negative side, a two-part study over a four-year period found that, although participants initially thought the program increased their awareness of organizational goals and improved communications between levels of management, eventually they came to feel that the program was a weak incentive to improve performance and that the appraisal part of the program had been used as a whip.[25] They also believed the program increased paperwork, overemphasized production, and failed to involve all levels of management. Another study also found that, although general impressions of MBO were positive, managers felt that it required too much paperwork.[26]

In one of the most exhaustive studies of MBO effectiveness, the conclusions of the author were not particularly encouraging. The study found that the more rigorous the research methods used to evaluate the program, the less effective MBO was shown to be. Case study examples appeared to place MBO in the most favorable light, while field studies indicated that whatever positive results were initially achieved by MBO programs were usually lost after about two years.[27]

One area of conflicting evidence regarding MBO needs to be resolved. In Chapters 3 and 4 it was noted that many studies have verified that goal setting increases motivation and also have emphasized the importance of goal setting in the management process. Why, then, does the research evidence fail to show that MBO programs are successful? The answer probably lies in the programs themselves. For most organizations, MBO is more than just goal setting. Also integrated into the programs are performance appraisals, salary reviews, and lack of training in goal setting itself, not to mention the potential effects of organizational politics. In any case, it is clear that more rigorous research into MBO is needed. Otherwise, it will never leave its present status as a popularized fad whose effectiveness is under a cloud of doubt.

## ☐ Evaluation of Sensitivity Training

In evaluating the effectiveness of sensitivity training, emphasis changes from variables such as profits and productivity to the more general criterion of "behavior change." This is because sensitivity training has a micro emphasis rather than a total organizational one. This does not mean that it does not have implications for the broader organization or that it cannot be used to develop large sections of organizations; but the fact remains that most efforts to evaluate sensitivity training have been concerned only with the immediate effects of the T-group experience on individual behavior. Thus, T-group training may be used for individuals, but its utility for the total organization is not yet clear. One of the reasons this problem exists is that the T-group experience is an artificial one; the behaviors learned may be either inappropriate for the organization, or the organizational environment may be unsupportive of the new behavior. Thus, even though T-groups may induce behavioral change, the changes may be short-lived when everyday work activities are resumed.

T-groups have been criticized as being "too effective" (i.e., they have a powerful influence on those involved in them). George Odiorne, one of the most vocal critics of T-group training, cites an extreme example in which

A slick brochure advertising a "Leader Training" course drew several dozen enrollees to a course. Those coming found themselves in T-group training. Shaken badly, two left early, and another broke into tears several months later describing his public humiliation to an interviewer. His T-group had voted him "the worst leader they would like to work for." The specificaion of their charge? He was "too wishy-washy." His job was procurement analyst and he was highly regarded by his superiors for his technical knowledge.[28]

As a general statement, it is probably fair to say that T-groups can cause behavioral change, but it is not yet clear whether (1) the overall change is positive or negative and (2) the changes are related to organizational performance. In a comprehensive review of the literature on T-groups, Dunnette and Campbell concluded that

Laboratory education has not been shown to bring about any marked change in one's standing on objective measures of attitudes, values, outlooks, interpersonal percep- tions, self-awareness, or interpersonal sensitivity. In spite of these essentially negative results on objective measures, individuals who have been trained by laboratory education measures are more likely to be seen as changing their job behavior than are individuals in similar job settings who have not been trained.[29]

## Box 15-5: Does Management Training Work?

Given the billions of dollars spent each year on management training of various sorts, does it pay off? That is, do managers actually improve their skills as a result of this training?

Researchers Joseph A. Olmstead and Devah R. Galloway of Human Resources Research Organization prepared a report on this exact question for the U.S. Bureau of Mines. Their conclusions were:

1. "Straight" instructional methods (lecture, discussion, case analysis) were effective at improving awareness and knowledge, but ineffective at changing behavior.
2. Changes in attitude can be achieved if the correct training methods are used.
3. Training can improve problem-solving skills.
4. Interpersonal skills can be improved but it requires much longer training time than is normally provided.
5. On the whole, no clear evidence exists that training affects the job performance of managers.

Source: *Training* (May 1983): 82.

Until there is more conclusive evidence regarding the impact of T-groups on variables such as profit and productivity, the effectiveness of such an OD tool must be viewed with caution.

## ☐ Evaluation of the Managerial Grid

In recognition of the measuring problems described earlier, as well as the fact that it is often difficult to convert behavioral science concepts into practice, an attempt was made to systematically evaluate the effectiveness of Blake and Mouton's Managerial Grid program in one company.[30] Overall, the analysis indicated that changes had occurred in four areas: (1) profits, (2) productivity, (3) practices and behavior, and (4) perceptions, attitudes, and values. The nature of these changes and some observations about them are discussed below.

**Profits**    During the first year after the Grid program had been implemented, profits rose substantially. However, attributing this improvement to the Grid program is difficult for two reasons: First, the firm routinely experienced fluctuating prices for both raw materials and the price of its finished goods. It would not be possible for an OD program to influence these noncontrollable factors. Second, the firm had laid off 600 workers during the period in question, and the associated reduction in personnel costs may have accounted for a substantial portion of the increase in profits.

**Productivity**    The most dramatic positive results were evident for the productivity aspect of company operations. Using 1960 as the base year (index = 100), productivity (calculated by dividing total production by the number of employees) increased from 103.9 in 1962 to 131.3 in 1963. Although it was during this time that 600 employees were laid off, the fact remains that output per employee increased. This is clearly a positive outcome, but consistent with our earlier remarks, the OD program is only one plausible explanation for the increased worker productivity.

**Practices and Behavior**    Data analysis indicated that noticeable changes in practices and behavior had occurred. These included changes in (1) promotional criteria (increased emphasis on younger, line personnel), (2) increased manager mobility (more internal transfers, indicating increased flexibility), and (3) a greater degree of decentralization (more decisions made by lower-level managers). The extent to which these changes are perceived as improvements depends on one's perspective. For example, with respect to (1), young line managers would probably rate the program highly whereas older staff specialists would not. The conclusion that these changes are desirable is a value judgment, not an objective conclusion. With respect to (3), whether increased decentralization is desirable is also a value judgment.

**Attitudes and Values**    To determine whether attitudes and values had been affected by the OD program, participants were asked to fill out questionnaires indicating their attitudes on work-related issues prior to the start of the program as well as one year later. These questionnaires were filled out at the second point in time (i.e., managers were asked at the second time period, before the start of the program). On balance, the results were very positive, with the respondents reporting improvements in (1) the way they worked with their boss, (2) the way their work group functioned, and (3) intergroup collaboration. The percentage of managers reporting improvement in each of these categories was 49 percent, 55 percent, and 61 percent, respectively. These findings support the general conclusion reported in Box 15-5. However, the approach itself is weak methodologically, since respondents were required to recall both present and prior attitudes at one point in time. A more appropriate methodology would have been to administer the attitude questionnaire *prior* to the OD program as well as *after* it.

Overall, these results suggest improvement in the functioning of the organization over the years studied. However, attributing these changes directly to the Grid program is difficult, since many other factors were at work simultaneously which could have influenced profits, employee attitudes, and productivity. Perhaps the most reasonable conclusion that can be drawn is that the Grid program either caused or was instrumental in causing some positive changes in the organization, but it is impossible to determine the *magnitude* of the causal relationship. Because of this, we do not know if the program was cost-effective (i.e., if the cost of the program was returned to the company in the form of increased profits).

## Box 15-6: Evaluating OD Programs

There are several problems that are encountered when companies try to evaluate OD programs. One problem is that many variables besides the actual OD program might cause improvements in organizational effectiveness. Another problem is that companies may be unwilling to set up an OD program in such a way that its impact can really be measured. This latter problem is one that is not normally mentioned when criticisms are made of OD programs. But we must recognize that the person in charge of the OD program would probably feel very threatened if it could be shown that the program was ineffective or, worse, was actually detrimental to the company. Not measuring the impact of the program makes it possible to argue that "the program probably had a positive effect."

While avoidance of measurement is a potential problem, it does not appear to happen frequently in practice. One review of thirty-five OD programs found that in the majority of the cases the effectiveness of the programs was rigorously measured.* In addition, the programs typically had an effect on both organizational processes (e.g., self-development) and organizational outcomes (e.g., profits).

*J. Porras and P. Berg, "The Impact of Organization Development," *Academy of Management Review* 3 (April 1978): 249–66.

In another company, researchers evaluated the effectiveness of phase two of the Grid program.[32] It was felt that this phase was the most crucial, since changes in behavior must occur before the remainder of the program can be successful. The researchers concluded that the Grid program failed for three reasons:

1. Individuals could not make the transference from the various leadership styles proposed by the Grid to critiquing their own behavior.
2. The gap between the new cultural values proposed by the Grid and the old cultural values of the organization was too great.
3. The larger organizational culture was not supportive of the new behaviors.

Because of these problems, the program was ultimately abandoned. However, this may be less of a criticism of the Grid program than it is of the organization's climate, since the organization did not meet the conditions necessary for OD success outlined at the beginning of this chapter. One could hardly expect *any* OD program to be effective if the prerequisites for success are not met.

## ☐ Conclusions About the Effectiveness of Organization Development Programs

Until more systematic methods are used to evaluate OD programs, problems like those noted previously will continue to plague evaluation efforts and seriously inhibit drawing conclusions about the effectiveness of OD approaches in general. What is needed to overcome these problems is for management and the OD consultant to do the following prior to the OD intervention:

1. *Decide on the variables which are of interest to management*—These might be very diverse and include such items as net profits, employee morale, competitive position in the industry, etc.
2. *Develop a systematic procedure for gathering data on the variables of interest*— This involves not only generating before and after measures of the variables but also setting up methods to take account of unexpected environmental influences which might occur during the OD intervention (e.g., the formation of a labor union or the imposition of new pollution standards by the government). These will have a direct impact on the variables of interest, and this impact must be assessed in order for a clear picture of the effectiveness of the OD intervention to emerge.
3. *The data gathered should be analyzed systematically to determine the effect of the OD intervention on the variables of interest*—This determination can be either qualitative or quantitative, but evaluative measures should be consistent with the variables being measured. For example, if an effort is made to change behavior, evaluative measures should be concerned with behaviors, not attitudes.
4. *Evaluation should be performed by an objective third party*—A neutral third party is most likely to be objective in (1) identifying the variables that should be

measured, (2) collecting the necessary data for measurement, and (3) evaluating the change in the variables.

While the above procedure does not allow totally certain conclusions to be drawn about the effectiveness of an OD program, it does represent a marked improvement over the way many OD interventions have been evaluated. In all cases, the organization should attempt to satisfy both the methodological requirement (conclusions can logically be made) and the feasibility requirement (the organization in question will be able to do it). If these two criteria are met, organizations will be in a better position to evaluate the effectiveness of their OD programs.[33]

Another area of organization development that needs more attention is prevention of "relapse," i.e., the tendency to revert to old behaviors following an intervention of some sort. In management training, for example, new behaviors may be adopted as a result of the training, but unless there is a follow-up strategy to maintain the new behaviors, there is a strong possibility that the new behaviors will slowly be lost. This suggests that organizations should spend at least an equal amount of time preventing relapse as they do in teaching the new behaviors.[34]

## ■ SUMMARY

Organization development is concerned with planned changes in organizations. This chapter has reviewed several micro and macro approaches to organization development and noted some general conditions that must be satisfied before planned change can occur. Three micro examples were discussed: job enrichment, management by objectives, and sensitivity training. Job enrichment is a program in which the organization attempts to increase the level of responsibility and challenge in employees' jobs. Although there is documented evidence that job enrichment can have a positive effect upon productivity, the approach must be used selectively. Not all people want enriched jobs, and the implementation process is critical to the program's success.

Management by objectives (MBO) is a program designed to integrate objectives from the top to the bottom of the organization. It is a system for encouraging managers and subordinates to share information about their jobs and performance objectives. Although MBO is a popular program in organizations, its general effectiveness has yet to be proven. MBO is, however, consistent with other research in organization behavior (e.g., goal setting).

Sensitivity training is a program designed to improve an individual's awareness of the impact of his or her behavior upon others. T-groups have declined in popularity recently, primarily because of the lack of evidence that the learning was transferable to the job.

Two macro approaches were reviewed: process consultation and the Managerial Grid. Process consultation involves using a third-party intervention to create a process through which the organization can deal with its problems and opportunities. Emphasis is upon gathering data and feeding it back to members of the organization for them to deal with. It is difficult to evaluate process consultation because of the wide variety of programs that are conducted using this method. The Managerial Grid is a popular model that is used for both leadership and conflict-management training. It uses a series of programs to progressively take an organization to a situation of open communications, supportive and production-oriented leadership styles, and a willingness to deal with conflict constructively.

The major weakness of most organizational programs is the difficulties in measuring their effectiveness. Many variables are operating simultaneously which makes it difficult to isolate the effect of a single intervention. Emphasis also needs to be placed upon the prevention of relapse, i.e., the unlearning of behaviors acquired in the organizational-development process.

## *Opening Incident Revisited—Nina Friesen*

After reading this chapter, Nina Friesen's dilemma should be clear. She would obviously be pleased that the company has made a sizable commitment to organization development, but there appear to be some nasty strings attached. Unless someone (likely Nina) does some sharp thinking very fast, there is a good chance the company will waste the $250,000 budget. Forgetting for the moment what Nina should do, let's first examine the problems the president has created.

First, he has not specified any particular problem he wants solved. He refers to noticing "several problems," and "taking the managers out of the dark ages," but these are not enough to design an organization development program. It is unlikely the program or training will do much good if it isn't directed at a specific problem or set of problems.

Second, the president wants tangible results. What type of results? We know that Nina could probably produce some attitude and knowledge change without much difficulty, but is this what the president wants? How does he intend that she measure results?

Third, the president is fairly optimistic about the time it takes to make a change in his organization. If there have been no developmental activities for some time, then it is unlikely that significant results will be achieved by next year. On the other hand, if he wants results by next year, Nina might give him these at some far greater cost (such as increased turnover).

And finally, the support Nina can anticipate is obviously weak. Although the president has *said* that he and his staff are behind her all the way, the fact is they will not be part of the program. This means there is a good chance that whatever good deeds Nina can pull off in her OD program will be lost quickly, since the senior managers will not likely be supportive of their changes.

What should Nina do? This is partly a question of strategy and partly a question of ethics. Based upon her knowledge of organization development programs, Nina will know that the chances of showing any tangible results within one year are slim. Even if she could accomplish something it would be hard to prove. Whether she should go ahead and try to give the president what he wants or tell him he is wasting his money is a choice she will have to make. Many a consultant has survived nicely by telling senior managers what they want to hear.

The strategic question is how she should go about attempting to achieve some measurable behavior change in the system. Here she will have to revert to her knowledge of the organization development process and put together a program that attempts to achieve the president's objectives.

Her first choice, however, should be to go back to the president with the very issues and concerns that have been raised here. She can then explain her concerns to the president and perhaps he can become more realistic about what $250,000 will buy him in human development.

## ■ REVIEW QUESTIONS

1. What is the main purpose of organization development?

2. How does organization development differ from other types of organizational change?

3. How does "action research" differ from hypothesis-testing research?

4. What are the major prerequisites for effective organization development programs?

5. Why is OD generally viewed as a long-run change strategy?

6. What types of organizational situations or problems lend themselves to organization development programs?

7. What are the differences between the micro and macro approaches to studying organization development?

8. What are the differences between job enlargement, job enrichment, and job rotation?

9. What are some useful ways of enriching jobs?

10. What are some of the reasons why job enrichment may not work?

11. What is the main purpose of an MBO program?

12. Discuss the limitations of MBO.

13. What is the purpose of T-groups? Their limitations?

14. What is the major goal of process consultation?

15. What is the major goal of the Managerial Grid program?

16. Why is it difficult to evaluate the effectiveness of OD programs?

# ■ EXERCISE 15-1: A CHANGE IN STYLE

The Sexton Company was a large and successful manufacturer of auto parts. The company had a policy of actively supporting its employees in any self-development programs they wanted to take. This support took the form of either (1) time off from work to attend seminars or (2) paying tuition for employees who wanted to attend evening courses at the local university. LuAnn Schmidt, the office manager of the Little Rock, Arkansas, office was known as "a real autocrat" by her subordinates. She had recently taken a fourteen-day seminar on "Improving Your Leadership Effectiveness," and upon her return, she called a meeting of her staff and told them in some detail what her experiences had been during the fourteen days. She concluded by saying, "I know I have been fairly strict in the past, but that is going to change. The program I have just taken convinced me that we will all benefit if I allow a little more flexibility in the way you perform your tasks."

1. Assuming Schmidt changes her style, what do you think will be the effects of this change?

2. Assuming she doesn't change, what do you think will be the effect?

3. Do you think Schmidt's behavior actually changed? Why or why not?

# ■ EXERCISE 15-2: THE CONCERNED FOREMEN

The Link Manufacturing Company employed 450 people (mostly blue-collar) and was located in a small town in Minnesota. Its president, James Link, recently attended a two-day organization development seminar in Minneapolis. He returned home quite enthusiastic about the potential of some of the techniques he had been exposed to. One week later, the fifteen front-line foremen in the factory received an interoffice memo summarizing the president's Minneapolis experience and stated that each of the foremen would be attending a three-day T-group session. After receiving their individual memos, the foremen consulted with one another about what they should do, since some of them felt unsure or uncomfortable about what was involved. After some discussion they decided to ask the president to let participation be voluntary. A meeting with the president was arranged and the foremen voiced their concerns. The president, upon hearing this, became fairly agitated and gave a lengthy speech about the value of "improving yourself." He concluded by saying that "both you and the company will benefit from your attendance at the T-group—it will increase your awareness of yourself, improve the relations between you and your subordinates, and will thus improve worker productivity and company profits."

1. What is your opinion of how the president handled the situation?

2. What assumptions are being made by each party?

3. How do you think the situation should have been handled?

# ■ ENDNOTES

1. W. H. French and C. H. Bell, "A Definition and History of Organization Development," *Academy of Management Proceedings* (1971): 146.

2. Richard Beckard, *Organization Development* (Reading, Mass.: Addison-Wesley, 1969) pp. 16–19.

3. Wendell French, "Organization Development: Objectives, Assumptions, and Strategies," *California Management Review* 12 (1969): 23–46.

4. D. A. Whitsett, "Where Are Your Unenriched Jobs?" *Harvard Business Review* 45 (January–February 1975): 74–80.

5. M. D. Kilbridge, "Reduced Costs Through Job Enlargement: A Case," *Journal of Business* 33 (1960): 357–62.

6. For some suggestions for dealing with union resistance to job enrichment, see M. Scott Myers, "Overcoming Union Resistance to Job Enrichment," *Harvard Business Review* 41 (May–June 1971): 37–49.

7. Elliott Jaques, *Equitable Payment*, (London: Heinemann Educational Books, Ltd.), 1970.

8. For a critical analysis of job enrichment, see Mitchell Fein, "The Myth of Job Enrichment," in *Humanizing the Workplace*, Roy P. Fairfield, ed., (Buffalo: Prometheus Books, 1974, pp. 71–78.

9. Robert Ford, "Job Enrichment Lessons for A.T.&T.," *Harvard Business Review*, January–February, 1973, pp. 96–106.

10. William J. Paul, Jr., Keith B. Robertson, and Frederick Herzberg, "Job Enrichment Pays Off," *Harvard Business Review*, March–April, 1969, pp. 61–78.

11. A. N. Turner and P. R. Lawrence, *Industrial Jobs and the Worker: An Investigation of Response to Task Attributes* (Boston: Harvard University Graduate School of Business Administration, 1965); see also M. R. Blood and C. L. Hulin, "Alienation, Environmental Characteristics, and Worker Responses," *Journal of Applied Psychology* 52 (1967): 284–90.

12. Peter Drucker, *The Practice of Management* (New York: Harper, 1954).

13. J. P. Campbell and M. D. Dunnette, "Effectiveness of T-Group Experiences in Managerial Training and Development," *Psychological Bulletin* 70 (1968) 73–104.

14. Edgar Schein, *Process Consultation: Its Role in Organization Development* (Reading, Mass.: Addison-Wesley, 1969), p. 9.

15. Schein, *Process Consultation*, p. 8.

16. Ibid., p. 78.

17. R. R. Blake, and J. S. Mouton, *The Managerial Grid* (Houston: Gulf, 1964).

18. Ibid., p. 318.

19. Ibid., pp. 266–85.

20. Robert Blake et al., "Breakthrough in Organization Development," *Harvard Business Review* 42 (1964): 133–55.

21. Blake and Mouton, *The Managerial Grid*, p. 318.

22. H. J. Bernardin and Kenneth Alvares, "The Managerial Grid as a Predictor of Conflict Resolution Method and Managerial Effectiveness," *Administrative Science Quarterly* 21 (March 1976): 84.

23. Edgar F. Huse and James L. Bowditch, *Behavior in Organizations* (Reading, Mass.: Addison-Wesley, 1973), p. 196.

24. Stephen J. Carroll, Jr. and Henry L. Tosi, "Goal Characteristics and Personality Factors in a Management-By-Objectives Program," *Administrative Science Quarterly* 15 (September 1970): 295–305.

25. The two studies are contained in Anthony P. Raia, "Goal Setting and Self-Control," *Journal of Management Studies* 2 (September 1965): 34–53; and Anthony P. Raia, "A Second Look at Management Goals and Controls," *California Management Review* 8 (Summer 1966): 49–58.

26. Henry L. Tosi and Stephen J. Carroll, "Managerial Reaction to Management By Objectives," *Academy of Management Journal* 11 (December 1966): 415–26.

27. Jack N. Kondrasuk, "Studies in MBO Effectiveness," *Academy of Management Review*, vol. 6, no. 3, 1981, pp. 419–30.

28. George Odiorne, "The Trouble with Sensitivity Training," *Training Directors Journal* 17 (October 1963): 12–19.

29. Marvin D. Dunnette and John P. Campbell, "Laboratory Education: Impact on People and Organizations," *Industrial Relations* 7 (October 1968): 23.

30. Blake et al., "Breakthrough in Organization Development."

31. This is calculated as follows: 56 percent of the increase in profits was accounted for by noncontrollable factors. Thus, 44 percent of the increase in profits was accounted for by reductions in controllable costs (costs which the Grid program could have reduced). Of the controllable cost savings, 69 percent came from the manpower reduction and 31 percent from improved operations procedures and high productivity per man hour. This fact reduces the maximum grid impact to 14 percent (31 percent of 44 percent).

32. S. R. Maxwell and M. G. Evans, "An Evaluation of Organizational Development: Three Phases of the Managerial Grid," *Journal of Business Administration* 5 (Fall 1973): 21–35.

33. For an in-depth analysis of the effectiveness of OD programs, see J. Porras and P. Berg, "The Impact of Organization Development," *Academy of Management Review* 3 (April 1978): 249–66.

34. One set of strategies for reducing relapse is contained in Robert D. Marx, "Relapse Prevention for Managerial Training: A Model For Maintenance of Behavior Change," *Academy of Management Review*, vol. 7, no. 3, 1982, pp. 433–41. Interestingly, the strategies recommended by the author are based upon strategies used to prevent relapse in addictive behaviors such as drinking, smoking, etc.

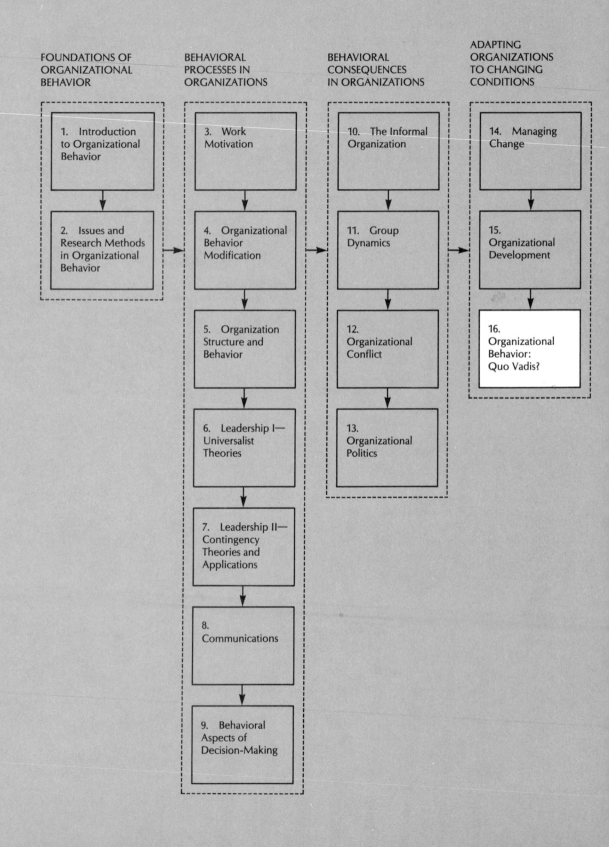

FOUNDATIONS OF
ORGANIZATIONAL
BEHAVIOR

BEHAVIORAL
PROCESSES IN
ORGANIZATIONS

BEHAVIORAL
CONSEQUENCES
IN ORGANIZATIONS

ADAPTING
ORGANIZATIONS
TO CHANGING
CONDITIONS

1. Introduction
to Organizational
Behavior

2. Issues and
Research Methods
in Organizational
Behavior

3. Work
Motivation

4. Organizational
Behavior
Modification

5. Organization
Structure and
Behavior

6. Leadership I—
Universalist
Theories

7. Leadership II—
Contingency
Theories and
Applications

8.
Communications

9. Behavioral
Aspects of
Decision-Making

10. The Informal
Organization

11. Group
Dynamics

12.
Organizational
Conflict

13.
Organizational
Politics

14. Managing
Change

15.
Organizational
Development

16.
Organizational
Behavior:
Quo Vadis?

# Organizational Behavior: Quo Vadis?

## ■ Learning Objectives

After reading and studying this chapter you should be able to:

☐ Describe the "simplicity-complexity" trend and give examples of how it has affected the field of organizational behavior.

☐ List the different philosophies of mankind and give illustrations of how the different philosophies have affected organizations.

☐ Explain the "consistency vs. effectiveness" dilemma.

☐ List the basic causes for the decline in the work ethic in our society.

☐ List and define the basic concepts that constitute the philosophy of Quality of Work Life (QWL).

☐ Describe the common misconceptions about QWL.

☐ Describe some common methods of improving QWL in organizations.

☐ Identify the major research considerations that are confronting organizational behavior.

☐ Define the "individual dignity" issue and point out its implications for the practice of management.

Chapter

# ■ KEY TERMS

Economic man

Social man

Self-actualizing man

Complex man

Work ethic

Worker alienation

Individual differences

Integrative research

Evaluation research

Individual dignity

Self-development

Quality of Work Life (QWL)

# ■ CHAPTER OUTLINE

I.  The Simplicity-Complexity Trend
    A.  Causal Relationships
    B.  Philosophies of Man
    C.  The Consistency versus Effectiveness Dilemma
    D.  Management Development
    E.  The Work Ethic

II.  Quality of Work Life
    A.  Philosophy of QWL
    B.  Misconceptions About QWL
    C.  Methods of Improving QWL

III.  Future Research Considerations
    A.  The Need for Integration
    B.  Applicability of Research
    C.  Evaluative Research

IV.  The Individual Dignity Issue

V.  A Final Comment

## *Opening Incident—Management in the Year 2000*

Imagine it's the year 2000. You have just finished college and are interviewing several companies for a job as a manager. On this particular day, you have an interview with the G & S Manufacturing Company, which employs about 2,000 people and manufactures home furnishings and related products. The interview consists of talking with the personnel manager and other senior managers in the company and taking a tour of the plant facilities.

During your interview with the personnel manager, Mr. Kirk, he describes the company and its operating philosophy: "We consider ourselves to be very 'people-oriented.' Everything we do here is built around the kind of people we have and what their needs are. If we have a problem, we involve the employees in the solution, get their ideas, and try to find a way to overcome it. Anyone who works here has to have the same philosophy. It's the way things are now."

At the end of the day you are collecting your thoughts, trying to put together a mental picture of this organization. The following facts about the organization stick out in your mind:

1. All of the workers are organized into autonomous work groups who work on a complete product. While groups number eight to twelve workers with about four to six different jobs in the group, there is considerable trading of jobs among the workers, since each person is usually able to do all of the jobs in the group.

2. The groups have no foreman. There is a "team leader" who is also part of the group. This person serves as a resource leader but does not have authority over the workers. If a problem arises, the team leader presents it to the group to solve.

3. While there are "good jobs" and "bad jobs" within each team, no one is assigned permanently to the jobs. For example, there are no janitors; everyone takes a turn at cleaning.

4. Screening of job applicants is also done by the team in cooperation with the personnel department.

5. The pay system is geared to the number of different jobs a person can perform, not seniority or type of job. Team members teach one another their jobs as well as members of other teams, so that the majority of workers in the plant earn the highest wage.

6. Workers are in charge of their own quality control, even to the point that they are occasionally sent to visit a customer who is having concerns about quality.

7. There are no set working hours except for a core of hours during the day and a requirement that employees work a minimum number of hours during each three-month period. Each team decides its own working schedule around the core.

8. The design of the plant minimizes differences among people. All have the same parking lot, restrooms, and eating facilities. Ample room is set aside for group activities and meetings.

9. There is a joint policy-making board that governs the total operation of the company. The workers elect representatives to sit on this board. While there are only three worker representatives on the twelve-person board, it is understood that any board member has the right to veto any proposal or decision. The board makes all of its decisions by consensus, not by majority vote.

10. The company policy toward fringe benefits allows each worker to decide what package of fringe benefits he or she wants. Many workers trade their paid sick leave for an extra week's vacation each year, provided, of course, that the team agrees to carry that person's load during their extra week off.

11. The company does have performance appraisal systems, but they are implemented by the work groups. All group members do a peer evaluation of other members and then these evaluations are discussed in group sessions.

12. There is also a variation of "management-by-objectives" in place. Once a year, a representative from each team attends a two-day retreat with all other managers to discuss the year's performance and set goals for the coming year.

As you review these facts, you wonder whether you have the necesssary skills to function in an organization like this. Or, perhaps more importantly, what are the skills necessary for an organization of this type?

In this concluding chapter we wish to examine briefly the field of organizational behavior and its role in the future. There is little doubt that the previous research in organizational behavior has been beneficial to both organizations and employees. However, organizational behavior is a dynamic discipline and researchers are continually pushing forward to new frontiers of knowledge. Organizations are also taking major initiatives in implementing innovative programs that would have been unheard of as little as ten or fifteen years ago. In this chapter we will attempt to capture the flavor of the dynamic nature of the field, as well as pull together some of the common themes of this book.

For those of you whose Latin is rusty, the phrase "Quo Vadis?" roughly translates into "Where from here?" In this chapter, we are going to attempt to outline where we go from here and what the future holds for organizational behavior. This requires that we make some relatively large leaps from what has been, up to now, largely descriptive material drawn from the efforts of scientists. In looking into the future, the process necessarily becomes less scientific and more a matter of interpretation, judgment, and values. The reader should keep in mind the discussion in Chapter 2 regarding descriptive, predictive, and prescriptive models in organizational behavior. As the chapter title suggests, we are now venturing into the predictive and prescriptive areas of organizational behavior, which tend to have the consistency of quicksand.

To look at the future, we will begin with the past. Although the field of organizational behavior is quite diverse, there are patterns that have emerged over time and we will use these patterns to project into the future. This will lead us into the application of that knowledge to actual organizations, a field of study known as Quality of Work Life (QWL). We will examine what is generally being done in QWL and suggest what this means for the future of organizations. Finally, we will explore some issues that arise out of past research and practice, since these will have to be resolved in the future.

# ■ THE SIMPLICITY-COMPLEXITY TREND

One of the major values of examining the past is to gather evidence on what might happen in the future. In studying social systems we are not looking so much for specific events that may or may not occur but, rather, for general *patterns* of behavior that may emerge from many different observations in different circumstances over substantial periods of time. Because this book has been primarily descriptive in nature, its content is primarily historical (i.e., we have described past managerial practices and research findings and generalized from these to current applications of the principles in organizations). In examining this descriptive material, a pattern seems to emerge which we believe is likely to be a major indicator of future managerial practices and theories about organizations. We label this the "simplicity–complexity" trend.

Our basic thesis is this: in examining the nature and development of management and organizational behavior theory over the last seventy-five years, it appears as though there is a trend from simplistic theories about people in organizations to more complex ones; a change away from the "one best way" philosophy of management to one which attempts to recognize individual differences; and a movement, strangely enough, away from the prescriptive approaches to organizational behavior to the more descriptive ones.

Some evidence of our contention is in order. In Chapter 3, a number of *motivation* theories were reviewed and evaluated. In comparing those theories it can generally be concluded that the more recent the development of the theory, the greater its complexity. For example, we have come the full gamut from relatively simplistic need theories (e.g., Maslow) to the more complex expectancy-type theories. The situation is similar for *leadership* proposals. Early (universalistic) theories of leadership, such as the trait approach, were relatively simplistic; more recent contingency proposals are much more complex and consider situational and individual differences. We have also learned that *organization structures* have evolved from the simple mechanistic structures of the early twentieth century to the more organic, complex structures of today, such as the matrix design. Also, both methods and patterns of *communication* in organizations have tended to become more complex as the need for information within the system has increased. The formation of *social groups* and the types of behavior these groups exhibit also reflect the increasing complexity of relationships that occur in organizations. In sum, all of the areas discussed in this book suggest that organizational behavior theory and practice are becoming more complex.

## ☐ Causal Relationships

A question of considerable importance concerns the causal relationships between the factors just mentioned. In other words, have individuals become more complex because organizations (or the environment) have become more complex, or vice versa? It should be clear that the relationship is not a simple one; because of the fundamental nature of social systems, there are multiple causal relationships operating. Probably the best examples of this multiple causality are the organization development programs that are common today. Since organization development is a method of changing organizations, we would hypothesize that emphasis in these programs should be upon the causal variables; however, if we examine the OD proposals which are most popular, we find a great deal of diversity in their emphasis. Many of these programs are directed at different types of causal variables, indicating the complexity of organizations. If, for example, structure was the sole determinant of behavior, our current approaches to organization development would be primarily structurally oriented. But as there are also organization development programs that deal with individuals, groups, processes, and clients, this is evidence that each variable must be viewed partly as a causal factor.

Another factor that must be considered is the improvement in social science research methods over the years. While workers of seventy-five years ago *may* have been more complex than the management theory at that time assumed, the state of the art in behavioral science research may have inhibited understanding of the nature and magnitude of the complexity. While people today are probably more complex in make-up and behavioral patterns than they were early in this century, the magnitude of these differences may be exaggerated by our more sophisticated research tools in use today.

These general comments lend support to the argument that the increasing complexity in organizational behavior theory is a function of the passage of time. A more specific discussion of certain issues will indicate how this complexity manifests itself in organizations. In the following sections we analyze the simplicity–complexity trend with respect to (1) philosophies of mankind, (2) consistency versus effectiveness in management, (3) management development, and (4) the work ethic.

## ☐ Philosophies of Man

During the last hundred years there have been substantial changes in the assumptions about human nature (see Figure 16-1).[1] In the first stage, referred to as "economic man," individuals were portrayed as rational people whose behavior was determined by the desire to maximize their economic position. This view of people had its roots in classical economic theory, wherein people were assumed to have perfect information, to examine all alternatives systematically, and to make the right (economic) decision. Much of the classical organization theory discussed in Chapter 5 is predicated on the assumptions contained in the economic man concept. While the extremes proposed by classical economic theory are unrealistic and oversimplified, it is nevertheless true that economic considerations were major influences on people's behavior at one time. The general

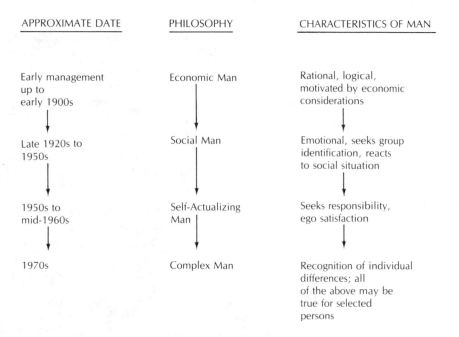

| APPROXIMATE DATE | PHILOSOPHY | CHARACTERISTICS OF MAN |
|---|---|---|
| Early management up to early 1900s | Economic Man | Rational, logical, motivated by economic considerations |
| Late 1920s to 1950s | Social Man | Emotional, seeks group identification, reacts to social situation |
| 1950s to mid-1960s | Self-Actualizing Man | Seeks responsibility, ego satisfaction |
| 1970s | Complex Man | Recognition of individual differences; all of the above may be true for selected persons |

**FIGURE 16-1. Development of Philosophies of Mankind**

principle, then, is that in times of economic scarcity (which characterized the earlier parts of this century) behavior is oriented more toward economic factors.

As increasing numbers of North American workers rose above the subsistence level, management theorists observed that people did not always react according to the logic or economics of the situation, but rather appeared to consider "nonlogical" aspects as well. Behavior appeared to be caused by factors such as affiliation needs, supervisory style, group norms, and social position in informal groups. This view gained strength with the Human Relations movement of the 1930s and retained its influence through the 1950s. This "social man" philosophy became very popular, and as a result, changes in management methods (human-relations training, participative management, employee counseling, etc.) were initiated.

As time passed, however, it became increasingly clear that the social man theory lacked predictive validity (i.e., there were a variety of employee attitudes and behaviors that could not be accounted for by the social man philosophy). The social man theory, therefore, gave way to the "self-actualizing man" theory of human behavior, which initially promised to resolve some of the predictive shortcomings of the social man perspective. In the self-actualizing philosophy, it was believed that people's desire for accomplishment, satisfaction, and individual dignity was of major importance. Accordingly, attention was directed toward developing ways of allowing workers to achieve feelings of satisfaction, achievement, and importance on the job. Emphasis shifted from the human relations philosophy of "treating employees better" to management strategies that would allow for workers' self-actualization in their jobs. As a result, programs such as job

## Box 16-1: Philosophies of Mankind and Organizational Behavior

It is no accident that our theories of organizational behavior have closely paralleled the general philosophies of human behavior identified in Figure 16-1. The chart below gives specific examples of this close relationship.

| Philosophy | Approximate Date | O.B. Theory |
|---|---|---|
| Economic man | early 1900s | Scientific Management<br>Bureacracy |
| Social man | late 1920s to 1950s | Human Relations theories:<br>    Communications<br>    Supportive management<br>    Informal organization<br>    Group behavior<br>    Counseling |
| Self-actualizing man | 1950s to mid-1960s | McGregor's X & Y<br>Herzberg's M-H theory<br>Participative management<br>Likert's System IV<br>Management by objectives<br>Maslow's need hierarchy<br>Decentralization |
| Complex man | 1960s to present | House's path–goal theory<br>Fiedler's leadership model<br>Vroom-Yetton leadership<br>    model<br>Expectancy theory<br>Behavior modification<br>Hersey-Blanchard<br>    situational leadership<br>    model<br>Matrix organization |

enrichment, management by objectives, and job rotation were instituted. This relatively sophisticated—but still simplistic—view of people still did not adequately account for observed behavior. Some workers did not respond positively to increased responsibility or to being allowed to participate in decision making or in setting their own objectives.

Perhaps more out of frustration than anything else, the philosophy of "the complex man" has developed. This view recognizes the importance of individual differences in behavior and includes parts of the three previous philosophies. It recognizes that, depending upon previous experiences, individuals can behave in a manner consistent with any one of the theories and that no particular theory can account for all behavior. The recognition of the complex man has the net effect of making the jobs of managers more difficult, the details of which are explored in the next section.

## ☐ The Consistency vs. Effectiveness Dilemma

While the recognition of the importance of individual differences in behavioral patterns has been a major step forward in the understanding of human behavior in organizations, it nevertheless presents some serious problems for the practicing manager. Perhaps the fundamental problem goes back to the basic nature of organizations as typified in bureaucratic organizational structures. It was noted in Chapter 5 that one of the major characteristics of bureaucratic organizations (and to varying degrees of all types of organizations) is the need to treat people, both clients and employees, equally. Yet, this need is in direct conflict with our knowledge that all people are different. So, on the one hand, we have the organization's need for efficient, consistent managerial decisions and, on the other, we have the individual's need for personal treatment. A common example of this dilemma occurs in unionized organizations: the union contract is designed to insure equal and consistent treatment of all members, yet management is frequently faced with requests from various employees for "special" treatment.

Individual managers are faced with a similar situation in their own work groups. They may prefer to manage their employees according to their needs (perhaps giving some employees more discretion in their work than others), which may result in the criticism that one person is being treated better than another. It is important to remember that, while the manager will perceive the treatment only as being "different," these differences may be perceived as "good" and/or "bad" because of the different perceptions held by employees. Consequently, honorable managerial intentions can backfire.

Unfortunately, we have no magic answer to resolve this consistency versus effectiveness dilemma. However, recognizing that its existence vastly complicates the decisions managers have to make is a useful insight. More important, we have every reason to believe that the forces causing the dilemma will increase and managers will face even more difficult problems in the future.

## ☐ Management Development

As the previous discussion suggests, the fact that organizations, employees, and the environment are changing and becoming more complex requires continual emphasis on management development. The quantity and importance of the behavioral science courses in university and community college curricula has increased significantly during the last several decades, as the need to understand the complexities of organizational life has become more apparent. We would certainly expect this emphasis to continue in the future. In addition, developmental activities such as seminars, training sessions, and retreats have been used with

# Box 16-2: What Would You Do?

You are the office manager with responsibility over one hundred secretarial, clerical, and administrative personnel located in one building. The staff is spread out over the building, generally working in groups of five to ten.

One day one of your male clerks approaches you in your office with a special request. He has just learned that his grandmother has died and he asks for some extra time off. The grandmother lived in a distant city where most of the other family members live. The family apparently has always looked up to your clerk as kind of the "family head" and is now looking to him to come and sort out the financial arrangements, as well as to provide some emotional support to the rest of the family. The grandmother practically raised your clerk after his father was killed in World War II and the mother had to go to work to support the family.

The company has a union which represents all administrative and clerical employees. The union contract specifies that bereavement pay will be given for a maximum of four days for the death of a member of the immediate family. "Immediate" is defined in the contract as a brother or sister, mother or father, wife or husband, son or daughter.

Your clerk tells you he is aware of the rule in the union contract but cannot afford to take the eight days he needs without pay. He asks you to pay him for the eight days he will miss and promises to make up the time after he returns by working evenings and weekends.

You know this employee fairly well. His immediate supervisor has always given him the highest ratings, and there are plans in the near future for his promotion into the supervisory ranks. You have no personal doubt that the time off would be made up should you grant his request. However, you have the following concerns:

(1) Granting the request may set a precedent which would lead to the union trying to put this policy into the next contract.

(2) Should anyone else find out what you did (and they most likely will), others will attempt similar requests for what you believe will be lesser reasons.

(3) You have turned down similar requests in the past which could result now in a series of grievances.

As far as you know, the union would support his request. What would you do?

increasing frequency. Both trends are indicative of the need for continually up-grading the level of skill and knowledge of practicing managers.

Taking our cue from current trends in learning theory, we can also predict some changes in the approaches to management development in the future. In addition to the formal training programs and seminars characteristic of many management development efforts today, it appears that training techniques are moving away from the lecture–discussion format and toward the more experiential forms of learning. In Chapter 1 it was noted that today's students of organizational behavior are having their traditional "content" courses supplemented with "process" types of learning (i.e., structured experiences allowing them actually to experience the concepts being taught). Basically, this approach helps students to learn from their experiences; since managers have a wealth of experiences at their disposal, training in this type of learning should prove to be valuable.

Once the experiential learning skills have been acquired, management development can change from reliance on an external source, such as a formal course or training program, to programs of *self-development* in which managers systematically analyze their experiences. Some headway is now being made in this area with such techniques as T-groups or other types of self-awareness programs. This is not to suggest that self-development will replace other external forms; improving managerial skills involves a blend of both the content and process approaches to learning.

---

### *Organizational Reality* 16-1
### *Retirement at Polaroid*

One of the more difficult issues facing companies today is the question of retirement policies. With human-rights legislation, many employees are resisting the mandatory retirement age and fighting to keep their jobs. With more and more employees reaching retirement age in the near future, this may become a more sticky problem.

Polaroid Corporation has found a way of overcoming this problem, and at the same time make better use of its human resources. The company believes that to sincerely assist older employees and to benefit from their skills and experience, the company must be prepared to introduce some flexibility into its work schedules and retirements.

Polaroid grants leaves of absence for an average of three months to employees so they can "rehearse" retirement. This way, employees can experience retirement without losing their jobs. When the leave is over, the employee can return to work or retire. Another concept of "phased retirement" allows older employees to reduce the number of hours worked daily, days worked each week, or the number of weeks worked each month.

At Polaroid, no employee is forced to retire. Every employee can choose early retirement at fifty-five or continue working past seventy. Evidence indicates that the new retirement program has been successful. The company discovered that many workers must leave their jobs entirely to discover they actually like what the job offers them. About one half of the employees who tried "rehearsal retirement" returned to work full-time.

---

Source: Joseph Perkins, "Polaroid Experimenting with Phased Retirement," *AMA International Forum* (April 1982): 31–33.

## □ **The Work Ethic**

A frequently heard lament of many managers today is, "People just don't want to work anymore." For managers in industrial organizations, this factor (usually manifested in high absenteeism and turnover) may be the most significant problem encountered in everyday operations. Although the situation described is generally attributed to younger workers, it is certainly not limited to this age group. We frequently hear criticisms directed at other types of workers who exhibit poor job attitudes and work habits. Armchair critics generally blame the "welfare state" for these behaviors, and the common remark heard is, "What this country needs is a good depression!" Assuming for the moment that this situation is as serious as some believe and that it indicates a trend for the future, it is important that we address the issue, utilizing our understanding of organizational behavior. A useful beginning point is the simplicity–complexity trend.

By now we should be aware that simplistic answers to complex problems are inappropriate. For example, it is highly unlikely that something as socially complex as a decline in the desire to work can be explained by something as simple as the welfare state. However, if we trace the development of our environment from the relatively simplistic society in the early part of this century to our current state of relative complexity, we can find some clues to some possible causes of behavior change.

**Diagnosis**   In the broadest sense, our society can be characterized today as one in which individuals have *more alternative behaviors* available to them than was formerly the case. The opportunity (if not the necessity) to make choices permeates our society all the way from childhood to adulthood. Today, younger people have comparatively more alternatives available to them, not only in terms of different *types* of behavior but also a wider *range* of choices within each type. Modern society presents more choices in such areas as schooling, religion, codes of dress, and consumer products, to name just a few. All of these alternatives are the product of our affluent and complex society. In comparison, as we go back in time we find that the opposite situation existed. People had fewer alternatives and ranges of behavior available, and decisions were therefore easier. It is ironic that the "good old days" we so often refer to were, in fact, times when fewer alternative behaviors existed from which to choose.

Organizations existing in an affluent, complex society are faced with two important problems relating to the work ethic. First, the work ethic has greater competition because people have a greater variety of activities that compete for their time. While level of wealth is certainly one important factor that allows individuals to do something other than work, there clearly are other factors influencing behavior, as evidenced by the fact that many wealthy people continue to engage in work activities and some poor people continually do not work. Perhaps another influence is the degree of safisfaction individuals receive from various activities. That is, given that one does not have to work in order to survive, then the pain-avoidance principle may operate, causing people to seek those activities that provide them with the most pleasure.

Second, individuals who in their early years have been conditioned through a complex society to expect a relatively high degree of choice in their lives (as many younger workers have been) are unlikely to find satisfaction in an organization that does not allow them the relative freedoms or alternatives to which they are accustomed. While this is partly related to job content, freedom and choice in organization is a function of many other organizational factors, such as types of supervision, motivation and control systems, and formal rules and prescriptions. If workers have been conditioned to expect considerable freedom in their lives, it is then unlikely they will obtain any real satisfaction from an organization that does not allow for a comparable number of alternative behaviors.[2]

The net effect of these two factors is that many of our current organizational practices reduce the attractiveness of the organization to the individual. Thus, it may be that the presumed decline in the work ethic observed over recent years has less to do with moral decay than it does with the increasing attractiveness of alternatives. Or, to put the matter in an organizational context, the fact that management methods have not kept pace with the increasing complexity of people has created considerable conflict between the individual and the organization. It is clear that in many ways organizations have not significantly changed their methods of management over the past several decades; in contrast, the environment in which these organizations function and the people produced by the environment have changed considerably.

We have noted previously that complex problems normally have complex causes. While the simplicity–complexity issue may explain the position of the work ethic in a general sense, it is difficult to suggest solutions until specific causes are detailed. The diagnosis of worker alienation by Richard Walton[3] is perhaps one of the most concise explanations of the conflict between the organization and the individual. It is based on the relationship between certain forces operating in our society and the characteristics of most organizations. The results of Walton's research are shown in Figure 16-2. His analysis describes a series of societal characteristics (such as the decline in the influence of the church, the need for egalitarian relationships, etc.) that are influential in determining behavior and also describes those organizational characteristics that are counter to these "natural" social processes. The result, shown at the top of Figure 16-2, is increased alienation of workers.

Another perspective on alienation is provided by Jerome M. Rosow, President of the Work America Institute, Inc. The Institute has conducted a considerable amount of research into QWL and Rosow suggests that the following six categories of attitude change have affected the quality of work life:[4]

1. *Challenge to authority.* Permissive society created a group of people who learned to question traditional values and goals. What began as a minority spread to a large proportion of the population and subsequently to the workplace, where workers questioned the authority of managers.
2. *Decline in confidence in institutions.* Public scandals in both business and government reduced trust and confidence in these important groups. Evidence

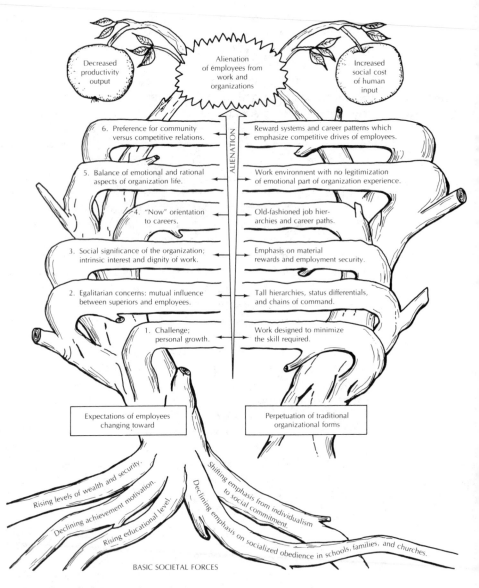

**FIGURE 16-2.   Diagnosis of Alienation in Organizations**

Source: Richard Walton, "How to Counter Alienation in the Plant," *Harvard Business Review* (November–December 1972): 70–81. Copyright © 1972 by the President and Fellows of Harvard College; all rights reserved.

of intentional pollution, discrimination, or other socially undesirable behavior were major factors. Watergate was the culmination of mistrust of government.

3. *Resistance to change.* Mistrust of organizations led to a resistance to innovation, particularly in the technological sense. Workers tired of having no input into

organizational change, yet always being the brunt of it. Change also created feelings of job insecurity.

4. *Changing attitudes toward work.* Traditional attitudes toward work were religious in nature. The Protestant ethic held that work was righteous and pleasure sinful. With the declining influence of the church, these attitudes have changed. Leisure activities have become more popular, partly because they avoid the problems employees experience at work.

5. *Work and family relationships.* The changing nature of marital and family relationships is also having an effect at work. There are more two-income families, more divorces, and more working-single-parent families. All of these place considerable stress on traditional work requirements.

6. *Faster societal than work place changes.* Many significant changes in society occurred over a relatively short period. Attitudes toward drugs, minorities, civil rights, sexual norms, and other social issues preceded changes in organizations' attitudes and behaviors toward the same things. These "new" attitudes place considerable pressure upon traditional organizational philosophy.

The research on employee attitudes confirms that alienation is increasing. One series of studies conducted over a twenty-five-year period showed that employees' attitudes toward their jobs and companies have steadily declined for the last fifteen years. For example, on the question, "How would you rate this company as a place to work compared with what it was when you started here," 40 percent of the workers responded "better now than it was" in 1960–64, compared to less than 20 percent in 1975–77. Although some attitudes had improved (such as attitudes toward quality of supervision), the general trend of the data was negative. Also, managers consistently had more positive attitudes than the hourly paid employees.[5]

**Toward Some Solutions**    What, then, can be done about worker alienation? Do we have the behavioral tools that will allow us to rekindle the work ethic in organizations? If not, what are our prospects? We feel that the approach one takes toward these problems will partly depend upon how one sees the source(s) of the problem. Based on our previous diagnosis, we can suggest both general and specific approaches that may be relevant for the future.

The major departing point for solutions depends upon the nature of the forces at work. It appears that many of the forces causing alienation are "givens" in the sense that they cannot be changed or eliminated. For example, the societal forces that operate to increase the number of alternatives available to individuals cannot be reversed—at least not by any purposeful force. Recogition of this fact is of major importance in determining strategy for change. Many managers spend countless frustrating hours trying to change people to fit the demands of the organization. This is generally an ineffective strategy since (1) we know that behavior conditioned over the long run does not change in the short run, (2) people tend to resent others forcing them to change their behavior, and (3) attempting to change behavior requires much effort and time. *Given this, perhaps a more*

## Box 16-3: Signs of an Outdated Manager

We've all heard of the "generation gap," the "good ole days," and other sayings that allude to the past and all its glory. People who constantly look backwards are generally people who cannot adapt to the present (historians excepted, perhaps). This may not be a bad characteristic generally, but in organizations this can be a sign of an outdated manager (i.e., one who constantly wishes things were different so that life would be easier). Below are some tell-tale signs to identify managers who may be outdated in their thinking:

1. "Back in the good ole days . . ."—One who longs for a return to times when everything was understood and compatible. Life was simple, complete, and under control.

2. "What this country needs is a good depression . . ."—This economic fatalist prays for some outside event to solve all managerial problems. It is based on the assumption that people no longer want to work, thus making the job of the manager impossible.

3. "I just can't understand why they do that . . ."—A statement often characteristic of an older manager made in reference to younger employees. Usually a sign not only of being outdated but also of extreme envy.

4. "We never did things like that back in . . ."—A variation of (1), most likely in response to a need for change in the organization.

5. "If they don't like it, they can go to . . ."—Usually the result of frustration caused by resistance of the workers to a management decision. This one often manifests itself as a way of proving how strong one is as a manager.

*appropriate strategy is to change organizations to fit individuals.* While it certainly is not easy to make changes in formal structures in order to accommodate different individuals, this strategy does have the significant advantage of moving *with* the natural social forces rather than *against* them.

The process of adapting organizations to the needs of individuals has received considerable attention in recent years. As Walton's analysis indicates, the costs of employee alienation are high and organizations are attempting to improve the relationship between work and human needs through a concept known as "quality of work life" (QWL) programs. In the following section we will examine the philosophy of QWL and give some examples of how QWL programs have been implemented.

## ☐   Quality of Work Life

Quality of work life (QWL) can be defined as ". . . the degree to which members of a work organization are able to satisfy important personal needs through their experiences in the organization."[6] A poor QWL would suggest that employees are not being fulfilled in their careers and likely tolerate their jobs only as a means to an economic end. Such individuals would have little loyalty to the organization and in extreme cases may actually engage in sabotage. The costs normally associated with a poor QWL are absenteeism, alcohol and drug abuse, personal stress, boredom on the job, and labor–management conflict.

**Philosophy of QWL** Although organization development is concerned with adapting organizations to the needs of the environment, the philosophy of QWL goes beyond this and its roots are much broader. The major difference between the two is their degrees of emphasis upon the organization versus the worker. Organization development still has its prime emphasis upon the organization and its functioning. QWL, on the other hand, holds that every person has the right to a job that satisfies his or her needs, and that organizations must adapt their management systems accordingly. Under the philosophy of OD, the satisfaction of the employee is a by-product; under QWL it is the major objective.

Given the general philosophy of QWL, it is not surprising that many different types of programs or practices could be used to meet the objective. To provide some idea of the breadth of QWL programs, the following list describes several areas that are of concern in QWL programs:

1. *Adequate and fair compensation.* To insure that compensation is not only equitable for the job, but is also above some minimum maintenance level.
2. *Safe and healthy working conditions.* Minimizes both physical and mental adverse conditions and pertains to hazards, noise, pollution, and visual annoyances.
3. *Development and growth of human capacities.* Focuses upon job design and the effective utilization of skills and abilities in jobs. Emphasis is upon the mental as well as the physical aspects of work.
4. *Growth and security.* Expands upon 3. above to insure that growth in job skills includes opportunity for job security.
5. *Social integration of people.* Includes acceptance of people without prejudice, greater egalitarianism, development of supportive primary work groups, and openness of interpersonal relations.
6. *Constitutionalism.* Insures that individual rights are protected and that due process is available for individual protection in grievances, appeals, etc.
7. *Protection of total life space.* Relates to upheavals in family due to job changes, undue expectations of employees that can adversely affect other aspects of their lives.
8. *Social relevance of work.* Broadens the concept of "satisfaction" from just the job itself to the role of the organization in society: its ethics, social value of its product line, responsibilities to the community, and congruence with social values.[7]

These eight features obviously cover a wide range of organizational experiences. In fact, one of the difficulties with the QWL concept is attempting to overcome the "systems effect" of the various experiences. Achieving a true quality environment would require the integration of many different aspects of organizational life which up to now have been viewed as "not the organization's problem." The supremacy of the organization itself must be questioned if the total philosophy of QWL is adopted. In the past, organizations have not been willing to make this adjustment. However, increased alienation may force the change if organizations are to survive and maintain their competitive position in the market.

**Misconceptions About QWL**    Like many organizational concepts, QWL means different things to different people. There has been a lack of clarity regarding the nature, purpose, and scope of QWL, so we will complete our understanding of it by pointing out what it is not.

1. *QWL is not just for first-line workers.* Problems of employee adjustment to the work environment occur at all levels. Also, improving QWL at the first level can have positive results upward, such as supervisors spending less time on discipline problems.
2. *QWL is not a "quick fix" for problems.* The process of overcoming barriers between labor and management, developing new work systems, and making major managerial and environmental changes cannot occur overnight. Many QWL programs do not show measurable improvements for years, and even then the improvements may be more intangible than bottom-line in nature.
3. *QWL is not a system for getting more out of workers.* The philosophy of QWL, as noted above, has a different value system compared to traditional organizational values. The shift in values requires additional (or equal) emphasis upon the needs of employees, which is viewed as largely independent of profits. Should QWL as well as profits be improved, that would be consistent with the QWL philosophy but not required of it.

---

## Organizational Reality   16-2
### Protecting Human Assets at Kawasaki

When sales slowed down at Kawasaki's Lincoln, Nebraska plant, ten production workers were no longer needed. Instead of laying them off, Kawasaki lent the employees to the city of Lincoln as temporary employees. The workers, however, continued to receive their pay from Kawasaki.

Robert C. Summers, personnel manager at the Lincoln plant, said continuing to pay the workers was in the company's and the employees' long-term interests. He said Kawasaki wanted to insure that workers returned to the assembly line when sales increased. The company's philosophy is that it is cheaper to retain experienced workers than to continually train new ones. According to Summers, the program eliminates the cost in time and money for training. In addition, veteran employees would immediately provide quality work at the desired level of productivity.

Source: "Management in Practice," *Management Review* (March 1982): 45–46.

4. *QWL is not anti-union.* Unions can feel threatened by QWL programs but the roots of those feelings are deeper than QWL itself, i.e., they are the result of years of experiences in dealing with management about many different employee-related matters. Ideally, unions can improve the effectiveness of QWL programs because of their representative role and communication opportunities with employees. However, both unions and management must change their traditional value systems for QWL programs to be effective.

## ☐ Methods of Improving QWL

The number and types of QWL programs are limited only by the creativity of the people involved. There are many standard approaches to improving QWL which are used by many organizations, and several ones unique to specific organizations. Here we will limit ourselves to some of the more common ways of improving life at work through the adaptation of management methods to the needs of employees.

**Work Schedules**   Diverse lifestyles and changing patterns of the labor force have generated a variety of new work patterns. Examples are *flex-time,* in which employees have some flexibility built around a core of required hours, and the *compressed workweek,* in which the normal workweek is compressed into fewer days. Minor alterations also occur, such as changing the hours of work to avoid major traffic patterns. There have also been special schedules to allow employees to attend to other matters, such as providing longer lunch breaks so that children can be attended to during school lunch periods.

**Industrial Hygiene**   Health and safety at the work place has also become a major QWL program for many organizations. Government pressure through legislation has no doubt increased the emphasis in this area. The right of employees to work in an environment free of unnecessary dangers and health hazards is widely accepted and many programs have been put in place. Safety committees are now common practice in many organizations, as are mechanisms to monitor potential health problems.

**Job Design**   As noted in the detailed discussion of job enrichment in Chapters 3 and 15, considerable attention has been given to the design of jobs to increase motivation, satisfaction, and productivity. Based upon the work of Frederick Herzberg, many companies are experimenting with methods of increasing the responsibility of jobs. It has been recognized that many jobs do not allow for personal growth and do not provide a feeling of responsibility and challenge.

In some instances it has been recognized that building in additional responsibility is, for all practical purposes, impossible. For example, jobs whose activities are mostly determined by technology would be very expensive to change. Assembly-line operations have considerable capital investment, and enrichment in the normal sense could be impossible. In these situations emphasis shifts to making the job environment as pleasant as possible, or to converting the job to one done

---

## Organizational Reality   16-3
### No Smoking at Radar Electric

Some companies have shown a strong concern for the general quality of the working environment. Not only is attention paid to normal health and safety problems, but also to areas previously ignored. Radar Electric, based in Seattle, Washington, implemented a no-smoking policy for its employees and customers in 1977 as part of an overall health program. It has turned out to be a money saver as well: employees save money by not buying cigarettes and, most significantly, absenteeism has dropped dramatically. A company study shows a 10 percent savings in janitorial costs as well.

When asked about the program's acceptability, President Warren McPherson said that the employees adjusted "surprisingly easily." It was more difficult to convince walk-in customers of the strict adherence to the no-smoking policy, but over time it has been accepted by almost everyone.

---

Source: "Smoke Signal," *Management Review* (June 1982): 44.

---

by a machine. Other approaches, such as job rotation, can also make boring jobs more acceptable.

**Participative Management**    Participative management is a method by which employees can have more say in the operation of the company. Although the intent is not to "turn the plant over to the employees," effective QWL does require employees to have an input in how the organization is managed. Evidence suggests that more and more "joint committees" (i.e., labor–management groups addressing QWL problems) are being established and their success suggests that these will become the norm in North American industry.[8]

Participative management can be a useful way of improving QWL because it can take so many different forms. Managers and supervisors can be trained in participation to increase its use at the lowest levels, special-purpose programs (e.g., employee-suggestion plans) can be instituted, and participation can occur in more formal settings such as placing employees on the board of directors or formalizing a "works council." Works councils differ from boards of directors in that they have no legal status but they provide a formal mechanism for employee input into policy decisions. In all cases, the programs are designed to increase the interest and commitment of employees by giving them some ownership of the system.

**Employee Counselling**    The negative by-products of a poor quality of work life can be serious, indeed. Not only can job performance be affected, but often an employee's personal life as well. Poor jobs and job environments can cause stress, frustration, anxiety, and a host of other psychological problems, often associated with alcoholism, drug abuse, or other serious effects. Many companies now accept that the physical and emotional problems of employees are part of the organization's responsibility. Efforts at dealing with such areas vary from training supervisors to spot alcoholism and drug abuse to instituting employee counselling programs. Some programs are also available to an employee's family members on the basis that quality of work life is affected if the employee is worried or upset about a family problem.

**Autonomous Work Groups**   One of the areas that has developed from the sociotechnical systems research is the concept of autonomous work groups. In considering only the technical factors of the job, the social needs and the functioning of the social group are ignored. Both the Hawthorne studies described in Chapter 1 and the sociotechnical systems research emphasized the need for understanding the influence that groups can have upon productivity.

The practical thrust of the systems research has been the use of autonomous (i.e., self-governing) work groups in place of individual effort. Where assembly lines used to exist, companies have begun to organize work around group efforts, with a team leader rather than a supervisor or foreman. Specialization of labor is minimized, so job design is affected as well. Groups can develop their own culture and adapt their behavior patterns to individual needs in the group. The autonomous work-group approach attempts to restore the family-like atmosphere in larger organizations by giving employees the opportunity to identify with a smaller group.

**Career Management**   The career management philosophy of QWL is similar to the well-known Japanese model. For many employees in Japan, a job is a career and they look to the organization as a source of stability and progression in their own careers.[9] In North America an individual's career has largely been seen as his or her own responsibility. This has resulted in considerable mobility, particularly in the lower ranks, as individuals have sought to better themselves and improve their job security. The conflict arose out of the expectation of loyalty by organizations but the unwillingness to take a major responsibility for career development and tenure.

While North American firms have yet to adopt the family orientation of many Japanese firms, many QWL programs have been implemented to overcome some of the previous problems. Retirement counseling, job relocation assistance, and general careeer counseling are some of the examples of QWL programs.

In addition, there are many innovative QWL programs in various organizations. Some examples are: company-operated day-care systems, employee sabbaticals, company-sponsored recreation facilities and programs, health programs such as stress management and physical fitness, and training programs to upgrade job skills. As would be expected, the nature and number of programs is almost endless, a factor which reflects the diverse needs of working people today.

These examples suggest that effective managerial strategies of the future will involve systems and policies that allow for the increased complexity of man within the constraints of the consistency–effectiveness dilemma discussed earlier. Those

> ## *Box 16-4: Fatigue and Quality of Work Life*
>
> Since physical factors are an important part of QWL, it is not surprising that considerable attention has been given to the length of the work day. In all this commotion, an interesting paradox emerges. On the one hand, QWL proponents are concerned about fatigue on the job, especially as it relates to health and safety factors. However, shorter work weeks (and therefore longer hours each day) have become a very popular work schedule and have also been incorporated into QWL programs.
>
> So what are the facts? Is there a danger in working longer than a typical eight-hour day? Not really, say researchers Jamal and Crawford. They did a study of people who work "extended hours" and concluded that there was a "near absence of patterned relationships between work patterns and undesirable outcomes. Moonlighters, overtimers, and (regular) employees all report similar levels of well-being, mental health, job stability, and performance."
>
> Source: Muhammad Jamal and Ronald L. Crawford, "Consequences of Extended Work Hours: A Comparison of Moonlighters, Overtimers, and Modal Employees," *Human Resource Management* (Fall 1981): 18–23.

strategies that allow for more individual choice, not only in job matters but in external matters as well, will be more effective than the unilateral systems that are characteristic of many organizations today. Because individuals have been conditioned by their early experiences in life to expect more freedom, organizations will likely be required to change to accommodate these expectations. In other words, the styles of management in the future will have to be such that organizational life will be more competitive with the alternatives available to most people.

## ■ FUTURE RESEARCH CONSIDERATIONS

At various places in this book we have alluded to some shortcomings in the current state of organizational behavior research. Without being too apologetic for the field, we believe it necessary to summarize these limitations and suggest some areas that need further attention.

### □ The Need for Integration

Although organizational behavior research has made significant strides in recent years, much of it is poorly integrated. Perhaps the best example of this is the existence of "separate" individual and group theories as we noted in Chapter 11. If we are to better understand influence processes in organizations, these approaches must be integrated. Another example is the emphasis received by the different areas of organizational behavior. Research efforts tend to concentrate on the separate areas of motivation, leadership, communication, etc., but little effort is made to integrate research findings in these areas into a complete theory of organization. There is evidence that we are making some progress in this area with contingency theories, and some of the current models of organization development are concerned with the total organization. But despite these few bright spots, organization behavior is still very much a discipline that needs considerable integration.

A major reason for the lack of emphasis on the integrative aspects of research is the difficulty of conducting viable experiments. The integrative approach requires that a large number of variables be accounted for and, unfortunately, many of these are uncontrollable. Consequently, integrative experiments are likely to suffer somewhat in their validity. These problems must be addressed, however, since the marginal utility of more studies in the separate areas decreases over time.

## ☐ Applicability of Research

Many of the major advances in organizational behavior research have been accomplished not by business researchers but by researchers in other fields such as psychology and sociology. We mentioned at the outset of this book that organizational behavior was essentially a stepchild discipline, since it is the amalgamation and application of other disciplines to the study of organizations. It is perhaps of some significance that the research efforts in the field have often come from the primary behavioral sciences areas rather than from the business scientists. Note, for example, that Skinner, Herzberg, Fiedler, and Maslow are all psychologists by training.

While there is nothing inherently wrong with the discipline crossover, it can generate some problems of perceived applicability and relevancy. Many psychological and sociological theories are tested in contrived laboratory situations that are artificial representations of the organizational world. The results are often open to the criticism of impracticality or irrelevancy. Perhaps the best example of this is the Skinnerian approach to behavior modification, which was originally developed in laboratory experiments using rats, mice, pigeons, and other animals. While most would agree with the effectiveness of Skinner's techniques with animals, many doubt their applicability to the real world.[10] Even laboratory experiments using human subjects are suspect because of the simplified environment that is present. It is difficult to convince a manager that "too much control" can cause maladaptive behavior if the data used to support this claim were generated in a laboratory experiment using college freshmen as subjects.

The alternative, of course, is to conduct experiments in actual organizational settings. While this is now done to some extent, many organizations are understandably reluctant to allow experimentation in the regular work situation. One reason is that such experiments can have repercussions beyond the experimental conditions. In the authors' personal experience, one company was reluctant to participate in a Skinnerian behavior modification experiment because managers were afraid that (1) if the experiment did work, the union would attempt to bargain the system into the next contract and that (2) if it didn't work, they would be worse off—in terms of the behavior they were trying to modify—than they were before the experiment. Their understandable position was, "We have to live here after you guys leave."

The middle ground between these two extremes should be obvious. While laboratory studies can be rightfully criticized as being artificial, it is under these controlled conditions that basic principles are developed; it then remains for the general principles to be further developed, modified, or scrapped when they are tested in the real world. Academicians need the understanding of the manager in developing theories, and a part of this understanding should be found in the willingness of organizations to allow some degree of experimentation. It is equally true that academic researchers should realize that managers are accountable to others for their performance, and this limits accessibility. In any event, the advancement of our knowledge about human behavior in organizations can come about more rapidly if greater cooperation and understanding between theoreticians and practitioners is achieved.

## ☐  Evaluative Research

One way of increasing the cooperation between the theory-construction portion of academic research and the problem orientation of most managers is through *evaluative research*. This is research resulting in judgments about the relative effectiveness of a course of action. For example, an organization may wish to implement some type of organization development activity; in order to obtain some measure of how effective the program has been, they may invite an outsider to conduct a research project on the program's effectiveness. This allows the researcher to use the scientific methods so important to theory construction and at the same time allows the organization to monitor a change that might otherwise be assumed by the organization to be satisfactory.

It is in this area of evaluative research that managers have a distinct advantage since they have access to the necessary data. But since managers are generally not trained in scientific research methods, the data are sometimes in the wrong form or have not been collected systematically, or interpretation is biased because of the vested interest of the people concerned. While academicians do not have the data, they presumably have the training to identify what type of data are needed to perform an evaluation and how to go about gathering it, and can shed some light on its interpretation because of their neutral position in the organization.

Perhaps the area with the greatest need for evaluative research is the QWL programs that are being implemented in many organizations. As noted earlier in this chapter, QWL has become a major focus of attention and firms are implementing all types of programs designed to improve QWL. Interestingly, there is relatively little known about the long-term effects of a complete QWL program. Some research has been conducted on certain programs (flex-time, for example), but it is extremely difficult to use traditional research methods on the innovative programs of QWL. Of course one reason for this difficulty is that, according to the philosophy of QWL, the employee's quality of work life is most important and needs satisfaction is a difficult concept to measure. Evaluating QWL is certainly a challenge to our traditional methods of organizational behavior research.

# ■ THE INDIVIDUAL DIGNITY ISSUE

In our introduction in Chapter 2 we raised an ethical issue concerning the use of knowledge about human behavior. It was noted that we could conceivably reach a level of knowledge through which it would be possible to influence behavior with a reasonable degree of consistency and predictability. This was described as moving from the descriptive to the predictive and finally to the prescriptive phase of organizational behavior. It is appropriate that now, having exposed the reader to the fundamentals of organizational behavior, we examine the issue again.

In one sense we are fortunate that in most areas of organizational behavior we have not yet reached the stage where prescription is the norm rather than the exception (although this still has not kept us from making prescriptive statements). In some areas, however, we are approaching the point where we should begin to be concerned about the nature and extent of the rights of a person (or group) to control the behavior of another person (or group). If we substitute the more palatable term *influence* for *control,* we can see that this is a major issue for the manager, since one of management's responsibilities is to influence the behavior of subordinates.

One technique that is receiving increasing attention in this area is reinforcement theory, discussed in Chapter 4. Scientifically, the principles of reinforcement theory have been well validated, although the applicability problems mentioned earlier are still lingering. Much of the evidence now available regarding the application of reinforcement theory to human behavior in organizations is less scientific, but the pattern is reasonably consistent with the laboratory evidence.

The psychologists have faced the individual dignity issue for quite some time, and their governing body has attempted to draft a policy statement about it. Unfortunately, the statement is so broad that it provides little guidance.[11]

It is perhaps because the issue is so philosophical that we have no solution or cogent remarks to clarify the problem. We do feel, however, that every manager should be aware that there are social limitations to the prerogatives of organizational influence. As the level of knowledge in behavioral science increases, this issue will assume increasing importance. Our concern derives in part from the historical evidence available on similar matters as well as our knowledge that any useful tool can be misused.

# ■ A FINAL COMMENT

One of the most persistent problems faced by teachers is the age-old question: "Is a little knowledge worse than none at all?" In some disciplines, such as history or calculus, the dangers associated with having a "little" knowledge are not very great to the average person. In the applied social sciences—management in particular—this concern is very real. In this book not only have we presented only a few of the many topics that can be included under the heading of organizational behavior, but we have also generally skimmed those topics. In each of the areas covered, it is not difficult to find complete books written on a topic we have analyzed only briefly. Fortunately, many readers will not have a major responsibility of using these concepts until they have also had a considerable amount of practical experience. As mentioned several times, we consider experience (providing one learns from the experiences) and textbook learning equally useful. Readers who may be using the textbook approach subsequent to their experiences will be in a position to temper their understanding of organizational behavior theory; this minimizes the risk that we will create educated fools. But regardless, it is important to note that a greater understanding of organizational behavior can (and should) be achieved by exploring the concepts presented here in greater depth. One of our primary purposes has been to encourage a continuing interest in organizational behavior so that personal development continues throughout one's managerial career. In this vein, we are reminded of Albert Schweitzer's statement:

"THE TRAGEDY OF LIFE IS WHAT DIES WITHIN A MAN WHILE HE STILL LIVES."

We hope you have been stimulated to avoid that fate.

## *Management in the Year 2000—Revisited*

The company described in the opening incident seems strange in comparison to many companies today. Is this just an idealistic representation of what companies might be like in the year 2000? To some extent, yes . . . but there is considerable evidence now that such management techniques may not be so far-fetched as one might first believe.

Although it would be rare to find all those characteristics in any single organization today, there are numerous companies that employ some of the methods already. In fact, several of the practices described in the opening incident are based upon an actual example of a plant owned by General Foods located in Topeka, Kansas. Richard Walton describes the operation of the plant in his article "How to Counter Alienation in the Plant."[12] The design and management of the company was based upon Walton's diagnosis of worker alienation, and the evidence suggests that it is a very effective method of managing. Other "new" techniques—such as joint policy-making boards—have been used in European firms for a number of years.

Assuming for the moment that this is the general direction for the future, then a proper appreciation for the types of managerial skills necessary is extremely important. It should be obvious that the traditional, autocratic methods of the past will be inappropriate, at least in most situations. This means that managers will have to have a greater appreciation for the more human approaches and will have to have the skills to match.

Although it may not be apparent at first glance, the situation described in the opening incident is not an example of management giving the plant away to the employees. Similarly, one should not conclude that in organizations of the future such things as control, standards, authority, etc., will be missing. The major difference between traditional and progressive organizations is the *source* of control; in traditional forms the source of control is the management and its authority; in the "human" forms of the future, control lies within the people employed, in conjunction with the controls derived from the right of private property. The managerial skill required to develop people to the point where self-control replaces imposed control is difficult indeed. The effective manager of the future will be the person who truly acquires the skill of "working through people."

# ■ REVIEW QUESTIONS

1. What are the implications of the simplicity–complexity trend for management practice?

2. How have our philosophies of mankind changed over the past century?

3. How does the existence of the "consistency versus effectiveness" dilemma make the manager's job more difficult?

4. What forces are present in society today that (1) attempt to increase the need for consistency of treatment and (2) attempt to increase the need for differential treatment?

5. What are some ways that management development may change in the future to accommodate the increasing complexity of man?

6. Why have we experienced a decline in the "work ethic" in recent years?

7. In what ways would organizations have to change to accommodate a declining work ethic?

8. What is the general purpose of QWL programs?

9. How is the philosophy of QWL different from other theories of managing people?

10. What are the common features of many QWL programs?

11. Why are we lacking a totally integrative theory of organizational behavior?

12. What steps can be taken to move toward such a theory?

13. Why are the findings of laboratory research sometimes not applicable to real life?

14. Why are real-life findings sometimes not applicable to creating theories?

15. What is the major role of evaluative research?

16. Of what importance is the "individual dignity issue" to the practicing manager?

# ■ EXERCISE 16-1: LETTER FROM A PRESIDENT

The following letter was written to a syndicated newspaper columnist in reply to a previous letter which had been published by the columnist.

Dear Columnist:

I am the president of a sizable business. I have never written to a newspaper in my life but now I feel compelled to present a rebuttal to the letter which you published from "An Employee." The headline on the employee's letter read "Dear Boss: When did you last say thanks for a job well done?"

I started from the bottom thirty years ago. Today I am "The Boss." I would like nothing better than to say, "Thank you for a job well done." But it's been a whale of a long time since I saw an employee who had earned the compliment.

This is indeed the age of the goof-off, the half-done job. People want two-hour lunches, thirty-minute coffee breaks and piped-in music. When they arrive late they blame the traffic or the weather. At closing time, come hell or high water, they run out the doors as if the building were burning.

I have interviewed a dozen young men since September. Do you know the questions they ask?

1. How much is the pay?
2. How much is the time off?
3. What is your retirement plan?

And now there is talk of a four-day week. For what? So they can spend more time drinking beer and watching TV?

Yes, I believe in saying thank you for a job well done but where are the employees who take pride in achievement and are willing to give the extra ounce? Young people complain that there are no opportunities anymore. There is more opportunity today than ever before but most of our kids don't recognize it because it is disguised as hard work! And they want no part of that!

. . . The Boss

1. Read the letter once or twice. Then write a number between 0 and 100 indicating how much you agree or disagree with the president: Use the following scale:

90–100 = "Hallelujah!"

70–89 = "Very near the truth . . . couldn't have said it better myself."

51–69 = "A lot of truth here . . ."

50 = "Some of it I agree with, some I dislike."

35–49 = "The guy's really got his problems . . . not much here I agree with."

Lower than

35 = "Pure trash! The guy's back in the Dark Ages."

Your instructor will compare the responses of the class.

2. What major values do you think the president holds?

3. What are the major strengths and weaknesses this letter reveals in the president?

# ■ EXERCISE 16-2: THE FATE OF ROMEO IN THE WORLD OF CASSIUS
## by Eugene J. Webb

It is hardly accidental that participative management expanded in the benign matrix of a nation reaching unprecedented levels of economic wealth and psychological comfort. The warm ambiance of sharing, the belief in the work setting's capacity to contribute to personal growth, and the evolution of the small collaborative group as a productive technology were all grounded in an American economy that had bolted forward from the moribund years of the 1930s. Giving, sharing, and caring are possible, even demanded, in a time of plenty. American wealth grew and American power grew. Abundance and security were, in turn, necessary conditions for the shift in management values most observers have noted.

The halcyon days are past. Spirited optimism is hard to sustain as we desperately hold on to the myth of a "temporary recession," when we observe Berlitz gearing up its Arabic capability, when neologisms like stagflation enter our language, and when even the French decide to give the United States $100,000,000 in a NATO relocation settlement.

A steady state world is the best that can be foreseen for most American organizations. Among candid friends, a common remark is, "I'm glad I got in this (university, business, agency) when I did." The question in previous decades was, "How can our department grow, develop, experiment?" while the issue today for most institutions is how to minimize the rot of decay.

How robust will the humanistic values inherent in participative management be when organizations struggle for their very survival? Can we preserve openness and concern for others when people are fighting to maintain their private empires, departments or even their jobs? What happens to shared power when economic conditions demand that new projects can't be funded and old ones cut back? Isn't it likely that a strong incentive will develop for members to play cover games, withhold information, build alliances and revert to power politics?

What does this mean about what we teach? For example, will the experientially based training values and the practices of humanistic psychology that are so central to many of our organizational behavior courses remain appropriate? I don't think the adolescent notion of "love conquering all" will win, but a more blurred middle-aged concept might. As professors in this arcane field, is it not more honest to stress the realities of power? As the organizational growth curve flattens or declines, we should expect an increase in compliance through fear, an upsurge in interdepartmental rivalries for scarce resources and a reduction in willingness to share information and feelings.

Creative teaching effort may come from an emphasis on intragroup accommodation to these new realities, with a focus on collaboration, and intergroup conflict and competition, with a focus on power and "arrangements." We are disposed to teach sharing, if for no other reason than that it's nicer to teach. Are we willing to teach the necessary power juggling and conscious manipulative tactics that might be necessary for our students to succeed and for worthwhile programs to survive?

My experience in talking with fellow professors is that we are not, as a group, comfortable in teaching power tactics. We become uneasy with the thought of arming a new generation of students with skills and values compatible to "go ye forth and manipulate." But even if I didn't know professors of organizational behavior (and some of my best friends are O.B. professors, even though I wouldn't want my daughter to marry one), the history of science suggests that inertia will rule.

Unfortunately, our ideology and instructional habits will lead us to continue to preach the doctrine that there should be an organizational coming together. Hopefully, in a nod to reality, we might also teach to count one's fingers after this joining of hands.

Source: *The Teaching of Organizational Behavior*, vol. 1, no. 1 (1974): 5–6. Reprinted with permission of author and publisher.

1.  This article was written over ten years ago as a suggestion regarding how organizational behavior courses might be taught to meet changing conditions in organizations. Comment on how the course you've just finished met the author's recommendations.

2.  Do you see any evidence that the world has changed according to the author's predictions?

# ■ ENDNOTES

1.  The reader should note how closely this development parallels Maslow's need hierarchy discussed in Chapter 3. Information for this diagram is taken from E. F. Schein, *Organizational Psychology*, 2nd edition (Englewood Cliffs, N.J.: Prentice-Hall): 55–75.

2.  This is a restatement of Chris Argyris' original thesis of the conflict between the mature personality and the demands of the formal organization. See Chris Argyris, *Personality and Organization*, (New York: Harper and Row, 1957).

3.  Richard Walton, "How to Counter Alienation in the Plant," *Harvard Business Review* (November-December, 1972): 70–81.

4.  Jerome M. Rosow, "Changing Attitudes to Work and Lifestyles," *Journal of Contemporary Business*, Vol. 8, No. 4 (1977).

5.  M. R. Cooper, B. S. Morgan, P. M. Foley, and L. B. Kaplan, "Changing Employee Values: Deepening Discontent?" *Harvard Business Review* (January-February, 1979): 117–125.

6.  J. Lloyd Suttle, "Improving Life at Work—Problems and Prospects," in J. Richard Hackman and J. Lloyd Suttle, eds., *Improving Life At Work* (Santa Monica: Goodyear Publishing Company, Inc., 1977: 4.

7.  Adapted from Richard Walton, "Quality of Working Life: What Is It?" *Sloan Management Review*, Vol. 15, No. 1 (Fall, 1973): 11–21.

8.  William L. Batt, Jr., and Edgar Weiberg, "Labor-Management Cooperation Today," *Harvard Business Review* (January-February, 1978): 96–104.

9.  William G. Ouchi, and Raymond L. Price, "Hierarchies, Clans, and Theory Z: A New Perspective on Organizational Development," *Organizational Dynamics* (Autumn, 1978): 25–44.

10.  We cannot resist the opportunity to reproduce a quote from a physiological psychology textbook that gives an interesting twist to our point:

> The investigators suggested that these results were consistent with the deficits of recent memory produced by bilateral ablations of the temporal lobe in man, a finding mentioned in Chapter 20, but, as we have seen, other experiments offer little encouragement for the idea that these human data can be extrapolated to mice.

From Peter M. Milner, *Physiological Psychology* (New York: Holt Rinehart, and Winston, 1970) p. 467.

11. Frederick H. Kanfer, "Issues and Ethics in Behavioral Manipulation," *Psychological Reports* 16 (1965).

12. Richard Walton, "How to Counter Alienation in the Plant," *Harvard Business Review* (November-December, 1972): 70–81.

# Comprehensive Cases

# Dilemma of a Young Manager[1]

"Where will it all end?" ponders Johnny Woods as he sits at his desk recalling the events of the past six weeks.

He thinks of what he studied about human relations in college. He wishes he had a workable and equitable solution to his problem.

Johnny thinks to himself, "I know I've been fair enough with those two guys—maybe, too fair at times. More than once I've jeopardized my job to protect them."

He momentarily remembers a question raised by one of his college buddies one day during the discussion of a case assigned in his personnel/human relations management course, "What if your subordinates don't like you?" Johnny wonders if being liked is really worth it and if being liked is the answer to his problem.

"Maybe," Johnny thinks, "Professor Bates can give me some advice as to how I might solve this problem."

Johnny decided to give Professor Bates a call and see if he could discuss this problem with the professor. Johnny called Professor Bates and he agreed to discuss Johnny's problem with him the next day.[2] The following is an account of Johnny's discussion of his problem with the professor.

## ☐ Events of the Past Six Weeks

Johnny Woods, age 24, started to work for the Futuristic Automotive Electrical Corporation six weeks ago immediately upon completing all the requirements for "A Certificate of Completion" in electrical theory and practice at The Community Technical Institute.[3] Johnny is the supervisor of the lathe-machines shop where he supervises the work of seven lathe operators. (Exhibit 1 presents a description of Johnny's job.) He has had problems with Billy Adams and Charles Pierce almost from his first day on the job. For instance, at the end of the first week on the job, Johnny overheard the following parts of a conversation among Mr. Adams, Mr. Pierce, and another of the lathe operators as he walked into the shower room this Friday morning:

ADAMS:  Those kids think they're just it! Why, I bet he isn't 20 years old. What do they teach these kids today—how to comb their sideburns? All that schoolboy ever thinks about is work.

---

1.  This case was prepared by Bill D. Fortune of the Texas A & M University System and Brian Belt of the University of Missouri–Kansas City as a basis for classroom discussion and not to illustrate either effective or ineffective handling of an administrative situation. The case was presented at a Southern Case Research Association workshop sponsored by the Harvard Business School.

2.  Professor Bates was the instructor of the personnel/human relations management course mentioned. Johnny took the course under Professor Bates at Lack University (LU), a four-year academic university. Johnny dropped out of LU during his junior year after making the decision to attend The Community Technical Institute located in his hometown.

3.  The Futuristic Automotive Electrical Corporation rebuilds automobile, truck, and farm tractor starters, generators, alternators, distributors, and voltage regulators that are marketed all across the United States. Its products are distributed primarily through automobile and truck parts and accessories shops. However, approximately 25% of its sales is to a national mail-order company. The corporation also provides machine-shop service, such as turning armatures, to local automobile and truck garages.

PIERCE: I remember when old man Jones had his [Johnny's] job.[4] He let us do our own thing. What's happening to the company when they'll let a kid come in here and boss around seven experienced machinists? Billy, you and me are at the top of our labor grade.

LAROQUE: Hey, you guys better shut up! Mr. Woods is standing over there. Let's go to work; it's time to punch in.

The following conversation ensued when Johnny conferred with his professor:

PROFESSOR BATES: How would you describe your relationship with the other lathe operators and with your boss, the general supervisor?

JOHNNY: I get along well with all the men except Adams and Pierce. With the exception of these two guys, everyone goes about doing his job without causing problems for me or anyone else. Adams and Pierce, no doubt, are good at their work. My boss seems to be satisfied with my work and the work of my shop. In fact, he complimented me several times for "getting the work out." But, I don't know how long this will last, if those two guys keep fouling things up for me.

PROFESSOR BATES: How would you characterize your boss?

JOHNNY: As I pointed out, he seems to be satisified with my work. However, when he interviewed me for this job, he emphasized several times that he takes "a hands-off approach" to the people who work under him. He said that he thinks a supervisor should be capable of handling his [the supervisor's] problems without intervention from him [the General Supervisor]. This is why I've tried to work out my own problems.

PROFESSOR BATES: Are there other events of the past six weeks you would like to discuss?

JOHNNY: Five times within the past six weeks, twice during my first week on the job, Billy Adams has been from 10-35 minutes late for work. Each time, I reminded him that it was important for all the men to be at work on time because of the high volume of work that had to be turned out by our shop in order to meet delivery dates set by Production Control. On each occasion, I told Adams that I saw no need to report his being late to the Personnel Office, as long as he was not late to work again.

Twice I have seen Adams leaving work early. Both times I checked his time card to see if he had punched out. He had not. On both occasions, I checked his time card again after 5 P.M., the shop's regular quitting time, to see if it had then been punched. As I suspected, someone had punched the time cards at 5 o'clock so that Adams' leaving early was not reflected on the cards. Although I realized that it was a Class A offense,[5] according to the existing labor contract, for a person to punch another employee's time card, I made no attempt to find out who punched the card. I have no evidence of it, but, I suspect Pierce of punching Adams' card. Again, although I have no evidence of it, I suspect the other lathe operators are aware of Adams' leaving early and having someone else punch his time card. I just have a feeling the others are aware; it's the way they act.

4. Mr. Jones held Johnny's job for eight years. Johnny was selected to replace Jones when he retired from the corporation.

5. A Class A offense is an infraction of company rules considered so serious as to warrant summary dismissal on the first offense, regardless of mitigating factors. Each of the seven lathe operators in Johnny's shop is a member of the United Automobile, Aircraft and Agricultural Implement Workers Union.

PROFESSOR BATES:    Johnny, are there other incidents similar to the ones you have just described?

JOHNNY:    Yeah, I'll tell you about a few of them.

Both Adams and Pierce have missed the last three biweekly safety meetings. In other words, they haven't attended a single safety meeting since I started to work here at Futuristic. I did not report their absence to either the General Supervisor, even though he is a stickler for safety, or to the Personnel Office. Each time I didn't think it would be necessary. After each of their first two absences, I reminded them of the company rule that requires their attendance at the safety meetings. They sounded so sincere each time when they told me they wouldn't miss another meeting and when they asked me please not to report them. I noticed at the last safety meeting that they were both absent again. Also, Mr. LaRoque was absent. He had never been absent before during my time here. The next morning I was able to catch Adams and Pierce in the shower room before work and after everyone else had left to go to the shop. I started out by asking them why they were absent from the safety meeting. Boy! Did they blow up! Pierce told me quite frankly that he had been working at Futuristic for three years and he already knew everything that was ever said at the meetings.

There are two more incidents I can tell you about.

One day, the manager of Stores, who fills requisitions for materials, parts, and hand tools called me and pointed out that Adams and Pierce had come to him several times requesting various hand tools without first having me sign the requisition forms, which I'm supposed to do. He very carefully explained to me, as if I didn't already know, that company policy required me to sign the requisition for all hand tools. This incident really made me look like a fool. I called this incident to the attention of Adams and Pierce. In no uncertain terms, Pierce was quick to tell me what I could do with the requisition forms.

But, wait until you hear about what happened yesterday a few hours before I called you, Professor Bates. After this incident, I just knew I had to ask someone for advice.

The bananas really hit the fan yesterday! It is company policy that working overtime be assigned to the men in the shop on a revolving basis. That is, each lathe operator in the shop works overtime in an emergency as his turn comes up. Well, yesterday I needed three men to work a few hours overtime in order to get out a rush order for one of the local garages. I checked the overtime schedule and found that Adams' name was among those persons whose turn it was to work overtime. I went to each of the three men just before quitting time and pointed out to them that we had to get out a rush order and that their names had come up to work overtime. [According to Johnny, he was informed of the rush order just a few minutes before he talked to the three lathe operators.] After a few seconds of the normal grumbling that always comes from the men who are asked to work overtime, the first two guys said they would work late. Adams' reaction was something else, though. He said he was tired and didn't want to work late. He turned and walked out of the shop. I had to get another guy to work in his place. Adams showed up for work this morning and acted as if nothing had happened.

PROFESSOR BATES:    Johnny, tell me something about the characteristics of Adams and Pierce.

JOHNNY:    Adams is 32 and Pierce is 29 years old. Adams has been with the company five years and Pierce, three years. Both of them are at the top of their labor grade. Both are high school graduates. Neither one of them is married, although I think Pierce used to be. I, quite naturally, would characterize them both as being smart alecks to say the least. That's about all I can tell you about them.

PROFESSOR BATES:   Was either of them a candidate for your job?

JOHNNY:   No. From what I've been able to pick up, neither one was interested in the job. Besides, my boss wanted a graduate of The Community Technical Institute for the job. So, I don't think there's any hard feelings because I got the job.

PROFESSOR BATES:   Johnny, tell me something about yourself.

JOHNNY:   As you know, my father has owned a machine shop and garage for more than 20 years. I started helping my father in the shop when I was about 10 years old. I learned to operate every machine in the shop—lathe, boring and honing machines, milling machines, valve grinding machines, and so on. I learned to completely rebuild any part of a car, truck, and tractor such as the motor, starter, generator, carburetor. You name it, and my father taught me how to rebuild it. However, I've always been most interested in automotive electronics. That's the reason I went to The Institute for formal training in electrical theory and practice. I learned things there in two years that I could never have learned in my father's shop. My interest in and desire to learn more about automotive electronics is what prompted me to take this job with Futuristic. Too, if I work up to General Supervisor, then I will have an opportunity to learn about the entire field of automotive electrical systems. I would like someday to be the owner-manager of my own shop. The experience I get at Futuristic will help me realize this long-run goal.

PROFESSOR BATES:   I gather you know a great deal about the technical side of your job. What would you say are your qualifications as a manager of people? That is, what are your qualifications as they pertain to the human side of your job?

JOHNNY:   As far as formal training goes, I had a course in working with people and a course in shop management at The Community Technical Institute. Also, I had your personnel/human relations course at LU. As a matter of fact, recalling some of the things we discussed in the course is what prompted me to call you.

PROFESSOR BATES:   Such as?

JOHNNY:   Well, things like Theory $X$ and Theory $Y$; role behavior and conflict; Chester Barnard's acceptance theory of authority; making unpopular decisions; and, taking disciplinary action.

PROFESSOR BATES:   What about practical experience in directing people?

JOHNNY:   This job with Futuristic is what I would consider to be the first job I've had where I am formally responsible for directing people. When I worked for my father, I helped him oversee the machinists and mechanics who worked in his shop. But, that's not quite the same as here at Futuristic. I guess I've got a lot to learn.

How do I solve this dilemma? I've only been here six weeks. What do I do? Do I take the problem to my hands-off boss who thinks I'm doing such a good job? Do I do nothing and jeopardize losing my job because I fail to meet production schedules or fail to carry out some other job responsibility? Maybe I should quit my job?

PROFESSOR BATES:   You've told me something about Billy Adams and Charles Pierce. What about the other lathe operators in your department? Is there anything you can tell me about them that might have a bearing on the resolution of your problem?

JOHNNY:   Not much. I've not had time in only six weeks to learn much about them. My job is not the kind that requires that I directly supervise and interact with the people in my department or shop. It's not really necessary; everyone knows his job and more or less takes his orders from the situation at hand. Also, because of the tight production schedules in my department, my men do not have a great deal of time away from their jobs so that I could get to know them better.

I do know that all the other lathe operators are married and have families and are older than I am. They all are experienced lathe machine operators. They seem to accept me. Other than this, there's not anything more I can tell you about them.

# ■ RESOLUTION OF THE PROBLEM

PROFESSOR BATES:   You alluded to your concern as to whether being liked was the answer to your problem. Do you think this is your problem? Why don't you reflect on all you've told me and then do the following, which should help to guide your thinking in determining a solution to your problem.

1. Define the problem(s).
2. Analyze the cause(s) of the problem.
3. Develop alternative ways of removing the causes and thus solving the problem. Remember that these alternatives should deal with causes, not symptoms of the problem.
4. Evaluate the alternatives, according to criteria such as these:
   a. How well does the alternative meet the corporation's objectives?
   b. How much time and organizational resources are required?
   c. Does the alternative conform to personal and organizational values for equitable and responsible behavior?
   d. What are the ramifications of each alternative?
   e. What is the probability of success?
5. Select an alternative.
6. Develop a detailed plan of implementing the solution to the problem. Who should do what? How? When?

# ■ EXHIBIT 1
# THE FUTURISTIC AUTOMOTIVE ELECTRICAL CORPORATION

**Position Description**

**Position:  Supervisor**
**Department:  Lathe-Machines shop**

Primary function: Under the supervision of the General Supervisor, supervises 7–12 (varies) lathe operators and through them provides the highest quality machine services that he is capable of to the entire plant.

Position content:
1. Seventy-five%: Performs supervisory duties as follows:
   a. Observes all work of subordinates to ascertain that the work conforms to work orders, as generated by Production Control.
   b. Supervises the machining of work pieces and directs the general work assignments made to his department.
   c. Schedules assignments as determined by work orders received from other activities and sees that tools, materials, equipment, and personnel are available as needed for best performance.
   d. Inspects equipment and tools to insure proper conditions and use; requests repairs as needed.

2. Ten%: Performs managerial duties as follows:
    a. Conducts safety meetings; revises work practices and equipment to alleviate hazards; sees that safety regulations are observed; procures, issues, or inspects individual safety equipment.
    b. Interprets standard practices and procedures for unusual conditions and checks for compliance with standard practices and procedures applying to machining activities.
    c. Initiates notices of employees' performance; reprimands for violations of regulations or for deficient work; participates in settlement of step-1 grievances; rates probationary employees.
    d. Transfers or promotes personnel to fill temporary vacancies in hourly positions; grants employees time off; prepares employee working schedules.
    e. Signs time cards; originates labor distribution; originates and signs Supervisor's accident reports, requests for medical attention, reports on unsafe practice or condition, safety charts, and safety meeting report.
3. Fifteen%: Performs technical and administrative duties as follows:
    a. Originates and signs work orders as needed for repair of equipment.
    b. Originates and signs material requisitions for supplies, tools, etc.
    c. Collaborates with various operating and maintenance personnel regarding work orders pertaining to jobs requiring services of Lathe-Machines Shop.
    d. Analyzes work orders and determines labor and equipment requirements for efficient operation. Assigns overtime according to company policy.

Working conditions:
1. Works day shift.
2. Works overtime during emergencies.
3. Subject to normal plant and Lathe-Machines Shop conditions.

# Hawkins' Knob Hill Plant

Mr. Kiplinger is plant manager of the Nob City division of the Hawkins Company. He was originally transferred to Nob City in 1960, from the home office in Altoona (Pennsylvania). He, his wife, and their four children reside in Nob City. Reporting directly to Mr. Kiplinger are his key staff officers, the office manager, the personnel and safety manager, and the production manager. Other supervisors include foremen who report directly to the production manager.

The workers have a certain set of expectations concerning their own rights and privileges. Some of these "privileges" are obvious, while others are rather subtle. One of the more widely held values on the part of the workers is what they call "leniency." The workers know they have a job to do and expect that, in the process of doing it, management will leave them alone. The main obligation they feel to the company is that of producing. Obedience to supervisors is displayed so long as it is directly related to a job to be done. Hostility is directed toward managment when discipline or forced obedience is exerted as a means of asserting the will of management. Conversely, the workers commend management when given certain privileges or when flexibility is shown in discipline.

"Job-shifting" provides another route for circumventing formal supervisory authority and is a type of vertical and horizontal mobility in the plant. Job-shifting is done by "bidding" for a vacancy in the plant, prompted either by desire for a job with higher status or as a means to escape an unpleasant foreman. The foremen resent this practice, since they feel that they should have the prerogative of choosing their own subordinates— and not the other way around.

A third right includes the use of company material for home repairs. The workers expect that they should have access to the company's finished product, either without charge or at a very large discount, and that company equipment should be made available for use in repairing broken down machinery or household furnishings.

One day Skip Kiplinger received a call from the home office notifying him that he could expect about two million dollars' worth of new equipment to be added to his plant's equipment, in conjunction with the addition of a new brake-lining product line. Along with the equipment addition, the home office notified Skip that they were transferring Louis Hirtmann from the plastics division in Pottstown to replace the retiring Ed Patterson as production manager. Hirtmann was a former Army officer and had an outstanding industrial record too. It was hoped by the board of directors that the change of leadership and the addition of equipment would add considerably to Hawkins' profit margin.

One of Hirtmann's first moves was to stop the practice of allowing workers to have access to company equipment and to reduce the discount given on the purchase of company-made equipment. He was able to do this after showing Kiplinger that several thousands of dollars in sales had been lost from abuse of this particular privilege, in the last year alone; some workers had resold company equipment at considerable profits. Another move was to eliminate the job-shifting policy and to replace it with a new seniority system. The new system was roundly applauded by foremen and other supervisory personnel, but workers became noticeably irritable and frustrated. Hirtmann believed that once an order was given, it was to be followed without question. Generally he paid attention to employee grievances only when they reached critical proportions.

Hirtmann made rounds every hour to check on the progress of the work flow. In the course of six months he instituted many technical changes designed to speed up production and reduce labor costs. These improvements were reflected in the profit margin: but during this six-month period, dissension had been building up, almost unnoticed tensions in the plant ran high, and employees were becoming very defensive. Dissatisfaction over the installment of new machinery became a focal point of the disruption. If the company could afford two million dollars for machinery, workers grumbled, it could afford higher wages.

About the eighth month Hirtmann was notified by the home office that he would attend a month-long managerial seminar in Chicago. Mr. Kiplinger decided to leave Hirtmann's post vacant in his absence, and to have each shift foreman be responsible for his particular shift with no further supervision.

Kiplinger learned through the foremen that the women on the first shift wanted their rest room painted and, because the room was exposed to the afternoon sun, they also asked for some shades and a fan. Without hesitation Kiplinger told the maintenance crew to go to work on the job. In addition he told the foremen to feel free to handle such minor grievances and requests on their own authority until Hirtmann returned.

Within the next week another request was presented. This time the workers complained about working a six-day week. Kiplinger considered the point and proposed that if production reached 20,000 pounds per day (a 5,000 pound increase), he could then institute a short shift on Saturday running from 7:30 A.M. to noon. Within a few days production reached the level indicated. Unfortunately, now Kiplinger was in a difficult position because the Altoona office demanded even more production to meet their orders. Kiplinger then had to go back to the workers and ask them to continue on the six-day schedule for another few days until the orders were filled. Although there was some grumbling, most of the workers continued to operate willingly. Within a week the press for more production was reduced so that it was possible to institute the promised short day on the following Saturday.

It had been the practice to blow a steam whistle in the plant at the beginning and end of the shift, as well as at five-minute rest periods and at lunch. One of the workers suggested that the company use the public address system instead. At first, employees ridiculed the new system but in a few days they took announcements as a matter of course; in one instance when the announcement was not made, the employees returned from lunch just the same. Later on in the month the announcements were dropped, yet the employees started and stopped work promptly.

Between the first and the last of the month the daily output of the plant had increased steadily from 25,000 pounds to about 33,000 pounds.

Kiplinger was puzzled. He could not understand why production was up 32 percent with no production manager present.

## Questions

1. Why do you think production was up by 32 percent with no production manager present?

2. How specifically do you think Hirtmann's actions influenced plant workers' "higher order needs"? The plant's hygienes?

3. Do you think Hirtmann's leadership style was appropriate for this situation?

4.  Do you think that giving employees more "freedom," as Kiplinger did, was viewed as an important "consequence" of good performance? Why? Why not?

5.  What would you do now if you were Kiplinger?

# Kilkenny Lumber Company

## Part 1*

The Kilkenny Lumber Company owned and managed a large tract of forest in the northeastern United States. The company employed a number of men to maintain the tract according to modern forestry practices. In rotation, various areas of the tract were annually harvested by removing mature trees. Each winter, in preparation for harvesting and when other forestry tasks were at a standstill, a timber-marking crew composed of eight to ten regular company employees traveled through a selected area designating the trees to be cut and estimating the usable volume of lumber. In the spring, contractors moved over the area removing the marked trees.

Tree marking required considerable timbering knowledge and judgment. Once a tree was designated as mature and economical for harvest, height and diameter were calculated, defects estimated, and volume calculated. This volume was recorded along with a number code for the tree and was subsequently used as a basis for payment from the contractor. The code number was painted on the tree itself, as an indication of permission for cutting by the contract crew.

Tree-marking errors were costly. Missed trees or improper postponement of cutting meant lost sales and poor contractor relations, the latter depending on the maximum density of mature trees for his profit. Incorrect volume calculations meant lost money to Kilkenny or costly arbitration with the contractor. Designation of immature trees for cutting also cost Kilkenny money, particularly since the harvesting cycle was extremely long.

Several procedures had been adopted to reduce the chance of marking errors. The crew formed a moving line, each man fifty feet away from the men on either side. A man's place in line was set by informal crew decision. The line was to keep within a predetermined strip of forest and the men kept in proper relation to each other by periodic shouts to determine relative positions and by supervisory observation. Supervisors also spent considerable time, particularly at the beginning of the winter, training the crew members to make judgments and measurements. Supervisors checked each man's work periodically to make sure it met standards. If not, additional training was given. If it still did not meet standards, the man was asigned to other work if it were available. Although there were no production quotas, the men were expected to keep up with the moving line and mark approximately the same number of trees. Despite occasional variations in terrain, disparity of work loads was not an issue.

Working conditions were arduous. Temperatures often fell below 0°F. Snow was heavy and often fell during working hours. The terrain was uneven and the men had to carry food and supplies on their backs. Generally the men had no opportunity to dry out or warm up during the twelve hours of daylight in which they worked.

The crew which began work in December, 1962 (see Table 1), had received timber-marking training, though, as usual, all the men worked at other tasks during the rest of the year. A brief period of further training had been carried out by the leader and his assistant before the crew began regular work. Past timber-marking experience indicated that a crew like this could easily mark timber with the desired accuracy and speed.

---

*This is a sequential case. Your instructor may want you to discuss Part 1 before you read succeeding parts, or he may want you to answer the questions provided and then continue on through the case. Copyright © 1963 by the President and Fellows of Harvard College.

This case was prepared by H. Swan under the direction of John B. Seiler as a basis for class discussion rather than to illustrate either effective or ineffective handling of an administrative situation. Reprinted by permission of the Harvard Business School.

The crew leader and his assistant were considered by Kilkenny management to be excellent foresters and teachers. In woodsman tradition, crew leaders were expected to carry out supervisory tasks and at the same time, turn out more individual marking than any one of their men. The leaders of this crew were able to live up to this tradition. Both leaders tended to allow the men privileges not strictly according to regulations, such as long lunch hours before a fire, early departures for home, and frequent work breaks, particularly when the weather was severe.

**TABLE 1. Kilkenny Lumber Company**

|  | TIMBER-MARKING CREW, 1962 | | | | |
| --- | --- | --- | --- | --- | --- |
| *Title* | *Rank** | *Pay Grade* | *Seniority* | *Age* | *Education* |
| Leader | Professional forester | 9 | 3 years | 25 | College degree |
| Assistant leader | Subprofessional forester | 7 | 30 years | 55 | College, 1 year |
| Crewman** | Professional forester | 7 | 6 years | 28 | College degree |
| Crewman** | Professional forester | 7 | 4 years | 26 | College degree |
| Crewman** | Professional forester | 5 | 3 years | 25 | College degree |
| Crewman | Subprofessional forester | 5 | 15 years | 38 | High school diploma |
| Crewman | Subprofessional forester | 5 | 1 year | 22 | College, 2 years |
| Crewman | Subprofessional forester | 3 | 4 years | 45 | High school diploma |

*Rank was attained by formal education, examination and experience. Professional foresters normally were responsible for maintenance of forest districts, often supervising crews of subprofessional foresters and other lower-ranking woodsmen.

**These three men had been assigned to this crew from a distant and organizationally separate district of Kilkenny's land. They were assigned to the crew because of lack of other work and were expected to gain new practical experience from the marking assignment. They customarily worked together in their home district. Unlike the rest of the crew, which lived near the district being marked, these men lived away from home on a subsistence and transportation allowance during the week.

**Predictions** From what I know of the tree-marking operation described in Part 1, I would predict that:

1. Productivity of the crew would be (high) (standard) (below standard). Explain the reasons for your prediction.
2. Crewmen would be (high) (moderately) (dis-) satisfied with their job. Explain why.
3. Group members would (get along well with each other) (get along with some but not others) (not get along well with each other). Explain why. If you predict the second alternative, state who you would predict would get along well and who would not.
4. Crewmen will, in terms of the given job description (do what they are supposed to do, no more or less) (do about what they are supposed to do and some other things as well) (not do many things they are supposed to do but will do other things). Explain your prediction. If you predict the second or third alternative, briefly describe "other things."
5. The group (or subgroups of the group) will have and/or develop the following beliefs and informal standards or norms about crew behavior. Explain why, taking care to identify the group or subgroups to which you refer in each instance.

# KILKENNY LUMBER COMPANY
## Part 2

The timber-marking crew split into two informal groups soon after work in the forest began. One group was composed of the three professional foresters who had been assigned to the crew from a distant district. They constantly complained about the weather, the inadequacy of equipment, and their leaders. They found the leader to be a taskmaster who worked them too hard, his assistant a busybody who was too fussy about quality. The quantity of work performed by these three ranged between one third and one half of that attained by the other crewmen who were considered to be performing at a normal pace. Efforts at retraining produced no change. Absences among the three were high and excuses, though plentiful, often proved to be fabricated. The three men kept to themselves, building their separate fire at lunch time.

The rest of the crew tended to stick together. Although some of these men lacked the skill and training possessed by the professional foresters, the men helped each other and production and quality were high. The leaders, feeling rejected by the three professional foresters, ate with the subprofessionals.

The leaders were angered by the three recalcitrant crewmen. They interpreted the latter's behavior as an attempt to be reassigned to a more pleasant job. Since no other positions were open and because the leaders disliked the thought of giving in to what they considered a play for preferential treatment, they told the three men they would have to stay out in the cold, work or not. Conditions did not improve.

**Postprediction Analysis**  Refer to your predictions at the end of Part 1. How closely do they match the information above? Do inaccuracies in your predicition reflect inadequate analysis? If so, explain the analytical failure. If not, what additional information would you have needed in Part 1 to improve your predictive accuracy and how would you have used that information?

# KILKENNY LUMBER COMPANY
## Part 3

After several weeks, the leaders decided on two alternative strategies to increase the productivity of the professional foresters. First, the three men would be dispersed along the line and placed near the leader and his assistant instead of congregating at the far end of the line and trailing off as they had chosen to do (see Figure 1).

If this strategy failed, the leader would assume responsibility for the professionals as a separate group away from the rest of the crew and hope to increase their production by close supervision.

### A. BEFORE CONTEMPLATED CHANGE:*

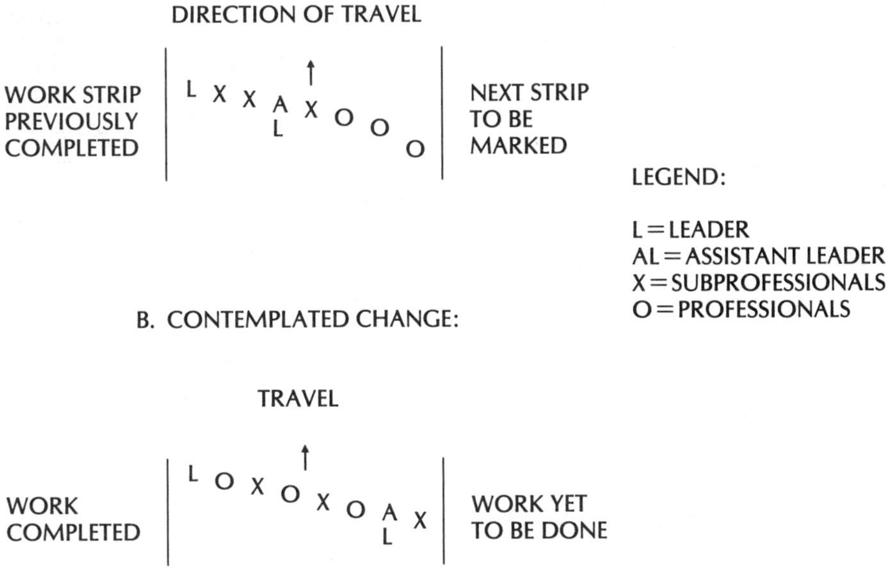

DIRECTION OF TRAVEL

WORK STRIP PREVIOUSLY COMPLETED | L X X A X O O / L X O O / O | NEXT STRIP TO BE MARKED

LEGEND:

L = LEADER
AL = ASSISTANT LEADER
X = SUBPROFESSIONALS
O = PROFESSIONALS

### B. CONTEMPLATED CHANGE:

TRAVEL

WORK COMPLETED | L O X O X O A X / L X | WORK YET TO BE DONE

**FIGURE 1.  Position in the Line of March**

**Note:** The unevenness of the line was compensated for by stopping forward progress before the end of the day and bringing the tail end of the line up to par with the leading edge.

**Predictions**   From Part 3 of the case, I would predict that:

1. The first strategy will be (successful) (partly successful) (unsuccessful). Explain why.
2. The second strategy (will) (will not) be attempted. If you predict the first alternative, the second strategy will be (successful) (partly successful) (unsuccessful). Explain why.
3. Some other strategy (will) (will not) be necessary. If you predict the first alternative explain what that strategy should be and why you expect it to succeed.

# ■ KILKENNY LUMBER COMPANY

## Part 4

Inserting the professional between other crew members served to slow the entire work line. Although quality did not suffer, productivity for the whole crew dropped off to a total figure lower than that previously achieved. Consequently, the second strategy was attempted. However, while the subprofessional crew resumed their former pace, the professionals moved even slower than they had under the initial arrangement. The leaders were at a loss to find a way to attain the productivity which they felt certain the crew members were capable of achieving.

**Postprediction Analysis**   Refer to your predictions at the end of Part 3. How closely do they match the information above? Do inaccuracies in your predictions reflect inadequate analysis? If so, explain the analytical failure. If not, what additional information would you have needed in Part 1 to improve your predictive accuracy and how would you have used that information?

# Carter Electric Company*

## Part 1

Carter Electric Company employed about 250 workers in its main plant which manu-factured and assembled various electrical fixtures, components, and accessories for many types of industrial and consumer products. Most of the manufacturing and assembly operations required unskilled labor with the exception of such positions as tool and die makers or machinists. The company plant consisted of four floors—including a basement—with a separate foreman in charge of each floor. Each foreman supervised anywhere from twenty-five to forty workers.

In some parts of the plant work was performed in assembly-line operations, but most workers worked either alone or in pairs. The one exception to this work layout was the Cord Room in which all the electrical cords used in the products were manufactured. This room was located in the basement of the factory and was physically separated from the rest of the floor by concrete block walls. Entrance into the Cord Room was through a single door that opened onto the rest of the factory floor. Because the Cord Room was separated from the foreman who was in charge of the basement operations, management placed a supervisor in the room called a "leadhand." The leadhand did not have the authority of a foreman and was a member of the same union as the employees. His main responsibility was to see that the work orders were completed on time and that the necessary supplies and equipment were available to the workers when needed. The foreman seldom entered the Cord Room unless requested by the leadhand. All ten of the employees in the Cord Room were female and most had been with Carter for several years. Most had worked in other parts of the factory before being transferred to the Cord Room. There were usually one or two new girls in the room and at certain peak produc-tion periods several additional girls would be hired on a temporary basis.

While the overall working conditions at Carter approximated that of most factories, the Cord Room differed in several respects. Because of its unique location in the base-ment, there were no windows. Thus, all the light provided came from the artificial over-head lighting. The room generally contained an odor that emanated from the "molding machine," a machine that melted plastic shavings into solid electrical plugs. This odor, plus the smell produced by the newly made rubber electrical cords, was always noticed by people entering the Cord Room. Although the machines in the Cord Room were not significantly noisier than those in other areas of the factory, the size of the room seemed to amplify the noise level. Most of the machines were run by compressed air and this made conversation difficult, especially during busy periods.

All the workers in the factory were paid a guaranteed hourly wage plus a bonus based upon productivity. The union contract specified that the company would share all pro-duction over 100% of standard on a 50-50 basis with employees. This would mean that if production for a given week was 110%, a worker earning an hourly rate of $4.00 per hour would receive instead $4.20 per hour (5% of $4.00 + $4.00). For purposes of computing the bonus rate, the factory was divided into five parts: first floor, second floor, third floor, basement, and the Cord Room. The Cord Room had been singled out as a separate area since it was easy to keep track of the group's production and their work had little relation to the other work performed in the basement.

---

*This is a sequential case. Your instructor may want you to discuss Part 1 before you read succeeding parts, or he may want you to answer the questions provided and then continue on through the case.

**Predictions for Part 1**   Given the information in Part 1, what would be your predictions regarding the following:

1. Morale of the Cord Room? (i) high (ii) medium (iii) low. Why?
2. Job satisfaction of Cord Room workers? (i) high (ii) medium (iii) low. Why?
3. The bonus paid to the Cord Room workers should be (i) higher than the other four groups (ii) lower than the other four groups (iii) about the same. Why?

# ■ CARTER ELECTRIC COMPANY
## Part 2

Carter maintained production records on a weekly basis since the bonus plan had been instituted four years previous. During this time the Cord Room continuously outproduced every other group in the factory. While the average productivity for the other groups was usually around 110%, the Cord Room consistently produced 120% of standard and on some occasions had reached 140%. Although the odors inside the Cord Room were occasionally offensive, most of the workers seemed to enjoy their surroundings. All considered the leadhand to be helpful, and while he was considered to be production-oriented in his attitudes, he was still considerate of the girls' needs and problems. It had become the custom on birthdays to "celebrate" and the birthday person always brought some type of food or snack from home for the rest of the group. Although all workers at Carter were allowed two fifteen-minute coffee breaks a day, the birthday celebrations never occurred during these periods or lunch hours. The parties seldom lasted more than one-half hour but were always confined to the Cord Room personnel since the regular foreman disapproved of such behavior.

Many of the jobs in the Cord Room were tedious as they either required extreme manual dexterity or were performed in unpleasant surroundings—such as near the molding machine which emitted the unpleasant odors. Even though the union contact specified certain wage levels for the different jobs, there was considerable switching around during the day between the girls to avoid one person having to be on an unpleasant job for an extended period of time. Although this switching was strictly prohibited by management, the leadhand never objected unless he knew the foreman would be visiting the Cord Room.

### Postprediction Analysis

1. Given the information in this part, how can you account for the behavior of the Cord Room personnel?
2. How close were your predictions? If inaccurate, was it because of a lack of information or faulty analysis?

# Diary of a National Guard Officer Candidate School Student

In the first week, the candidates were civilians in every sense. Having just arrived from civilian life they found themselves in an atmosphere of constraint and exacting regimentation. As a result, practically every individual personality trait had to be either suppressed so that it could not be detected or else transformed into organizational identification. Only three members of an initial group of 107 men had any prior experience which might have been helpful in the situation. These three had just returned from Korean combat.

The few remaining members of the group who had military experience found it impossible to utilize former training. The incompatibility of the situation with prior models of expectations was quickly evident. By the end of the fourteenth day, over twenty-five candidates had returned to home units. At the end of the twenty-second week, fifty-one of the original 107 graduated.

Although the estimates were not complete, information provided by a postschool club of officers showed the forty-three of the graduates had been promoted in the first three years since their graduation (although my colleague was not among them). A majority of them had received commendation for their service to their home guard units and none had indicated any intention of giving up their roles as National Guard Officers.

What was the state of an organizational structure which, on the one hand, was highly effective in producing a desirable state of persisting officer effectiveness and, on the other hand, took a high toll of apparently well-qualified candidates? Perhaps a few of the anecdotes given in the following diary will suggest an answer to these questions.

# I

Sometimes all that kept me going on those twenty mile night marches was my hate for the "redbirds" (upperclassmen). They would double-time us the first five miles or so with rifles over our heads and twenty-pound packs clutching at our tails in the direction of that infernal range of mountains. By the time we hit the first foothills, our feet were numb and we were soaked with sweat. Then we would settle down to a murderous grind to the top of that damned rocky trail. All the time the "redbirds" harassed us.

Some said they made it on dogged determination; many didn't. On hot summer nights sick men would fall out on the trail, and we weren't allowed to help them. I know that what really kept me going was my hate for some "redbird" skipping lightly along without pack or rifle. I would watch him pick on some fellow about to stumble senseless into the ditch, and become so filled with hate for that particular bastard that I wasn't conscious of my exhaustion. With each step I conceived of a new plan for splitting his skull if he so much as said a word to me. I remember one night in particular, drooling and snarling like an animal while trying to get at one of those _____, but instead I tripped and cut my shin.

Reproduced with permission of Michael Schwartz from his Ph. D. thesis, pp. 7–12, University of Illinois, 1962. Data for case provided by Doyle Kent Rice.

We always reached the top somehow, where we were allowed to rest three minutes— as some wit said, "whether we need it or not."

I never remembered much about the return trip. All we could think of was the milk and orange juice we could buy if we were able to get it down before getting sick or passing out on the cots.

The grass-picking detail early Sunday morning was a kind of pleasure. At least we could rest. That same "redbird" would come around me and screech at me in his obnoxious command voice. This time I would hasten over to report—resolute that every inflection, every word, every minute property of my actions in his presence would be beyond reproach. But something was always wrong—I was reminded for the thousandth time that I was a disgrace to the uniform. I would beat a deflated retreat, wondering if I would ever improve. I did improve, but never enough; sometimes an entire week would pass without any serious offenses; then I would get twenty demerits because I had been lacking in attention to some detail like the arrangement of toothbrushes in my squad's footlockers for Saturday inspection. I could have pointed out that forty items were flawlessly arranged, but that too was against the code. That and every Saturday night I was back on the punitive march.

# II

In the ninth week the Tac decided that the experimental NG OCS class should be sent into the field on a tactical mission. One of the members of the second platoon was on detail after supper one night and overheard the Tac commander in a telephone conversation making arrangements to send three platoons of "aggressor redbirds" out to take the NG slouches by surprise.

We were waiting for them. A happier, more alert complement of trainees never went into the field. (We even had prearranged bird whistle signals—Daniel Boone vintage.) What followed was one of the most satisfying, though somewhat sadistic, experiences of my military career. At dark, the Tac officer inspected our positions and then retired to the main camp—saying that he would return later. We knew his mission was to instruct the "redbirds" on our position. We quickly shifted from our line of defense into a semicircle forward of the original line, but this time we didn't dig fox holes—we left a few decoys in the supposed position to smoke occasional cigarettes. We hid in clumps of underbrush or lay silently in tall grass. There was even some possibility we would give ourselves away by arguing over who had the most right to jump which "redbird." We were a terribly antagonistic group of men—and worse, we had just been certified in the school of infighting. The more conservative (and favored) NGs would only sanction the use of judo and fists on the "birds." In some sense they had become our leaders because we complied.

The upperclassmen never knew what hit them. Three squads of their left platoon cautiously approached our end platoon in a flanking movement. But they weren't the aggressors, we were! We fell on them as they moved unsuspectingly into our midst. Jim was with us then. I shall never forget the near human screech with which he sounded the attack. It was difficult to remember the details of the following melee. I do remember the shock of later discovering the victim whose lower arm I had snapped in a judo lock was one of the few "redbirds" that I had any feeling for as a human being. The next morning almost a fifth of the entire upper class was in the post hospital. Many others were on limited duty. The Tac remained silent about the entire incident, but they cracked down on us in every conceivable way. The so-called dreaded "shuffle" began. Every night for seven days we were ordered to move each night into an empty barracks. We usually had about an hour to perform this impossible shuffle. Since we were nevertheless expected to have perfectly flawless bunk areas the following morning we would risk being caught out of bed to work on these nasty little details until three or four in the morning. It was during this period that I learned to sleep with my eyes open. Kern Sumal set an enviable record. He was able to get thirteen hours of sleep during the ordeal. The average was about seven hours. As a result, thirteen more candidates were eliminated for reasons of physical exhaustion. We knew we were paying a horrible price, but no one would admit regret for having found a legitimate vehicle for the expression of our antagonism. By the end of the ordeal, neither the regular "redbirds" nor their replacements seemed to have any real interest in harassing us after that. About the twelfth week OCS command cut an order stating that since NG classes were being trained for reserve commands, it would not be necessary for such limited status personnel to sustain a practical exercise in unit defense against simulated "aggressor troops."

## III

My first and most overwhelming impression of life at OCS was that there were no situations which could be classified as pleasurable. The first few weeks I couldn't escape an awareness of deep-seated anxiety mixed with a vicious resentment that not only my every mannerism but also certain private domains of my personality were subject to destructive criticism. I remember a sort of private platitude became my foremost rule for every thought and action. It went something like this—"If you can be flexible enough in your overt action, you can beat this bunch of damned idiots at their own games without seriously changing your basic self"—it was a cruel game of constant pretense, one in which I was not entirely successful, however. Perhaps I did change in many superficial respects. At any rate, almost the entire superstructure of my personality had to be cut away in order for me to survive and protect myself from external threat. I learned to pacify my frustration in hundreds of minute and animal-like ways. The definition of the situation had been reduced to the fact that I was nothing more than a bit of human organism which had a mind and stubborn drive to conquer previously unsuspected tricks that OCS might have in store. I also discovered that there were many previously undetected pleasures available. When I was not plotting the readjustment of my actions, I indulged in minute physiological sensations. I suppose a certain amount of masochism was unavoidable. I learned to enjoy everything from taking the boots off my tired feet to the nightly inspection of a corrupted sore on my kneecap which refused to heal.

Certainly these simple rewards were not sufficient to have committed one to survival of the course. I suppose the fact that it would have been shameful to go home to my unit as a failure had some bearing on my desire to remain. However, I don't remember using this argument much. Instead, since I had committed myself to the school as a means of supporting my wife for the summer months, I knew I couldn't let her down. Naturally, from the very first, letters from my wife were a source of considerable comfort, although I fear that the correspondence was very one-sided. The few letters I wrote to her were full of self-pity and complaints. At more critical moments, I would telephone her. Nor do I feel that my case was any more than average. The average telephone bill for members of the platoon each month was twenty-five or thirty dollars. For that matter I didn't share my complaints without being detected. Unfortunately, I was silent most of the time.

Somehow it didn't occur to me until the last few weeks that the eight to twelve hours a day we spent in the classroom were somewhat of a pleasure. At least in contrast to the icy atmosphere we experienced every moment when not in class, this was a holiday. With a few exceptions, the school instructors were willing to forego at least some of the OCS techniques of rigid constraint. Their only concern was that we learned the materials presented. The question often arose as to how we were able to perform satisfactorily when we were never given the opportunity to study outside the classroom. The answer was that the average classroom was a sort of escape from the tyrannical and punitive effects of the OCS training measures. Many of our instructors were West Point graduates, and in contrast to the surly OCS crowd, they seemed to set a more desirable model of military efficiency. And more important, they occasionally acted human by giving advice and encouragement. They even allowed us to violate some of the OCS restrictions. The general opinion was that these were genuine officers who were capable of leading us without benefit of dictatorial methods. Perhaps the real situation was that their task was made easy for them. OCS candidates came to the classroom searching for any form of stimuli which was presented in a manner that suggested personal freedom was allowed. And this freedom is exactly what we received in the classroom. The men often stated that they would "do anything for some of the school officers." Moreover, in the often-raised question, "Whom would you rather be in combat with?" the school officers were always the favorite. Needless to say, much of what was really more important in the way of officer personality was effectively copied in the classroom.

**Question for Discussion**    While it is true that the above remarks cannot in any sense be called reliable social data, the question is what can these data show about the effectiveness-producing potential of an organization?

# Center City Engineering Department

The Engineering Department of Center City employed approximately 1,000 people, all of whom worked under the provisions of the Civil Service System. Of these employees, about 100 worked in the Design Division. Parker Nolton, an Associate Engineer, had been employed in the Design Division for 19 years and was known personally by virtually everyone in the division, if not in Center City itself. Nolton had held the position of Associate Engineer for seven years on a provisional basis only, for he had never been able to pass the required civil service examinations to gain permanent appointment to this grade, although he had taken them often. Many of his co-workers felt that his lack of formal engineering education prevented him from passing the examinations, but Nolton felt that his failures were the result of his tendency to "tighten up" when taking an examination. Off the job, Nolton was extremely active in civic affairs and city-sponsored recreational programs. During the past year, for example, he had been president of the High School Parent Teacher's Association, captain of the bowling team sponsored by the Engineering Department in the Municipal Bowling League, and a member of the Managing Committee of the Center City Little League.

As Center City grew and the activities of the Engineering Department expanded to keep pace with this growth, younger men were hired into the Department in relatively large numbers. Among those hired were Ralph Boyer and Doug Worth. Both of these young men were graduate engineers, and had accepted the positions with the Engineering Department after fulfilling their military obligations. Ralph Boyer had been an officer in the Army Corps of Engineers. In order to give the new men opportunities to achieve permanent status in the Civil Service System, examinations were scheduled with greater frequency than they had been in the past. Nolton's performance on the examinations continued to be unsatisfactory. The new men, however, passed the exams for successively higher positions with flying colors. Ralph Boyer in particular experienced marked success in these examinations and advanced rapidly. Three years after his initial employment, he was in charge of a design group within the Design Division. Parker Nolton, in the meantime, had been shifted from the position of a project engineer to that of the purchase order coordinator. The position of purchase order coordinator was more limited in scope than that of a project engineer, although the responsibilities of the position were great. He continued to be classified as an Associate Engineer, however.

Ralph Boyer continued his successful career and soon qualified for the position of Senior Engineer. A new administrative group that had been created to meet the problems that arose in the Design Division because of the expanding activities of the Engineering Department was placed under his direction. Doug Worth, too, was successful in his examinations and was shortly promoted to the grade of Associate Engineer and transferred into the administrative group headed by Ralph Boyer.

One of the functions under the new administrative group was that of purchase order coordination. This relationship required that Parker Nolton report to Ralph Boyer. Nolton, however, chose to ignore the new organizational structure and dealt directly with the

Chief Engineer, an arrangement which received the latter's tacit approval. Nolton was given a semiprivate office and the services of a Junior Engineer to assist him in his activities. His assistant, John Palmer, soon requested a transfer on the grounds that he had nothing to do, and there was no need for anyone in this position. Nolton, on the other hand, always appeared to be extremely busy and was continually requesting additional manpower and assistance to help him with the coordination of purchase orders.

Some four months after the organizational changes noted above had taken place, the Chief Engineer left the company and his replacement, Stan Matson, was appointed from within the division. Matson was the logical successor to the position; his appointment came as no surprise and was well received by all the employees. His appointment was shortly followed by the assignment of Ralph Boyer to a special position which took him completely out of the Design Division. Doug Worth was assigned to the position thus vacated, Supervisor of the Administrative Group, and consequently inherited the supervision of Parker Nolton's activities. This assignment, initially made on a provisional basis, was soon made permanent when Worth passed the required examinations and was awarded the grade of Senior Engineer. Doug Worth had never worked closely with Parker Nolton but had been on cordial terms with him since his arrival in the Engineering Department. He had had contact with Nolton in several recreational activities in which they both had participated.

During the months which followed, Parker Nolton continued his direct reporting relationship with the Chief Engineer, now in the person of Stan Matson, and never consulted or advised Doug Worth regarding the progress of his activities as purchase order coordinator. His former assistant, John Palmer, had been transferred and had been replaced by an engineering aide. Both the aide and Nolton appeared to be busy most of the time, and Nolton was still requesting more manpower for his activity through formal channels. When occasions arose which required that Doug Worth check on Nolton's activities, he was always forced to go to Nolton's office for information. Nolton always claimed to be too busy to leave his own office. During the conversations which occurred when Worth visited Nolton, Nolton frequently gave the impression that he regarded Worth's activities and interest as superfluous. Several times he suggested that in future situations Worth just send the inquiring party directly to him if questions arose about his activities. He often made the comment that he knew everyone in the department, and often it was better to handle many situations informally rather than through channels.

Doug Worth was concerned with Nolton's attitude, for he did not feel that he could effectively carry out his responsibilities as Supervisor of the Administrative Group if he did not know the current status of activities in all of the functions under his control. Consequently, he attempted to gain more cooperation from Nolton by approaching the subject at times when the two men were engaged in common off-hours recreational activities. These attempts were uniformly unsuccessful. Nolton always quickly brought the conversation around to the standing of the bowling team, the progress of the P.T.A., or any other unrelated subject close at hand.

After several attempts to talk with Nolton in a friendly way off the job, Worth concluded that the situation as it currently stood was intolerable. While he realized he must do something, Worth felt he understood Nolton's attitude and reactions and was sympathetic. After all, Nolton had been in the department for years and had been relatively successful. He knew all the "ropes" and had many friends. Worth reflected that it must be a blow to a man like Nolton to have to report to young, relatively inexperienced men. Worth had faced similar problems during his military career, when he had more experienced men many years his senior under his command. After much thought, he decided his best approach would be to appeal to Nolton in a very direct manner for a greater degree of cooperation. Thus, Worth approached Nolton on the job and suggested that they have a talk in his private office where they would not be disturbed by all the activity in Nolton's office. Nolton protested that he could not take time away from his duties. Worth was firm, however, and Nolton reluctantly agreed to come to Worth's office, protesting all the way that he really could not spare the time.

During his opening remarks to what Worth had planned as a sympathetic discussion of the situation, Worth referred to "the normal relationship between a man and his superior." Nolton's reaction was violent. He stated that he didn't regard any young upstart as a "superior," especially his. He told Worth to run his own office and to let him, Nolton, run his. He concluded by stating, "If you haven't anything more to say, I would like to get back to my office where important work is being neglected." Worth, realizing that nothing more could be accomplished in the atmosphere which prevailed, watched in silence as Nolton left.

Doug Worth subsequently reported his latest conversation with Nolton to Stan Matson, the Chief Engineer. He also related the events which had led to this conversation. In concluding his remarks, he stated that he could no longer take responsibility for Nolton's actions, because Nolton would neither accept his guidance, nor advise him of the state of his work. Matson's reply to this last statement was "Yes, I know." This was the only comment Matson made during the interview, although he listened intently to Worth's analysis of the situation.

At the next meeting of the Supervisory Staff of which Worth was a member but Nolton was not, Worth proposed that Nolton be transferred to the position of Design Drafting Engineer, in effect a demotion. As Worth was explaining the reasons for his proposed action regarding Nolton, one of the other members of the Supervisory Staff interrupted to proclaim very heatedly that Nolton was "one of the pillars of the entire Engineering Department," and that he would be violently opposed to the demotion of "so fine a man." Following this interruption, a very heated, emotional discussion ensued concerning the desirability of demoting Nolton.

During this discussion Stan Matson remained silent; yet he reflected that he probably should take some action during the meeting regarding the Nolton situation.

# Savemore Food Store 5116[1]

The Savemore Corporation is a chain of four hundred retail supermarkets located primarily in the Northeastern section of the United States. Store 5116 employs over fifty persons, all of whom live within suburban Portage, New York, where this store is located.

Wally Shultz served as general manager of store 5116 for six years. Last April he was transferred to another store in the chain. At that time the employees were told by the district manager, Mr. Finnie, that Wally Shultz was being promoted to manage a larger store in another township.

Most of the employees seemed unhappy to lose their old manager. Nearly everyone agreed with the opinion that Shultz was a "good guy to work for." As examples of his desirability as a boss the employees told how Wally had frequently helped the arthritic porter with his floor mopping, how he had shut the store five minutes early each night so that certain employees might catch their busses, of a Christmas party held each year for employees at his own expense, and his general willingness to pitch in. All employees had been on a first-name basis with the manager. About half of them had begun work with the Savemore Corporation when the Portage store was opened.

Wally Shultz was replaced by Clark Raymond. Raymond, about twenty-five years old, was a graduate of an Ivy League college and had been with Savemore a little over one year. After completion of his six-month training program, he served as manager of one of the chain's smaller stores before being advanced to store 5116. In introducing Raymond to the employees, Mr. Finnie stressed his rapid advancement and the profit increase that occurred while Raymond had charge of his last store.

I began my employment in store 5116 in early June. Mr. Raymond was the first person I met in the store, and he impressed me as being more intelligent and efficient than the managers I had worked for in previous summers at other stores. After a brief conversation concerning our respective colleges, he assigned me to a cash register, and I began my duties as a checker and bagger.

In the course of the next month I began to sense that relationships between Raymond and his employees were somewhat strained. This attitude was particularly evident among the older employees of the store, who had worked in store 5116 since its opening. As we all ate our sandwiches together in the cage (an area about twenty feet square in the cellar fenced in by chicken wire, to be used during coffee breaks and lunch hours), I began to question some of the older employees as to why they disliked Mr. Raymond. Laura Morgan, a fellow checker about forty years of age and the mother of two grade-school boys, gave the most specific answers. Her complaints were:

1. Raymond had fired the arthritic porter on the grounds that a porter who "can't mop is no good to the company."
2. Raymond had not employed new help to make up for normal attrition. Because of this, everybody's work load was much heavier than it ever had been before.
3. The new manager made everyone call him "mister . . . he's unfriendly."
4. Raymond didn't pitch in. Wally Shultz had, according to Laura, helped people when they were behind in their work. She said that Shultz had helped her bag on rushed

Reprinted by permission of John W. Hennessey, Jr., The Amos Tuck School of Business Administration, Dartmouth College.

1. At the time of this case, the author, a college student, was employed for the summer as a checker and stockboy in store 5116.

Friday nights when a long line waited at her checkout booth, but "Raymond wouldn't lift a finger if you were dying."

5. Employees were no longer let out early to catch busses. Because of the relative infrequency of this means of transportation, some employees now arrived home up to an hour later.

6. "Young Mr. Know-it-all with his fancy degree . . . takes all the fun out of this place."

Other employees had similar complaints. Gloria, another checker, claimed that, ". . . he sends the company nurse to your home every time you call in sick." Margo, a meat wrapper, remarked, "Everyone knows how he's having an affair with that new bookkeeper, he hired to replace Carol when she quit." Pops Devery, head checker who had been with the chain for over ten years, was perhaps the most vehement of the group. He expressed his views in the following manner: "That new guy's a real louse . . . got a mean streak a mile long. Always trying to cut corners. First it's not enough help, then no overtime, and now, come Saturday mornings, we have to use boxes[2] for the orders 'til the truck arrives. If it wasn't just a year 'til retirement, I'd leave. Things just aren't what they used to be when Wally was around." The last statement was repeated in different forms by many of the other employees. Hearing all this praise of Wally, I was rather surprised when Mr. Finnie dropped the comment to me one morning that Wally had been demoted for inefficiency, and that no one at store 5116 had been told this. It was important that Mr. Shultz save face, Mr. Finnie told me.

A few days later, on Saturday of the busy weekend preceding the July Fourth holiday, store 5116 again ran out of paper bags. However, the delivery truck did not arrive at ten o'clock, and by 10:30 the supply of cardboard cartons was also low. Mr. Raymond put in a hurried call to the warehouse. The men there did not know the whereabouts of the truck but promised to get an emergency supply of bags to us around noon. By eleven o'clock, there were no more containers of any type available, and Mr. Raymond reluctantly locked the doors to all further customers. The twenty checkers and packers remained in their respective booths, chatting among themselves. After a few minutes, Mr. Raymond requested that they all retire to the cellar cage because he had a few words for them. As soon as the group was seated on the wooden benches in the chicken wire enclosed area, Mr. Raymond began to speak, his back to the cellar stairs. In what appeared to be an angered tone, he began, "I'm out for myself first, Savemore second, the customer third, and you last. The inefficiency in this store has amazed me from the moment I arrived here . . ."

At about this time I noticed Mr. Finnie, the district manager, standing at the head of the cellar stairs. It was not surprising to see him at this time because he usually made three or four unannounced visits to the store each week as part of his regular supervisory procedure. Mr. Raymond, his back turned, had not observed Finnie's entrance.

Mr. Raymond continued, "Contrary to what seems to be the opinion of many of you, the Savemore Corporation is not running a social club here. We're in business for just one thing . . . to make money. One way that we lose money is by closing the store on Saturday morning at eleven o'clock. Another way that we lose money is by using a 60-pound paper bag to do the job of a 20-pound bag. A 60-pound bag costs us over 2 cents apiece; a 20-pound bag costs less than a penny. So when you sell a couple of quarts of

---

2. The truck from the company warehouse bringing merchandise for sale and store supplies normally arrived at ten o'clock Saturday mornings. Frequently, the stock of large paper bags would be temporarily depleted. It was then necessary to pack orders in cardboard cartons until the truck was unloaded.

milk or a loaf of bread, don't use the big bags. Why do you think we have four different sizes anyway? There's no great intelligence or effort required to pick the right size. So do it. This store wouldn't be closed right now if you'd used your common sense. We started out this week with enough bags to last 'til Monday . . . and they would have lasted 'til Monday if you'd only used your brains. This kind of thing doesn't look good for the store, and it doesn't look good for me. Some of you have been bagging for over five years . . . and you ought'a be able to do it right by now . . ." Mr. Raymond paused and then said, "I trust I've made myself clear on this point."

The cage was silent for a moment, and then Pops Devery, the head checker, spoke up: "Just one thing, Mis-tuh Raymond. Things were running pretty well before you came around. When Wally was here we never ran out'a bags. The customers never complained about overloaded bags or the bottoms falling out before you got here. What're you gonna tell somebody when they ask for a couple of extra bags to use in garbage cans? What're you gonna tell somebody when they want their groceries in a bag, and not a box? You gonna tell them the manager's too damn cheap to give 'em bags? Is that what you're gonna tell 'em? No sir, things were never like this when Wally Shultz was around. We never had to apologize for a cheap manager who didn't order enough then. What'ta you got to say to that, Mis-tuh Raymond?"

Mr. Raymond, his tone more emphatic, began again. "I've got just one thing to say to that, Mr. Devery, and that's this: store 5116 never did much better than break even when Shultz was in charge here. I've shown a profit better than the best he ever hit in six years every week since I've been here. You can check that fact in the book upstairs any time you want. If you don't like the way I'm running things around here, there's nobody begging you to stay . . ."

At this point, Pops Devery interrupted and, looking up the stairs at the district manager, asked, "What about that, Mr. Finnie? You've been around here as long as I have. You told us how Wally got promoted 'cause he was such a good boss. Supposin' you tell this young fellar here what a good manager is really like? How about that, Mr. Finnie?"

A rather surprised Mr. Raymond turned around to look up the stairs at Mr. Finnie. The manager of store 5116 and his checkers and packers waited for Mr. Finnie's answer.

# Dominion Acceptance Company Limited*

In May 1973 Mr. B. L. Keast, Atlantic regional manager of operations for Dominion Acceptance Company Limited, faced a number of personnel and operating procedures decisions directly affecting the operations of the Moncton, New Brunswick, branch of D.A.C. Earlier in the year changes in the management staffing of the Moncton branch had been made, and after three months the results of these changes were being evaluated in order to make adequate permanent changes in the Moncton operation. As the problems which had led to the changes had been of a particularly serious nature, it was imperative that Mr. Keast thoroughly examine the possible effects of any changes, as well as the causes of the problems arising earlier. In doing so he was compelled to consider the viewpoints of the Moncton branch manager, Mr. Ronald Snell, Snell's current assistant manager, Mr. Alex DeCoste, his previous assistant manager, Mr. Jerry MacDonald and the rest of the Moncton staff. In addition he recognized the importance of keeping the Moncton operation consistent with the other branches in his region as well as with national D.A.C. policy.

## ☐ Background

D.A.C. was one of the largest finance companies in Canada. Its primary business was the acceptance of conditional sales contracts from customers who had purchased customer goods. D.A.C. then paid the retailer while the customer paid D.A.C. in monthly installments. In addition to this retail financing, D.A.C. also made loans to firms either to begin or expand existing businesses. The company was entirely Canadian-owned, and operated on a national basis. Regional offices were located in five major Canadian cities, viz., Halifax, Montreal, Toronto, Winnipeg and Vancouver. Branch offices were located in most cities and some towns serving as district shopping centres. Atlantic region branch staff sizes varied from 3–40 depending on the population of the market being served and the amount of money loaned.

Corporate headquarters were in Toronto and functioned as a central policy-making and administrative centre. Head office established specific policies and procedures regarding loans, branch control, and reporting methods, as well as personnel policies and administrative procedures designed to ensure consistent coast-to-coast operations. To obtain consistency, D.A.C. had in 1968 prepared and distributed to each branch a detailed procedures manual which, in addition to the above policies, prescribed office procedures and provided detailed job descriptions for all branch positions. In the manual the policy of aggressively seeking new profitable accounts was stressed.

The regional manager of operations (RMO) functioned as the intermediary between corporate headquarters and the branches in their respective regions. As with the Halifax RMO, all RMOs had as their primary source of information regarding branch operations the monthly statistics prepared for them by each branch. The format was prescribed by the procedures manual (including the due date of the third of each month covering the previous month's operations) and consisted of statistics on the number and dollar value of accounts, collections made, total branch expenses for the month, and overdue accounts

---

*Case material prepared by Mr. William J. MacNeil under the direction of W. H. Cooper, assistant professor of business administration, St. Francis Xavier University, Antigonish, N.S., Canada. Reprinted by permission of Professor Cooper.

by age. As part of the computer analysis of branch operations, the RMO compiled this data into a regional report comparing all branches in the region and sent copies to each branch as well as to Toronto. Each branch manager could therefore regularly compare his performance against the other individual branches as well as with the region as a whole.

In his evaluation of branch operations and the resulting report Mr. Keast placed emphasis on the control of payments. The percentage of accounts 30 or more days late was the key evaluation variable, and he expected the collection departments in each branch to give special attention to such deficient accounts. The Atlantic region's average delinquency rate was 3 percent. Branch managers were generally quite sensitive about their office's delinquency rate and how their rate compared with other branches in the region, as shown in the monthly RMOs' report.

In addition to the monthly reports, the RMO conducted a yearly visit to each branch (without prior notice being given) to perform several kinds of inspection and audits. The RMO and his staff inspected the accounts and credit records, performed employee evaluations of the manager and assistant manager, and if time allowed, reviewed the manager's evaluations of the other staff members. As each manager hired his own staff and operated his branch with some autonomy, the results of the monthly and annual evaluations were of particular importance in judging the manager and his staff's ability.

## ☐ The February Inspection

Mr. Keast's inspection in June 1972 had rated the Moncton branch's overall performance as slightly below average. The July 1972 and subsequent monthly reports began to show a steadily increasing delinquency rate and a decrease in the dollar value as well as in the number of accounts. By January 1973 the delinquency rate stood at 8 percent and the number of customer accounts had fallen from 3,500 in June 1972 to 3,000. This performance decline was significantly poorer than the other branches in southern New Brunswick. After repeated requests for explanations and unsatisfactory responses, Mr. Keast decided to make his 1973 visit much earlier in the year, and hence on February 14 he arrived in Moncton at 7:15 A.M. Upon entering the airport terminal Mr. Keast and his staff assistant were surprised to find Mr. Snell queuing up for a ticket on the 7:35 A.M. departure for Toronto. An embarrassed Snell explained that he had some personal business in Hamilton but that it was not urgent and could be delayed, particularly in light of the unexpected annual inspection of the branch which was to be conducted that day.

Traveling to the branch from the airport Snell explained: "I've been finding it tough to do much to control our late accounts. We've a poor clientele, my assistant isn't qualified, and the girls we've been getting to keep our account records up-to-date have not worked out. I know it makes the branch look poor, but you know I've tried. I think in a couple of months we'll have the office turned around and be back among the regional leaders where we belong." Keast listened politely and expressed concern that something must be done soon to improve the Moncton operations. "If your staff is not up to the job, maybe we can fix that, but as far as customers go, you've got as good an economic area here as Scott does in Fredericton and Angus in St. John. Anyhow, you certainly have a lot more snow here than we do down in Halifax. Let's see how things are looking in the office." Arriving downtown, Keast and his assistant spent the next few hours going over the account cards and other financial records.

Things did not look good. Over 20 account cards had been found which were over 90 days past due (the January report had shown a total of 12 such accounts), and no note of contact between the office and the customer could be found for most of them for the past 60 days. The office was in disarray, the filing system in chaos, key records and papers took some time to locate, and the customer account clerks seemed unfamiliar with much of the routine office procedure. Keast finished the morning going over the personnel files and noted that the turnover rate for clerical personnel was high, absenteeism a problem, and a key staff member (the accounts supervisor) had been fired a month ago and had not been replaced. Leaving his assistant to tabulate the results of the morning's inspection, Keast took a by now very worried-looking Snell to lunch at Cy's. He intended to utilize lunch to do the performance appraisal and to suggest several courses of action that might be taken to remedy the Moncton problems. He was disturbed and somewhat surprised by what they had uncovered in their morning's work.

The bleak view of the Petitcodiac River at low tide which was visible from the restaurant window provided an appropriate backdrop to their luncheon conversation. Keast began: "Look Ron, you're over $5 million outstanding and $400,000 of that is overdue. We can't find half of what we're looking for in your records, and no one seems to know what they're doing. You admit yourself that things are out of hand." "But Mr. Keast, I've told you that I know we're having problems, but I think it is up to me to solve them. I've been the manager here for eight years, and I promise that within six months we'll have everything back to normal."

Toying with his lobster thermidor, Keast considered what he should and could do. He had certainly given Snell ample notice of dissatisfaction with the branch's operation, and the prospect for improvement seemed dim. On the other hand, Snell had a long record of satisfactory work with only one year of poor operation. He had been manager of the Moncton branch for eight years and had the longest stay of any branch manager in the region, as well as the longest service of any of the current staff at that branch. Keast thought that this visit had impressed on all the Moncton staff the alarm with which their performance was viewed by him. Weighing this, Keast advised Snell that "the inspection this morning has convinced me that changes have to be made. I think you knew this. You have worked well in the past, but it looks to me that you may need some help in bringing the turnaround about." Snell agreed that he needed help. Keast continued: "My assistant worked at the Halifax branch before he became my assistant at regional. You met him this morning. What do you think of him?" Snell responded in a noncommittal fashion saying, "He certainly seems efficient and gets right to the problem without fooling around. He seems fine. Why?" "Well, Ron, you suggested that Jerry MacDonald isn't doing his job the way you'd like him to. I'll see him this afternoon for his performance appraisal, and I propose to offer him a field salesman position in Prince Edward Island. I would like to replace him temporarily with my assistant, Alex DeCoste," Stunned at this suggestion, Snell could only nod. He had half expected to be fired himself.

Before returning to the office Keast told Snell that this move was only temporary and would last for three months. At the end of that time he would return to Moncton and reinspect the branch. Both expressed the hope that the results would warrant a rerating of the branch from poor to at least satisfactory.

On returning to the office Keast spent half an hour with Jerry MacDonald, explaining the reasons for the changes and his new reponsibilities. Jerry was 40 years old and had once been the branch manager in Edmundston, New Brunswick, before coming to Moncton. His performance in Edmundston had resulted in his becoming assistant manager at the Moncton branch. Since then he had not shown much interest in becoming a branch manager again. He accepted the proposed change calmly. Keast then met with Snell and DeCoste, and they discussed the changes that would have to be made in order to eliminate the current operating problems. DeCoste made several suggestions regarding collections, personnel training, and new business, which were greeted with mild interest by Snell. They agreed to explore these ideas more fully when DeCoste returned February 19 to assume his new duties. Keast and DeCoste then left the Moncton branch to catch their return flight to Halifax. On the return flight Keast impressed upon DeCoste the importance of getting the Moncton branch back in shape, not only for the sake of the branch's health, but also because other branch managers in the region were keenly interested in how Keast would handle the situation.

## ☐ Changes

Returning the following Monday, DeCoste and Snell met briefly and exchanged pleasantries. Snell then formally introduced him to the rest of the staff, some of whom DeCoste had met the previous Wednesday. Most of the staff gave DeCoste a warm greeting. The staff consisted of three collection officers, a cashier/cash journal clerk, and three file clerk/typists (a fourth had quit a week earlier). The accounts supervisor position remained unfilled. (See Exhibit 1 for an organizational chart of the Moncton branch.) Snell and DeCoste then returned to discuss the changes that needed to be made.

As with all the D.A.C. branches which had both a manager and an assistant manager, the Moncton manager's job description prescribed his primary duties as that of seeking

**EXHIBIT 1. Organization Chart: February 19, 1973**

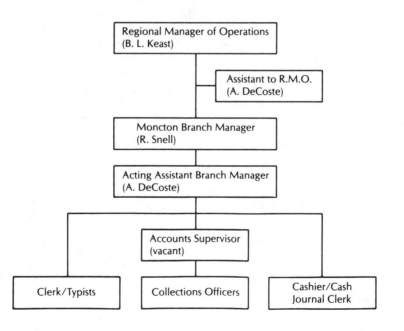

new customers (both consumer and commercial), promoting sales, and performing all public relations duties. These duties called for significant amounts of field work, and as a result the daily supervision of office work was assigned to the assistant manager. DeCoste would assume all responsibilities for directing and appraising office personnel and acting as liaison between the staff and the manager where necessary. In the Monday meeting the two men agreed that DeCoste would run the office as his job description indicated but that any significant changes and decisions that DeCoste might make would be thoroughly discussed with Snell before making them.

On the afternoon of the 19th, DeCoste met with the collections staff and explained the changes to be made in the collection of past due and current accounts. The collection officers were to have all the accounts pulled which were 60 or more days overdue and resolve these accounts according to procedures set forth in the procedures manual. Once these were settled, they would then focus their attention on the next most critical group, the 30 to 60 days overdue accounts. It was agreed that these 250 accounts would be processed in two weeks' time. DeCoste promised that a replacement for the previously fired accounts supervisor would be on the job within two weeks. In the meantime he designated the most senior of the officers as the temporary chief of this concerted effort.

That afternoon DeCoste met with the three clerk/typists and spent the rest of the day reorganizing the filing system and instructing them in the standard procedures for keeping account records current. This procedure consisted of the dating of all payments on the reverse of the customer's account card and the daily pulling of all account cards whose payments were due that day. These cards were then placed at the back of the "accounts payable" file. When accounts were paid, the cashier/journal clerk noted this on the card and placed them in the "to file" box, to be filed by the clerk/typists. Two of the girls claimed to have never been trained in these procedures and made reference to account cards which had been handled somewhat carelessly in the past. It was hoped that this systematic customer accounts method would reduce the number of customer complaints.

By the end of February the office had begun to operate more smoothly than it had for some time. The office now had its full complement of staff, morale had improved, the number of uncollected overdue accounts had been reduced to 100, and DeCoste felt progress was being made. However, new problems were beginning to arise.

## ☐ March

The first problem arose at the end of the month. The February report was due March 3rd, which meant that the actual completion date would be Thursday, the 1st. It was DeCoste's responsibility to complete the task and on Wednesday he asked the staff (exclusive of Mr. Snell) to work overtime compiling data for the report. This request met with loud disapproval. The staff claimed that this had not been the practice for some time, and when it had been, the staff had had to buy their own supper. Mr. Snell had ended the policy of D.A.C. paying for the dinner, claiming that it was too costly, and the evening work at month's end ended shortly thereafter. The procedure manual stipulated that agreement to work overtime once a month was a condition of employment and the D.A.C. would pay for any expenses (including meals) incurred as a result.

Another problem related to an informal practice which had existed for some time. Between Keast's inspection visit and DeCoste's arrival as assistant manager, Snell had instructed all the staff that coffee breaks were to be eliminated. Snell continued to take a break twice a day in the coffee shop next door. On two occasions after his arrival, DeCoste accompanied Snell on his coffee break. On both occasions Snell belittled the staff, complaining about their ineptness, criticized his previous assistant manager, and complained that after 18 years of service with the company they had forgotten about him. The staff began to sneak in thermoses of tea and coffee for use during Snell's regular visits to the coffee shop.

A third problem began occurring immediately after DeCoste's arrival. Arguments between staff members began to occur over who was to do what. Snell would hear these disputes, come out of his office, and immediately direct the employees involved to do the tasks in the manner he indicated, all of this before DeCoste could act to resolve the dispute. On these occasions Snell referred to the need to run an efficient office.

An additional problem began during DeCoste's second week at Moncton. One of the collection officers approached him regarding a raise, pointing out that the last raise he had had was 18 months ago and it was for only $3 per week, raising him to $118. Alex checked the employee's personnel file and found he had not been appraised since the time of his last raise, despite the fact that it was D.A.C. policy to perform employee reviews annually on the anniversary of their employment. A raise seemed warranted to Alex as the officer was making $500 below the average for collection officers in the region with similar lengths of service, although there was a considerable range in salaries throughout the region. DeCoste approached Snell but was told that no raises would be granted until the rating of the branch was judged satisfactory by the RMO. He claimed the employee was being overpaid now and referred to the outstanding accounts problem. DeCoste responded, "Look, Mr. Snell, I've examined all the personnel files for all our staff and have found the rates of pay to be well below the D.A.C. rates in the Atlantic region and our staff knows this. I think we need to catch up on our raises. I know Jerry MacDonald left this to you, but you're too busy as it is and we're way overdue on the annual appraisals. As it is now, none of the staff knows why they have not had raises and that includes Jerry before he left." Snell's response was short and repeated his claim that no raises would be approved until the branch shaped up. DeCoste was sure that Keast had given Snell no directions regarding salary changes. After this conversation of the 27th Alex informed the employee that he was trying to get a raise of $10 a week approved and that a strong showing on the outstanding collections would improve his case.

Finally, DeCoste noted that he had inherited a staff who had grown accustomed to going to Snell with any operating problems. This practice had been tacitly approved by Jerry MacDonald, who had become used to having Mr. Snell in the office most of the time and left most matters of consequence for Snell to deal with. MacDonald had not, however, refrained from joining in on the jokes made about Snell on the rare occasions when he was out of the office.

## ☐ The May Inspection

During the February–April period the monthly reports showed the branch's improvement in its accounts collections. The delinquency rate for April 1973 was down to 4 percent and only one clerk/typist had quit. Some of the administrative and operations problems had been resolved, but the problems of raises, office supervision by Snell, and the coffee breaks prohibitions remained while the number of accounts had continued to fall. Keast had requested a private report from DeCoste regarding the Moncton operations and had received it at the end of April. In it he made observations regarding the various administrative and operating problems and also noted his own frustration in his current position.

Keast was to arrive on May 7 and the Moncton staff anticipated his arrival with varying mixtures of anxiety, hope, and fascination. Keast's own view of the May visit was one of realizing that there was more involved than the health of the Moncton branch. Keast had tried carefully to consider all the factors regarding the Snell case in light of the current branch control system and the branch manager's job. Keast also had to keep in mind Snell's long service record, his welfare and that of the Moncton staff, as well as the health of the total Moncton operations and its place in the region. On the May 7, 7:30 A.M. flight, he reviewed what he intended to say at that meeting. The weather had improved since his last flight to Moncton and he hoped the Moncton operation would continue similarly to improve.

# Blair, Inc.*

The information for this case was obtained from Mr. Burton L. Davis, a recent employee of Blair, Inc.

Burton Davis started work last September as a mechanical engineer in the engine and motor division of the Blair Company, a large multiple-industry corporaton. The division, with 400 employees, was the principal employer in Midland. Formed four years ago, the division designed and manufactured small gasoline-combustion engines used in lawn mowers, motor scooters, snow throwers, portable saws, and power plants. Recently, the division had begun to turn out small electric motors. Division sales were currently $6 million.

Davis, seven years out of Purdue, had previously worked as an automotive engineer for two major automobile manufacturers and had excellent references from both. His salary at Blair was $950 per month.

He found that the engineering offices were new, of modern design, and air-conditioned. Supporting personnel in drafting, machine shop, and laboratory were adequate, and excellent physical facilities were available. Fringe benefits were at or above the industry level. For instance, Davis was promised a two-week vacation before completing a full year of service. His moving expenses were paid in full, in addition to $500 for an earlier trip to locate suitable housing. His travel expenses had also been covered when he came to Midland to interview the division chief engineer, Charles Lyons, and the corporate executive personnel director.

Burton Davis was assigned to the design and development department (see Exhibit 1 for partial organization chart). Four of the six other engineers had no work experience with other employers (which was also true of the chief engineer) and had been with the company from two to thirteen years.

Davis was assigned a numbered space in the main parking lot and was given a decal for his car window. Only the first three rows in this lot were reserved by number. Employment was high at the time, and the only space available was one vacated by a draftsman who had just resigned (see Exhibits 2 and 2A).

Davis soon noticed that more than half of those who parked in the two parking areas adjacent to the engineering offices were people he would not have expected to have more favorable parking locations than the engineers (see locations 6A and 6B, Exhibit 2A). Talking with his fellow engineers, he found they also thought it strange and had been irritated about it for some time.

The following personnel parked in these areas where space was reserved by name: C. Lyons, B. Swensen, J. Schomer, G. Tully, J. Barmeier, W. Wright, L. Stewart, S. Bonura, T. Michaels, V. Doran, and H. O'Brien. O'Brien was a disabled draftsman who used crutches—all agreed he deserved this location. Most engineers also agreed that Barmeier should park there; although his title was chief draftsman, he functioned almost as an assistant chief engineer and had been with the company for 20 years.

The engineering group felt strongly that Wright, Stewart, Bonura, Michaels, and Doran should not have parking privileges in a more desirable area than their own. Wright, assistant chief draftsman, supervised three drafting checkers and was seen constantly at

*Copyright J. L. Kellogg Graduate School of Management, Northwestern University. Reproduced by permission.

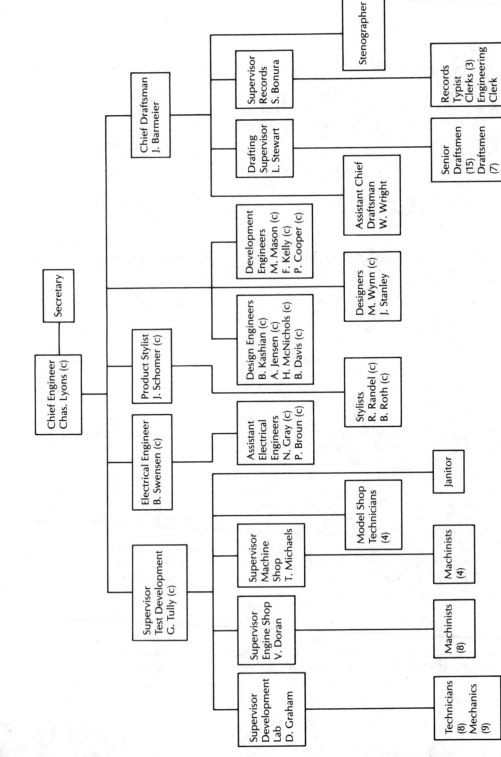

**EXHIBIT 1.  Partial Organization Chart: Engine and Motor Division**

(c) = College degree

Barmeier's elbow. The engineers called them "The Bobbsey twins." Stewart supervised some 20 draftsmen. In the engineers' view, his job consisted mainly of handing out time-cards and paychecks. Draftsmen were allocated among the engineers and rarely changed assignments. Stewart usually asked the engineers to fill out job-rating sheets for the draftsmen since he had no basis for appraising their performance. Bonura supervised several office clericals. Michaels of the machine shop and Doran of the engine shop were called supervisors, but the engineering group felt that "foremen" was a more accurate term.

Arnold Jensen (eight years with the company) and Paul Cooper (two years with Blair and two with Ellington Electronics) told Davis they were glad to find someone else concerned about this situation. Other engineers agreed but were reluctant to make an issue of it. One of them told Davis he might be considered a "rabbler-rouser" if he talked too much about it.

From what Davis could determine, everyone had parked in the main lot until a few years back. Then two sections of grass were removed to make the small parking areas (6A and 6B in Exhibit 2A).

Since there wasn't room to include Lyons, Swensen, Schomer, Tully, Barmeier, and all the engineers, Lyons said that rather than draw a line among them he would not have any of the engineers park there. Instead, all "direct" supervisors were given reserved slots, which just filled the space in the new area. Some engineers felt that Barmeier may have influenced this decision. Technically, the engineers were not "direct" supervisors, although they might have as many as ten people (draftsmen, typists, and so on) working under their control at one time.

Davis knew that every company had irritations with which one learned to live. However, as the weather grew worse, he walked through the unpaved gravel lot (which developed many holes in winter), plodded along the street (there was no sidewalk), and still halfway from the entrance, watched others drive in, park near the engineering offices, and enter before he reached the door.

Other things began to disturb him about his position. He found that Barmeier and Wright, without his approval, changed drawings he had released from Engineering.

There were three blank boxes on each engineering drawing. The draftsman would initial the "drawn by" space; the checker, the "checked by"; and the engineer, the "approved by." Lyons usually also initialed the last box, which provided room for two sets of initials. A few months after Davis had started work, Wright started erasing the engineer's initials from the "approved" box, entered his own, and told the engineers to initial after the checker's in the middle box. Jensen and Davis immediately told Wright that he could put his own initial after the checkers's, since he was supposed to be the checker's supervisor and they were the engineers in charge of the project. Davis told Wright, "If you feel otherwise about it, let's go to Lyons right now." Wright immediately agreed to initial after the checker.

Some time after this incident, a sign reading "Authorized Personnel Only" appeared on the door to the blueprint records storage room where Bonura and the clerks worked. Barmeier told the engineering group that the purpose of this was to avoid disturbing the overworked print girls and that the sign applied to all draftsmen and engineers. Although the engineers protested, Barmeier refused to change his stand. Lyons came by during the argument and moved the group into the conference room. The engineers explained that they often needed information from a tracing; a quick glance was enough before returning it to the file. Under the new system, they would have to order a print and wait to get the information. Lyons agreed with the engineers. Davis, Jensen, and Cooper were particularly pleased. Jensen said later, "At last *we* won something around here."

**EXHIBIT 2.    Index to Plant Layout in Exhibit 2A**

1. Main office door—visitors only.
2. Division administration.
3. Entrance—all administrative and engineering employees.
4. Entrance—factory employees.
5. Entrance—engineering labs (not an employee entrance).
6. Parking—engineering personnel, reserved by name.
7. Parking—administrative personnel, reserved by number.
8. Parking—most of the engineers, reserved by number.
9. Parking—most of the draftsmen, reserved by number.
10. Parking—Burton Davis, reserved by number.
11. Engineering gate—open all day.
12. Truck loading dock.
13. Paved empty space (could park eight cars).
14. Storage area (could park ten cars).
15. Storage area (could park five cars).
16. Storage area (could park ten cars).
17. Parking—supervisor of development lab, later supervisor of test and development also.
18. Parking—engineering station wagon and pickup truck.

It gradually became apparent to Davis that Lyons planned most of the engineering for his engineers. When assigning a new project, he would suggest the handling of it in such detail that all chance of creative or original work was eliminated. He frequently went out in the drafting room and told layout draftsmen how he wanted things done. Sometimes he even failed to bring the responsible engineer in on the discussion.

No engineering meetings were held. The only regular meeting was a "production" meeting for which the division manager and his plant manager came to Lyons's office. Lyons was the only engineer in the meetings, although he often stepped out to get a drawing or to get a question answered from a design or developmental engineer whose project was under discussion at the time. On the rare occasions when an engineer *was* called into the meeting, it was without any advance warning, so that he was frequently unable to furnish the desired information on the spot. Barmeier, Wright, and Bonura sat in on all meetings. Since these were the only regular conferences, discussions inevitably went beyond production problems and dealt with new products and plans as well. The sales manager and the corporate director of engineering attended some of the meetings. To find out what was going on, the engineers relied on the grapevine or were forced to ask Barmeier, Wright, or Bonura. They rarely talked with Lyons except when he was giving them ideas on how he thought they should do their jobs.

Dissatisfaction grew among the engineers, although several still felt there was nothing to be gained by "stirring things up." Davis felt that if Lyons realized the extent of the developing morale problem he would try to do something about it.

One evening he had an opportunity to talk to Lyons alone. He made it clear that he thought the situation was becoming critical. He told Lyons what he thought were the main points: The generally low status of the engineers and the feeling they had that they were not given enough responsibility. Davis pointed out that the parking situation was one of the main symbols of the engineers' status since it was a visible method of ranking. Lyons seemed uncomfortable throughout the discussion but said that he would think

**EXHIBIT 2A.**

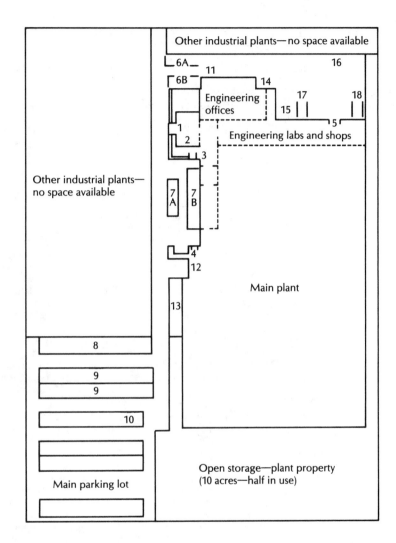

about it. Davis told Lyons that he was speaking only for himself but was sure his feelings were shared by most of the others. On leaving, Davis gave Lyons a reprint of an article on morale and suggested it might be of value.[1]

As months passed, no perceptible changes were made.[2] George Dunlop was hired to supervise the engineers with the title of "chief, design and development" and with the design and development engineers and the designers reporting to him. They had formerly

---

1. A portion of the article is reproduced in Exhibit 3.
2. During this period Burton Davis typed a memo and circulated it informally among individuals in the division (see Exhibit 4).

**EXHIBIT 3**

| Indicator area | High morale exists when— | Low morale exists when— |
|---|---|---|
| 1. The company | Lines of responsibility and authority are clear; coordination good; line staff teamwork generally productive; organization structure is flexible; managers can get to right official when necessary. | Authority overlaps; organizational structure is too complex; company has too many layers of review; communication breakdowns are frequent; reorganizations don't add up; committees interfere. |
| 2. Company-division practices | Good rapport exists among managers; agreements are honored; people know where they stand and how they are doing; policies are clearly and quickly communicated; reward system is fair and current. | There's too much paperwork; managers have to beat the system; excessive rivalry exists among the departments; deadlines don't mean a thing; it is hard to get needed information; ideas die on vine. |
| 3. Decisions | Decisions are tied in well to policies and plans; managers get chance to participate in decision making; delegation is adequate; bad decisions are withdrawn when necessary; accountability is clear. | Decisions are too slow, poorly timed; subordinate has little chance to participate in the making of decisions; delegation is meager; decisions unduly influenced by tradition; real issues are evaded. |
| 4. Leadership | Staff meetings are well run and produce results; boss keeps subordinates informed of policies and plans affecting them; people know the scope of their responsibilities; boss shows dignity and fairness. | Assignments and orders of boss are unclear; people have to work without knowing policy limitations; boss sets unreasonable deadlines; too many attempts are made at regimentation; standards fall. |
| 5. Group climate | Team takes pride in its performance; people will go to bat for each other; professional aims, standards are high; grievances of a member are heard; overall quality of group output is high-grade. | Too many cliques exist; favoritism is shown some; work output is inadequate; one person dominates the group; bickering is common; there are recurrent rule violations; professional standards are low. |
| 6. Job conditions | Managers find sufficient challenge in their jobs; abilities of people are utilized well; employees able to express their views; performance standards are realistic; workers get recognition when deserved. | It's difficult to get a job done; ideas put aside too often, too fast; people have to break rules to get action; boredom and restlessness are prevalent; pay scales lag behind the rates in other firms. |
| 7. Status | Job privileges are modest but good; management is receptive to an employee's views; talents are utilized; employees enjoy higher status in community because of their association with the company. | Favored few get recognition; opportunities for development are restricted; criticisms far exceed compliments; people must look out for themselves; firm has too many dead-end jobs. |

Source: Adapted from Nathaniel Stewart, "You Can Keep Morale High," *Nation's Business,* March 1963. Reprinted by permission.

reported directly to Lyons. (Dunlop parked in the engineering lot: Tully was moved to the rear with Graham, area #17 on Exhibit 2A—actually a more desirable spot, only 10 feet from a door.) Before Dunlop arrived, Lyons held a meeting with all salaried personnel to explain the decision to bring in a man from outside. He said that he thought the position could have been filled from within the company but that Edward King, the corporate director of engineering, thought that a man with considerable experience was needed. Davis considered it interesting that Lyons was only 34.

**EXHIBIT 4**

---

*Office Memo*

**ENGINE AND MOTOR ENGINEERING SECTION**

*To:*  "Supervisory" Personnel

*Subject:*  Fitness Program

Going along with the present Washington administration's emphasis on hiking as a means of improving the fitness of the American people, it is suggested that those Blair employees now parking near the building exchange parking places with the engine and motor section *engineers*. The engineers are in splendid shape from their long hikes and feel that it is only fair to share this conditioning. After a suitable "building-up" period, a rotation system will be worked out to insure the retention of all the fitness benefits.

*The Personnel Department*

---

Dunlop was 48 years old and had worked as an executive engineer for National Motors, for Burling Aircraft, and for Duval Maufacturing. Lyons mentioned that people might wonder why a man with this background would come here. He explained that Dunlop liked small towns and enjoyed this type of work and that money was not that important to him. Davis commented later to Jensen that "executive engineer" at National Motors meant a big job and that Dunlop must have had a real setback somewhere along the way. The engineers considered it significant that Dunlop was placed in charge of seven engineers with the draftsmen and technicians still reporting to others. Moreover, Barmeier was still next to Lyons with no intermediary. They also noted that Dunlop had not been given the title of assistant chief engineer.

Several engineers with long experience with the firm believed they should have been candidates for the job. Other engineers thought Dunlop might become a useful go-between for them. They saw that Barmeier took care of *his* people and Tully took care of *his*. Perhaps the engineers now had someone to put in a few good words for them. Dunlop seemed, at first, to be a much better administrator than Lyons. At least, the engineers felt he "talked a good game." They began to tell him about things they felt needed improvement or correction. But after two months it became apparent that Dunlop had not recommended any changes to Lyons. It appeared to Davis and others that he was loathe to tell Lyons anything that might be disturbing. The engineers felt that he was "running scared."

Davis suggested to Jensen and Cooper that talking to Dunlop was not unlike a session with a psychiatrist. You talked about your problems and felt better even though nothing really changed. Whenever anyone returned from a talk with Dunlop, a colleague would ask, "Did you have a nice couch session?"

As the small group talked about their problems, the situation became almost unbearable to Davis. There was considerable talk of other jobs, and occasionally one of the men would have an interview with another firm. Finally, Davis, Jensen, and Cooper decided to approach Lyons in a group. They had decided that they would all leave anyway unless changes were made. This "group action" was distasteful to them, but they felt that it was the only way to get Lyons to realize he had a real problem to face. There seemed to be little to lose.

Following are some of the comments made by the engineers and Lyons as they talked in the chief engineer's office one evening after work:

ENGINEER:   We feel a little silly talking about this, but since it does bother us and affects our morale, we feel you should know.

ENGINEER:   The parking position ranks everyone, whether or not you believe it does.

LYONS:   Where you park doesn't have anything to do with the way I rank you.

ENGINEER:   We feel that as highly paid college graduates who actually do the creative work we should rank above "assistant chief draftsmen" and "foremen."

ENGINEER:   Specifically, we feel that we should rank ahead of Wright, Stewart, Bonura, Doran, and Michaels.

LYONS:   Do you feel you are better than those people?

ENGINEER:   In terms of working for this company, yes. We would certainly be harder to replace. In any case, ranking is inevitable; we would like to think that you agree with us on where we rank.

LYONS:   You know that you make much more money than those people, don't you?

ENGINEER:   Yes, which is another reason for keeping the other symbols of rank in the same order.

ENGINEER:   Salary is not a problem. We do not feel overpaid or underpaid in our present jobs.

ENGINEER:   Whether or not *you* feel this is a problem, the fact that *we* feel it is a problem *makes* it a problem, by definition.

ENGINEER:   The fact that parking ranks us in status actually affects our job efficiency as it relates to others. We have more trouble "getting things done" if we don't have the status to back it up.

ENGINEER:   Saying that status symbols are unimportant doesn't make them go away. We live with status symbols all the time; unless they are distorted from the way most people expect to see them, they go unnoticed. Only when the symbol system gets out of line does it become a problem. This means that to have a smoothly functioning organization, an administrator has to consider status symbols and make every attempt to allocate them as his subordinates expect him to.

ENGINEER:   Doran and Michaels are foremen, no matter what fancy names they are called. Stewart is the drafting supervisor and should rank under us, but Barmeier and Wright are doing engineering work. If you want to rank them above us that is your decision, but their titles should be changed. A chief draftsman and his assistant should never rank above any engineer. The situation is similar to the army, where a master sergeant may have many years of experience and be valuable, but he does not outrank the greenest second lieutenant.

ENGINEER:   We note that you have the closest space to the door in the lots near engineering, and the division manager has the space closest to the door in the administration lot. Isn't it logical that the No. 2 ranking people have the next spaces, and so on down the line? That's the way almost everyone looks at it.

ENGINEER:   We don't care *where* we actually park. The question is *who* parks where. If everyone had the same long walk, there would be no problem.

ENGINEER:   Locating our parking spaces more conveniently without changing the relative status of the spaces will be no solution at all.

LYONS:   But where can I find more parking space?

ENGINEERS:   We think there are a number of areas that could be used, but some effort would be required. There is unused space in front of the plant (13 in Exhibit 2A), or space could be made available by moving some of the stored materials from the area east of Engineering (14, 15, and 16 in Exhibit 2A). Even if you can't find space for improved parking for everyone, engineers should park in that lot. Not necessarily the three of us, but *engineers.*

ENGINEER: The fact that you don't or can't trust us with more responsibility affects our morale and job interest also.

LYONS: But I do give as much responsibility as possible.

ENGINEER: But you act as if you don't really trust us.

LYONS: It's not that I don't trust you; it's just that I want to see the job done right.

As the talk ended, Lyons appeared to be disturbed and concerned. He said that he would think about what had been said and would see if there was anything that he could do.

Nevertheless, the three engineers were sure that Lyons had not really understood them. In spite of their emphasis on "not where, but *who,*" they sensed that the chief engineer believed that all they wanted was better, closer parking places. They felt he didn't understand their desire for more responsibility, either; he seemed to think they had all the responsibility they had a right to expect. They agreed that his comment on "doing the job right" demonstrated how little effect they had had.

They predicted that any solution that Lyons might devise would be unsatisfactory. They wondered if they should take any other steps or just wait and hope that Lyons had more understanding than they suspected. They realized that if the solution was unsatisfactory it was the end of the road. They could hardly start the process all over again.

# The Crown Fastener Company

During the summer between his junior and senior years at Dartmouth College, Edgar Hagan took a job as a student trainee with the Crown Fastener Company, a medium-sized manufacturer and distributor of nuts and bolts. The training program Hagan was placed in consisted of four weeks in the company warehouse, four weeks in the company factory, and two weeks in the company offices. There were five students in the program, all of whom had the understanding that they would receive jobs as salesmen with the company after two summers in the program.

On the first day of work, all five of the trainees met in the office of John Cusick, the superintendent of the warehouse. Cusick was a man in his middle thirties, a former decorated navy veteran, and a graduate of Dartmouth College. After outlining the work program for the next four weeks and assigning each of the trainees to a specific department for the first two weeks, he offered this advice to them: "Fellows, I would be very careful in my relationships with the employees here if I were you. The majority of the people here are a pretty crude bunch. Their work is pretty much physical and routine in nature; as a result, we can afford to hire men of generally low intelligence. They're all . . . from the slums, and they're tough customers. So watch out for your valuables, and don't start any trouble with them."

For the first two weeks, Hagan was assigned to the sixth floor, in the hexagon nut department, under the supervision of Guido Bovanni, a man who had been with the company since its inception twenty-two years before. Bovanni, a short but extremely powerful man, spoke in broken English and had quite a difficult time reading any material with which he was not previously familiar. When Cusick introduced Hagan to Bovanni, he said: "Guido, this is Edgar Hagan, a college trainee who'll be with us for the summer. I've decided to have him work here for the first two weeks, and I'd like you to teach him all you know about nuts. Give him all the odd jobs you have so he'll get experience with as many different types of nuts as possible. Well, good luck, Hagan. We'll get together again soon."

After Cusick left, Bovanni said to Hagan: "A college boy, eh! I'll learn you about nuts, but I'll do it my way. Cusick thinks I can learn you in two weeks what I've learned in twenty years. Christ! Don't pay no attention to him. We'll start you helping the packers so you can work with the nuts we ship most of. You'll be lucky if you can learn them in two weeks. Then each day, I'll try to learn you a few of the nuts we don't see very often."

Hagan was amazed that each of the nine employees in the hexagon nut department quickly told him almost the same thing as soon as he was alone with them. Typical of these comments was this statement by Ted Grant, an elderly packer: "If I were you, I'd stay on the good side of Guido. He's one hell of a good foreman and really knows his stuff. He can teach you more about nuts and bolts than any guy in this place. Work hard for him, and you'll get along swell here."

Hagan did his best to follow this advice and soon found that Bovanni was spending more and more time with him. He was very surprised when on Friday, Bovanni said: "Grab your lunch, and let's go eat across the street." Bovanni regularly ate his lunch in a little bar across from the warehouse with a group of about seven other foremen. The conversation ranged from families to sport but soon settled on Cusick. Hagan was amazed at this because he, a newcomer, was there, and interpreted this to mean that Bovanni must have spoken to the men, saying that he was o.k. It was quickly obvious that Bovanni was the leader among this group; and when he summed up the conversation in the following manner, everyone seemed in complete agreement with him: "Cusick tries hard. He's tried to improve things here, but he hasn't had the experience. He must be able to handle Charley Crown,* though; look at the money he's got us for new equipment. But Christ, then he screws up and buys the wrong stuff. He just don't know what to do and won't listen when we tell him."

On Friday of Hagan's first week, Cusick issued a bulletin stating that all forms used in the routing of materials in the warehouse would be changed to a slightly more complicated type on which material locations could be designated more precisely. The bulletin was handed out to all warehouse employees with their pay envelopes at the close of work Friday. Included was a group of the new forms. The bulletin simply stated that the change was to be made and requested that each man familiarize himself with the new forms over the weekend so that he could use them correctly on Monday. The men just took the material and stuffed it into their pockets in their haste to catch their streetcars home.

On Monday morning, everyone in the hexagon nut department quickly went to work distributing the backlog of materials that had been delivered on Saturday, making a note of each shipment's ultimate location. As was the practice in this department, all of the department personnel met at Bovanni's desk at 10:30 A.M. to give this information to Bovanni so that he could copy it onto the formal forms which went to the office for inventory control. Bovanni claimed he used this procedure so that all the forms would be uniformly filled out and not mutilated by the men carrying them around as they worked. It was quite obvious, however, that his main purpose for insisting on this procedure was that he wanted to know where every shipment on his floor was located, so that when orders came through from the office, he could tell the men exactly where the material ordered was located, from memory. Hagan was constantly amazed by Bovanni's ability to remember exactly where, within each tier and row, a certain shipment was located. This ability had been built up over a period of years, and Bovanni was obviously quite proud of it.

At the Monday morning meeting, there was a considerable difference of opinion among the various department personnel as to how the locations should be entered on the new forms. Bovanni insisted that it should be done in the same manner as before, where the aisle and tier of each shipment were recorded, while most of the other men protested that additional information as to the exact location within each aisle and tier should be noted. Bovanni argued that this would provide unnecessary detail and would only confuse things. He was quite adamant about this, and the other men quickly acceded to his point of view.

The next morning, Cusick came up to the sixth floor and walked directly to Bovanni's desk. He said in quite a loud voice: "Guido, you're filling out the forms all wrong. Didn't you read the notice? You're still doing it the old way, and that's just what we're trying to get away from. Do you think we would go to all this trouble only to have things done in the same old way? Now you've really got the office all fouled up. We need new forms on all the materials you received yesterday. You'd better get at it right away so they can make orders out on some of that material."

---

*The president of the Crown Fastener Company.

Guido was sitting at his desk, looking up a catalogue number, while Cusick was talking to him. He was obviously getting madder and madder as Cusick spoke. Finally, he broke in.

**Guido Bovanni:**    Look, Mr. Cusick, this department never had no trouble with its locations before. We've been getting along fine. Why do you have to foul up by making us change everything? I've been running this department for one hell of a long time, and I guess to Christ I know as much about it as you do. Why don't you handle the top brass and let me handle my department? As long as I get the work done, what do you care how I do it? When those orders come through, I'll be able to find those kegs just like I always have.

**John Cusick:**    That's the trouble with you Guido; you only think of yourself. I've made this change in the entire warehouse. You're the only one bitching about it. From now on, the office wants a complete record of exactly where everything is. Now, dammit, as long as I'm running this warehouse, we're going to do it my way!

**Bovanni** *(getting madder all the time):*    Listen, Cusick, you may run this warehouse, but I run this floor. Nobody really needs to know those locations except me, and you know it. The way we're doing things here works fine, and you know it. Why pick on me? Why don't you go climb on some of the other boys that don't get their work done? Why come nosing around here telling me how to do my job?

# Hausser Food Products Company

Brenda Cooper, the southeastern regional sales manager for the Hausser Food Products (HFP) Company, expressed her concern to a researcher from a well-known eastern business school.

> I think during the past year I've begun to make some progress here, but the situation is a lot more difficult than I thought when I first arrived. Our current methods of selling products just are not adequate, and the people in the field don't seem interested in coming up with new ideas or approaches to selling.

## ☐ Background

Hausser Food Products Company is a leading producer and marketer of infant foods in the United States. The company manufactures and markets a whole line of foods for the infant market, including strained meats, vegetables, fruits, and combination dishes. The product line includes foods that are completely strained, for infants, as well as foods that are partially strained or chopped, for children 6 months of age and older. HFP has traditionally been the leader in this field. The company has no other major product lines. Its products are known for their high quality and its name is well-known to most consumers.

HFP owns its production and warehousing facilities. Its well-developed distribution network provides direct delivery of products to the warehouses and stores of most major food chains. The smallest segment of its market is composed of a limited number of institutions for children that purchase HFP products in bulk.

HFP has had a long history in the infant food business. Traditionally the market leader, it has over the years maintained a market share of approximately 60 percent. During the 1960s, the firm experienced rapid expansion and growth. The number of different types of infant food products increased tremendously to keep up with increasing demand for a greater number of foods and a greater variety of products. From the mid-1960s to the mid-1970s, growth in sales approached 15 percent compounded yearly.

During the past few years, HFP has faced a greatly changing market for infant foods. The sudden decrease in the birth rate brought about major changes in the whole infant food business, and projections of sales had to be altered drastically. In addition, the new concern about food additives, including flavorings, dyes, and preservatives, also had its impact on the baby food market. Many consumer advocates argued that mothers would be much safer in making their own baby foods, rather than purchasing the commercially prepared products, such as those manufactured by HFP. Finally, competition in the baby food market also increased with private brands competing on the basis of price against the nationally advertised brand names.

These changing conditions had been viewed with great alarm by the top management of HFP. The drop in growth of sales (to 3 percent in the most recent year) was accompanied by an even greater drop in earnings, as management felt itself faced with unused plant and warehouse capacity. Management is currently concerned with looking for new ways to stimulate demand for HFP products as well as with the longer-range problem of finding other complementary products to develop and market.

## ☐ **Marketing Organization**

In 1975 a researcher from a major business school became involved in studying the marketing organization of HFP as part of a larger-scale research project. His inquiries led him to look closely at the sales department and to investigate some of the problems that were being experienced here.

The marketing function at HFP is directed by a vice president for marketing, who reports directly to the president of HFP. (See Exhibit 1 for a partial organization chart.)

**EXHIBIT 1.    Partial Chart of Formal Organization Structure of Hausser Food Products**

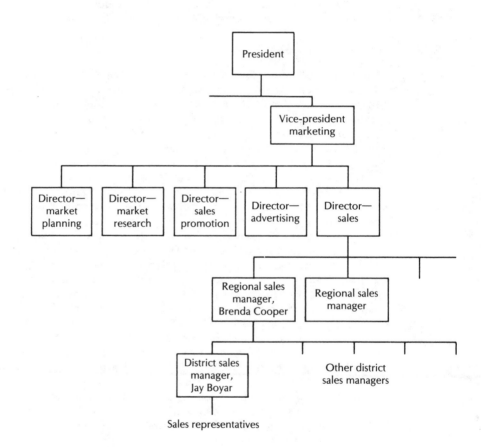

The vice president for marketing has five functional directors reporting to him. Each director is responsible for one of the major areas of marketing activity, including market research, market planning, sales promotion, advertising, and sales. The sales department, which has been the focus of much recent concern, is headed by the director of sales. This person directs selling activities in the entire United States. The country is divided into seven major regions, each of which has a regional sales manager. Regions are further divided into districts—each district may include a range of geographic areas, from several states to part of a city, depending upon the particular location. The district manager heads the HFP sales team for each district. The sales team has the ultimate job of selling HFP products to customers, offering promotions, maintaining contact with the customers, ensuring adequate shelf space, etc.

A key element in the marketing organization is the regional sales manager position. This position has been an entry position for many bright, aggressive, and well-trained young people who subsequently have risen to high-level positions within the company. The current president of the company, the vice-president for marketing, and three of the five marketing directors began their careers at HFP as regional sales managers.

Brenda Cooper, the southeastern regional sales manager, is fairly typical of the kind of person placed in that position. Brenda entered an MBA program immediately after graduation from one of the best women's colleges in the country. Majoring in marketing, she did extremely well in business school and graduated near the top of her class. Upon graduation she received many job offers and took a position as an assistant product manager in a large nonfood consumer products company. During 4 years at that firm, she performed extremely well both in the management of existing products and in the launching of new products. By the end of her fourth year, however, she was becoming restless and, seeing no opportunities for quick advancement, decided to accept an offer to become a regional sales manager at HFP. The salary was attractive, and she would receive a potentially large bonus based on the profit performance of the entire company. What also attracted Brenda was the possibility of advancement within the company; she had heard that many of the senior staff had started in the regional manager position. At the end of her first year, Brenda is still very much concerned about doing well in her job; in particular, she is adjusting to her role as a manager, with six district managers reporting to her.

## ☐ Sales Plan

Much of the activity of the regional managers centers around the yearly sales plan. The sales plan is essentially a budget that includes projections of sales, expenses, and profit. It serves as the basic yardstick against which the performance of regional managers is measured.

Each year the sales plan is developed through a multistage process, as follows.

1. The director of market planning projects sales for the coming year. At the same time, the director of sales asks the regional managers for their projections of sales for the next year. These projections are usually extrapolations of previous-year figures with adjustments for major changes in the market year, if any.
2. The directors of market planning and sales, along with their staffs, negotiate to resolve the differences that usually exist between their two projections (market planning always tends to be higher). Out of these negotiations emerges the sales plan for the coming year. This plan includes budgeted expenditures for promotions, advertising, expenses, and so forth, as well as projected sales volume and profit.

3. The sales director allocates portions of the sales plan to each of the regional managers, who are responsible for meeting the plan within their own region. Regional managers, in turn, allocate parts of the plan to each of their district sales managers and teams.
4. The district managers receive the plan in the form of sales targets and expense budgets for the coming year. The district manager typically receives a relatively low base salary combined with a relatively large yearly bonus, which is based entirely on the performance of the sales team, measured against the sales plan. At the end of the year, the district manager is also given a pool of bonus dollars, also based on team performance against plan, to be distributed to the individual salespeople. Salespeople also receive relatively low base salaries and look to their yearly bonuses as a major source of income.

## ☐  Problems of Regional Sales Managers

As part of the investigation, the researcher visited Brenda Cooper in her Atlanta office. After describing the operations of her region, Brenda began to talk about some of her problems.

> We in HFP are currently wrestling with the problem of a very mature product line. Top management has begun to see the critical need to diversify, in other words to hedge our bets with some other lines of products which are not dependent upon a steadily increasing birth rate. They have been talking about some interesting and exciting things, but any new product is still a few years away from being introduced . . . . In the meantime, it is the job of us out here in the field to come up with new ideas to help keep up sales of our existing product line. I think there must be better ways of selling our product and I am sure that there are new things that we can do to get much more performance out of the line than we are seeing now. The problem is that the best ideas usually come in from the field, from the salespeople themselves, and we really have had very little from our sales teams. They seem content to continue to let the products sell themselves and just keep the shelves stocked, as they have for years. I just don't get any new ideas or approaches from my sales teams.

Brenda and the researcher then reviewed the sales figures for her region, in particular the sales performance of the different areas. Brenda noted:

> Look here at Jay Boyar and his group in Florida. This is a prime example of the kind of problem I am facing. While we have been facing decreasing growth in sales, and actual drop off of sales some places, Jay's group consistently comes in at 10 percent above the sales plan. I've been down there and met with them and I've talked with Jay numerous times, but I can't figure out how they do it. They must be doing something that could be used in other places, but every time I ask how they do it I get very vague answers, such as, "Well, we work very hard down here" or "We work together as a group; that's how we are able to do well." I'm sure it must be more than that, but I can't seem to get them to open up.

## ☐  Visit to the Florida Sales Team

Intrigued with the Florida figures, the researcher arranged an extensive visit (during January and February) with the Florida sales team. The researcher was given a letter of introduction from the vice president for marketing. This letter explained that the researcher was collecting background information for a major research project that would be of help to the company, that any information collected would be confidential, and that the sales team should provide any needed assistance.

At first Jay Boyar and his group made no attempt to hide their suspicion of the researcher. Slowly, however, as the researcher spent numerous days in the field, riding the Florida roads with each salesperson, they began to trust him and reveal how they felt about their jobs and the company. (See Exhibit 2 for a listing of the staff of the Florida Sales team).

David Berz, the unofficial assistant team manager, talked at length about why he liked his job.

> What I really like is the freedom. I'm really my own boss most of the time. I don't have to be sitting in an office for the whole day, with some supervisor hanging over my shoulder and looking at all of my work. I get to be outside, here in the car, doing what I like to be doing—being out in the world, talking to people, and making the sale.

Neil Portnow, who had been with the company longer than the other team members, commented on the group:

> This is really a great bunch of guys to work with. I've been with a couple of different groups, but this is the best. I've been together with Dave and Jay for about 15 years now and I wouldn't trade it for anything. Jay is really one of us; he knows that we know how to do our jobs and he doesn't try to put a lot of controls on us. We go about doing the job the way we know is best and that is OK with Jay.
>
> The guys are also good because they help you out. When I was sick last year, they all pitched in to cover my territory so that we could make our plan plus 10 percent without reporting my illness to the company. They can also be hard on someone who doesn't realize how things work here. A few years back, when one of the young guys, Fred, came on with us, he was all fired up. He was going to sell baby food to half the mothers in Florida, personally! He didn't realize that you have to take your time and not waste your effort for the company. The other guys gave him a little bit of a hard time at first—he found his orders getting lost and shipments being changed—but when he finally came to his senses, they treated him great and showed him the ropes.

Picking up on the references to "the company," the researcher asked Neil to talk more about HFP as a place to work:

> It's all pretty simple: the company is out to screw the salespeople. Up in Atlanta and New York, all they are concerned about is the numbers, meeting the plan no matter

**EXHIBIT 2.  Staff of the Florida Sales Team**

| Name | Position | Age | Years with HFP | Education |
|------|----------|-----|------|-----------|
| Jay Boyar | District sales manager | 52 | 30 | High school |
| David Berz | Salesperson (assistant manager) | 50 | 30 | High school |
| Neil Portnow | Salesperson | 56 | 36 | High school |
| Alby Siegel | Salesperson | 49 | 18 | ½ yr college |
| Mike Wolly | Salesperson | 35 | 12 | 2 yr college |
| John Cassis | Salesperson | 28 | 4 | BA |
| Fred Hopengarten | Salesperson | 30 | 3 | BA |

what. The worst thing is if you work hard, meet the plan, and then keep going so you can earn some decent money. Then they go and change the plan next year. They increase the sales quota so that you have to work harder just to earn the same money! It just doesn't pay to bust your ass . . . .

The people in Atlanta also want all kinds of paperwork: sales reports, call reports, all kinds of reports. If you filled out all of the things that they want you to fill out, you'd spend all your time doing paperwork and no time selling, looking for new accounts, making cold calls, or any of the things that a salesperson really is supposed to do if he's going to keep on top of his area.

As the researcher talked with the other salespeople, he found general agreement with Neil's views on the company. Alby Siegel added:

The biggest joke they got going is the suggestion plan. They want us to come up with new ideas about how the company should make more money. The joke of it is, if you come up with an idea that, for instance, makes the company a couple of hundred thousand profit across the country, they are generous enough to give you $500. That's the top figure, $500 for your idea. That amount of money is an insult . . . .

One thing you have to remember is that in one way or another, we're all in this for the money. Despite what they say, it's not the greatest thing to be out on the road all of the time, staying in motels, fighting the competition. But it's worth it because I can earn more money doing this job than anything else I could do. I can live better than most "professionals" with their college degrees . . . . Jay is pretty good about the money thing too. He makes sure that we get our bonus, year in and year out and he keeps the people in Atlanta from taking our bonus checks away from us. He's not management—he's one of us. You can really tell it during the team meetings. Once every 2 months we all meet in Tampa and spend a day going over the accounts and talking about ideas for selling. We spend the whole day in this hotel room, working, and then we go out and spend the whole night on the town, usually drinking. Jay is one of us . . . . Many is the night that I've helped carry him back to the hotel.

After about 4 weeks with the team, the researcher participated in one of the bi-monthly team meetings. During lunch, Jay came over to him and began to talk:

Listen, I need to talk over something with you before we start the afternoon meeting. We trust you so we're going to let you in on our little discovery. You may have noticed that we aren't doing so badly, and you're right. The reason is a little finding made by Alby about 3 years ago. He was out in one of the stores and he noticed that a lot of people buying our products were not mothers of young children, but old people! We started looking around and we began to notice that a lot of older people were buying HFP jars. We talked with some of them and it turns out that they like our stuff, particularly those people who have all kinds of teeth problems.

Since then we've developed a very lucrative trade with a number of the old folks's homes, and we've been able to sell to them through some of the supermarkets who are located in areas where there is a larger older population. It's a great new piece of the market: it takes the pressure off us to make plan, and we don't even have to push it very hard to keep making plan and about 10 percent.

We've also been pretty successful in keeping Atlanta from finding out. If they knew, they'd up our plan, leaving us no time to sell, no time to develop new customers, no time to make cold calls, or anything. This way we use this new area as a little cushion, and it helps us to stay on top of our territory. I had to tell you because we'll be talking about the old people this afternoon. The boys seem to think you are OK, so I'm trusting you with it. I hope I'm not making a mistake telling you this.

## ☐  **Back in Atlanta**

Soon after the Tampa meeting, the researcher left the Florida sales team and returned to New York. On the way back, he made a final brief visit with Brenda Cooper. He found her even more concerned about her problems.

> I'm getting all kinds of pressure from New York to jack up my sales in the region. They are pushing me to increase the plan for the next year. I really am beginning to feel that my job is on the line on this one. If I can't come up with something that is good in the coming year, the future for me at HFP looks bleak.
>
> At the same time, I'm getting flack from my district managers. They all say that they're running flat out as is and they can't squeeze any more sales out of the district than they already are. Even Jay Boyer is complaining that he may not make plan if we have another increase next year. At the same time, he always seems to pull out his 10 percent extra by the end of the year; I wonder what they're really doing down there.

# Bill French, Accountant

Bill French picked up the phone and called his boss, Wes Davidson, controller of Duo-Products Corporation. "Say, Wes, I'm all set for the meeting this afternoon. I've put together a set of break-even statements that should really make the boys sit up and take notice—and I think they'll be able to understand them, too." After a brief conversation about other matters, the call was concluded and French turned to his charts for one last checkout before the meeting.

French had been hired six months earlier as a staff accountant. He was directly responsible to Davidson and, up to the time of this case, had been doing routine types of analysis work. French was an alumnus of a liberal arts undergraduate school and graduate business school, and was considered by his associates to be quite capable and unusually conscientious. It was this latter characteristic that had apparently caused him to "rub some of the working guys the wrong way," as one of his co-workers put it. French was well aware of his capabilities and took advantage of every opportunity that arose to try to educate those around him. Wes Davidson's invitation for French to attend an informal manager's meeting had come as some surprise to others in the accounting group. However, when French requested permission to make a presentation of some break-even data, Davidson acquiesced. The Duo-Products Corporation had not been making use of this type of analysis in its review or planning programs.

Basically, what French had done was to determine the level of operation at which the company must operate in order to break even. As he phrased it, "The company must be able to sell at least a sufficient volume of goods so that it will cover all of the variable costs of producing and selling the goods; further, it will not make a profit unless it covers the fixed, or nonvariable, costs as well. The level of operation at which total costs (that is, variable plus nonvariable) are just covered is the break-even volume. This should be the lower limit in all of our planning."

The acounting records had provided the following information that French used in constructing his chart:

Plant Capacity—2,000,000 units
Past Year's Level of Operations—1,500,000 units
Average Unit Selling Price—$1.20
Total Fixed Costs—$520,000
Average Variable Unit Cost—$0.75

From this information, he observed that each unit contributed $0.45 to fixed overhead after covering the variable costs. Given total fixed costs of $520,000, he calculated that 1,155,556 units must be sold in order to break even. He verified this conclusion by calculating the dollar sales volume that was required to break even. Since the variable costs per unit were 62.5 percent of the selling price, French reasoned that 37.5 percent of every sales dollar was left available to cover fixed costs. Thus, fixed costs of $520,000 require sales of $1,386,667 in order to break even.

When he constructed a break-even chart to present the information graphically, his conclusions were further verified. The chart also made it clear that the firm was operating at a fair margin over the break-even requirements, and that the profits accruing (at the rate of 37.5 percent of every sales dollar over break even) increased rapidly as volume increased (see Exhibit 1).

**EXHIBIT 1.   Duo-Products Corporation's Break-Even Chart — Total Business**

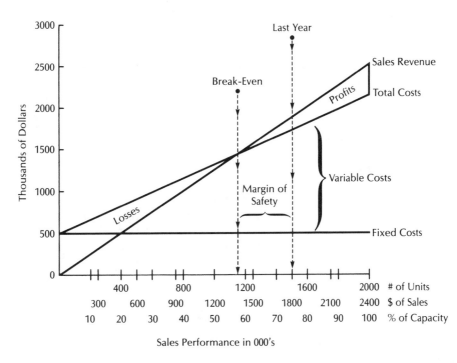

Break-Even Volume = 1,156,000 units, or
$1,387,000

Shortly after lunch, French and Davidson left for the meeting. Several representatives of the manufacturing departments were present, as well as the general sales manager, two assistant sales managers, the purchasing officer, and two men from the product engineering office. Davidson introduced French to the few men that he had not already met and then the meeting got under way. French's presentation was the last item on Davidson's agenda, and in due time the controller introduced French, explaining his interest in cost control and analysis.

French had prepared enough copies of his chart and supporting calculations so that they could be distributed to everyone at the meeting. He described carefully what he had done and explained how the chart pointed to a profitable year, dependent on meeting the volume of sales activity that had been maintained in the past. It soon became apparent that some of the participants had known in advance what French planned to discuss; they had come prepared to challenge him and soon had taken control of the meeting. The following exchange ensued (see Exhibit 3 at end of case for a checklist of participants with their titles):

COOPER *(Production Control):*  You know, Bill, I'm really concerned that you haven't allowed for our planned changes in volume next year. It seems to me that you should have allowed for the sales department's guess that we'll boost sales by 20 percent, unit-wise. We'll be pushing 90 percent of what we call capacity then. It sure seems that this would make quite a difference in your figuring.

FRENCH:  That might be true, but as you can see, all you have to do is read the cost and profit relationship right off the chart for the new volume. Let's see—at a million-eight units we'd . . . .

WILLIAMS *(Manufacturing):*  Wait a minute, now!!! If you're going to talk in terms of 90 percent of capacity, and it looks like that's what it will be, you damn well better note that we'll be shelling out some more for the plant. We've already got okays on investment money that will boost your fixed costs by ten thousand dollars a month, easy. And that may not be all. We may call it 90 percent of plant capacity, but there are a lot of places where we're just full up and we can't pull things up any tighter.

COOPER:  See, Bill? Fred Williams is right, but I'm not finished on this bit about volume changes. According to the information I've got here—and it came from your office—I'm not sure that your break-even chart can really be used even if there were to be no changes next year. Looks to me like you've got average figures that don't allow for the fact that we're dealing with three basic products. Your report here [see Exhibit 2] on costs, according to product lines, for last year makes it pretty clear that the "average" is way out of line. How would the break-even point look if we took this on an individual product basis?

**EXHIBIT 2.  Duo-Products Corporation's Product Class Cost Analysis (Normal Year)**

|  | Aggregate | "A" | "B" | "C" |
|---|---|---|---|---|
| Sales at Full Capacity (units) | 2,000,000 | | | |
| Actual Sales Volume (units) | 1,500,000 | 600,000 | 400,000 | 500,000 |
| Unit Sales Price | $1.20 | $1.67 | $1.50 | $0.40 |
| Total Sales Revenue | $1,800,000 | $1,000,000 | $600,000 | $200,000 |
| Variable Cost per Unit | $0.75 | $1.25 | $0.625 | $0.25 |
| Total Variable Cost | $1,125,000 | $ 750,000 | $250,000 | $125,000 |
| Fixed Costs | $ 520,000 | $ 170,000 | $275,000 | $ 75,000 |
| Net Profit | $ 155,000 | $  80,000 | $ 75,000 | —0— |
| Ratios: | | | | |
|    Variable Cost to Sales | .63 | .75 | .42 | .63 |
|    Variable Income to Sales | .37 | .25 | .58 | .37 |
|    Utilization of Capacity | 75.0% | 30.0% | 20.0% | 25.0% |

FRENCH:    Well, I'm not sure. Seems to me that there is only one break-even point for the firm. Whether we take it product by product or in total, we've got to hit that point. I'll be glad to check for you if you want, but . . .

BRADSHAW *(Asst. Sales Mgr.):*    Guess I may as well get in on this one, Bill. If you're going to do anything with individual products, you ought to know that we're looking for a big swing in our product mix. Might even start before we get into the new season. The "A" line is really losing out, and I imagine that we'll be lucky to hold two-thirds of the volume there next year. Wouldn't you buy that, Arnie? *[Agreement from the General Sales Manager]* That's not too bad, though, because we expect that we should pick up the 200,000 that we lose, and about a quarter million units more, over in "C" production. We don't see anything that shows much of a change in "B." That's been solid for years and shouldn't change much now.

WINETKI *(Gen. Sales Mgr.):*    Bradshaw's called it about as we figure it, but there's something else here too. We've talked about our pricing on "C" enough, and now I'm really going to push our side of it. Ray's estimate of maybe half a million—four hundred fifty thousand I guess it was—up on "C" for next year is on the basis of doubling the price with no change in cost. We've been priced so low on this item that it's been a crime—we've got to raise, but good, for two reasons. First, for our reputation; the price is out of line class-wise and is completely inconsistent with our quality reputation. Second, if we don't raise the price, we'll be swamped and we can't handle it. You heard what Williams said about capacity. The way the whole "C" field is exploding, we'll have to answer to another half million units in unsatisfied orders if we don't jack that price up. We can't afford to expand that much for this product.

At this point, Hugh Fraser, administrative assistant to the president, walked up toward the front of the room from where he had been standing near the rear door. The discussion broke for a minute, and he took advantage of the lull to interject a few comments.

FRASER:    This has certainly been enlightening. Looks like you fellows are pretty well up on this whole operation. As long as you're going to try to get all of the things together that you ought to pin down for next year, let's see what I can add to help you.

Number One: Let's remember that everything that shows in the profit area here on Bill's chart is divided just about evenly between the government and us. Now, for last year we can read a profit of about $150,000. Well, that's right. But we were left with half of that, and then paid out dividends of $50,000 to the stockholders. Since we've got an anniversary year coming up, we'd like to put out a special dividend of about 50 percent extra. We ought to hold $25,000 in for the business, too. This means that we'd like to hit $100,000 *after* the costs of being governed.

Number Two: From where I sit, it looks like we're going to have to talk with the union again, and this time it's liable to cost us. All the indications are—and this isn't public—that we may have to meet demands that will boost our production costs—what do you call them here, Bill—variable costs—by 10 percent across the board. This may kill the bonus dividend plans, but we've got to hold the line on past profits. This means that we can give that much to the union only if we can make it in added revenues. I guess you'd say that that raises your break-even point, Bill—and for that one I'd consider the company's profit to be a fixed cost.

Number Three: Maybe this is the time to think about switching our product emphasis. Arnie Winetki may know better than I which of the products is more profitable. You check me out on this, Arnie—and it might be a good idea for you and Bill French to get together on this one, too. These figures that I have (Exhibit 2] make it look like the percentage contribution on line "A" is the lowest of the bunch. If we're losing volume there as rapidly as you sales folks say, and if we're as hard pressed for space as Fred Williams has indicated, maybe we'd be better off grabbing some of that big demand for "C" by shifting some of the facilities over there from "A." That's all I've got to say. Looks to me like you've all got plenty to think about.

DAVIDSON:   Thanks, Hugh. I sort of figured that we'd get wound up here as soon as Bill brought out his charts. This is an approach that we've barely touched, but as you can see, you've all got ideas that have got to be made to fit here somewhere. I'll tell you what we should do. Bill, suppose you rework your chart and try to bring into it some of the points that were made here today. I'll see if I can summarize what everyone seems to be looking for.

First of all, I have the idea buzzing around in the back of my mind that your presentation is based on a rather important series of assumptions. Most of the questions that were raised were really about those assumptions; it might help us all if you try to set the assumptions down in black and white so that we can see just how they influence the analysis.

Then, I think that Cooper would like to see the unit sales increase taken up, and he'd also like to see whether there's any difference if you base the calculations on an analysis of individual product lines. Also, as Bradshaw suggested, since the product mix is bound to change, why not see how things look if the shift materialized as Sales has forecast.

Arnie Winetki would like to see the influence of a price increase in the "C" line, Fred Williams looks toward an increase in fixed manufacturing costs of ten thousand a month, and Hugh Fraser has suggested that we should consider taxes, dividends, expected union demands, and the question of product emphasis.

I think that ties it all together. Let's hold off on our next meeting, fellows, until Bill has time to work this all into shape.

With that, the participants broke off into small groups and the meeting disbanded. Bill French and Wes Davidson headed back to their offices, and French, in a tone of concern, asked Davidson, "Why didn't you warn me about the hornet's nest I was walking into?"

"Bill, you didn't ask!"

## EXHIBIT 3.   Duo-Products Corporation's List of Participants in the Meeting

| |
|---|
| Bill French — Staff Accountant |
| Wes Davidson — Controller |
| John Cooper — Production Control |
| Fred Williams — Manufacturing |
| Ray Bradshaw — Assistant Sales Manager |
| Arnie Winetki — General Sales Manager |
| Hugh Fraser — Administrative Assistant to President |

# United Mutual Insurance Company: "Anyone for Coffee?"

The United Mutual Insurance Company was organized in 1939 by Paul and James Taylor. Since its organization, these two men have maintained active personal direction of the company. The company is located in Kansas City, Missouri, and writes all forms of automobile and general casualty insurance. At the present time United Mutual is represented by more than 2,000 agents located in Wisconsin, Illinois, Iowa, Missouri, Kentucky, and Colorado, and it has thirty-two field managers and eighty claims adjusters working out of forty-seven offices. The company has grown steadily since it was founded.

The home office of United Mutual has about 425 employees of which approximately 75 percent are women. Due primarily to marriage and family obligations of many of the women, annual labor turnover is 25 to 30 percent. There has been a mild labor shortage in Kansas City the past few years which has made it difficult to obtain secretaries, typists, and file clerks. Of the 425 persons in the home office, about 100 are supervisory employees. The term "supervisory employees" or "supervisors" in this company refers to those persons who do not have to punch clocks and do not receive overtime pay. It includes people who direct the work of others, and also some technical and professional people such as lawyers and underwriters. An organization chart of the persons primarily involved in this case is shown in Figure 1.

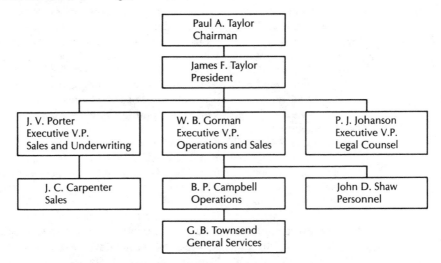

**FIGURE 1. Current Organization Chart Showing Top Positions in United Mutual Insurance Company**

This case begins about five years ago. At that time the company allowed one coffee break of fifteen minutes in the morning and a similar break in the afternoon. Employees went to the cafeteria for their break. At this time both Gorman and Townsend had some responsibility for the coffee break. Gorman had general responsibility for control of the break, because he was in charge of general operations in the home office. Townsend had responsibility for the cafeteria and payroll (for example, should a clerk have her time docked for overstaying her break?). He also acted unofficially as personnel director.

Gradually many of the supervisory employees started taking advantage of the coffee break and overstaying their time in the cafeteria. When the nonsupervisory employees saw what was happening, they also started to take longer coffee breaks than were authorized. Before many months had passed, most all of the employees were taking longer breaks than were allotted. When Townsend and Gorman questioned several of the supervisory employees as to why they spend so much time during coffee breaks when they knew that only fifteen minutes were authorized, the standard reply was; "We were discussing business problems of United Mutual," or "We were having a meeting, so we actually were working."

It is probable that many overstayed coffee breaks actually were informal business meetings, because most of the supervisors were either underwriters, claim adjusters, or operations supervisors, and daily meetings of some of these people were common to discuss their business problems. There was, of course, no way to prove which discussions were social and which were informal business meetings. One thing seemed sure. It was almost impossible to get nonsupervisory employees to believe that supervisors were actually working during coffee hour; so Gorman told the supervisors that they had to keep within their fifteen minutes in order to set an example for the rest of the employees. They failed to heed his words and the coffee break continued to be violated. To add to the complication, too many employees were coming to the cafeteria at the same time, which resulted in much congestion and waiting to get their coffee.

In an effort to keep the coffee break limited to fifteen minutes, Townsend started staying in the cafeteria during the complete coffee hour and watching for offenders who stayed over the time limit. He in turn reported the offenders to department heads, who were supposed to take the action necessary to ensure that their employees obeyed the coffee-period time limit. For the next few months employees observed the fifteen-minute coffee period very closely with few exceptions. Then the department heads again became lax, and nonsupervisory, as well as supervisory, employees began exceeding the time limit on coffee periods.

Again Gorman and Townsend went into consultation, and this time they came up with the idea of installing bells in the cafeteria. These bells were then installed and were adjusted to ring every ten minutes. Considering that it took a few minutes for each employee to get from his office to the cafeteria. Gorman and Townsend felt that ten minutes in the cafeteria was the maximum time that could be allowed in order to still stay within the limits of the fifteen-minute coffee period. Schedules were set up by the department heads so that employees were *supposed* to arrive at the cafeteria when the bells rang and they would stay until the bells rang again, at which time they were supposed to leave. Townsend noted that the bells did keep some employees in the cafeteria for only ten minutes, but it was very difficult to synchronize the various groups. People were sifting into and out of the cafeteria all the time and not according to the schedule for which the bells were adjusted. Also, when one group was leaving the cafeteria, another group was scheduled to enter, which added to the congestion. The general opinion among some employees was that the bells made them feel "like they were in prison cells" and could not get out until the bells rang. Others thought the bells very irritating and said it was impossible to enjoy the coffee period. It was soon evident that the bells were not solving the coffee-period problem, but since no better solution was offered, the bells remained, and employees continued to complain about them.

Three years ago top management realized that United Mutual was expanding to the extent that there was definite need for a personnel director to handle the coffee-break problem as well as the increasing number of other personnel problems existing within the home office. Therefore, in July of that year John Shaw was hired as personnel director of United Mutual. Shaw had sixteen years experience in personnel work and was highly regarded in local personnel circles. Soon after his arrival at United Mutual, the current personnel problems were explained to him, and, of course, one of these problems was the coffee break. Shaw soon found out for himself that employees were taking more than their allotted time during coffee periods. The president wanted something done to remedy the situation, and this problem was given to Shaw.

He tackled the problem rapidly and directly. In his own words, "I made periodic checks with all of the department heads concerning the coffee hour and found what their reactions were. I told the department heads to keep check on the employees under their jurisdiction and to try to keep the coffee break confined within the fifteen-minute period."

Shaw soon found out that the bells were ineffective and unpopular. He had them removed from the cafeteria. A few executives approached Shaw and suggested that the coffee periods be discontinued. He countered with the following argument: "The labor shortage in our city is critical at the present time. We have twenty-five vacancies within the company and yet you want me to discontinue the coffee periods and, as a result, perhaps lose more employees."

In December of Shaw's first year top management asked him to justify his stand that the coffee hour was necessary and, if he could justify it, to provide a remedy to the problem. Shaw gave the following reasons why the coffee periods should be continued:

1. A coffee break helps new employees make friends with people in their own and other departments. United Mutual has a 25 to 30 percent labor turnover each year, so several new employees are coming to the company every week.
2. By having a coffee break there is a cross-pollination of ideas and this prevents stratification and cliques.
3. A coffee break will give renewed vigor to the employees and this will result in greater productivity.
4. The nature of detailed work and mental activity is so confining that people need a respite from their routines.

After much deliberation and consultation, Shaw arrived at a solution for the coffee break and submitted it to the top executives. They approved it, including his proposal that coffee be furnished free to employees. Free coffee was first given on March 23 by means of a routine announcement in the cafeteria. The remainder of Shaw's proposal was put into effect by a memorandum issued on March 31 by Shaw to all home office employees of United Mutual, as shown in Figure 2.

The memorandum was well received by most of the employees. The work week was cut from thirty-nine hours, thirty-five minutes, to thirty-eight hours, forty-five minutes. Employees who smoked enjoyed the privilege that was given them by the memorandum.

*United Mutual Insurance Company Memorandum*

Subject:  Changes in Working, Lunch, and Rest Period Schedules
To:        All Home Office Department Heads and Employees
From:     Personnel

Effective April 4, the working schedule of the office will be as follows: 8:00 A.M. to 12:00 noon.

Forty-minute lunch periods will be scheduled at five regular intervals.

*Fifteen-minute* morning *rest periods* will be scheduled at five regular intervals. The working day will end at 4:25 P.M.

This new working schedule reduces the workday by ten minutes and makes an overall workweek of 38.75 hours. We feel sure that employees will welcome this change since it will help to avoid further the evening traffic congestion and facilitate bus and trolley connections.

The morning rest period will be scheduled from 9:30 A.M. through 10:25 A.M. Departments will be scheduled at ten-minute intervals. *Fifteen minutes will be allowed for each employee, which includes travel time to and from the cafeteria.* It is important that employees adhere to the schedule listed below since the principal reason for staggering is to eliminate confusion and congestion and to improve service in the cafeteria. It will be the responsibility of department heads to make certain that employees follow the asssigned schedules. Following is the morning rest period schedule for all departments.

[The schedule is omitted.]

Where stand-by telephone service is required, department heads will exercise discretion in keeping their operation staffed during the morning rest and lunch periods.

In keeping with the national trend in offices, smoking will be permitted at the working desk by all employees. We know that employees will exercise discretion in respect to both safety requirements and office etiquette.

With the reduction of the workweek by fifty minutes and the provision for the new smoking privilege, we feel that the afternoon rest period is unnecessary. The cafeteria will be closed after the last lunch group has been served.

3/31/—
JDS:RG

**FIGURE 2.   Memorandum to Employees**

Shaw believed that everything would have turned out all right if United Mutual had been remodeling and adding to its building at that time (see Figure 3).

As can be seen from the diagram, this construction meant that all employees from the North Building had to walk outside and around the center building in order to get to the cafeteria for the coffee period. Employees on the third floor took as long as six to seven minutes to reach the cafeteria, which caused their break to extend beyond the fifteen-minute limitation. In the ensuing months, department heads became slack in enforcing the memorandum issued by Shaw, and employees again started taking more time than was allotted to them. Most department heads had their department split into two sections. One section was to go for their coffee and the other section was to wait until the first

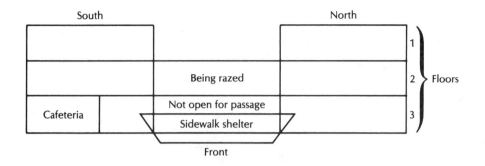

**FIGURE 3.  United Mutual Building During Remodeling**

section returned. The only trouble was that the second section was not waiting for the first section to return before they left. The result was mass confusion in the cafeteria. Groups did not come on the regular schedule, and when they did come, they stayed over the fifteen minutes. Shaw conferred with all the department heads and told them that if the practice of long coffee breaks continued in the future, there was a strong possibility of not having any coffee breaks at all.

One department head realized the seriousness of the problem and issued a memorandum to all his employees explaining why time limits must be observed by everyone. Gorman liked the memorandum and had Shaw send copies to all supervisors.

Early last year United Mutual's management decided that an opinion survey might help solve some of the personnel problems encountered by the company. In this survey approximately sixty employees complained about the coffee period. Many of them didn't drink coffee and wanted to know why coffee was free while the rest of the liquid refreshments were not. There were some complaints about not having an afternoon coffee break in addition to the morning break. Shaw conferred with the vice-president, Gorman, and they decided to offer free tea and cocoa as well as free coffee to employees, but the practice of only one coffee break each day would be continued. Shaw informed all department heads that the coffee break was still only fifteen minutes and in the morning only, but that cocoa and tea were free to employees beginning June 1. He also mentioned that this free coffee, tea, and cocoa would cost United Mutual $400 a month, and in order for this coffee break to be continued, employees would have to restrict their coffee break to the time mentioned in the memorandum, which was fifteen minutes.

In October of last year the building was finished and employees could walk through the building again to get to the cafeteria. A new middle section had been added to the building, and considerably more space existed for all employees. Also an elevator was installed for the convenience of all employees.

The coffee break in the morning was continued, and employees seemed to like the free coffee, tea, and cocoa. In fact, they liked it so much that most of them started taking second cups and overstaying their allotted fifteen minutes. In an effort to remind employees that the coffee break was still only fifteen minutes, Shaw had table napkins printed showing a friendly clock tapping two employees on their shoulders and reminding them, "Coffee break is fifteen minutes."

The napkins were removed from the table once or twice a week so that employees would not get a "routine feeling" about the napkins and would know that they were there for a purpose. The napkins served a very useful purpose as many of the employees did limit their coffee break to fifteen minutes, but there still were several (mostly supervisory employees) who continued to break the time limit on the coffee period.

Recently the case interviewer began a study of the coffee problem at United Mutual. On his first random visit to coffee hour he made the following observations:

1. Although the coffee break wasn't scheduled to start until 9:30, approximately thirty-five persons were in the cafeteria prior to that time.
2. At 9:35 A.M. there were approximately two hundred employees in the cafeteria when there should have been only seventy-five to one hundred. This resulted in much congestion, and when the 9:45 group came to coffee, there weren't enough clean cups due to the overflow at 9:30.
3. At 9:45 when the first group of employees was supposed to have left the cafeteria, approximately 25 percent still remained.
4. On the basis of spot checks it appeared that about 90 percent of the clerical employees obeyed the fifteen-minute coffee-break rule and the other 10 percent were just a few minutes over the limit. Spot checks of several supervisors showed that they spent anywhere from fifteen minutes to over an hour in the cafeteria. Typical examples are one supervisor who stayed in the cafeteria for twenty-two minutes and another who stayed approximately thirty minutes. One supervisor spent an hour and ten minutes in the cafeteria.
5. A check of two departments revealed that in each the second section left for coffee hour before the first section returned.

Shaw feels that a problem still exists at United Mutual concerning the coffee period. The current action which Shaw is taking is to revise the coffee-hour schedule in order to prevent congestion and achieve better control. Neither Gorman nor Shaw is sure what else should be done, if anything.

### Study Guides

1. Appraise management's handling of the problems that developed in this case.

2. At the end of the case what are the key problems, if any? What are the alternatives to choose from? What would you do in the role of Gorman? What would you do if you were Shaw?

### Role-playing Situations

1. In the role of Shaw, arrange to discuss this case with Gorman.

2. In the role of Gorman, call in Shaw to instruct him to improve the coffee-break situation.

# The City National Bank

## Part I*

The Transit Department of the City National Bank was located on the sixth floor of the bank building and contained eleven full-time and seven part-time employees. The main task of the department was the collection of deposits from the tellers, "proving" the deposits on IBM Proof Machines, and distributing the cancelled checks to correspondent banks with whom the bank dealt. Proving a deposit involved adding up the checks to see if the balance shown was correct and forwarding the checks to the proper banks. The proof machines consisted of a ten-key adding machine keyboard and a large drum inside the machine; by punching buttons that rotated the drum, the operator was able to simultaneously prove the deposit, as well as sort the checks to their proper place. While most anyone could operate a machine after only a one-day training period, it took considerable time to build up the speed necessary to be an efficient operator.

The machines were normally operated by the eleven full-time employees, all of whom were women. The part-time employees, all males and mostly college students from a nearby university, performed mostly support roles and only ran the proof machine in peak periods or when one of the full-time operators was not available. The head proof machine served to collect all the data during the day from the other machines and served as a summary unit for the day's operations. No deposits were run through this machine. The supervisor of the unit had been with the bank for ten years and supervisor of this group for three years.

The layout of the department is pictured in Figure 1. Machines were placed in rows facing the supervisor's desk. The head proof machine was located closest to the supervisor since there was constant communication between the head proof operator and the supervisor during the day. The other machines were referred to as Machine 1, Machine 2, Machine 3, etc. and similarly, the operators were referred to by numbers. As a general rule, the machines were organized according to seniority, with the most senior operator having Machine No. 1, and so on down through the other operators. At the lower machine numbers, when an operator quit and a new one was hired, the other operators moved to the next highest machine so the newest operator always occupied Machine No. 11.

Work came to the department through messenger boys who placed stacks of deposits on the supervisor's desk for sorting and distribution to the operators. The supervisor generally tried to give the more experienced operators the most difficult items, generally referred to as "junk" by the operators because the checks tended to be from a variety of different banks and were drawn for complicated amounts. The "gravy" deposits were generally given to the newer operators as these deposits were easier to balance since they contained relatively fewer checks from a small number of different banks, and the checks tended to have a lot of zeroes in them.

**Questions for Analysis**  Given the data in Part I, make the following predictions:

1. The group's morale would be (A) high, (B) medium, or (C) low? Why?

2. The informal group structure would be (A) ill-defined (B) rigidly defined? Why?

---

*This is a sequential case. Your instructor may wish you to analyze only this part before going further.

3. The productivity of the group would be considered by management to be (A) high (B) medium (C) low? Why?

4. Subgroups (A) *would* (B) *would not* form. Why?

5. There (A) *would* (B) *would not* be conflicts between group members.

The table shows the distribution of seniority, pay grades, and average daily productivity within the work unit.

| Worker | Machine | Seniority | Pay Level | Average Daily Productivity* |
|--------|---------|-----------|-----------|------------------------------|
| 1 | 1 | 11 yrs. | 10 | 13,500 items |
| 2 | 2 | 8 yrs. | 9 | 13,000 items |
| 3 | 3 | 5 yrs. | 7 | 11,000 items |
| 4 | 4 | 4 yrs. | 7 | 11,200 items |
| 5 | 5 | 2 yrs. | 4 | 9,000 items |
| 6 | 6 | 1 yr. | 3 | 9,000 items |
| 7 | 7 | 1 yr. | 3 | 9,000 items |
| 8 | 8 | 9 mo. | 2 | 8,000 items |
| 9 | 9 | 8 mo. | 2 | 7,000 items |
| 10 | 10 | 6 mo. | 1 | 7,500 items |
| 11 | 11 | 11 wks. | 1 | 3,000 items |

*Productivity for new workers was lower partly because they were often assigned to other tasks during slack periods. Senior workers generally ran machines all the time.

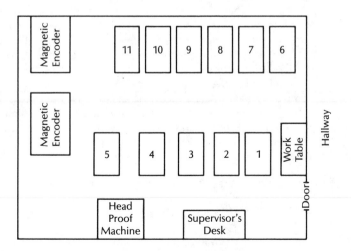

**FIGURE 1.   Diagram of the Transit Department**

# THE CITY NATIONAL BANK

## Part II*

The Transit Department had a reputation throughout the bank for being a well-organized, productive unit. Morale was generally high among the workers, particularly those with high seniority. There was considerable competition among the senior women to see who could run the most items during the day, although it was commonly recognized that Operator No. 1 was the fastest. The senior women also took considerable pride in their work and often joked during the day about who was producing the most work. Operator No. 1 generally requested all the "junk" work since processing these difficult deposits, while at the same time maintaining her top production record, gave her considerable satisfaction.

The total group was generally split into two informal groups: the older, more senior employees, and the newer, less skilled employees. While there was no animosity between the two, there were considerable differences in day-to-day behaviors, aspirations, and productivity. Generally speaking, the women ate in pairs, always matched up with workers of their own group. Most of the younger women did not aspire to be permanent operators and were working only until they got married or until a better job came along. They tended not to build up to the speed of the senior operators, mostly because they lacked the competitive spirit of the senior workers. Nevertheless, their performance was generally satisfactory.

The status hierarchy of the group was quite explicit and generally followed lines of seniority—and hence, productivity, although this trend became more obscure in the junior ranks. The senior operators referred to themselves in daily conversation by their machine number and most had given their machines names such as "Mabel," "Tessie," etc. The supervisor was reluctant to disrupt any of these informal behaviors. Operator No. 1 tended to dominate the work group and was always put in charge of training new operators.

**Postprediction Analysis** How closely does the information above conform to your previous predictions? If there are differences, can they be accounted for by faulty analysis? Lack of information? How would you change your analysis in light of the above?

---

*This is a sequential case. Your instructor may wish you to answer these questions before proceeding further.

# THE CITY NATIONAL BANK
## Part III*

For some time, bank officials, in consultation with the Transit Department manager, had been considering the purchase of newer equipment for the department. Many banks were moving into magnetic encoding of checks and deposits, which greatly enhanced their capacity to process these items with a minimum of manual efforts and mistakes. The IBM proof machines had been in the department for fifteen years and were technologically incapable of placing magnetic ink characters on checks and deposits. As a temporary measure, the bank purchased several "encoding machines" which would encode items with dollar amounts and account numbers but it was considered highly inefficient since each item had to be processed twice before it could be sent to data processing. Within a year's time, the bank decided to purchase several NCR proof machines which had the capability of proving, sorting, and encoding items in one operation.

The NCR machines were significantly different from the older IBM ones. Instead of the ten-key adding machine keyboard, they had full keyboards with a set of keys nine high and thirteen wide (only nine keys were needed vertically since the machine automatically inserted a zero if a key was not punched). NCR representatives showed bank officials data illustrating that these newer machines were faster than the previous ones not only because of the machines' ability to perform multiple operations but also because the operator had fewer keys to punch. Their research had shown that the majority of figures on bank items are zeros, a number that must be punched on a ten-key adding machine keyboard. On the NCRs, however, a ten dollar item could be inserted after punching only the "one" key in the fourth column.

The bank decided that the changeover from the old machines to the new should occur slowly and that one machine at a time would be introduced to the department. NCR agreed to provide the training necessary for the operators on the bank's premises.

### Predictions

1. If you were the supervisor, who would you give the first machine to? Why?

2. If this failed, what would be your next strategy? Why?

---

*This is a sequential case. Your instructor may wish you to answer these questions before proceeding further.

# THE CITY NATIONAL BANK
## Part IV

The supervisor decided that the first machine should go to Operator No. 1. Upon informing her of this, she went into a tantrum and said she couldn't understand why the IBMs could not do the job, as they had done fine with them for fifteen years. She pointed out that they had already purchased the special encoding machines and with them, using the IBMs would be more than satisfactory. She tried the "new" keyboard of the NCR and felt that it was highly inefficient, particularly on the "junk" deposits she ran which contained many checks with a variety of complex amounts. She proceeded to prove several times to the supervisor that she could run a deposit faster on the IBM than she could on the NCR.

### Postprediction Analysis

1. Refer to your strategies in Part III. How did your analysis match what is described here? If there is a difference, why did it occur? Faulty analysis? Lack of information?

2. What would you do now? Why?

# East End General Hospital

East End General Hospital is a well-established general hospital in an eastern suburb of the community. The administrator is close to retirement, has had some concerns about the organization, and before retiring would like to make some recommendations to the board of directors.

To accomplish this, he has engaged the services of a management consulting firm, of which you are a part, to do the following:

☐ Study the existing organization as an effective structure for achievement of the hospital's objectives.
☐ Recommend plans for changes and improvements.
☐ Define responsibilities.

The objectives of the hospital were described to the consultants as follows:

1. To provide the highest quality of patient care to the community.
2. To maintain and enlarge its school of nursing program.
3. To operate the hospital in an efficient manner at reasonable and lowest possible costs.

The initial findings of the consulting team are summarized below as a basis for you to make recommendations and identify and establish improvement plans.

Organization charts and position descriptions were available only for the office manager's staff and the three key nursing directors. Therefore, a chart was prepared to show the hospital's existing organization (see Figure 1).

Most positions reported directly to the administrator. The chart reflects the administrator's pattern of management. Decision-making powers are held very tightly by the administrator. There is little delegation of responsibility and authority. Department heads receive little opportunity to participate in decisions affecting their departments. They tend to avoid the administrator whenever possible.

Despite the administrator's autocratic approach to management, the quality of patient care is high. This is partially due to the competence and dedication of department heads and their staff. Another significant reason is the number of informal relationships which have developed over the last two or three years in the process of planning the work to be done and in solving day-to-day problems. Here are the three most important examples:

1. The office manager exercised considerable influence over all other department heads who approached him voluntarily rather than trying to contact the busy administrator. Over several years, the office manager had developed smooth-running, routine office systems conforming to commission requirements. The office now ran itself through two competent supervisors. This meant the office manager was free to discuss problems with other department heads and to pursue a university hospital administration program.

---

2. The director of nursing had established excellent rapport with several other department heads on a day-to-day working relationship such as C.S.R., admitting, out-patient, physiotherapy, and social work.
3. The laundry manager had made considerable improvements in his department. Automated equipment and new systems and machine layout have resulted in a dramatic increase in quality and timeliness of service and an impressive decrease in costs. With the laundry operating on a near-automated basis, the laundry manager has often been observed assisting personnel and supervisors in housekeeping, maintenance, boiler-room, elevators and security with their duties.

Unfortunately, there are a number of problems which seem to be in conflict with the hospital's objectives as listed above. The administrator has always felt he was controlling effectively the purchase of food, drugs, supplies, etc., by signing every purchase requisition. However, food costs per patient meal and drug costs were much higher than in comparable hospitals. Large inventories of supplies and drugs were maintained. There was little discount buying and bulk purchasing.

On several occasions, the board of directors had become deeply involved in personnel problems. This has had a frustrating effect on department heads.

Despite the reportedly high quality of patient care, nursing personnel complained about the inadequate support they received from housekeeping, dietary, pharmacy, and other departments. They indicated that this prevented them from devoting more time to patient care and bedside nursing.

The director of nursing described the many difficulties involved in integrating the nursing education program with nursing services—despite a cooperative relationship between the two assistants. Inadequate attention to student nurses on ward duty is a repeated criticism.

All of the above findings prompted the consultants to analyze the impact of the hospital's total organization on the patient. It was decided that the organization's effectiveness could be viewed through the work performed by nurses. Therefore, a technique known as "work sampling" was selected.

Under the guidance of a consulting specialist, a committee of nursing staff observed a representative number of nursing personnel activities. The results of this study are revealed in Table 1.

As a team of management consultants, with the findings described above, you are now in a position to:

☐ Discuss the effectiveness of the existing organization.
☐ Plan the broad structure of an improved organization.
☐ Develop plans for solving problems and identifying potential improvements.

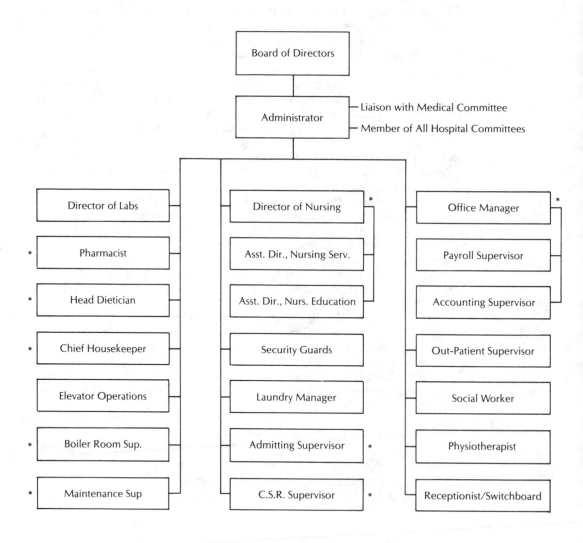

*Designates purchasing activities.

**FIGURE 1.   Organization Chart, East End General Hospital**

**TABLE 1.   Study Results—All Observations, East End General Hospital**

| Category | Percentage |
|---|---|
| 1.  Accompany doctor on rounds | 5 |
| 2.  Work on patient charts | 3 |
| 3.  Medication | 2 |
| 4.  Treatment of patients | 3.5 |
| 5.  Personal patient care other than treatment | 15 |
| 6.  Admitting and discharging | 2 |
| 7.  Telephoning relatives of patients | 1 |
| 8.  Instructions to student nurses | 1 |
| 9.  Checking diet slips | 3 |
| 10. Checking and serving food trays | 10 |
| 11. Miscellaneous paperwork | 9 |
| 12. Telephoning other departments | 0.5 |
| 13. Leaving ward to get drugs | 10 |
| 14. Leaving ward to get supplies | 4 |
| 15. Work direction to maids and cleaners | 4 |
| 16. Cleaning rooms and making beds | 10 |
| 17. Work direction to other personnel | 1 |
| 18. Conversation | 6 |
| 19. Walking | 4 |
| 20. Personal time with other activities | 6 |
| | 100 |

# Index